Leave No One Behind –
Behind the SDG of India

Leave No One Behind – Behind the SDG of India

Reflection of the SDGs in the Indian Constitution

Dr. Sanjoy Sarkar

GYAN

ISBN: 978-81-212-2196-2

Published, 2021

Published by

Gyan Publishing House
5, Ansari Road
Daryaganj, New Delhi-110002
Phone: 011-47034999, 9811692060
www.gyanbooks.com
E-mail: books@gyanbooks.com

Printed at: Gyan Press, Delhi.

This page for –

MY

Father, Late Srishtidhar Sarkar &
Late Father-in-Law, Bimalendu Mukherjee;
Mother, Smt. Kamala Sarkar &
Mother-in-Law, Smt. Manimala Mukherjee

AND

Daughter Srinjeeta & Wife Jayasree

DEDICATION

This book is dedicated to Professor Samir Kumar Dasgupta, the teacher of teachers. The teacher who had taught me the way to read along with interpretation of the social issues during my training of doing research on Sociology of Development. He is no more in the living world. I had a last talk to him on the day of Teacher's day 2020. He is the man who has guided and inspired me; he is the man who has pick me from the last bench of the class within a lot of his bright students. Then he had introduced me in the world of development studies by his motivational talk and training. Lastly, it must be say that, he is the man for whose motivational talk has pushed me, as a result I come at my present position from the back bench of the class room. I am proud to being a student of such a figure in the field of sociology.

[Born: June 6, 1949 – Death: September 9, 2020]

Note: Photo credit, Dr. Koushik Chattopadhyay, Assistant Professor of SNH College, Farakka, West Bengal (Research Scholar of Professor Samir Dasgupta).

Contents

Preface

Since the beginning of my academic carrier and as a trainee of development studies I am trying to read the development initiatives. The journey from Millennium Development Goals (MDGs) to Sustainable Development Goals (SDGs) has seems to me a more objective and strategic than others. In the other side, India have a Constitution which is more dynamic and it is been adopting by amending all the issues related to citizen's rights, duties and obligations to the nation in due time.

No doubt, the approach of the MDGs-SDGs and the Constitution of India are 'inclusive' in nature; the MDGs-SDGs are for an 'inclusive world' and the Constitution of India is for 'inclusive India'. When I was reading the *SDG India Index Baseline Report, 2018*, its idea, agenda and scope repeatedly diverted me to the Constitution of India. The author has started to read the Constitution of India again and again.

From this point of time, I am feeling that, there is strong influence of 'Peace, Justice and Strong Institutions' to execute the agenda of any development initiatives, whatever it national or international spheres.

The SDG India Index Baseline Report, 2018 reported that India scored '71' in the SDG-16, that is 'Peace, Justice and Strong Institutions'.

It seems to me, this score could be a measuring parameter of other goals included in the SDGs. In this book I am trying to assess the performance of India with '71' score in the 'Peace, Justice and Strong Institutions'. Because, the agenda of SDGs is made for a better world for the future generation and all the agenda of SDGs has to be completed by 2030.

Finally, on the basis of India's performance of each SDG, I have tried to highlight how much efficiently effective role to be required in 22 chapters of this book and trying to highlighted how the Constitution of India could monitor the issue for the future generation of India.

Chapter Summary/Overview of the Book

In chapter – 1, the author tried grasp the tune of SDGs as resolved in the United Nation's General Assembly through the short assessment of MDGs and explored the essence of SDG in the contemporary world along with especial emphasis on India.

In Chapter – 2, the author tried to elaborate the role of peace in achievements. As per the theoretical as well as empirical observations of the term 'peace', I am tried to grasp the position of India in overall peace-making to measure India's performance of SDGs through the mirror of SDG India Index Baseline Report, 2018.

In Chapter – 3, tried to give a look into the provisions to accelerate the success of SDGs in the Constitution of India and tried to link the Articles, Schedules and Lists of the Constitution of India to the SDGs according to the links as reported in the SDG India Index Baseline Report, 2018.

In Chapter – 4, according to the tune of the SDGs, SDG-17, that is partnership of the goals, is a vital tool of achieving SDG's targets; in this regard the author tried to summarize a report on performance of India on the SDGs to grasp reality of SDGs in India and elaborate the present situation on India. Here, in this chapter, the author tried to elaborate the methods of presentation of the book.

In Chapter-5, the author tried to elaborate the UN, SDG targets, indicators; indicators, data source and computational approach framed by the NITI *Aayog*; Indian Constitutional provisions to accelerate the success of the SDG-1; policies initiative, authorities of the policies and performance of India and remaining UN, SDG targets and indicators of India on SDG-1, No Poverty.

In Chapter-6, the author tried to elaborate the UN, SDG targets, indicators; indicators, data source and computational approach framed by the NITI *Aayog*; Indian Constitutional provisions to accelerate the success of the SDG-2; policies initiative, authorities of the policies and performance of India and remaining UN, SDG targets and indicators of India on SDG-2, Zero Hunger.

In Chapter-7, the author tried to elaborate the UN, SDG targets, indicators; indicators, data source and computational approach framed by the NITI *Aayog*; Indian Constitutional provisions to accelerate the success of the SDG-3; policies initiative, authorities of the policies and performance of India and remaining UN, SDG targets and indicators of India on SDG-3, Good Health and Well-being.

In Chapter-8, the author tried to elaborate the UN, SDG targets, indicators; indicators, data source and computational approach framed by the NITI *Aayog*; Indian Constitutional provisions to accelerate the success of the SDG-4; policies initiative, authorities of the policies and performance of India and remaining UN, SDG targets and indicators of India on SDG-4, Quality Education.

In Chapter-9, the author tried to elaborate the UN, SDG targets, indicators; indicators, data source and computational approach framed by the NITI *Aayog*; Indian Constitutional provisions to accelerate the success of the SDG-5; policies initiative, authorities of the policies and performance of India and remaining UN, SDG targets and indicators of India on SDG-5, Gender Equality.

In Chapter-10, the author tried to elaborate the UN, SDG targets, indicators; indicators, data source and computational approach framed by the NITI *Aayog*; Indian Constitutional provisions to accelerate the success of the SDG-6; policies initiative, authorities of the policies and performance of India and remaining UN, SDG targets and indicators of India on SDG-6, Clean Water and Sanitation.

In Chapter-11, the author tried to elaborate the UN, SDG targets, indicators; indicators, data source and computational approach framed by the NITI *Aayog*; Indian Constitutional provisions to accelerate the success of the SDG-7; policies initiative, authorities of the policies and performance of India and remaining UN, SDG targets and indicators of India on SDG-7, Affordable and Clean Energy.

In Chapter-12, the author tried to elaborate the UN, SDG targets, indicators; indicators, data source and computational approach framed by the NITI *Aayog*; Indian Constitutional provisions to accelerate the success of the SDG-8; policies initiative, authorities of the policies and performance of India and remaining UN, SDG targets and indicators of India on SDG-8: SDG, Decent Work and Economic Growth.

In Chapter-13, the author tried to elaborate the UN, SDG targets, indicators; indicators, data source and computational approach framed by the NITI *Aayog*; Indian Constitutional provisions to accelerate the success of the SDG-9; policies initiative, authorities of the policies and performance of India and remaining UN, SDG targets and indicators of India on SDG-9, Industry, Innovation and Infrastructure.

In Chapter-14, the author tried to elaborate the UN, SDG targets, indicators; indicators, data source and computational approach framed by the NITI *Aayog*; Indian Constitutional provisions to accelerate the success of the SDG-10; policies initiative, authorities of the policies and performance of India and remaining UN, SDG targets and indicators of India on SDG-10, Reduce Inequality.

In Chapter-15, the author tried to elaborate the UN, SDG targets, indicators; indicators, data source and computational approach framed by the NITI *Aayog*; Indian Constitutional provisions to accelerate the success of the SDG-11; policies initiative, authorities of the policies and performance of India and remaining UN, SDG targets and indicators of India on SDG-11, Sustainable Cities and Communities.

In Chapter-16, the author tried to elaborate the UN, SDG targets, indicators; Indian Constitutional provisions to accelerate the success of the SDG-12; policies initiative, authorities of the policies and remaining UN, SDG targets and indicators of India on SDG-12, Sustainable Consumption and Production.

In Chapter-17, the author tried to elaborate the UN, SDG targets, indicators; Indian Constitutional provisions to accelerate the success of the SDG-13; policies initiative, authorities of the policies and remaining UN, SDG targets and indicators of India on SDG-13, Climate Action.

In Chapter-18, the author tried to elaborate the UN, SDG targets, indicators; Indian Constitutional provisions to accelerate the success of the SDG-13; policies initiative, authorities of the policies and remaining UN, SDG targets and indicators of India on SDG-14, Life Bellow Water.

In Chapter-19, the author tried to elaborate the UN, SDG targets, indicators; indicators, data source and computational approach framed by the NITI *Aayog*; Indian Constitutional provisions to accelerate the success of the SDG-15; policies initiative, authorities of the policies and performance of India and remaining UN, SDG targets and indicators of India on SDG-15, Life and Land.

In Chapter-20, the author tried to elaborate the UN, SDG targets, indicators; indicators, data source and computational approach framed by the NITI *Aayog*; Indian Constitutional provisions to accelerate the success of the SDG-16; policies initiative, authorities of the policies and performance of India and remaining UN, SDG targets and indicators of India on SDG-16, Peace, Justice and Strong Institutions.

In Chapter-21, the author tried to elaborate the UN, SDG targets, indicators; Indian Constitutional provisions to accelerate the success of the SDG-17; policies initiative, authorities of the policies and remaining UN, SDG targets and indicators of India on SDG-17, Partnerships for the Goals.

In Chapter-22, is elaborated the concluding remarks on the performance of the Government of India in the SDGs along with the suggestions to the Indian citizens for the future generation.

Abbreviations

AAY	:	*Antoydaya Anna Yojana*
ACROSS	:	Atmosphere and Climate Research – Modelling, Observing Systems and Services
ADIP	:	Assistance to Disabled Persons for purchase of Fitting Devices
AIM	:	Atal Innovation Mission
AMRUT	:	Atal Mission for Rejuvenation and Urban Transformation
APY	:	*Atal* Pension *Yojana*
ART	:	Antiretroviral Therapy
ASEAN	:	Association of South-East Asian Nations
ASER	:	Annual Status of Education Report
AUSC	:	Advanced Ultra Super Critical
AYUSH	:	Ayurveda, Yoga & Naturopathy, Unani, siddha and Homeopathy
BADP	:	Border Area Development Programme
BMI	:	Body Mass Index
BRICSAM	:	Brazil, Russia, India, China, South Africa, the ASEAN states, Mexico
CAGR	:	Combine Annual Growth Rate
CAS	:	Cooperation, Assistance and Sharing
CBDT	:	Central Board of Direct Taxes
CPCB	:	Central Pollution Control Board
CSS	:	Central Sector Schemes
DAC	:	Development Assistance Committee
DADF	:	Department of Animal Husbandry, Dairying & Fisheries
DAY	:	*Deen Dayal Antyodaya Yojana*

DAY	:	NRLM - *Deendayal Antyodaya Yojana*-National Rural Livelihood Mission
DBT	:	Direct Benefit Transfer
DDRS	:	*Deendayal* Disabled Rehabilitation Scheme
DDU-GKY	:	*Deen Dayal Upadhyaya Grameen Kaushalya Yojana*
DFS	:	Department of Financial Services
DIPP	:	Department for Promotion of Industry and International Trade
DMD	:	Dedicated Ministries or the Departments
DRR	:	Disaster Risk Reduction
DSPV	:	Decentralized Solar Photovoltaic
DUGKY	:	*Deendayal Upadhyay Grameen Kaushalya Yojana*
EAP	:	Technical Education Quality Improvement Programme
ECI	:	Election Commission of India
ECOSOC	:	United Nations Economic and Social Council
EVS	:	Environmental Science
FAO	:	Food and Agriculture Organization
FDI	:	Foreign Direct Investment
FIES	:	Food Insecurity Experience Scale
GDP	:	Gross Domestic Product
GGGI	:	Global Green Growth Institute
GGSDI	:	Green Growth and Sustainable Development in India
GHI	:	Global Hunger Index
GNI	:	Gross National Income
GPs	:	Gram Panchayats
GST	:	Goods and Services Tax
HRIDAY	:	National Heritage City Development and Augmentation *Yojana*
IAEG-SDGs	:	Inter-Agency and Expert Group on SDG Indicators
ICDS	:	Integrated Child Development Services
ICSSR	:	India Council of Social Science Research
ICT	:	Information and Communications Technology
IDSP	:	Integrated Disease Surveillance Programme
IESS	:	India Energy Security Scenarios

IHR	:	International Health Regulations
ILO	:	International Labour Organization
IMD	:	India Meteorological Department
IMF	:	International Monetary Fund
ISRO	:	Indian Space Research Organisation
LDCs	:	Least Developed Countries
LED	:	Light Emitting Diode
LESS	:	Labour and Employment Statistical System
LGBTQ	:	Lesbian, Gay, Bisexual, Transgender and Queer
LPG	:	Liquefied Petroleum Gas
MDGs	:	Millennium Development Goals
MDM	:	Mid-day Meal
MDWS	:	Ministry of Drinking Water and Sanitation
MEF&CC	:	Ministry of Forest, Environment and Climate Change
MGNREGS	:	Mahatma Gandhi National Rural Employment Guarantee Scheme
MGNRGEA	:	Mahatma Gandhi National Rural Employment Guarantee Act
MH&FW	:	Ministry of Health and Family Welfare
MHA	:	Ministry of Home Affairs
MHRD	:	Ministry of Human Resource Development
MHUA	:	Ministry of Housing and Urban Affairs
MIDH	:	Mission for Integrated Development of Horticulture
MIIUS	:	Modified Industrial Infrastructure Upgradation Scheme
MIS-PSS	:	Market Intervention Scheme and Price Support Scheme
MMDA	:	Modified Market Development Assistance
MMR	:	Maternal Mortality Ratio
MPLADS	:	Member of Parliament Local Area Development Scheme
MRD	:	Ministry of Rural Development
MRTS	:	Mass Rapid Transit System
MSDP	:	Multi Sectoral Development Programme for Minorities
MSMEs	:	Micro, Small and Medium Enterprises
NAMP	:	National Air Quality Monitoring Programme
NAPCC	:	National Action Plan on Climate Change

NCERT	:	National Council of Educational Research and Training
NCRB	:	National Crime Record Bureau
NCRMP	:	National Cyclone Risk Mitigation Project
NCS	:	National Career Services
NDCs	:	National Determined Contributions
NDMP	:	National Disaster Management Plan
NEIDS	:	North East Industrial Development Scheme
NERLP	:	North East Region Livelihood Project
NERUDP	:	North Eastern Regional Urban Development Project
NFHS	:	National Family Health Survey
NGO	:	Non-Governmental Organization
NHM	:	National Health Mission
NIEPI	:	National Institute of Education Planning and Implementation
NIF	:	National Information Network
NITI	:	National Institution for Transforming India
NLM	:	National Livestock Mission
NMAET	:	National Mission on Agriculture Extension & Technology
NMEEE	:	National Mission for Enhanced Energy Efficiency
NMGI	:	National Mission for a Green India
NMHP	:	National Mental Health Programme
NMOOP	:	National Mission on Oilseeds & Oil Palm
NMSA	:	National Mission for Sustainable Agriculture
NMSH	:	National Mission on Sustainable Habitats
NMSH	:	National Mission on Sustainable Habitats
NMSHE	:	National Mission for Sustaining the Himalayan Ecosystem
NMSKCC	:	National Mission on Strategic Knowledge on Climate Change
NNM	:	National Nutrition Mission
NNS	:	National Nutrition Strategy
NP	:	Negative Performance
NPCDCS	:	National Programme for Prevention and Control of Cancer, Diabetes, Cardiovascular Diseases and Stroke
NPP	:	National Perspective Plan

NRCP	:	National River Conservation Programme
NRDWP	:	National Rural Drinking Water Programme
NRHM	:	National Rural Health Mission
NRLM	:	National Rural Livelihood Mission
NRRDO	:	National Rural Roads Development Organisation
NRWDP	:	National Rural Drinking Water Programme
NSAP	:	National Social Assistance Programme
NSIGSE	:	National Scheme for Incentive to Girl Child for Secondary Education
NSM	:	National Solar Mission
NSS	:	National Service Scheme
NSSO	:	National Sample Survey Organization
NUHM	:	National Urban Health Mission
NULM	:	National Urban Livelihood Mission
NWM	:	National Water Mission
NWQSM	:	National Water Quality Sub-Mission
ODA	:	Official Development Assistance
ODF	:	Open Defecation Free
OSTORMS	:	Ocean Services, Technology, Observations, Resources, Modelling and Science
PCBs	:	Pollution Control Committees
PDS	:	Public Distribution System
PMAW	:	*Pradhan Mantri Awas Yojana*
PMAY	:	*Pradhan Mantri Awas Yojana*
PMEGP	:	Prime Minister's Employment Generation Programme
PMFBY	:	*Pradhan Mantri Fasal Bima Yojana*
PMGSY	:	*Pradhan Mantri Gram Sadak Yojana*
PMJAY	:	*Pradhan Mantri Jan Aarogya Yojana*
PMJSBY	:	*Pradhan Mantri Jeevan Suraksha Beema Yojana*
PMKSY	:	*Pradhan Mantri Krishi Sinchayee Yojana*
PMMMNMTT	:	*Pandit Madan Mohan Malaviya* National Mission on Teachers and Teaching
PMMSK	:	*Pradhan Mantri Mahila Shakti Kendra*
PMMVY	:	*Mantri Matru Vandana Yojana*
PMMY	:	*Pradhan Mantri Mudra Yojana*

PMSBY : *Pradhan Mantri Suraksha Bima Yojana*
PMVVY : *Pradhan Mantri Vaya Vandana Yojana*
PP : Positive Performance
PPP : Public-Private Partnership
PRAGATI : Providing Assistance for Girls' Advancement in Technical Education Initiative
PVTGs : Vulnerable Tribal Groups
PwD : Persons with Disabilities
RGI : Registrar General of India
RGSA : *Rashtriya Gram Swaraj Abhiyan*
RKVY : *Rashtriya Krishi Vikas Yojana*
RMSA : *Rashtriya Madhyamik Shiksha Abhiyan*
RNTCP : Revised National Tuberculosis Control Programme
ROMS : Real-time Out-come Based Monitoring Systems
RSOC : Rapid Survey on Children
RTE : Right to Education
SAARC : South Asian Association for Regional Cooperation
SAGE : Seismology and Geosciences
SARDP-NE : Special Accelerated Road Development Programme for North Eastern Region
SC : Scheduled Caste
SCA to TSS : Special Central Assistance to Tribal Sub-Scheme
SCBs : Scheduled Commercial Banks
SCM : Smart Cities Mission
SCP : Sustainable Consumption and Production
SCSP : Scheduled Caste Sub Plan
SDGs : Sustainable Development Goals
SECC : Socio-Economic Caste Census
SETU : Self Employment and Talent Utilization
SIDs : Small Island Developing States
SPCBs : State Pollution Control Boards
SPV : Solar Photovoltaic
SRRI : Social and Rural Research Institute
SSA : *Sarva Shiksha Abhiyan*
ST : Scheduled Tribe

STEP	:	Support to Training and Employment Programme
TB	:	Tuberculosis
TE	:	Teacher Education
TERI	:	The Energy and Resources Institute
TFM	:	Technology Facilitation Mechanism
TSP	:	Tribal Sub Plan
UHC	:	- Universal Health Coverage
UIDAI	:	Unique Identity Authority of India
UNCTAD	:	UN Conference on Trade and Development
UNFCCC	:	United Nations Framework Convention on Climate Change
UNHRC	:	United Nations Human Rights Commission
UNHRC	:	United Nations Human Rights Commission
USTAAD	:	Upgrading Skills and Training in Traditional Arts / Crafts for Development
UTs	:	Union Territories
VNR	:	Voluntary National Reviews
w. e. f	:	With Effect From
WASH	:	Water, Sanitation and Hygiene
WEF	:	Walk Free Foundation
WNTA	:	*Wada Na Todo Abhiyan (Don't Break Your Promise)*
WTO	:	World Trade Organization

Acknowledgements

At first I want to express my sincere gratitude to my teachers who has given their valuable time to me in different stage of learning. I am thankful to the teachers of *Muratipur Prathamic Vidyalaya, Charswarati,* and the Teachers of *Pannalal Institution*, Kalyani, Nadia. I am expressing my sincere gratitude to my *tutor Anil Da, Foni Da, Babu Da, Dilip Da, Swapan Da, Pradip Da, Swapam Da* and *Brindaban* Sir along with the students, scholars, staffs and the teachers of Sociology Department, namely Professor M. Mukherjee, Professor P. K. Majumder, Professor P. K. Sen, Professor D. Sengupta, Professor S. Sen, Professor S. Manna, Professor A. Mukhopdhyay, Professor P. S. De along with Sri Sujan Bhttyacharya (Late), Sri Nemai Duttaand Sri Rabin Biswas (1997-2010), University of Kalyani.

I would like to express my sincere gratitude to the staffs engaged with design, promotion, marketing officials, editors, reviewers associate with the of Gyan Publishing House. I am an escapist in family matter; I had never filled any desired expectation in due time to any of the family member even others. It is their greatness, they tolerate me. It is a great privilege and I have taken the opportunity to give a thanks to all of them for their patience and their power of toleration. For all kind of academic activities I am especially thankful to my beloved 10 years old daughter Srinjeeta, wife Jayasree, my 70 years old mother and mother-in-law. They are being borne all the negligence from my side. This work is ultimately a production of negligence, the time I have got for the work from the negligence, finally has helped a lot to complete this work. I am hopeful, they will excuse me.

It is privilege to express my sincere gratitude to the IIT, Kharagpur for giving me the opportunity to attend the course on *'Research Methodology for Rural Social Sciences'* in 2006; MPISSR, Ujjain for giving me the opportunity to attend the course on *'Capacity Building Programme for Social Science Faculty Members / Researchers'* in 2015 and GIDS, Lucknow for giving me the opportunity to attend the course on *'Capacity Building Programme for Social Science Faculty Members'* in 2017.

I am extending gratitude to the all the past and present Students of Sociology Department; Principal, Dr. Sareojendra Nath Kar; Teacher-in-Charge, Dr. Somnath Bandyopadhyay; Dr. Animesh Andrew Lulam Rai, Head of the Sociology Department; Dr. Krishna Dey & Late Bipasha Sinha of the Sociology Department; Dr. Sanat Kumar Biswas, Librarian; Dr. Ahasan Ali, Associate Professor of Bengali; Dr. Sushmita Banaerjee, Associate Professor of Bengali; Sri Kalidas Mukherjee, Associate Professor of Commerce; Sri Hirak Roy, Associate Professor of Commerce; Dr. Arindam Chakraborty, Head of the Commerce Department; Dr. Shilpi Basak, Assistant Professor of English; Asit Da, Priyanka Di, Gourisankar, Subrata, Bibhas, Manosij, Annapurna, Soma (both), Rini, Tuhin (both), Arup (Laltu), Tarak, Hadu (Prolay), Bijoy Da and all other teaching and non-teaching Staffs of my college, Sudhiranjan Lahiri Mahavidyalaya for their spontaneous help, cooperation, support and encouragement and providing a good working environment.

I am also thankful to Dr. Jawleswar Ghosh, Government approved faculty of Haringhata Mahavidyalaya, West Bengal; Dr. Debasis Mallick, Associate Professor of Haringhata Mahavidyalaya, West Bengal; Dr. Koushik Chattopadhyay, Assistant Professor of SNH College, Farakka, West Bengal; Dr. Sudeshna Chanda, Assistant Professor, Kazi Nazru Mahavidyalaya, Agartala, Tripura, Shri Subir Das, Deputy Librarian, BCKV, West Bengal; Dr. Animseh Biswas, Assistant Professor of GIDS, Lucknow; Librarian and Staffs of SIPRD, Kalyani for their spontaneous support and encouragement.

It will be great injustice if I forget to acknowledge my root of origin, that is Jogendranath Colony, Kalyani, Nadia, West Bengal -741235, I am thankful to all the residents irrespective of their age and gender. Late Lochan Tahkur, was a civil engineer, one among the friend and mentor of my student life from my village, I am missing him for his unexpected death in a cardiac arrest. I am expressing my cordial respect to his soul. I am still connected with my few mates of primary, secondary and higher secondary schools, I thanks all of them. I cannot forget the boarders of Banyan Hostel of University of Kalyani, where the seeds of higher learning has planted to my mind by the boarders. The boarders of Research Scholars Hall of University of Kalyani has nurtured the learner's mind of a sociology researcher - thanks to all.

A major time of my adulthood I have spent with *Kalyani Natya Charcha Kendra* (a Theatre Group) leaded by leading academic elites of

Kalyani Town during 1997-2002. The group has as an academically influential institution to me, I am expressing my sincere gratitude to all the members of this theatre group.

Finally, I am expressing my special thanks to Dr. Swarup Bose, Dr. Prajjal Dutta, Dr. Bimal Mandal of West Bengal Higher Education Services and Sri Surajit Mondal along with other close friends of my locality, schools and university for mind refreshing moment at the Tea Stall of Basu Da, beside Central Park Kalyani. Thanks to Dr. Bibhas Guha, Faculty of NSOU; Dr. Biswamber Mondal, Faculty of University of Kalyani; Kunal Chakrabort (Political Science), Dr. Pratay Debnath (Mathematics, Banyan Hall, University of Kalyani); Dr. Alok Chandra Samal (Environmental Science,), Dr. Nithar Ranjan Madhu, Dr. Surajit Pathak, Dr. Sujoy Bag (Zoology); Dr Sovan Kanti Singha (Chemistry); Dr. Sanjib Chattopadhyay (Botany) of Research Scholar Hostel, University of Kalyani. I am thankful to the people who has criticised me in different point of time of my life. I believe that, the power of accepting criticism may open-up a new avenue to decorate the life-order. So, I am thanking in advance. I am extending my cordial thanks to the people who will take an effective role to decorate the life-order of future generation by reading this book to decorate the life-order of future generation. The author is humbly expecting all kinds of academic criticism.

List of Tables

Chapter – I

Introduction

Global leaders has been committed to create a better world for the future generations, this commitment framed as like an umbrella with multiple sticks to uphold the humanity. The first initiative in the 21st century entitled as Millennium Development Goals (MDGs), which was started a global effort to tackle the indignity of poverty in 2000. The MDGs were established as measurable and universally-agreed objectives for tackling extreme poverty, hunger, preventing deadly diseases, and expanding primary education to all children, among other development priorities.

For the last 15 years of the 21st century, the MDGs drove progress in several important areas, such as reducing income poverty, providing much needed access to water and sanitation, driving down child mortality and drastically improving maternal health. They has also kick-started a global movement for free primary education, inspiring countries to invest for their future generations. Most significantly, the MDGs has made huge strides in combatting HIV/AIDS and other treatable diseases such as malaria and tuberculosis. But different reports on the MDGs has bound to reframe further such kind of policy by considering the limitations as well as the barriers to achieved the target of the MDGs and in the other side considered the occurrences of all kinds of changes, such as socio-economic, socio-political, socio-demographic, socio-technological, socio-urbanization, socio-industrialization and the socio-environmental all over the world, which resulted by increasing human stress as well as strain throughout the world and finally this initiative entitled as Sustainable Development Goals (SDGs).

So, it has been expected that, the coming generation will lead a stress less as well as a decent life in all respect with dignity irrespective of their root of origin. This tune of leading life was farmed in the United Nations General Assembly Summit in September, 2015 with presence of 193

Member States. The summit was resolved with a vision towards poverty eradication; quality education; decent work; reduce inequality; gender equality; human health and sanitation to urban settlements and to safeguarding the global ecosystems on which humanity depends for its survival by 2030, literally as well as popularly the approach known as SDGs. The SDGs are a bold universal set of 17 Goals and 169 targets to help, organise and streamline development actions for greater achievement of human wellbeing, while *'leaving no one behind'* by 2030. The initiatives under the agenda of SDGs are the part of transforming our world for the future generation. No doubt, this is an international social inclusion approach of achieving peace by the people of the people and for the people, who are in margin.

SDGs have light as well as shade of its own approach. Basically, it offered opportunities as well as challenges for developing countries to bring long-time, the developing countries has bound to meet a high cost to implement the agenda of SDGs. Because, the socio-anthropological evidences of different nations are different in historical experiences, demographic compositions, cultural traditions, mode of governances and its polity, mode of technological achievement and base of economy are varied. These common varied natures of 193 Member States has jointly committed to achieve a single headed agenda entitled SDG composed by a set of 17 goals and 169 targets for greater achievement of human wellbeing by 2030. In this approach, India has played a prominent role in the formulation of SDGs and much of the India's national development agenda has mirrored in the SDGs (NITI Aayog 2018).

Since the beginnings of MDGs in 2000 the world even having the commonalities with the problems and varied in historical experiences, demographic compositions, cultural traditions, mode of governances and its polity and base of economy; though the nations' achievement was limited for other reasons, which are also reflected in the SDGs when it has been framed. If we look into the SDG-16, which entitled, *peace, justice and strong institutions* that aimed to developing effective, accountable and transparent institutions at all levels top promote peaceful and inclusive societies for sustainable development, provide access to justice for all and build effective, accountable and inclusive institutions at all levels and in SDG-17, *partnerships for the Goals* that was aimed to strengthen the means of implementation and revitalize the global partnership for sustainable development - these goals are basically the weakness of the implementing countries, which has assessed in the end of the MDGs and then included in the SDGs as tools of success and measurable as well.

So, sustainable development is basically based on peace, stability, human rights, and effective governance based on the rule of law. We are living in a world, which is increasingly divided as well as stratified; like socially, economically, politically divided and some countries are having the nature of cultural stratification, like Indian caste system. Some regions has enjoying sustained peace, security and prosperity, while others has fall into seemingly endless cycles of conflict and violence. This is by no means inevitable and must be addressed to the achievement of the SDGs.

High levels of armed violence and insecurity has a destructive impact on a country's development, affecting economic growth and often resulting in long-standing grievances that can last for generations. Sexual violence, crime, exploitation and torture are also prevalent where there is conflict or no rule of law, and countries must take measures to protect those most at risk.

The SDGs has also aimed to significantly reduce all forms of violence, and work with governments and communities to find lasting solutions to conflict and insecurity. Strengthening the rule of law and promoting human rights is keys to this process, as is reducing the flow of illicit arms and strengthening the participation of developing countries in the institutions of global governance.

So, the success of the SDGs were depended on the achievement of the SDG-16, *Peace, Justice and Strong Institutions,* which was aimed to developing effective, accountable and transparent institutions at all levels top promote peaceful and inclusive societies for sustainable development, provide access to justice for all and build effective, accountable and inclusive institutions at all levels. The success of rest of the SDGs; such as SDG-1 to SDG-15 and SDG-17 are depends on SDG-16, so there is an association of success among SDG-16 with rest of the SDGs which are SDG-1 to SDG-15 and SDG-17. So, it is assumed that, the success of the SDG-16 will be reflected in the rest of the SDGs. In this initiative the author has trying to draw a relation, with the SDG-16 among rest of the SDGs that is SDG-1 to SDG-15 and SDG-17 through the mirror of the *SDG India Index Baseline Report,* 2018, published by NITI *Aayog*, Government of India. The initiative has been explored by the expected performance, actual performance and performance differences, when SDG-16, *Peace, Justice and Strong Institutions* was measured and fixed along with other SDGs that is SDG-1 to SDG-11 and SDG-15; expecting the analysis of the SDG *India Index Baseline Report,* 2018 in this tune will help to frame immediate action plan to achieve the SDGs global agenda by 2030. Along with that, the author tried to grasp the overall

SDGs with the Constitutional provisions of India, that is provisions under the Articles and Schedules of the Indian Constitution, which are linked with the individual SDGs for a holistic understanding of the initiatives of *Peace, Justice and Strong Institutions* (SDG-16) in India has perceiving since adoption of the Indian Constitution.

1.1. The Millennium Development Goals to the Sustainable Development Goals

As we know that, SDGs were born at the United Nations Conference on Sustainable Development in Rio de Janeiro in 2012. The objective was to produce a set of universal goals that meet the urgent environmental, political and economic challenges facing our world. The SDGs replaced the MDGs, which was started a global effort in 2000 to tackle the indignity of poverty. The MDGs established measurable, universally-agreed objectives for tackling extreme poverty and hunger, preventing deadly diseases, and expanding primary education to all children, among other development priorities. For 15 years, the MDGs has drove progress in several important areas, reduced income poverty, provided much needed access to water and sanitation, driving down child mortality and drastically improved the maternal health. The MDGs are also kick-started a global movement for free primary education, inspiring countries to invest in their future generations. Most significantly, the MDGs made huge strides in combatting HIV/AIDS and other treatable diseases such as malaria and tuberculosis (UNDP 2012).

1.2. Achievements of the Millennium Development Goals

As per the report, more than 1 billion people have been lifted out of extreme poverty since 1999 child mortality has dropped by more than half; the number of out of school children has dropped by more than half and HIV/AIDS infections has fell by almost 40 percent since 2000. These legacy and achievements of the MDGs has provided valuable lessons and experience to begin work on the new goals. Because, the jobs are remains unfinished for millions of people around the world. The world leader has thought, it need to go the last mile on end hunger, achieving full gender equality, improving health services and getting every child into school beyond primary. In this regard the SDGs are also an urgent call to shift the world into a more sustainable path than the past.

The SDGs has a bold commitment to finish what the world has started and tackle some of the more pressing challenges which has been facing the contemporary world today. All the 17 SDGs are interconnect, which means, the success in one affects the success for others. Dealing with the threat of climate change impacts how we manage our fragile natural resources, achieving gender equality or better health helps eradicate poverty, and fostering peace and inclusive societies will reduce inequalities and help economies prosper. In short, this is the greatest chance by which we able to improve the life of our future generations.

The SDGs has coincided with another historic agreement reached in 2015 at the COP21 Paris Climate Conference. Together with the Sendai Framework for Disaster Risk Reduction, signed in Japan in March 2015, these agreements has provided a set of common standards and achievable targets to reduce carbon emissions, manage the risks of climate change and natural disasters, and to build back better after a crisis.

In these global circumstances, it may be called, the SDGs are unique in nature, because they cover issues that affect us all. They reaffirm our international commitment to end poverty, permanently, everywhere. They are ambitious in making sure no one is left behind. More importantly, they involve us all to build a more sustainable, safer, more prosperous planet for all humanity (UNDP 2012).

The MDGs has produced the most successful anti-poverty movement in history and will serve as the jumping-off point for the new sustainable development agenda to be adopted this year. The MDG Report 2015 has found that the 15-year effort to achieve the eight aspirational goals set out in the Millennium Declaration in 2000 was largely successful across the globe, while acknowledging shortfalls that remain. The data and analysis presented in the report show that with targeted interventions, sound strategies, adequate resources and political will, even the poorest can make progress. The final MDG report confirms that goal-setting can lift millions of people out of poverty, empower women and girls, improve health and well-being, and provide vast new opportunities for better lives.

The number of people now living in extreme poverty has declined from 1.9 billion in 1990 to 836 million in 2015; the number of people in the working middle class, living on more than $4 a day, nearly tripled between 1991 and 2015. The proportion of undernourished people in the developing regions dropped by almost half since 1990; the number of out-of-school children of primary school age worldwide fell by almost half, to an estimated 57 million in 2015, down from 100 million in 2000; gender parity in primary school has been achieved in the majority of countries. The mortality rate of children under-five was cut by more than half since 1990; since 1990, maternal mortality fell by 45 percent worldwide; over 6.2 million malaria deaths have been averted between

2000 and 2015. New HIV infections fell by approximately 40 percent between 2000 and 2013; by June 2014, 13.6 million people living with HIV were receiving antiretroviral therapy (ART) globally, an immense increase from just 800,000 in 2003. Between 2000 and 2013, tuberculosis prevention, diagnosis and treatment interventions saved an estimated 37 million lives. Worldwide 2.1 billion people have gained access to improved sanitation; globally, 147 countries have met the MDG drinking water target, 95 countries have met the MDG sanitation target and 77 countries have met both. Official development assistance from developed countries increased 66 percent in real terms from 2000 and 2014, reaching $135.2 billion (UNDP 2017).

1.3. The Sustainable Development Goals

The reports has aimed to describe global development in 2015, looking back 15 years at the trends and positive forces during the Millennium Development Goal (MDG) era and assessing the main challenges for the coming 15 years. The 2030 Sustainable Development Agenda is of unprecedented scope and ambition, applicable to all countries, and goes well beyond the MDGs. While poverty eradication, health, education, and food security and nutrition remain priorities, the Sustainable Development Goals (SDGs) comprise a broad range of economic, social and environmental objectives, and has offered the prospect of more peaceful and inclusive societies. Progress towards the MDGs, on the whole, has been remarkable, including, for instance, poverty reduction, education improvements and increased access to safe drinking-water. Progress on the three health goals and targets has also been considerable. Globally, the HIV, tuberculosis (TB) and malaria epidemics were "turned around", child mortality and maternal mortality decreased greatly (53% and 44%, respectively, since 1990), despite falling short of the MDG targets. During the MDG era, many global progress records were set. The MDGs have gone a long way to changing the way we think and talk about the world, shaping the international discourse and debate on development, and have also contributed to major increases in development assistance. However, several limitations of the MDGs have also become apparent, including a limited focus, resulting in verticalization of health and disease programmes in countries, a lack of attention to strengthening health systems, the emphasis on a "one-size-fits-all" development planning approach, and a focus on aggregate targets rather than equity. The 17 goals and 169 targets, including one specific goal for health with 13 targets, of the new development agenda integrate the three dimensions of sustainable development around people, planet, prosperity, peace and partnership. The health goal is broad; *"Ensure healthy lives and promote well-being for all at all ages"*. Health has a central place as a major contributor to and beneficiary of sustainable development policies. There are many linkages between the health goal and other goals and targets; reflecting the integrated approach that is underpinning the SDGs. Universal health coverage (UHC), one of the 13 health goal targets, provides an overall framework for the implementation of a broad and ambitious health agenda in all countries. Monitoring and review of progress will be a critical element of the SDGs. An indicator framework is still being developed and is scheduled to be adopted in 2016. An overview of the SDGs are analysed to justify the cause to MDGs to SDGs. In the following, the author has tried to analyse the magnitudes of individual SDG to drag its immediate relevancies to implement accordingly; unless we will not be in a position to face the future generation with a smile – which is the essence of 'peace'; on which rest of the activities may rest.

1.3.1. SDG-1: No Poverty: Poverty is the socio-economic reflection of the society which allows us to call, lack of basic human needs to survive with dignity. So we have to address the numbers with this feature from each of the societal units for the sake of future generations. Presently, eradicating poverty in all its forms remains one of the greatest challenges facing humanity. While the number of people living in extreme poverty dropped by more than half between 1990 and 2015, too many are still struggling for the most basic human needs.

As of 2015, about 736 million people still lived on less than US$1.90 a day; many lack food, clean drinking water and sanitation. Rapid growth in countries such as China and India has lifted millions out of poverty, but progress has been uneven. Women are more likely to be poor than men because they have less paid work, education, and own less property.

Progress has also been limited in other regions, such as South Asia and sub- Saharan Africa, which account for 80 percent of those living in extreme poverty. New threats brought on by climate change, conflict and food insecurity, mean even more work is needed to bring people out of poverty.

The SDGs are a bold commitment to finish what we has started, and end poverty in all forms and dimensions by 2030. This involves targeting the most vulnerable, increasing basic resources and services, and supporting communities affected by conflict and climate-related disasters.

Globally, 736 million people still live in extreme poverty; 10 percent of the world's population live in extreme poverty, down from 36 percent in 1990; 1.3 billion people live in multidimensional poverty; 50 percent that is half of all people living in poverty are under 18; 1 person in every 10 is extremely poor and 80 percent of people living on less than $1.90 are in South Asia and sub-Saharan Africa (UNDP 2016: SDG 1).

1.3.2. SDG-2: Zero Hunger: Can you imagine a child sipping the breast of a dead mother in the first quarter of 21st century? Here, in the era of digitalization, both are undernourished, the mother is dead and the child is struggling for survival. Although, the number of undernourished people has dropped by almost half in the past two decades because of rapid economic growth and increased agricultural productivity. Many developing countries that used to suffer from famine and hunger can now meet their nutritional needs. Central and East Asia, Latin America and the Caribbean have all made huge progress in eradicating extreme hunger.

Unfortunately, extreme hunger and malnutrition remains a huge barrier to development in many countries. There are 821 million people estimated to be chronically undernourished as of 2017, often as a direct consequence of environmental degradation, drought and biodiversity loss. Over 90 million children under five are dangerously underweight. Undernourishment and severe food insecurity appear to be increasing in almost all regions of Africa, as well as in South America.

The SDGs has aimed to end all forms of hunger and malnutrition by 2030, making sure all people–especially children–have sufficient and nutritious food all year. This involves promoting sustainable agricultural, supporting small-scale farmers and equal access to land, technology and markets. It also requires international cooperation to ensure investment in infrastructure and technology to improve agricultural productivity.

In this regard, the global data explored that the number of undernourished people reached 821 million in 2017; in 2017 Asia accounted for nearly two thirds, 63 percent, of the world's hungry; nearly 151 million children under five, 22 percent, were still stunted in 2017; more than 1 in 8 adults is obese; 1 in 3 women of reproductive age is anaemic and 26 percent of workers are employed in agriculture (UNDP 2016: SDG 2).

1.3.3. SDG-3: Good Health and Well-being: The good health and well-being are varied by man to man, by land, by soil, by source of water, by environment, by economy, by type of work with duration and security, by health care facilities provided and the by the social institutions; and all are interlinked by nature. The world has made great progress against several leading causes of death and disease. Life expectancy has increased dramatically; infant and maternal mortality rates have declined, we've turned the tide on HIV and malaria deaths have halved.

Good health is essential to sustainable development and the 2030 agenda reflects the complexity and interconnectedness of the two. It takes into account widening economic and social inequalities, rapid urbanization, threats to the climate and the environment, the continuing burden of HIV and other infectious diseases, and emerging challenges such as non-communicable diseases. Universal health coverage will be integral to achieving SDG-3, ending poverty and reducing inequalities. Emerging global health priorities not explicitly included in the SDGs, including antimicrobial resistance, also demand action.

But the world is off-track to achieve the health-related SDGs. Progress has been uneven, both between and within countries. There's a 31-year gap between the countries with the shortest and longest life expectancies. In the other side, some countries have made impressive gains, national averages hide that many are being left behind. Multi-sectoral, rights-based and gender-sensitive approaches are essential to address inequalities and to build good health for all.

Globally, at least 400 million people have no basic healthcare, and 40 percent lack social protection; more than 1.6 billion people live in fragile settings where protracted crises, combined with weak national capacity to deliver basic health services, present a significant challenge to global health; by the end of 2017, 21.7 million people living with HIV were receiving antiretroviral therapy, yet more than 15 million people are still waiting for treatment; within every 2 seconds someone aged 30 to 70 years dies prematurely from non-communicable diseases - cardiovascular disease, chronic respiratory disease, diabetes or cancer; 7 million people die every year from exposure to fine particles in polluted air and more than one of every three women have experienced either physical or sexual violence at some point in their life resulting in both short- and long-term consequences for their physical, mental, and sexual and reproductive health (UNDP 2016: SDG 3).

1.3.4. SDG-4: Quality Education: As we know the education is the foundation of a nation and it has the power to accelerate development. Spread of education is depends upon teachers, students, supporting environment and the good as well as wise role of authorities who frame the seeds of education with appropriate methods according with dynamic demands of time. The spread of education enable to solve many of the issues as addressed in the SDGs. Since 2000, there has been enormous progress in achieving the target of universal primary education. The total enrolment rate in developing regions reached 91 percent in 2015, and the worldwide number of children out of school has dropped by almost half. There has also been a dramatic increase in literacy rates, and many more girls are in school than ever before. These are all remarkable successes.

Progress has also been tough in some developing regions due to high levels of poverty, armed conflicts and other emergencies. In Western Asia and North Africa, ongoing armed conflict has seen an increase in the number of children out of school. This is a worrying trend. While Sub-Saharan Africa made the greatest progress in primary school enrolment among all developing regions – from 52 percent in 1990, up to 78 percent in 2012 – large disparities still remain. Children from the poorest households are up to four times more likely to be out of school than those of the richest households. Disparities between rural and urban areas also remain high.

Achieving inclusive and quality education for all is reaffirms the belief that education is one of the most powerful and proven vehicles for sustainable development. This goal ensures that all girls and boys complete free primary and secondary schooling by 2030. It also aims to provide equal access to affordable vocational training, to eliminate gender and wealth disparities, and achieve universal access to a quality higher education.

It has been reported that, the enrolments in primary education in developing countries have reached 91 percent; still, 57 million primary-aged children remain out of school, more than half of them in sub-Saharan Africa; in developing countries, one in four girls is not in school; 50 percent that is about half of all out-of-school children of primary school age live in conflict-affected areas; 103 million youth worldwide lack basic literacy skills, and more than 60 percent of them are women and 6 out of 10 children and adolescents are not achieving a minimum level of proficiency in reading and math UNDP 2016: SDG 4).

1.3.5. SDG-5: Gender Equality: Is the culture of silence is imposed by society or is naturally adopted by women since their girlhood? Whatever the causes of silence of women, is it a healthy practice for overall societal development? Ignorance, various kinds of restrictions, movement and limit them in logical debate are trained since their childhood socialization process. For the sake of dignified healthy future generation, it is the time to restrict its consequences and the call is come from the United Nation's SDG's 5th goal entitled as 'gender equality'. Ending all discrimination against women and girls is not only a basic human right, it's crucial for sustainable future; it is proven that empowering women and girls help economic growth and development at all level.

UNDP has made gender equality as the central to its work and have experienced remarkable progress in the past 20 years. There are more girls in school now compared to 15 years ago, and most regions have reached gender parity in primary education.

But although there are more women than ever in the labour market, there are still large inequalities in some regions, with women systematically denied the same work rights as men. Sexual violence and exploitation, the unequal division of unpaid care and domestic work, and discrimination in public office all remain huge barriers. Climate change and disasters continue to have a disproportionate effect on women and children, as do conflict and migration.

It is vital to give women equal rights land and property, sexual and reproductive health, and to technology and the internet. Today there are more women in public office than ever before, but encouraging more women leaders will help achieve greater gender equality.

Statistically, women earn only 77 cents for every dollar that men get for the same work; 1 in 3 or 35 percent of women have experienced physical and/or sexual violence; women represent just 13 percent of agricultural landholders; almost 750 million women and girls alive today were married before their 18th birthday; two thirds of developing countries have achieved gender parity in primary education and only 24 percent of national parliamentarians were women as of November 2018, a small increase from 11.3 percent in 1995 (UNDP 2016: SDG 5).

1.3.6. SDG-6: Clean Water and Sanitation: Water is counted as the lifeline of civilization for its various use; it is proved in the recorded history of world's rich as well as old civilization and all are based on water connectivity from agriculture, its marketing and communication as well. In other side water is denoted as synonym of life. The availability and purity of the water for healthy life which are also associated with sanitation and good health, which is under threat. Can we imagine a society without the clean water? Water scarcity affects more than 40 percent of people, an alarming figure that is projected to rise as temperatures do. Although 2.1 billion people has improved water sanitation since 1990, dwindling drinking water supplies are affecting every continent. More and more countries are experiencing water stress, and increasing drought and desertification is already worsening these trends. By 2050, it is projected that at least one in four people will suffer recurring water shortages. Safe and affordable drinking water for all by 2030 requires we invest in adequate infrastructure, provide sanitation facilities, and encourage hygiene. Protecting and restoring water-related ecosystems is essential.

Ensuring universal safe and affordable drinking water involves reaching over 800 million people who lack basic services and improving accessibility and safety of services for over two billion. In 2015, 4.5 billion people lacked safely managed sanitation services and 2.3 billion lacked even basic sanitation.

It has been explored that the 71 percent of the global population, 5.2 billion people, had safely-managed drinking water in 2015, but 844 million people still lacked even basic drinking water; 39 percent of the global population, 2.9 billion people, had safe sanitation in 2015, but 2.3 billion people still lacked basic sanitation. 892 million people practiced open defecation; 80 percent of wastewater goes into waterways without adequate treatment; water stress affects more than 2 billion people, with this figure projected to increase; 80 percent of countries have laid the foundations for integrated water resources management and the world has lost 70 percent of its natural wetlands over the last century (UNDP 2016: SDG 6).

1.3.7. SDG-7: Affordable and Clean Energy: Energy is considered as the engine of civilization; the concept of progress was to innovate the components which are enable to generate energy from the natural resource; world demands of energy are increasing according with its population and so called development; now the sustainable development remind us to use the environment or the natural resources as the source of energy by considering the survival of future generation by innovate the way to provide affordable and clean energy to all. Between 2000 and 2016, the number of people with electricity increased from 78 to 87 percent, and the numbers without electricity has dipped to just below one billion; yet as the population continues to grow, so will the demand for cheap energy, and an economy reliant on fossil fuels is creating drastic changes to our climate; investing in solar, wind and thermal power, improving energy productivity, and ensuring energy for all is vital if we are to achieve SDG-7 by 2030. Expanding infrastructure and upgrading technology to provide clean and more efficient energy in all countries will encourage growth and help the environment.

Globally one in 7 people still lacks electricity, and most of them live in rural areas of the developing world; energy is the main contributor to climate change, it produces around 60 percent of greenhouse gases; more efficient energy standards could reduce building and industry electricity consumption by 14 percent; more than 40 percent of the world's population that is 3 billion rely on polluting and unhealthy fuels for cooking; hopefully as of 2015, more than 20 percent of power was generated through renewable sources and the renewable energy sector employed a record 10.3 million people in 2017 (UNDP 2016: SDG 7).

1.3.8. SDG-8: Decent Work and Economic Growth: Here again, we have to start with the essence of quality education; education process must be framed in accordance with the global societal demands and its changes for all. Then the SDG-8's agenda of decent work will be filled and subsequently it will reflect in the economic growth by reducing poverty, hunger, inequalities etc. and increasing investment in health care, innovation and infrastructures as per contemporary demands as well. Over the past 25 years the number of workers living in extreme poverty has declined dramatically, despite the lasting impact of the 2008 economic crisis and global recession. In developing countries, the middle class now makes up more than 34 percent of total employment – a number that has almost tripled between 1991 and 2015.

However, as the global economy continues to recover we are seeing slower growth, widening inequalities, and not enough jobs to keep up with a growing labour force. According to the International Labour Organization, more than 204 million people were unemployed in 2015.

The SDGs promote sustained economic growth, higher levels of productivity and technological innovation. Encouraging entrepreneurship and job creation are keys to this, as are effective measures to eradicate forced labour, slavery and human trafficking. With these targets in mind, the goal is to achieve full and productive employment, and decent work, for all women and men by 2030.

The reports has pointed that, an estimated 172 million people worldwide were without work in 2018 - an unemployment rate of 5 percent; as a result of an expanding labour force, the number of unemployed is projected to increase by 1 million every year and reach 174 million by 2020 and some 700 million workers lived in extreme or moderate poverty in 2018, with less than US$3.20 per day.

Women's participation in the labour force stood at 48 per cent in 2018, compared with 75 percent for men. Around 3 in 5 of the 3.5 billion people in the labour force in 2018 were men. Overall, 2 billion workers were in informal employment in 2016, accounting for 61 per cent of the world's workforce and many more women than men are underutilized in the labour force that is 85 million compared to 55 million (UNDP 2016: SDG 8).

1.3.9. SDG-9: Industry, Innovation and Infrastructure: Considering the tune of SDGs which has framed by the United Nations, for the sake of dignified life for the future generation, we have to redesign the imagination of innovation of scientific, technological as well as industrial development and upgradation in accordance with the sustainable development agenda and developed infrastructures as what it is demanding. Investment in infrastructure and innovation are crucial drivers of economic growth and development. With over half the world population now living in cities, mass transport and renewable energy are becoming ever more important, as are the growth of new industries and information and communication technologies. The technological progress is also key to finding lasting solutions to both economic and environmental challenges, such as providing new jobs and promoting energy efficiency. Promoting sustainable industries and investing in scientific research and innovation are all important ways to facilitate sustainable development.

More than 4 billion people still do not have access to the internet, and 90 percent are from the developing world. Bridging this digital divide is crucial to ensure equal access to information and knowledge, as well as foster innovation and entrepreneurship.

Worldwide, 2.3 billion people lack access to basic sanitation; in some low-income African countries, infrastructure constraints cut businesses' productivity by around 40 percent; 2.6 billion people in developing countries do not have access to constant electricity; more than 4 billion people still do not have access to the internet; 90 percent of them are in the developing world ; the renewable energy sectors currently employ more than 2.3 million people; the number could reach 20 million by 2030 and in developing countries, barely 30 percent of agricultural products undergo industrial processing, compared to 98 percent high-income countries (UNDP 2016: SDG 9).

1.3.10. SDG-10: Reduced Inequalities: Where from the process of reducing inequalities will be start? In a socially stratified society like India, where each and every ascribed social position of people protected by the Constitution; and the incident of undignified remarks and behaviour on using public facilities are taking place even in the highest academic institutions and it mirrored in even in the economic differences as well, named as 'social class'. Income inequality is on the rise, the richest 10 percent have up to 40 percent of global income whereas the poorest

10 percent earn only between 2 to 7 percent. If we take into account population growth inequality in developing countries, inequality has increased by 11 percent. Income inequality has increased in nearly everywhere in recent decades, but at different speeds. It's lowest in Europe and highest in the Middle East.

These widening disparities require sound policies to empower lower income earners, and promote economic inclusion of all regardless of sex, race or ethnicity. Income inequality requires global solutions; this involves improving the regulation and monitoring of financial markets and institutions, encouraging development assistance and foreign direct investment to regions where the need is greatest. Facilitating the safe migration and mobility of people is also considered as key to bridging the widening divide.

Globally, in 2016, 22 percent of global income was received by the top 1 percent compared with 10 percent of income for the bottom 50 percent; in 1980, the top one percent had 16 percent of global income. The bottom 50 percent had 8 percent of income; this kind of economic inequality is largely driven by the unequal ownership of capital. Since 1980, very large transfers of public to private wealth occurred in nearly all countries. The global wealth share of the top 1 percent was 33 percent in 2016. Under "business as usual", the top 1 percent global wealth will reach 39 percent by 2050; women spend, on average, twice as much time on unpaid housework as men and women have as much access to financial services as men in just 60 percent of the countries assessed and to land ownership in just 42 percent of the countries assessed (UNDP 2016: SDG 10).

1.3.11. SDG-11: Sustainable Cities and Communities: Globally the cities are the composed with heterogeneous people with different educational backgrounds, economic class, professions, skills, caste, cultures and religions as well; and it is increasing by population in a limited urban area; this trend forced to widen the urban space to destroy agriculture as well as green fields and the local water land of the adjacent urban areas. These features of growing cities pushed the world leaders to think differently and has produced a global agenda in the SDGs entitled as sustainable cities and communities. The evidence explored that, more than half of population of the world live in cities and has projected that by 2050, two-thirds of all humanity that is 6.5 billion people will be urban inhabitants. Sustainable development cannot be achieved without significantly transforming the way we build and manage our urban spaces; rapid growth of cities has resulted of rising populations and increasing migration has led to a boom in mega-cities, especially in the developing world, and slums are becoming a more significant feature of urban life.

Making cities sustainable means creating career and business opportunities, safe and affordable housing, and building resilient societies and economies. It involves investment in public transport, creating green public spaces, and improving urban planning and management in participatory and inclusive ways.

The global scenario explored that in 2018, 4.2 billion people, 55 percent of the world's population, lived in cities; by 2050, the urban population is expected to reach 6.5 billion; cities occupy just 3 percent of the Earth's land but account for 60 to 80 percent of energy consumption and at least 70 percent of carbon emissions. 828 million people are estimated to live in slums, and the number is rising; in 1990, there were 10 cities with 10 million people or more, by 2014, the number of mega-cities rose to 28, and was expected to reach 33 by 2018. In the future, 9 out of 10 mega-cities will be in the developing world; in the coming decades, 90 percent of urban expansion will be in the developing world and the economic role of cities is significant. They generate about 80 percent of the global GDP (UNDP 2016: SDG 11).

1.3.12. SDG-12: Responsible Consumption and Production: Previously, the necessity of human needs are widely campaign; now the call is for consume as per your needs, so that crisis can be addressed. In other way almost all the production of human needs are somehow produced by using or destroying our own ecology which must retain in a balance position for the present and for the future generation, it is the tune of this global agenda. Achieving economic growth and sustainable development requires that we urgently reduce our ecological footprint by changing the way we are producing and consume goods and resources. Agriculture is the biggest user of water worldwide, and irrigation now claims close to 70 percent of all freshwater for human use. The efficient management of our shared natural resources, and the way we dispose of toxic waste and pollutants, are important targets to achieve this goal. Encouraging industries, businesses and consumers to recycle and reduce waste is equally important, as has supporting the developing countries to move towards more sustainable patterns of consumption by 2030.

A large share of the world population is still consuming far too little to meet even their basic needs. Halving the per capita of global food waste at the retailer and consumer levels is also important for creating more efficient production and supply chains. This can help with food security, and shift us towards a more resource efficient economy.

Globally 1.3 billion tonnes of food is wasted every year, while almost 2 billion people go hungry or undernourished; the food sector accounts for around 22 percent of total greenhouse gas emissions, largely from the conversion of forests into farmland. Globally, 2 billion people are overweight or obese; only 3 percent of the world's water is fresh which is drinkable and humans are using it faster than nature can replenish it; if people everywhere switched to energy efficient lightbulbs, the world would save US$120 billion annually and one-fifth of the world's final energy consumption in 2013 was from renewable sources (UNDP 2016: SDG 12).

1.3.13. SDG-13: Climate Action: Till the day the world unable to explore any way to restore the changed climate;. it is stigmatized as the irresponsible consumption and production for profit and luxury of the world civilization. There is no country that is not experiencing the drastic effects of climate change. Greenhouse gas emissions are more than 50 percent higher than in 1990. Global warming is causing long-lasting changes to our climate system, which threatens irreversible consequences if we do not act.

The annual average economic losses from climate-centric disasters are in the hundreds of billions of dollars. This is not to mention the human impact of geo-physical disasters, which are 91 percent climate-centric, and which between 1998 and 2017 killed 1.3 million people, and left 4.4 billion injured. The goal aims to mobilize US$100 billion annually by 2020 to address the needs of developing countries to both adapt to climate change and invest in low-carbon development.

Supporting vulnerable regions will directly has contributed not only to SDG-13 but also to the other SDGs. These actions must also go hand in hand with efforts to integrate disaster risk measures, sustainable natural resource management, and human security into national development strategies. It is still possible, with strong political will, increased investment, and using existing technology, to limit the increase in global mean temperature to 2^0C above pre-industrial levels, aiming at 1.5°C, but this requires urgent and ambitious collective action.

Globally, as of 2017 humans are estimated to have caused approximately 1.0°C of global warming above pre-industrial levels: the Sea levels have risen by about 20 cm that is 8 inches since 1880 and are projected to rise another 30 to 122 cm or 1 to 4 feet by 2100. To limit warming to 1.5C, global net CO2 emissions must drop by 45% between 2010 and 2030, and reach net zero around 2050; climate pledges under The Paris Agreement cover only one third of the emissions reductions needed to keep the world below 2°C. Bold climate action could trigger at least US$26 trillion in economic benefits by 2030 and the energy sector alone will create around 18 million more jobs by 2030, focused specifically on sustainable energy (UNDP 2016: SDG 13).

1.3.14. SDG-14: Life below Water: Livelihood as well as the economic activities of the most of the marginal people are based on water by performing fishing and agricultural production. The irresponsible consumption and production for profit and luxury along with changed climate changed the economic fertility of the dependents of these areas with its chemistry. The world's oceans and their temperature, chemistry, currents and life – has driven global systems that make the Earth habitable for humankind. How we manage this vital resource is essential for humanity as a whole, and to counter balance the effects of climate change. Over three billion people depend on marine and coastal biodiversity for their livelihoods. However, today we are seeing 30 percent of the world's fish stocks overexploited, reaching below the level at which they can produce sustainable yields.

Oceans also absorb about 30 percent of the carbon dioxide produced by humans, and we are seeing a 26 percent rise in ocean acidification since the beginning of the industrial revolution. Marine pollution, an overwhelming majority of which comes from land-based sources, is reaching alarming levels, with an average of 13,000 pieces of plastic litter to be found on every square kilometre of ocean. This SDG has aimed to sustainably manage and protect marine and coastal ecosystems from pollution, as well as address the impacts of ocean acidification. Enhancing conservation and the sustainable use of ocean-based resources through international law will also help mitigate some of the challenges facing our oceans.

Globally, the ocean covers three quarters of the Earth's surface and represents 99 percent of the living space on the planet by volume; the ocean contains nearly 200,000 identified species, but actual numbers may lie in the millions; as much as 40 percent of the ocean is heavily affected by pollution, depleted fisheries, loss of coastal habitats and other human activities; the ocean absorbs about 30 percent of carbon dioxide produced by humans, buffering the impacts of global warming; more than 3 billion people depend on marine and coastal biodiversity for their livelihoods and the market value of marine and coastal resources and industries is estimated at US$3 trillion per year, about 5 percent of global GDP (UNDP 2016: SDG 14).

1.3.15. SDG-15: Life on Land: The dignified living is depends on the uses of land; degradation of it has produced unemployment to food crisis as well. The agenda of reduce hunger and poverty and health and wellbeing are very much liked with this agenda and the agenda also has reflected in climate action. Human life is depends on the earth as much as the ocean for our sustenance and livelihoods. Plant life provides 80 percent of our human diet, and we rely on agriculture as an important economic resource and means of development. Forests account for 30 percent of the earth's surface, providing vital habitats for millions of species and important sources for clean air and water; as well as being crucial for combating climate change.

Today we are seeing unprecedented land degradation, and the loss of arable land at 30 to 35 times the historical rate. Drought and desertification is also on the rise each year, amounting to the loss of 12 million hectares and affects poor communities globally. Of the 8,300 animal breeds known, 8 percent are extinct and 22 percent are at risk of extinction.

The SDG-15 has aimed to conserve and restore the use of terrestrial ecosystems such as forests, wetlands, drylands and mountains by 2030. Halting deforestation is also vital to mitigating the impact of climate change. Urgent action must be taken to reduce the loss of natural habitats and biodiversity which are part of our common heritage.

Globally, around 1.6 billion people depend on forests for their livelihoods; forests are home to more than 80 percent of all terrestrial species of animals, plants and insects; 2.6 billion people depend directly on agriculture for their livelihoods; nature based climate solutions can contribution about a third of the CO2 reductions needed by 2030; the value of ecosystems to human livelihoods and well-being is $US125 trillion per year and mountain regions provide 60 to 80 percent of the earth's fresh water (UNDP 2016: SDG 15).

1.3.16. SDG-16: Peace, Justice and Strong Institutions: The debate on the issue may go on, that the, effective governance can produce efficient executives or the effective executives can produce efficient governance; but for the sake of stable society, which is one among other basic criteria of sustainable development, to uphold peace, justice and strong institutions of its own is depends on effective governance along with effective as well as efficient executives of any country; its elements must be well established as well as decentralized. As we know, without peace, stability, human rights, and effective governance based on the rule of law we cannot hope for sustainable development. We live in a world that is increasingly divided. Some regions enjoy sustained peace, security and prosperity, while others fall into seemingly endless cycles of conflict and violence. This is by no means inevitable and must be addressed.

High levels of armed violence and insecurity have a destructive impact on a country's development, affecting economic growth and often resulting in long-standing grievances that can last for generations. Sexual violence, crime, exploitation and torture are also prevalent where there is conflict or no rule of law, and countries must take measures to protect those most at risk.

The SDG-16 has aimed to significantly reduce all forms of violence, and work with governments and communities to find lasting solutions to conflict and insecurity. Strengthening the rule of law and promoting human rights is keys to this process, as is reducing the flow of illicit arms and strengthening the participation of developing countries in the institutions of global governance.

Globally, by the end of 2017, 68.5 million people had been forcibly displaced by persecution, conflict, violence or human rights violations; there are at least 10 million stateless people who have been denied nationality and its related rights; corruption, bribery, theft and tax evasion cost developing countries US$1.26 trillion per year; 49 countries lack laws protecting women from domestic violence; in 46 countries, women now hold more than 30 percent of seats in at least one chamber of national government and 1 billion people cannot prove who they are, and are legally 'invisible'. This includes an estimated 625 million children who were not registered at birth (UNDP 2016: SDG 16).

1.3.17. SDG-17: Partnerships for the Goals: Cooperation, assistance and sharing (CAS) are the fundamental responsibilities of all the stakeholder in all respect which has been included in the SDGs within and between the countries to achieve its targets and indicators as stated by United Nations. The SDGs can only be realized with strong global partnerships and cooperation. Official Development Assistance (ODA) remained steady but below target, at US$147 billion in 2017. While humanitarian crises brought on by conflict or natural disasters continue to demand more financial resources and aid. Many countries also require Official Development Assistance to encourage growth and trade.

The world is more interconnected than ever. Improving access to technology and knowledge is an important way to share ideas and foster innovation. Coordinating policies to help developing countries manage their debt, as well as promoting investment for the least developed, is vital for sustainable growth and development.

The goals aim to enhance North-South and South-South cooperation by supporting national plans to achieve all the targets. Promoting international trade, and helping developing countries increase their exports is all part of achieving a universal rules-based and equitable trading system that is fair and open and benefits all.

The UN Conference on Trade and Development (UNCTAD) says achieving SDGs will require US$5 trillion to $7 trillion in annual investment; total Official Development Assistance reached US$147.2 billion in 2017; in 2017, international remittances totalled US$613 billion; 76 percent of it went to developing countries; in 2016, 6 countries met the international target to keep Official Development Assistance at or above 0.7 percent of gross national income; sustainable and responsible investments represent high-potential sources of capital for SDGs; as of 2016, US$18.2 trillion was invested in this asset class and the bond market for sustainable business is growing. In 2018 global green bonds reached US$155.5billion, up 78 percent from previous year (UNDP 2016: SDG 17).

There is no confusion or debate about aiming or selecting goals of the SDGs, the SDGs goals are resolved from the experiences of the MDGs. The priorities are given on the emerging issues for sustainable development as well as way of implementation. The tools and methods of work has selected as the goal of SDGs; but almost all the SDG's goals are somehow interlinked with each other; so the achievement or the success of individual SDG's goal to be reflected or influenced the linked SDG or SDGs. So, methodologically all the SDGs are varied; so how the success to be measured? From this perspective we need a 'unit' to measure the SDG's achievement or success. The SDGs sets SDG-17 that is, '*Partnerships for the Goals*'. That is, SDGs can only be realized with strong global partnerships and cooperation; and it depends on the SDG-16 that is, '*Peace, Justice and Strong Institutions*'; and without peace, stability, human rights, and effective governance based on the rule of law, we cannot hope for sustainable development. We live in a world that is increasingly divided and stratified. Some regions enjoy sustained peace, security and prosperity, while others fall into seemingly endless cycles of conflict and violence. This is by no means inevitable and must be addressed. To address the SDG-16 and 17, a country must have a liberal legal support from which a country can address for the tools of the strong global and local partnerships and cooperation as well as the peace, stability, human rights, and effective governance. India have it, in the next section the author is discussing about the peace, justice and strong institution to analyse the SDGs achievement, that is expected performance, actual performance and performance differences, when SDG–16, *Peace, Justice and Strong Institutions* was measured and fixed along with other SDGs that is SDG-1 to SDG-11 and SDG-15; expecting the analysis of the SDG *India Index Baseline Report,* 2018 in this tune will help to framing immediate action plan to be needed to achieving the SDGs global agenda by 2030. Along with that, the author has tried to grasp the overall SDGs with the Constitutional provisions of India that is the Articles and Schedules of the Constitution, which are linked with the individual SDGs for a holistic understanding of the initiatives of *Peace, Justice and Strong Institutions* (SDG–16) in India is perceiving.

Chapter – II

The Peace as the Key to Achieve the Sustainable Development Goals

Generally the word, peace is a concept of societal friendship and harmony in the absence of hostility and violence. In a social sense, peace is commonly used to mean a lack of conflict and freedom from fear of violence between individuals or heterogeneous groups. Throughout the history world leaders have used peace making diplomacy to establish a certain type of behavioural restraint that has resulted in the establishment of regional peace or economic growth through various forms of agreements or peace treaties. Such behavioural restraint has often resulted in the reduction of conflicts, greater economic interactivity, and consequently substantial prosperity. The avoidance of war or violent hostility can be the result of thoughtful active listening and communication that enables greater genuine mutual understanding and therefore compromise. Leaders often has benefited tremendously from the prestige of peace talks and treaties that can result in substantially has enhanced popularity.

"Psychological peace", such as a peaceful thinking and emotions are perhaps less well defined yet often a necessary precursor to establishing "behavioural peace." Peaceful behaviour sometimes results from a "peaceful inner disposition." Some have expressed the belief that peace can be initiated with a certain quality of inner tranquillity that does not depend upon the uncertainties of daily life for its existence. In this regard, here it would be justified by quoting the words of Dalai Lama *"World peace must develop from inner peace. Peace is not just mere absence of violence. Peace is, I think, the manifestation of human compassion (*Dalai Lama 2018)*"*. The acquisition of such a "peaceful internal disposition" for oneself and others can contribute to resolving of otherwise seemingly irreconcilable competing interests. Because psychological peace can be important to behavioural peace, leaders sometimes deescalate conflicts through compliments and generosity. Small gestures of rhetorical and actual generosity have been shown in psychological research to often result in larger levels of reciprocal generosity and even virtuous circles of generosity. Such benevolent selfless behaviour can eventually become a pattern that may become a lasting basis for improved relations between individuals and groups of people. Peace talks often start without preconditions and preconceived notions, because they are more than just negotiating opportunities. They place attention on peace itself over and above what may have been previously perceived as the competing needs or interests of separate individuals or parties to elicit peaceful feelings and therefore produce benevolent behavioural results. Peace talks are sometimes also uniquely important learning opportunities for the individuals or parties involved.

Epistemologically, the Anglo-French term *Pes* itself comes from the Latin *pax*, meaning "peace, compact, agreement, treaty of peace, tranquillity, absence of hostility, harmony." The English word came into use in various personal greetings from c.1300 as a translation of the Hebrew word shalom, which, according to Jewish theology, comes from a Hebrew verb meaning 'to be complete, whole' (Jeff A. Benner 2018). Although 'peace' is the usual translation, however, it is an incomplete one, because *'shalom,'* which is also cognate with the Arabic *salaam*, has multiple other meanings in addition to peace, including justice, good health, safety, well-being, prosperity, equity, security, good fortune, and friendliness, as well as simply the greetings, "hello" and "goodbye". At a personal level, peaceful behaviours are kind, considerate, respectful, just, and tolerant of others' beliefs and behaviours — tending to manifest goodwill. The term-'peace' originates most recently from the Anglo-French *pes,* and the Old French *pais*, meaning "peace, reconciliation, silence, agreement" (Etymonline 2015).

This latter understanding of peace can also pertain to an individual's introspective sense or concept of her or himself, as in being "at peace" in one's own mind, as found in European references from c.1200. The early English term is also used in the sense of "quiet", reflecting calm, serene, and meditative approaches to family or group relationships that avoid quarrelling and seek tranquillity — an absence of disturbance or agitation.

In many languages, the word for peace is also used as a greeting or a farewell, for example the Hawaiian word *aloha*, as well as the Arabic word *salaam*. In English the word peace is occasionally used as a farewell, especially for the dead, as in the phrase *rest in peace*.

Wolfgang Dietrich in his research project which led to the book *The Palgrave International Handbook of Peace Studies* (Dietrich 2011) maps the different meanings of peace in different languages and from different regions across the world. Later, in his *Interpretations of Peace in History and Culture* (Dietrich Wolfgang 2012), he grouped the different meanings of peace into five peace families: Energetic/Harmony, Moral/Justice, Modern/Security, Postmodern/Truth, and Trans-rational, a synthesis of the positive sides of the four previous families and the society.

So, the word peace have individual, societal, national to transnational implications. Literally the word composed of justice, good health, safety, well-being, prosperity, equity, security, good fortune, and friendliness, as well as simply the greetings, "hello" and "goodbye". Here, the author trying to restricted the analyses, in tune, that is role of the Government of India to achieve peace in the individual as well as the societal level through the mirror SDG India Index Baseline Report, 2018.

Peace is intended and has to achieve by variety of cost to the individual to the international level. In the contemporary world, generally the word peace is an expected situation of equilibrium to an individual, to a country and to the world; at the same way it is a dynamic in nature. Because, after offering a common environment, resources and time, many of the individuals and the nations are unable to meet the peace as was targeted and it reflected in the world system. In this regard the head of the family to the head of nations are framing plans after plans to achieve peace within their limitations. By searching the barriers of achieving the peace; pointed the targets, methods and time – the head of the nations committed to increase overall human wellbeing by 2030. So, expected that, the coming generation will lead a stress less as well as a decent life in all respect with dignity irrespective of their root of origin – this tune of leading life was farmed in the United Nations General Assembly Summit in September, 2015 with the presence of 193 Member States. The summit has resolved with a vision towards poverty eradication, quality education; decent work, reduce inequality, gender equality, human health and sanitation to urban settlements and to safeguarding the global ecosystems on which humanity depends for its survival by 2030, literally as well as popularly the approach known as Sustainable Development Goals (SDGs). The SDGs are a bold universal set of 17 Goals and 169 targets to help organise and streamline development actions for greater achievement of human wellbeing, while leaving no one behind – by 2030. They are a part of transforming our world: the 2030 Agenda for Sustainable Development. No doubt, this is an international social inclusion approach of achieving peace by the people of the people and for the people from the marginalized in all forms.

SDGs have light as well as shade of its own approach. Basically, it offered opportunities as well as challenges for developing countries, to bring long-time, the developing countries bound to meet a high cost to implement the approach. Because, the socio-anthropological evidences of different nations are different in historical experiences, demographic compositions, cultural traditions, mode of governances and its polity and base of economy are varied. By considering such variations of the 193 Member States committed to achieve a single headed agenda entitled SDG composed by a set of 17 goals and 169 targets for greater achievement of human wellbeing by 2030. In this approach, India played a prominent role in the formulation of SDGs and much of the country's National Development Agenda is mirrored in the SDGs (NITI *Aayog* 2018). This section will analyse India in general through the mirror of world views on peace.

2.1. The World Views of Peace

The famous book on peace study by Johan Galtung (Galtung 1967) entitled *Theories of Peace - A Synthetic Approach to Peace Thinking* has published by International Peace Research Institute, Oslo. The book is based on comprehensive and relatively exhaustive survey of thinking about peace. In the introduction of the book he explored three directions of "peace".

First of all there is the old idea of peace as a synonym for stability or equilibrium. This conception of peace also refers to internal states of a human being, the person who is at peace with himself. It also covers the "law and order" concept, in other words the idea of a predictable social order even if this order is brought about by means of force and the threat of force. In general this concept does not exclude violence, since the soldier can have peace with himself on the battlefield.

Then there is the idea of peace as the absence of organized collective violence, in other words violence between major human groups; particularly nations, but also between classes and between racial and ethnic groups because of the magnitude internal wars can have. We shall refer to this type of peace as negative peace. …. (Galtung 1967).

And then there is a third concept of peace which is less clearly defined. This is peace as a synonym for all other good things in the world community, particularly cooperation and integration between human groups, with less emphasis on the absence of violence. We shall refer to it as positive peace (Galtung 1967).

Again, *Positive Peace Report 2018: Analysing the Factors that Sustain Peace* (IEP 2018) published by Institute for Economics and Peace (IEP) generalized few points from the findings of their initiative these are as:-

Positive Peace is defined as the attitudes, institutions and structures that create and sustain peaceful societies; these same factors also lead to many other positive outcomes that society feels are important, such as economic strength, resilience and well-being; therefore, positive peace creates the optimum environment for human potential to flourish; the most peaceful countries in the world perform strongly on all eight pillars of positive peace; high positive peace countries are more likely to maintain stability, adapt, and recover from shocks as they overcome their challenges; countries that are high in positive peace are more likely to maintain high levels of peace and the level of positive peace is a country's best long-term indicator of how peaceful a country is likely to be.

2.2. The Pillars of the Peace

Institute for Economics and Peace (IEP) has explored eight key factors, or pillars, that comprise positive peace, these are:

2.2.1. Well-functioning Government: A well-functioning government delivers high-quality public and civil services, engenders trust and participation, demonstrates political stability and upholds the rule of law.

2.2.2. Sound Business Environment: The strength of economic conditions as well as the formal institutions that support the operation of the private sector. Business competitiveness and economic productivity are both associated with the most peaceful countries.

2.2.3. Equitable Distribution of Resources: Peaceful countries tend to ensure equity in access to resources such as education, health and, to a lesser extent, equity in income distribution.

2.2.4. Acceptance of the Rights of Others: Peaceful countries often have formal laws that guarantee basic human rights and freedoms and the informal social and cultural norms that relate to behaviours of citizens.

2.2.5. Good Relations with Neighbours: Peaceful relations with other countries are as important as good relations between groups within a country. Countries with positive external relations are more peaceful and tend to be more politically stable, have better functioning governments, are regionally integrated and have lower levels of organised internal conflict.

2.2.6. Free Flow of Information: Free and independent media disseminates information in a way that leads to greater knowledge and helps individuals; business and civil society make better decisions. This leads to better outcomes and more rational responses in times of crisis.

2.2.7. High Levels of Human Capital: A skilled human capital base reflects the extent to which societies educate citizens and promote the development of knowledge, thereby improving economic productivity, care for the young, political participation and social capital.

2.2.8. Low Levels of Corruption: In societies with high levels of corruption, resources are inefficiently allocated, often leading to a lack of funding for essential services and civil unrest. Low corruption can enhance confidence and trust in institutions (IEP 2018).

From the above perspective of 'peace', in the next section I will try to touch the spirit of 'peace' making initiatives that already India performed and have.

2.3. Peace – the Physical and Social Components in India

Global geography map pointed that, India situated in the South Asia, institutionally known as the Republic of India 7th largest by area that is 3,287,263km^2 ; 2nd population with more than 1.3 billion and the world's largest along with most popular democracy in the world. Territorially the country bounded by the Indian Ocean on the south, the Arabian Sea on the southwest, and the Bay of Bengal on the southeast, it shares land borders with Pakistan to the west; China, Nepal, and Bhutan to the northeast; and Bangladesh and Myanmar to the east. In the Indian Ocean, India is in the vicinity of Sri Lanka and the Maldives and Andaman and Nicobar Islands share a maritime border with Thailand and Indonesia.

Historically, the country was the home to the urban Indus Valley Civilisation of the 3rd millennium BCE. In the following millennium, the oldest scriptures associated with Hinduism began to be composed. Social stratification, based on caste, emerged in the first millennium BCE and the Buddhism and Jainism arose. Early political consolidations took place under the *Maurya* and *Gupta* empires; later peninsular Middle Kingdoms influenced cultures as far as Southeast Asia. In the medieval era, Judaism, Zoroastrianism, Christianity, and Islam arrived, and Sikhism emerged, all adding to the region's diverse culture. Much of the north fell to the Delhi Sultanate; the south was united under the *Vijayanagara* Empire. The economy expanded in the 17th century in the Mughal Empire. In the mid-18th century, the subcontinent came under British East India Company rule, and in the mid-19th under British Crown rule. A nationalist movement emerged in the late 19th century, which later, under Mahatma Gandhi, was noted for nonviolent resistance and led to India's independence in 1947.

After the independence in 1947, the administrative institutions of India are a federation with a parliamentary system has been governed under the Constitution of India, which serves as the country's supreme legal document. It is a constitutional republic and representative democracy, in which "majority rule is tempered by minority rights protected by law". Federalism in India defines the power distribution between the union, or central, government and the states as well as union territories. The government abides by constitutional checks and balances. The Constitution of India, which came into effect on 26 January 1950 (Metcalf 2006), states in its preamble that India is sovereign, socialist, secular, democratic republic (Dutt 1998). India's form of government, traditionally described as "quasi-federal" with a strong centre and weak states (Wheare 1980) has grown increasingly federal since the late 1990s as a result of political, economic, and social changes (Sinha 2004), (Echeverri-Gent 2002).

2.4. Functioning of the Government of India

The Government of India comprises three Institutional branches, namely executive, legislature and judiciary -

2.4.1. Executive: The President of India is the ceremonial head of state (B. K. Sharma 2007), 2007) who is elected indirectly for a five-year term by an electoral college comprising members of national and state legislatures (B. K. Sharma 2007), (Gledhill 1970). The Prime Minister of India is the head of government and exercises most executive power (R. Sharma 1950). Appointed by the president (Sinha 2004), the prime minister is by convention supported by the party or political alliance having a majority of seats in the lower house of parliament (R. Sharma 1950). The executive of the Indian government consists of the president, the vice president, and the Union Council of Ministers - with the cabinet being its executive committee - headed by the prime minister. Any minister holding a portfolio must be a member of one of the houses of parliament (B. K. Sharma 2007). In the Indian parliamentary system, the executive is subordinate to the legislature; the prime minister and his or her council are directly responsible to the lower house of the parliament. The civil servants act as permanent executives and all decisions of the executive are implemented by them.

2.4.2. Legislature: The legislature of India is the bicameral parliament. Operating under a Westminster-style parliamentary system, it comprises an upper house called the Rajya Sabha or the Council of States and a lower house called the Lok Sabha or the House of the People (Gledhill 1970). The Rajya Sabha is a permanent body of 245 members who serve staggered six-year terms. Most are elected indirectly by the state and union territorial legislatures in numbers proportional to their state's share of the national population. All of the Lok Sabha's 545 members are directly elected by popular vote; they represent single-member constituencies for five-year terms. The remaining two members are nominated by the president from among the Anglo-Indian community, in case the president decides that they are not adequately represented (B. K. Sharma 2007).

2.4.3. Judiciary: India has a three-tier unitary independent judiciary comprising the Supreme Court, headed by the Chief Justice of India, 24 High Courts, and a large number of trial courts (Neuborne 2003). The Supreme Court has original jurisdiction over cases involving fundamental rights and over disputes between states and the centre and has appellate jurisdiction over the high courts. It has the power to both strike down union or state laws which contravene the constitution (Sripati 1998), and invalidate any government action it deems unconstitutional (Pylee 2003).

India is a federal union comprising 29 states and 7 union territories (Library of Congress 2004). All states, as well in addition to the union territories of Puducherry and the National Capital Territory of Delhi, have elected legislatures and governments following on the Westminster system of governance. The remaining five union territories are directly ruled by the centre through appointed administrators. In 1956, under the States Reorganisation Act, states were reorganised on a linguistic basis. Since then, their structure has remained largely unchanged. Each state or union territory is further divided into administrative districts. The districts are further divided into tehsils and ultimately into villages.

2.5. Economy and Business Environment of India

Economically India is fast growing and one among the world developing countries. According to the International Monetary Fund (IMF), the Indian economy in 2017 was nominally worth US$2.611 trillion; it is the 6th largest economy by market exchange rates, and is, at US$9.459 trillion, the 3rd largest by purchasing power parity, or PPP (Business Standard 2020). With its average annual GDP growth rate of 5.8% over the past two decades, and reaching 6.1% during 2011–12, India is one of the world's fastest-growing economies (Nayak, Goldar and Agrawal 2010). However, The International Monetary Fund (IMF) data shows that India became the world's fifth-largest economy in 2019, surpassing the UK and France. The latest IMF data, however, puts India back in the sixth position in 2020, and further down to no 7 in 2021 (Business Standard, 2020). Until 1991, all Indian governments followed protectionist policies that were influenced by socialist economics. Widespread state intervention and regulation largely walled the economy off from the outside world. An acute balance of payments crisis in 1991 forced the nation to liberalise its economy (Wolpert 2003). Over the past two decades, India has moved away from its former dirigiste model and become a market-based economy. This process started in the mid-1980s and gathered substantial momentum at the beginning of the 1990s (OECD 2007). Since then it has slowly moved towards a free-market system by emphasising both foreign trade and direct investment inflows (Gargan 1992). India has been a member of WTO since 1st January 1995 (WTO 2016).

2.5.1. Labour Force in India: Contemporary India is a homeland of all round skilled work force. The 471.7-million-worker Indian labour force is the world's 2nd largest, as of 2020 (The World Bank 2021). The service sector has makes up 55.6% of GDP, the industrial sector 26.3% and the agricultural sector 18.1%. India's foreign exchange remittances of US$70 billion in 2014, the largest in the world, contributed to its economy by 25 million Indians working in foreign countries (Sherani 2015). Major agricultural products include rice, wheat, oilseed, cotton, jute, tea, sugarcane, and potatoes. Major industries include textiles, telecommunications, chemicals, pharmaceuticals, biotechnology, food processing, steel, transport equipment, cement, mining, petroleum, machinery, and software. The integration of domestic economy through the twin channels of trade and capital flows has seen acceleration over the last two decades as India's GDP reached Rs. 203.39 trillion (US$ 2.88 trillion) in 2019–20 (Provisional estimates at current prices). Simultaneously, the per capita income also nearly trebled during these years. India's trade and external sector had a significant impact on the GDP growth as well as expansion in per capita income (IBEF 2021). In 2008, India's share of world trade was 1.68% and estimated that India will be 5% share of global trade by 2020 (The Times of India 2009). In 2011, India was the world's 10th largest importer and the 19th largest exporter. Major exports include petroleum products, textile goods, jewellery, software, engineering goods, chemicals, and leather manufactures. Major imports include crude oil, machinery, gems, fertiliser, and chemicals. Between 2001 and 2011, the contribution of petrochemical and engineering goods to total exports grew from 14% to 42% (The Economist 2011). India was the 2nd largest textile exporter after China in the world in the calendar year 2013.

Averaging an economic growth rate of 7.5% for several years prior to 2007, India has more than doubled its hourly wage rates during the first decade of the 21st century. Some 431 million Indians have left poverty since 1985; India's middle classes are projected to number around 580 million by 2030 (*Bonner 2010*). Though ranking 51st in global competitiveness, India ranks 17th in financial market sophistication, 24th in the banking sector, 44th in business sophistication, and 39th in innovation, ahead of several advanced economies, as of 2010 (Schwab 2010). With 7 of the world's top 15 information technology outsourcing companies based in India, the country is viewed as the second-most favourable outsourcing destination after the United States, as of 2009 (Niraj 2009). India's consumer market, the world's 7th largest, is expected to become 5th largest by 2030. The other major spending force in India's new consumer market is the global Indians, earning more than 1 million rupees ($21,882, or $118,000, taking into account the cost of living). These are senior corporate executives, large business owners, high-end professionals, politicians and big agricultural-land owners. Today there are just 1.2 million global Indian households accounting for some 2 trillion rupees in spending power. But a new breed of ferociously upwardly mobile Indians is emerging—young graduates of India's top colleges who can command large salaries from Indian and foreign multinationals. Their tastes are indistinguishable from those of prosperous young Westerners—many own high-end luxury cars and wear designer clothes, employ maids and full-time cooks, and regularly vacation abroad. By 2025, there will be 9.5 million Indians in this class and their spending power will hit 14.1 trillion rupees—20 percent of total Indian consumption (Diana 2007). However, hardly 2% of Indians pay income taxes. The number of taxpayers in India is reported 1.46 crore, as confirmed by the Central Board of Direct Taxes (CBDT) in a tweet. This is a small number when you take the total population of 130 crore into perspective. CBDT further clarified that one crore taxpayer reported income between the range of Rs 5-10 lakh, while only 46 lakh reported over Rs 10 lakh (Sharma 2021).

2.5.2. Consumer Market in India: According to a 2011 PricewaterhouseCoopers (PwC) report, the world economy could more than double in size by 2050, for outstripping population growth, due to continued technology-driven productivity improvement. As a result, six of the seven largest economies in the world are projected to be emerging economies in 2050 led by China 1st, India 2nd and Indonesia 4th (PWC

2017). India's GDP at purchasing power parity could overtake that of the United States by 2045. During the next four decades, Indian GDP is expected to grow at an annualised average of 8%, making it potentially the world's fastest-growing major economy until 2050. The report highlights key growth factors: a young and rapidly growing working-age population; growth in the manufacturing sector because of rising education and engineering skill levels; and sustained growth of the consumer market driven by a rapidly growing middle-class. The World Bank cautions that, for India to achieve its economic potential, it must continue to focus on public sector reform, transport infrastructure, agricultural and rural development, removal of labour regulations, education, energy security, and public health and nutrition.

According to the Worldwide Cost of Living Report 2017 released by the Economist Intelligence Unit (EIU) which was created by comparing more than 400 individual prices across 160 products and services, four of the cheapest cities of the world were in India; these are Bangalore 3rd, Chennai 6th, Mumbai 7th and New Delhi 10th (The Economist 2017).

2.5.3. Industries of India: India's telecommunication industry, the world's fastest-growing, added 227 million subscribers during the period 2010–11 and after the third quarter of 2017, India surpassed the US to become the second largest smartphone market in the world after China (Khan 2017).

The Indian automotive industry is the world's 2nd fastest growing, increased domestic sales by 26% during 2009–10 and exports by 36% during 2008–09 (Express India 2009). India's capacity to generate electrical power is 300 gigawatts, of which 42 gigawatts is renewable. At the end of 2011, the Indian IT industry employed 2.8 million professionals, generated revenues close to US$100 billion equalling 7.5% of Indian GDP and contributed 26% of India's merchandise exports.

In recent years, 13 out of 23 industry groups in the manufacturing sector shows positive growth in India. India's industrial production (base year 2011-12=100) improved 4.3% in July 2019, while showing acceleration in growth from four-month low of 1.2% in June 2019. However, the industrial production growth for June 2019 has been revised downwards to 1.2% from 2.0% as reported provisionally.

The manufacturing sector output rose 4.2%, while showing improvement in growth from 0.2% increase in June 2019. The mining sector production growth also improved to 4.9% in July 2019. On the other hand, the electricity generation growth has moderated to four-month low of 4.8% in July 2019.

As per the use-based classification, the output of capital goods continued to decline for seventh straight month at 7.1% in July 2019, while the output of intermediate goods improved at record high pace of 13.9% for current base year data in July 2019 driving overall industrial production growth. The infrastructure/ construction goods growth rebounded 2.1%, while the output of primary goods also rose at improved pace of 3.5%. Within the consumer durables, the output of consumer non-durables increased 8.3%, but that of consumer durables dipped 2.7% in July 2019 (Business Standard 2019).

2.6. International Relations and Strategy of India

India maintain a good relation with other countries to maintain world peace. Since its independence in 1947, India has maintained cordial relations with most nations. In the 1950s, it strongly supported decolonisation in Africa and Asia has played a lead role in the Non-Aligned Movement (Rothermund 2000). In the late 1980s, the Indian military twice intervened abroad at the invitation of neighbouring countries; a peace-keeping operation in Sri Lanka between 1987 and 1990; and an armed intervention to prevent a 1988 coup *d'état* attempt in the Maldives. India has tense relations with neighbouring Pakistan; the two nations have gone to war four times: in 1947, 1965, 1971, and 1999. Three of these wars were fought over the disputed territory of Kashmir, while the fourth, the 1971 war, followed from India's support for the independence of Bangladesh (Gilbert 2002). After waging the 1962 Sino-Indian War and the 1965 war with Pakistan, India pursued close military and economic ties with the Soviet Union; by the late 1960s, the Soviet Union was its largest arms supplier (S. R. Sharma 1999).

Aside from ongoing special relationship with Russia (Times Now News 2018), India has wide-ranging defence relations with Israel and France. In recent years, it has played key roles in the South Asian Association for Regional Cooperation (SAARC) and the World Trade Organization (WTO). The nation has provided 100,000 military and police personnel to serve in 35 UN peace-keeping operations across four continents. It participates in the East Asia Summit, the G8+5, and other multilateral forums. India has close economic ties with South America, Asia, and Africa; it pursues a "Look East" policy that seeks to strengthen partnerships with the Association of South-East Asian Nations (ASEAN), Japan, and South Korea that revolve around many issues, but especially those involving economic investment and regional security (Sisodia and Naidu 2005).

China's nuclear test of 1964, as well as its repeated threats to intervene in support of Pakistan in the 1965 war, convinced India to develop nuclear weapons (Perkovich 2001). India conducted its first nuclear weapons test in 1974 and carried out further underground testing in 1998. Despite criticism and military sanctions, India has signed neither the Comprehensive Nuclear-Test-Ban Treaty nor the Nuclear Non-Proliferation Treaty, considering both to be flawed and discriminatory (Kumar 2010).

Since the end of the Cold War, India has increased its economic, strategic, and military co-operation with the United States and the European Union (Behera 2012). In 2008, a civilian nuclear agreement was signed between India and the United States. Although India possessed nuclear weapons at the time and was not party to the Nuclear Non-Proliferation Treaty, it received waivers from the International Atomic Energy Agency and the Nuclear Suppliers Group, ending earlier restrictions on India's nuclear technology and commerce. As a consequence, India became the sixth *de facto* nuclear weapons state. India subsequently signed co-operation agreements involving civilian nuclear energy with Russia, France, the United Kingdom, and Canada.

2.7. Measures to Sovereignty in India

To protect the nation from external threats, the Indian Constitution given the authority to the President of India as the supreme commander of the nation's armed forces; with 1.395 million active troops, they compose the world's 2nd largest military. It comprises the Indian Army, the Indian Navy, the Indian Air Force, and the Indian Coast Guard. The official Indian defence budget for 2011 was US$36.03 billion, or 1.83% of GDP (Behera 2011). For the fiscal year spanning 2012–2013, US$40.44 billion was budgeted. According to a 2008 SIPRI report, India's annual military expenditure in terms of purchasing power stood at US$72.7 billion (Freman and Elisabeth 2008). In 2011, the announcement of a country's annual defence expenditure is as much about geo-political signalling as about budgeting. From New Delhi, where the government announced a 12% increase in defence spending in its annual budget 2011-2012, here is the big message: notwithstanding our focus on development and social justice; and despite the still uncertain international economic climate, India will spend what is needed for an acceptable level of security (Shukla 2011). As of 2012, India is the world's largest arms importer; between 2007 and 2011, it accounted for 10% of funds spent on international arms purchases. Much of the military expenditure was focused on defence against Pakistan and countering growing Chinese influence in the Indian Ocean. In May 2017, the Indian Space Research Organisation (ISRO) launched the South Asia Satellite, a gift from India to its neighbouring SAARC countries (Deccan Herald 2015). In October 2018, India signed a US$5.43 billion (over Rs 400 billion) agreement with Russia to procure four S-400 Triumf surface-to-air missile defence systems, Russia's most advanced long-range missile defence system (The Times of India 2018).

2.8. Socio-economic Challenges in India

Despite good administrative institutions, good international relations and economic growth during recent decades, India continues to face variety of socio-economic challenges. In 2006, India contained the largest number of people living below the World Bank's international poverty line of US$1.25 per day (World Bank 2006), the proportion having decreased from 60% in 1981 to 42% in 2005 under its later revised poverty line, it was 21% in 2011 (World Bank 2011). The number of hungry people has declined in India with its score on the Global Hunger Index improving to 55th position in 2014 due to progress made in addressing underweight in children, says a report and 30.7% of India's children are under the age of five are underweight (The Economic Times, 2014). Again, in the 2020 Global Hunger Index (GHI), India ranks 94th out of the 107 countries with sufficient data to calculate 2020 GHI scores. With a score of 27.2, India has a level of hunger that is serious (GHI 2020).

In addition to this, Prime Minister Narendra Modi in his *Mann ki Baat* session said that the entire month of September will be observed as '*Poshan Maah'* i.e. 'Nutrition month' even amidst the pandemic. He recalled the maxim – "*Yatha Annam Tatha Mannam,*" which means that mental and intellectual development is directly related to the quality of our food intake. Keeping this in mind, let's look at the nutritional status of the nation in detail.

India is one of the world's largest producers of milk & pulses and ranks as the second-largest producer of rice, wheat, sugarcane, groundnut, vegetables, fruits, and cotton, as per the Food and Agriculture Organization (FAO) of the United Nations. Despite the status, 14 per cent of India's population is undernourished, according to 'The State of Food Security and Nutrition in the World, 2020' report.

The report states 189.2 million people are undernourished in India and 34.7 per cent of the children aged under five in India are stunted. It further reports that 20 per cent of India's children under the age of 5 suffer from wasting, meaning their weight is too low for their height (Shob 2020). The Mid-Day Meal Scheme attempts to lower these rates.

The Global Slavery Index by human rights organisation Walk Free Foundation said the number was 1.4% of India's population, the fourth highest among 167 countries with the largest proportion of slaves. "Existing research suggests all forms of modern slavery continue to exist in India, including inter-generational bonded labour, forced child labour, commercial sexual exploitation, forced begging, forced recruitment into non-state armed groups and forced marriage," said Grace Forrest, co-founder of the Australia-based foundation. The survey said an estimated 45.8 million people are living in modern slavery globally and 58% of them are concentrated in India, China, Pakistan, Bangladesh and Uzbekistan. The report coincided with the Centre unveiling a draft bill that envisages punishment for gangs involved in human trafficking and scrutiny of placement agencies, many of which are accused of forcing children into bonded labour and prostitution (Hindustan Times, 2016). According to the 2011 census, there were 10.1 million child labourers in the country, a decline of 2.6 million from 12.6 million child labourers in 2001 (ILO 2017).

Since 1991, economic inequality between India's states has consistently grown; the per-capita net state domestic product of the richest states in 2007 was 3.2 times that of the poorest (Pal and Ghosh 2007). India's rank has slipped six places to 86th among 180 countries in corruption perception index (CPI) in 2020. For 2020, Transparency International (TI)'s Corruption Perception Index (CPI) was released on Thursday. The index, which ranks 180 countries and territories by their perceived levels of public sector corruption according to experts and business people, uses a scale of 0 to 100, where 0 is highly corrupt and 100 is very clean (The Economic Times 2021).

2.9. Demographics of India

Demographic features of India are historically quite plural in nature. India is the 2nd most populated country in the world with nearly a 5th that is 17.74% of the world's population. According to the 2017 revision of the World Population Prospects (UN-DESA-PD 2017), the population stood at 1,324,171,354.

During 1975–2010 the population doubled to 1.2 billion. The Indian population reached the billion marks in 1998. India is projected to be the world's most populous country by 2024 (The Times of India 2017) surpassing the population of China. It is expected to become the first political entity in history to be home to more than 1.5 billion people by 2030, and its population is set to reach 1.7 billion by 2050. Its population growth rate is 1.13%, ranking 112th in the world in 2017 (The World Bank 2019). India has more than 50% of its population below the age of 25 and more than 65% below the age of 35. It is expected that, in 2020, the average age of an Indian will be 29 years, compared to 37 for China and 48 for Japan; and, by 2030, India's dependency ratio should be just over 0.4 (Basu 2007).

2.10. Socio-anthropological Features of India

A total of 2,504 Y-DNA haplotypes, representing 50 different ethnic groups in the Indian subcontinent (Matsoukas 2018) and every major religion has represented, as are four major families of languages (Indo-European, Dravidian, Austroasiatic and Sino-Tibetan languages).

Further complexity is lent by the great variation that occurs across this population on social parameters such as income and education. Only the continent of Africa exceeds the linguistic, genetic and cultural diversity of the nation of India. The sex ratio is 944 females for 1000 males (2016) (940 per 1000 in 2011 (Registrar General & Census Commissioner 2011). This ratio has been showing an upwards trend for the last two decades after a continuous decline in the last century.

The 2011 census reported that the religion in India with the largest number of followers was Hinduism (79.80% of the population), followed by Islam (14.23%); the remaining were Christianity (2.30%), Sikhism (1.72%), Buddhism (0.70%), Jainism (0.36%) and others religion and not stated religion are 0.9% (Registrar General & Census Commissioner 2011). A country with a Hindu majority, India is estimated to have the third largest Muslim population in the world and a Christian population of over 25 million. The current two-term Prime Minister is Sikh, the past president is Muslim, and the head of the national governing alliance is Catholic. Buddhist, Christian, Hindu, Muslim, Sikh, and Parsi holidays are recognized as public holidays. India also has an independent judiciary, independent media, and a dynamic civil society. In recent years, the national government and several state governments have taken positive steps to improve religious freedom, including increasing support for governmental bodies that provide financial support for minority groups and programs (USCIRF 2012).

Indian cultural history spans more than 4,500 years (Kuipe 2010). During the Vedic period (c1700-c500 BCE), the foundations of Hindu philosophy, mythology, theology and literature were laid, and many beliefs and practices which still exist today, such as *dhárma*, *kárma*, *yóga*, and *moksha*, were established (Kuipe 2010). India is notable for its religious diversity, with Hinduism, Buddhism, Sikhism, Islam, Christianity, and Jainism among the nation's major religions (*Heehs, 2002).* The predominant religion, Hinduism, has been shaped by various historical schools of thought, including those of the *Upanishads* (*Deutsch, 1969)*, the *Yoga Sutras*, the *Bhakti* movement (Heehs 2002), and by Buddhist philosophy (Nakamura 1999).

Traditional Indian society is sometimes defined by social hierarchy. The Indian caste system embodies much of the social stratification and many of the social restrictions found in the Indian subcontinent. Social classes are defined by thousands of endogamous hereditary groups, often termed as *jatis*, or "castes". India declared untouchability to be illegal in 1947 and has since enacted other anti-discriminatory laws and social welfare initiatives. At the workplace in urban India and in international or leading Indian companies, the caste related identification has pretty much lost its importance (Messner 2009).

Family values are important in the Indian tradition, and multi-generational patriarchal joint families have been the norm in India, though nuclear families are becoming common in urban areas (Makar 2007). An overwhelming majority of Indians, with their consent, have their marriages arranged by their parents or other elders in the family (Medora 2003). Marriage is thought to be for life (*Medora, 2003),* and the divorce rate is extremely low (Jones 2005). As of 2001, just 1.6 percent of Indian women were divorced but this figure was rising due to their education and economic independence (Jones 2005). Child marriages are common, especially in rural areas; many women wed before reaching 18, which is their legal marriageable age (Cullen-Dupont 2009).

Half a million girls a year are being aborted in India, equal to the total number of girls born in the UK. The scale of sex selection in Asia is extraordinary, yet it has not attracted the attention it deserves in the west. This is the age of "missing women" - an estimated 30 to 70 million of them. The number of girls born has dropped significantly because of sex selective abortions, and the sex imbalance has been aggravated by higher mortality rates as boys receive better care. The very vagueness of the figures indicates how poorly understood this massive phenomenon is – quite apart from the still limited analysis of the impact the resulting sex imbalance will have on the development of countries such as India and China. In May, there was widespread concern in India as the results of the 2011 census revealed a sharp deterioration of the sex ratio. Many attributed the growing gap to a powerful lobby of doctors and commercial interests who sell ultrasound machines; both make profits from the illegal, multimillion dollar sex selection procedures Female infanticide and female foeticide in the country have caused a discrepancy in the sex ratio, as of 2005 it was estimated that there were 50 million more males than females in the nation (The Guardian 2011). However, from 2011 has shown improvement in the gender ratio. The payment of dowry, although illegal, remains widespread across class lines in India. In 2019, reported dowry death cases in India amounted to more than 7.1 thousand. This was a gradual decrease from the 2014, in which this number was approximately 8.5 thousand. The dowry system in India incorporates payments in the form of capital, durable goods, real estate among others, made to the bridegroom from the family of the bride as a condition for marriage (Statista 2021). Deaths resulting from dowry, mostly from bride burning, are on the rise, despite stringent anti-dowry laws (Pereira 2013).

Many of Indian festivals are religious in origin. The best known included *Diwali, Ganesh Chaturthi, Thai Pongal, Holi, Durga Puja, Eid-ul-Fitr, Bakra-Id*, *Christmas*, and *Vaisakhi*. India has three national holidays which are observed in all states and union territories – Republic Day, Independence Day and Gandhi Jayanti. Other sets of holidays, varying between nine and twelve, are officially observed in individual states.

The Constitution of India is a dynamic as well as documented institution for India as well as for the Indian; for the demands of the time or the emerging situations it has enacted and modified by its own power and the Constitution of India exercise its power to "*constitute India into a Sovereign Socialist Secular Democratic Republic and to secure to all its citizens*" (India 1950/2015). The SDGs are the demands of the global change and its emergent situations, the issues of the SDGs has composed for overcoming varied threat to the human civilization; which are to be achieved to maintain sustainability of the world within 2030. India has committed to play a major role to the success of the SDGs in India by which India could be reduce the major socio-economic threat of the world on the issues designed in the SDGs. The Constitution of India, by nature it has adopted the laws to tackle the changes for Indian. This drive could a step forward to "*constitute India into a Sovereign Socialist Secular Democratic Republic and to secure to all its citizens*". In the next chapter, author has trying to draw the linked Constitutional provisions with the SDG's for making India up-to-date for the future generation.

Chapter – III

The Constitution of India – The Dynamic Peace Making Institution

At the beginning, the author is humbly submitting that he is not a Constitution expert nor a development planner; a researcher of social science has been trained to explore the gaps in between the published data, literatures and from different ICSSR sponsored Research Methodology Training Programmes, financially supported by the India Council of Social Science Research (ICSSR), India. This initiative is a products of the Research Methodology Training Programmes from where from where the author have gained most of his research expertise. Practically, from the varied nature of emergent global data on dignified life throughout the world the United Nations General Assembly was bound to frame the targets and indicators of the SDGs. This initiative have multiple vision, such as poverty eradication, quality education; decent work, reduce inequality, gender equality, human health and sanitation to urban settlements and to safeguarding the global ecosystems on which humanity depends for its survival. All of these have to be achieve by 2030. In a humanistic point of view, the approach is known as Sustainable Development Goals (SDGs). No doubt, this is a global inclusive approach. In the other side, *"We the people of India, having solemnly resolved to constitute India into a Sovereign Socialist Secular Democratic Republic and to secure to all its citizens: justice, social, economic and political; liberty of thought, expression, belief, faith and worship; equality of status and of opportunity; and to promote among them all fraternity assuring the dignity of the individual and the unity and integrity of the nation; in our Constituent Assembly this twenty-sixth day of November, 1949, do hereby adopt, enact and give to ourselves this Constitution* (India 1950/ 2015)" - this is the Preamble of The Indian Constitution. It was resolved and adopted in 26th November, 1949 in the *Constituent Assembly*, to *"constitute India into a Sovereign Socialist Secular Democratic Republic and to secure to all its citizens: justice, social, economic and political; liberty of thought, expression, belief, faith and worship; equality of status and of opportunity; and to promote among them all fraternity assuring the dignity of the individual and the unity and integrity of the nation* (India 1950/2015)*"*.

Now, we are in the era of SDGs, the basic question is, after 71 years of adoption of the Indian Constitution, how much constitute India as it was resolved? Are there any methods to measure? Yes, in the beginning of the 70nd years of adoption of the Constitution of India, the Government of India has published a document entitled *"SDG India Index - Baseline Report, 2018*", by the NITI *Aayog.* Here, the author is like to say that, what India thinks in the 1949, the world thinks it more than 50 years later in the name of MDGs and then MDGs through United Nations. Because, if we go through the Constitution of India, we find there are ample options in the name *Articles* in the form of *Rights, Schedules, Clauses, Order, Sections* to constitute India as it is reflected in the targeted SDGs to create a better world for the future generations. In the following section the author has trying to draw a link between the *Articles* of the Indian Constitution and the SDGs. Here in this regard the author has captured the parts of the Indian Constitution which has been touched in the spirit of SDGs.

3.1. The Indian Constitutional Provisions to address Sustainable Development Goals

Part-III of the Constitution of India has detailed about the Fundamental Rights of its citizen; that is "*The Fundamental Rights - Right to Equality*"**.** The Article-12, defined the spirit of the Part-III of the Constitution of India; in this Part, unless the context otherwise requires, - 'the State' includes the Government and Parliament of India and the Government and the Legislature of each of the States and all local or other authorities within the territory of India or under the control of the Government of India.

The Article-13 has directed and clarified about Part-III of the Constitution of India; "Laws inconsistent with or in derogation of the fundamental rights - (1) All laws in force in the territory of India immediately before the commencement of this Constitution, in so far as they are inconsistent with the provisions of this Part, shall, to the extent of such inconsistency, be void. (2) The State shall not make any law which takes away or abridges the rights conferred by this Part and any law made in contravention of this clause shall, to the extent of the contravention, be void. (3) In this article, unless the context otherwise requires, - (a) "law" includes any Ordinance, order, bye-law, rule, regulation, notification, custom or usage having in the territory of India the force of law; (b) "laws in force" includes laws passed or made by a Legislature or other competent authority in the territory of India before the commencement of this Constitution and not previously repealed, notwithstanding that any such law or any part thereof may not be then in operation either at all or in particular areas. (4) Nothing in this article shall apply to any amendment of this Constitution made under Article 368" (Article-368: Power of Parliament to amend the Constitution and procedure therefor).

Right to Equality

Article-14: *"The State shall not deny to any person equality before the law or the equal protection of the laws within the territory of India".-*

Inferences: the Article-14 is a provision to promote 'Gender Equality' (SDG-5), 'Decent Work and Economic Growth' (SDG-8); 'Industry, Innovation and Infrastructure' (SDG-9); 'Reduced Inequalities' (SDG-10), 'Sustainable Cities and Communities' (SDG-11), 'Sustainable Consumption and Production' (SDG-12), 'Climate Action' (SDG-13) and 'Life and Land' (SDG-15); ultimately this Article is the strong tools to achieve as well as a builder of the 'Peace, Justice and Strong Institutions' (SDG-16) in the country.

Article-15: *"Prohibition of discrimination on grounds of religion, race, caste, sex or place of birth".*

(1) The State shall not discriminate against any citizen on grounds only of religion, race, caste, sex, place of birth or any of them.

(2) No citizen shall, on grounds only of religion, race, caste, sex, place of birth or any of them, be subject to any disability, liability, restriction or condition with regard to—

(a) access to shops, public restaurants, hotels and places of public entertainment;

(b) the use of wells, tanks, bathing *ghats*, roads and places of public resort maintained wholly or partly out of State funds or dedicated to the use of the general public.

(3) Nothing in this article shall prevent the State from making any special provision for women and children.

(4) Nothing in this article or in clause (2) of article 29 shall prevent the State from making any special provision for the advancement

of any socially and educationally backward classes of citizens or for the Scheduled Castes and the Scheduled Tribes[1].

(5) Nothing in this article or in sub-clause (*g*) of clause (1) of article 19 shall prevent the State from making any special provision, by law, for the advancement of any socially and educationally backward classes of citizens or for the Scheduled Castes or the Scheduled Tribes in so far as such special provisions relate to their admission to educational institutions including private educational institutions, whether aided or unaided by the State, other than the minority educational institutions referred to in clause (1) of Article - 30[2].

Inferences: this part of the Article-15, that are as subsection 1, 2-a and b, 3, 4 and 5 are the provisions for equality, in this ground the Article-15 is the base of the SDG-16, entitled as 'Peace, Justice and Strong Institutions' in India; and to making special provision, the State would enable to promote advancement of any socially and educationally backward classes of citizens or for the Scheduled Castes and the Scheduled Tribes, which gradually open the scope of promote 'Quality Education (SDG-4), 'Decent Work and Economic Growth' (SDG-8), 'Gender Equality' (SDG-5); 'Reduce Poverty' (SDG-1), 'Hunger' (SDG-2), 'Good Health and Well-being' (SDG-3), 'Affordable and Clean Energy (SDG-7), 'Decent Work and Economic Growth' (SDG-8), 'Industry, Innovation and Infrastructure' (SDG-9) and 'Reduced Inequality' (SDG-10).

After achieving the above SDGs, the citizens of India ultimately will try to search for better option of life, which may be reflected in the 'Good Health and Wellbeing' (SDG-3), 'Clean Water and Sanitation' (SDG-6), 'Affordable and Clean Energy' (SDG-7), 'Industry Innovation and Infrastructure' (SDG-9), 'Sustainable Cities and Communities' (SDG-11), 'Sustainable Consumption and Production' (SDG-12), 'Climate Action' (SDG-13), 'Life Below Water' (SDG-14), 'Life on Land' (SDG-15) and 'Partnerships for the Goals' (SDG-17); ultimately this Article and its sections are the strong tools to achieve as well as build the 'Peace, Justice and Strong Institutions' (SDG-16) in the country.

Article-16: *"Equality of opportunity in matters of public employment".*

1. There shall be equality of opportunity for all citizens in matters relating to employment or appointment to any office under the State.

2. No citizen shall, on grounds only of religion, race, caste, sex, descent, place of birth, residence or any of them, be ineligible for, or discriminated against in respect of, any employment or office under the State.
3. Nothing in this article shall prevent Parliament from making any law prescribing, in regard to a class or classes of employment or appointment to an office (under the Government of, or any local or other authority within, a State or Union territory, any requirement as to residence within that State or Union territory[3] prior to such employment or appointment.
4. Nothing in this article shall prevent the State from making any provision for the reservation of appointments or posts in favour of any backward class of citizens which, in the opinion of the State, is not adequately represented in the services under the State.

(4A). Nothing in this article shall prevent the State from making any provision for reservation (in matters of promotion, with consequential seniority, to any class[4] or classes of posts in the services under the State in favour of the Scheduled Castes and the Scheduled Tribes which, in the opinion of the State, are not adequately represented in the services under the State[5].

(4B). Nothing in this article shall prevent the State from considering any unfilled vacancies of a year which are reserved for being filled up in that year in accordance with any provision for reservation made under clause (4) or clause (4A) as a separate class of vacancies to be filled up in any succeeding year or years and such class of vacancies shall not be considered together with the vacancies of the year in which they are being filled up for determining the ceiling of fifty percent reservation on total number of vacancies of that year[6].

5. Nothing in this article shall affect the operation of any law which provides that the incumbent of an office in connection with the affairs of any religious or denominational institution or any member of the governing body thereof shall be a person professing a particular religion or belonging to a particular denomination.

Inferences: Subsection (1) to (5) of the Article-16 has been directly reflected in the SDG-16, entitled as 'Peace, Justice and Strong Institutions' which will promote decent work and economic growth (SDG-8); and it will promote 'Gender Equality' (SDG-5), 'Decent Work and Economic

Growth' (SDG-8) and 'Reduced Inequality' (SDG-10), which gradually open the scope of promote 'Quality Education' (SDG-4), 'Decent Work and Economic Growth' (SDG-8), 'Gender Equality' (SDG-5); 'Reduced Poverty' (SDG-1), 'Hunger' (SDG-2), 'Reduced Inequality' (SDG-10).

After achieving the above SDGs, the citizens of India ultimately will try to search for better option of life, which may reflected in the 'Good Health and Wellbeing' (SDG-3), 'Clean Water and Sanitation' (SDG-6), 'Affordable and Clean Energy' (SDG-7), 'Industry Innovation and Infrastructure' (SDG-9), 'Sustainable Cities and Communities' (SDG-11), 'Sustainable Consumption and Production' (SDG-12), 'Climate Action' (SDG-13), 'Life Below Water' (SDG-14), 'Life on Land' (SDG-15) and 'Partnerships for the Goals' (SDG-17).

Article-17: *"Abolition of Untouchability: "Untouchability" is abolished and its practice in any form is forbidden. The enforcement of any disability arising out of "Untouchability" shall be an offence punishable in accordance with law".*

Inferences: Article-17 is a provision to promote 'Gender Equality' (SDG-5) and to 'Reduced Inequalities' (SDG-10). Proper implementation of this Article will reduce all forms of inequality and ultimately this Article is one of the strongest tool to achieve as well as build the 'Peace, Justice and Strong Institutions' (SDG-16) in the country.

Article-18: *"Abolition of titles".*

(1) No title, not being a military or academic distinction, shall be conferred by the State.

(2) No citizen of India shall accept any title from any foreign State.

(3) No person who is not a citizen of India shall, while he holds any office of profit or trust under the State, accept without the consent of the President any title from any foreign State.

(4) No person holding any office of profit or trust under the State shall, without the consent of the President, accept any present, emolument, or office of any kind from or under any foreign State.

Inferences: Subsection (1) to (4) of Article-18 are the provisions to promote 'Gender Equality' (SDG-5) and to 'Reduced Inequalities' (SDG-10). Proper implementation of this Article will reduce all forms of inequality.

Right to Freedom

Article-19: Protection of certain rights regarding freedom of speech, etc.

1. All citizens shall have the right—
   (a) To freedom of speech and expression;
   (b) To assemble peaceably and without arms;
   (c) To form associations or unions [or co-operative societies][7];
   (d) To move freely throughout the territory of India;
   (e) To reside and settle in any part of the territory of India[8];
   (f) Sub-clause (f)[9] omitted and
   (g) To practise any profession, or to carry on any occupation, trade or business.
2. Nothing in sub-clause *(a)* of clause (1) shall affect the operation of any existing law, or prevent the State from making any law, in so far as such law imposes reasonable restrictions on the exercise of the right conferred by the said sub-clause in the interests of (the sovereignty and integrity of India[10], the security of the State, friendly relations with foreign States, public order, decency or morality, or in relation to contempt of court, defamation or incitement to an offence[11].
3. Nothing in sub-clause *(b)* of the said clause shall affect the operation of any existing law in so far as it imposes, or prevent the State from making any law imposing, in the interests of (the sovereignty and integrity of India or[9] public order, reasonable restrictions on the exercise of the right conferred by the said sub-clause.
4. Nothing in sub-clause (*c*) of the said clause shall affect the operation of any existing law in so far as it imposes, or prevent the State from making any law imposing, in the interests of (the sovereignty and integrity of India or[9] public order or morality, reasonable restrictions on the exercise of the right conferred by the said sub-clause.
5. Nothing in (sub-clauses *(d)* and (*e*)[12] of the said clause shall affect the operation of any existing law in so far as it imposes, or prevent the State from making any law imposing, reasonable restrictions on the exercise of any of the rights conferred by the said sub-clauses either in the interests of the general public or for the protection of the interests of any Scheduled Tribe.
6. Nothing in sub-clause (*g*) of the said clause shall affect the operation of any existing law in so far as it imposes, or prevent

the State from making any law imposing, in the interests of the general public, reasonable restrictions on the exercise of the right conferred by the said sub-clause, and, in particular, (nothing in the said sub-clause shall affect the operation of any existing law in so far as it relates to, or prevent the State from making any law relating to,—

(i) The professional or technical qualifications necessary for practising any profession or carrying on any occupation, trade or business, or

(ii) The carrying on by the State or by a corporation owned or controlled by the State, of any trade, business, industry or service, whether to the exclusion, complete or partial, of citizens or otherwise[13].

Inferences: Subsections (a) to (e) of Article-19-1 has been reflected in the SDG-16, entitled as 'Peace, Justice and Strong Institutions' and proper implementation of this part will reduce inequality (SDG-10) and *Article 19-1.(g)* reflected in 'Decent Work and Economic Growth' (SDG-8) and 'Industry Innovation and Infrastructure' (SDG-9). Again proper implementations of this part will promote 'Quality Education' (SDG-4), 'Gender Equality' (SDG-5), 'Reduce Poverty' (SDG-1), 'Reduced Hunger' (SDG-2), 'Reduced Inequality' (SDG-10), 'Sustainable Consumption and Production' (SDG-12), and 'Climate Action' (SDG-13).

Again, subsections (2) to (6) of the Article-19 is reflected in the SDG-16, entitled as 'Peace, Justice and Strong Institutions' and proper implementation of the part will increase 'Decent Work & Economic Growth' (SDG-8), 'Industry Innovation and Infrastructure' (SDG-9) and wide the 'Partnerships for the Goals' (SDG-17).

Article-20: *"Protection in respect of conviction for offences"*.

(1) No person shall be convicted of any offence except for violation of a law in force at the time of the commission of the act charged as an offence, nor be subjected to a penalty greater than that which might have been inflicted under the law in force at the time of the commission of the offence.

(2) No person shall be prosecuted and punished for the same offence more than once.

(3) No person accused of any offence shall be compelled to be a witness against himself.

Inferences: Subsections (1), (2) and (3) of Article-20 has been reflected in the SDG-16, entitled as 'Peace, Justice and Strong Institutions' and proper implementation of the this part will promote 'Gender Equality' (SDG-5) as well as 'Reduce Inequalities' (SDG-10).

Article-21: *"Protection of life and personal liberty".*

No person shall be deprived of his life or personal liberty except according to procedure established by law.

Inferences: Article-21 has been reflected in the SDG-16, entitled as 'Peace, Justice and Strong Institutions' and proper implementation of the part will promote 'Good Health and Well-being' (SDG-3), 'Gender Equality' (SDG-5), 'Clean Water and Sanitation' (SDF-6), 'Affordable and Clean Energy (SDG-7), 'Decent Work and Economic Growth' (SDG-8), 'Industry, Innovation and Infrastructure' (SDG-9), 'Reduced Inequalities' (SDG-10), 'Sustainable Cities and Communities' (SDG-11), 'Sustainable Consumption and Production' (SDG-12),'Climate Action' (SDG-13) and 'Life bellow Water' (SDG-14).

Right to Education

Article-21A: *"Right to education"* - The State shall provide free and compulsory education to all children of the age of six to fourteen years in such manner as the State may, by law, determine[14].

Inferences: Article 21-A has been reflected in the SDG-4, entitled as 'Quality Education' and proper implementation of the this part will promote 'Gender Equality' (SDG-4), 'Affordable and Clean Energy (SDG-7), 'Decent Work and Economic Growth'(SDG-8), and 'Reduced Inequalities' (SDG-10); this promotion will reduce the 'Poverty' (SDG-1), 'Hunger' (SDG-2); finally promote the 'Good Health & Wellbeing' (SDG-3) and 'Clean Water and Sanitation' (SDG-6).

After achieving the above SDGs, the citizens of India ultimately will try to search for better option of life, which may reflected in the 'Gender Equality' (SDG-5), 'Clean Water and Sanitation' (SDG-6), 'Affordable and Clean Energy' (SDG-7), 'Industry Innovation and Infrastructure' (SDG-9), 'Sustainable Cities and Communities' (SDG-11), 'Sustainable Consumption and Production' (SDG-12), 'Climate Action' (SDG-13), 'Life Below Water' (SDG-14), 'Life on Land' (SDG-15), 'Peace, Justice and Strong Institutions' (SDG-16) and 'Partnerships for the Goals' (SDG-17).

Article-22: *"Protection against arrest and detention in certain cases".*

(1) No person who is arrested shall be detained in custody without being informed, as soon as may be, of the grounds for such arrest nor shall he be denied the right to consult, and to be defended by, a legal practitioner of his choice.

(2) Every person who is arrested and detained in custody shall be produced before the nearest magistrate within a period of twenty-four hours of such arrest excluding the time necessary for the journey from the place of arrest to the court of the magistrate and no such person shall be detained in custody beyond the said period without the authority of a magistrate.

(3) Nothing in clauses (1) and (2) shall apply -

  (a) To any person who for the time being is an enemy alien; or

  (b) To any person who is arrested or detained under any law providing for preventive detention.

(4) No law providing for preventive detention shall authorise the detention of a person for a longer period than three months unless[15] —

  (*a*) An Advisory Board consisting of persons who are, or have been, or are qualified to be appointed as, Judges of a High Court has reported before the expiration of the said period of three months that there is in its opinion sufficient cause for such detention:

  Provided that nothing in this sub-clause shall authorise the detention of any person beyond the maximum period prescribed by any law made by Parliament under sub-clause (*b*) of clause (7); or

  (*b*) Such person is detained in accordance with the provisions of any law made by Parliament under sub-clauses (*a*) and (*b*) of clause (7)

(5) When any person is detained in pursuance of an order made under any law providing for preventive detention, the authority making the order shall, as soon as may be, communicate to such person the grounds on which the order has been made and shall afford him the earliest opportunity of making a representation against the order.

(6) Nothing in clause (5) shall require the authority making any such order as is referred to in that clause to disclose facts which such authority considers to be against the public interest to disclose.

(7) Parliament may by law prescribe—

(*a*) The circumstances under which, and the class or classes of cases in which, a person may be detained for a period longer than three months under any law providing for preventive detention without obtaining the opinion of an Advisory Board in accordance with the provisions of sub-clause (*a*) of clause (4)[16];

(*b*) The maximum period for which any person may in any class or classes of cases be detained under any law providing for preventive detention[17]; and

(*c*) The procedure to be followed by an Advisory Board in an inquiry under sub-clause (*a*) of clause (4)[18].

Inferences: Subsections (1) to (7) of the Article-22 has been reflected in the SDG-16, entitled as 'Peace, Justice and Strong Institutions' and proper implementation of the *Article* will all forms of inequality that is 'Reduced Inequalities' (SDG-10).

Right against Exploitation

Article-23: *"Prohibition of traffic in human beings and forced labour".*

(1) Traffic in human beings and *beggar* and other similar forms of forced labour are prohibited and any contravention of this provision shall be an offence punishable in accordance with law.

(2) Nothing in this article shall prevent the State from imposing compulsory service for public purposes, and in imposing such service the State shall not make any discrimination on grounds only of religion, race, caste or class or any of them.

Inferences: Subsections (1) and (2) of Article-23 has been reflected in the *SDG-16,* entitled as 'Peace, Justice and Strong Institutions' and proper implementation of the *Article* will promote 'Gender Equality' (SDG-5), 'Decent Work and Economic Growth' (SDG-8) as well as 'Reduce Inequalities' (SDG-10).

Article 24: *"Prohibition of employment of children in factories, etc".*

No child below the age of fourteen years shall be employed to work in any factory or mine or engaged in any other hazardous employment.

Inferences: The Article-24 has been reflected in the *SDG-16,* entitled as 'Peace, Justice and Strong Institutions' and proper implementation of the *Article* will promote 'Gender Equality' (SDG-5), 'Decent Work and Economic Growth' (SDG-8) as well as 'Reduce Inequalities' (SDG-10).

Right to Freedom of Religion

Article-25: *"Freedom of conscience and free profession, practice and propagation of religion"* -

(1) Subject to public order, morality and health and to the other provisions of this Part, all persons are equally entitled to freedom of conscience and the right freely to profess, practise and propagate religion.

(2) Nothing in this article shall affect the operation of any existing law or prevent the State from making any law—

(*a*) Regulating or restricting any economic, financial, political or other secular activity which may be associated with religious practice;

(*b*) Providing for social welfare and reform or the throwing open of Hindu religious institutions of a public character to all classes and sections of Hindus.

Explanation I.—the wearing and carrying of *kirpans* shall be deemed to be included in the profession of the Sikh religion.

Explanation II.—In sub-clause (*b*) of clause (2), the reference to Hindus shall be construed as including a reference to persons professing the Sikh, Jaina or Buddhist religion, and the reference to Hindu religious institutions shall be construed accordingly.

Inferences: Subsections (1) and (2)-(a) and (b) of Article-25 has been reflected in the SDG-16, entitled as 'Peace, Justice and Strong Institutions' and proper implementation of the Article will 'Reduced Inequalities' (SDG-10).

Article-26: *"Freedom to manage religious affairs"* -

Subject to public order, morality and health, every religious denomination or any section thereof shall have the right—

(*a*) To establish and maintain institutions for religious and charitable purposes;

(*b*) To manage its own affairs in matters of religion;

(*c*) To own and acquire movable and immovable property; and

(*d*) To administer such property in accordance with law.

Inferences: Subsections (a) to (d) of Article-26 has been reflected in the SDG-16, entitled as 'Peace, Justice and Strong Institutions' and proper implementation of the *Article* will 'Reduced Inequalities' (SDG-10).

Article-27: *"Freedom as to payment of taxes for promotion of any particular religion"* -

No person shall be compelled to pay any taxes, the proceeds of which are specifically appropriated in payment of expenses for the promotion or maintenance of any particular religion or religious denomination.

Inferences: The Article-27 has been reflected in the SDG-16, entitled as 'Peace, Justice and Strong Institutions' and proper implementation of the *Article* will 'Reduced Inequalities' (SDG-10).

Article-28: *"Freedom as to attendance at religious instruction or religious worship in certain educational institutions"* -

(1) No religious instruction shall be provided in any educational institution wholly maintained out of State funds.

(2) Nothing in clause (1) shall apply to an educational institution which is administered by the State but has been established under any endowment or trust which requires that religious instruction shall be imparted in such institution.

(3) No person attending any educational institution recognised by the State or receiving aid out of State funds shall be required to take part in any religious instruction that may be imparted in such institution or to attend any religious worship that may be conducted in such Institution or in any premises attached thereto unless such person or, if such person is a minor, his guardian has given his consent thereto.

Inferences: Subsections (1) to (3) of Article-28 has been reflected in the SDG-16, entitled as 'Peace, Justice and Strong Institutions' and proper implementation of the *Article* will promote 'Quality Education (SDG-4), 'Gender Equality' (SDG-5) and 'Reduced Inequalities' (SDG-10).

Cultural and Educational Rights

Article-29: *"Protection of interests of minorities"*-

(1) Any section of the citizens residing in the territory of India or any part thereof having a distinct language, script or culture of its own shall have the right to conserve the same.

(2) No citizen shall be denied admission into any educational institution maintained by the State or receiving aid out of State

funds on grounds only of religion, race, caste, language or any of them.

Inferences: Subsections (1) and (2) of Article-29 has been reflected in the SDG-16, entitled as 'Peace, Justice and Strong Institutions' and proper implementation of the Article will promote 'Quality Education (SDG-4), 'Decent Work and Economic Growth' (SDG-8) and 'Reduced Inequalities' (SDG-10).

Article-30: *"Right of minorities to establish and administer educational institutions"* -

(1) All minorities, whether based on religion or language, shall have the right to establish and administer educational institutions of their choice.

(1A) In making any law providing for the compulsory acquisition of any property of an educational institution established and administered by a minority, referred to in clause (1), the State shall ensure that the amount fixed by or determined under such law for the acquisition of such property is such as would not restrict or abrogate the right guaranteed under that clause[19].

(2) The State shall not, in granting aid to educational institutions, discriminate against any educational institution on the ground that it is under the management of a minority, whether based on religion or language

Inferences: Subsections (1), (1A) and (2) of Article-30 has been reflected in the *SDG-16,* entitled as 'Peace, Justice and Strong Institutions' and proper implementation of the *Article* will promote 'Quality Education (SDG-4), 'Gender Equality' (SDG-5) and 'Reduced Inequalities' SDG-10

Article-31: *"Right to Property" the Compulsory acquisition of property repealed by the Constitution (Forty-fourth Amendment) Act,* 1978, *s.* 6 *(w.e.f.* 20-6-1979), omitted by the Constitution[20].

Saving of Certain Laws[21]

Article-31A[22]: *"Saving of laws providing for acquisition of estates, etc".*

(1) Notwithstanding anything contained in article 13, no law providing for[23] —

(*a*) The acquisition by the State of any estate or of any rights therein or the extinguishment or modification of any such rights, or (*b*) The taking over of the management of any property by the State for a limited period either in the public interest or in order to secure the proper management of the property, or

(*c*) The amalgamation of two or more corporations either in the public interest or in order to secure the proper management of any of the corporations, or

(*d*) The extinguishment or modification of any rights of managing agents, secretaries and treasurers, managing directors, directors or managers of corporations, or of any voting rights of shareholders thereof, or

(*e*) The extinguishment or modification of any rights accruing by virtue of any agreement, lease or licence for the purpose of searching for, or winning, any mineral or mineral oil, or the premature termination or cancellation of any such agreement, lease or licence, shall be deemed to be void on the ground that it is inconsistent with, or takes away or abridges any of the rights conferred by article 14 or article 19[24]:

Provided that where such law is a law made by the Legislature of a State, the provisions of this article shall not apply thereto unless such law, having been reserved for the consideration of the President, has received his assent:

Provided further that where any law makes any provision for the acquisition by the State of any estate and where any land comprised therein is held by a person under his personal cultivation, it shall not be lawful for the State to acquire any portion of such land as is within the ceiling limit applicable to him under any law for the time being in force or any building or structure standing thereon or appurtenant thereto, unless the law relating to the acquisition of such land, building or structure, provides for payment of compensation at a rate which shall not be less than the market value thereof[25].

(2) In this article,—

(*a*) The expression "estate" shall, in relation to any local area, have the same meaning as that expression or its local equivalent has in the existing law relating to land tenures in force in that area and shall also include[26] —

(*i*) Any *jagir, inam* or *muafi* or other similar grant and in the States of Tamil Nadu[27] and Kerala, any *janmam* right;

(*ii*) Any land held under *ryotwari* settlement;

(*iii*) any land held or let for purposes of agriculture or for purposes ancillary thereto, including waste land, forest land, land for pasture or sites of buildings and other structures occupied by cultivators of land, agricultural labourers and village artisans;

(*b*) The expression "rights", in relation to an estate, shall include any rights vesting in a proprietor, sub-proprietor, under-proprietor, tenure-holder, [*raiyat, under-raiyat*] or other intermediary and any rights or privileges in respect of land revenue[28].

Article-31B: *"Validation of certain Acts and Regulations"* -

Without prejudice to the generality of the provisions contained in article 31A, none of the Acts and Regulations specified in the Ninth Schedule nor any of the provisions thereof shall be deemed to be void, or ever to have become void, on the ground that such Act, Regulation or provision is inconsistent with, or takes away or abridges any of the rights conferred by, any provisions of this Part, and notwithstanding any judgment, decree or order of any court or Tribunal to the contrary, each of the said Acts and Regulations shall, subject to the power of any competent Legislature to repeal or amend it, continue in force[29].

Article-31C: *"Saving of laws giving effect to certain directive principles"*[30] -

Notwithstanding anything contained in Article-13, no law giving effect to the policy of the State towards securing (all or any of the principles laid down in Part IV[31] shall be deemed to be void on the ground that it is inconsistent with, or takes away or abridges any of the rights conferred by article 14 or article 19[32]; *and no law containing a declaration that it is for giving effect to such policy shall be called in question in any court on the ground that it does not give effect to such policy*[33]:

Provided that where such law is made by the Legislature of a State, the provisions of this article shall not apply thereto unless such law, having been reserved for the consideration of the President, has received his assent.

Article-31D: "*Saving of laws in respect of anti-national activities"* - *Repealed by the Constitution (Forty-third Amendment) Act,* 1977, *s.* 2 (*w.e.f.* 13-4-1978)[34].

Right to Constitutional Remedies

Article-32: *"Remedies for enforcement of rights conferred by this Part"* -

(1) The right to move the Supreme Court by appropriate proceedings for the enforcement of the rights conferred by this Part is guaranteed.

(2) The Supreme Court shall have power to issue directions or orders or writs, including writs in the nature of *habeas corpus, mandamus,* prohibition, *quo warranto* and *certiorari,* whichever may be appropriate, for the enforcement of any of the rights conferred by this Part.

(3) Without prejudice to the powers conferred on the Supreme Court by clauses (1) and (2), Parliament may by law empower any other court to exercise within the local limits of its jurisdiction all or any of the powers exercisable by the Supreme Court under clause (2).

(4) The right guaranteed by this article shall not be suspended except as otherwise provided for by this Constitution.

Article-32A: *"Constitutional validity of State laws not to be considered in proceedings under article 32"*[35]*; Repealed by the Constitution (Forty-third Amendment) Act,* 1977, Section - 3 *(w.e.f.* 13-4-1978).

Article-33: *"Power of Parliament to modify the rights conferred by this Part in their application to Forces, etc"*[36] -

Parliament may, by law, determine to what extent any of the rights conferred by this Part shall, in their application to, -

(*a*) The members of the Armed Forces; or

(*b*) The members of the Forces charged with the maintenance of public order; or

(*c*) Persons employed in any bureau or other organisation established by the State for purposes of intelligence or counter intelligence; or

(*d*) Persons employed in, or in connection with, the telecommunication systems set up for the purposes of any Force, bureau or organisation referred to in clauses (*a*) to (*c*), be restricted or abrogated so as to ensure the proper discharge of their duties and the maintenance of discipline among them.

Article-34: *"Restriction on rights conferred by this Part while martial law is in force in any area"* -

Notwithstanding anything in the foregoing provisions of this Part, Parliament may by law indemnify any person in the service of the Union or of a State or any other person in respect of any act done by him in connection with the maintenance or restoration of order in any area within the territory of India where martial law was in force or validate any sentence passed, punishment inflicted, forfeiture ordered or other act done under martial law in such area.

Article-35: *"Legislation to give effect to the provisions of this Part"* -

Notwithstanding anything in this Constitution, -

(*a*) Parliament shall have, and the Legislature of a State shall not have, power to make laws -

(*i*) With respect to any of the matters which under clause (3) of article 16, clause (3) of article 32, article 33 and article 34 may be provided for by law made by Parliament; and

(*ii*) For prescribing punishment for those acts which are declared to be offences under this Part; and Parliament shall, as soon as may be after the commencement of this Constitution, make laws for prescribing punishment for the acts referred to in sub-clause (*ii*);

(*b*) Any law in force immediately before the commencement of this Constitution in the territory of India with respect to any of the matters referred to in sub-clause (*i*) of clause (*a*) or providing for punishment for any act referred to in sub-clause (*ii*) of that clause shall, subject to the terms thereof and to any adaptations and modifications that may be made therein under article 372, continue in force until altered or repealed or amended by Parliament.

Explanation - In this article, the expression "law in force" has the same meaning as in Article 372.

Inferences: Article-31 is the *"Right to Property"* it is the *Compulsory acquisition of property repealed by the Constitution;* Article-31A, Saving of laws providing for acquisition of estates, etc.; Article-31B - Validation of certain Acts and Regulations; Article-31C, Saving of laws giving effect to certain directive principles; Article-31D "*Saving of laws in respect of anti-national activities"* Repealed by the *Constitution*; Article-32, Remedies for enforcement of rights conferred by this Part; Article-32A, *Constitutional validity of State laws not to be considered in proceedings under article* 32 *Repealed by the Constitution*; Article-33, Power of Parliament to modify the rights conferred by this Part in their application to Forces, etc; Article-34, Restriction on rights conferred by this Part while martial law is in force in any area and Article-35, Legislation to give effect to the provisions of this Part are the basic Constitutional protective Articles which enable .... *to constitute India into a Sovereign Socialist Secular Democratic Republic and to secure to all its citizens: justice, social, economic and political; liberty of thought, expression, belief, faith and worship; equality of status and of opportunity; and to promote among them all fraternity assuring the dignity of the individual and the unity and integrity of the nation.....* (Government of India, 2015) are has been reflected in the SDG-16, entitled as 'Peace, Justice and Strong Institutions'.

PART-IV: Directive Principles of State Policy

Part-IV of the Constitution of India detailed about the Directive Principles of State Policy. The Article-36, defined the spirit of the Part-IV that is; *"In this Part, unless the context otherwise requires, "the 'State' has the same meaning as in Part III"* of the Constitution of India; and Article-37, clarify the Directive Principles of State Policy, that is *"Application of the principles contained in this Part"*- The provisions contained in this Part shall not be enforceable by any court, but the principles therein laid down are nevertheless fundamental in the governance of the country and it shall be the duty of the State to apply these principles in making laws.

Article-38: *"State to secure a social order for the promotion of welfare of the people"*.

(1) The State shall strive to promote the welfare of the people by securing and protecting as effectively as it may a social order in which justice, social, economic and political, shall inform all the institutions of the national life[37].

(2) The State shall, in particular, strive to minimise the inequalities in income, and endeavour to eliminate inequalities in status, facilities and opportunities, not only amongst individuals but also amongst groups of people residing in different areas or engaged in different vocations[38].

Inferences: Subsections (1) and (2) of Article-38 has been reflected in the *SDG-16,* entitled as 'Peace, Justice and Strong Institutions' and proper implementation of the this Article will promote to 'Reduce Poverty' (SDG-1), 'Reduce Hunger' (SDG-2), 'Good Health and Wellbeing' (SDG-3) 'Quality Education' (SDG-4), 'Gender Equality'

(SDG-5), 'Clean Water and Sanitation' (SDG-6), 'Affordable and Clean Energy' (SDG-7), 'Decent Work and Economic Growth' (SDG-8), 'Industry Innovation and Infrastructure' (SDG-9), 'Reduced Inequalities' (SDG-10), 'Sustainable Cities and Communities' (SDG-11), 'Sustainable Consumption and Production' (SDG-12), 'Climate Action' (SDG-13), 'Life Below Water' (SDG-14), 'Life on Land' (SDG-15) and 'Partnerships for the Goals' (SDG-17).

Article-39: *"Certain principles of policy to be followed by the State. The State shall, in particular, direct its policy towards securing"* —

(*a*) That the citizens, men and women equally, have the right to an adequate means of livelihood;

(*b*) That the ownership and control of the material resources of the community are so distributed as best to sub-serve the common good;

(*c*) That the operation of the economic system does not result in the concentration of wealth and means of production to the common detriment;

(*d*) That there is equal pay for equal work for both men and women;

(*e*) That the health and strength of workers, men and women, and the tender age of children are not abused and that citizens are not forced by economic necessity to enter avocations unsuited to their age or strength;

(*f*) That children are given opportunities and facilities to develop in a healthy manner and in conditions of freedom and dignity and that childhood and youth are protected against exploitation and against moral and material abandonment[39].

Inferences: Subsections of (a) to (f) of Article-39 has been reflected in the *SDG-16,* entitled as 'Peace, Justice and Strong Institutions' and proper implementation of the this *Article* will promote to 'Reduce Poverty' (SDG-1), 'Reduce Hunger' (SDG-2), 'Gender Equality' (SDG-5), 'Clean Water and Sanitation' (SDG-6), 'Affordable and Clean Energy (SDG-7), 'Decent Work and Economic Growth' (SDG-8), 'Industry Innovation and Infrastructure' (SDG-9), 'Reduced Inequalities' (SDG-10), 'Schedules of the Constitution of India' (SDG-11), Sustainable Consumption and Production (SDG-12), 'Climate Action' (SDG-13), and 'Life bellow Water' (SDG-14).

Article-39A: *"Equal justice and free legal aid".*

The State shall secure that the operation of the legal system promotes justice, on a basis of equal opportunity, and shall, in particular, provide free legal aid, by suitable legislation or schemes or in any other way, to ensure that opportunities for securing justice are not denied to any citizen by reason of economic or other disabilities[40].

Inferences: Article-39A has been reflected in the *SDG-16,* entitled as 'Peace, Justice and Strong Institutions' and proper implementation of the this *Article* will promote to "Reduce Poverty' (SDG-1), 'Reduce Hunger' (SDG-2), 'Gender Equality' (SDG-5), 'Decent Work and Economic Growth' (SDG-8), 'Industry, Innovation and Infrastructure' (SDG-9), 'Reduced Inequalities' (SDG-10), 'Schedules of the Constitution of India' (SDG-11), and Sustainable Consumption and Production (SDG-12), Sustainable Consumption and Production (SDG-12), 'Climate Action' (SDG-13) and 'Life bellow Water' (SDG-14).

Article-40: *"Organisation of village panchayats".*

The State shall take steps to organise village panchayats and endow them with such powers and authority as may be necessary to enable them to function as units of self-Government.

Inferences: Article-40 has been reflected in the *SDG-16,* entitled as 'Peace, Justice and Strong Institutions' and proper implementation of the *Article* will promote to 'Gender Equality' (SDG-5), and 'Reduced Inequalities' (SDG-10).

Article-41: *"Right to work, to education and to public assistance in certain cases".*

The State shall, within the limits of its economic capacity and development, make effective provision for securing the right to work, to education and to public assistance in cases of unemployment, old age, sickness and disablement, and in other cases of undeserved want.

Inferences: Article-41 has been reflected in the *SDG-16,* entitled as 'Peace, Justice and Strong Institutions' and proper implementation of the this *Article* will promote to 'Reduce Poverty' (SDG-1), 'Reduce Hunger' (SDG-2), 'Good Health and Wellbeing' (SDG-3) 'Quality Education' (SDG-4), 'Gender Equality' (SDG-5), 'Clean Water and Sanitation' (SDG-6), 'Affordable and Clean Energy (SDG-7), 'Decent Work and Economic Growth' (SDG-8), 'Industry, Innovation and Infrastructure' (SDG-9), 'Reduced Inequalities' (SDG-10 Sustainable Consumption and Production (SDG-12), 'Climate Action' (SDG-13), 'Life bellow Water' (SDG-14) and 'Life and Land'.

Article-42: *"Provision for just and humane conditions of work and maternity relief".*

The State shall make provision for securing just and humane conditions of work and for maternity relief.

Inferences: Article-42 has been reflected in the *SDG-16,* entitled as 'Peace, Justice and Strong Institutions' and proper implementation of the *Article* will promote to 'Reduce Poverty' (SDG-1), 'Reduce Hunger' (SDG-2), 'Good Health and Wellbeing' (SDG-3), 'Gender Equality' (SDG-5), 'Clean Water and Sanitation' (SDG-6), 'Affordable and Clean Energy (SDG-7), 'Decent Work and Economic Growth' (SDG-8), 'Industry, Innovation and Infrastructure' (SDG-9), 'Reduced Inequalities' (SDG-10), Sustainable Consumption and Production (SDG-12) and 'Climate Action' (SDG-13).

Article-43: *"Living wage, etc. for workers".*

The State shall endeavour to secure, by suitable legislation or economic organisation or in any other way, to all workers, agricultural, industrial or otherwise, work, a living wage, conditions of work ensuring a decent standard of life and full enjoyment of leisure and social and cultural opportunities and, in particular, the State shall endeavour to promote cottage industries on an individual or co-operative basis in rural areas.

Inferences: Article-43 has been reflected in the *SDG-16,* entitled as 'Peace, Justice and Strong Institutions' and proper implementation of the this *Article* will directly promote to 'Decent Work and Economic Growth' (SDG-8) and this SDG results in 'Reduce Poverty' (SDG-1), 'Reduce Hunger' (SDG-2), promote 'Good Health and Wellbeing' (SDG-3) 'Quality Education' (SDG-4), 'Gender Equality' (SDG-5), 'Clean Water and Sanitation' (SDG-6), 'Affordable and Clean Energy (SDG-7), 'Industry, Innovation and Infrastructure' (SDG-9), 'Reduced Inequalities' (SDG-10), Sustainable Consumption and Production (SDG-12), 'Climate Action' (SDG-13) and 'Life bellow Water' (SDG-14).

Article-43A: *"Participation of workers in management of industries".*

The State shall take steps, by suitable legislation or in any other way, to secure the participation of workers in the management of undertakings, establishments or other organisations engaged in any industry[41].

Inferences: Article-43A has been reflected in the *SDG-16,* entitled as 'Peace, Justice and Strong Institutions' and proper implementation of the *Article* will promote to 'Gender Equality' (SDG-5), 'Decent Work and Economic Growth' (SDG-8), 'Industry, Innovation and

Infrastructure' (SDG-9), 'Reduced Inequalities' (SDG-10), 'Climate Action' (SDG-13); 'Life bellow Water' (SDG-14) and 'Partnerships for the Goals' (SDG-17).

Article-43B: *"Promotion of cooperative societies".*

The State shall endeavour to promote voluntary formation, autonomous functioning, democratic control and professional management of co-operative societies[42].

Inferences: Article 43B has been reflected in the *SDG-16,* entitled as 'Peace, Justice and Strong Institutions' and proper implementation of the *Article* will promote to 'Gender Equality' (SDG-5), 'Decent Work and Economic Growth' (SDG-8), 'Industry, Innovation and Infrastructure' (SDG-9), 'Reduced Inequalities' (SDG-10) and Sustainable Consumption and Production (SDG-12).

Article 44; *"Uniform civil code for the citizens. The State shall endeavour to secure for the citizens a uniform civil code throughout the territory of India".*

Inferences: Article-44 has been reflected in the SDG-16, entitled as 'Peace, Justice and Strong Institutions' and proper implementation of the Article will promote to 'Gender Equality' (SDG-5), 'Decent Work and Economic Growth' (SDG-8), 'Industry, Innovation and Infrastructure' (SDG-9), 'Reduced Inequalities' (SDG-10), Sustainable Consumption and Production (SDG-12), 'Climate Action' (SDG-13) and 'Life bellow Water' (SDG-14).

Article-45: *"Provision for early childhood care and education to children below the age of six years".*

The State shall endeavour to provide early childhood care and education for all children until they complete the age of six years[43].

Inferences: Article-45 has been reflected in the SDG-16, entitled as 'Peace, Justice and Strong Institutions' and proper implementation of the Article will promote to 'Reduce Hunger' (SDG-2), 'Good Health and Wellbeing' (SDG-3) 'Quality Education' (SDG-4), 'Gender Equality' (SDG-5), 'Clean Water and Sanitation' (SDG-6), 'Decent Work and Economic Growth' (SDG-8), 'Reduced Inequalities' (SDG-10), 'Sustainable Cities and Communities' (SDG-11), Sustainable Consumption and Production (SDG-12) and 'Climate Action' (SDG-13).

Article-46: *"Promotion of educational and economic interests of Scheduled Castes, Scheduled Tribes and other weaker sections".*

The State shall promote with special care the educational and economic interests of the weaker sections of the people, and, in particular, of the Scheduled Castes and the Scheduled Tribes, and shall protect them from social injustice and all forms of exploitation.

Inferences: Article-46 has been reflected in the SDG-16, entitled as 'Peace, Justice and Strong Institutions' and proper implementation of the this Article will promote to 'Reduce Poverty' (SDG-1), 'Reduce Hunger' (SDG-2), 'Quality Education' (SDG-4), 'Gender Equality' (SDG-5), 'Affordable and Clean Energy (SDG-7), 'Decent Work and Economic Growth' (SDG-8), 'Industry, Innovation and Infrastructure' (SDG-9), 'Reduced Inequalities' (SDG-10), 'Sustainable Cities and Communities' (SDG-11), Sustainable Consumption and Production (SDG-12), 'Life and Land' (SDG-15) and 'Partnerships for the Goals' (SDG-17).

Article-47: *"Duty of the State to raise the level of nutrition and the standard of living and to improve public health"*.

The State shall regard the raising of the level of nutrition and the standard of living of its people and the improvement of public health as among its primary duties and, in particular, the State shall endeavour to bring about prohibition of the consumption except for medicinal purposes of intoxicating drinks and of drugs which are injurious to health.

Inferences: Article-47 has been reflected in the SDG-16, entitled as 'Peace, Justice and Strong Institutions' and proper implementation of the Article will promote to 'Reduce Poverty' (SDG-1), 'Reduce Hunger' (SDG-2), 'Good Health and Wellbeing' (SDG-3), 'Gender Equality' (SDG-5), 'Clean Water and Sanitation' (SDG-6), 'Affordable and Clean Energy (SDG-7), 'Decent Work and Economic Growth' (SDG-8), 'Reduced Inequalities' (SDG-10), 'Sustainable Cities and Communities' (SDG-11), Sustainable Consumption and Production (SDG-12), 'Climate Action' (SDG-13) and, 'Life and Land' (SDG-15) and 'Life bellow Water (SDG-14).

Article-48: *"Organisation of agriculture and animal husbandry"*.

The State shall endeavour to organise agriculture and animal husbandry on modern and scientific lines and shall, in particular, take steps for preserving and improving the breeds, and prohibiting the slaughter, of cows and calves and other milk and draught cattle.

Inferences: Article-48 has been reflected in the SDG-16, entitled as 'Peace, Justice and Strong Institutions' and proper implementation of the this Article will promote to 'Reduce Hunger' (SDG-2), 'Good Health and Wellbeing', 'Decent Work and Economic Growth' (SDG-8), 'Industry,

Innovation and Infrastructure' (SDG-9), 'Reduced Inequalities' (SDG-10), 'Sustainable Cities and Communities' (SDG-11), 'Sustainable Consumption and Production' (SDG-12), 'Climate Action' (SDG-13) and 'Life and Land' (SDG-15).

Article-48A: *"Protection and improvement of environment and safeguarding of forests and wild life".*

The State shall endeavour to protect and improve the environment and to safeguard the forests and wild life of the country[44].

Article-49: *"Protection of monuments and places and objects of national importance".*

It shall be the obligation of the State to protect every monument or place or object of artistic or historic interest, declared by or under law made by Parliament[45] to be of national importance, from spoliation, disfigurement, destruction, removal, disposal or export, as the case may be.

Inferences: Article-48A and Article-49 has been reflected in the SDG-16, entitled as 'Peace, Justice and Strong Institutions' and proper implementation of the Article will promote to 'Affordable and Clean Energy (SDG-7), 'Decent Work and Economic Growth' (SDG-8), 'Industry, Innovation and Infrastructure' (SDG-9), 'Schedules of the Constitution of India' (SDG-11), Sustainable Consumption and Production (SDG-12), 'Climate Action' (SDG-13), 'Life bellow Water (SDG-14), and Life on Land (SDG-15).

Article-50: *"Separation of judiciary from executive".*

The State shall take steps to separate the judiciary from the executive in the public services of the State.

Article-51: *"Promotion of international peace and security".* The State shall endeavour to -

(*a*) Promote international peace and security;

(*b*) Maintain just and honourable relations between nations;

(*c*) Foster respect for international law and treaty obligations in the dealings of organised peoples with one another; and

(*d*) Encourage settlement of international disputes by arbitration.

Inferences: Article-50 and all the subsections of the Article-51 has been reflected in the overall SDG, the Articles are resolved the internal and external disputes to uphold the humanity and peace in the national and international level.

PART-IVA[46]: Fundamental Duties

Part-IVA of the Constitution of India detailed about the *"Fundamental Duties"* of every citizen in India.

Article-51A: It shall be the duty of every citizen of India—

(*a*) To abide by the Constitution and respect its ideals and institutions, the National Flag and the National Anthem;

(*b*) To cherish and follow the noble ideals which inspired our national struggle for freedom;

(*c*) To uphold and protect the sovereignty, unity and integrity of India;

(*d*) To defend the country and render national service when called upon to do so;

(*e*) To promote harmony and the spirit of common brotherhood amongst all the people of India transcending religious, linguistic and regional or sectional diversities; to renounce practices derogatory to the dignity of women;

(*f*) To value and preserve the rich heritage of our composite culture;

(*g*) To protect and improve the natural environment including forests, lakes, rivers and wild life, and to have compassion for living creatures;

(*h*) To develop the scientific temper, humanism and the spirit of inquiry and reform;

(*i*) To safeguard public property and to abjure violence;

(*j*) To strive towards excellence in all spheres of individual and collective activity so that the nation constantly rises to higher levels of endeavour and achievement;

(*k*) Who is a parent or guardian to provide opportunities for education to his child or, as the case may be, ward between the age of six and fourteen years[47].

Inferences: Subsections (a) to (j) of the Article-51A has been reflected in the overall SDG, here the Constitution of India prescribed duties of its citizen to *constitute India into a Sovereign Socialist Secular Democratic Republic and to secure to all its citizens: justice, social, economic and political; liberty of thought, expression, belief, faith and worship; equality of status and of opportunity; and to promote among them all fraternity assuring the dignity of the individual and the unity and integrity of the nation...* (India 1950/2015), the better performance of duties by the citizens able to strong the SDG-16, entitled as 'Peace, Justice and Strong Institutions'.

Again, the better performance of the part of Article-51A (g) will create better options for the future generations; which will reflected in the SDG-15, that is 'Life and Land'; SDG-13 'Climate Action'; and it will promote 'Good Health and Wellbeing' (SDG-3), 'Gender Equality' (SDG-5), 'Clean Water and Sanitation' (SDG-6), 'Affordable and Clean Energy (SDG-7), 'Decent Work and Economic Growth' (SDG-8), 'Industry, Innovation and Infrastructure' (SDG-9), 'Reduced Inequalities' (SDG-10), 'Schedules of the Constitution of India' (SDG-11), 'Sustainable Consumption and Production' (SDG-12), 'Climate Action' (SDG-13), 'Life Below Water' (SDG-14), 'Life and Land' (SDG-15) and 'Partnerships for the Goals' (SDG-17). The *(k)* of Article 51A directly promote the 'Quality Education' (SDG-4).

PART-IX[48]: The Panchayats

Part-IX of the Constitution of India detailed about the *Panchayats* System in India. The Article-243, defined the spirit of the Part-IX, these are as -

Article-243: In this Part, unless the context otherwise requires,—

(*a*) "District" means a district in a State;

(*b*) "Gram Sabha" means a body consisting of persons registered in the electoral rolls relating to a village comprised within the area of Panchayat at the village level;

(*c*) "Intermediate level" means a level between the village and district levels specified by the Governor of a State by public notification to be the intermediate level for the purposes of this Part;

(*d*) "Panchayat" means an institution (by whatever name called) of self-government constituted under Article - 243B, for the rural areas;

(*e*) "Panchayat area" means the territorial area of a Panchayat;

(*f*) "Population" means the population as ascertained at the last preceding census of which the relevant figures have been published;

(*g*) "Village" means a village specified by the Governor by public notification to be a village for the purposes of this Part and includes a group of villages so specified.

Article-243A: *"Gram Sabha"* -

A Gram Sabha may exercise such powers and perform such functions at the village level as the Legislature of a State may, by law, provide.

Article-243B: *"Constitution of Panchayats"*-

(1) There shall be constituted in every State, Panchayats at the village, intermediate and district levels in accordance with the provisions of this Part.

(2) Notwithstanding anything in clause (1), Panchayats at the intermediate level may not be constituted in a State having a population not exceeding twenty lakhs.

Article-243C: *"Composition of Panchayats"* -

(1) Subject to the provisions of this Part, the Legislature of a State may, by law, make provisions with respect to the composition of Panchayats: Provided that the ratio between the population of the territorial area of a Panchayat at any level and the number of seats in such Panchayat to be filled by election shall, so far as practicable, be the same throughout the State.

(2) All the seats in a Panchayat shall be filled by persons chosen by direct election from territorial constituencies in the Panchayat area and, for this purpose, each Panchayat area shall be divided into territorial constituencies in such manner that the ratio between the population of each constituency and the number of seats allotted to it shall, so far as practicable, be the same throughout the Panchayat area.

(3) The Legislature of a State may, by law, provide for the representation—

(*a*) of the Chairpersons of the Panchayats at the village level, in the Panchayats at the intermediate level or, in the case of a State not having Panchayats at the intermediate level, in the Panchayats at the district level;

(*b*) Of the Chairpersons of the Panchayats at the intermediate level, in the Panchayats at the district level;

(*c*) Of the members of the House of the People and the members of the Legislative Assembly of the State representing constituencies which comprise wholly or partly a Panchayat area at a level other than the village level, in such Panchayat;

(*d*) Of the members of the Council of States and the members of the Legislative Council of the State, where they are registered as electors within—

(*i*) A Panchayat area at the intermediate level, in Panchayat at the intermediate level;

(*ii*) A Panchayat area at the district level, in Panchayat at the district level.

(4) The Chairperson of a Panchayat and other members of a Panchayat whether or not chosen by direct election from territorial constituencies in the Panchayat area shall have the right to vote in the meetings of the Panchayats.

(5) The Chairperson of—

(*a*) A Panchayat at the village level shall be elected in such manner as the Legislature of a State may, by law, provide; and

(*b*) A Panchayat at the intermediate level or district level shall be elected by, and from amongst, the elected members thereof.

Article-243D: *"Reservation of seats"*.

(1) Seats shall be reserved for — (*a*) the Scheduled Castes; and (*b*) the Scheduled Tribes, in every Panchayat and the number of seats so reserved shall bear, as nearly as may be, the same proportion to the total number of seats to be filled by direct election in that Panchayat as the population of the Scheduled Castes in that Panchayat area or of the Scheduled Tribes in that Panchayat area bears to the total population of that area and such seats may be allotted by rotation to different constituencies in a Panchayat.

(2) Not less than one-third of the total number of seats reserved under clause (1) shall be reserved for women belonging to the Scheduled Castes or, as the case may be, the Scheduled Tribes.

(3) Not less than one-third (including the number of seats reserved for women belonging to the Scheduled Castes and the Scheduled Tribes) of the total number of seats to be filled by direct election in every Panchayat shall be reserved for women and such seats may be allotted by rotation to different constituencies in a Panchayat.

(4) The offices of the Chairpersons in the Panchayats at the village or any other level shall be reserved for the Scheduled Castes, the

Scheduled Tribes and women in such manner as the Legislature of a State may, by law, provide:

Provided that the number of offices of Chairpersons reserved for the Scheduled Castes and the Scheduled Tribes in the Panchayats at each level in any State shall bear, as nearly as may be, the same proportion to the total number of such offices in the Panchayats at each level as the population of the Scheduled Castes in the State or of the Scheduled Tribes in the State bears to the total population of the State:

Provided further that not less than one-third of the total number of offices of Chairpersons in the Panchayats at each level shall be reserved for women:

Provided also that the number of offices reserved under this clause shall be allotted by rotation to different Panchayats at each level.

(5) The reservation of seats under clauses (1) and (2) and the reservation of offices of Chairpersons (other than the reservation for women) under clause (4) shall cease to have effect on the expiration of the period specified in Article 334.

(6) Nothing in this Part shall prevent the Legislature of a State from making any provision for reservation of seats in any Panchayat or offices of Chairpersons in the Panchayats at any level in favour of backward class of citizens.

Inferences: All the sections and subsections of Article-243, Article-243A, Article-243B, Article-243C and Article-243D has been reflected in the SDG-16, entitled as 'Peace, Justice and Strong Institutions' and proper implementation of the Article will promote to 'Reduced Inequalities' (SDG-10) and 'Partnerships for the Goals' (SDG-17).

PART-IXA[49]: The Municipalities

Part-IXA of the Constitution of India detailed about the Municipalities in India. The Article-243P, defined the spirit of the Part IX, these are as -

Article 243P: In this Part, unless the context otherwise requires,—

(*a*) "Committee" means a Committee constituted under article 243S;

(*b*) "District" means a district in a State;

(*c*) "Metropolitan area" means an area having a population of ten lakhs or more, comprised in one or more districts and consisting of two or more Municipalities or Panchayats or other contiguous areas, specified by the Governor by public notification to be a Metropolitan area for the purposes of this Part;

(*d*) "Municipal area" means the territorial area of a Municipality as is notified by the Governor;

(*e*) "Municipality" means an institution of self-government constituted under article 243Q;

(*f*) "Panchayat" means a Panchayat constituted under article 243B;

(*g*) "Population" means the population as ascertained at the last preceding census of which the relevant figures have been published.

Article 243Q: (1) There shall be constituted in every State,—

(*a*) A Nagar Panchayat (by whatever name called) for a transitional area, that is to say, an area in transition from a rural area to an urban area;

(*b*) A Municipal Council for a smaller urban area; and

(*c*) A Municipal Corporation for a larger urban area, in accordance with the provisions of this Part:

Provided that a Municipality under this clause may not be constituted in such urban area or part thereof as the Governor may, having regard to the size of the area and the municipal services being provided or proposed to be provided by an industrial establishment in that area and such other factors as he may deem fit, by public notification, specify to be an industrial township.

(2) In this article, "a transitional area", "a smaller urban area" or "a larger urban area" means such area as the Governor may, having regard to the population of the area, the density of the population therein, the revenue generated for local administration, the percentage of employment in non-agricultural activities, the economic importance or such other factors as he may deem fit, specify by public notification for the purposes of this Part.

Article 243R: (1) Save as provided in clause (2), all the seats in a Municipality shall be filled by persons chosen by direct election from the territorial constituencies in the Municipal area and for this purpose each Municipal area shall be divided into territorial constituencies to be known as wards.

(2) The Legislature of a State may, by law, provide -

(*a*) For the representation in a Municipality of -

(*i*) Persons having special knowledge or experience in Municipal administration;

(*ii*) The members of the House of the People and the members of the Legislative Assembly of the State representing constituencies which comprise wholly or partly the Municipal area;

(*iii*) The members of the Council of States and the members of the Legislative Council of the State registered as electors within the Municipal area;

(*iv*) The Chairpersons of the Committees constituted under clause (5) of article 243S:

Provided that the persons referred to in paragraph (*i*) shall not have the right to vote in the meetings of the Municipality; (*b*) the manner of election of the Chairperson of a Municipality.

Article 243S: *"Constitution and composition of Wards Committees, etc."* -

(1) There shall be constituted Wards Committees, consisting of one or more wards, within the territorial area of a Municipality having a population of three lakhs or more.

(2) The Legislature of a State may, by law, make provision with respect to -

(*a*) The composition and the territorial area of a Wards Committee;

(*b*) The manner in which the seats in a Wards Committee shall be filled.

(3) A member of a Municipality representing a ward within the territorial area of the Wards Committee shall be a member of that Committee.

(4) Where a Wards Committee consists of -

(*a*) One ward, the member representing that ward in the Municipality; or

(*b*) Two or more wards, one of the members representing such wards in the Municipality elected by the members of the Wards Committee, shall be the Chairperson of that Committee.

(5) Nothing in this article shall be deemed to prevent the Legislature of a State from making any provision for the constitution of Committees in addition to the Wards Committees.

Article 243T: "Reservation of seats".

(1) Seats shall be reserved for the Scheduled Castes and the Scheduled Tribes in every Municipality and the number of seats so reserved shall bear, as nearly as may be, the same proportion to the total number of seats to be filled by direct election in that Municipality as the population of the Scheduled Castes in the Municipal area or of the Scheduled Tribes in the Municipal area bears to the total population of that area and such seats may be allotted by rotation to different constituencies in a Municipality.

(2) Not less than one-third of the total number of seats reserved under clause (1) shall be reserved for women belonging to the Scheduled Castes or, as the case may be, the Scheduled Tribes.

(3) Not less than one-third (including the number of seats reserved for women belonging to the Scheduled Castes and the Scheduled Tribes) of the total number of seats to be filled by direct election in every Municipality shall be reserved for women and such seats may be allotted by rotation to different constituencies in a Municipality.

(4) The offices of Chairpersons in the Municipalities shall be reserved for the Scheduled Castes, the Scheduled Tribes and women in such manner as the Legislature of a State may, by law, provide.

(5) The reservation of seats under clauses (1) and (2) and the reservation of offices of Chairpersons (other than the reservation for women) under clause (4) shall cease to have effect on the expiration of the period specified in Article 334.

(6) Nothing in this Part shall prevent the Legislature of a State from making any provision for reservation of seats in any Municipality or offices of Chairpersons in the Municipalities in favour of backward class of citizens.

Inferences: All the sections and subsections of Article-243P, Article-243Q, Article-243R, Article-243S and Article-243T has been reflected in the *SDG-16,* entitled as 'Peace, Justice and Strong Institutions' and proper implementation of the *Article* will promote to 'Reduced Inequalities' (SDG-10) and 'Partnerships for the Goals' (SDG-17).

PART-XIII: Trade, Commerce and Intercourse within the Territory of India

Part-XIII of the Constitution of India detailed about the Trade, Commerce and Intercourse within the Territory of India.

Article-301: *"Freedom of trade, commerce and intercourse".*

Subject to the other provisions of this Part, trade, commerce and intercourse throughout the territory of India shall be free.

Inferences: Article-301 has been reflected in the SDG-16, entitled as 'Peace, Justice and Strong Institutions' and proper implementation of the Article will directly promote to 'Gender Equality' (SDG-5), 'Decent Work and Economic Growth' (SDG-8), 'Industry Innovation and Infrastructure' (SDG-9), 'Reduced Inequalities' (SDG-10), 'Sustainable Consumption and Production' (SDG-12) and 'Life bellow Water' (SDG-14).

Article-302: *"Power of Parliament to impose restrictions on trade, commerce and intercourse".*

Parliament may by law impose such restrictions on the freedom of trade, commerce or intercourse between one State and another or within any part of the territory of India as may be required in the public interest.

Inferences: Article-302 has been reflected in the SDG-16, entitled as 'Peace, Justice and Strong Institutions' and proper implementation of the Article will directly promote to peaceful environment of 'Decent Work and Economic Growth' (SDG-8), 'Industry Innovation and Infrastructure' (SDG-9), 'Reduced Inequalities' (SDG-10), 'Sustainable Consumption and Production' (SDG-12), 'Climate Action' (SDG-13) and 'Life bellow Water' (SDG-14).

Article-303: *"Restrictions on the legislative powers of the Union and of the States with regard to trade and commerce".*

(1) Notwithstanding anything in Article 302, neither Parliament nor the Legislature of a State shall have power to make any law giving, or authorising the giving of, any preference to one State over another, or making, or authorising the making of, any discrimination between one State and another, by virtue of any entry relating to trade and commerce in any of the Lists in the Seventh Schedule.

(2) Nothing in clause (1) shall prevent Parliament from making any law giving, or authorising the giving of, any preference or making, or authorising the making of, any discrimination if it is declared by such law that it is necessary to do so for the purpose of dealing with a situation arising from scarcity of goods in any part of the territory of India.

Inferences: Subsections (1) and (2) of Article-303 has been reflected in the SDG-16, entitled as 'Peace, Justice and Strong Institutions' and proper implementation of the Article will directly promote to peace full environment of 'Decent Work and Economic Growth' (SDG-8), 'Industry Innovation and Infrastructure' (SDG-9), 'Reduced Inequalities' (SDG-10), 'Sustainable Consumption and Production' (SDG-12), 'Climate Action' (SDG-13) and 'Life bellow Water' (SDG-14).

Article-304: *"Restrictions on trade, commerce and intercourse among States".*

Notwithstanding anything in article 301 or article 303, the Legislature of a State may by law -

(*a*) Impose on goods imported from other States or the Union territories[50] any tax to which similar goods manufactured or produced in that State are subject, so, however, as not to discriminate between goods so imported and goods so manufactured or produced; and

(*b*) Impose such reasonable restrictions on the freedom of trade, commerce or intercourse with or within that State as may be required in the public interest:

Provided that no Bill or amendment for the purposes of clause (*b*) shall be introduced or moved in the Legislature of a State without the previous sanction of the President.

Article-305 *"Saving of existing laws and laws providing for State monopolies".*

Nothing in articles 301 and 303 shall affect the provisions of any existing law except in so far as the President may by order otherwise direct; and nothing in article 301 shall affect the operation of any law made before the commencement of the Constitution (Fourth Amendment) Act, 1955, in so far as it relates to, or prevent Parliament or the Legislature of a State from making any law relating to, any such matter as is referred to in sub-clause (*ii*) of clause (6) of article 19[51].

Inferences: Article 304 and Article 305 has been reflected in the SDG-16, entitled as 'Peace, Justice and Strong Institutions' and proper implementation of this Article will directly promote to peaceful environment of 'Decent Work and Economic Growth' (SDG-8), 'Industry Innovation and Infrastructure' (SDG-9), 'Reduced Inequalities' (SDG-10), 'Sustainable Consumption and Production' (SDG-12), 'Climate Action' (SDG-13), 'Life bellow Water' (SDG-14) and 'Life and Land' (SDG-15).

Article-306: *"Power of certain States in Part B of the First Schedule to impose restrictions on trade and commerce" Repealed by the Constitution (Seventh Amendment) Act,* 1956, *Section* - 29 *and Schedule.*

Article-307: *"Appointment of authority for carrying out the purposes of articles 301 to 304".*

Parliament may by law appoint such authority as it considers appropriate for carrying out the purposes of articles 301, 302, 303 and 304, and confer on the authority so appointed such powers and such duties as it thinks necessary.

Inferences: Article 306 and Article 307 has been reflected in the SDG-16, entitled as 'Peace, Justice and Strong Institutions' and proper implementation of the Article will directly promote to peaceful environment of 'Decent Work and Economic Growth' (SDG-8), 'Industry Innovation and Infrastructure' (SDG-9), 'Reduced Inequalities' (SDG-10), 'Sustainable Consumption and Production' (SDG-12), 'Climate Action' (SDG-13), 'Life bellow Water' (SDG-14) and 'Life and Land' (SDG-15).

PART-XIV, Services under the Union and the States, Chapter-I, Services

Part-XIV, 'Chapter-I – Services' of the Constitution of India detailed about the 'Services under the Union and the States'. In the Article 308 – there is an 'Interpretation' "In this Part, unless the context otherwise requires, the expression "State" (does not include the State of Jammu and Kashmir[52].

Article-309: *"Recruitment and conditions of service of persons serving the Union or a State".*

Subject to the provisions of this Constitution, Acts of the appropriate Legislature may regulate the recruitment, and conditions of service of persons appointed, to public services and posts in connection with the affairs of the Union or of any State:

Provided that it shall be competent for the President or such person as he may direct in the case of services and posts in connection with the affairs of the Union, and for the Governor[53] of a State or such person as he may direct in the case of services and posts in connection with the affairs of the State, to make rules regulating the recruitment, and the conditions of service of persons appointed, to such services and posts until provision in that behalf is made by or under an Act of the appropriate Legislature under this article, and any rules so made shall have effect subject to the provisions of any such Act.

Article-310: *"Tenure of office of persons serving the Union or a State".*

(1) Except as expressly provided by this Constitution, every person who is a member of a defence service or of a civil service of the Union or of an all-India service or holds any post connected with defence or any civil post under the Union holds office during the pleasure of the President, and every person who is a member of a civil service of a State or holds any civil post under a State holds office during the pleasure of the Governor of the State.

(2) Notwithstanding that a person holding a civil post under the Union or a State holds office during the pleasure of the President or, as the case may be, of the Governor of the State, any contract under which a person, not being a member of a defence service or of an all-India service or of a civil service of the Union or a State, is appointed under this Constitution to hold such a post may, if the President or the Governor, as the case may be, deems it necessary in order to secure the services of a person having special qualifications, provide for the payment to him of compensation, if before the expiration of an agreed period that post is abolished or he is, for reasons not connected with any misconduct on his part, required to vacate that post.

Article-311: *"Dismissal, removal or reduction in rank of persons employed in civil capacities under the Union or a State".*

(1) No person who is a member of a civil service of the Union or an all-India service or a civil service of a State or holds a civil post under the Union or a State shall be dismissed or removed by an authority subordinate to that by which he was appointed.

(2)[54] No such person as aforesaid shall be dismissed or removed or reduced in rank except after an inquiry in which he has been informed of the charges against him and given a reasonable opportunity of being heard in respect of those charges[55]:

(Provided that where it is proposed after such inquiry, to impose upon him any such penalty, such penalty may be imposed on the basis of the evidence adduced during such inquiry and it shall not be necessary to give such person any opportunity of making representation on the penalty proposed:

Provided further that this clause shall not apply)[56] -

(*a*) where a person is dismissed or removed or reduced in rank on the ground of conduct which has led to his conviction on a criminal charge; or

(*b*) where the authority empowered to dismiss or remove a person or to reduce him in rank is satisfied that for some reason, to be recorded by that authority in writing, it is not reasonably practicable to hold such inquiry; or

(*c*) where the President or the Governor, as the case may be, is satisfied that in the interest of the security of the State it is not expedient to hold such inquiry.

(3) If, in respect of any such person as aforesaid, a question arises whether it is reasonably practicable to hold such inquiry as is referred to in clause (2), the decision thereon of the authority empowered to dismiss or remove such person or to reduce him in rank shall be final.

Article-312: *"All-India Services"*.

(1) Notwithstanding anything in (Chapter VI of Part VI or Part XI)[57], if the Council of States has declared by resolution supported by not less than two-thirds of the members present and voting that it is necessary or expedient in the national interest so to do, Parliament may by law provide for the creation of one or more all-India services (including an all-India judicial service) [82] common to the Union and the States, and, subject to the other provisions of this Chapter, regulate the recruitment, and the conditions of service of persons appointed, to any such service.

(2) The services known at the commencement of this Constitution as the Indian Administrative Service and the Indian Police Service shall be deemed to be services created by Parliament under this article.

(3) The all-India judicial service referred to in clause (1) shall not include any post inferior to that of a district judge as defined in article 236[58].

(4) The law providing for the creation of all-India judicial service aforesaid may contain such provisions for the amendment of Chapter VI of Part VI as may be necessary for giving effect to the provisions of that law and no such law shall be deemed to be an amendment of this Constitution for the purposes of article 368.

Article-312A: *"Power of Parliament to vary or revoke conditions of service of officers of certain services"*[59].

(1) Parliament may by law—

(*a*) vary or revoke, whether prospectively or retrospectively, the conditions of services as respects remuneration, leave and pension and the rights as respects disciplinary matters of persons who, having been appointed by the Secretary of State or Secretary of State in Council to a civil service of the Crown in India before the commencement of this Constitution, continue on and after the commencement of the Constitution (Twenty-eighth Amendment) Act, 1972, to serve under the Government of India or of a State in any service or post;

(*b*) vary or revoke, whether prospectively or retrospectively, the conditions of service as respects pension of persons who, having been appointed by the Secretary of State or Secretary of State in Council to a civil service of the Crown in India before the commencement of this Constitution, retired or otherwise ceased to be in service at any time before the commencement of the Constitution (Twenty-eighth Amendment) Act, 1972:

Provided that in the case of any such person who is holding or has held the office of the Chief Justice or other Judge of the Supreme Court or a High Court, the Comptroller and Auditor-General of India, the Chairman or other member of the Union or a State Public Service Commission or the Chief Election Commissioner, nothing in sub-clause (*a*) or sub-clause (*b*) shall be construed as empowering Parliament to vary or revoke, after his appointment to such post, the conditions of his service to his disadvantage except in so far as such conditions of service are applicable to him by reason of his being a person appointed by the Secretary of State or Secretary of State in Council to a civil service of the Crown in India.

(2) Except to the extent provided for by Parliament by law under this article, nothing in this article shall affect the power of any Legislature or other authority under any other provision of this Constitution to regulate the conditions of service of persons referred to in clause (1).

(3) Neither the Supreme Court nor any other court shall have jurisdiction in—

(*a*) Any dispute arising out of any provision of, or any endorsement on, any covenant, agreement or other similar instrument which was entered into or executed by any person referred to in clause (1), or arising out of any letter issued to such person, in relation to his appointment to any civil service of the Crown in India or his continuance in service under the Government of the Dominion of India or a Province thereof;

(*b*) Any dispute in respect of any right, liability or obligation under article 314 as originally enacted.

(4) The provisions of this article shall have effect notwithstanding anything in article 314 as originally enacted or in any other provision of this Constitution.

Article-313: *"Transitional provisions"*.

Until other provision is made in this behalf under this Constitution, all the laws in force immediately before the commencement of this Constitution and applicable to any public service or any post which continues to exist after the commencement of this Constitution, as an all-India service or as service or post under the Union or a State shall continue in force so far as consistent with the provisions of this Constitution.

Article-314: *Provision for protection of existing officers of certain services;* Repealed by the Constitution (Twenty-eighth Amendment) Act, 1972, s. 3 (w.e.f. 29-8-1972)[60].

CHAPTER-II: Public Service Commissions

Article-315: *"Public Service Commissions for the Union and for the States"*.

(1) Subject to the provisions of this article, there shall be a Public Service Commission for the Union and a Public Service Commission for each State.

(2) Two or more States may agree that there shall be one Public Service Commission for that group of States, and if a resolution to that effect is passed by the House or, where there are two Houses, by each House of the Legislature of each of those States, Parliament may by law provide for the appointment of a Joint State Public Service Commission (referred to in this Chapter as Joint Commission) to serve the needs of those States.

(3) Any such law as aforesaid may contain such incidental and consequential provisions as may be necessary or desirable for giving effect to the purposes of the law.

(4) The Public Service Commission for the Union, if requested so to do by the Governor of a State, may, with the approval of the President, agree to serve all or any of the needs of the State.

(5) References in this Constitution to the Union Public Service Commission or a State Public Service Commission shall, unless the context otherwise requires, be construed as references to the Commission serving the needs of the Union or, as the case may be, the State as respects the particular matter in question.

Article-320: *"Functions of Public Service Commissions"*.

(1) It shall be the duty of the Union and the State Public Service Commissions to conduct examinations for appointments to the services of the Union and the services of the State respectively.

(2) It shall also be the duty of the Union Public Service Commission, if requested by any two or more States so to do, to assist those States in framing and operating schemes of joint recruitment for any services for which candidates possessing special qualifications are required.

(3) The Union Public Service Commission or the State Public Service Commission, as the case may be, shall be consulted -

(*a*) on all matters relating to methods of recruitment to civil services and for civil posts;

(*b*) on the principles to be followed in making appointments to civil services and posts and in making promotions and transfers from one service to another and on the suitability of candidates for such appointments, promotions or transfers;

(*c*) on all disciplinary matters affecting a person serving under the Government of India or the Government of a State in a civil capacity, including memorials or petitions relating to such matters;

(*d*) on any claim by or in respect of a person who is serving or has served under the Government of India or the Government of a State or under the Crown in India or under the Government of an Indian State, in a civil capacity, that any costs incurred by him in defending legal proceedings instituted against him in respect of acts done or purporting to be done in the execution of his duty should be paid out of the Consolidated Fund of India, or, as the case may be, out of the Consolidated Fund of the State;

(*e*) on any claim for the award of a pension in respect of injuries sustained by a person while serving under the Government of India or the Government of a State or under the Crown in India or under the Government of an Indian State, in a civil capacity, and any question as to the amount of any such award, and it shall be the duty of a Public Service Commission to advise on any matter so referred to them and on any other matter which the President, or, as the case may be, the Governor of the State, may refer to them:

Provided that the President as respects the all-India services and also as respects other services and posts in connection with the affairs of the Union, and the Governor, as respects other services and posts in connection with the affairs of a State, may make regulations specifying the matters in which either generally, or in any particular class of case or in any particular circumstances, it shall not be necessary for a Public Service Commission to be consulted.

(4) Nothing in clause (3) shall require a Public Service Commission to be consulted as respects the manner in which any provision referred to in clause (4) of article 16 may be made or as respects the manner in which effect may be given to the provisions of article 335.

(5) All regulations made under the proviso to clause (3) by the President or the Governor of a State shall be laid for not less than fourteen days before each House of Parliament or the House or each House of the Legislature of the State, as the case may be, as soon as possible after they are made, and shall be subject to such modifications, whether by way of repeal or amendment, as both Houses of Parliament or the House or both Houses of the Legislature of the State may make during the session in which they are so laid.

PART-XIVA[61]: Tribunals

Part-XIVA, of the Constitution of India detailed about the 'Tribunals' for the adjudication of disputes and complaints on the following issues.

Article-323A: "Administrative tribunals".

(1) Parliament may, by law, provide for the adjudication or trial by administrative tribunals of disputes and complaints with respect to recruitment and conditions of service of persons appointed to public services and posts in connection with the affairs of the Union or of any State or of any local or other authority within the territory of India or under the control of the Government of India or of any corporation owned or controlled by the Government.

(2) A law made under clause (1) may—

(*a*) Provide for the establishment of an administrative tribunal for the Union and a separate administrative tribunal for each State or for two or more States;

(*b*) Specify the jurisdiction, powers (including the power to punish for contempt) and authority which may be exercised by each of the said tribunals;

(*c*) Provide for the procedure (including provisions as to limitation and rules of evidence) to be followed by the said tribunals;

(*d*) Exclude the jurisdiction of all courts, except the jurisdiction of the Supreme Court under article 136, with respect to the disputes or complaints referred to in clause (1);

(*e*) Provide for the transfer to each such administrative tribunal of any cases pending before any court or other authority immediately before the establishment of such tribunal as would have been within the jurisdiction of such tribunal if the causes of action on which such suits or proceedings are based had arisen after such establishment;

(*f*) Repeal or amend any order made by the President under clause (3) of article 371D; (*g*) contain such supplemental, incidental and consequential provisions (including provisions as to fees) as Parliament may deem necessary for the effective functioning of, and for the speedy disposal of cases by, and the enforcement of the orders of, such tribunals.

(3) The provisions of this article shall have effect notwithstanding anything in any other provision of this Constitution or in any other law for the time being in force.

Article-323B: *"Tribunals for other matters"*.

(1) The appropriate Legislature may, by law, provide for the adjudication or trial by tribunals of any disputes, complaints, or offences with respect to all or any of the matters specified in clause (2) with respect to which such Legislature has power to make laws.

(2) The matters referred to in clause (1) are the following, namely:—

(*a*) Levy, assessment, collection and enforcement of any tax;

(*b*) Foreign exchange, import and export across customs frontiers;

(*c*) Industrial and labour disputes;

(*d*) Land reforms by way of acquisition by the State of any estate as defined in article 31A or of any rights therein or the extinguishment or modification of any such rights or by way of ceiling on agricultural land or in any other way;

(*e*) Ceiling on urban property;

(*f*) Elections to either House of Parliament or the House or either House of the Legislature of a State, but excluding the matters referred to in article 329 and article 329A;

(*g*) Production, procurement, supply and distribution of food-stuffs (including edible oilseeds and oils) and such other goods as the President may, by public notification, declare to be essential goods for the purpose of this article and control of prices of such goods;

(*h*) Rent, its regulation and control and tenancy issues including the right, title and interest of landlords and tenants[62];

(*i*)[63] Offences against laws with respect to any of the matters specified in sub-clauses (*a*) to (*h*)[64] and fees in respect of any of those matters;

(*j*)[65] any matter incidental to any of the matters specified in sub-clauses (*a*) to 4 (*i*)[66].

(3) A law made under clause (1) may—

(*a*) Provide for the establishment of a hierarchy of tribunals;

(*b*) Specify the jurisdiction, powers (including the power to punish for contempt) and authority which may be exercised by each of the said tribunals;

(*c*) Provide for the procedure (including provisions as to limitation and rules of evidence) to be followed by the said tribunals;

(*d*) Exclude the jurisdiction of all courts, except the jurisdiction of the Supreme Court under article 136, with respect to all or any of the matters falling within the jurisdiction of the said tribunals;

(*e*) Provide for the transfer to each such tribunal of any cases pending before any court or any other authority immediately before the establishment of such tribunal as would have been within the jurisdiction of such tribunal if the causes of action on which such suits or proceedings are based had arisen after such establishment;

(*f*) Contain such supplemental, incidental and consequential provisions (including provisions as to fees) as the appropriate Legislature may deem necessary for the effective functioning of, and for the speedy disposal of cases by, and the enforcement of the orders of, such tribunals.

(4) The provisions of this article have effect notwithstanding anything in any other provision of this Constitution or in any other law for the time being in force.

Explanation - In this article, "appropriate Legislature", in relation to any matter, means Parliament or, as the case may be, a State Legislature competent to make laws with respect to such matter in accordance with the provisions of Part XI.

Inferences: All the sections and subsections of Article-309, Article-310, Article-311, Article-312, Article-313, Article-314, Article-315, Article-320, Article-323A and Article-323B has been reflected in the *SDG-16,* entitled as 'Peace, Justice and Strong Institutions' and proper implementation of the this *Article* will promote to 'Reduce Poverty' (SDG-1), 'Reduce Hunger' (SDG-2), 'Good Health and Wellbeing' (SDG-3) 'Quality Education' (SDG-4), 'Gender Equality' (SDG-5), 'Clean Water and Sanitation' (SDG-6), 'Affordable and Clean Energy' (SDG-7), 'Decent Work and Economic Growth' (SDG-8), 'Industry Innovation and Infrastructure' (SDG-9), 'Reduced Inequalities' (SDG-10), 'Sustainable Cities and Communities' (SDG-11), 'Sustainable Consumption and Production' (SDG-12), 'Climate Action' (SDG-13), 'Life Below Water' (SDG-14), 'Life on Land' (SDG-15) and 'Partnerships for the Goals' (SDG-17).

PART-XV: Elections

Part-XV, of the Constitution of India detailed about the 'Elections', the relevant part of this part analysed as -

Article-325: *"No person to be ineligible for inclusion in, or to claim to be included in a special, electoral roll on grounds of religion, race, caste or sex".*

There shall be one general electoral roll for every territorial constituency for election to either House of Parliament or to the House or either House of the Legislature of a State and no person shall be ineligible for inclusion in any such roll or claim to be included in any special electoral roll for any such constituency on grounds only of religion, race, caste, sex or any of them.

Article-326: *"Elections to the House of the People and to the Legislative Assemblies of States to be on the basis of adult suffrage".*

The elections to the House of the People and to the Legislative Assembly of every State shall be on the basis of adult suffrage; that is to say, every person who is a citizen of India and who is not less than (eighteen years)[67] of age on such date as may be fixed in that behalf by or under any law made by the appropriate Legislature and is not otherwise disqualified under this Constitution or any law made by the appropriate Legislature on the ground of non-residence, unsoundness of mind, crime or corrupt or illegal practice, shall be entitled to be registered as a voter at any such election.

PART-XVI: Special Provisions Relating to Certain Classes

Part-XVI, of the Constitution of India detailed about the 'Special Provisions Relating to Certain Classes', the relevant part of this part analysed as -

Article-330: *"Reservation of seats for Scheduled Castes and Scheduled Tribes in the House of the People".*

(1) Seats shall be reserved in the House of the People for—

- (*a*) The Scheduled Castes;
- (*b*) The Scheduled Tribes except the Scheduled Tribes in the autonomous districts of Assam[68]; and
- (*c*) The Scheduled Tribes in the autonomous districts of Assam.

(2) The number of seats reserved in any State or Union territory[69] for the Scheduled Castes or the Scheduled Tribes under clause

(1) shall bear, as nearly as may be, the same proportion to the total number of seats allotted to that State or Union territory in the House of the

People as the population of the Scheduled Castes in the State or Union territory[91] or of the Scheduled Tribes in the State or Union territory or part of the State or Union territory, as the case may be, in respect of which seats are so reserved, bears to the total population of the State or Union territory.

(3). Notwithstanding anything contained in clause (2), the number of seats reserved in the House of the People for the Scheduled Tribes in the autonomous districts of Assam shall bear to the total number of seats allotted to that State a proportion not less than the population of the Scheduled Tribes in the said autonomous districts bears to the total population of the State[70].

Article-331: *"Representation of the Anglo-Indian community in the House of the People".*

Notwithstanding anything in article 81, the President may, if he is of opinion that the Anglo-Indian community is not adequately represented in the House of the People, nominate not more than two members of that community to the House of the People.

Article-332: *"Reservation of seats for Scheduled Castes and Scheduled Tribes in the Legislative Assemblies of the States".*

(1) Seats shall be reserved for the Scheduled Castes and the Scheduled Tribes, (except the Scheduled Tribes in the autonomous districts of Assam)[71], in the Legislative Assembly of every State[72].

(2) Seats shall be reserved also for the autonomous districts in the Legislative Assembly of the State of Assam.

(3) The number of seats reserved for the Scheduled Castes or the Scheduled Tribes in the Legislative Assembly of any State under clause (1) shall bear, as nearly as may be, the same proportion to the total number of seats in the Assembly as the population of the Scheduled Castes in the State or of the Scheduled Tribes in the State or part of the State, as the case may be, in respect of which seats are so reserved, bears to the total population of the State.

(3A)[73] Notwithstanding anything contained in clause (3), until the taking effect, under article 170, of the re-adjustment, on the basis of the first census after the year 2026[74], of the number of seats in the Legislative Assemblies of the States of Arunachal Pradesh, Meghalaya, Mizoram and Nagaland, the seats which shall be reserved for the Scheduled Tribes in the Legislative Assembly of any such State shall be,—

(*a*) if all the seats in the Legislative Assembly of such State in existence on the date of coming into force of the Constitution (Fifty-seventh Amendment) Act, 1987 (hereafter in this clause referred to as the existing Assembly) are held by members of the Scheduled Tribes, all the seats except one;

(*b*) in any other case, such number of seats as bears to the total number of seats, a proportion not less than the number (as on the said date) of members belonging to the Scheduled Tribes in the existing Assembly bears to the total number of seats in thc cxisting Assembly.

(3B)[75] Notwithstanding anything contained in clause (3), until the re-adjustment, under article 170, takes effect on the basis of the first census after the year 2026[98], of the number of seats in the Legislative Assembly of the State of Tripura, the seats which shall be reserved for the Scheduled Tribes in the Legislative Assembly shall be, such number of seats as bears to the total number of seats, a proportion not less than the number, as on the date of coming into force of the Constitution (Seventy second Amendment) Act, 1992, of members belonging to the Scheduled Tribes in the Legislative Assembly in existence on the said date bears to the total number of seats in that Assembly.

(4) The number of seats reserved for an autonomous district in the Legislative Assembly of the State of Assam shall bear to the total number of seats in that Assembly a proportion not less than the population of the district bears to the total population of the State.

(5) The constituencies for the seats reserved for any autonomous district of Assam shall not comprise any area outside that district[76].

(6) No person who is not a member of a Scheduled Tribe of any autonomous district of the State of Assam shall be eligible for election to the Legislative Assembly of the State from any constituency of that district[77]:

Provided that for elections to the Legislative Assembly of the State of Assam, the representation of the Scheduled Tribes and non-Scheduled

Tribes in the constituencies included in the Bodoland Territorial Areas District, so notified, and existing prior to the constitution of the Bodoland Territorial Areas District, shall be maintained[78].

Article-333: *"Representation of the Anglo-Indian community in the Legislative Assemblies of the States".*

Notwithstanding anything in article 170, the Governor of a State may, if he is of opinion that the Anglo-Indian community needs representation in the Legislative Assembly of the State and is not adequately represented therein, nominate one member of that community to the Assembly[79].

Article-334: *"Reservation of seats and special representation to cease after seventy years"[80].*

Notwithstanding anything in the foregoing provisions of this Part, the provisions of this Constitution relating to—

(*a*) The reservation of seats for the Scheduled Castes and the Scheduled Tribes in the House of the People and in the Legislative Assemblies of the States; and

(*b*) The representation of the Anglo-Indian community in the House of the People and in the Legislative Assemblies of the States by nomination shall cease to have effect on the expiration of a period of seventy years[102] from the commencement of this Constitution:

Provided that nothing in this article shall affect any representation in the House of the People or in the Legislative Assembly of a State until the dissolution of the then existing House or Assembly, as the case may be.

Article-335: *"Claims of Scheduled Castes and Scheduled Tribes to services and posts".*

The claims of the members of the Scheduled Castes and the Scheduled Tribes shall be taken into consideration, consistently with the maintenance of efficiency of administration, in the making of appointments to services and posts in connection with the affairs of the Union or of a State.

Provided that nothing in this article shall prevent in making of any provision in favour of the members of the Scheduled Castes and the Scheduled Tribes for relaxation in qualifying marks in any examination or lowering the standards of evaluation, for reservation in matters of promotion to any class or classes of services or posts in connection with the affairs of the Union or of a State.

Article-336: *"Special provision for Anglo-Indian community in certain services".*

(1) During the first two years after the commencement of this Constitution, appointments of members of the Anglo-Indian community to posts in the railway, customs, postal and telegraph services of the Union shall be made on the same basis as immediately before the fifteenth day of August, 1947.

During every succeeding period of two years, the number of posts reserved for the members of the said community in the said services shall, as nearly as possible, be less by ten percent than the numbers so reserved during the immediately preceding period of two years:

Provided that at the end of ten years from the commencement of this Constitution all such reservations shall cease.

(2) Nothing in clause (1) shall bar the appointment of members of the Anglo-Indian community to posts other than, or in addition to, those reserved for the community under that clause if such members are found qualified for appointment on merit as compared with the members of other communities.

Article-337: *"Special provision with respect to educational grants for the benefit of Anglo-Indian community".*

During the first three financial years after the commencement of this Constitution, the same grants, if any, shall be made by the Union and by each State for the benefit of the Anglo-Indian community in respect of education as were made in the financial year ending on the thirty-first day of March, 1948.

During every succeeding period of three years the grants may be less by ten per cent than those for the immediately preceding period of three years:

Provided that at the end of ten years from the commencement of this Constitution such grants, to the extent to which they are a special concession to the Anglo-Indian community, shall cease:

Provided further that no educational institution shall be entitled to receive any grant under this article unless at least forty percent of the annual admissions therein are made available to members of communities other than the Anglo-Indian community.

Article-338: *"National Commission for Scheduled Castes"*[81].

(1) There shall be a Commission for the Scheduled Castes to be known as the National Commission for the Scheduled Castes.

(2) Subject to the provisions of any law made in this behalf by Parliament, the Commission shall consist of a Chairperson, Vice-Chairperson and three other Members and the conditions of service and tenure of office of the Chairperson, Vice-Chairperson and other Members so appointed shall be such as the President may by rule determine[82].

(3) The Chairperson, Vice-Chairperson and other Members of the Commission shall be appointed by the President by warrant under his hand and seal.

(4) The Commission shall have the power to regulate its own procedure.

(5) It shall be the duty of the Commission -

(*a*) To investigate and monitor all matters relating to the safeguards provided for the Scheduled Castes[83] under this Constitution or under any other law for the time being in force or under any order of the Government and to evaluate the working of such safeguards;

(*b*) To inquire into specific complaints with respect to the deprivation of rights and safeguards of the Scheduled Castes;

(*c*) To participate and advise on the planning process of socio-economic development of the Scheduled Castes and to evaluate the progress of their development under the Union and any State;

(*d*) To present to the President, annually and at such other times as the Commission may deem fit, reports upon the working of those safeguards;

(*e*) To make in such reports recommendations as to the measures that should be taken by the Union or any State for the effective implementation of those safeguards and other measures for the protection, welfare and socio-economic development of the Scheduled Castes; and

(*f*) To discharge such other functions in relation to the protection, welfare and development and advancement of the Scheduled Castes as the President may, subject to the provisions of any law made by Parliament, by rule specify.

Article-338A: *"National Commission for Scheduled Tribes"*[84].

(1) There shall be a Commission for the Scheduled Tribes to be known as the National Commission for the Scheduled Tribes.

(5) It shall be the duty of the Commission -

(*a*) To investigate and monitor all matters relating to the safeguards provided for the Scheduled Tribes under this Constitution or under any other law for the time being in force or under any order of the Government and to evaluate the working of such safeguards;

(*b*) To inquire into specific complaints with respect to the deprivation of rights and safeguards of the Scheduled Tribes;

(*c*) To participate and advise on the planning process of socio-economic development of the Scheduled Tribes and to evaluate the progress of their development under the Union and any State;

(*d*) To present to the President, annually and at such other times as the Commission may deem fit, reports upon the working of those safeguards;

(*e*) To make in such reports recommendations as to the measures that should be taken by the Union or any State for the effective implementation of those safeguards and other measures for the protection, welfare and socio-economic development of the Scheduled Tribes; and

(*f*) To discharge such other functions in relation to the protection, welfare and development and advancement of the Scheduled Tribes as the President may, subject to the provisions of any law made by Parliament, by rule specify.

Article-340: Appointment of a Commission to investigate the conditions of backward classes.

Article-341: *"Scheduled Castes"*

(1) The President may with respect to any State or Union territory, and where it is a State, after consultation with the Governor thereof, by public notification[85], specify the castes, races or tribes or parts of or groups within castes, races or tribes which shall for the purposes of this Constitution be deemed to be Scheduled Castes in relation to that State or Union territory, as the case may be.

(2) Parliament may by law include in or exclude from the list of Scheduled Castes specified in a notification issued under clause (1) any caste, race or tribe or part of or group within any caste, race or tribe, but save as aforesaid a notification issued under the said clause shall not be varied by any subsequent notification.

Article-342: *"Scheduled Tribes"*

(1) The President may with respect to any State or Union territory, and where it is a State· after consultation with the Governor thereof, by public notification, specify the tribes or tribal communities or parts of or groups within tribes or tribal communities which shall for the purposes of this Constitution be deemed to be Scheduled Tribes in relation to that State or Union territory, as the case may be.

(2) Parliament may by law include in or exclude from the list of Scheduled Tribes specified in a notification issued under clause (1) any tribe or tribal community or part of or group within any tribe or tribal community, but save as aforesaid a notification issued under the said clause shall not be varied by any subsequent notification.

Article-350A: *"Facilities for instruction in mother-tongue at primary stage".*

It shall be the endeavour of every State and of every local authority within the State to provide adequate facilities for instruction in the mother-tongue at the primary stage of education to children belonging to linguistic minority groups; and the President may issue such directions to any State as he considers necessary or proper for securing the provision of such facilities[86].

Article-350B: *"Special Officer for linguistic minorities".*

(1) There shall be a Special Officer for linguistic minorities to be appointed by the President.

(2) It shall be the duty of the Special Officer to investigate all matters relating to the safeguards provided for linguistic minorities under this Constitution and report to the President upon those matters at such intervals as the President may direct, and the President shall cause all such reports to be laid before each House of Parliament, and sent to the Governments of the States concerned.

Article-351: *"Directive for development of the Hindi language".*

It shall be the duty of the Union to promote the spread of the Hindi language, to develop it so that it may serve as a medium of expression for all the elements of the composite culture of India and to secure its enrichment by assimilating without interfering with its genius, the forms, style and expressions used in Hindustani and in the other languages of India specified in the Eighth Schedule, and by drawing, wherever necessary or desirable, for its vocabulary, primarily on Sanskrit and secondarily on other languages.

Inferences: All the sections and subsections of Articles-325, Articles-326, Articles-333, Articles-334, Articles-335, Articles-336, Articles-337, Articles-338, Articles-338A, Articles-340, Articles-341, Articles-342, Articles-350A, 350B and Articles-351has been reflected in the SDG-16, entitled as 'Peace, Justice and Strong Institutions' and proper implementation of the this Article will directly promote to 'Gender Equality' (SDG-5) as well as 'Reduced Inequalities' (SDG-10).

PART-XIX: Miscellaneous

Article-364: *"Special provisions as to major ports and aerodromes".*

(1) Notwithstanding anything in this Constitution, the President may by public notification direct that as from such date as may be specified in the notification—

(*a*) Any law made by Parliament or by the Legislature of a State shall not apply to any major port or aerodrome or shall apply thereto subject to such exceptions or modifications as may be specified in the notification, or

(*b*) any existing law shall cease to have effect in any major port or aerodrome except as respects things done or omitted to be done before the said date, or shall in its application to such port or aerodrome have effect subject to such exceptions or modifications as may be specified in the notification.

(2) In this article—

(*a*) "major port" means a port declared to be a major port by or under any law made by Parliament or any existing law and includes all areas for the time being included within the limits of such port;

(*b*) "Aerodrome" means aerodrome as defined for the purposes of the enactments relating to airways, aircraft and air navigation.

Article-365: *"Effect of failure to comply with, or to give effect to, directions given by the Union".*

Where any State has failed to comply with, or to give effect to, any directions given in the exercise of the executive power of the Union under any of the provisions of this Constitution, it shall be lawful for the President to hold that a situation has arisen in which the Government of the State cannot be carried on in accordance with the provisions of this Constitution.

Inferences: All the sections and subsections of Articles-364, and Articles-365 are reflected in the SDG-16, entitled as 'Peace, Justice and Strong Institutions' and proper implementation of the Article will promote to 'Decent Work and Economic Growth' (SDG-8) and 'Industry Innovation and Infrastructure' (SDG-9).

Seventh Schedule (Article 246)

In the Article-246 of the Constitution of India, there are three List, which specify the limitations of responsibilities of *'Union'* (List-I-Union List), *'State'* (List-II-State List) and the list of both *'Union'* and *'State'* 'List-III—Concurrent List', that means, these listed responsibilities had been performing by Union, that is Government of India from List-I; the List-II had been performing by the all 'State', that Government of the individual States; and the List-III entitled as 'Concurrent List' had been jointly performing by the Government of India and the State Governments.

List-I: Union List

1. Defence of India and every part thereof including preparation for defence and all such acts as may be conducive in times of war to its prosecution and after its termination to effective demobilisation.

2. Naval, military and air forces; any other armed forces of the Union.

2A. Deployment of any armed force of the Union or any other force subject to the control of the Union or any contingent or unit thereof in any State in aid of the civil power; powers, jurisdiction, privileges and liabilities of the members of such forces while on such deployment[87].

3. Delimitation of cantonment areas, local self-government in such areas, the constitution and powers within such areas of cantonment authorities and the regulation of house accommodation (including the control of rents) in such areas.

4. Naval, military and air force works.

5. Arms, firearms, ammunition and explosives.

6. Atomic energy and mineral resources necessary for its production.

7. Industries declared by Parliament by law to be necessary for the purpose of defence or for the prosecution of war.

8. Central Bureau of Intelligence and Investigation.

9. Preventive detention for reasons connected with Defence, Foreign Affairs, or the security of India; persons subjected to such detention.

10. Foreign affairs; all matters which bring the Union into relation with any foreign country.

11. Diplomatic, consular and trade representation.

12. United Nations Organisation.

13. Participation in international conferences, associations and other bodies and implementing of decisions made thereat.

14. Entering into treaties and agreements with foreign countries and implementing of treaties, agreements and conventions with foreign countries.

15. War and peace.

16. Foreign jurisdiction.

17. Citizenship, naturalisation and aliens.

18. Extradition.

19. Admission into, and emigration and expulsion from, India; passports and visas.

20. Pilgrimages to places outside India.

21. Piracies and crimes committed on the high seas or in the air; offences against the law of nations committed on land or the high seas or in the air.

Inferences: The Sections of Article 246, Listed 1 to 21 of 7th Schedule, List-I has been directly reflected in the SDG-16, entitled as 'Peace, Justice and Strong Institutions', which means, for the sake of 'peace' in the national as well as in the international level from the perspective of territory of India, the 'Union' that is Government of India is the authorized authority to take actions.

22. Railways.

23. Highways declared by or under law made by Parliament to be national highways.

24. Shipping and navigation on inland waterways, declared by Parliament by law to be national waterways, as regards mechanically propelled vessels; the rule of the road on such waterways.

25. Maritime shipping and navigation, including shipping and navigation on tidal waters; provision of education and training for the mercantile marine and regulation of such education and training provided by States and other agencies.

26. Lighthouses, including lightships, beacons and other provision for the safety of shipping and aircraft.

27. Ports declared by or under law made by Parliament or existing law to be major ports, including their delimitation, and the constitution and powers of port authorities therein.

28. Port quarantine, including hospitals connected therewith; seamen's and marine hospitals.

29. Airways; aircraft and air navigation; provision of aerodromes; regulation and organisation of air traffic and of aerodromes; provision for aeronautical education and training and regulation of such education and training provided by States and other agencies.

30. Carriage of passengers and goods by railway, sea or air, or by national waterways in mechanically propelled vessels.

31. Posts and telegraphs; telephones, wireless, broadcasting and other like forms of communication.

Inferences: The sections of Article-246, Listed 22 to 31 of 7th Schedule, List-I has been directly reflected in the SDG-8, entitled as Decent Work and Economic Growth as well as SDG-9, entitled as 'Industry Innovation and Infrastructure', which means, for the sake of 'Decent Work and Economic Growth' (SDG-8), 'Industry Innovation and Infrastructure' (SDG-9), 'Reduced Inequality' (SDG-10), 'Sustainable Cities and Communities' (SDG-11), 'Sustainable Consumption and Production' (SDG-12), 'Climate Action' (SDG-13), 'Life bellow Water' (SDG-14), 'Life and Land' (SDG-15) and 'Partnership of the Goals'(SDG-17); which means, in the national as well as in the international level from the perspective of territory of India, the 'Union' that is Government of India is the authorized authority to take actions; ultimately these Numbers of the List I, that is Union List of the 7th Schedule are the strong tools to achieve as well as build the 'Peace, Justice and Strong Institutions' (SDG-16) in the country.

32. Property of the Union and the revenue therefrom, but as regards property situated in a State subject to legislation by the State, save in so far as Parliament by law otherwise provides.

33.[88] List I, Union List-33, Entry *33* omitted by the Constitution.

34. Courts of wards for the estates of Rulers of Indian States.

35. Public debt of the Union.

36. Currency, coinage and legal tender; foreign exchange.

37. Foreign loans.

38. Reserve Bank of India.

39. Post Office Savings Bank.

40. Lotteries organised by the Government of India or the Government of a State.

41. Trade and commerce with foreign countries; import and export across customs frontiers; definition of customs frontiers.

42. Inter-State trade and commerce.

43. Incorporation, regulation and winding up of trading corporations, including banking, insurance and financial corporations but not including co-operative societies.

44. Incorporation, regulation and winding up of corporations, whether trading or not, with objects not confined to one State, but not including universities.

45. Banking.

46. Bills of exchange, cheques, promissory notes and other like instruments.

47. Insurance.

48. Stock exchanges and futures markets.

49. Patents, inventions and designs; copyright; trade-marks and merchandise marks.

50. Establishment of standards of weight and measure.

51. Establishment of standards of quality for goods to be exported out of India or transported from one State to another.

Inferences: The sections of Article 246, Listed 32 and 34 to 51 of 7th Schedule, List-I has been directly reflected in the SDG-8, entitled as 'Decent Work and Economic Growth', 'Industry Innovation and

Infrastructure' (SDG-9), 'Reduced Inequality' (SDG-10), 'Sustainable Consumption and Production' (SDG-12), 'Climate Action' (SDG-13), 'Life and Land' (SDG-15) and 'Partnership of the Goals' (SDG-17); which means, for the sake of above issues in the national as well as in the international level from the perspective of territory of India, the 'Union' that is Government of India is the authorized authority to take actions; ultimately these Numbers of the List I, that is Union List of the 7th Schedule are the strong tools to achieve as well as build the 'Peace, Justice and Strong Institutions' (SDG-16) in the country.

52. Industries, the control of which by the Union is declared by Parliament by law to be expedient in the public interest.

53. Regulation and development of oilfields and mineral oil resources; petroleum and petroleum products; other liquids and substances declared by Parliament by law to be dangerously inflammable.

54. Regulation of mines and mineral development to the extent to which such regulation and development under the control of the Union is declared by Parliament by law to be expedient in the public interest.

Inferences: The sections of Article 246, Listed 52 to 54 of 7th Schedule, List-I has been directly reflected in the SDG-8, entitled as Decent Work and Economic Growth as well as 'Industry Innovation and Infrastructure' (SDG-9), 'Reduced Inequality (SDG-10), 'Sustainable Cities and Communities' (SDG-11), 'Sustainable Consumption and Production' (SDG-12), 'Climate Action' (SDG-13) and 'Life bellow Water' (SDG-14) and 'Life and Land' (SDG-15; which means, for the sake of above issues in the national as well as in the international level from the perspective of territory of India, the 'Union' that is Government of India is the authorized authority to take actions; ultimately these Numbers of the List I, that is Union List of the 7th Schedule are the strong tools to achieve as well as build the 'Peace, Justice and Strong Institutions' (SDG-16) in the country.

55. Regulation of labour and safety in mines and oilfields.

56. Regulation and development of inter-State rivers and river valleys to the extent to which such regulation and development under the control of the Union is declared by Parliament by law to be expedient in the public interest.

57. Fishing and fisheries beyond territorial waters.

58. Manufacture, supply and distribution of salt by Union agencies; regulation and control of manufacture, supply and distribution of salt by other agencies.

59. Cultivation, manufacture, and sale for export, of opium.

60. Sanctioning of cinematograph films for exhibition.

61. Industrial disputes concerning Union employees.

Inferences: The sections of Article 246, Listed 55 to 61 of 7th Schedule, List-I has been directly reflected in the SDG-3, 'Good Health and Wellbeing', SDG-8, entitled as 'Decent Work and Economic Growth', SDG-9, entitled as 'Industry Innovation and Infrastructure' and SDG-10 entitled as 'Reduced Inequalities' which means, for the sake of 'Good Health and Wellbeing' (SDG-3), 'Decent Work and Economic Growth' (SDG-8) , 'Industry Innovation and Infrastructure' (SDG-9), Reduced Inequalities' (SDG-10), 'Sustainable Cities and Communities' (SDG-11), 'Sustainable Consumption and Production' (SDG-12) 'Climate Action' (SDG-13), 'Life bellow Water' (SDG-14) and 'Life and Land' (SDG-15), in the national as well as in the international level from the perspective of territory of India, the 'Union' that is Government of India is the authorized authority to take actions; ultimately these Numbers of the List I, that is Union List of the 7th Schedule are the strong tools to achieve as well as build the 'Peace, Justice and Strong Institutions' (SDG-16) in the country.

62. The institutions known at the commencement of this Constitution as the National Library, the Indian Museum, the Imperial War Museum, the Victoria Memorial and the Indian War Memorial, and any other like institution financed by the Government of India wholly or in part and declared by Parliament by law to be an institution of national importance.

63. The institutions known at the commencement of this Constitution as the Benares Hindu University, the Aligarh Muslim University and the Delhi University; the University established in pursuance of article 371E[89]; any other institution declared by Parliament by law to be an institution of national importance.

64. Institutions for scientific or technical education financed by the Government of India wholly or in part and declared by Parliament by law to be institutions of national importance.

65. Union agencies and institutions for—

(*a*) Professional, vocational or technical training, including the training of police officers; or

(*b*) The promotion of special studies or research; or (*c*) scientific or technical assistance in the investigation or detection of crime.

66. Co-ordination and determination of standards in institutions for higher education or research and scientific and technical institutions.

67. Ancient and historical monuments and records, and archaeological sites and remains, declared by or under law made by Parliament to be of national importance.

68. The Survey of India, the Geological, Botanical, Zoological and Anthropological Surveys of India; Meteorological organisations.

69. Census.

Inferences: The sections of Article 246, Listed 62 to 69 of 7th Schedule, List-I has been directly reflected in the 'Quality Education' (SDG-4), 'Gender Equality' (SDG-5), 'Affordable and Clean Energy (SDG-7), 'Decent Work and Economic Growth' (SDG-8), 'Industry Innovation and Infrastructure (SDG-9)', 'Reduced Inequalities' (SDG-10), 'Sustainable Cities and Communities' (SDG-11), 'Sustainable Consumption and Production' (SDG-12), 'Climate Action' (SDG-13), 'Life bellow Water' (SDG-14) and 'Life and Land' (SDG-15) and 'Partnership of the Goals' (SDG-17); which means, for the sake of 'Quality Education, Gender Equality, Decent Work and Economic Growth , Industry Innovation and Infrastructure and Reduced Inequalities' in the national as well as in the international level from the perspective of territory of India, the 'Union' that is Government of India is the authorized authority to take actions; ultimately these Numbers of the List I, that is Union List of the 7th Schedule are the strong tools to achieve as well as build the 'Peace, Justice and Strong Institutions' (SDG-16) in the country.

70. Union Public Service; All-India Services; Union Public Service Commission.

71. Union pensions, that is to say, pensions payable by the Government of India or out of the Consolidated Fund of India.

72. Elections to Parliament, to the Legislatures of States and to the offices of President and Vice-President; the Election Commission.

73. Salaries and allowances of members of Parliament, the Chairman and Deputy Chairman of the Council of States and the Speaker and Deputy Speaker of the House of the People.

74. Powers, privileges and immunities of each House of Parliament and of the members and the Committees of each House; enforcement of attendance of persons for giving evidence or producing documents before committees of Parliament or commissions appointed by Parliament.

75. Emoluments, allowances, privileges, and rights in respect of leave of absence, of the President and Governors; salaries and allowances of the Ministers for the Union; the salaries, allowances, and rights in respect of leave of absence and other conditions of service of the Comptroller and Auditor-General.

76. Audit of the accounts of the Union and of the States.

77. Constitution, organisation, jurisdiction and powers of the Supreme Court (including contempt of such Court), and the fees taken therein; persons entitled to practise before the Supreme Court.

78. Constitution and organisation (including vacations[90]) of the High Courts except provisions as to officers and servants of High Courts; persons entitled to practise before the High Courts.

79. Extension of the jurisdiction of a High Court to, and exclusion of the jurisdiction of a High Court from, any Union territory.

80. Extension of the powers and jurisdiction of members of a police force belonging to any State to any area outside that State, but not so as to enable the police of one State to exercise powers and jurisdiction in any area outside that State without the consent of the Government of the State in which such area is situated; extension of the powers and jurisdiction of members of a police force belonging to any State to railway areas outside that State.

81. Inter-State migration; inter-State quarantine.

Inferences: The sections of Article 246, Listed 70 to 78 and 80, 81 of 7th Schedule, List-I has been directly reflected in the SDG-16, entitled as 'Peace, Justice and Strong Institutions', which means, for the sake 'justice' in the national as well as in the international level from the perspective of territory of India, the 'Union' that is Government of India is the authorized authority to take actions on 70 – 81 of the List-I.

82. Taxes on income other than agricultural income.

83. Duties of customs including export duties.

84. Duties of excise on tobacco and other goods manufactured or produced in India except—

(*a*) Alcoholic liquors for human consumption.

(*b*) Opium, Indian hemp and other narcotic drugs and narcotics, but including medicinal and toilet preparations containing alcohol or any substance included in sub-paragraph (*b*) of this entry.

85. Corporation tax.

86. Taxes on the capital value of the assets, exclusive of agricultural land, of individuals and companies; taxes on the capital of companies.

87. Estate duty in respect of property other than agricultural land.

88. Duties in respect of succession to property other than agricultural land.

89. Terminal taxes on goods or passengers, carried by railway, sea or air; taxes on railway fares and freights.

90. Taxes other than stamp duties on transactions in stock exchanges and futures markets.

91. Rates of stamp duty in respect of bills of exchange, cheques, promissory notes, bills of lading, letters of credit, policies of insurance, transfer of shares, debentures, proxies and receipts.

92. Taxes on the sale or purchase of newspapers and on advertisements published therein.

92A. Taxes on the sale or purchase of goods other than newspapers, where such sale or purchase takes place in the course of inter-State trade or commerce[91].

92B. Taxes on the consignment of goods (whether the consignment is to the person making it or to any other person), where such consignment takes place in the course of inter-State trade or commerce.

Inferences: The sections of Article 246, Listed 82 to 92B of 7th Schedule List-I has been directly reflected in the 'Quality Education' (SDG-4), 'Gender Equality' (SDG-5), 'Affordable and Clean Energy (SDG-7), 'Decent Work and Economic Growth' (SDG-8), 'Industry Innovation and Infrastructure (SDG-9)', 'Reduced Inequalities' (SDG-10), 'Sustainable Cities and Communities' (SDG-11), 'Sustainable Consumption and Production' (SDG-12) and 'Life bellow Water' (SDG-14); which means, for the sake of 'Quality Education, Gender Equality, Decent Work and Economic Growth , Industry Innovation and Infrastructure and Reduced Inequalities' in the national as well as in the international level from the perspective of territory of India, the 'Union' that is Government of India is the authorized authority to take actions; ultimately these Numbers of the List I, that is Union List of the 7th Schedule are the strong tools to achieve as well as build the 'Peace, Justice and Strong Institutions' (SDG-16) in the country.

92C. Taxes on services[92].

93. Offences against laws with respect to any of the matters in this List.

94. Inquiries, surveys and statistics for the purpose of any of the matters in this List.

95. Jurisdiction and powers of all courts, except the Supreme Court, with respect to any of the matters in this List; admiralty jurisdiction.

96. Fees in respect of any of the matters in this List, but not including fees taken in any court.

97. Any other matter not enumerated in List II or List III including any tax not mentioned in either of those Lists.

Inferences: The sections of Article 246, Listed 93 to 97 of 7th Schedule, List-I are directly reflected in the SDG-16, entitled as 'Peace, Justice and Strong Institutions', which means, for the sake 'peace' and 'justice' in the national as well as in the international level from the perspective of territory of India, the 'Union' that is Government of India is the authorized authority to take actions on 70 – 81 of the List-I.

List-II: State List

1. Public order (but not including the use of any naval, military or air force or any other armed force of the Union or of any other force subject to the control of the Union or of any contingent or unit thereof in aid of the civil power[93]).

2. Police (including railway and village police) subject to the provisions of entry 2A of List-I[94].

3. Officers and servants of the High Court; procedure in rent and revenue courts; fees taken in all courts except the Supreme Court[95].

4. Prisons, reformatories, Borstal institutions and other institutions of a like nature, and persons detained therein; arrangements with other States for the use of prisons and other institutions.

5. Local Government, that is to say, the constitution and powers of municipal corporations, improvement trusts, district boards, mining settlement authorities and other local authorities for the purpose of local self-Government or village administration.

Inferences: The sections of Article-246, Listed 1 to 5 of 7th Schedule, List-II are directly reflected in the SDG-16, entitled as 'Peace, Justice and Strong Institutions', which means, for the sake of 'peace' and 'justice' within the territorial area of the State, that is, the 'State Government' is the authorized authority to take actions.

6. Public health and sanitation; hospitals and dispensaries.

Inferences: The section of Article-246, Listed 6 of the 7th Schedule, List-II has been directly reflected in the SDG-10, entitled as 'Good Health and Wellbeing' and SDG-6, entitled as 'Clean Water and Sanitation', 'Clean and affordable Energy' (SDG-7) and then to 'Reduce Poverty' (SDG-1), 'Zero Hunger' (SDG-2), 'Gender Equality' (SDG-5), 'Reduced Inequality' (SDG-10), 'Sustainable Cities and Communities' (SDG-11), Sustainable Consumption and Production' (SDG-12), 'Climate Action' (SDG-13), 'Life bellow Water' (SDG-14) and 'Partnership of the Goals'(SDF-17), which means, for the sake of public health and sanitation; hospitals and dispensaries within the territorial area of the State, that is, the 'State Government' is the authorized authority to take actions; ultimately these Numbers of the List II, that is State List of the 7th Schedule are the strong tools to achieve as well as build the 'Peace, Justice and Strong Institutions' (SDG-16) in the country.

7. Pilgrimages, other than pilgrimages to places outside India.

Inferences: The section of Article-246, Listed 7 of the 7th Schedule, List-II has been directly reflected in the SDG-10, entitled as 'Reduced Inequalities' which means, for the sake of creating as well as preserving and protecting equal opportunity for religious and cultural values within the territorial area of the State, that is, the 'State Government' is the authorized authority to take actions in this regard.

8. Intoxicating liquors, that is to say, the production, manufacture, possession, transport, purchase and sale of intoxicating liquors.

Inferences: The section of Article 246, Listed 8 of the 7th Schedule, List-II has been reflected in the SDG-8, entitled as 'Decent Work and Economic Growth' and 'Industry Innovation and Infrastructure' (SDG-9) and 'Sustainable Cities and Communities' (SDG-11) which means, for the sake of creating dignified economic opportunity within the territorial area of the State, that is, the 'State Government' is the authorized authority to take actions in this regard; ultimately these Numbers of the List II, that is State List of the 7th Schedule are the strong tools to achieve as well as build the 'Peace, Justice and Strong Institutions' (SDG-16) in the country.

9. Relief of the disabled and unemployable.

Inferences: The section of Article-246, Listed 9 of the 7th Schedule, List-II has been directly reflected in the SDG-3, entitled as 'Good Health and Well-being', 'Decent Work and Economic Growth' (SDG-8), 'Industry Innovation and Infrastructure' (SDG-9), 'Reduced Inequalities' (SDG-10) and it will 'Reduce Poverty' (SDG-1), 'Reduce Hunger' (SDG-2),

'Clean and affordable Energy' (SDG-7; 'Gender Equality' and 'Sustainable Consumption and Production' (SDG-12); which means, for the sake of creating equal dignified opportunity for the disabled and unemployable persons within the territorial area of the State, that is, the 'State Government' is the authorized authority to take actions in this regard; ultimately these Numbers of the List II, that is State List of the 7th Schedule are the strong tools to achieve as well as build the 'Peace, Justice and Strong Institutions' (SDG-16) in the country.

10. Burials and burial grounds; cremations and cremation grounds.

Inferences: The section of Article-246, Listed 10 of the 7th Schedule, List-II is directly reflected in the SDG-3, entitled as 'Reduced Inequalities' and 'Sustainable Cities and Communities' (SDG-11) and 'Climate Action' (SDG-13) which means, for the sake of creating as well as preserving and protecting equal opportunity for the religious groups to performing rituals after death within the territorial area of the State, that is, the 'State Government' is the authorized authority to take actions in this regard; ultimately these Numbers of the List II, that is State List of the 7th Schedule are the strong tools to achieve as well as build the 'Peace, Justice and Strong Institutions' (SDG-16) in the country.

11. Entry 11 omitted[96].

12. Libraries, museums and other similar institutions controlled or financed by the State; ancient and historical monuments and records other than those (declared by or under law made by Parliament) to be of national importance.

Inferences: The section of Article-246, Listed 12 of the 7th Schedule, List-II has been reflected in the SDG-4, entitled as 'Quality Education', 'Gender Equality' (SDG-5), 'Reduced Inequalities' (SDG-10), 'Sustainable Cities and Communities' (SDG-11) and 'Partnership of the Goals'(SDF-17) which means, for the sake of creating as well as preserving and protecting historical records for the future generation within the territorial area of the State, that is, the 'State Government' is the authorized authority to take actions in this regard; ultimately these Numbers of the List II, that is State List of the 7th Schedule are the strong tools to achieve as well as build the 'Peace, Justice and Strong Institutions' (SDG-16) in the country.

13. Communications, that is to say, roads, bridges, ferries, and other means of communication not specified in List I; municipal tramways; ropeways; inland waterways and traffic thereon subject to the provisions of List I and List III with regard to such waterways; vehicles other than mechanically propelled vehicles.

Inferences: The section of Article-246, Listed 13 of the 7th Schedule, List-II has been reflected in the 'Decent Work and Economic Growth' (SDG-8), 'Industry Innovation and Infrastructure' (SDG-9), 'Reduced Inequalities' (SDG-10); 'Sustainable Cities and Communities' (SDG-11), 'Sustainable Consumption and Production' (SDG-12), 'Climate Action' (SDG-13), 'Life bellow Water' (SDG-14), 'Life and Land' (SDG-15) and 'Partnership of the Goals'(SDF-17); which means, for the sake of creating, preserving and protecting the mode of communications within the territorial area of the State, that is, the 'State Government' is the authorized authority to take actions in this regard; ultimately these Numbers of the List II, that is State List of the 7th Schedule are the strong tools to achieve as well as build the 'Peace, Justice and Strong Institutions' (SDG-16) in the country.

14. Agriculture, including agricultural education and research, protection against pests and prevention of plant diseases.

15. Preservation, protection and improvement of stock and prevention of animal diseases; veterinary training and practice.

16. Pounds and the prevention of cattle trespass.

17. Water, that is to say, water supplies, irrigation and canals, drainage and embankments, water storage and water power subject to the provisions of entry 56 of List I.

18. Land, that is to say, rights in or over land, land tenures including the relation of landlord and tenant, and the collection of rents; transfer and alienation of agricultural land; land improvement and agricultural loans; colonization.

19. Entry 19 omitted[97].

20. Entry 20 omitted[97].

21. Fisheries.

Inferences: The sections of Article-246, Listed 14 to 18 and 21 of the 7th Schedule, List-II has been directly reflected in the SDG-4, entitled as 'Quality Education' (SDG-4); 'Reduce Poverty' (SDG-1); 'Reduce Hunger' (SDG-2); 'Good Health and Wellbeing' (SDG-3); 'Clean Water and Sanitation' (SDG-6), 'Decent Work and Economic Growth' (SDG-8); 'Industry Innovation and Infrastructure' (SDG-9), 'Reduced Inequalities' (SDG-10); 'Sustainable Cities and Communities' (SDG-11), 'Sustainable Consumption and Production' (SDG-12); 'Climate Action' (SDG-13), 'Life bellow Water' (SDG-14), 'Life on Land' (SDG-15) and ultimately to the 'Peace, Justice and Strong Institutions' (SDG-16) which means, for the sake above listed activities that is 14 to 18 and 21within the territorial area of the State, that is, the 'State Government' is the authorized authority to take actions in this regard; ultimately these Numbers of the List-II, that is State List of the 7th Schedule are the strong tools to achieve as well as build the 'Peace, Justice and Strong Institutions' (SDG-16) in the country.

22. Courts of wards subject to the provisions of entry 34 of List-I; encumbered and attached estates.

23. Regulation of mines and mineral development subject to the provisions of List-I with respect to regulation and development under the control of the Union.

24. Industries subject to the provisions of (entries 7 and 52[98]) of List-I.

25. Gas and gas-works.

26. Trade and commerce within the State subject to the provisions of entry 33 of List-III.

27. Production, supply and distribution of goods subject to the provisions of entry 33 of List-III.

28. Markets and fairs.

29. Entry 29 omitted[97].

30. Money-lending and money-lenders; relief of agricultural indebtedness.

31. Inns and inn-keepers.

32. Incorporation, regulation and winding up of corporations, other than those specified in List-I, and universities; unincorporated trading, literary, scientific, religious and other societies and associations; co-operative societies.

33. Theatres and dramatic performances; cinemas subject to the provisions of entry 60 of List-I; sports, entertainments and amusements.

34. Betting and gambling.

35. Works, lands and buildings vested in or in the possession of the State.

Inferences: The sections of Article-246, Listed 22 to 28 and 30 to 35 of the 7th Schedule, List-II are directly reflected in the SDG-16, entitled as 'Peace, Justice and Strong Institutions' and these are promote to 'Decent Work and Economic Growth'(SDG-8); 'Clean and affordable Energy'

(SDG-7), 'Industry Innovation and Infrastructure' (SDG-9), 'Reduced Inequalities' (SDG-10), 'Sustainable Cities and Communities' (SDG-11), 'Sustainable Consumption and Production' (SDG-12), 'Climate Action' (SDG-13), 'Life bellow Water' (SDG-14), 'Life and Land' (SDG-15) and 'Partnership of the Goals'(SDF-17) which means, for the sake above listed that is 22 to 28 and 29 to 35 activities within the territorial area of the State, that is, the 'State Government' is the authorized authority to take actions in this regard; ultimately these Numbers of the List II, that is State List of the 7th Schedule are the strong tools to achieve as well as build the 'Peace, Justice and Strong Institutions' (SDG-16) in the country.

36. Entry 29 omitted[99].

37. Elections to the Legislature of the State subject to the provisions of any law made by Parliament.

38. Salaries and allowances of members of the Legislature of the State, of the Speaker and Deputy Speaker of the Legislative Assembly and, if there is a Legislative Council, of the Chairman and Deputy Chairman thereof.

39. Powers, privileges and immunities of the Legislative Assembly and of the members and the committees thereof, and, if there is a Legislative Council, of that Council and of the members and the committees thereof; enforcement of attendance of persons for giving evidence or producing documents before committees of the Legislature of the State.

40. Salaries and allowances of Ministers for the State.

41. State public services; State Public Service Commission.

42. State pensions, that is to say, pensions payable by the State or out of the Consolidated Fund of the State.

43. Public debt of the State.

44. Treasure trove.

45. Land revenue, including the assessment and collection of revenue, the maintenance of land records, survey for revenue purposes and records of rights, and alienation of revenues.

46. Taxes on agricultural income.

47. Duties in respect of succession to agricultural land.

48. Estate duty in respect of agricultural land.

49. Taxes on lands and buildings.

50. Taxes on mineral rights subject to any limitations imposed by Parliament by law relating to mineral development.

51. Duties of excise on the following goods manufactured or produced in the State and countervailing duties at the same or lower rates on similar goods manufactured or produced elsewhere in India:—

(*a*) Alcoholic liquors for human consumption;

(*b*) Opium, Indian hemp and other narcotic drugs and narcotics; but not including medicinal and toilet preparations containing alcohol or any substance included in sub-paragraph (*b*) of this entry.

52. Taxes on the entry of goods into a local area for consumption, use or sale therein.

53. Taxes on the consumption or sale of electricity.

54. Taxes on the sale or purchase of goods other than newspapers, subject to the provisions of entry 92A of List I[100].

55. Taxes on advertisements other than advertisements published in the newspapers (and advertisements broadcast by radio or television)[101].

56. Taxes on goods and passengers carried by road or on inland waterways.

57. Taxes on vehicles, whether mechanically propelled or not, suitable for use on roads, including tramcars subject to the provisions of entry 35 of List III.

58. Taxes on animals and boats.

59. Tolls.

60. Taxes on professions, trades, callings and employments.

61. Capitation taxes.

62. Taxes on luxuries, including taxes on entertainments, amusements, betting and gambling.

63. Rates of stamp duty in respect of documents other than those specified in the provisions of List I with regard to rates of stamp duty.

64. Offences against laws with respect to any of the matters in this List.

65. Jurisdiction and powers of all courts, except the Supreme Court, with respect to any of the matters in this List.

66. Fees in respect of any of the matters in this List, but not including fees taken in any court.

Inferences: The sections of Article 246, Listed 37 to 66 of the 7th Schedule, List-II has been directly reflected in the SDG-16, entitled as 'Peace, Justice and Strong Institutions' and these are promote to 'Decent Work and Economic Growth'(SDG-8); 'Industry Innovation and Infrastructure' (SDG-9) and 'Life and Land' (SDG-15); which means, for the sake above listed that is 37 to 66 activities within the territorial area of the State, that is, the 'State Government' is the authorized authority to take actions in this regard; ultimately these Numbers of the List II, that is State List of the 7th Schedule are the strong tools to achieve as well as build the 'Peace, Justice and Strong Institutions' (SDG-16) in the country.

List-III: Concurrent List

1. Criminal law, including all matters included in the Indian Penal Code at the commencement of this Constitution but excluding offences against laws with respect to any of the matters specified in List I or List II and excluding the use of naval, military or air forces or any other armed forces of the Union in aid of the civil power.

2. Criminal procedure, including all matters included in the Code of Criminal Procedure at the commencement of this Constitution.

3. Preventive detention for reasons connected with the security of a State, the maintenance of public order, or the maintenance of supplies and services essential to the community; persons subjected to such detention.

4. Removal from one State to another State of prisoners, accused persons and persons subjected to preventive detention for reasons specified in entry 3 of this List.

5. Marriage and divorce; infants and minors; adoption; wills, intestacy and succession; joint family and partition; all matters in respect of which parties in judicial proceedings were immediately before the commencement of this Constitution subject to their personal law.

6. Transfer of property other than agricultural land; registration of deeds and documents.

7. Contracts, including partnership, agency, contracts of carriage, and other special forms of contracts, but not including contracts relating to agricultural land.

8. Actionable wrongs.

9. Bankruptcy and insolvency.

10. Trust and Trustees.

11. Administrators—general and official trustees.

11A. Administration of justice; constitution and organisation of all courts, except the Supreme Court and the High Courts[102].

12. Evidence and oaths; recognition of laws, public acts and records, and judicial proceedings.

13. Civil procedure, including all matters included in the Code of Civil Procedure at the commencement of this Constitution, limitation and arbitration.

14. Contempt of court, but not including contempt of the Supreme Court.

15. Vagrancy; nomadic and migratory tribes.

Inferences: The sections of Article-246, Listed 1 to 15 of the 7th Schedule, List-III has been directly reflected in the SDG-16, entitled as 'Peace, Justice and Strong Institutions' which means, for the sake above listed that is 1 to 15 activities within the territorial area of the State jointly with Union or specific Order or Directions, Laws, Acts, etc. on specific issue will followed by the 'State Government' to take actions in this regard; ultimately these Numbers of the List III, that is Concurrent List of the 7th Schedule are the strong tools to achieve as well as build the 'Peace, Justice and Strong Institutions' (SDG-16) in the country.

16. Lunacy and mental deficiency, including places for the reception or treatment of lunatics and mental deficient.

Inferences: The section of Article-246, Listed 16 of the 7th Schedule, List-III has been directly reflected in the SDG-3, entitled as 'Good Health and Wellbeing', 'Reduced Inequalities' (SDG-10); 'Sustainable Cities and Communities' (SDG-11) and 'Sustainable Consumption and Production' (SDG-12); which means, for the sake above listed activity within the territorial area of the State jointly with Union or specific Order or Directions, Laws, Acts, etc. on specific issue will followed by the 'State Government' to take actions in this regard; ultimately these Numbers of the List III, that is Concurrent List of the 7th Schedule are the strong tools to achieve as well as build the 'Peace, Justice and Strong Institutions' (SDG-16) in the country.

17. Prevention of cruelty to animals.

17A. Forests[103].

17B. Protection of wild animals and birds.

18. Adulteration of foodstuffs and other goods.

19. Drugs and poisons, subject to the provisions of entry 59 of List I with respect to opium.

Inferences: The sections of Article-246, Listed 17 to 19 of the 7th Schedule, List-III has been directly reflected in the SDG-13, entitled as 'Climate Action' and 'Water and Sanitation' (SDG-6), 'Decent Work and Economic Growth' (SDG-8), 'Sustainable Consumption and Production' (SDG-12) and 'Climate Action' (SDG-13) and 'Life on Land' (SDG-15) which means, for the sake above listed activity within the territorial area of the State jointly with Union or specific Order or Directions, Laws, Acts, etc. on specific issue will followed by the 'State Government' to take actions in this regard; ultimately these Numbers of the List III, that is Concurrent List of the 7th Schedule are the strong tools to achieve as well as build the 'Peace, Justice and Strong Institutions' (SDG-16) in the country.

20. Economic and social planning.

20A. Population control and family planning[104].

21. Commercial and industrial monopolies, combines and trusts.

22. Trade unions; industrial and labour disputes.

23. Social security and social insurance; employment and unemployment.

24. Welfare of labour including conditions of work, provident funds, employers' liability, workmen's compensation, invalidity and old age pensions and maternity benefits.

Inferences: The sections of Article-246, Listed 20 to 24 of the 7th Schedule, List-III has been directly reflected in the SDG-16, entitled as 'Peace, Justice and Strong Institutions' and it promote to take actions on 'Reduced Poverty' (SDG-1); 'Reduce Hunger' (SDG-2); 'Good Health and Wellbeing' (SDG-3); 'Quality Education' (SDG-4); 'Gender Equality' (SDG-5); 'Clean Water and Sanitation' (SDG-6); 'Affordable and Clean Energy' (SDG-7); 'Decent Work and Economic Growth' (SDG-8); 'Industry Innovation and Infrastructure' (SDG-9); 'Reduced Inequalities' (SDG-10); 'Sustainable Cities and Communities' (SDG-11), 'Sustainable Consumption and Production' (SDG-12), 'Climate Action' (SDG-13 and 'Life bellow Water' (SDG-14)); which means, for the sake above listed that is 20 to 24 activities within the territorial area of the State jointly with Union or specific Order or Directions, Laws, Acts, etc. on specific issue will followed by the 'State Government' to take actions in this regard.

25. Education, including technical education, medical education and universities, subject to the provisions of entries 63, 64, 65 and 66 of List I; vocational and technical training of labour[105].

26. Legal, medical and other professions.

Inferences: The sections of Article-246, Listed 25 to 26 of the 7th Schedule, List-III has been directly reflected in the SDG-4, entitled as 'Quality Education' and it promote to take actions on 'Reduced Poverty' (SDG-1); 'Reduce Hunger' (SDG-2); 'Good Health and Wellbeing' (SDG-3); 'Gender Equality' (SDG-5); 'Clean Water and Sanitation' (SDG-6); 'Affordable and Clean Energy' (SDG-7); 'Decent Work and Economic Growth' (SDG-8); 'Industry Innovation and Infrastructure' (SDG-9); 'Reduced Inequalities' (SDG-10); 'Sustainable Cities and Communities' (SDG-11); 'Sustainable Consumption and Production' (SDG-12), 'Climate Action' (SDG-13), 'Life bellow Water' (SDG-14), 'Life and Land' (SDG-15) and 'Partnership of the Goals'(SDF-17) that ultimately promote to develop 'Peace, Justice and Strong Institutions' (SDG-16) which means, for the sake above listed that is 25 to 26 activities within the territorial area of the State jointly with Union or specific Order or Directions, Laws, Acts, etc. on specific issue will followed by the 'State Government' to take actions in this regard.

27. Relief and rehabilitation of persons displaced from their original place of residence by reason of the setting up of the Dominions of India and Pakistan.

28. Charities and charitable institutions, charitable and religious endowments and religious institutions.

Inferences: The sections of Article-246, Listed 27 to 28 of the 7th Schedule, List-III has been directly reflected in the SDG-16, entitled as 'Peace, Justice and Strong Institutions' which means, for the sake above listed that is 27 to 28 activities within the territorial area of the State jointly with Union or specific Order or Directions, Laws, Acts, etc. on specific issue will followed by the 'State Government' to take actions in this regard.

29. Prevention of the extension from one State to another of infectious or contagious diseases or pests affecting men, animals or plants.

30. Vital statistics including registration of births and deaths.

Inferences: The sections of Article-246, Listed 29 to 30 of the 7th Schedule, List-III has been reflected in the SDG-16, entitled as 'Peace,

Justice and Strong Institutions'; it promotes directly to 'Good Health and Wellbeing' (SDG-3); 'Clean and affordable Energy' (SDG-7), 'Decent Work and Economic Growth' (SDG-8), 'Industry Innovation and Infrastructure' (SDG-9), 'Reduced Inequality' (SDG-10), 'Sustainable Cities and Communities' (SDG-11); 'Sustainable Consumption and Production' (SDG-12); 'Climate Action' (SDG-13); 'Life on Land' (SDG-15); 'Partnership of the Goals'(SDF-17); 'No Poverty' (SDG-1) and 'Zero Hunger' (SDG-2) which means, for the sake above listed that is 29 to 30 activities within the territorial area of the State jointly with Union or specific Order or Directions, Laws, Acts, etc. on specific issue will followed by the 'State Government' to take actions in this regard.

31. Ports other than those declared by or under law made by Parliament or existing law to be major ports.

32. Shipping and navigation on inland waterways as regards mechanically propelled vessels, and the rule of the road on such waterways, and the carriage of passengers and goods on inland waterways subject to the provisions of List I with respect to national waterways.

33. Trade and commerce in, and the production, supply and distribution of[106], —

(*a*) the products of any industry where the control of such industry by the Union is declared by Parliament by law to be expedient in the public interest, and imported goods of the same kind as such products;

(*b*) Foodstuffs, including edible oilseeds and oils;

(*c*) Cattle fodder, including oilcakes and other concentrates;

(*d*) Raw cotton, whether ginned or unginned, and cotton seed; and

(*e*) Raw jute.

33A. Weights and measures except establishment of standards[107].

34. Price control.

35. Mechanically propelled vehicles including the principles on which taxes on such vehicles are to be levied.

36. Factories.

37. Boilers.

38. Electricity.

39. Newspapers, books and printing presses.

40. Archaeological sites and remains other than those (declared by or under law made by Parliament to be of national importance.

41. Custody, management and disposal of property (including agricultural land) declared by law to be evacuee property.

42. Acquisition and requisitioning of property[108].

43. Recovery in a State of claims in respect of taxes and other public demands, including arrears of land-revenue and sums recoverable as such arrears, arising outside that State.

44. Stamp duties other than duties or fees collected by means of judicial stamps, but not including rates of stamp duty.

45. Inquiries and statistics for the purposes of any of the matters specified in List-II or List-III.

46. Jurisdiction and powers of all courts, except the Supreme Court, with respect to any of the matters in this List.

47. Fees in respect of any of the matters in this List, but not including fees taken in any court.

> **Inferences:** The sections of Article-246, Listed 31 to 47 of the 7th Schedule, List-III has been directly reflected in the SDG-16, entitled as 'Peace, Justice and Strong Institutions' and it promote to take actions on 'Clean Water and Sanitation' (SDG-6), 'Affordable and Clean Energy' (SDG-7); 'Decent Work and Economic Growth' (SDG-8); 'Industry Innovation and Infrastructure' (SDG-9); 'Reduced Inequalities' (SDG-10); 'Sustainable Cities and Communities' (SDG-11); 'Sustainable Consumption and Production' (SDG-12), 'Climate Action' (SDG-13), 'Life and Land' (SDG-15) and ultimately to develop 'Peace, Justice and Strong Institutions' (SDG-16) which means, for the sake above listed that is 25 to 26 activities within the territorial area of the State jointly with Union or specific Order or Directions, Laws, Acts, etc. on specific issue will followed by the 'State Government' to take actions in this regard.

243G. Powers, authority and responsibilities of Panchayats. Subject to the provisions of this Constitution, the Legislature of a State may, by law, endow the Panchayats with such powers and authority as may be necessary to enable them to function as institutions of self-government and such law may contain provisions for the devolution of powers and responsibilities upon Panchayats at the appropriate level, subject to such conditions as may be specified therein, with respect to—
(*a*) the preparation of plans for economic development and social justice;

(*b*) the implementation of schemes for economic development and social justice as may be entrusted to them including those in relation to the matters listed in the Eleventh Schedule.

ELEVENTH SCHEDULE[109] (Article 243G)

1. Agriculture, including agricultural extension.

2. Land improvement, implementation of land reforms, land consolidation and soil conservation.

3. Minor irrigation, water management and watershed development.

4. Animal husbandry, dairying and poultry.

5. Fisheries.

Inferences: The sections of Article-243G, Listed 1 to 5 of the 11th Schedule has been reflected in the 'Reduced Poverty' (SDG-1); 'Reduce Hunger' (SDG-2); 'Good Health and Wellbeing' (SDG-3); 'Gender Equality' (SDG-5), 'Clean Water and Sanitation' (SDG-6); 'Clean and affordable Energy' (SDG-7), 'Decent Work and Economic Growth' (SDG-8); 'Industry Innovation and Infrastructure' (SDG-9), 'Reduced Inequalities' (SDG-10); 'Sustainable Consumption and Production' (SDG-12); 'Climate Action' (SDG-13), 'Life bellow Water' (SDG-14) and 'Life and Land' (SDG-15) which means, for the sake of community development within the territorial area of a *Panchayat* is authorized to take actions from the above mentioned listed activities; ultimately these Numbers of the 11th Schedule, provide by Article 243G are the strong tools to achieve as well as build the 'Peace, Justice and Strong Institutions' (SDG-16) in the country.

6. Social forestry and farm forestry.

7. Minor forest produce.

Inferences: The sections of Article 243G, Listed 6 to 7 of the 11th Schedule has been reflected in the 'Reduce Hunger' (SDG-2); 'Good Health and Wellbeing' (SDG-3); 'Clean and affordable Energy' (SDG-7), 'Reduced Inequalities' (SDG-10); 'Sustainable Consumption and Production' (SDG-12); 'Climate Action' (SDG-13) and 'Life and Land' (SDG-15) which means, for the sake of community development within the territorial area of a Panchayat is authorized to take actions from the above mentioned listed activities; ultimately these Numbers of the 11th Schedule, provide by Article 243G are the strong tools to achieve as well as build the 'Peace, Justice and Strong Institutions' (SDG-16) in the country.

8. Small scale industries, including food processing industries.
9. Khadi, village and cottage industries.

Inferences: The sections of Article-243G, Listed 8 to 9 of the 11th Schedule has been reflected in the 'Reduce Hunger' (SDG-2); 'Gender Equality'(SDG-5), 'Decent Work and Economic Growth' (SDG-8); 'Industry Innovation and Infrastructure' (SDG-9); 'Reduced Inequalities' (SDG-10); 'Sustainable Consumption and Production' (SDG-12); 'Climate Action' (SDG-13) and 'Life and Land' (SDG-15) which means, for the sake of community development within the territorial area of a Panchayat is authorized to take actions from the above mentioned listed activities; ultimately these Numbers of the 11th Schedule, provide by Article 243G are the strong tools to achieve as well as build the 'Peace, Justice and Strong Institutions' (SDG-16) in the country.

10. Rural housing.
11. Drinking water.
12. Fuel and fodder.

Inferences: The sections of Article-243G, Listed 10 to 12 of the 11th Schedule has been reflected in the 'Reduced Poverty' (SDG-1); 'Reduce Hunger' (SDG-2); 'Gender Equality', (SDG-5), 'Good Health and Wellbeing' (SDG-3); 'Clean Water and Sanitation' (SDG-6), 'Clean and affordable Energy' (SDG-7), 'Decent Work and Economic Growth' (SDG-8), 'Industry Innovation and Infrastructure' (SDG-9) and 'Reduced Inequalities' (SDG-10); 'Sustainable Consumption and Production' (SDG-12) and 'Climate Action' (SDG-13); which means, for the sake of community development within the territorial area of a Panchayat is authorized to take actions from the above mentioned listed activities; ultimately these Numbers of the 11th Schedule, provide by Article 243G are the strong tools to achieve as well as build the 'Peace, Justice and Strong Institutions' (SDG-16) in the country.

13. Roads, culverts, bridges, ferries, waterways and other means of communication.
14. Rural electrification, including distribution of electricity.
15. Non-conventional energy sources.
16. Poverty alleviation programme.

Inferences: The sections of Article-243G, Listed 13 to 16 of the 11th Schedule has been reflected in the 'Affordable and Clean Energy' (SDG-7); 'Decent Work and Economic Growth' (SDG-8); 'Industry

Innovation and Infrastructure' (SDG-9); 'Reduced Inequalities' (SDG-10); 'Sustainable Consumption and Production' (SDG-12); 'Climate Action' (SDG-13), 'Life bellow Water' (SDG-14), 'Life and Land' (SDG-15), 'Gender Equality' (SDG-3), 'Reduced Poverty' (SDG-1) and 'Reduced Hunger' (SDG-2) which means, for the sake of community development within the territorial area of a Panchayat is authorized to take actions from the above mentioned listed activities; ultimately these Numbers of the 11th Schedule, provide by Article 243G are the strong tools to achieve as well as build the 'Peace, Justice and Strong Institutions' (SDG-16) in the country.

17. Education, including primary and secondary schools.

18. Technical training and vocational education.

19. Adult and non-formal education.

20. Libraries.

21. Cultural activities.

22. Markets and fairs.

Inferences: The sections of Article-243G, Listed 17 to 22 of the 11th Schedule has been reflected in the 'Reduce Hunger' (SDG-2); 'Quality Education' (SDG-4) it ultimately promote to 'Gender Equality' (SDG-5); 'Clean and affordable Energy' (SDG-7), 'Decent Work and Economic Growth' (SDG-8); 'Industry Innovation and Infrastructure' (SDG-9) and 'Reduced Inequalities' (SDG-10), 'Sustainable Consumption and Production' (SDG-12), 'Climate Action' (SDG-13) and 'Life bellow Water' (SDG-14) and 'Life and Land' (SDG-15); which means, for the sake of community development within the territorial area of a Panchayat is authorized to take actions from the above mentioned listed activities; ultimately these Numbers of the 11th Schedule, provide by Article 243G are the strong tools to achieve as well as build the 'Peace, Justice and Strong Institutions' (SDG-16) in the country.

23. Health and sanitation, including hospitals, primary health centres and dispensaries.

24. Family welfare.

25. Women and child development.

26. Social welfare, including welfare of the handicapped and mentally retarded.

27. Welfare of the weaker sections, and in particular, of the Scheduled Castes and the Scheduled Tribes.

28. Public distribution system.

29. Maintenance of community assets.

Inferences: The sections of Article-243G, Listed 23 to 29 of the 11th Schedule has been reflected in the 'Reduced Poverty' (SDG-1); 'Reduced Hunger' (SDG-2); 'Gender Equality', 'Good Health and Wellbeing' (SDG-3); 'Gender Equality' (SDG-5); 'Decent Work and Economic Growth' (SDG-8), 'Industry Innovation and Infrastructure' (SDG-9), 'Reduced Inequalities' (SDG-10), 'Sustainable Consumption and Production' (SDG-12) and 'Climate Action' (SDG-13); 'Life and land' (SDG-15) and it ultimately to the 'Peace, Justice and Strong Institutions' (SDG-16) which means, for the sake of community development within the territorial area of a Panchayat is authorized to take actions from the above mentioned listed activities; ultimately these Numbers of the 11th Schedule, provide by Article 243G are the strong tools to achieve as well as build the 'Peace, Justice and Strong Institutions' (SDG-16) in the country.

243W. Powers, authority and responsibilities of Municipalities, etc. Subject to the provisions of this Constitution, the Legislature of a State may, by law, endow— (*a*) the Municipalities with such powers and authority as may be necessary to enable them to function as institutions of self-government and such law may contain provisions for the devolution of powers and responsibilities upon Municipalities, subject to such conditions as may be specified therein, with respect to— (*i*) the preparation of plans for economic development and social justice; (*ii*) the performance of functions and the implementation of schemes as may be entrusted to them including those in relation to the matters listed in the Twelfth Schedule; (*b*) the Committees with such powers and authority as may be necessary to enable them to carry out the responsibilities conferred upon them including those in relation to the matters listed in the Twelfth Schedule.

TWELFTH SCHEDULE[110] (Article 243W)

1. Urban planning including town planning.

2. Regulation of land-use and construction of buildings.

Inferences: The sections of Article-243W, Listed 1 to 2 of the 12th Schedule has been reflected in the 'Reduced Poverty' (SDG-1); 'Reduced Hunger' (SDG-2), 'Good Health and Well-being' (SDG-3), 'Gender Equality' (SDG-5), 'Clean Water and Sanitation' (SDG-6), 'Clean and affordable Energy' (SDG-7), 'Decent Work and Economic Growth' (SDG-8), 'Industry Innovation and Infrastructure' (SDG-9), 'Reduced

Inequalities' (SDG-10); 'Sustainable Cities and Communities' (SDG-11), 'Climate Action' (SDG-13), 'Life bellow Water' (SDG-14) and 'Life and Land' (SDG-15); which means, for the sake of development within the territorial area of a Municipality is authorized to take actions from the above mentioned listed activities; ultimately these Numbers of the 12th Schedule, provide by Article 243TG are the strong tools to achieve as well as build the 'Peace, Justice and Strong Institutions' (SDG-16) in the country.

3. Planning for economic and social development.

Inferences: The section of Article-243W, Listed 3 of the 12th Schedule has been reflected in the 'Reduced Poverty' (SDG-1); 'Reduced Hunger' (SDG-2), 'Good Health and Well-being' (SDG-3), 'Gender Equality' (SDG-5), 'Clean Water and Sanitation' (SDG-6), 'Clean and affordable Energy' (SDG-7), 'Decent Work and Economic Growth' (SDG-8); 'Industry Innovation and Infrastructure' (SDG-9); 'Reduced Inequalities' (SDG-10), 'Sustainable Cities and Communities' (SDG-11), 'Climate Action' (SDG-13), 'Life bellow Water' (SDG-14) and 'Life and Land' (SDG-15); which means, for the sake of development within the territorial area of a Municipality is authorized to take actions from the above mentioned listed activities; ultimately the Number of the 12th Schedule, provide by Article 243TG are the strong tools to achieve as well as build the 'Peace, Justice and Strong Institutions' (SDG-16) in the country.

4. Roads and bridges.

5. Water supply for domestic, industrial and commercial purposes.

6. Public health, sanitation conservancy and solid waste management.

7. Fire services.

Inferences: The sections of Article-243W, Listed 4 to 7 of the 12th Schedule has been reflected in the 'Reduced Poverty' (SDG-1); 'Reduced Hunger' (SDG-2), 'Good Health and Wellbeing' (SDG-3); 'Gender Equality' (SDG-5), 'Clean Water and Sanitation' (SDG-6); 'Clean and affordable Energy' (SDG-7), 'Decent Work and Economic Growth' (SDG-8), 'Industry Innovation and Infrastructure' (SDG-9), 'Reduced Inequalities' (SDG-10); 'Sustainable Cities and Communities' (SDG-11), 'Climate Action' (SDG-13) , 'Life bellow Water' (SDG-14) and 'Life and Land' (SDG-15); which means, for the sake of development within the territorial area of a Municipality is authorized to take actions from the above mentioned listed activities.

8. Urban forestry, protection of the environment and promotion of ecological aspects.

Inferences: The sections of Article-243W, Listed 8 of the 12th Schedule has been reflected in the 'Reduced Hunger' (SDG-2), 'Good Health and Wellbeing' (SDG-3); 'Gender Equality' (SDG-5), 'Clean and affordable Energy' (SDG-7), 'Industry Innovation and Infrastructure' (SDG-9), 'Reduced Inequalities' (SDG-10); 'Sustainable Cities and Communities' (SDG-11); 'Climate Action ' (SDG-13); 'Life bellow Water' (SDG-14), and 'Life on Land' (SDG-15) which means, for the sake of development within the territorial area of a Municipality is authorized to take actions from the above mentioned listed activities; ultimately these Numbers of the 12th Schedule, provide by Article 243TG are the strong tools to achieve as well as build the 'Peace, Justice and Strong Institutions' (SDG-16) in the country.

9. Safeguarding the interests of weaker sections of society, including the handicapped and mentally retarded.

10. Slum improvement and upgradation.

11. Urban poverty alleviation.

Inferences: The sections of Article-243W, Listed 9 to 11 of the 12th Schedule has been reflected in the 'Reduced Poverty' (SDG-1); 'Reduced Hunger' (SDG-2); 'Good Health and Wellbeing' (SDG-3); 'Gender Equality' (SDG-5); 'Clean Water and Sanitation' (SDG-6), 'Clean and affordable Energy' (SDG-7), 'Decent Work and Economic Growth' (SDG-8), 'Reduced Inequalities' (SDG-10), 'Sustainable Cities and Communities' (SDG-11), 'Climate Action' (SDG-13), 'Life bellow Water' (SDG-14) and 'Life and Land' (SDG-15); which means, for the sake of development within the territorial area of a Municipality is authorized to take actions from the above mentioned listed activities.

12. Provision of urban amenities and facilities such as parks, gardens, playgrounds.

13. Promotion of cultural, educational and aesthetic aspects.

14. Burials and burial grounds; cremations, cremation grounds; and electric crematoriums.

Inferences: The sections of Article-243W, Listed 12 to 14 of the 12th Schedule has been reflected in the 'Reduced Inequalities' (SDG-10), 'Sustainable Cities and Communities' (SDG-11) and 'Life and Land' (SDG-15); which means, for the sake of development within the territorial area of a Municipality is authorized to take actions from the above mentioned listed activities; ultimately these Numbers of the 12th Schedule, provide by Article 243TG are the strong tools to achieve as well as build the 'Peace, Justice and Strong Institutions' (SDG-16) in the country.

15. Cattle pounds; prevention of cruelty to animals.

Inferences: The sections of Article-243W, Listed 15 of the 12th Schedule areas been reflected in the 'Sustainable Cities and Communities' (SDG-11), 'Climate Action' (SDG-13) and 'Life and Land' (SDG-15); which means, for the sake of development within the territorial area of a Municipality is authorized to take actions from the above mentioned listed activities.

16. Vital statistics including registration of births and deaths.

Inferences: The section of Article-243W, Listed 16 of the 12th Schedule has been reflected in the 'Reduced Poverty' (SDG-1); 'Reduced Hunger' (SDG-2); 'Good Health and Wellbeing' (SDG-3); 'Quality Education' (SDG-4); 'Gender Equality' (SDG-5); 'Clean Water and Sanitation' (SDG-6); 'Affordable and Clean Energy' (SDG-7); 'Decent Work and Economic Growth' (SDG-8); 'Industry Innovation and Infrastructure' (SDG-9); 'Reduced Inequalities' (SDG-10); 'Reduced Inequalities' (SDG-10); 'Sustainable Cities and Communities' (SDG-11); 'Sustainable Consumption and Production' (SDG-12); 'Climate Action' (SDG-13); 'Life Below Water' (SDG-14); 'Life and Land' (SDG-15) and 'Partnerships for the Goals' (SDG-17) which means, for the sake of development within the territorial area of a Municipality is authorized to take actions from the above mentioned listed activities; ultimately these Numbers of the 12th Schedule, provide by Article 243TG are the strong tools to achieve as well as build the 'Peace, Justice and Strong Institutions' (SDG-16) in the country.

17. Public amenities including street lighting, parking lots, bus stops and public conveniences.

Inferences: The section of Article-243W, Listed 17 of the 12th Schedule has been reflected in the 'Sustainable Cities and Communities' (SDG-11) and 'Climate Action' (SDG-13) which means, for the sake of development within the territorial area of a Municipality is authorized to take actions from the above mentioned listed activities; ultimately these Numbers of the 12th Schedule, provide by Article 243TG are the strong tools to achieve as well as build the 'Peace, Justice and Strong Institutions' (SDG-16) in the country.

18. Regulation of slaughter houses and tanneries.

Inferences: The section of Article-243W, Listed 17 of the 12th Schedule has been reflected in the 'Industry Innovation and Infrastructure' (SDG-9), 'Sustainable Cities and Communities' (SDG-11), 'Climate Action' (SDG-13) and 'Life and Land' (SDG-15) which means, for the sake of development within the territorial area of a Municipality is authorized to take actions from the above mentioned listed activities; ultimately the Number of the 12th Schedule, provide by Article 243TG are the strong tools to achieve as well as build the 'Peace, Justice and Strong Institutions' (SDG-16) in the country.

Notes

1. Added by the Constitution (First Amendment) Act, 1951, Sections-2. Article-15, Clause (4); *"Nothing in this article or in clause (2) of article 29 shall prevent the State from making any special provision for the advancement of any socially and educationally backward classes of citizens or for the Scheduled Castes and the Scheduled Tribes".*
2. Inserted by the Constitution (Ninety-third Amendment) Act, 2005, Sections - 2, (w.e.f. 20-1-2006). Article-15, Clause (5) *"Nothing in this article or in sub-clause (g) of clause (1) of article 19 shall prevent the State from making any special provision, by law, for the advancement of any socially and educationally backward classes of citizens or for the Scheduled Castes or the Scheduled Tribes in so far as such special provisions relate to their admission to educational institutions including private educational institutions, whether aided or unaided by the State, other than the minority educational institutions referred to in clause (1) of Article – 30".*
3. Clause 5 Substituted by the Constitution (Seventh Amendment) Act, 1956, Sections - 29 and Schedule, for "under any State specified in the First Schedule or any local or other authority within its territory, any requirement as to residence within that State". Article-16, Clause (3). Nothing in this article shall prevent Parliament from making any law prescribing, in regard to a class or classes of employment or appointment to an office *(under the Government of, or any local or other authority within, a State or Union territory, any requirement as to residence within that State or Union territory* prior to such employment or appointment.
4. Inserted by the Constitution (Seventy-seventh Amendment) Act, 1995, Sections - 2. Article-16, Clause (4A), *"Nothing in this article shall prevent the State from making any provision for reservation (in matters of promotion, with consequential seniority, to any class".*
5. Substituted by the Constitution (Eighty-fifth Amendment) Act, 2001, Sections - 2, for certain words (w.e.f. 17-6-1995). Article-16, Clause (4A), "or classes of posts in the services under the State in favour of the Scheduled Castes and the Scheduled Tribes which, in the opinion of the State, are not adequately represented in the services under the State".
6. 2000: Inserted by the Constitution (Eighty-first Amendment) Act, 2000, Sections - 2 (w.e.f. 9-6-2000). Article-16, Clause (4B), *"Nothing in this article*

shall prevent the State from considering any unfilled vacancies of a year which are reserved for being filled up in that year in accordance with any provision for reservation made under clause (4) or clause (4A) as a separate class of vacancies to be filled up in any succeeding year or years and such class of vacancies shall not be considered together with the vacancies of the year in which they are being filled up for determining the ceiling of fifty percent reservation on total number of vacancies of that year".

7. 2011: Inserted by the Constitution (Ninety-seventh Amendment) Act, 2011, Sections - 2 (w.e.f. 8-2-2012). Article-19 - 1 (c). *"to form associations or unions [or co-operative societies"* .
8. Sub-clause *(f)* omitted by the Constitution (Forty-fourth Amendment) Act, 1978, Sections - 2 (w.e.f. 20-6-1979). Article-19 – 1 (f).
9. Clause *(f)* omitted by s. 2, *ibid.* (w.e.f. 20-6-1979).
10. Inserted by the Constitution (Sixteenth Amendment) Act, 1963, Sections - 2. Article-19, Clause 2, *"the security of the State, friendly relations with foreign States, public order, decency or morality, or in relation to contempt of court, defamation or incitement to an offence".*
11. Substituted by the Constitution (First Amendment) Act, 1951, Sections - 3, for Clause (2) (with retrospective effect). Article-19, v Clause 2, *"Nothing in sub-clause (a) of clause (1) shall affect the operation of any existing law, or prevent the State from making any law, in so far as such law imposes reasonable restrictions on the exercise of the right conferred by the said sub-clause in the interests of (the sovereignty and integrity of India".*
12. Substituted by the Constitution (Forty-fourth Amendment) Act, 1978, Sections - 2, for "sub-clauses *(d)*, *(e)* and *(f)*" (w.e.f. 20-6-1979). Article-19, Clause 5, *"Nothing in (sub-clauses (d) and (e) of the said clause shall affect the operation of any existing law in so far as it imposes, or prevent the State from making any law imposing, reasonable restrictions on the exercise of any of the rights conferred by the said sub-clauses either in the interests of the general public or for the protection of the interests of any Scheduled Tribe".*
13. Substituted by the Constitution (First Amendment) Act, 1951, Sections - 3, for certain words. Article-19, Clause 6, *"nothing in the said sub-clause shall affect the operation of any existing law in so far as it relates to, or prevent the State from making any law relating to,- (i) the professional or technical qualifications necessary for practising any profession or carrying on any occupation, trade or business, or (ii) the carrying on by the State, or by a corporation owned or controlled by the State, of any trade, business, industry or service, whether to the exclusion, complete or partial, of citizens or otherwise".*
14. Inserted by the Constitution (Eighty-sixth Amendment) Act, 2002, Sections - 2 (w.e.f. 1-4-2010). Article-21A, *"The State shall provide free and compulsory education to all children of the age of six to fourteen years in such manner as the State may, by law, determine.*
15. Article-22, Clause (4), shall stand substituted by the Constitution (Forty-fourth Amendment) Act, 1978, s. 3 (date yet to be notified). "*No law providing for preventive detention shall authorise the detention of a person for a longer period than two months unless an Advisory Board constituted in accordance with the*

recommendations of the Chief Justice of the appropriate High Court has reported before the expiration of the said period of two months that there is in its opinion sufficient cause for such detention: Provided that an Advisory Board shall consist of a Chairman and not less than two other members, and the Chairman shall be a serving Judge of the appropriate High Court and the other members shall be serving or retired Judges of any High Court: Provided further that nothing in this clause shall authorise the detention of any person beyond the maximum period prescribed by any law made by Parliament under sub-clause (a) of clause (7). Explanation.—In this clause, "appropriate High Court" means,— (i) in the case of the detention of a person in pursuance of an order of detention made by the Government of India or an officer or authority subordinate to that Government, the High Court for the Union territory of Delhi; (ii) in the case of the detention of a person in pursuance of an order of detention made by the Government of any State (other than a Union territory), the High Court for that State; and (iii) in the case of the detention of a person in pursuance of an order of detention made by the administrator of a Union territory or an officer or authority subordinate to such administrator, such High Court as may be specified by or under any law made by Parliament in this behalf".

16. Article-22, Clause (7), Sub-clause (*a*) shall stand omitted by the Constitution (Forty-fourth Amendment) Act, 1978, Section - 3 (which is yet not in force, date to be notified later on). *"(a) the circumstances under which, and the class or classes of cases in which, a person may be detained for a period longer than three months under any law providing for preventive detention without obtaining the opinion of an Advisory Board in accordance with the provisions of sub-clause (a) of clause (4)".*
17. Article-22, Clause (7), Sub-clause (*b*) shall stand re-lettered as sub-clause (*a*) by Section - 3, (date yet to be notified). *"the maximum period for which any person may in any class or classes of cases be detained under any law providing for preventive detention".*
18. Article-22-Clause (7), Sub-clause (*c*) the words, letter and figure in brackets shall stand substituted as "clause 4" by s. 3, (date yet to be notified), "(*c*) the procedure to be followed by an Advisory Board in an inquiry under sub-clause (*a*) of clause (4)".
19. Section - 4 (w.e.f. 20-6-1979). *"In making any law providing for the compulsory acquisition of any property of an educational institution established and administered by a minority, referred to in clause (1), the State shall ensure that the amount fixed by or determined under such law for the acquisition of such property is such as would not restrict or abrogate the right guaranteed under that clause".*
20. Article-31, *"Right to Property" the Compulsory acquisition of property repealed by the Constitution (Forty-fourth Amendment) Act,* 1978, *s.* 6 *(w.e.f.* 20-6-1979), omitted by the Constitution.
21. Inserted by the Constitution (Forty-second Amendment) Act, 1976, Section - 3 (w.e.f. 3-1-1977); *Saving of Certain Laws.*
22. Article 31A, Inserted by the Constitution (First Amendment) Act, 1951, Section - 4 (with retrospective effect).

23. Article 31A, Substituted by the Constitution (Fourth Amendment) Act, 1955, Section - 3, for Clause (1) (with retrospective effect).
24. Article 31A, Clause (1)-e, Substituted by the Constitution (Forty-fourth Amendment) Act, 1978, Section - 7, for "article 14, article 19 or article 31" (w.e.f. 20-6-1979); *"the extinguishment or modification of any rights accruing by virtue of any agreement, lease or licence for the purpose of searching for, or winning, any mineral or mineral oil, or the premature termination or cancellation of any such agreement, lease or licence, shall be deemed to be void on the ground that it is inconsistent with, or takes away or abridges any of the rights conferred by article 14 or article 19".*
25. Article 31A, Clause (1)-e, Inserted by the Constitution (Seventeenth Amendment) Act, 1964, Section – 2; *"Provided further that where any law makes any provision for the acquisition by the State of any estate and where any land comprised therein is held by a person under his personal cultivation, it shall not be lawful for the State to acquire any portion of such land as is within the ceiling limit applicable to him under any law for the time being in force or any building or structure standing thereon or appurtenant thereto, unless the law relating to the acquisition of such land, building or structure, provides for payment of compensation at a rate which shall not be less than the market value thereof".*
26. Article 31A, Substituted by the Constitution (Seventeenth Amendment) Act, 1964, Section – 2 for sub-clause (*a*) (with retrospective effect); *"the expression "estate" shall, in relation to any local area, have the same meaning as that expression or its local equivalent has in the existing law relating to land tenures in force in that area and shall also include".*
27. Article 31A, Substituted by the Madras State (Alteration of Name) Act, 1968 (53 of 1968), Section – 4, for "Madras" (w.e.f. 14-1-1969).
28. Article 31A, Inserted by the Constitution (Fourth Amendment) Act, 1955, Section – 3, Clause-2-b (with retrospective effect); *"the expression "rights", in relation to an estate, shall include any rights vesting in a proprietor, sub-proprietor, under-proprietor, tenure-holder, [raiyat, under-raiyat] or other intermediary and any rights or privileges in respect of land revenue".*
29. Article 31B, Inserted by the Constitution (First Amendment) Act, 1951, Section – 5; Validation of certain Acts and Regulations – *"Without prejudice to the generality of the provisions contained in article 31A, none of the Acts and Regulations specified in the Ninth Schedule nor any of the provisions thereof shall be deemed to be void, or ever to have become void, on the ground that such Act, Regulation or provision is inconsistent with, or takes away or abridges any of the rights conferred by, any provisions of this Part, and notwithstanding any judgment, decree or order of any court or Tribunal to the contrary, each of the said Acts and Regulations shall, subject to the power of any competent Legislature to repeal or amend it, continue in force".*
30. Article 31C - Inserted by the Constitution (Twenty-fifth Amendment) Act, 1971, Section – 3 (w.e.f. 20-4-1972); *"Saving of laws giving effect to certain directive principles".*
31. Article 31C, Substituted by the Constitution (Forty-second Amendment) Act, 1976, Section – 4, for "the principles specified in clause (*b*) or clause (*c*) of

article 39" (w.e.f. 3-1-1977). Section-4 has been declared invalid by the Supreme Court in *Minerva Mills Ltd. and Others vs. Union of India and Others* (1980) 2 S.C.C. 591.

32. Article 31C, Substituted by the Constitution (Forty-fourth Amendment) Act, 1978, Section – 8, for "article 14, article 19 or article 31" (w.e.f. 20-6-1979).

33. Article 31C, In *Kesavananda Bharati vs. The State of Kerala,* (1973) Supp. S.C.R. 1, the Supreme Court held the provision in italics to be invalid; *"and no law containing a declaration that it is for giving effect to such policy shall be called in question in any court on the ground that it does not give effect to such policy".*

34. Article 31D, Inserted by the Constitution (Forty-second Amendment) Act, 1976, Section – 5 (w.e.f. 3-1-1977). *Saving of laws in respect of anti-national activities Repealed by the Constitution (Forty-third Amendment) Act,* 1977, Section – 2 (*w.e.f.* 13-4-1978).

35. Article 32A, Inserted by the Constitution (Forty-second Amendment) Act, 1976, Section – 6, (w.e.f. 1-2-1977). *Constitutional validity of State laws not to be considered in proceedings under article* 32 *Repealed by the Constitution (Forty-third Amendment) Act,* 1977, *s.* 3 *(w.e.f.* 13-4-1978).

36. Article 33, Substituted by the Constitution (Fiftieth Amendment) Act, 1984, Section – 2, for Article 33; "*Power of Parliament to modify the rights conferred by this Part in their application to Forces, etc".*

37. Article 38 renumbered as Clause (1) thereof by the Constitution (Forty-fourth Amendment) Act, 1978, Section - 9 (w.e.f. 20-6-1979); *"State to secure a social order for the promotion of welfare of the people".*

38. Article 38 Inserted as Clause (2) thereof by the Constitution (Forty-fourth Amendment) Act, 1978, Section - 9 (w.e.f. 20-6-1979); "The State shall, in particular, strive to minimise the inequalities in income, and endeavour to eliminate inequalities in status, facilities and opportunities, not only amongst individuals but also amongst groups of people residing in different areas or engaged in different vocations".

39. Article 39 (f), Substituted by the Constitution (Forty-second Amendment) Act, 1976, Section - 7, for Clause (*f*) (w.e.f. 3-1-1977).

40. Article 39A, Inserted by the Constitution (Forty-second Amendment) Act, 1976, Section - 8, (w.e.f. 3-1-1977); *"Equal justice and free legal aid". "The State shall secure that the operation of the legal system promotes justice, on a basis of equal opportunity, and shall, in particular, provide free legal aid, by suitable legislation or schemes or in any other way, to ensure that opportunities for securing justice are not denied to any citizen by reason of economic or other disabilities".*

41. Article 43A, Inserted by the Constitution (Forty-second Amendment) Act, 1976, Section - 9 (w.e.f. 3-1-1977); *"Participation of workers in management of industries". "The State shall take steps, by suitable legislation or in any other way, to secure the participation of workers in the management of undertakings, establishments or other organisations engaged in any industry".*

42. Article 43B, Inserted by the Constitution (Ninety-seventh Amendment) Act, 2011, Section - 3, (w.e.f. 15-2-2012); "Promotion of cooperative societies. *"The State*

shall endeavour to promote voluntary formation, autonomous functioning, democratic control and professional management of co-operative societies".

43. Article 45, Substituted by the Constitution (Eighty-sixth Amendment) Act, 2002, Section - 3, for art. 45 (w.e.f. 1-4-2010), "Provision for early childhood care and education to children below the age of six years". "The State shall endeavour to provide early childhood care and education for all children until they complete the age of six years".
44. Article 48A, Inserted by the Constitution (Forty-second Amendment) Act, 1976, Section - 10 (w.e.f. 3-1-1977); "Protection and improvement of environment and safeguarding of forests and wild life". "The State shall endeavour to protect and improve the environment and to safeguard the forests and wild life of the country".
45. Article 49, Substituted by the Constitution (Seventh Amendment) Act, 1956, Section - 27, for "declared by Parliament by law"; "Protection of monuments and places and objects of national importance". "It shall be the obligation of the State to protect every monument or place or object of artistic or historic interest, declared by or under law made by Parliament to be of national importance, from spoliation, disfigurement, destruction, removal, disposal or export, as the case may be".
46. *Part IVA of the Indian Constitution* is Inserted by the Constitution (Forty-second Amendment) Act, 1976, Section - 11 (w.e.f. 3-1-1977).
47. Article 51A, (k), Inserted by the Constitution (Eighty-sixth Amendment) Act, 2002, Section - 4 (w.e.f. 1-4-2010); *"who is a parent or guardian to provide opportunities for education to his child or, as the case may be, ward between the age of six and fourteen years".*
48. *Part IX of the Indian Constitution* is Inserted by the Constitution (Seventy-third Amendment) Act, 1992, Section - 2 (w.e.f. 24-4-1993). Original Part IX was omitted by the Constitution (Seventh Amendment) Act, 1956, Section - 29 and Schedule.
49. *Part IXA of the Indian Constitution* is Inserted by the Constitution (Seventy-fourth Amendment) Act, 1992, Section - 2 (w.e.f. 1-6-1993).
50. Article 304A, Inserted by the Constitution (Seventh Amendment) Act, 1956, Section - 29 and Schedule; "*the Union territories*".
51. Article 305, Substituted by the Constitution (Fourth Amendment) Act, 1955, Section - 4, for art. 305; "Saving of existing laws and laws providing for State monopolies". "Nothing in articles 301 and 303 shall affect the provisions of any existing law except in so far as the President may by order otherwise direct; and nothing in article 301 shall affect the operation of any law made before the commencement of the Constitution (Fourth Amendment) Act, 1955, in so far as it relates to, or prevent Parliament or the Legislature of a State from making any law relating to, any such matter as is referred to in sub-clause (*ii*) of clause (6) of Article 19".
52. Part XIV, 'Chapter I – Services' of the Constitution of India detailed about the 'Services under the Union and the States'. In the Article 308 – there is an 'Interpretation' "In this Part, unless the context otherwise requires, the expression "State" (does not include the State of Jammu and Kashmir; Substituted by the

Constitution (Seventh Amendment) Act, 1956, Section - 29 and Schedule, for "means a State specified in Part A or Part B of the First Schedule".

53. The words "or *Rajpramukh*" omitted by the Constitution (Seventh Amendment) Act, 1956, Section - 29 and Schedule.
54. Substituted by the Constitution (Fifteenth Amendment) Act, 1963, Section - 10, for clauses (2) and (3).
55. Certain words omitted by the Constitution (Forty-second Amendment) Act, 1976, Section - 44 (w.e.f. 3-1-1977).
56. Substituted by the Constitution (Forty-second Amendment) Act, 1976, Section - 44, for certain words (w.e.f. 3-1-1977).
57. Substituted by the Constitution (Forty-second Amendment) Act, 1976, Section - 45, for "Part XI" (w.e.f. 3-1-1977).
58. Inserted by the Constitution (Forty-second Amendment) Act, 1976, Section - 45, (w.e.f. 3-1-1977).
59. Inserted by the Constitution (Twenty-eighth Amendment) Act, 1972, s. 2 (w.e.f. 29-8-1972).
60. Inserted by the Constitution (Twenty-eighth Amendment) Act, 1972, Section - 2 (w.e.f. 29-8-1972).
61. Inserted by the Constitution (Forty-second Amendment) Act, 1976, Section - 46 (w.e.f. 3-1-1977).
62. Inserted by the Constitution (Seventy-fifth Amendment) Act, 1993, Section - 2 (w.e.f. 15-5-1994).
63. Sub-clauses (*h*) and (*i*) re-lettered as sub-clauses (*i*) and (*j*) by the Constitution (Seventy-fifth Amendment) Act, 1993, Section - 2 (w.e.f. 15-5-1994).
64. Substituted by the Constitution (Seventy-fifth Amendment) Act, 1993, Section - 2 for "(*g*)" (w.e.f. 15-5-1994).
65. Sub-clauses (*h*) and (*i*) re-lettered as sub-clauses (*i*) and (*j*) by the Constitution (Seventy-fifth Amendment) Act, 1993, Section - 2 (w.e.f. 15-5-1994).
66. Substituted by the Constitution (Seventy-fifth Amendment) Act, 1993, Section - 2 for "(*h*)" (w.e.f. 15-5-1994).
67. Article 326, Substituted by the Constitution (Sixty-first Amendment) Act, 1988, Section - 2, for *"twenty-one years"*.
68. Article 330 – 1 (b), Substituted by the Constitution (Fifty-first Amendment) Act, 1984, Section - 2, for sub-clause (*b*) (w.e.f. 16-6-1986); *"the Scheduled Tribes except the Scheduled Tribes in the autonomous districts of Assam"*.
69. Article 330 – 2, Inserted by the Constitution (Seventh Amendment) Act, 1956, Section - 29 and Schedule; "Union territory".
70. Article 330 – 3, Inserted by the Constitution (Thirty-first Amendment) Act, 1973, Section – 3; *"Notwithstanding anything contained in clause (2), the number of seats reserved in the House of the People for the Scheduled Tribes in the autonomous districts of Assam shall bear to the total number of seats allotted to that State a proportion not less than the population of the Scheduled Tribes in the said autonomous districts bears to the total population of the State"*.

71. Article 332 – 1, Substituted by the Constitution (Fifty-first Amendment) Act, 1984, Section - 3, for certain words (w.e.f. 16-6-1986); *"except the Scheduled Tribes in the autonomous districts of Assam"*.
72. Article 332 – 1, The words and letters "specified in Part A or Part B of the First Schedule" omitted by the Constitution (Seventh Amendment) Act, 1956, Section - 29 and Schedule; *"in the Legislative Assembly of every State"*.
73. Article 332 – 3A, Inserted by the Constitution (Fifty-seventh Amendment) Act, 1987, Section - 2 (w.e.f. 21-9-1987); *"Notwithstanding anything contained in clause (3), until the re-adjustment, under article 170, takes effect on the basis of the first census after the year (2026)"*.
74. Article 332 – 3A, Substituted by the Constitution (Eighty-fourth Amendment) Act, 2001, Section - 7, for "2000", "2026".
75. Article 332 – 3B, Inserted by the Constitution (Seventy-second Amendment) Act, 1992, Section – 2, (w.e.f. 5-12-1992).
76. Article 332 – 5, Certain words omitted by the North-Eastern Areas (Reorganisation) Act, 1971 (81 of 1971), Section -71(w.e.f. 21-1-1972).
77. Article 332 – 5, Certain words omitted by the North-Eastern Areas (Reorganisation) Act, 1971 (81 of 1971), Section -71(w.e.f. 21-1-1972).
78. Article 332 – 6, Inserted by the Constitution (Ninetieth Amendment) Act, 2003, Section – 2; *"Provided that for elections to the Legislative Assembly of the State of Assam, the representation of the Scheduled Tribes and non-Scheduled Tribes in the constituencies included in the Bodoland Territorial Areas District, so notified, and existing prior to the constitution of the Bodoland Territorial Areas District, shall be maintained"*.
79. Article 332, Substituted by the Constitution (Twenty-third Amendment) Act, 1969, Section - 4, for "nominate such number of members of the community to the Assembly as he considers appropriate"; *"nominate one member of that community to the Assembly"*.
80. Article 334 (b), Substituted by the Constitution (Ninety-fifth Amendment) Act, 2009, Section - 2, for "sixty years" (w.e.f. 25-1-2010); *"seventy years"*.
81. Article 338, Substituted by the Constitution (Eighty-ninth Amendment) Act, 2003, Section - 2, for the marginal heading (w.e.f. 19-2-2004); *"National Commission for Scheduled Castes"*.
82. Article 338 (1), Substituted by the Constitution (Eighty-ninth Amendment) Act, 2003, Section - 2, for clauses (1) and (2) (w.e.f. 19-2-2004); *"There shall be a Commission for the Scheduled Castes to be known as the National Commission for the Scheduled Castes"*.
83. Article 338 (5)-(a), The words "and Scheduled Tribes" omitted the Constitution (Eighty-ninth Amendment) Act, 2003, Section - 2, (w.e.f. 19-2-2004).
84. Article 338A, Inserted by the Constitution (Eighty-ninth Amendment) Act, 2003, Section - 3 (w.e.f. 19-2-2004).
85. *See* the Constitution (Scheduled Castes) Order, 1950 (C.O. 19), the Constitution (Scheduled Castes) (Union Territories) Order, 1951 (C.O. 32), the Constitution (Jammu and Kashmir) Schedued Castes Order, 1956 (C.O. 52), the Constitution (Dadra and Nagar Haveli) Schedued Castes Order, 1962 (C.O. 64), the

Constitution (Pondicherry) Scheduled Castes Order, 1964 (C.O. 68), the Constitution (Goa, Daman and Diu) Scheduled Castes Order, 1968 (C.O. 81) and the Constitution (Sikkim) Scheduled Castes Order, 1978 (C.O. 110).

86. Article 350A, Inserted by the Constitution (Seventh Amendment) Act, 1956, Section – 21; *"It shall be the endeavour of every State and of every local authority within the State to provide adequate facilities for instruction in the mother-tongue at the primary stage of education to children belonging to linguistic minority groups; and the President may issue such directions to any State as he considers necessary or proper for securing the provision of such facilities".*

87. Article 246, Seventh Schedule – List I, Union List-2A, Inserted by the Constitution (Forty-second Amendment) Act, 1976, Section –57 (w.e.f. 3-1-1977); *"Deployment of any armed force of the Union or any other force subject to the control of the Union or any contingent or unit thereof in any State in aid of the civil power; powers, jurisdiction, privileges and liabilities of the members of such forces while on such deployment".*

88. Article 246, Seventh Schedule – List I, Union List-33, Entry *33* omitted by the Constitution (Seventh Amendment) Act, 1956, Section – 26.

89. *"The institutions known at the commencement of this Constitution as the Benares Hindu University, the Aligarh Muslim University and the Delhi University; the University established in pursuance of article 371E; any other institution declared by Parliament by law to be an institution of national importance.*

90. Article 246, Seventh Schedule – List I, Union List-78 Inserted by the Constitution (Fifteenth Amendment) Act, 1963, Section –12 (with retrospective effect); *"Constitution and organisation (including vacations) of the High Courts except provisions as to officers and servants of High Courts; persons entitled to practise before the High Courts".*

91. Article 246, Seventh Schedule – List I, Union List-92A, Inserted by the Constitution (Sixth Amendment) Act, 1956, Section – 2; *"Taxes on the sale or purchase of goods other than newspapers, where such sale or purchase takes place in the course of inter-State trade or commerce".*

92. Article 246, Seventh Schedule – List I, Union List-92C, Inserted by the Constitution (Eighty-eighth Amendment) Act, 2003, Section – 4 (which is yet not in force, date to be notified later on); *"Taxes on services".*

93. Article 246, Seventh Schedule – List II, State List-1, Substituted by the Constitution (Forty-second Amendment) Act, 1976, Section – 57, for certain words (w.e.f. 3-1-1977) [126]; *"Public order (but not including the use of any naval, military or air force or any other armed force of the Union or of any other force subject to the control of the Union or of any contingent or unit thereof in aid of the civil power)".*

94. Article 246, Seventh Schedule – List II, State List-2, Substituted by the Constitution (Forty-second Amendment) Act, 1976, Section – 57, for entry 2 (w.e.f. 3-1-1977); *"Police (including railway and village police) subject to the provisions of entry 2A of List I".*

95. Article 246, Seventh Schedule – List II, State List-3, Certain words omitted by the Constitution (Forty-second Amendment) Act, 1976, Section – 57, (w.e.f.

3-1-1977); *"Officers and servants of the High Court; procedure in rent and revenue courts; fees taken in all courts except the Supreme Court"*.

96. Article 246, Seventh Schedule – List II, State List-11, Entry *11* omitted by the Constitution (Forty-second Amendment) Act, 1976, Section – 57, (w.e.f. 3-1-1977).

97. Article 246, Seventh Schedule – List II, State List-19, 20 and 29, Entries *19, 20* and 29 omitted by the Constitution (Forty-second Amendment) Act, 1976, Section – 57, (w.e.f. 3-1-1977).

98. Article 246, Seventh Schedule – List II, State List-24, Substituted by the Constitution (Seventh Amendment) Act, 1956, Section – 28, for "entry 52"; *"Industries subject to the provisions of (entries 7 and 52) of List I"*.

99. Article 246, Seventh Schedule – List II, State List-36, Entry *36* omitted by the Constitution (Seventh Amendment) Act, 1956, Section – 26.

100. Article 246, Seventh Schedule – List II, State List-54, Substituted by the Constitution (Sixth Amendment) Act, 1956, Section – 2, for entry 54; *"Taxes on the sale or purchase of goods other than newspapers, subject to the provisions of entry 92A of List I"*.

101. Article 246, Seventh Schedule – List II, State List-55, Inserted by the Constitution (Forty-second Amendment) Act, 1976, Section – 57 (w.e.f. 3-1-1977); *"Taxes on advertisements other than advertisements published in the newspapers (and advertisements broadcast by radio or television)"*.

102. Inserted by the Constitution (Forty-second Amendment) Act, 1976, s. 57 (w.e.f. 3-1-1977).

103. Inserted by the Constitution (Forty-second Amendment) Act, 1976, s. 57 (w.e.f. 3-1-1977).

104. Inserted by the Constitution (Forty-second Amendment) Act, 1976, s. 57 (w.e.f. 3-1-1977).

105. Article 246, Seventh Schedule – List III, Concurrent List-25, Substituted by the Constitution (Forty-second Amendment) Act, 1976, Section – 57, for entry 25 (w.e.f. 3-1-1977); *"Education, including technical education, medical education and universities, subject to the provisions of entries 63, 64, 65 and 66 of List I; vocational and technical training of labour"*.

106. Article 246, Seventh Schedule – List III, Concurrent List-33, Substituted by the Constitution (Third Amendment) Act, 1954, Section – 2, for entry 33: *"Trade and commerce in, and the production, supply and distribution of"*, — *(a)* *"the products of any industry where the control of such industry by the Union is declared by Parliament by law to be expedient in the public interest, and imported goods of the same kind as such products"*; (*b*) *"foodstuffs, including edible oilseeds and oils"*; (*c*) *"cattle fodder, including oilcakes and other concentrates"*; (*d*) *"raw cotton, whether ginned or unginned, and cotton seed"*; and (*e*) *"raw jute"*.

107. Article 246, Seventh Schedule – List III, Concurrent List-33A, Inserted by the Constitution (Forty-second Amendment) Act, 1976, Section – 57 (w.e.f. 3-1-1977); *"Weights and measures except establishment of standards"*.

108. Article 246, Seventh Schedule – List III, Concurrent List-42, Substituted by the Constitution (Seventh Amendment) Act, 1956, Section – 26, for entry 42; *"Acquisition and requisitioning of property"*.
109. Article 243G, Eleventh Schedule, Added by the Constitution (Seventy-third Amendment) Act, 1992, Section – 4 (w.e.f. 24-4-1993).
110. Article 243W, Twelfth Schedule, Added by the Constitution (Seventy-fourth Amendment) Act, 1992, Section – 4 (w.e.f. 1-6-1993).

Chapter – IV

An Observation of Civil Society on SDGs

After 2015 or since 2016, there are many books and reports has differently explored about the SDGs in India such as *'Sustainable Development and India: Convergence of Law, Economics, Science, and Politics'* (Nagar 2018); *'Lessons in Sustainable Development from Bangladesh and India'* (Simi Mehta 2018); *'Development and Ecological Sustainability in India: Possibilities for the Post-2015 Framework'* (Kothari 2018); *'Annual Report 2017-2018 of GAIL'* (GAIL 2018), *'India and Sustainable Development Goals: The Way Forward'* by Research and Information System for Developing Countries (UN-RIS 2016); *'Millennium Development Goals – Final Country Report of India'* (MoSPI 2017); *'Green Growth and Sustainable Development in India'* (TERI-GGGI 2015), *'Voluntary National Review Report on Implementation of Sustainable Development Goals'* (NITI Aayog 2017) presented to the United Nations High Level Political Forum 2017, by the NITI *Aayog*, Government of India – all the books and reports are relevant for its concept and way of presentation.

Without blaming other, SDGs are fully composed of individual's that is citizen's responsibility, which demands individual awareness, inclusive participation of the citizens and it has a need to convey the gaps to respective administrative levels of a country. In the other side, it demands cooperation, assistance and sharing (CAS) within own country and between other countries. Which has been reflected in the name of SDG-17 'partnership of the goals'. In this regard, the following exploration will encourage the citizens to take a stand in favour of SDG as a citizen of India. It demands, because, our country has been played a vital role to include such of its issues in the agenda of United Nation's Sustainable Development Goals (SDGs), which to be achieved by 2030 and the Indian Constitution guided us as a citizen of India. We must decide, unless we will not be in a position to face the future generation with a smile.

Sustainable Development Goals Agenda 2030: India 2017–A Civil Society Report, Coordinated by *'Wada Na Todo Abhiyan'* (WNTA) in English *'Don't Break Your Promise'* summarized that, the 17 Goals of the 2030 Agenda for Sustainable Development - adopted by 193 nations in September 2015 at the UN Summit - officially came into force on 1 January 2016. While ambitious and universal in nature, they have, in princi-ple, charted out a path for nations to achieve development that is fair; equitable; inclusive and environment friendly. Human and environmental rights underpin the foundation of the SDGs that demand robust and integrated actions nationally, recognizing the role of different actors in the process.

The SDGs being interdependent in nature; require actions at all levels to attain the development outcomes. In the Glob-al South context, it is only logical to deduce that much is desired of the emerging economies of the world (BRICSAM nations), which account for highest proportion of poorest communities. And with the rising Gross Domestic Product (GDP), India accounts for the largest number of people living below international poverty line, with 30 per cent (nearly 800 million) of its population living under $1.90 a day (World Bank 2013).

Poverty is more than lack of income or resources, it includes social discrimination and exclusion, lack of basic services, such as education, health, water and sanitation, and lack of participation in decision making. These 'durable inequal-ities' perpetuate acute poverty, limiting the life options of historically marginalised communities. The recent Credit Suisse report shows that the richest 1 per cent Indians now own 58.4 per cent of the country's wealth. In a country where more than half the households are dependent on land (agriculture had 48.9 per cent of employment share in 2011-12), its distribution is highly unequal. The visible fiscal and economic inequalities are undercut by gross social inequalities based on identity and social status, viz. caste, ethnicity, religion, region, age and gender.

National and state level statistics testify to the trends of exclusion from land ownership and agriculture. Census data reveals that in the 10-year period between Census 2001 and Census 2011, there were nearly 9 million less cultivators in India. The number of landless agricultural workers in the country rose from 106.7 million in 2001 to 144.3 million in 2011. Further, landlessness is highest among Dalits (57.3 per cent), Muslims (52.6 per cent) and women headed (56.8 per cent) households, castigating them to work as agricultural labourers, and to face the spectre of depressed and unequal wages or to be expelled altogether to join the massive migration to the cities. Constituting only 8 per cent of the population, the Tribals shouldered 55 percent of the development induced displacement till 1995, and not much has bucked the trend to date. There is also a growing trend of feminization of agricultural labour, but only 13.6 per cent households are headed by women, owning 7.17 per cent of total productive land. Even where they report ownership of productive land there is the question of who controls the use of such land.

Besides, in India, employment generation is abysmally low even during the periods of high growth rate. The youth population, is therefore, either getting into unskilled /informal labour sector where scope for economic betterment is too narrow.

The decline in agricultural investments that started in the 1980s is continuing till date. A total of 12, 602 farmer sui-cides were reported officially, with Maharashtra topping the list with 4,291 suicides, followed by Karnataka 1,569, Telangana 1,400, Madhya Pradesh 1,290, Chhattisgarh 954, Andhra Pradesh 916 and Tamil Nadu 606 farmer suicides. Togeth-er, these seven states accounted for 87.5% (11,026) of total 12,602 suicides in the farming sector in the country. The per capita availability of land has declined from 0.5 hectares in 1951 to 0.15 hectares in 2011, with shrunken agriculture, and related insecurities due to commercialization, natural disasters and climate vagaries.

India released the first National Disaster Management Plan (NDMP) in June 2016. While the Indian Government has embarked upon building urban infrastructure across the country and develops 100 smart cities over the coming years, it is important for cities and infrastructure being built to consider the topography of the area and its vulnerability to various hazards.

One of the fundamental problems is the lack of appropriate vulnerability assessment mechanism. Most of the state plans are based on the Vulnerability Atlas of India. While these provide macro level analysis, it leaves out the slow onset disasters such as droughts and sea level rise. In 2016, 255,923 villages across 10 states suffered severe drought, which impacted food security and access to water, resulting in acute indebtedness. And despite the known vulnerability of India to various disasters, most of the mitigation programmes so far are designed as responsive/ reactive, and not resilience centric.

Appropriate infrastructure for India Meteorological Department (IMD), rainfall and weather monitoring stations, lack of forecasts providing information down to the village level rather than giving it for regions, and lack of IMD and ISRO information in a user-friendly and understandable manner remains the need of the states. Issues like migration, indebtedness, and livelihood regeneration are yet to be considered as a part of climate change and Disaster Risk Reduction (DRR) planning in the government policies; which will make the approach to sustainable cities and communities comprehensive and risk resilience focused (SDG-11).

As far as the local governments are concerned, they have almost no role in managing climate change and disasters. The 73rd and 74th Constitutional Amendment Act, 1992, which aimed at empowering local rural and urban authorities including the right to raise resources, pursue social justice policies and contribute to economic development, largely remains unimplemented. This is ironical as world over these are local governments who are leading the transition of cities.

Lack of jobs in rural areas and low returns on agriculture have only created a pool of seasonal migrants flowing into urban centres, settling down in slums working in casual/unorganized sector or being rendered homeless. The Govern-ment is implementing its National Rural Drinking Water Programme through the concerned ministries for ensuring drinking water to people in the rural and urban areas. There are several programmes run by the Government around river development and rejuvenation of Ganga River in India. Despite all this, there are still 76 million people who do not have access to safe drinking water in India today.

Absorption into the unorganised sector fuelled rather by distress than by choice hides huge underemployment. In a situation where even the formal sector is being in formalised in the form of contract labour, the working conditions range from insecure to precarious to near or total bondage, impacting health and wellbeing of the workers adversely.

As it stands now, government spending on health is around 30 per cent of the total expenditure on health in India, while 62.4 per cent of the total expenditure is borne out of pocket. In such a scenario, wage labourers sometimes prefer private health services to save a day's wage being lost to long waits in the government hospitals. This demonstrates the poor quality of healthcare in India and the disproportionate burden that it imposes on the poor and the marginalised. India does not yet explicitly recognise a national minimum social security cover.

In the 2017-2018 Union Budget, the Finance Minister announced an allocation of Rs. 48,000 crores to the Mahatma Gandhi National Rural Employment Guarantee Scheme (MGNREGS), which is the highest allocation to the scheme ever. But this is only a 1 per cent increase from the Rs. 47,499 crores (revised estimate or RE) in 2016-17. Furthermore, expenditure for 2016-17 (as on 1 February) is Rs. 53,594 crores which indicates a massive shortfall. The absence or poor quality of social security provisions, both in coverage and quantum, has further intensified the impoverishment of the poor in India. Government records show that under the MGNREGS, Rs. 441 crore worth of compensation was due to the workers against delayed wages in financial year 2016-17.

Health spending by the Central government remains at only 0.3 per cent of the GDP out of a total 1.3 per cent of GDP spent by the states and Centre together. In fact, the total spending is a far cry from the 3 per cent of GDP which is widely accepted to be the minimum level required to achieve reasonable universal health coverage.

As per the data of Rapid Survey on Children (RSOC) of the Ministry of Women and Child Development, about 44 % of the adolescent girls could be classified as severely thin. This prevalence increases further when we look at socially excluded groups like Scheduled Caste (SC) (46.4%) and Scheduled Tribes (ST) (45%); with highest number of severely thin adolescent girls amongst the lowest income quartile (47.9 %). The states with high rates of stunting include Chhattisgarh, Madhya Pradesh, Bihar, Jharkhand, Assam, Gujarat and Meghalaya. Bihar tops the list with 49.4 % of children in age group of 0-59 months stunted.

The numbers of women in the reproductive age group of 15-49 years with lower than normal Body Mass Index (BMI) reduced from 35 % in 2005-06 to 22.9 % in 2015-16 as recorded in the last two rounds of National Sample Survey Office (NSSO). Almost 52 % of women in rural areas were as anaemic as 45.7 % women reported anaemic in urban areas.

The National Health Policy 2017 talks of "strategic purchasing", which indicates a push towards privatisation. Tracking progress towards the SDG-3 targets will require a robust and reliable monitoring system, as well as a strong account-ability mechanism, both of which are currently lacking.

Close attention needs to be paid to inequities in health indicators as well as provision of services, especially along lines of caste, class, religion and geographical location, and specific concerns of marginalized groups especially Dalits, Tri-bals, religious minorities and women must be taken into account in the designing and provisioning of health services.

To attain Goal-4 on the quality education, India will have to increase its spending to 6 % of the GDP on education as compared to the current 3.5% spending. The government, in the previous three years, has made impressive strides with its national campaign of *Swachh Bharat*, and according to the ASER 2016, there has been improvement in the number of schools with toilets but, even now nearly 200,000 are running without toilets. These conditions push children, especial-ly girls to drop out, besides bringing children at risk of illnesses that can be avoided if provided for Water, Sanitation and Hygiene requirements. The Union Budget has ignored effective implementation of the Right to Education, and a meagre increase in the *Sarva Shiksha Abhiyan's* budget – by Rs 1,000 crores – is far from helping the meaningful imple-mentation of the Act and achievement of SDG-4.

The progress of the community is measured by the degree of progress which women have achieved. India ranks 88th out of 186 countries in the list on number of women parliamentarians with 18.5 percent of women appointed in ministerial positions as of January 1, 2017 (Sengupta 2017). There are only five ministers (18.5 %) in the Cabinet, and only 8 states having more than 10% of women members in the Legislative Assemblies; 12% of parliamentarians constitute only 12%. The Lok Sabha and Rajya Sabha have only 11.8 % and 11 % representation of women, respectively. Reservation of 33% for women in the government has improved representation of women in urban and rural areas, but their voice and participation remain tethered. In the armed forces, women only constitute 5.4 %. However, induction of women fighter pilots is a positive step towards gender equality. The 68th Round of National Sample Survey (2011-12) por-trays that the labour force participation rate of women in India, dropped from 42.7 % in 2004-05 to 31.2% in 2011-12. The Global Wage Gap Report (ILO 2016) informs that the proportion of women in India represent no more than 10–15 percent of wage earners. World Economic Forum (WEF 2016) reports that only less than 9% of the firms have female representation in the top management. Only 58.75% of females are literate as compared to 62.31% among the males. The figures for SC and ST women are 56.5% and 49.4% respectively. Overall, Muslim women's participation in employment is significantly low. State response to poor outcomes for religious minorities has been one of either complete denial or of lip service.

India recorded 644 incidents of communal violence in 2016, compared to 751 in 2015, and 703 recorded in 2014. The number of larger incidents may have come down, but there are many small incidents as low-intensity violence and polarisation along communal lines is increasing. Similarly, the NCRB lists 45,003 cases of atrocities against SCs and 10,914 against STs with a conviction rate of 27.6 in both the cases in 2015. Although better reporting is a reason for higher numbers in the recent years, the low rate of conviction is a dampener in this struggle to access justice. This will be a major threat to the attainment of peace and justice (SDG-16) for India if not contained through preventive actions.

The National Crime Records Bureau (NCRB) recorded A total of 51, 56,172 cognizable crimes comprising 32, 25,701 Indian Penal Code (IPC) crimes and 19, 30,471 Special & Local Laws (SLL) crimes were registered in 2019. It shows an increase of 1.6% in registration of cases over 2018 (50, 74,635 cases). Crime rate registered per lakh population has increased marginally from 383.5 in 2018 to 385.5 in 2019. During 2019, registration of cases under IPC has increased by 3.0% whereas SLL crimes have declined marginally by 0.6% over 2018. Percentage share of IPC was 62.6% while percentage share of SLL cases was 37.4% of total cognizable crimes during 2019.

A total of 4, 05,861 cases of crime against women were registered during 2019, showing an increase of 7.3% over 2018 (3, 78,236 cases). Majority of cases under crime against women under IPC were registered under 'Cruelty by Husband or His Relatives' (30.9%) followed by 'Assault on Women with Intent to Outrage her Modesty' (21.8%), 'Kidnapping & Abduction of Women' (17.9%) and 'Rape' (7.9%). The crime rate registered per lakh women population is 62.4 in 2019 in comparison with 58.8 in 2018. A total of 1, 48,185 cases of crime against children were registered during 2019, showing an increase of 4.5% over 2018 (1, 41,764 cases). In percentage terms, major crime heads under 'Crime Against Children' during 2019 were Kidnapping & Abduction (46.6%) and Protection of Children from Sexual Offences Act, 2012 (35.3%) including child rape. The crime rate registered per lakh children population is 33.2 in 2019 in comparison with 31.8 in 2018. A total of 32,235 cases have been registered against Juveniles during 2019, depicting a small increase of 2.0% over 2018 (31,591 cases). The crime rate also depicts a small increase from 7.1 in 2018 to 7.2 in 2019. A total of 38,685 juveniles were apprehended in 32,235 cases, out of which 35,214 juveniles were apprehended under cases of IPC and 3,471 juveniles were apprehended under cases of SLL during 2019. Majority of juveniles in conflict with law apprehended under IPC & SLL crimes were in the age group of 16 years to 18 years (75.2%) (29,084 out of 38,685) during 2019. A total of 27,696 cases were registered for committing crime against Senior Citizens (aged above 60 years), showing an increase of 13.7% in registration over 2018 (24,349 cases). The increase is mainly due to increase in registration of Theft cases. Crime head-wise cases revealed that simple hurt with 21.8% (6,042 cases) formed the highest chunk of cases of crimes against Senior Citizens followed by Theft with 17.9% (4,971 cases) and FCF (Forgery, Cheating & Fraud) with 10.0% (2,758 cases) during 2019. A total of 45,935 cases were registered for committing crime against Scheduled Castes (SCs), showing an increase of 7.3% over 2018 (42,793 cases). Crime rate registered showed an increase from 21.2 in 2018 to 22.8 in 2019. Crime head-wise cases revealed that simple hurt with 28.9% (13,273 cases) formed the largest chunk of cases of crimes/atrocities against Scheduled Castes (SCs) during 2019. It was followed by cases under SC/ST (Prevention of Atrocities) Act with 9.0% (4,129 cases) and cases under Rape with 7.6% (3,486 cases). A total of 8,257 cases were registered for committing crime against Scheduled Tribes (STs), showing an increase of 26.5% over 2018 (6,528 cases). Crime rate registered increased from 6.3 in 2018 to 7.9 in 2019. Crime head-wise cases revealed that simple hurt (1,675 cases) formed the highest number of cases of crimes/atrocities against Scheduled Tribes (STs) accounting for 20.3% during 2019, it was followed by rape with 13.4% (1,110 cases) and assault on women with intent to outrage her modesty with 10.7% (880 cases) (NCRB 2019).

These trends must be rigorously altered to stay true to the SDG-5.

The LGBT Community remains most discriminated and excluded from public services and society. Section 377 of the Indian Penal Code continues to criminalise sexual minorities. Their basic existence to live a fearless life is under big threat. Government's refusal to vote in the United Nations Human Rights Commission's (UNHRC) resolution to set up the office of an independent expert to end discrimination against LGBTQ people shows their stand on the LGBTQ rights.

Gender inequalities have curbed progress of women in India, while caste has played an important role in exclusion of a community which consist of more than 201 million people in the country. Religious minorities, differently abled and people with different sexual orientation have faced similar discrimination in their socio-economic and political aspects of life. The intersectionality of these social groups has seen the further exclusion and inequalities to another spec-trum.

The elderly population of age 60 and above is another marginalised and silenced group which is fast growing in India. Their population jumped 35.5 percent - from 7.6 crores in 2001 to 10.3 crores in 2015. The *Elder Abuse* study by HelpAge India (HelpAge India 2020) revealed1 in 3 older people reported abuse within the family ranging from physical abuse to verbal abuse Moreover, according to the Crime in India 2014 report by the NCRB, there is a significant increase in crime against older people who are considered soft targets.

The SDGs cannot accrue benefits to these communities with a conventional headcount approach to poverty. The indi-cators, therefore, need to adopt a holistic approach, which evaluates access of marginalised and vulnerable communities to quality basic services, and disaggregates data to assess progress made regarding all dimensions of poverty. There is a need to ensure that public policies that contribute towards achieving SDGs are governed by the principles of intersectionality that can be measured by predetermined indices. Hence, reducing inequalities within the country and communities (SDG-10); points categorically towards socio-economic and political equity and erasing of any discrimi-natory mechanisms which propels inequality among the people which the Government of India must work hard upon.

The Government must ensure engagement and influence of people's representatives in planning and implementation for realization of SDGs by instituting oversight function for Parliamentarians in the enactment of legislation and adop-tion of budgets, as envisioned by the SDG General Assembly Resolution.

From the above challenging perspectives of the SDGs in India along with the SDG India Index, baseline Report, 2018, the author has been assumed that, as a citizen of India, irrespective of the Socio-economic, socio-political, socio-administrative; political-administrative and the political-executives status have must to play that vital role along with India, which India was committed in United Nations General Assembly in 2015 by 2030. For achieving this citizen's goal, Indian Constitution is along with the citizens of India to create a dignified as well as decent future for the future generation with its dynamic nature in the changing scenario of the world and its own. As I mentioned earlier, I will try to analyse this peace making initiative through the mirror of SDG-16 entitled as 'peace, justice and strong institution' reported and measured or standardized by the SDG India Index, baseline Report, 2018 (NITI Aayog 2018).

4.1. SDGs Index of India in Achieving Peace

As per SDG India Index, baseline Report, 2018, SDG India Index does not currently cover goals 12, 13 and 14 largely on account of unavailability of comparable data across States and UTs. Further, SDG-17 is also not included given that indicators have not been identified by National Information Network (NIF). Selection of indicators is based on the criteria that emphasises availability, coverage across States and UTs and ownership by the ministries.

The indicators focus largely on data sources emerging from central official statistical system and the respective union ministries and departments, schemes and their data sources have not been tapped for this exercise.

Assigning equal weightage for all indicators across all Goals may lead to biased results. Additionally, some indicators may be less relevant to some States. For example, indicators like the *Mahatma Gandhi National Rural Employment Guarantee Act* (MGNRGEA), *Pradhan Mantri Gram Sadak Yojana* (PMGSY) have less relevance in states like Punjab and Haryana because they have already been performing better on these targets. Thus, their progress on these schematic indicators will seem less in comparison to other states but it does not signify that these states are poor performers. Given the equal significance of all Goals, equal weights have been assigned to all the considered SDGs.

So, the exclusion of goals, selection bias, indicators emerging from the states schemes are not included, limitation of equal weightage and missing data are the reported features of evaluating of the Sustainable Development Goals (SDGs) in India. Like other parts of the world, India also experienced economic growth as well as people were lifted out of poverty in between Millennium Development Goals (MDGs) and Sustainable Development Goals. However, new set of challenges arose, especially mentioned in the agenda of Sustainable Development Goals. In many parts, the benefits of the growth were not equally distributed. Rapid economic growth in many parts of India coincided with an equally rapid increase in energy consumption, depletion of natural resources and other material inputs to the point where the increase in economic welfare – after accounting for the side-effects of the growth, such as environmental degradation was considerably less than the growth in incomes.

Despite good administrative institutions, good international relations and economic growth during recent decades, according to the SDG India index Report 2018, indexed indicator of India under the SDG-1 that is 'no poverty', the raw data explored that, India continues with 21.92% live below poverty line; 28.7% of in India have at least one member covered under a health insurance or health scheme; 84.75 % of people who demanded employment under MGNREGA were provided employment in rural India and 36.4% eligible beneficiaries received maternity benefits and 10 homeless households for every 100000 households.

Indexed indicator of India under the SDG-2 that is 'zero hunger', the raw data explored that, one rural household is covered under PDS for every low income rural household where monthly income of highest earning less than Rs. 5000; 38.4% Children aged under 5 in India are stunted; 50% of pregnant women aged between 15-49 years are anaemic in India and 2509 Kg per Hectare annual agricultural productivity of wheat, rice & coarse cereals.

Indexed indicator of India under the SDG-3 that is 'good health and well-being', the raw data explored that, Maternal Mortality Ratio 130 per 100000 live births; for every 1000 live births 50 children under 5 years die; 62% immunization cover among children aged 12 - 23 months, target 1000; annually 138 cases of Tuberculosis noticed per 1 lakh population and 221 Governmental Health Workers per 100000 persons, Kerala has the highest rate 762, target of India is 550.

Indexed indicator of India under the SDG-4 that is 'quality education, the raw data explored that, 73.83% of eligible children are enrolled into school at elementary and Secondary Level; 54.69% students of class 5 able to respond correctly on learning outcomes in Language, Mathematics and Environmental Science; 44.58% students of class 8 able to respond correctly on learning outcomes in Language, Mathematics, Science and Social Sciences; 2.97 % children among Age Group 6 - 13 are out of school; average annual drop-out rate at Secondary Level is 17.06%; 81.15% teachers in India are professionally qualified and roughly 70% of Indian School have 30:1 Pupils: Teacher Ratio.

Indexed indicator of India under the SDG-5 that is 'gender equality', the raw data explored that, 898 females are born for every 1000 Males; earnings of females 70% of that of males; one in three women have experienced spousal violence; 8.7% of seats won by women in the General Elections to State Legislative Assembly; 32% female labour force participation rate of that of men and 54% of women in the age group of 15-49 years using modern method of family planning.

Indexed indicator of India under the SDG-6 that is 'clean water and sanitation', the raw data explored that, 71.8 of population having safe and adequate drinking water in rural areas; 82.72% of rural households with individual household toilets; 32% districts in the country are open defecation free; 37.58% sewage treatment capacity of urban India of total generated sewage and 62% annual ground water withdrawal against net annual availability;

Indexed indicator of India under the SDG-7 that is 'affordable and clean energy', the raw data explored that, 95% households in India have access to electricity; 43.8 % households in India use clean cooking fuels, such as electricity, LPG or natural and biogas and renewable sources constitute 17.51% of total installed generating capacity of electricity.

Indexed indicator of India under the SDG-8 that is 'decent work and economic growth', the raw data explored that, 6.5% annual GDP growth rate in India; 64 persons are average unemployed among per 1000 population in India; 99.99 % households in the country have bank accounts and 16.84 bank ATMs available in the country for per 100000 population.

Indexed indicator of India under the SDG-9 that is 'industry, innovation and infrastructures', the raw data explored that, 47.38% of rural habitations are connected with all-weather roads; 83 mobile connections for per 100 persons in rural and urban area; 33 internet subscribers per 100 population in India and 42.43% Gram Panchayats are covered under Bharat Net.

Indexed indicator of India under the SDG-10 that is 'reduced inequalities', the raw data explored that, in urban India 1.41 that is 10% times of the richest households spend 1.41 times more of the poorest 40% of the households on monthly consumption; In rural India 0.92 that is 10% times of the households spend 0.92 times more of the bottom 40% of the households on monthly consumption; 0.64% labour force participation rate to male labour force participation rate and 77.67% utilized from the total welfare fund allocated towards Scheduled Caste was utilized and 82.98% utilized from the total welfare fund allocated towards Scheduled Tribes was utilized.

Indexed indicator of India under the SDG-11 that is 'sustainable cities and communities', the raw data explored that, 3.2% houses completed under PNYA (U) Scheme of 5.41% urban households live in slums; 73.58% of wards collecting 100% of the waste through door to door collection across India and 24.8% of the generated waste in India gets treated.

Indexed indicator of India under the SDG-15 that is 'life and land', the raw data explored that, 21.54% of total land area in India covered under forest; extent of water bodies within forests 18.24 between 2005 & 2015; Between 2015 & 2017, 6778 SQ-KM forest cover increased nationally and 20% in population of wild elephants in India.

Indexed indicator of India under the SDG-16 that is 'peace justice and strong institution', the raw data explored that, India reported

24 cognizable crimes, 2.4 murders against children per 100000 population; 13 courts per 100000 population; 34 corruption cases reported crimes per 1 crore population and 88.3% of births get registered and 90 of population covered under AADHAR, it provided universal identity.

From the above reality, the author has tried to draw a methodology of its own to grasp the gap in the initiative taken by the government to meet the target of the SDGs which was measured by United Nations General Assembly. Are the components has been reflected in the provisions of the Indian Constitution or not? Secondly, has tried to measure the expected performance of India in SDGs (as per available raw data) through the mirror of SDG-16 entitled as 'peace, justice and strong institution' which was reported and measured or standardized by the SDG India Index, baseline Report, 2018 (NITI Aayog 2018). The author has assume that, the way of analysis in this book able to will explore the ways to prepare for required from the citizens of India to being a partner of the SDGs and it could be give a scope to face the future generation with a smile.

4.2. Methodology

The leaders of the world committed to create a better world for the future generations by implementing the SDGs by 2030; on the other side the independent India framed and adopted its dynamic Constitution of India in 26th January of 1952 "....to *constitute India into a Sovereign Socialist Secular Democratic Republic and to secure to all its citizens: justice, social, economic and political; liberty of thought, expression, belief, faith and worship; equality of status and of opportunity; and to promote among them all fraternity assuring the dignity of the individual and the unity and integrity of the nation....* (India 1950/2015)". Both are the prescriptions of increasing human wellbeing. From these perspectives, in this initiative, the author has tried to assess the achievement towards increasing of human wellbeing in the era of Sustainable Development Goals (SDGs) through the parameter of SDG-16, that is peace, justice and strong institutions. Part from that, the author has tried to point out the provisions within the Constitution of India which has been reflected in the SDGs.

In this connection, at first the author has tried to –

- Reviewed the present world situations and its supporting data on SDGs from different research articles, reports, news and websites;
- Tried to pick the provisions of SDGs which has been reflected in the Constitution of India (only the reflected parts has been

tried to take for analysis from Constitution of India as on 9th November, 2015);

- As the SDGs are implemented since 1st January, 2016; the author has tried to give a review the provision of SDGs in the Constitution of India updated and published as on 9th November, 2015 to explore the dynamism of the Indian Constitution.
- After, review of the SDG India Index Baseline Report 2018; the author has been used the raw data to assess the performance of India in SDGs.
- The author has assumed that the *"Peace, Justice and Strong Institution"* are the pre conditions of achievement, so he has used the Indian score on SDG-16, that *Peace, Justice and Strong Institutions* as the parameter of measure the performance of India in SDGs.
- Reviewed basic literatures on the 'peace' and its elements.
- Draw the inference of the Articles; Schedule and Lists of the Indian Constitution, the author tried to follow the inter-linked among the SDGs.
- Explored inference of the expected performance, the author used the equation as –

  It is assumed that, 'Peace, Justice and Strong Institutions' are the pre-conditions of achievement;

  Here, Expected Performance = India SDG 16 Score × (UN target of this SDG ÷100); and

  Performance Difference = (Expected Performance - Performance of India).

- To draw the responsibilities; as the citizen of India, the author separated the uncaptured as of SDG India Index Baseline Report, 2018 of UN-SDG's indicators of each individual SDG.
- Concluded this initiative by evaluating the performance as of SDG India Index Baseline Report, 2018 and the equation drawn by the author to justify; why, when, to whom and how to place finger as a citizen of India for the sake of the decent as well as dignified life of the future generation.

Because, the SDGs has aimed to significantly reduce all forms of violence, and work with governments and communities to find lasting solutions to conflict and insecurity. Strengthening the rule of law and promoting human rights is keys to this process, as is reducing the flow of illicit arms and strengthening the participation of developing countries in the institutions of global governance.

So, the success of the SDGs has been based on the achievement of the SDG–16, *Peace, Justice and Strong Institutions* that aimed to developing effective, accountable and transparent institutions at all levels top promote peaceful and inclusive societies for sustainable development, provide access to justice for all and build effective, accountable and inclusive institutions at all levels. The success of rest of the SDGs that is SDG-1 to SDG -15 and SDG – 17 are depends on SDG – 16, so expecting there is a relation or association among SDG – 16 with rest of the SDGs that is SDG-1 to SDG -15 and SDG-17. So, the success of the SDG–16 reflected in the rest of the SDGs. In this initiative I am trying to draw the inferences among SDG-16 with rest of the SDGs that is SDG-1 to SDG-1 and SDG-15 to SDG-16 through the mirror of the *SDG India Index Baseline Report,* 2018, published by NITI *Aayog*, Government of India. The author has thinks the initiative will give a direction to all the stakeholders of India about what and how much we have devote for the dignified decent life for our future generations by 2030 when such a rich as well as dynamic Constitutional provisions provided by India.

Chapter – V

Initiative and Performance of India in SDG-1, No Poverty

The global agenda of SDG-1 is entitled as 'No Poverty' which was aimed to end poverty in all its forms and from everywhere. Ending poverty in all its forms from everywhere implies, focusing on complete eradication of extreme poverty; the level globally measured as people living on less than $1.25 a day, as well as paying attention to other determinants that influence poverty such as socio-economic, cultural, political and environmental factors.

The SDG-1, was also aimed to reduce, at least by half, the proportion of men, women and children of all ages, living in poverty in all its dimensions according to national definitions. It calls for continuous monitoring including monitoring progress in social protection and inequality. Further, it has emphasised on creating sound policy frameworks, mobilisation of resources from a variety of sources and implementing nationally appropriate social protection systems that ensure equal rights; and access to basic services and economic resources.

Poverty manifests itself in diminished opportunities for livelihood and quality education, lack of access to resources, social discrimination and exposure and vulnerability to extreme climate events.

5.1. The Global Targets and Indicators for SDG-1

The global indicator framework was developed by the Inter-Agency and Expert Group on SDG Indicators (IAEG-SDGs) and agreed to, as a practical starting point at the 47th session of the UN Statistical Commission held in March 2016. The report of the Commission, which included the global indicator framework, was then taken note of by ECOSOC at its 70th session in June 2016. The global targets and the indicator of this SDG are tabled (Table no-01) bellow –

Table No. 1: UNDP-DDGs Targets and Indicators of SDG-1

Table No-01: SDG-1, End poverty in all its forms everywhere[1]	
Targets	***Indicators***
1.1: By 2030, eradicate extreme poverty for all people everywhere, currently measured as people living on less than $1.25 a day.	1.1.1: Proportion of population below the international poverty line, by sex, age, employment status and geographical location (urban/rural).
1.2: By 2030, reduce at least by half the proportion of men, women and children of all ages living in poverty in all its dimensions according to national definitions.	1.2.1: Proportion of population living below the national poverty line, by sex and age.
	1.2.2: Proportion of men, women and children of all ages living in poverty in all its dimensions according to national definitions.
1.3: Implement nationally appropriate social protection systems and measures for all, including floors, and by 2030 achieve substantial coverage of the poor and the vulnerable.	1.3.1: Proportion of population covered by social protection floors/systems, by sex, distinguishing children, unemployed persons, older persons, persons with disabilities, pregnant women, new-borns, work-injury victims and the poor and the vulnerable.
1.4: By 2030, ensure that all men and women, in particular the poor and the vulnerable, have equal rights to economic resources, as well as access to basic services, ownership and control over land and other forms of property, inheritance, natural resources, appropriate new technology and financial services, including microfinance.	1.4.1: Proportion of population living in households with access to basic services.
	1.4.2: Proportion of total adult population with secure tenure rights to land, with legally recognized documentation and who perceive their rights to land as secure, by sex and by type of tenure.
1.5: By 2030, build the resilience of the poor and those in vulnerable situations and reduce their exposure and vulnerability to climate-related extreme events and other economic, social and environmental shocks and disasters	1.5.1: Number of deaths, missing persons and persons affected by disaster per 100,000 people [a].
	1.5.2: Direct disaster economic loss in relation to global gross domestic product (GDP) [a].
	1.5.3: Number of countries with national and local disaster risk reduction strategies [a].
1.a: Ensure significant mobilization of resources from a variety of sources, including through enhanced development cooperation, in order to provide adequate and predictable means for developing countries, in particular least developed countries, to implement programmes and policies to end poverty in all its dimensions.	1.a.1: Proportion of resources allocated by the government directly to poverty reduction programmes.
	1.a.2: Proportion of total government spending on essential services (education, health and social protection).
1.b: Create sound policy frameworks at the national, regional and international levels, based on pro-poor and gender-sensitive development strategies, to support accelerated investment in poverty eradication actions.	1.b.1: Proportion of government recurrent and capital spending to sectors that disproportionately benefit women, the poor and vulnerable groups.
Note: [a] - An open-ended intergovernmental expert working group on indicators and terminology relating to disaster risk reduction established by the General Assembly (resolution 69/284) is developing a set of indicators to measure global progress in the implementation of the Sendai Framework. These indicators will eventually reflect the agreements on the Sendai Framework indicators.	

1. Data Source: SDG India Index Baseline Report, 2018, NITI *Aayog*, Government of India, New Delhi.

5.2. Interlinkage of SDG-1 with other SDGs

The nature of formation of SDGs are interlinked with each other (NITI Aayog 2018). This section is presenting the linkage of the SDG-1 to other SDGs, that is, the success of this SDG habitually will influence the success of the linked SDGs; according to the SDG India Index, Baseline Report, 2018, the SDG-1 linked with the following SDGs -

SDG-2, that is *Zero Hunger*, which aims to end all forms of malnutrition and ensures access to safe, nutritious and sufficient food for all, in particular the poor and vulnerable, and support small scale food producers.

SDG-3, is *Good Health and Well-being*, which aims to end epidemics and preventable deaths and achieve universal health coverage, including financial risk protection and access to quality essential health care services, medicines and vaccines for all.

SDG-4, is *Quality Education* that aims to ensure that all girls and boys complete free, equitable and quality primary and secondary education leading to relevant and effective learning outcomes, including technical and vocational skills for employment, decent jobs and entrepreneurship.

SDG-5, is *Gender Equality* as Goal 1 emphasises creation of gender sensitive development strategies, and equal rights and access to economic resources, as well as ownership and control over land and other forms of property, inheritance, natural resources and financial resources, including microfinance.

SDG-6, is *Clean Water and Sanitation*, which aims to achieve universal and equitable access to safe and affordable drinking water and sanitation and hygiene for all.

SDG-7, is *Affordable and Clean Energy* that aims to ensure universal access to affordable, reliable and modern energy services.

SDG-8, is *Decent Work and Economic Growth* which aims to promote development oriented policies that support productive activities, decent job creation, entrepreneurship, and encourage the formalization and growth of micro-, small - and medium-sized enterprises through access to financial services.

SDG-10, is *Reduced Inequalities* that aims to adopt policies, especially fiscal wage and social protection policies and progressively achieve and sustain income growth of the bottom 40 percent of the population at a rate higher than the national average, leading to greater equality.

SDG-11, is *Sustainable Cities and Communities* which aims to ensure access for all to adequate, safe and affordable housing and basic services and upgrade slums, and significantly reduce the numbers of deaths and people affected by disasters, with focus on protecting the poor and vulnerable.

SDG-13, is *Climate Action* which aims to develop resilience and adaptive capacity of the poor to climate related hazards and natural disasters.

SDG-15, *Life on Land* which aims to mobilize significant resources from all sources and at all levels, and integrate ecosystem and biodiversity values into national and local planning, development processes, poverty reduction strategies and accounts.

SDG-16, *Peace, Justice and Strong Institutions* that aims to developing effective, accountable and transparent institutions at all levels.

5.3. The National Context of SDG-1

As per the nature of developmental initiatives of independent India, India has framed and implementing a comprehensive development strategy to end poverty in all its forms. The strategy encompasses focussing on economic growth, supporting poverty alleviation programmes, providing gainful employment, strengthening livelihood opportunities and improving access to basic services, particular for the socio-economically disadvantaged and vulnerable sections of the population. This is supported by providing institutional platforms, technology support and access to financial services.

It is the clear that poverty eradication requires pursuing dual objectives of pulling people out of poverty and sustaining poverty escapes. While social assistance programmes and schemes that provide basic needs help in achieving the first objective, inclusive economic growth and skill development provide opportunities for achieving the second objective.

The Government of India has initiated various programmes to tackle chronic poverty, increase access to basic services, provide social protection, sustain poverty escapes, and generate gainful employment.

Anti-poverty programmes like MGNREGA and the National Rural Livelihood Mission, *Deendayal Upadhyay Grameen Kaushalya Yojana* focus on generating employment, skill employability among the poor.

Social security programmes have been helping build resilience and reduce exposure to vulnerabilities. These programmes include the

National Social Assistance Programmes (NSAP) which provides pension to the elderly, widowed and differently-abled individuals. The *Pradhan Mantri Jeevan Jyoti Beema Yojana* (PMJJBY) and *Pradhan Mantri Jeevan Suraksha Beema Yojana* (PMJSBY) that facilitate access to life insurance and personal accident insurance, and the recently launched health insurance programme, *Ayushman Bharat.*

Programmes like Mission *Antyodaya*, National Food Security Mission, *Poshan Abhiyan, Swachh Bharat Mission, Pradhan Mantri Awas Yojana* (PMAY), *Pradhan Mantri Ujjawala Yojana, Pradhan Mantri Jan Dhan Yojana* (PMJDY) etc. aim at ensuring access to basïc services to the vulnerable sections. These interventions are expected to yield better results over time in terms of alleviation of poverty.

All above initiatives has been reflected in the process of reducing poverty in India. According to the SDG India Index Base Line Report, 2018 (NITI Aayog 2018), over the last two decades there have been large advancements in economic growth and poverty reduction. According to the Tendulkar Committee estimates, poverty rate in India declined 18 percent between 1993-94 and 2004-05; and further declined by 41 percent in 2004-05 to 2011-12, 21.9 percent of India's population was below the poverty line.

The improved economic performance coupled with concerted interventions by the government towards poverty eradication has led to decline in poverty rates across all economic, social and religious groups at the national level and in all States.

Important policy initiatives has been taken up and a number of outcome-based and well-targeted programmes and schemes are being executed at national, State and local levels, such as the Mahatma Gandhi National Rural Employment Generation Act (MGNREGA) *Pradhan Mantri Jeevan Jan Dhan Yojana* (PMJDY) *and Deendayal Antyodaya Yojana* of *Pradhan Mantri* National Rural and Urban Livelihood Mission.

A significant initiative to address the agenda of "leaving no one behind" and tackling poverty in all its dimensions is to use data from the Socio-Economic Caste Census (SECC) 2011, which measures different forms of deprivation for identifying beneficiaries for different development programmes. This aids better targeting to the households that are most deprived on a range of indicators.

Recent economic reforms has focused on fiscal consolidation, inflation targeting, improved governance all around, accelerated infrastructure development, and further liberalization of foreign direct investment, closure of sick units in the public sector and curbing of corruption.

Implementation of *Aadhaar Act* (for providing unique identity); Insolvency and Bankruptcy Act, Goods and Services Tax steps in strengthening the fiscal management of the economy and for bringing transparency. As a result, today, India is one of the fastest growing major economies of the world.

As per report of the poverty rate of India, it gives us hope, that is to say we can achieve the target of the SDG-1 by 2030. As per the Tendulkar Committee estimates, 21.92 percent of the Indian population were living below the poverty line 2011-12. According to these estimates, seven States and five Union Territories have already achieved the national target of reducing the poverty rates to below 10.95 percent by 2030. Goa among the States and Andaman and Nicobar Islands among the Union Territories (UT) had the lowest poverty rates at 5.09 percent and 1 percent respectively.

When we look into the reported Health Insurance Coverage status of India, it pained us; but we can say it is started, expecting we will devote our best to achieve the target by 2030. As per report, 28.7 percent of households in India have at least one member covered under a health insurance or health scheme. The national target is to cover 100 percent of the households in India by 2030. No State or UT has achieved this target as yet. Andhra Pradesh at 74.6 percent has the highest coverage in the country.

The MGNREG Act, 2005 has accelerated the eradication of poverty agenda in India with dignity that is the workers were paid by creating social capital, works are guaranteed by the Union. The MGNREG Act, 2005 aims to provide hundred days of guaranteed wage employment in every financial year to every rural household whose adult member volunteers' to do unskilled manual work. 84.75 percent of people who demanded employment under this Act were provided the same in the 2017-18, the data is looking positive to reduce poverty in India.

The Maternity Benefits is a one among the social protection measures framed by the Government of India. The report of NFHS-4, 36.4 percent of the eligible beneficiaries in India receive social protection benefits under the maternity benefits. The country aims to achieve full coverage by 2030. All States and UTs are yet to achieve this national target. Odisha has the highest coverage in India with 72.6 percent of eligible beneficiaries receiving maternity benefits.

Homelessness is an indicator of SDG agenda, its aim to be achieved by 2030. Report explored that almost ten in every ten thousand households in India are homeless. The target is to eliminate homelessness by 2030. The Union Territory of Lakshadweep Island is the first in India to have achieved this target. Arunachal Pradesh is the top performing among States and is very close to achieving the national target with current homelessness at only 0.23 homeless households for every ten thousand households.

In the next part, the author has tried to visualized the performance level of India through the SDG's targets and the SDG India Index Base Line Report, 2018 along with the Constitutional provisions in India to explore citizen's responsibility along with the its institutions through the mirror of indexed score on 'peace, justice and strong institutions' (SDG-16).

5.4. SDG-1 Targets, National Indicators and Target Values of India

India in its SDG India Index Base Line Report, 2018 (NITI Aayog 2018), India had measured the performance of India on the goal of 'No Poverty', India has identified five national level indicators, which captured three (1.2, 1.3 and 1.4) out of seven UN's SDG targets for 2030. These indicators had selected on the basis of availability of data at national level; these are in Table no-02.

Table No. 2: SDG-1 Targets, National Indicators and Target Values of India

SDG-1 Global Target	*Indicator Selected for SDG India Index*	*National Target Value for 2030*
1.2: By 2030, reduce at least by half the proportion of men, women and children of all ages living in poverty in all its dimensions according to national definitions.	1. Percentage of population living below National Poverty line	10.95
1.3: Implement nationally appropriate social protection system and measure for all, including floors and by 2030 achieve substantial coverage of the poor and the vulnerable.	2. Percentage of households with any usual member covered by any health scheme or health insurance.	100
	3. Persons provided employment as a percentage of persons who demanded employment under MGNREGA	100
	4. Proportion of the population (out of total eligible population) receiving social protection benefits under Maternity Benefits.	100

(Contd...)

1.4: By 2030, ensure that all men and women, in particular the poor and the vulnerable, have equal rights to economic resources, as well as access to basic services, ownership and control over land and other forms of property, inheritance, natural resources, appropriate new technology and financial services, including microfinance.	5. Number of homeless households per 10,000 households	0

Source: (NITI Aayog 2018).

5.5. Indian's SDG-1 Index Indicators, Data Source and Interpretations

The NITI *Aayog*, Government of India had collected required data from different government agencies to capture the UN-SDG's target indicators as well as framed its own indicators to justify the achievement of the SDGs. Apart from that the NITI *Aayog* had developed the computational approach of the disaggregated data as per valid methods along with the parameters of the performance; in the following tables (Table no-03, Table no-04, Table no-05, Table no-06 and Table no-07) shows the details of the above issue to develop a sense of progress of the SDG-1, entitled as 'No Poverty'.

Table No. 3: SDG-1, Indian Indicator-1

SDG-1: No Poverty	**Indicator-1: Percentage of population living below national poverty line.**
Indicator data source	NITI *Aayog* [Tendulkar Committee estimates]
Computation approach	Directly from data source
Data period (year)	2011-2012
States/UTs covered	35
Data periodicity	Non-periodic
Relevant UN target	1.2: By 2030, reduce at least by half the proportion of men, women and children of all ages living in poverty in all its dimensions according to national definitions.
Relevant UN indicator	1.2.1: Proportion of population living below the national poverty line, by sex and age
Relevant MoSPI indicator	1.1.1: Proportion of population living below the National poverty line
Indicator interpretation	Higher value means lower performance (-)

Source: (NITI Aayog 2018).

Table No. 4: SDG-1, Indian Indicator-2

SDG-1: No Poverty	***Indicator-2: Percentage of households with any usual member covered by any health scheme or health insurance***
Indicator data source	Ministry of Health and Family Welfare (National Family Health Survey-4)
Computation approach	Directly from data source
Data period (year)	2015-2016
States/UTs covered	36
Data periodicity	3 years
Relevant UN target	1.3: Implement nationally appropriate social protection system and measure for all, including floors and by 2030 achieve substantial coverage of the poor and the vulnerable.
Relevant UN indicator	1.3.1: Proportion of population covered by social protection floors/ systems by sex, distinguishing children, unemployed persons, older persons, persons with disabilities, pregnant women, new-borns, work-injury victims and the poor and the vulnerable.
Relevant MoSPI indicator	1.3.1: Percentage of households with any usual member covered by any health scheme or health insurance.
Indicator interpretation	Higher value means higher performance (+)

Source: (NITI Aayog 2018).

Table No. 5: SDG-1, Indian Indicator-3

SDG-1: No Poverty	**Indicator-3: Persons provided employment as a percentage of persons who demanded employment under Mahatma Gandhi National Rural Employment Guarantee Act (MGNREGA).**
Indicator data source	Ministry of Rural Development (MGNREGA Progress Report)
Computation approach	(Persons provided employment under divided MGNREGA ÷ Person demanded employment under MGNREGA) × 100
Data period (year)	2017-25018
States/UTs covered	32
Data periodicity	Annual
Relevant UN target	1.3: Implement nationally appropriate social protection system and measure for all, including floors and by 2030 achieve substantial coverage of the poor and the vulnerable.
Relevant UN indicator	1.3.1: Proportion of population covered by social protection floors/ systems by sex, distinguishing children, unemployed persons, older persons, persons with disabilities, pregnant women, new-borns, work-injury victims and the poor and the vulnerable
Relevant MoSPI indicator	1.3.3: Proportion of the population (out of total eligible population) receiving social protection benefits under (MGNREGA).
Indicator interpretation	Higher value means higher performance (+)

Source: (NITI Aayog 2018).

Table No. 6: SDG-1, Indian Indicator-4

SDG-1: No Poverty	Indicator-4: Proportion of the population (out of total eligible population) receiving social protection benefits under Maternity Benefits (%).
Indicator data source	Ministry of Health and Family Welfare (National Family Health Survey-4)
Computation approach	Directly from data source
Data period (year)	2015-2016
States/UTs covered	36
Data periodicity	3 years
Relevant UN target	1.3: Implement nationally appropriate social protection system and measure for all, including floors and by 2030 achieve substantial coverage of the poor and the vulnerable.
Relevant UN indicator	1.3.1: Proportion of population covered by social protection floors/ systems by sex, distinguishing children, unemployed persons, older persons, persons with disabilities, pregnant women, new-borns, work-injury victims and the poor and the vulnerable.
Relevant MoSPI indicator	1.3.5: Proportion of the population (out of total eligible population) receiving social protection benefits under Maternity Benefits.
Indicator interpretation	Higher value means higher performance (+)

Source: (NITI Aayog 2018).

Table No. 7: SDG-1, Indian Indicator-5

SDG-1: No Poverty	Indicator-5: Number of homeless households per 10,000 households.
Indicator data source	Numerator: Ministry of Rural Development (Socio-economic Caste Census), Denominator: Ministry of Home Affairs (Census, 2011)
Computation approach	Number of homeless households per 10,000 households calculated as – (Number of homeless households ÷ total number of households) × 10000
Data period (year)	2015-2012
States/UTs covered	36
Data periodicity	10 years
Relevant UN target	1.4: By 2030, ensure that all men and women, in particular the poor and the vulnerable, have equal rights to economic resources, as well as access to basic services, ownership and control over land and other forms of property, inheritance, natural resources, appropriate new technology and financial services, including microfinance.
Relevant UN indicator	Not Applicable
Relevant MoSPI indicator	1.4.4: Proportion of homeless population to total population
Indicator interpretation	Higher value means lower performance (-)

Source: (NITI Aayog 2018).

5.6. Provisions of the Indian Constitution for SDG-1

The spirit of the unity in this diverse country, India is secured by its great Constitution; the Constitution of India not only secured its unity, announced a vision in the Preamble in the beginning of its Articles included in the Indian Constitution, *"We the people of India, having solemnly resolved to constitute India into a Sovereign Socialist Secular Democratic Republic and to secure to all its citizens: justice, social, economic and political; liberty of thought, expression, belief, faith and worship; equality of status and of opportunity; and to promote among them all fraternity assuring the dignity of the individual and the unity and integrity of the nation; in our Constituent Assembly this twenty-sixth day of November, 1949, do hereby adopt, enact and give to ourselves this Constitution* (India 1950/2015)". The mode of orientation of the Indian Constitution and the sustainable development goals of the contemporary time has given us an opportunity to make a link between these two visions of development and the author has been trying to make the link.

As we know the sustainable development goals are interlinked, that means the success or failure of one is to be affected to other SDGs. From this perspective, this section presents the provisions in the Indian Constitution to eradicate poverty which has been reflected in the sustainable development agenda entitled as SDG-1, No Poverty. The linked Constitutional provisions are in the following Table no-08 -

Table No. 8: Provisions in Indian Constitution for SDG-1

SDG-1 and the Linked Articles and Schedules of the Constitution of India
Article 15-(2).(a), Article 15-(4) and (5), Article 16-(1) to (5), Article 19-1.(a) to (g), Article 21A, Article 38-(1) and (2), Article 39-(a) to (f), Article 39A, Article 41, Article 42, Article 43, Article 46, Article 47, Article 309, Article 310, Article 311, Article 312, Article 313, Article 314, Article 315, Article 320, Article 323A and Article 323B.
Article 246-Seventh Schedule, List-I: Union List No: 12, 15, 55, 65, 65, 66, 68, 69, and 94 List-II: State List No: 6, 9, 14 to 18, 21, 23 and27. List-III: Concurrent List No: 24, 25, 26 and 30.
Article 243G: Eleventh Schedule: Powers, Authority and Responsibilities of Panchayats. Schedule No: 1, 2, 3, 4, 5, 10, 11, 12, 16, 17, 18, 19, 23, 25, 26, 27 and 28. Article 243W: Twelfth Schedule: Powers, Authority and Responsibilities of Municipalities. Schedule No: 1, 3, 6, 9, 11 and 16.

Source: The Constitution of India, 2015 as on 9th November, 2015.

5.7. Policies of the Government of India for Targets of the SDG-1

According to the SDG India Index Base Line Report, 2018 (NITI Aayog 2018), India is proactive to achieve the target of the UN's SDGs. The Government of India has initiated as well as implemented various policies to capture the indicators of the targets of each individual SDG. On the moment of preparation of SDG India Index Base Line Report, 2018, on the basis of the availability of the disaggregated data, the NITI *Aayog* framed India's own indicators of the targets of each individual SDG. For the SDG-1, that is 'No Poverty', the NITI *Aayog* framed five indicators; which capture three out of seven UNs SDG targets. As per the report, 68 dedicated policies or schemes are in action to achieve three targets (1.2, 1.3 and 1.4) of the UN's SDG-1 under the leadership and monitoring of 12 dedicated Ministries or the Departments. The policies or schemes to achieve the targets of SDG-1 and the concerned dedicated Ministries and the Departments are detailed in the - Table no-09.

Table No. 9: Policies Initiated by the Indian Government for Targets of SDG-1

Target of SDG-1: End poverty in all its forms everywhere.	
Target: 1.1: By 2030, eradicate extreme poverty for all people everywhere, currently measured as people living on less than $1.25 a day.	
Centrally Sponsored /Central Sector Schemes (CSS)	Concerned Ministries/ Departments
1. Mahatma Gandhi National Rural Employment Guarantee Act (MGNREGA) 2. *Deen Dayal Antyodaya Yojana* (DAY) -National Rural Livelihood Mission (NRLM) 3. *Pradhan Mantri Awaas Yojana - Gramin* 4. National Social Assistance Programme (NSAP)	Ministry of Rural Development
5. Market Intervention Scheme and Price Support Scheme (MIS-PSS)	Agriculture and Cooperation
6. *Deen Dayal Antyodaya Yojana* (DAY) - National Urban Livelihood Mission (NULM) 7. *Pradhan Mantri Awaas Yojana* -Urban	Ministry of Housing and Urban Affairs
8. Development of Skills (Umbrella Scheme)	Skill Development & Entrepreneurship
9. Prime Minister Employment Generation Programme (PMEGP)	Micro, Small and Medium Enterprises
10. *Pradhan Mantri Rojgar Protsahan Yojana* 11. Employment Promotion Scheme	Ministry of Labour and Employment
12. Umbrella Programme for Development of Scheduled Castes and Other Vulnerable Groups 13. Special Central Assistance to Tribal Sub-Scheme (SCA to TSS) 14. Assistance to Disabled Persons for purchase of Fitting Devices (ADIP)	Ministry of Social Justice and Empowerment
15. Umbrella Programme for Development of Minorities	Ministry of Minority Affairs
16. Umbrella Programme for Development of Scheduled Tribes,	Ministry of Tribal Affairs
17. *Pradhan Mantri Jan Dhan Yojana* 18. *Pradhan Mantri Jeevan Jyoti Bima Yojana* 19. *Pradhan Mantri Suraksha Bima Yojana* (PMSBY) 20. *Atal Pension Yojana* (APY) 21. *Pradhan Mantri Vaya Vandana Yojana* (PMVVY)	Ministry of Finance

Target: 1.2: By 2030, reduce at least by half the proportion of men, women and children of all ages living in poverty in all its dimensions accord-to the national definitions.	
Centrally Sponsored /Central Sector Schemes (CSS)	Concerned Ministries/ Departments
1. Mahatma Gandhi National Rural Employment Guarantee Act (MGNREGA) 2. *Deen Dayal Antyodaya Yojana* (DAY) -National Rural Livelihood Mission (NRLM) 3. *Pradhan Mantri Awaas Yojana - Gramin* 4. National Social Assistance Programme (NSAP)	Ministry of Rural Development
5. Market Intervention Scheme and Price Support Scheme (MIS-PSS)	Agriculture and Cooperation
6. *Pradhan Mantri Jan Dhan Yojana* 7. *Pradhan Mantri Jeevan Jyoti Bima Yojana* 8. *Pradhan Mantri Suraksha Bima Yojana* (PMSBY) 9. *Atal Pension Yojana* (APY) 10. *Pradhan Mantri Vaya Vandana Yojana* (PMVVY)	Ministry of Finance
11. *Deen Dayal Antyodaya Yojana* (DAY) - National Urban Livelihood Mission (NULM) 12. *Pradhan Mantri Awaas Yojana* - Urban	Ministry of Housing and Urban Affairs
13. Development of Skills (Umbrella Scheme)	Skill Development and Entrepreneurship,
14. Prime Minister Employment Generation Programme (PMEGP)	Micro, Small and Medium Enterprises
15. *Pradhan Mantri Rojgar Protsahan Yojana* 16. Employment Promotion Scheme	Ministry of Labour and Employment
17. Umbrella Programme for Development of Scheduled Castes and Other Vulnerable Groups 18. Special Central Assistance to Tribal Sub-Scheme (SCA to TSS) 19. Assistance to Disabled Persons for purchase of Fitting Devices (ADIP)	Ministry of Social Justice and Empowerment
20. Umbrella Programme for Development of Minorities	Ministry of Minority Affairs
21. Umbrella Programme for Development of Scheduled Tribes,	Ministry of Tribal Affairs

Target: 1.3: Implement nationally appropriate social protection systems and measures for all, including floors and by 2030 achieve substantial coverage of the poor and the vulnerable	
Centrally Sponsored /Central Sector Schemes (CSS)	Concerned Ministries/ Departments
1. Mahatma Gandhi National Rural Employment Guarantee Act (MGNREGA) 2. *Deen Dayal Antyodaya Yojana* (DAY) 3. National Rural Livelihood Mission (NRLM) 4. National Social Assistance Programme (NSAP) 5. *Pradhan Mantri Awaas Yojana-Gramin*	Ministry of Rural Development
6. *Deen Dayal Antyodaya Yojana* (DAY) 7. National Urban Livelihood Mission (NULM)	Ministry of Housing and Urban Affairs
6. Assistance to Disabled Persons for purchase of Fitting Devices (ADIP) 7. Integrated Programme for Senior Citizens	Ministry of Social Justice and Empowerment
8. National Health Mission 9. *Ayushman Bharat* (National Health Protection Mission)	Health and Family Welfare

(Contd...)

10. Umbrella Integrated Child Development Services (ICDS) Scheme	Ministry of Women and Child Development
11. Creation of National Platform of Unorganized Workers and allotment of an *Aadhaar* numbers 12. *Bima Yojana* for Unorganized Workers 13. Labour Welfare Scheme	Ministry of Labour and Employment
14. *Pradhan Mantri Jan Dhan Yojana* 15. *Pradhan Mantri Jeevan Jyoti Bima Yojana* 16. *Pradhan Mantri Suraksha Bima Yojana* (PMSBY) 17. *Atal Pension Yojana* (APY) 18. *Pradhan Mantri Vaya Vandana Yojana* (PMVVY)	Ministry of Finance
19. Special Schemes for Welfare of Minorities	Ministry of Minority Affairs
20. *Vanbandhu Kalyan Yojana*	Ministry of Tribal Affairs
21. Relief and Rehabilitation for Migrants and Repatriates 22. Freedom Fighters (pension and other benefits)	Ministry of Home Affairs
Target: 1.4: By 2030, ensure that all men and women, in particular the poor and the vulnerable, have equal rights to economic resources, as well as access to basic services, ownership and control over land and other forms of property, inheritance, natural resources, appropriate new technology and financial services, including microfinance	
Centrally Sponsored /Central Sector Schemes (CSS)	Concerned Ministries/ Departments
1. *Deen Dayal Antyodaya Yojana* (DAY) 2. National Rural Livelihood Mission (NRLM) 3. National Urban Livelihood Mission (NULM) 4. *Pradhan Mantri Awaas Yojana* (Rural) 5. *Shyama Prasad Mukherjee* RURBAN Mission 6. *Pradhan Mantri Gram Sadak Yojana* (PMGSY) 7. National Social Assistance Programme (NSAP)	Ministry of Rural Development
8. Nation Rural Drinking Water Programme 9. *Swachh Bharat Mission* (Rural)	Drinking Water and Sanitation
10. *Deen Dayal Antyodaya Yojana* (DAY) 11. National Urban Livelihood Mission (NULM) 12. AMRUT (Atal Mission for Rejuvenation and Urban Transformation) 13. *Swachh Bharat Mission* (Urban) 14. *Pradhan Mantri Awaas Yojana* (Urban)	Ministry of Housing and Urban Affairs
15. *Pradhan Mantri Jan Dhan Yojana* 16. *Pradhan Mantri MUDRA Yojana* 17. Credit Guarantee Fund for providing guarantee to loans extended under *Pradhan Mantri Mudra Yojana* 18. *Pradhan Mantri Jeevan Jyoti Bima Yojana* 19. *Pradhan Mantri Suraksha Bima Yojana* (PMSBY) 20. *Atal Pension Yojana* (APY) 21. *Pradhan Mantri Vaya Vandana Yojana* (PMVVY)	Ministry of Finance
22. Umbrella Programme for Development of Scheduled Castes, OBCs and Other Vulnerable Groups	Ministry of Social Justice and Empowerment
23. Umbrella Programme for Development of Minorities including Development of Minorities - Multi Sectoral Development Programme for Minorities (MSDP)	Ministry of Minority Affairs
24. Umbrella Programme for Development of Scheduled Tribes 25. Equity Support to the National/State Scheduled Tribes Finance and Development Corporation for Financial support to tribal entrepreneurs	Ministry of Tribal Affairs

(*Contd...*)

26. Relief and Rehabilitation for Migrants and Repatriates 27. Freedom Fighters (pension and other benefits)	Ministry of Home Affairs
28. *Deendayal Upadhyaya Gram Jyoti Yojana* (DDUGJY) 29. *Pradhan Mantri Sahaj Bijli Har Ghar Yojana – "Saubhagya"* (Rural & Urban)	Ministry of Power
30. *Rashtriya Gram Swaraj Abhiyan* (RGSA)	Ministry of *Panchayati* Raj
31. LPG Connection to poor households – UJJWALA	Ministry of Petroleum and Natural Gas
Target: 1.5: By 2030, build the resilience of the poor and those in vulnerable situations and reduce their exposure and vulnerability to climate-related extreme events and other economic, social and environmental shocks and disasters	
Centrally Sponsored /Central Sector Schemes (CSS)	Concerned Ministries/ Departments
1. Infrastructure of Disaster Management 2. National Cyclone Risk Mitigation Project (NCRMP) 3. Other Disaster Management Schemes	Ministry of Home Affairs
4. River Basin Management 5. Flood Management & Border Areas Programme 6. Development of Water Resources Information System	Ministry of Water Resource, Rural Development & Green Revolution
7. Atmosphere and Climate Research Modelling, Observing Systems and Services (ACROSS) 8. Ocean Services, Technology, Observations, Resources, Modelling and Science (OSTORMS) 9. Seismology and Geosciences (SAGE)	Earth Sciences
10. Design & Development of Applications for EO, Communication, Disaster Management, etc.	Space
Target: 1.a: Ensure significant mobilization of resources from a variety of sources, including through enhanced development cooperation, in order to provide adequate and predictable means for a developing countries, in particular least developed countries, to implement programmes and policies to end poverty in all its dimensions.	
Centrally Sponsored /Central Sector Schemes (CSS)	Concerned Ministries/ Departments
1. *Sarva Shiksha Abhiyan*, 2. National Programme of Mid Day Meal in Schools (MDM) 3. *Rashtriya Madhyamik Shiksha Abhiyan*, 4. Strengthening of Teacher Training Institutions 5. *Pandit Madan Mohan Malaviya* National Mission on Teachers and Teaching (PMMMNMTT) 6. National Scheme for Incentive to Girl Child for Secondary Education (NSIGSE) 7. Interest subsidy and contribution for Guarantee Funds 8. Scholarship for College & University Students	Ministry of Human Resource Development
9. Pre- & post-matric scholarships for SC, OBC and other vulnerable groups 10. Pre-matric Scholarship to students with disabilities	Ministry of Social Justice and Empowerment
11. Umbrella Programme for Development of ST communities including • pre- & post-matric scholarships for ST students & • *Vanbandhu Kalyan Yojana*	Ministry of Tribal Affairs
12. Umbrella Programme for Development of Minorities including pre- & post-matric scholarships for Minority students	Ministry of Minority Affairs

(*Contd...*)

Target: 1.b: Create sound policy frameworks at the national, regional and international levels, based on pro-poor and gender-sensitive development strategies, to support accelerated investment in poverty eradication actions	
	Ministry of Rural Development, Ministry of Housing and Urban Affairs, Ministry of Human Resource Development, Ministry of External Affairs, Ministry of Social Justice and Empowerment, Ministry of Tribal Affairs, Ministry of Minority Affairs

Source: (NITI Aayog 2018).

5.8. Initiatives, Expectation and Performance of Government of India in SDG-1

According to the SDG India Index Base Line Report, 2018 (NITI Aayog 2018), to achieving the target of the UN's SDG-1, the Government of India had framed five indicators; which captured three out of seven UNs SDG targets. The Government of India reported that, 68 dedicated policies or schemes are in action to achieve three targets (1.2, 1.3 and 1.4) of the UN's SDG-1 under the leadership and monitoring of 12 dedicated Ministries or the Departments. The SDG-1 indicators are -

SDG_1_1: Percentage of population living below national poverty line.

SDG_1_2: Percentage of households with any usual member covered by any health scheme or health insurance.

SDG_1_3: Persons provided employment as a percentage of persons who demanded employment under Mahatma Gandhi National Rural Employment Guarantee Act (MGNREGA).

SDG_1_4: Proportion of the population (out of total eligible population) receiving social protection benefits under Maternity Benefits (%).

SDG_1_5: Number of homeless households per 10,000 households.

Table No. 10: India's SDG-16=71 and the Performances in SDG-1

SDG India Indicators	SDG-1-1	SDG-1-2	SDG-1-3	SDG-1-4	SDG-1-5
UN Target of this SDG	11	100	100	100	0
Performance of India	21.92	28.7	84.75	36.4	10.39
India SDG 16 Score	71	71	71	71	71
Expected Performance, When SDG-16=71	7.81	71	71	71	0
Indicator Interpretation	Value High - Performance Low	Value High - Performance High	Value High - Performance High	Value High - Performance High	Value High - Performance Low
Performance Difference, When SDG 16=71	-14.11	-42.33	+13.75	-34.6	-10.39
Data Source: NITI *Aayog*, 2018 and Inference drawn by the author.					

Inference: It was assumed that, 'Peace, Justice and Strong Institutions' are the pre-conditions of achievement.

Here, Expected Performance = India SDG 16 Score (UN target of this SDG / 100) and

Performance Difference = (Expected Performance - Performance of India)

From the above conditions it is explored in the table no-10.

For the SDG_1_1: That is 'Percentage of population living below national poverty line', here performance of India is negatively differed (21.92) from its expected score 7.81 when SDG-16 score is 71 and here performance have to reduce to a level of 14.11 from the present performance. So India have to devote its tools of 'Peace, Justice and Strong Institutions' in a better way for a better score. Here the performance difference is -14.11.

SDG_1_2: That is 'Percentage of households with any usual member covered by any health scheme or health insurance', here performance of India is negatively differed (28.7) from its expected score is 71 when SDG-16 score is 71 and here performance have to increase to a level of 42.33 from the present performance. So India have to devote its tools of 'Peace, Justice and Strong Institutions' in a better way for a better score. Here the performance difference is -42.33.

SDG_1_3: That is 'Persons provided employment as a percentage of persons who demanded employment under Mahatma Gandhi National Rural Employment Guarantee Act (MGNREGA)', here performance of India is positively differed (84.75) from its expected score 71, when SDG-16 score is 71 and here performance level have to hold and increase to a far better score from 84.75. Here the performance difference is -13.75.

SDG_1_4: That is 'Proportion of the population (out of total eligible population) receiving social protection benefits under Maternity Benefits (%)', here performance of India is negatively differed (36.4) from its expected score 71 when SDG-16 score is 71 and here performance have to increase to a level of 34.6 from the present performance. So India have to devote its tools of 'Peace, Justice and Strong Institutions' in a better way for a better score. Here the performance difference is -34.6.

SDG_1_5: That is 'Number of homeless households per 10,000 households', here performance of India is negatively differed (10.39) from its expected score '0' when SDG-16 score is 71 and here performance have to decrease to a level of '0' from the present performance. So India have to devote its tools of 'Peace, Justice and Strong Institutions' in a better way for a better score. Here the performance difference is -10.39.

5.9. Government of India's Remaining Targets and the Indicators for SDG-1

As we know that, on the basis of the availability of the disaggregated data, the NITI *Aayog* had framed India's own indicators of the targets of each individual SDG. For the SDG-1, that is 'No Poverty', the NITI *Aayog* had framed five indicators; which captured two (1.2.1 and 1.3.1) of twelve indicators of the seven UNs SDG targets. As per the report, 68 dedicated policies or schemes are in action to achieve three targets (1.2, 1.3 and 1.4) of the UN's SDG-1; the remaining indicators of the UN's SDG-1 is to be achieve by 2030. The remaining lists of targets along with the indicators of SDG-1 are detailed in Table no-11.

Table No-11: Government of India's Remaining Targets and the Indicators for SDG-1

India's Remaining Targets and the Indicators for SDG-1	
Targets	***Indicators***
1.1: By 2030, eradicate extreme poverty for all people everywhere, currently measured as people living on less than $1.25 a day [iv].	1.1.1: Proportion of population below the international poverty line, by sex, age, employment status and geographical location (urban/rural) [iv].
1.2: By 2030, reduce at least by half the proportion of men, women and children of all ages living in poverty in all its dimensions according to national definitions [i].	1.2.1: Proportion of population living below the national poverty line, by sex and age [ii].
	1.2: Proportion of men, women and children of all ages living in poverty in all its dimensions according to national definitions [iii].
1.3: Implement nationally appropriate social protection systems and measures for all, including floors, and by 2030 achieve substantial coverage of the poor and the vulnerable [ii].	1.3.1: Proportion of population covered by social protection floors/systems, by sex, distinguishing children, unemployed persons, older persons, persons with disabilities, pregnant women, new-borns, work-injury victims and the poor and the vulnerable [ii].
1.4: By 2030, ensure that all men and women, in particular the poor and the vulnerable, have equal rights to economic resources, as well as access to basic services, ownership and control over land and other forms of property, inheritance, natural resources, appropriate new technology and financial services, including microfinance [iii].	1.4.1: Proportion of population living in households with access to basic services [iv].
	1.4.2: Proportion of total adult population with secure tenure rights to land, with legally recognized documentation and who perceive their rights to land as secure, by sex and by type of tenure [iv].

(*Contd...*)

1.5: By 2030, build the resilience of the poor and those in vulnerable situations and reduce their exposure and vulnerability to climate-related extreme events and other economic, social and environmental shocks and disasters [iv].	1.5.1: Number of deaths, missing persons and persons affected by disaster per 100,000 people [a, iv].
	1.5.2: Direct disaster economic loss in relation to global gross domestic product (GDP) [a, iv].
	1.5.3: Number of countries with national and local disaster risk reduction strategies [a, iv].
1.a: Ensure significant mobilization of resources from a variety of sources, including through enhanced development cooperation, in order to provide adequate and predictable means for developing countries, in particular least developed countries, to implement programmes and policies to end poverty in all its dimensions [iv].	1.a.1: Proportion of resources allocated by the government directly to poverty reduction programmes [iv].
	1.a.2: Proportion of total government spending on essential services (education, health and social protection) [iv].
1.b: Create sound policy frameworks at the national, regional and international levels, based on pro-poor and gender-sensitive development strategies, to support accelerated investment in poverty eradication actions [iv].	1.b.1: Proportion of government recurrent and capital spending to sectors that disproportionately benefit women, the poor and vulnerable groups [iv].

Notes of the Table:

[a] - An open-ended intergovernmental expert working group on indicators and terminology relating to disaster risk reduction established by the General Assembly (resolution 69/284) is developing a set of indicators to measure global progress in the implementation of the Sendai Framework. These indicators will eventually reflect the agreements on the Sendai Framework indicators.

i. Not captured all the indicators.
ii. Target indicators captured and analysed.
iii. Only the target captured.
iv. Remaining.

The Ministries and the Departments associate with the indicators of this SDG such as Agriculture and Cooperation, Drinking Water and Sanitation, Earth Sciences, Finance, Health and Family Welfare, Home Affairs, Housing and Urban Affairs, Human Resource Development, Labour and Employment, Micro, Small and Medium Enterprises, Ministry of Petroleum and Natural Gas and Minority Affairs have to concentrate to monitor on the above issues to achieve the target by 2030 through the provisions of Indian Constitution such as Article 15-(2).(a), Article 15-(4) and (5), Article 16-(1) to (5), Article 19-1.(a) to (g), Article 21A, Article 38-(1) and (2), Article 39-(a) to (f), Article 39A, Article 41, Article 42, Article 43, Article 46 and Article 47, Article 309, Article 310, Article 311, Article 312, Article 313, Article 314, Article 315, Article 320, Article 323A and Article 323B; Article 246 - Seventh Schedule, List-I-Union List 12, 15, 55, 65, 65, 66, 68, 69, and 94; List-II-State List No 6, 9, 14 to

18, 21, 23 and 27; List-III-Concurrent List No - 24, 25, 26 and 30; Article 243G - Eleventh Schedule - Powers, Authority and Responsibilities of Panchayats – Schedule No – 1,2, 3, 4, 5, 10, 11, 12, 16, 17, 18, 19, 23, 25, 26, 27 and 28; Article 243W - Twelfth Schedule - Powers, Authority and Responsibilities of Municipalities - Schedule No – 1, 3, 6, 9, 11 and 16; if we could not monitor, we would not be able to stand in front of the future generation with a smile.

Chapter – VI

Initiative and Performance of India in SDG-2, Zero Hunger

The global agenda of SDG-2 is entitled as 'Zero Hunger' which aimed to end hunger by achieving food security and improved nutrition and promotes sustainable agriculture. Eliminating hunger is fundamental to ensuring human development. Goal-2 was aimed to end all forms of hunger and malnutrition by 2030; making sure all people-especially children has access to sufficient and nutritious food all year round. It seeks to end all forms of malnutrition, double agricultural productivity and ensure sustainable food production systems.

The food security is influence by number of factors, including those that determine food availability - domestic food production and the capacity to import food, as well as determinants of food access, utilization and vulnerability. Although India has surpluses of wheat and rice stocks, improving access, utilization and reducing vulnerability remain a significant challenge. Access is determined by purchasing power of the households or access to government programmes. Additionally, it is also determined by inequalities such as gender inequalities with women eating last and least. Malnutrition caused by number of factors such as quality of food, sanitation and quality of water. Vulnerability to shocks and disasters too influenced food security.

6.1. The Global Targets and Indicators for SDG-2

The global indicator framework was developed by the Inter-Agency and Expert Group on SDG Indicators (IAEG-SDGs) and agreed to, as a practical starting point at the 47th session of the UN Statistical Commission held in March 2016. The report of the Commission, which was included the global indicator framework and taken note of by ECOSOC at its 70th session in June 2016. The global targets and the indicator of this SDG are tabled (Table no-12) bellow –

Table No. 12: UNDP-DDGs Targets and Indicators of SDG-2

Goal-2, End hunger, achieves food security and improved nutrition and promotes sustainable agriculture[1]

Targets	*Indicators*
2.1: By 2030, end hunger and ensure access by all people, in particular the poor and people in vulnerable situations, including infants, to safe, nutritious and sufficient food all year round.	2.1.1: Prevalence of undernourishment.
	2.1.2: Prevalence of moderate or severe food insecurity in the population, based on the Food Insecurity Experience Scale (FIES).
2.2: By 2030, end all forms of malnutrition, including achieving, by 2025, the internationally agreed targets on stunting and wasting in children under 5 years of age, and address the nutritional needs of adolescent girls, pregnant and lactating women and older persons.	2.2.1: Prevalence of stunting (height for age <-2 standard deviation from the median of the World Health Organization (WHO) Child Growth Standards) among children under 5 years of age.
	2.2.2-Prevalence of malnutrition (weight for height >+2 or <-2 standard deviation from the median of the WHO Child Growth Standards) among children under 5 years of age, by type (wasting and overweight).
2.3: By 2030, double the agricultural productivity and incomes of small-scale food producers, in particular women, indigenous peoples, family farmers, pastoralists and fishers, including through secure and equal access to land, other productive resources and inputs, knowledge, financial services, markets and opportunities for value addition and non-farm employment.	2.3.1: Volume of production per labour unit by classes of farming/pastoral/forestry enterprise size.
	2.3.2: Average income of small-scale food producers, by sex and indigenous status.
2.4: By 2030, ensure sustainable food production systems and implement resilient agricultural practices that increase productivity and production, that help maintain ecosystems, that strengthen capacity for adaptation to climate change, extreme weather, drought, flooding and other disasters and that progressively improve land and soil quality.	2.4.1: Proportion of agricultural area under productive and sustainable agriculture.
2.5: By 2020, maintain the genetic diversity of seeds, cultivated plants and farmed and domesticated animals and their related wild species, including through soundly managed and diversified seed and plant banks at the national, regional and international levels, and promote access to and fair and equitable sharing of benefits arising from the utilization of genetic resources and associated traditional knowledge, as internationally agreed.	2.5.1: Number of plant and animal genetic resources for food and agriculture secured in either medium or long-term conservation facilities.
	2.5.2: Proportion of local breeds classified as being at risk, not-at-risk or at unknown level of risk of extinction.

(*Contd...*)

1. Data Source: SDG India Index Baseline Report, 2018, NITI *Aayog*, Government of India, New Delhi.

2.a: Increase investment, including through enhanced international cooperation, in rural infrastructure, agricultural research and extension services, technology development and plant and livestock gene banks in order to enhance agricultural productive capacity in developing countries, in particular least developed countries.	2.a.1: The agriculture orientation index for government expenditures.
	2.a.2: Total official flows (official development assistance plus other official flows) to the agriculture sector.
2.b: Correct and prevent trade restrictions and distortions in world agricultural markets, including through the parallel elimination of all forms of agricultural export subsidies and all export measures with equivalent effect, in accordance with the mandate of the Doha Development Round.	2.b.1: Producer Support Estimate.
	2.b.2: Agricultural export subsidies.
2.c: Adopt measures to ensure the proper functioning of food commodity markets and their derivatives and facilitate timely access to market information, including on food reserves, in order to help limit extreme food price volatility.	2.c.1: Indicator of food price anomalies.

6.2. Interlinkage of SDG-2 with other SDGs

This section presents the linkage of the SDG-2 to other SDGs, that is, the success of this SDG habitually will influence the success of the linked SDGs; according to the SDG India Index, Baseline Report, 2018 (NITI Aayog 2018), the SDG-2 linked with the following SDGs -

SDG-1, that is *No Poverty*, which aims to reduce poverty in all its dimensions, which includes ensuring access to safe, nutritious and sufficient food all year round, particularly for the poor.

SDG-3, is *Good Health and Well-being*, which aims to end epidemics and preventable deaths and achieve universal health coverage, including financial risk protection and access to quality essential health care services, medicines and vaccines for all.

SDG-4, is *Quality Education* that aims to ensure that all girls and boys complete free, equitable and quality primary and secondary education leading to relevant and effective learning outcomes, including technical and vocational skills for employment, decent jobs and entrepreneurship.

SDG-5, is *Gender Equality* as Goal 1 emphasises creation of gender sensitive development strategies, and equal rights and access to economic resources, as well as ownership and control over land and other forms of property, inheritance, natural resources and financial resources, including microfinance.

SDG-6, is *Clean Water and Sanitation*, which aims to achieve universal and equitable access to safe and affordable drinking water and sanitation and hygiene for all.

SDG-7, is *Affordable and Clean Energy* that aims to ensure universal access to affordable, reliable and modern energy services.

SDG-8, is *Decent Work and Economic Growth* which aims to promote development oriented policies that support productive activities, decent job creation, entrepreneurship, and encourage the formalization and growth of micro-, small - and medium-sized enterprises through access to financial services.

SDG-10, is *Reduced Inequalities* that aims to adopt policies, especially fiscal wage and social protection policies and progressively achieve and sustain income growth of the bottom 40 percent of the population at a rate higher than the national average, leading to greater equality.

SDG-12, *Sustainable Consumption and Production* aiming to halve per capita global food waste at consumer level and reduce food losses along production and supply chains.

SDG-13, is *Climate Action* which aims to develop resilience and adaptive capacity of the poor to climate related hazards and natural disasters.

6.3 The National Context of SDG-2

For the SDG-2, India has aimed for 2030 is to end hunger and malnutrition by ensuring that quality food is accessible to all, to meet their nutritional needs for a healthy life. Ending hunger and malnutrition demands resilient food production systems and sustainable agricultural practices. Additionally, it requires ensuring equitable access to nutritious food by all, improving sanitation and hygiene, and reducing vulnerability to shocks and disasters.

Despite the gains in reducing poverty rate, India is saddled with high levels of malnutrition, anaemia, stunting and wasting. According to the National Family Health Survey (NFHS-4), almost half of pregnant Indian women aged between 15 and 49 years are anaemic, and more than one-thirds of women have a low Body Mass Index (BMI). Among children younger than age five 38.4 percent have low height-for-age and 21 percent have low weight-for-age. Food security and nutrition pose a challenge in India because of a number of factors such as inadequate access to food, structural inequalities (gender, caste and social groups), lack of water and sanitation, micronutrient deficiencies and illiteracy.

India has targeted initiatives, both at the national as well as State level, aiming to achieve this Goal. The National Food Security Act, 2013, which mandates provision of food grains to nearly 75 percent of the population in rural areas and 50 percent of the population in urban areas at affordable prices (Rs. 3, Rs. 2 and Rs. 1 for per KG rice, wheat and coarse grains respectively under the Targeted Public Distribution System. Under the Integrated Child Development Scheme (ICDS), supplementary nutrition is provided to pregnant women, lactating mothers and children below 6 years of age. The recently launched *Poshan Abhiyaan* or the National Nutrition Mission has brought in renewed focus and synergized efforts to battle stunting, wasting, anaemia and malnutrition among children. Initiatives like the National Mission on Sustainable Agriculture and E-NAM are promoting sustainable food production systems and ensuring proper functioning of the food commodity markets. Schemes like the Mid-Day-Meal focus on reducing malnutrition among school children, thereby encouraging enrolment in schools.

Working towards ending hunger and all forms of malnutrition, India has undertaken various initiatives that are strongly aligned with the targets outlined under this goal. The government has various nutrition related policies, and is implementing different programmes and schemes. National Nutrition Strategy (NNS) aimed to accelerate the decline of malnutrition in India. The National Nutrition Mission (NNM) monitors growth of children, as well as checks the pilferage of food rations provided at *Aanganwadi* Centres. *POSHAN Abhiyaan,* launched in 2017-18, aimed to reduce stunting, under-nutrition, anaemia, and low-birth-weight-babies through synergy and convergence among different programmes, better monitoring and improved community mobilisation. Another scheme called *Antoydaya Anna Yojana* (AAY) aimed to provide food at subsidized prices to poor families. Further, Integrated Child Development Scheme (ICDS) envisages comprehensive early childhood care and development by focusing on the children in the age-group 0-6 years, pregnant women and adolescent girls. Mid-day Meal (MDM) scheme aims to improve nutritional levels among school children which also has a direct and positive impact on enrolment, retention and attendance in schools. Under the *Pradhan Mantri Matru Vandana Yojana* (PMMVY), Rs.6, 000 is transferred directly to bank accounts of pregnant women for availing better facilities for their delivery.

In addition to these, there are several agriculture related policies, programmes and schemes. The National Mission on Agriculture Extension and Technology enables delivery of appropriate technologies and improved agronomic practices for farmers. The National Mission on Sustainable Agriculture and the National Food Security Mission aims to enhance agricultural productivity, and the *Pradhan Mantri Krishi Sinchayee Yojana* (PMKSY) aims to improve water use efficiency.

To reducing hunger, India provide food subsidy to all the poor citizens of India. Roughly one rural household is covered under the Public Distribution System (PDS) for every rural household where the monthly income of the highest earning member is less than Rs. 5000 as per Socio-Economic-Caste Census 2011. Manipur among the States and Delhi among the Union Territories have recorded best performance for this indicator at 1.36 and 1.29 respectively.

Stunting children is a headache of India for different factor, it start from under-age marriage of mother and it accelerate illiteracy to poverty. As per report, 38.4 percent of children under 5 years of age are categorized as stunted in India. The aim is to reduce this to 21.03 percent by 2030. The only States to have achieved this target are Kerala and Goa. No UT has achieved this target as yet. Andaman and Nicobar Islands have the lowest rate of stunting among the UTs at 23.3 percent.

Anaemia among women is a burning issue, which must be address immediately. As per report, almost half of pregnant women aged between 15 and 49 years are anaemic in India. This rate is much above the national target of 23.57 percent to be achieved by 2030. While Kerala is the only State in India to have reduced this rate to below the national target, Sikkim is very near to achieving this target with current rate at 23.6 percent. Puducherry performed the best among UTs at 26 percent.

Agricultural productivity to be increased along with its population trends, secondly the income inequality to be reduced to increase the required purchasing of foods. India currently produces 2,509 kg of agricultural produce of rice, wheat and coarse grains from 1 Ha of land annually. India aims to double this by 2030 to 5,018kg/Ha. While no State or UT in India has achieved this target as yet, the UT of Chandigarh is nearing the targeted productivity with current levels at 4,600kg/Ha. Following suite is Punjab with annual productivity of 4,297kg/Ha.

In the next part of this chapter we tried to visualized the performance level of India through the SDG's targets and the SDG India Index Base Line Report, 2018 (NITI Aayog 2018) along with the Constitutional provisions in India to explore citizen's responsibility along with the its institutions through the mirror of indexed score on 'peace, justice and strong institutions' (SDG-16).

6.4. SDG-1 Targets, National Indicators and Target Values of India

India in its SDG India Index Base Line Report, 2018 (NITI Aayog 2018), India had measured the performance of India on the goal of 'Zero Hunger', India had identified five national level indicators, which captured three (2.1, 2.2 and 2.3) out of the eight UN's SDG targets for 2030. These indicators have been selected based on availability of data at national level; these are in Table no-13.

Table No. 13: UNDP-SDG-2, Targets, Indicators Selected and Target Value of India

SDG-2 Targets, National Indicators and Target Values of India		
SDG-2 Global Target	***Indicator Selected for SDG India Index***	***National Target Value for 2030***
2.1: By 2030, end hunger and ensure access by all people, in particular the poor and people in vulnerable situations, including infants, to safe, nutritious and sufficient food all year round.	1. Ratio of rural households covered under public distribution system to rural households where monthly income of highest earning member is less than Rs.5, 000.	1.29
2.2: By 2030, end all forms of malnutrition, including achieving, by 2025, the internationally agreed targets on stunting and wasting in children under five years of age and address the nutritional needs of adolescent girls, pregnant and lactating women, and older persons.	2. Percentage of children under age 5 years who are stunted.	21.03
	3. Percentage of pregnant women aged 15 - 49 years who are anaemic (11.0/dl)%	23.57
2.3: By 2030 doubles the agricultural productivity and the incomes of small-scale food producers, particularly women, indigenous peoples, family farmers, pastoralists and fishers including through secure and equal access to land, other productive resources and inputs, knowledge, financial services markets and opportunities value addition and non-farm employment.	4. Rice, wheat and coarse cereals Produced Annually unit area (Kg/Ha) %.	5,018.44

Source: (NITI Aayog 2018).

6.5. Indian's SDG-2 Index Indicators, Data Source and Interpretations

The NITI *Aayog*, Government of India had collected the required data from different government agencies to capture the UN SDG's target indicators as well as framed its own indicators to justify the achievement of the SDGs. Apart from that the NITI *Aayog* had developed the computational approach of the disaggregated data as per valid methods along with the parameters of the performance; in the following tables (Table no-14, Table no-15, Table no-16, and Table no-17) shows the details of the above issue to develop a sense of progress of the SDG-2, entitled as 'Zero Hunger'.

Table No. 14: SDG-2, Indian Indicator-1

SDG-2: Zero Hunger	**Indicator-1: Ratio of rural households covered under public distribution system to rural households where monthly income of highest earning member is less than Rs.5, 000.**
Indicator data source	Numerator: Planning Commission Planning Commission estimates based on National Sample Survey Organization (NSSO), Consumption Expenditure Survey data] Denominator: [SECC].
Computation approach	Percentage of rural households covered under PDS ÷ Proportion of rural households where monthly income of highest earning member is less than Rs. 5000.
Data period (year)	2011-2012
States/UTs covered	36
Data periodicity	10 years
Relevant UN target	2.1: By 2030, end hunger and ensure access by all people, in particular the poor and people in vulnerable situations, including infants, to safe, nutritious and sufficient food all year round.
Relevant UN indicator	2.1.2: Prevalence of moderate or severe food insecurity in the population, based on the Food Insecurity Experience Scale (FIES).
Relevant MoSPI indicator	2.1.2: Proportion of population (marginalized and vulnerable) with access to food grains at subsidized prices
Indicator interpretation	Higher value means higher performance (+)

Source: (NITI Aayog 2018).

Table No. 15: SDG-2, Indian Indicator-2

SDG-2: Zero Hunger	**Indicator-2: Percentage of children under age 5 years who are stunted.**
Indicator data source	Ministry of Health and Family Welfare (National Health Family Survey – 4)
Computation approach	Directly from data source
Data period (year)	2015-2016
States/UTs covered	36

(Contd...)

Data periodicity	3 years
Relevant UN target	2.2: By 2030, end all forms of malnutrition, including achieving, by 2025, the internationally agreed targets on stunting and wasting in children under 5 years of age, and address the nutritional needs of adolescent girls, pregnant and lactating women and older persons.
Relevant UN indicator	2.2.1: Prevalence stunting (height for <-2 standard deviation from the median of the World Health Organization [WHO] Child Growth Standards) among children under five years of age.
Relevant MoSPI indicator	2.2.1: Percentage of children under age 5 years who are stunted
Indicator interpretation	Higher value means lower performance (-)

Source: (NITI Aayog 2018).

Table No. 16: SDG-2, Indian Indicator-3

SDG-2: Zero Hunger	**Indicator-3: Percentage of pregnant women aged 15-49 years are anaemic (11.0g/dl)**
Indicator data source	Ministry of Health and Family Welfare (National Health Family Survey – 4)
Computation approach	Directly from data source
Data period (year)	2015-2016
States/UTs covered	34
Data periodicity	3 years
Relevant UN target	2.2: By 2030, end all forms of malnutrition, including achieving, by 2025, the internationally agreed targets on stunting and wasting in children under 5 years of age, and address the nutritional needs of adolescent girls, pregnant and lactating women and older persons.
Relevant UN indicator	NA
Relevant MoSPI indicator	2.2.1: Percentage of pregnant women aged 15-49 years are anaemic (11.0g/dl)
Indicator interpretation	Higher value means lower performance (-)

Source: (NITI Aayog 2018).

Table No. 17: SDG-2, Indian Indicator-4

SDG-2: Zero Hunger	**Indicator-4: Rice, wheat and coarse cereals produced annually per unit area (Kg/Ha).**
Indicator data source	Ministry of Agriculture and Farmers Welfare, Ministry Report
Computation approach	Total rice, wheat and coarse cereals produced annually ÷ Total agricultural area under rice, wheat and coarse cereals.
Data period (year)	2015-2016
States/UTs covered	36
Data periodicity	Annual
Relevant UN target	2.3: By 2030, double the agricultural productivity and incomes of small-scale food producers, in particular women, indigenous people, family farmers, pastoralists and fishers including through secure and equal access to land, other productive resources and inputs, knowledge, financial services, markets and opportunities for value addition and non-farm employment.

(*Contd...*)

Relevant UN indicator	NA
Relevant MoSPI indicator	2.3.1: Volume of production per labour unit by classes of farming/pastoral/ forestry enterprise size.
Indicator interpretation	Higher value means higher performance (+)

6.6. Provisions of the Indian Constitution for SDG-2

The spirit of the unity in this diverse country, India is secured by its great Constitution; the Constitution of India not only secured its unity, announced a vision in the Preamble in the beginning of its Articles included in the Indian Constitution, "*We the people of India, having solemnly resolved to constitute India into a Sovereign Socialist Secular Democratic Republic and to secure to all its citizens: justice, social, economic and political; liberty of thought, expression, belief, faith and worship; equality of status and of opportunity; and to promote among them all fraternity assuring the dignity of the individual and the unity and integrity of the nation; in our Constituent Assembly this twenty-sixth day of November, 1949, do hereby adopt, enact and give to ourselves this Constitution* (India 1950/2015)". The mode of orientation of the Indian Constitution and the sustainable development goals of the contemporary time are given us an opportunity to make a link between these two visions of development and the author is trying to make the link.

As we know the sustainable development goals are interlinked, that means the success or failure of one is affected to other SDGs. From this perspective, this section presents the provisions in the Indian Constitution to eradicate poverty as reflected in the sustainable development agenda entitled as SDG-2, Zero Hunger. The linked Constitutional provisions are in the following Table no-18 -

Table No. 18: Provisions in Indian Constitution for SDG-2

SDG-2 and the Linked Articles and Schedules of the Constitution of India
Article 15-(2).(a), Article 15-(4) and (5), Article 16-(1) to (5), Article 19-1.(a) to (g), Article 21A, Article 38-(1) and (2), Article 39-(a) to (f), Article 39A, Article 41, Article 42, Article 43, Article 45, Article 46, Article 47, Article 48, Article 309, Article 310, Article 311, Article 312, Article 313, Article 314, Article 315, Article 320, Article 323A and Article 323B.
Article 246: Seventh Schedule, List-I: Union List No: 12, 15, 55, 65, 66, 68, 69 and 94. List-II: State List No: 6, 9, 14 to 18, 21, 23 and 27. List-III: Concurrent List No: 24, 25, 26 and 30.
Article 243G: Eleventh Schedule: Powers, Authority and Responsibilities of Panchayats. Schedule No: 1, 2, 3, 4, 5, 6, 8, 9, 10, 11, 12, 16, 17, 18, 19, 23, 24, 25, 26, 27, 28 and 29. Article 243W: Twelfth Schedule: Powers, Authority and Responsibilities of Municipalities. Schedule No: 1, 3, 6, 8, 9, 10, 11 and 16.

Source: The Constitution of India, 2015 as on 9th November, 2015.

6.7. Policies of the Government of India for Targets of the SDG-2

According to the SDG India Index Base Line Report, 2018 (NITI Aayog 2018), India is proactive to achieve the target of the UN's SDGs. The Government of India initiated as well as implemented various policies to capture the indicators of the targets of each individual SDG. On the moment of preparation of SDG India Index Base Line Report, 2018, on the basis of the availability of the disaggregated data, the NITI *Aayog* framed India's own indicators of the targets of each individual SDG. For the SDG-2, that is 'Zero Hunger', the NITI *Aayog* framed four indicators; which capture three out of eight UNs SDG targets. As per the report, 37 dedicated policies or schemes are in action to achieve three targets (2.1, 2.2 and 2.3) of the UN's SDG-2 under the leadership and monitoring of 15 dedicated Ministries or the Departments. The policies or schemes to achieve the targets of SDG-2 and the concerned dedicated Ministries and the Departments are detailed in the - Table no-19.

Table No. 19: Policies Initiated by the Indian Government for Targets of SDG-1

SDG-2, Zero Hunger	
SDG-2: End hunger, achieve food security and improved nutrition and promote sustainable agriculture.	
Target: 2.1: By 2030, end hunger and ensure access by all people, in particular the poor and people in vulnerable situations, including infants, to safe, nutritious and sufficient food all year round.	
Centrally Sponsored /Central Sector Schemes (CSS)	Concerned Ministries/ Departments
1. Food subsidy (procurement, transport, distribution, etc.)	Ministry of Consumers Affairs Food and Public Distribution
2. Umbrella Integrated Child Development Services (*Anganwadi* Services, National Nutrition Mission, Scheme for Adolescent Girls, Child Protection Services and, National Creche Mission 3. *Pradhan Mantri Matru Vandana Yojana* (PMMVY)	Ministry of Women and Child Development
4. National Programme of Mid-Day Meal in Schools (MDM)	Ministry of Human Resource Development
Target: 2.2: By 2030, end all forms of malnutrition, including achieving, by 2025, the internationally agreed targets on stunting and wasting in children under 5 years of age, and address the nutritional needs of adolescent girls, pregnant and lactating women and older person	
Centrally Sponsored /Central Sector Schemes (CSS)	Concerned Ministries/ Departments
1. Umbrella Integrated Child Development Services (*Anganwadi* Services, National Nutrition Mission, Scheme for Adolescent Girls, Child Protection Services and, National Creche Mission) 2. *Pradhan Mantri Matru Vandana Yojana* (PMMVY)	Ministry of Women and Child Development
3. National Programme of Mid-Day Meal in Schools (MDM)	Ministry of Human Resource Development
4. National Health Mission	Ministry of Health & Family Welfare

(*Contd...*)

5. National AYUSH Mission	AYUSH
6. Biotechnology Research & Development	Department of Science & Technology
Target: 2.3: By 2030, double the agricultural productivity and incomes of small-scale food producers, in particular women, indigenous peoples, family farmers, pastoralists and fishers, including through secure and equal access to land, other productive resources and inputs, knowledge, financial services, markets and opportunities for value addition and non-farm employment.	
Centrally Sponsored /Central Sector Schemes (CSS)	Concerned Ministries/ Departments
1. Green Revolution umbrella scheme, including: *Rashtriya Krishi Vikas Yojana* (RKVY); and *Krishi Unnati* Schemes, Mission for Integrated Development of Horticulture (MIDH), Integrated Scheme on Agriculture Census & Statistics, Integrated Scheme on Agriculture Cooperation, Integrated Scheme on Agricultural Marketing, National Food Security Mission, National Mission on Oilseeds & Oil Palm (NMOOP), National Mission for Sustainable Agriculture (NMSA), and National Mission on Agriculture Extension & Technology (NMAET). 2. *Pradhan Mantri Krishi Sinchayee Yojana* 3. *Pradhan Mantri Fasal Bima Yojana* (PMFBY) 4. White Revolution (the umbrella scheme includes National Livestock Mission (NLM), National Programme for Bovine Breeding and Dairy Development, and Livestock Health and Disease Control Programme. 5. Blue Revolution (includes schemes related inland and marine fisheries) 6. Crop Science 7. Animal Science 8. Fishery science 9. Interest subsidy for short term credit of farmers 10. Sub-mission on agriculture mechanisation	Agriculture and Cooperation
11. *Pradhan Mantri Krishi Sinchayee Yojana* (accelerated irrigation benefits) programme & command area development programme	Ministry of Water Resource, Ministry of Rural Development &Green Revolution,
12. Nutrient-Based Subsidy 13. Urea Subsid	Ministry of Chemicals and Fertilisers
14. *Pradhan Mantri MUDRA Yojana*	Ministry of Finance
15. Digital India Land Record Modernization Programme	Department of Land Resources
16. Biotechnology Research & Development	Department of Science and Technology
Target: 2.4: By 2030, ensure sustainable food production systems and implement resilient agricultural practices that increase productivity and production, that help maintain ecosystems, that strengthen capacity for adaptation to climate change, extreme weather, drought, flooding and other disasters and that progressively improve land and soil quality.	
Centrally Sponsored /Central Sector Schemes (CSS)	Concerned Ministries/ Departments
1. Green Revolution, the umbrella scheme, includes: *Rashtriya Krishi Vikas Yojana* (RKVY); and *Krishi Unnati* Schemes Mission for Integrated Development of Horticulture (MIDH), Integrated Scheme on Agriculture Census & Statistics, Integrated	Agriculture & Cooperation,

(*Contd*...)

1. Green Revolution, the umbrella scheme, includes: *Rashtriya Krishi Vikas Yojana* (RKVY); and *Krishi Unnati* Schemes Mission for Integrated Development of Horticulture (MIDH), Integrated Scheme on Agriculture Census & Statistics, Integrated Scheme on Agriculture Cooperation, Integrated Scheme on Agricultural Marketing, National Food Security Mission, National Mission on Oilseeds & Oil Palm (NMOOP), National Mission for Sustainable Agriculture (NMSA), and National Mission on Agriculture Extension & Technology (NMAET) 2. *Pradhan Mantri Krishi Sinchayee Yojana* 3. Natural Resource Management	Agriculture & Cooperation,
4. River Basin Management 5. Development of Water Resources Information System	Ministry of Water Resource, Ministry of Rural Development &Green Revolution,
Target: 2.5: By 2020, maintain the genetic diversity of seeds, cultivated plants and farmed and domesticated animals and their related wild species, including through soundly managed and diversified seeds and plant banks at the national, regional and international levels, and promote access to and fair and equitable sharing of benefits arising from the utilization of genetic resources and associated traditional knowledge, as internationally agreed.	
1. Sub- Mission on Seed and Planting Material (under NMAET under the umbrella programme on Green Revolution) 2. Crop Science 3. Horticulture 4. Animal Science 5. Fishery Science	Agriculture & Cooperation
6. *Vanbandhu Kalyan Yojana*	Ministry of Tribal Affairs
Target: 2.a: Increase investment, including through enhanced international cooperation, in rural infrastructure, agricultural research and extension services, technology development and plant and livestock gene banks in order to enhance agricultural productive capacity in developing countries, in particular least developed countries.	
1. Green Revolution, the umbrella scheme, includes: *Rashtriya Krishi Vikas Yojana* (RKVY); and *Krishi Unnati* Schemes Mission for Integrated Development of Horticulture (MIDH), Integrated Scheme on Agriculture Census & Statistics, Integrated Scheme on Agriculture Cooperation, Integrated Scheme on Agricultural Marketing, National Food Security Mission, National Mission on Oilseeds & Oil Palm (NMOOP), National Mission for Sustainable Agriculture (NMSA), and National Mission on Agriculture Extension & Technology (NMAET) 2. *Pradhan Mantri Krishi Sinchayee Yojana* 3. White Revolution	Agriculture & Cooperation
4. *Gram Sadak Yojana*	Rural Development
5. River Basin Management 6. Development of Water Resources Information System	Ministry of Water Resource, Ministry of Rural Development &Green Revolution,

(*Contd*...)

7. Agricultural Education 8. Agricultural Extension	Department of Agricultural Research and Education
	Ministry of Commerce, Ministry of External Affairs
Target: 2.b: Correct and prevent trade restrictions and distortions in world agricultural markets, including through the parallel elimination of all forms of agricultural export subsidies and all export measures with equivalent effect, in accordance with the mandate of the Doha Development Round.	
Centrally Sponsored /Central Sector Schemes (CSS)	Concerned Ministries/ Departments
	Ministry of Commerce
Target: 2.c: Adopt measures to ensure the proper functioning of food commodity markets and their derivatives and facilitate timely access to market information, including on food reserves, in order to help limit extreme food price volatility.	
Centrally Sponsored /Central Sector Schemes (CSS)	Concerned Ministries/ Departments
1. Green Revolution (Agriculture Marketing and allied interventions) 2. Market Intervention Scheme and Price Support Scheme (MIS-PSS)	Agriculture & Cooperation
3. Price Stabilisation Fund	Ministry of Consumers Affairs Food and Public Distribution
4. *Pradhan Mantri Kisan Sampada Yojana*	Food Processing Industries

Source: (NITI Aayog 2018).

6.8. Initiatives, Expectation and Performance of Government of India in SDG-2

According to the SDG India Index Base Line Report, 2018 (NITI Aayog 2018), to achieving the target of the UN's SDG-2, the Government of India has framed four indicators. The Government of India reported that, 37 dedicated policies or schemes are in action to achieve three targets (2.1, 2.2 and 2.3) of the UN's SDG-2 under the leadership and monitoring of 15 dedicated Ministries or the Departments. The SDG-2 indicators are –

SDG_2_1: Ratio of rural households covered under public distribution system to rural households where monthly income of highest earning member is less than Rs.5, 000.

SDG_2_2: Percentage of children under age 5 years who are stunted.

SDG_2_3: Percentage of pregnant women aged 15 - 49 years who are anaemic (11.0/dl).

SDG_2_4: Ratio of rice, wheat and coarse cereals Produced Annually unit area (Kg/Ha).

Table No. 20: India's SDG-16=71 and the Performances in SDG-2

SDG India Indicators	SDG_2_1	SDG_2_2	SDG_2_3	SDG_2_4
UN Target of this SDG	1.29	21.03	23.57	5018.44
Performance of India	1.01	38.4	50.3	2509.22
India SDG 16 Score	71	71	71	71
India SDG Mean Score	57	57	57	57
Expected Performance, When SDG 16=71	0.92	14.93	16.73	3563.10
Indicator Interpretation	Value High - Performance High	Value High - Performance Low	Value High - Performance Low	Value High - Performance High
Performance Difference, When SDG 16=71	+0.09	-23.47	-33.57	-1053.88
Data Source: NITI *Aayog*, 2018 and Inference drawn by the author.				

Inference: It was assumed that, 'Peace, Justice and Strong Institutions' are the pre-conditions of achievement.

Here, Expected Performance = India SDG 16 Score (UN target of this SDG / 100) and

Performance Difference = (Expected Performance - Performance of India)

From the above conditions it is explored in the table no-20.

For the SDG_2_1: That is 'Ratio of rural households covered under public distribution system to rural households where monthly income of highest earning member is less than Rs.5, 000', here the performance of India is positively differed (1.01) from its expected score 0.92, when SDG-16 score is 71 and here performance level have to hold and increase to a far better score. Here the performance difference is +0.92.

SDG_2_2: That is 'Percentage of children under age 5 years who are stunted', here the performance of India is negatively differed (38.4) from its expected score 14.93 when SDG-16 score is 71 and here performance have to reduce to a level of 23.47 from the present performance. So India have to devote its tools of 'Peace, Justice and Strong Institutions' in a better way for a better score. Here the performance difference is -23.47.

SDG_2_3: That is 'Percentage of pregnant women aged 15 - 49 years who are anaemic (11.0/dl)', here the performance of India is negatively differed (50.3) from its expected score 16.73 when SDG-16 score is 71 and here performance have to reduce to a level of 33.57 from the present performance. So India have to devote its tools of 'Peace, Justice and Strong Institutions' in a better way for a better score. Here the performance difference is -23.57.

SDG_2_4: That is 'Ratio of rice, wheat and coarse cereals Produced Annually unit area (Kg/Ha)', here the performance of India is negatively differed (2509.22) from its expected score 3563.10 when SDG-16 score is 71 and here performance have to increase to a level of 1053.88 of rice, wheat and coarse cereals Produced Annually unit area (Kg/Ha) from the present performance. So India have to devote its tools of 'Peace, Justice and Strong Institutions' in a better way for a better score. Here the performance difference is -1053.88.

6.9. Government of India's Remaining Targets and the Indicators for SDG-2

As we know that, on the basis of the availability of the disaggregated data, the NITI *Aayog* had framed India's own indicators of the targets of each individual SDG. For the SDG-2, that is 'Zero Hunger', the NITI *Aayog* had framed four indicators; which captured three (2.1.2, 2.2.1 and 2.3.1) of fourteen indicators of the eight UNs SDG targets. As per the report, 37 dedicated policies or schemes are in action to achieve three targets (2.1, 2.2 and 2.3) of the UN's SDG-2; the remaining indicators of the UN's SDG-2 is to be achieve by 2030. The remaining lists of targets along with the indicators of SDG-2 are detailed in Table no-21.

Table No. 21: Government of India's Remaining Targets and the Indicators for SDG-2

India's Remaining Targets and the Indicators for SDG-2	
Targets	***Indicators***
2.1: By 2030, end hunger and ensure access by all people, in particular the poor and people in vulnerable situations, including infants, to safe, nutritious and sufficient food all year round [i].	2.1.1: Prevalence of undernourishment [3].
	2.1.2: Prevalence of moderate or severe food insecurity in the population, based on the Food Insecurity Experience Scale (FIES) [ii].
2.2: By 2030, end all forms of malnutrition, including achieving, by 2025, the internationally agreed targets on stunting and wasting in children under 5 years of age, and address the nutritional needs of adolescent girls, pregnant and lactating women and older persons [i].	2.2.1: Prevalence of stunting (height for age <-2 standard deviation from the median of the World Health Organization (WHO) Child Growth Standards) among children under 5 years of age [ii].
	2.2.2: Prevalence of malnutrition (weight for height >+2 or <-2 standard deviation from the median of the WHO Child Growth Standards) among children under 5 years of age, by type (wasting and overweight) [iii].
2.3: By 2030, double the agricultural productivity and incomes of small-scale food producers, in particular women, indigenous peoples, family farmers, pastoralists and fishers, including through secure and equal access to land, other productive resources and inputs, knowledge, financial services, markets and opportunities for value addition and non-farm employment [i].	2.3.1: Volume of production per labour unit by classes of farming/pastoral/forestry enterprise size [ii].
	2.3.2: Average income of small-scale food producers, by sex and indigenous status [iii].

(*Contd*...)

2.4: By 2030, ensure sustainable food production systems and implement resilient agricultural practices that increase productivity and production, that help maintain ecosystems, that strengthen capacity for adaptation to climate change, extreme weather, drought, flooding and other disasters and that progressively improve land and soil quality [iii].	2.4.1: Proportion of agricultural area under productive and sustainable agriculture [iii].
2.5: By 2020, maintain the genetic diversity of seeds, cultivated plants and farmed and domesticated animals and their related wild species, including through soundly managed and diversified seed and plant banks at the national, regional and international levels, and promote access to and fair and equitable sharing of benefits arising from the utilization of genetic resources and associated traditional knowledge, as internationally agreed [iii].	2.5.1: Number of plant and animal genetic resources for food and agriculture secured in either medium or long-term conservation facilities [iii]. 2.5.2: Proportion of local breeds classified as being at risk, not-at-risk or at unknown level of risk of extinction [iii].
2.a: Increase investment, including through enhanced international cooperation, in rural infrastructure, agricultural research and extension services, technology development and plant and livestock gene banks in order to enhance agricultural productive capacity in developing countries, in particular least developed countries [iii].	2.a.1: The agriculture orientation index for government expenditures [iii]. 2.a.2: Total official flows (official development assistance plus other official flows) to the agriculture sector [iii].
2.b: Correct and prevent trade restrictions and distortions in world agricultural markets, including through the parallel elimination of all forms of agricultural export subsidies and all export measures with equivalent effect, in accordance with the mandate of the Doha Development Round [iii].	2.b.1: Producer Support Estimate [iii]. 2.b.2: Agricultural export subsidies [iii].
2.c: Adopt measures to ensure the proper functioning of food commodity markets and their derivatives and facilitate timely access to market information, including on food reserves, in order to help limit extreme food price volatility [iii].	2.c.1: Indicator of food price anomalies [iii].
Notes of the Table: i. Not captured all the indicators. ii. Target indicators captured and analysed. iii. Remaining.	

The Ministries and the Departments associate with indicators of this SDG such as Agriculture & Cooperation, AYUSH, Chemicals and Fertilisers, Consumers Affairs Food and Public Distribution, Department of Agricultural Research and Education, Department of Land Resources, Finance, Food Processing Industries, Health & FW, HRD, MoWR, RD&GR, Rural Development, Science & Technology, Tribal Affairs and

Women & Child Development have to concentrate to monitor on the above issues to achieve the target by 2030 through the provisions of Indian Constitution such as Article 15-(2).(a), Article 15-(4) and (5), Article 16-(1) to (5), Article 19-1.(a) to (g), Article 21A, Article 38-(1) and (2), Article 39-(a) to (f), Article 39A, Article 41, Article 42, Article 43, Article 45, Article 46, Article 47, Article 48, Article 309, Article 310, Article 311, Article 312, Article 313, Article 314, Article 315, Article 320, Article 323A and Article 323B; Article 246 - Seventh Schedule; List-I-Union List 12, 15, 55, 65, 66, 68, 69 and 94; List-II-State List No 6, 9, 14 to 18, 21, 23 and 27; List-III-Concurrent List No-24, 25, 26 and 30; Article 243G - Eleventh Schedule - Powers, Authority and Responsibilities of Panchayats – Schedule No – 1, 2, 3, 4, 5, 6, 8, 9, 10, 11, 12, 16, 17, 18, 19, 23, 24. 25, 26, 27, 28 and 29 and Article 243W - Twelfth Schedule - Powers, Authority and Responsibilities of Municipalities - Schedule No – 1, 3, 6, 8, 9, 10, 11 and 16 - if we could not monitor, we would not be able to stand in front of the future generation with a smile.

Chapter – VII

Initiative and Performance of India in SDG-3, Good Health and Well-being

The global agenda of goal-3 is entitled as 'Good Health and Well-being' which aimed to ensure that people enjoy a level of health that enables them to lead a socially and economically productive life. It was aimed also to end preventable deaths across all ages from communicable and non-communicable diseases and illness caused by air, water and soil pollution and contamination. Sensitive and ensure that all learners acquire knowledge and skills needed to promote sustainable development.

It was also aimed to achieve universal health coverage, including financial risk, access to quality essential health care services and access to safe, effective, quality and affordable essential medicines. It also calls for a renewed focus on mental health issues.

7.1. The Global Targets and Indicators for SDG-3

The global indicator framework was developed by the Inter-Agency and Expert Group on SDG Indicators (IAEG-SDGs) and agreed to, as a practical starting point at the 47th session of the UN Statistical Commission held in March 2016. The report of the Commission, which included the global indicator framework, was then taken note of by ECOSOC at its 70th session in June 2016. The global targets and the indicator of this SDG are tabled (Table no-22) bellow –

Table No. 22: UNDP-DDGs Targets and Indicators of SDG-3

SDG-3, Ensure healthy lives and promote well-being for all at all ages[1]	
Targets	***Indicators***
3.1: By 2030, reduce the global maternal mortality ratio to less than 70 per 100,000 live births.	3.1.1: Maternal mortality ratio.
	3.1.2: Proportion of births attended by skilled health personnel.

(*Contd...*)

3.2: By 2030, end preventable deaths of new-borns and children under 5 years of age, with all countries aiming to reduce neonatal mortality to at least as low as 12 per 1,000 live births and under-5 mortality to at least as low as 25 per 1,000 live births.	3.2.1: Under-five mortality rate.
	3.2.2: Neonatal mortality rate.
3.3: By 2030, end the epidemics of AIDS, tuberculosis, malaria and neglected tropical diseases and combat hepatitis, water-borne diseases and other communicable diseases.	3.3.1: Number of new HIV infections per 1,000 uninfected population, by sex, age and key populations.
	3.3.2: Tuberculosis incidence per 1,000 populations.
	3.3.3: Malaria incidence per 1,000 populations.
	3.3.4: Hepatitis B incidence per 100,000 populations.
	3.3.5: Number of people requiring interventions against neglected tropical diseases.
3.4: By 2030, reduce by one third premature mortality from non-communicable diseases through prevention and treatment and promote mental health and well-being.	3.4.1: Mortality rate attributed to cardiovascular disease, cancer, diabetes or chronic respiratory disease.
	3.4.2: Suicide mortality rate.
3.5: Strengthen the prevention and treatment of substance abuse, including narcotic drug abuse and harmful use of alcohol.	3.5.1: Coverage of treatment interventions (pharmacological, psychosocial and rehabilitation and aftercare services) for substance use disorders.
	3.5.2: Harmful use of alcohol, defined according to the national context as alcohol per capita consumption (aged 15 years and older) within a calendar year in litres of pure alcohol.
3.6: By 2020, halve the number of global deaths and injuries from road traffic accidents.	3.6.1: Death rate due to road traffic injuries.
3.7: By 2030, ensure universal access to sexual and reproductive health-care services, including for family planning, information and education, and the integration of reproductive health into national strategies and programmes.	3.7.1: Proportion of women of reproductive age (aged 15-49 years) who have their need for family planning satisfied with modern methods.
	3.7.2: Adolescent birth rate (aged 10-14 years; aged 15-19 years) per 1,000 women in that age group.
3.8: Achieve universal health coverage, including financial risk protection, access to quality essential health-care services and access to safe, effective, quality and affordable essential medicines and vaccines for all.	3.8.1: Coverage of essential health services (defined as the average coverage of essential services based on tracer interventions that include reproductive, maternal, new-born and child health, infectious diseases, non-communicable diseases and service capacity and access, among the general and the most disadvantaged population).
	3.8.2: Number of people covered by health insurance or a public health system per 1,000 populations.
3.9: By 2030, substantially reduce the number of deaths and illnesses from hazardous chemicals and air, water and soil pollution and contamination.	3.9.1: Mortality rate attributed to household and ambient air pollution.
	3.9.2: Mortality rate attributed to unsafe water, unsafe sanitation and lack of hygiene (exposure to unsafe Water, Sanitation and Hygiene for All (WASH) services).
	3.9.3: Mortality rate attributed to unintentional poisoning.

(*Contd...*)

3.a: Strengthen the implementation of the World Health Organization Framework Convention on Tobacco Control in all countries, as appropriate.	3.a.1: Age-standardized prevalence of current tobacco use among persons aged 15 years and older.
3.b: Support the research and development of vaccines and medicines for the communicable and non-communicable diseases that primarily affect developing countries, provide access to affordable essential medicines and vaccines, in accordance with the Doha Declaration on the TRIPS Agreement and Public Health, which affirms the right of developing countries to use to the full the provisions in the Agreement on Trade-Related Aspects of Intellectual Property Rights regarding flexibilities to protect public health, and, in particular, provide access to medicines for all.	3.b.1: Proportion of the population with access to affordable medicines and vaccines on a sustainable basis.
	3.b.2: Total net official development assistance to medical research and basic health sectors.
3.c: Substantially increase health financing and the recruitment, development, training and retention of the health workforce in developing countries, especially in least developed countries and small island developing States.	3.c.1: Health worker density and distribution.
3.d: Strengthen the capacity of all countries, in particular developing countries, for early warning, risk reduction and management of national and global health risks.	3.d.1: International Health Regulations (IHR) capacity and health emergency preparedness.

7.2. Interlinkage of SDG-3 with other SDGs

This section presents the linkage of the SDG-3 to other SDGs, that is, the success of this SDG habitually will influence the success of the linked SDGs; according to the SDG India Index, Baseline Report, 2018 (NITI Aayog 2018), the SDG-3 linked with the following SDGs –

SDG-1, that is *No Poverty*, which aims to reduce poverty in all its dimensions, which includes ensuring access to safe, nutritious and sufficient food all year round, particularly for the poor.

SDG-2, that is *Zero Hunger*, which aims to end all forms of malnutrition and ensures access to safe, nutritious and sufficient food for all, in particular the poor and vulnerable, and support small scale food producers.

SDG-4, is *Quality Education* that aims to ensure that all girls and boys complete free, equitable and quality primary and secondary education leading to relevant and effective learning outcomes, including technical and vocational skills for employment, decent jobs and entrepreneurship.

SDG-5, is *Gender Equality* as Goal 1 emphasises creation of gender sensitive development strategies, and equal rights and access to economic resources, as well as ownership and control over land and other forms of property, inheritance, natural resources and financial resources, including microfinance.

SDG-6, is *Clean Water and Sanitation*, which aims to achieve universal and equitable access to safe and affordable drinking water and sanitation and hygiene for all.

SDG-10, is *Reduced Inequalities* that aims to adopt policies, especially fiscal wage and social protection policies and progressively achieve and sustain income growth of the bottom 40 percent of the population at a rate higher than the national average, leading to greater equality.

SDG-11, is *Sustainable Cities and Communities* which aims to ensure access for all to adequate, safe and affordable housing and basic services and upgrade slums, and significantly reduce the numbers of deaths and people affected by disasters, with focus on protecting the poor and vulnerable.

SDG-12, *Sustainable Consumption and Production* aiming to halve per capita global food waste at consumer level and reduce food losses along production and supply chains.

7.3. The National Context of SDG-3

The volume of stunt children will not be a strong future of any capital growth unit of the globe. National aspirations for economic growth cannot be achieved without a healthy and productive population. Economic and social advancements can neither be secure nor sustainable unless sufficient investments are made to protect and promote the health and well-being for all at, all ages. Thus, maintaining good health is important for individuals to lead a better life and is critical for a nation's development.

While sustained efforts have to be made for India to achieve the targets set under Goal 3, the country has made impressive gains on key indicators. The maternal mortality ration has declined 130 in 2014-16 from 254 in 2004-06. Under 5, mortality in 2015-16 was 50 down from 74 in 2005-06. *Ayushman Bharat* and *POSHAN Abhiyan* are two of the most comprehensive and recent programmes of the Government of India to promote good health.

The Government of India has been actively working to cover every aspect of Goal-3 and strengthen the health sector in the country. The various initiatives of the Government cover many dimensions of the goal, which include reducing mortality, reducing spread of communicable and non- communicable diseases and ensuring universal health coverage.

The National Health Mission (NHM), which encompasses two sub-missions - National Rural Health Mission (NRHM) and National Urban Health Mission (NUHM), aims to provide universal access to health care by strengthening systems, institutions and human resource capabilities. *AYUSHMAN BHARAT - Pradhan Mantri Jan Aarogya Yojana* (PMJAY) is a National Health Protection scheme which aims to provide coverage of up to 5 lakh rupees per family per year for secondary and tertiary care hospitalization, covering 10 crore poor and vulnerable families (approximately 50 crore beneficiaries). *Mission Indradhanush* aims to increase full immunization coverage in India to at least 90 percent children by December 2018.

For non- communicable diseases control, a number of schemes are in place. Revised National Tuberculosis Control Programme (RNTCP) aimed to improve the success rate of treatment among sensitive Tuberculosis (TB) cases. National Leprosy Eradication Programme aims to reduce leprosy cases. Integrated Disease Surveillance Programme (IDSP) aims to monitor disease trends and to detect and respond to outbreaks in early rising phase. National Mental Health Programme (NMHP) aims to improve the access of mental healthcare services. National Programme for control of blindness aims to reduce the cases of blindness. National Programme for Prevention and control of cancer, diabetes, cardiovascular diseases and stroke (NPCDCS) aims to reduce premature mortality and morbidity from these diseases.

The Maternal Mortality Ratio (MMR) in India stands at 130 per 1 lakh live births. The SDG target is to reduce the MMR less than 70 per 1 lakh live births by 2030. Three States namely Kerala, Maharastra and Tamil Nadu have achieved this target with MMR of 41, 61 and 66 per 1 lakh live births respectively.

In the case of under-five mortality rate, for every thousand live births in India, 50 children under 5 years die. The national target is to bring this rate down to 11 per thousand live births by 2030. Kerala is the only State to have achieved this. Goa among the States, and Andaman and Nicobar Islands among the UTs are nearing the target with current under mortality rates at 13 per thousand live births each.

The immunization coverage in children of India reported that, the 62 percent of children aged 12-23 months are fully immunized (BCG, Measles and three doses of prevalent vaccines). The national target is to increase this rate to 100 percent. No State or Union Territories has yet achieved this target. Highest immunization coverage is observed in Punjab

(89 percent) among the States and Puducherry (91 percent) among the Union Territories.

The reported figure is about 138 cases of tuberculosis are noted annually per 1 lakh persons in the country. The national target is to completely eradicate tuberculosis by 2025. The lowest incidence of tuberculosis is noted in Tripura (44 cases per 1 lakh population) among the States and in Lakshadweep Island (70 cases per 1 lakh population) among the Union Territories.

In the case of all kind of Health workforce, there are roughly 221 government physicians, nurses and midwives per 1 lakh of population in India. This rate is the highest in Kerala at about 762. Delhi is the best performing among the UTs with about 344 health workers per 1 lakh population.

In the next part of this chapter we tried to visualized the performance level of India through the SDG's targets and the SDG India Index Base Line Report, 2018 along with the Constitutional provisions in India to explore citizen's responsibility along with the its institutions through the mirror of indexed score on 'peace, justice and strong institutions' (SDG-16).

7.4. SDG-3 Targets, National Indicators and Target Values of India

India in its SDG India Index Base Line Report, 2018, India had measured the performance of India on the goal of 'Good Health and well-being', India had identified five national level indicators, which captured four (3.1, 3.2, 3.3 and 3.8) out of the thirteen UN's SDG targets for 2030. These indicators have been selected based on availability of data at national level these are in Table no-23.

Table No. 23: SDG-3 Targets, National Indicators and Target Values of India

SDG-3 Targets, National Indicators and Target Values of India		
SDG-3 Global Target	**Indicator Selected for SDG India Index**	**National Target Value for 2030**
3.1: By 2030, reduces the global maternal mortality ratio to less than 70 per 100,000 live births.	1. Maternal Mortality Ratio.	70
3.2: By 2030, end preventable deaths of new-borns and children under 5 years of age, with all countries aiming to reduce neonatal mortality to at least as low as 12 per, 1000 live births and under-5 mortality to at least as low as 25 per 1,000 live births.	2. Under five years mortality rate per 1,000 live births.	11

(*Contd...*)

	3. Percentage of children aged 12 -23 months fully immunized (BCG, Measles and three doses of Pentavalent vaccine).	100
3.3: By 2030, end the epidemics of AIDS, tuberculosis, malaria and neglected tropical diseases and combat hepatitis, water-borne diseases and other communicable diseases.	4. Annual notification of Tuberculosis cases per 1 lakh population.	0
3.8: By 2030, achieve universal health coverage, including financial risk protection, access to quality essential health-care services and access to safe, effective, quality and affordable essential medicines and vaccines for all.	5. Number of governmental physicians, nurses and midwives per 1, 00,000 populations.	550

Source: (NITI Aayog 2018).

7.5. Indian's SDG-3 Index Indicators, Data Source and Interpretations

The NITI *Aayog*, Government of India had collected required data from different government agencies to capture the UN SDG's target indicators as well as framed its own indicators to justify the achievement of the SDGs. Apart from that the NITI *Aayog* had developed the computational approach of the disaggregated data as per valid methods along with the parameters of the performance; in the following tables (Table no-24, Table no-25, Table no-26, Table no-27 and Table no-28) shows the details of the above issue to develop a sense of progress of the SDG-3, entitled as 'Good Health and Well-being'.

Table No. 24: SDG-3, Indian Indicator-1

SDG-3: Good Health and Well-being	**Indicator-1:** Maternal Mortality Ratio.
Indicator data source	Ministry of Home Affairs [Sample Registration System]
Computation approach	Directly from data source
Data period (year)	2014-2016
States/UTs covered	19
Data periodicity	3 years
Relevant UN target	3.1: By 2030, reduce the global maternal mortality ratio to less than 70 per 100,000 live Births.
Relevant UN indicator	3.1.1: Maternal mortality ratio.
Relevant MoSPI indicator	3.1.1: Maternal mortality ratio.
Indicator interpretation	Higher value means lower performance (-).

Source: (NITI Aayog 2018).

Table No. 25: SDG-3, Indian Indicator-2

SDG-3: Good Health and Well-being	**Indicator-2:** Maternal Mortality Ratio.
Indicator data source	Ministry of Home Affairs [Sample Registration System]
Computation approach	Directly from data source
Data period (year)	2041-2016
States/UTs covered	35
Data periodicity	3 years
Relevant UN target	3.2: By 2030, end preventable deaths of new-borns and children under 5 years of age, with all countries aiming to reduce neonatal mortality to at least as low as 12 per, 1000 live births and under-5 mortality to at least as low as 25 per 1,000 live births.
Relevant UN indicator	3.2.1: Under-5 mortality rate.
Relevant MoSPI indicator	3.2.1: Under-5 mortality rate.
Indicator interpretation	Higher value means lower performance (-).

Source: (NITI Aayog 2018).

Table No. 26: SDG-3, Indian Indicator-3

SDG-3: Good Health and Well-being	**Indicator-3:** Percentage of children aged 12 -23 months fully immunized (BCG, Measles and three doses of Pentavalent vaccine).
Indicator data source	Ministry of Home Affairs [Sample Registration System]
Computation approach	Directly from data source
Data period (year)	2041-2016
States/UTs covered	36
Data periodicity	3 years
Relevant UN target	3.2: By 2030, end preventable deaths of new-borns and children under 5 years of age, with all countries aiming to reduce neonatal mortality to at least as low as 12 per, 1000 live births and under-5 mortality to at least as low as 25 per 1,000 live births.
Relevant UN indicator	NA
Relevant MoSPI indicator	3.2.3: Percentage of children aged 12-23 months fully immunized (BCG, Measles and three doses Pentavalent vaccine).
Indicator interpretation	Higher value means higher performance (+)

Table No. 27: SDG-3, Indian Indicator-4

SDG-3: Good Health and Well-being	**Indicator-4:** Annual notification of Tuberculosis cases per 1 lakh population.
Indicator data source	Ministry of Home Affairs [Sample Registration System]
Computation approach	Directly from data source
Data period (year)	2041-2016
States/UTs covered	36
Data periodicity	Annual
Relevant UN target	3.3: By 2030, end the epidemics of AIDS, tuberculosis, malaria and neglected tropical diseases and combat hepatitis, water-borne diseases and other communicable diseases.
Relevant UN indicator	3.3.2: Tuberculosis incidence per 100,000 populations.
Relevant MoSPI indicator	3.3.2: Tuberculosis incidence per 100,000 populations.
Indicator interpretation	Higher value means lower performance (-)

Source: (NITI Aayog 2018).

Table No. 28: SDG-3, Indian Indicator-5

SDG-3: Good Health and Well-being	**Indicator-5:** Number of governmental physicians, nurses and midwives per 1, 00,000 populations.
Indicator data source	Ministry of Home Affairs [Sample Registration System]
Computation approach	Directly from data source
Data period (year)	2041-2016
States/UTs covered	35
Data periodicity	3 Years
Relevant UN target	3.8: By 2030, achieve universal health coverage, including financial risk protection, access to quality essential health-care services and access to safe, effective, quality and affordable essential medicines and vaccines for all.
Relevant UN indicator	NA
Relevant MoSPI indicator	3.8.8: Total physicians, nurses and midwives per 10000 population
Indicator interpretation	Higher value means higher performance (+)

Source: (NITI Aayog 2018).

7.6. Provisions of the Indian Constitution for SDG-3

The spirit of the unity in this diverse country, India is secured by its great Constitution; the Constitution of India not only secured its unity, announced a vision in the Preamble in the beginning of its Articles included in the Indian Constitution, *"We the people of India, having solemnly resolved to constitute India into a Sovereign Socialist Secular Democratic Republic and to secure to all its citizens: justice, social, economic and political; liberty of thought, expression, belief, faith and worship; equality of status and of opportunity; and to promote among them all fraternity assuring the dignity of the individual and the unity and integrity of the nation; in our Constituent Assembly this twenty-sixth day of November, 1949, do hereby adopt, enact and give to ourselves this Constitution* (India 1950/2015)". The mode of orientation of the Indian Constitution and the sustainable development goals of the contemporary time are given us an opportunity to make a link between these two visions of development and the author is trying to make the link.

As we know the sustainable development goals are interlinked, that means the success or failure of one is affected to other SDGs. From this perspective, this section presents the provisions in the Indian Constitution to eradicate poverty as reflected in the sustainable development agenda entitled as SDG-3, Good Health and Well-being. The linked Constitutional provisions are in the following Table no-29 -

Table No-29: Provisions in Indian Constitution for SDG-3

SDG-3 and the Linked Articles and Schedules of the Constitution of India
Article 15-(2).(a), Article 15-(3), (4) and (5), Article 16-(1) to (5), Article 21A, Article 38-(1) and (2), Article 41, Article 42, Article 43, Article 45, Article 47, Article 48, Article 51A (g), Article 309, Article 310, Article 311, Article 312, Article 313, Article 314, Article 315, Article 320, Article 323A and Article 323B.
Article 246: Seventh Schedule, List-I Union List: 12, 15, 55, 65, 66, 68, 69 and 94. List-II: State List No: 6, 9, 14 to 17, 21 and 23. List-III: Concurrent List No: 19, 20, 20A, 24, 25, 26 and 30.
Article 243G: Eleventh Schedule: Powers, Authority and Responsibilities of Panchayats. Schedule No: 3, 6, 7, 8, 10, 11, 12, 16, 17 and 23 to 29. Article 243W: - Twelfth Schedule: Powers, Authority and Responsibilities of Municipalities. Schedule No: 1, 3, 4, 5, 6, 8, 9, 10, 11 and 16.

Source: The Constitution of India, 2015 as on 9th November, 2015.

7.7. Policies of the Government of India for Targets of the SDG-3

According to the SDG India Index Base Line Report, 2018, India is proactive to achieve the target of the UN's SDGs. The Government of India initiated as well as implemented various policies to capture the indicators of the targets of each individual SDG. On the moment of preparation of SDG India Index Base Line Report, 2018, on the basis of the availability of the disaggregated data, the NITI *Aayog* framed India's own indicators of the targets of each individual SDG. For the SDG-3, that is 'Good Health and Well-being'; the NITI *Aayog* framed five indicators; which capture four out of thirteen UNs SDG targets. As per the report, 45 dedicated policies or schemes are in action to achieve four targets (3.1, 3.2, 3.3 and 3.8) of the UN's SDG-3 under the leadership and monitoring of 19 dedicated Ministries or the Departments. The policies or schemes to achieve the targets of SDG-3 and the concerned dedicated Ministries and the Departments are detailed in the - Table no-30.

Table No. 30: Policies Initiated by the Indian Government for Targets of SDG-3

SDG-3, Good Health and Well-being
SDG-3: Good Health and Well-being, which aims to end epidemics and preventable deaths and achieve universal health coverage, including financial risk protection and access to quality essential health care services, medicines and vaccines for all the SDG linked with the SDGs – 1, 2, 4, 5, 6, 10, 11 and 12.
Target: 3.1: By 2030, reduce the global maternal mortality ratio to less than 70 per 100,000 live births.

(*Contd...*)

Centrally Sponsored /Central Sector Schemes (CSS)	Concerned Ministries/ Departments
1. National Health Mission (NRHM RCH Flexible Pool including Health System Strengthening, Routine Immunisation Programme, National Iodine Deficiency programme, Pulse Polio Immunisation Disorders Control Programme etc., National Urban Health Mission – Flexible Pool) 2. Human Resources for Health & Medical Education	Ministry of Family & Health Welfare
3. National AYUSH Mission	AYUSH
4. Umbrella ICDS 5. *Pradhan Mantri Matru Vandana Yojana* (PMMVY)	Ministry of Women and Child Development
Target: 3.2: By 2030, end preventable deaths of new-borns and children under 5 years of age, with all countries aiming to reduce neonatal mortality to at least as low as 12 per 1,000 live births and under-5 mortality to at least as low as 25 per 1,000 live births.	
Centrally Sponsored /Central Sector Schemes (CSS)	Concerned Ministries/ Departments
1. National Health Mission (NRHM RCH Flexible Pool including Health System Strengthening, Routine Immunisation Programme, National Iodine Deficiency programme, Pulse Polio Immunisation Disorders Control Programme etc., National Urban Health Mission – Flexible Pool) 2. Mission *Indradhanush*	Ministry of Family & Health Welfare
3. National AYUSH Mission	AYUSH
4. Umbrella ICDS	Ministry of Women and Child Development
Target: 3.3: By 2030, end the epidemics of AIDS, tuberculosis, malaria and neglected tropical diseases and combat hepatitis, water-borne diseases and other communicable diseases.	
Centrally Sponsored /Central Sector Schemes (CSS)	Concerned Ministries/ Departments
1. NHM - Flexible Pool for Communicable Diseases 2. National AIDS Control Programme	Ministry of Family & Health Welfare
3. National AYUSH Mission	AYUSH
4. *Swachh Bharat Mission* (SBM) – Rural 5. National Rural Drinking Water programme	Drinking Water and Sanitation
6. *Swachh Bharat* Mission (SBM) – Rural 7. Atal Mission for Rejuvenation and Urban Transformation (AMRUT)	Ministry of Housing and Urban Affairs
8. *Shyama Prasad Mukherjee* RURBAN Mission	Ministry of Rural Development
9. *Pradhan Mantri Ujjwala Yojana*	Ministry of Petroleum & Natural Gas
10. *Pradhan Mantri Kisan* SAMPADA *Yojana*	Food Processing Industries
11. Special Central Assistance to Tribal Sub Scheme 12. Umbrella Programme for Development of Scheduled Tribes	Ministry of Tribal Affairs
Target: 3.4: By 2030, reduce by one third premature mortality from non-communicable diseases through prevention and treatment and promote mental health and well- being.	
Centrally Sponsored /Central Sector Schemes (CSS)	Concerned Ministries/ Departments
1. NHM- Flexible Pool for Non-Communicable Diseases, Injury and Trauma 2. NHM-Human Resources for Health & Medical Education 3. NHM-Strengthening of State Drug Regulatory System.	Ministry of Family & Health Welfare
4. National AYUSH Mission	AYUSH

(*Contd*...)

5. Special Central Assistance to Tribal Sub Scheme 6. Umbrella Programme for Development of Scheduled Tribes	Ministry of Tribal Affairs
Target: 3.5: Strengthen the prevention and treatment of substance abuse, including narcotic drug abuse and harmful use of alcohol.	
Centrally Sponsored /Central Sector Schemes (CSS)	Concerned Ministries/ Departments
1. Scheme for Prevention of Alcoholism and Substance (Drugs) Abuse	Ministry of Social Justice & Empowerment
2. National AYUSH Mission	AYUSH
3. Police Infrastructure (Narcotics Control Bureau, etc.)	Ministry of Home Affairs
Target: 3.6: By 2020, halve the number of global deaths and injuries from road traffic accidents.	
Centrally Sponsored /Central Sector Schemes (CSS)	Concerned Ministries/ Departments
1. Road Safety Schemes (Publicity and awareness generation, NHARSS-National Highways Accident Relief Service Project, Institute of Driving Training and Research, etc.)	Ministry of Road Transport & Highways
2. National Health Mission	Ministry of Family & Health Welfare
3. National AYUSH Mission	AYUSH
Target: 3.7: By 2030, ensure universal access to sexual and reproductive healthcare services, including for family planning, information and education, and the integration of reproductive health into national strategies and programmes.	
Centrally Sponsored /Central Sector Schemes (CSS)	Concerned Ministries/ Departments
1. National Health Mission (RCH Flexible Pool) 2. National AYUSH Mission	Ministry of Family & Health Welfare AYUSH
3. Umbrella ICDS	Ministry of Women and Child Development
Target: 3.8: Achieve universal health coverage, including financial risk protection access to quality essential health-care services and access to safe effective quality and affordable essential medicines and vaccines for all.	
Centrally Sponsored /Central Sector Schemes (CSS)	Concerned Ministries/ Departments
1. National Health Protection Scheme (*Ayushman Bharat*) 2. National Health Mission (RCH Flexible Pool) 3. National Health Mission (Flexible Pool for communicable diseases) 4. National Health Mission (Flexible Pool for non-communicable diseases) 5. National AIDS Control Programme 6. Medical treatment of CGHS pensioners (PORB) 7. NHM-Human Resources for Health & Medical Education	Ministry of Family & Health Welfare
8. National AYUSH Mission	AYUSH
9. Umbrella ICDS	Ministry of Women and Child Development
10. Umbrella Programme for Development of STs & Minorities	Tribal Affairs
11. Umbrella Programme for Development of Minorities including Development of Minorities - Multi Sectoral Development Programme for Minorities (MSDP).	Ministry of Minority Affairs
12. *Jan Aushudhi* Scheme	Ministry of Chemicals & Fertilizers

(*Contd*...)

<table>
<tr><td colspan="2">Target: 3.9: By 2030 substantially reduce the number of deaths and illnesses from hazardous chemicals and air, water and soil pollution and contamination.</td></tr>
<tr><td>Centrally Sponsored /Central Sector Schemes (CSS)</td><td>Concerned Ministries/ Departments</td></tr>
<tr><td>1. Environment Protection, Management and Sustainable Development (Pollution Abatement)
2. Decision Support conservation skills and System for Environmental Policy, Planning and Outcome Evaluation</td><td>MoEF&CC</td></tr>
<tr><td>3. Urban Transport including Metro Projects, UT Planning Scheme & Capacity Building</td><td>Ministry of Housing and Urban Affairs</td></tr>
<tr><td>4. National River Conservation Programme
5. Research & Development and Implementation of National Water Mission</td><td>Ministry of Water Resources, River Development & Ganga Rejuvenation</td></tr>
<tr><td>6. Development of Major and Minor Ports</td><td>Ministry of Shipping</td></tr>
<tr><td colspan="2">Target: 3.a: Strengthen the implementation of the World Health Organization Framework Convention on Tobacco Control in all countries, as appropriate.</td></tr>
<tr><td>Centrally Sponsored /Central Sector Schemes (CSS)</td><td>Concerned Ministries/ Departments</td></tr>
<tr><td>1. National Tobacco Control Programme</td><td>Ministry of Family & Health Welfare</td></tr>
<tr><td colspan="2">Target: 3.b: Support the research and development of vaccines and medicines for the communicable and non-communicable diseases and that primarily affect developing countries, provide access to affordable essential medicines and vaccines, in accordance with the Doha Declaration on the TRIPS Agreement and Public Health, which affirms the right to developing countries to use to the full the provisions in the Agreement on Trade-Related Aspects of Intellectual Property Rights regarding flexibilities to protect public health, and, in particular, provide access to medicines for all.</td></tr>
<tr><td>Centrally Sponsored /Central Sector Schemes (CSS)</td><td>Concerned Ministries/ Departments</td></tr>
<tr><td>1. National Health Mission
2. Setting up of a Network of Laboratories for Managing Epidemics and National Calamities
3. Development of Infrastructure for Promotion of Health Research</td><td>Family & Health Welfare</td></tr>
<tr><td>4. National AYUSH Mission and allied schemes related to pharmaceuticals</td><td>AYUSH</td></tr>
<tr><td>5. Innovation, Technology Development and Deployment
6. Biotechnology Research &Development</td><td>Science & Technology</td></tr>
<tr><td>7. National Institutes of Pharmaceutical Education and Research (NIPERs)</td><td>Chemicals & Fertilizers</td></tr>
<tr><td colspan="2">Target: 3.c: Substantially increase health financing and the recruitment, development, training and retention of the health workforce in developing countries, especially in least developed countries and small island developing States.</td></tr>
<tr><td>Centrally Sponsored /Central Sector Schemes (CSS)</td><td>Concerned Ministries/ Departments</td></tr>
<tr><td>1. NHM - Human Resources for Health & Medical Education
2. Human Resource & Capacity Development</td><td>Family & Health Welfare</td></tr>
<tr><td>3. Umbrella ICDS</td><td>Women and Child Development</td></tr>
<tr><td>Target: 3.d: Strengthen the capacity of all countries, in particular developing countries, for early warning, risk reduction and management of national and global health risks.</td><td>Health & FW,
AYUSH</td></tr>
</table>

Source: (NITI Aayog 2018).

7.8. Initiatives, Expectation and Performance of Government of India in SDG-3

According to the SDG India Index Base Line Report, 2018 (NITI Aayog 2018), to achieving the target of the UN's SDG-3, the Government of India has framed five indicators. The Government of India reported that, 45 dedicated policies or schemes are in to achieve four targets (3.1, 3.2, 3.3 and 3.8) of the UN's SDG-3 under the leadership and monitoring of 19 dedicated Ministries or the Departments. The SDG-3 indicators are –

SDG_3_1: Maternal mortality ratio.

SDG_3_2: Under five years mortality rate per 1,000 live births.

SDG_3_3: Percentage of children aged 12 -23 months fully immunized (BCG, Measles and three doses of Pentavalent vaccine).

SDG_3_4: Annual notification of Tuberculosis cases per 1 lakh population.

SDG_3_5: Number of governmental physicians, nurses and midwives per 1, 00,000 populations.

Table No. 31: India's SDG-16=71 and the Performances in SDG-3

	SDG_3_1	SDG_3_2	SDG_3_3	SDG_3_4	SDG_3_5
UN Target of this SDG	70	11	100	0	549.96
Performance of India	130	50	62	138.33	220.96
India SDG-16 Score	71	71	71	71	71
India SDG Mean Score	57	57	57	57	57
Expected Performance, When SDG-16=71	49.7	7.81	71	0	390.47
Indicator Interpretation	Value High - Performance Low	Value High - Performance Low	Value High - Performance High	Value High - Performance Low	Value High - Performance High
Performance Difference, When SDG-16=71	-80.3	-42.19	-9	-138.33	-169.51

Data Source: NITI *Aayog*, 2018 and Inference drawn by the author.

Inference: It was assumed that, 'Peace, Justice and Strong Institutions' are the pre-conditions of achievement.

Here, Expected Performance = India SDG 16 Score (UN target of this SDG / 100) and

Performance Difference = (Expected Performance - Performance of India)

From the above conditions it is explored in the table no-31.

For the SDG_3_1: That is 'Maternal mortality ratio', here the performance of India is negatively differed (130) from its expected score 49.7, when SDG-16 score is 71 and here performance have to reduce to a level of 80.3 from the present performance. So India have to devote its tools of 'Peace, Justice and Strong Institutions' in a better way for a better score. Here the performance difference is -80.3.

For the SDG_3_2: That is 'Under five years mortality rate per 1,000 live births', here the performance of India is negatively differed (50) from its expected score 7.81, when SDG-16 score is 71 and here performance have to reduce to a level of 42.19 from the present performance. So India have to devote its tools of 'Peace, Justice and Strong Institutions' in a better way for a better score. Here the performance difference is -42.19.

For the SDG_3_3: That is 'Under five years mortality rate per 1,000 live births', here the performance of India is negatively differed (62) from its expected score 71, when SDG-16 score is 71 and here performance have to increase to a level of 9 from the present performance. So India have to devote its tools of 'Peace, Justice and Strong Institutions' in a better way for a better score. Here the performance difference is -9.

For the SDG_3_4: That is 'Annual notification of Tuberculosis cases per 1 lakh population', here the performance of India is negatively differed (138.33) from its expected score '0', when SDG-16 score is 71 and here performance have to reduce to a level of '0' from the present performance. So India have to devote its tools of 'Peace, Justice and Strong Institutions' in a better way for a better score. Here the performance difference is -138.33.

For the SDG_3_5: That is 'Number of governmental physicians, nurses and midwives per 1, 00,000 populations', here the performance of India is negatively differed (220.96) from its expected score 390.47, when SDG-16 score is 71 and here performance have to increase to a level of 169.51 from the present performance. So India have to devote its tools of 'Peace, Justice and Strong Institutions' in a better way for a better score. Here the performance difference is -169.59.

7.9. Government of India's Remaining Targets and the Indicators for SDG-3

As we know that, on the basis of the availability of the disaggregated data, the NITI *Aayog* had framed India's own indicators of the targets of each individual SDG. For the SDG-3, that is 'Good Health and Well-being', the NITI *Aayog* had framed five indicators; which captured three (3.1.1, 3.2.1 and 3.3.2) of twenty six indicators of the thirteen UNs SDG targets. As per the report, 45 dedicated policies or schemes are in action to achieve four targets (3.1, 3.2, 3.3 and 3.8) of the UN's SDG-3; the remaining indicators of the UN's SDG-3 is to be achieve by 2030. The remaining lists of targets along with the indicators of SDG-3 are detailed in Table no-32.

Table No. 32: Government of India's Remaining Targets and the Indicators for SDG-3

India's Remaining Targets and the Indicators for SDG-3	
Targets	**Indicators**
3.1: By 2030, reduce the global maternal mortality ratio to less than 70 per 100,000 live births [i].	3.1.1: Maternal mortality ratio [ii].
	3.1.2: Proportion of births attended by skilled health personnel [iv].
3.2: By 2030, end preventable deaths of new-borns and children under 5 years of age, with all countries aiming to reduce neonatal mortality to at least as low as 12 per 1,000 live births and under-5 mortality to at least as low as 25 per 1,000 live births [i].	3.2.1: Under-five mortality rate [ii].
	3.2.2: Neonatal mortality rate [iv].
3.3: By 2030, end the epidemics of AIDS, tuberculosis, malaria and neglected tropical diseases and combat hepatitis, water-borne diseases and other communicable diseases [i].	3.3.1: Number of new HIV infections per 1,000 uninfected population, by sex, age and key populations [iv].
	3.3.2: Tuberculosis incidence per 1,000 population [ii].
	3.3.3: Malaria incidence per 1,000 populations [iv].
	3.3.4: Hepatitis B incidence per 100,000 populations [iv].
	3.3.5: Number of people requiring interventions against neglected tropical diseases [iv].
3.4: By 2030, reduce by one third premature mortality from non-communicable diseases through prevention and treatment and promote mental health and well-being [iv].	3.4.1: Mortality rate attributed to cardiovascular disease, cancer, diabetes or chronic respiratory disease [iv].
	3.4.2: Suicide mortality rate [iv].
3.5: Strengthen the prevention and treatment of substance abuse, including narcotic drug abuse and harmful use of alcohol [iv].	3.5.1: Coverage of treatment interventions (pharmacological, psychosocial and rehabilitation and aftercare services) for substance use disorders [iv].
	3.5.2: Harmful use of alcohol, defined according to the national context as alcohol per capita consumption (aged 15 years and older) within a calendar year in litres of pure alcohol [iv].
3.6: By 2020, halve the number of global deaths and injuries from road traffic accidents [iv].	3.6.1: Death rate due to road traffic injuries [iv].

(Contd...)

Target	Indicator
3.7: By 2030, ensure universal access to sexual and reproductive health-care services, including for family planning, information and education, and the integration of reproductive health into national strategies and programmes [iv].	3.7.1: Proportion of women of reproductive age (aged 15-49 years) who have their need for family planning satisfied with modern methods [iv].
	3.7.2: Adolescent birth rate (aged 10-14 years; aged 15-19 years) per 1,000 women in that age group [iv].
3.8: Achieve universal health coverage, including financial risk protection, access to quality essential health-care services and access to safe, effective, quality and affordable essential medicines and vaccines for all [iii].	3.8.1: Coverage of essential health services (defined as the average coverage of essential services based on tracer interventions that include reproductive, maternal, new-born and child health, infectious diseases, non-communicable diseases and service capacity and access, among the general and the most disadvantaged population) [iv].
	3.8.2: Number of people covered by health insurance or a public health system per 1,000 populations [iv].
3.9: By 2030, substantially reduce the number of deaths and illnesses from hazardous chemicals and air, water and soil pollution and contamination [iv].	3.9.1: Mortality rate attributed to household and ambient air pollution [4].
	3.9.2: Mortality rate attributed to unsafe water, unsafe sanitation and lack of hygiene (exposure to unsafe Water, Sanitation and Hygiene for All (WASH) services) [iv].
	3.9.3: Mortality rate attributed to unintentional poisoning [iv].
3.a.: Strengthen the implementation of the World Health Organization Framework Convention on Tobacco Control in all countries, as appropriate [iv].	3.a.1: Age-standardized prevalence of current tobacco use among persons aged 15 years and older [iv].
3.b.: Support the research and development of vaccines and medicines for the communicable and non-communicable diseases that primarily affect developing countries, provide access to affordable essential medicines and vaccines, in accordance with the Doha Declaration on the TRIPS Agreement and Public Health, which affirms the right of developing countries to use to the full the provisions in the Agreement on Trade-Related Aspects of Intellectual Property Rights regarding flexibilities to protect public health, and, in particular, provide access to medicines for all [iv].	3.b.1: Proportion of the population with access to affordable medicines and vaccines on a sustainable basis [iv].
	3. b.2: Total net official development assistance to medical research and basic health sectors [iv].
3.c.: Substantially increase health financing and the recruitment, development, training and retention of the health workforce in developing countries, especially in least developed countries and small island developing States [iv].	3.c.1: Health worker density and distribution [iv].
3.d.: Strengthen the capacity of all countries, in particular developing countries, for early warning, risk reduction and management of national and global health risks [iv].	3.d.1: International Health Regulations (IHR) capacity and health emergency preparedness [iv].

(*Contd...*)

Notes of the Table:

i. Not captured all the indicators.
ii. Target indicators captured and analysed.
iii. Only the target captured.
iv. Remaining.

The Ministries and the Departments associate with indicators of this SDG such as, YUSH, Chemicals & Fertilizers, Drinking Water and Sanitation, Family & Health Welfare, Food Processing Industries, Home Affairs, Housing and Urban Affairs, Minority Affairs, MoEF&CC, National AYUSH Mission, Petroleum & Natural Gas, Road Transport & Highways, Rural Development, Science & Technology, Shipping, Social Justice & Empowerment, Tribal Affairs, Water Resources, River Development & Ganga Rejuvenation and Women and Child Development have to concentrate to monitor on the above issues to achieve the target by 2030 through the provisions of Indian Constitution such as Article 15-(2).(a), Article 15-(3), (4) and (5), Article 16-(1) to (5), Article 21A, Article 38-(1) and (2), Article 41, Article 42, Article 43, Article 45, Article 47, Article 48, Article 51A (g), Article 309, Article 310, Article 311, Article 312, Article 313, Article 314, Article 315, Article 320, Article 323A and Article 323B; Article 246 - Seventh Schedule, List-I-Union List No 12, 15, 55, 65, 66, 68, 69 and 94; List-II-State List No 6, 9, 14 to 17, 21 and 23; List-III-Concurrent List No 19, 20, 20A, 24, 25, 26 and 30; Article 243G - Eleventh Schedule - Powers, Authority and Responsibilities of Panchayats – Schedule No – 3, 6, 7, 8, 10, 11, 12, 16, 17 and 23 to 29 and Article 243W - Twelfth Schedule - Powers, Authority and Responsibilities of Municipalities - Schedule No – 1, 3, 4, 5, 6, 8, 9, 10, 11 and 16 - if we could not monitor, we would not be able to stand in front of the future generation with a smile.

Chapter – VIII

Initiative and Performance of India in SDG-4, Quality Education

The global agenda of SDG-4 is entitled as *Quality Education* that aimed to ensure inclusive and equitable quality education and promote lifelong learning opportunities for all; that is, all girls and boys complete free, equitable and quality primary and secondary education leading to relevant and effective learning outcomes, including technical and vocational skills for employment, decent jobs and entrepreneurship.

Education is the foundation of any society on which dreams of economic growth and development are built. Its role is not only limited to boosting economic growth by enhancing skills and opening up opportunities for sustainable livelihoods, but also to enable people to lead a life of dignity.

The SDG-4 was aimed to ensure inclusive, equitable and quality education for all, including technical and vocational training by providing lifelong learning opportunities, so as to achieve substantial adult literacy and numeracy. It also aims to build and upgrade education facilities that are child, disability and gender sensitive and ensure that all learners acquire knowledge and skills needed to promote sustainable development.

8.1. The Global Targets and Indicators for SDG-4

The global indicator framework was developed by the Inter-Agency and Expert Group on SDG Indicators (IAEG-SDGs) and agreed to, as a practical starting point at the 47th session of the UN Statistical Commission held in March 2016. The report of the Commission, which included the global indicator framework, was then taken note of by ECOSOC at its 70th session in June 2016. The global targets and the indicator of this SDG are tabled (Table no-33) bellow –

Table No. 33: UNDP-DDGs Targets and Indicators of SDG-4

SDG-4, Ensure inclusive and equitable quality education and promote lifelong learning opportunities for all[1]	
Targets	**Indicators**
4.1: By 2030, ensure that all girls and boys complete free, equitable and quality primary and secondary education leading to relevant and effective learning outcomes.	4.1.1: Proportion of children and young people: (a) in grades 2/3; (b) at the end of primary; and (c) at the end of lower secondary achieving at least a minimum proficiency level in (i) reading and (ii) mathematics, by sex.
4.2: By 2030, ensure that all girls and boys have access to quality early childhood development, care and pre-primary education so that they are ready for primary education.	4.2.1: Proportion of children under 5 years of age who are developmentally on track in health, learning and psychosocial well-being, by sex.
	4.2.2: Participation rate in organized learning (one year before the official primary entry age), by sex.
4.3: By 2030, ensure equal access for all women and men to affordable and quality technical, vocational and tertiary education, including university.	4.3.1: Participation rate of youth and adults in formal and non-formal education and training in the previous 12 months, by sex.
4.4: By 2030, substantially increase the number of youth and adults who have relevant skills, including technical and vocational skills, for employment, decent jobs and entrepreneurship.	4.4.1: Proportion of youth and adults with information and communications technology (ICT) skills, by type of skill.
4.5: By 2030, eliminate gender disparities in education and ensure equal access to all levels of education and vocational training for the vulnerable, including persons with disabilities, indigenous peoples and children in vulnerable situations.	4.5.1: Parity indices (female/male, rural/urban, bottom/top wealth quintile and others such as disability status, indigenous peoples and conflict affected, as data become available) for all education indicators on this list that can be disaggregated.
4.6: By 2030, ensure that all youth and a substantial proportion of adults, both men and women, achieve literacy and numeracy.	4.6.1: Percentage of population in a given age group achieving at least a fixed level of proficiency in functional (a) literacy and (b) numeracy skills, by sex.
4.7: By 2030, ensure that all learners acquire the knowledge and skills needed to promote sustainable development, including, among others, through education for sustainable development and sustainable lifestyles, human rights, gender equality, promotion of a culture of peace and non-violence, global citizenship and appreciation of cultural diversity and of culture's contribution to sustainable development.	4.7.1: Extent to which (i) global citizenship education and (ii) education for sustainable development, including gender equality and human rights, are mainstreamed at all levels in: (a) national education policies, (b) curricula, (c) teacher education and (d) student assessment.
4.a: Build and upgrade education facilities that are child, disability and gender sensitive and provide safe, non-violent, inclusive and effective learning environments for all.	4.a.1: Proportion of schools with access to: (a) electricity; (b) the Internet for pedagogical purposes; (c) computers for pedagogical purposes; (d) adapted infrastructure and materials for students with disabilities; (e) basic drinking water; (f) single sex basic sanitation facilities; and (g) basic handwashing facilities (as per the WASH indicator definitions).

(Contd...)

1. Data Source: SDG India Index Baseline Report, 2018, NITI *Aayog*, Government of India, New Delhi.

4.b: By 2020, substantially expand globally the number of scholarships available to developing countries, in particular least developed countries, small island developing States and African countries, for enrolment in higher education, including vocational training and information and communications technology, technical, engineering and scientific programmes, in developed countries and other developing countries.	4.b.1: Volume of official development assistance flows for scholarships by sector and type of study.
4.c: By 2030, substantially increase the supply of qualified teachers, including through international cooperation for teacher training in developing countries, especially least developed countries and small island developing States.	4.c.1: Proportion of teachers in: (a) pre-primary; (b) primary; (c) lower secondary; and (d) upper secondary education who have received at least the minimum organized teacher training (e.g. pedagogical training) pre-service or in-service required for teaching at the relevant level in a given country.

8.2. Interlinkage of SDG-4 with other SDGs

This section presents the linkage of the SDG-4 to other SDGs, that is, the success of this SDG habitually will influence the success of the linked SDGs; according to the SDG India Index, Baseline Report, 2018 (NITI Aayog 2018), the SDG-4 linked with the following SDGs –

SDG-1, that is *No Poverty*, which was aimed to reduce poverty in all its dimensions, which includes ensuring access to safe, nutritious and sufficient food all year round, particularly for the poor.

SDG-2, that is *Zero Hunger*, which aims to end all forms of malnutrition and ensures access to safe, nutritious and sufficient food for all, in particular the poor and vulnerable, and support small scale food producers.

SDG-3, is *Good Health and Well-being*, which aims to end epidemics and preventable deaths and achieve universal health coverage, including financial risk protection and access to quality essential health care services, medicines and vaccines for all.

SDG-5, is *Gender Equality* as Goal 1 emphasises creation of gender sensitive development strategies, and equal rights and access to economic resources, as well as ownership and control over land and other forms of property, inheritance, natural resources and financial resources, including microfinance.

SDG-6, is *Clean Water and Sanitation*, which aims to achieve universal and equitable access to safe and affordable drinking water and sanitation and hygiene for all.

SDG-8, is *Decent Work and Economic Growth* which aims to promote development oriented policies that support productive activities, decent job creation, entrepreneurship, and encourage the formalization and growth of micro-, small - and medium-sized enterprises through access to financial services.

SDG-9, is *Industry, Innovation and Infrastructure* aims at building quality, reliable and resilient infrastructures. It further aims at promoting resource-use efficiency and greater adoption of clean and environmentally sound technologies and industrial processes, to support economic development and human well-being. Investment in innovation is an important pillar of this goal.

SDG-10, is *Reduced Inequalities* that aims to adopt policies, especially fiscal wage and social protection policies and progressively achieve and sustain income growth of the bottom 40 percent of the population at a rate higher than the national average, leading to greater equality.

SDG-12, *Sustainable Consumption and Production* aiming to halve per capita global food waste at consumer level and reduce food losses along production and supply chains.

SDG-13, is *Climate Action* which aims to develop resilience and adaptive capacity of the poor to climate related hazards and natural disasters.

8.3. The National Context of SDG-4

Education is a fundamental right that empowers people and ensures that they are able to lead a productive life in a globalising world. Recognising this, the Government of India amended the Constitution to include the Right of Children to Free and Compulsory Education (RTE) Act, 2009. It acknowledges that every child has a right to full time elementary education of satisfactory and equitable quality in a formal school. Further, the national and State governments have various schemes and programmes to ensure that children from the vulnerable sections of the societies enrol in and attend schools. Two of the many schemes, namely *Sarva Shiksha Abhiyan* and the Mid-day Meal scheme have had a huge impact and success in the country. The Mid-day Meal scheme is aimed at increasing enrolment in primary schools as well as improving the nutritional status of primary school children. *Sarva Shiksha Abhiyan*, on the other hand, aims to universalise elementary education across the country.

The Government of India recognises the challenges faced by the education sector in the country and has come up with innovative programmes that address the various needs and issues. The Union Budget 2018-19 has proposed to treat school education holistically without segmentation from pre-nursery to Class 12. To achieve this, a comprehensive programme, *Samagra Shiksha*, has been envisaged with the aim of improving effectiveness of and providing equal educational opportunities to all. It has subsumed three previously existing schemes: *Sarva Shiksha Abhiyan* (SSA), *Rashtriya Madhyamik Shiksha Abhiyan* (RMSA) and Teacher Education (TE). The objective is also to enhance use of digital technology in education through smart classrooms, digital boards and Direct to Home channels. Digital initiatives like *Shala Kosh, Shagun, Shaala Saarthi* are also helping promote technology in the education sector.

Sarva Shiksha Abhiyan, launched in 2000-2001continues to be India's main programme for universal elementary education. The interventions under SSA include building of school infrastructure, provisioning for teachers, periodic teacher training and academic resource support, making available learning resources for children like text books, computers, libraries, etc. To ensure equal learning opportunities for all, including girls and the poor, residential schools for girls known as *Kasturba Gandhi Balika Vidyalayas* have been set up, and local level accountability has been established by engaging with community based organizations. The Mid-day Meal scheme is aimed at increasing enrolment in primary schools as well as improving the nutritional status of primary school children.

The country moved to a right-based education framework with the implementation of Right of Children to Free and Compulsory Education (RTE) Act, 2009. The right casts legal obligation on the Central and State governments to provide and ensure admission, attendance and completion of elementary education by all children in the 6-14 age group. In addition, to improve access to secondary education, *Rashtriya Madhyamik Shiksha Abhiyan* was launched in 2009 to achieve an enrolment rate of 75 percent at secondary school level by providing a secondary school within reasonable distance of habitation.

As per report the Adjusted Net Enrolment Ratio at Elementary (Class 1-8) and Secondary (Class 9-10) schools in India is 75.83 percent. All States/UTs are yet to achieve the target of 100 percent enrolment. Among the States, Tripura has the highest enrolment ratio of 94.72 percent, while Delhi leads the UTs with an enrolment ratio of 92.95 percent.

On the account of student proficiency in Class 5 and 8, 54.69 percent of responses on Language, Mathematics and Environmental Science (EVS) were attempted correctly by Class 5 students across the country.

This percentage stood at 44.58 percent for Class 8 students when assessed Language, Mathematics, Science and Social Sciences.

Only 2.97 percent of children in the age-group 6-13 years are out of school in India. Seventeen States/Union Territories have achieved the national target of reducing this rate to two percent. Himachal Pradesh and Puducherry perform the best among States and Union Territories respectively.

The average annual dropout rate at secondary level is a major threat to quality education even having the government initiatives along with the RTE. In India, there still 17.06 of school students are dropout at Secondary level I n India, against the 2030 target of reducing this rate to below 10 percent. Three States - Himachal Pradesh, Punjab and Tamil Nadu and two Union Territories – Andaman and Nicobar Islands and Lakshadweep Islands have already achieved the 2030 target of reducing the dropout rate to 10 percent or less.

India having 81.15 percent of school teachers in India are professionally qualified for their job. The national target for 2030 is to have all teachers to be professionally qualified Delhi has already achieved this milestone. Not far are Gujrat, Maharashtra and Puducherry.

70.43 percent of elementary and secondary schools in India have achieved a Pupil Teacher Ratio of less than or equal to 30. The 2030 national target is to have 100 percent schools providing at least one teacher for 30 students. UT of Lakshadweep Islands has already achieved this target.

In the next part of this chapter we tried to visualized the performance level of India through the SDG's targets and the SDG India Index Base Line Report, 2018 along with the Constitutional provisions in India to explore citizen's responsibility along with the its institutions through the mirror of indexed score on 'peace, justice and strong institutions' (SDG-16).

8.4. SDG India Index of SDG-4, Quality Education

India in its SDG India Index Base Line Report, 2018 (NITI Aayog 2018), India had measured the performance of India on the goal of 'Quality Education, India had identified seven national level indicators, which captured two (4.1 and 4.c) out of the ten UN's SDG targets for 2030. These indicators have been selected based on availability of data at national level; these are in Table no-34.

Table No. 34: SDG-4 Targets, National Indicators and Target Values of India

SDG-4 Global Target	Indicator Selected for SDG India Index	National Target Value for 2030
4.1: By 2030, ensure that all girls and boys complete free, equitable and quality primary and secondary education leading to relevant and effective learning outcomes.	1. Adjusted Net Enrolment Ratio at Elementary (Class 1-8) and Secondary (Class (9-10) School.	100
	2. Percentage corrects responses on Learning Outcomes in Language, Mathematics and Environmental Science (EVS) for Class – 5 Students.	67.89
	3. Percentage corrects responses on Learning Outcomes in Language, Mathematics, Science and Social Science for Class 8 students.	57.17
	4. Percentage of children in the Age-group 6-13 who are out of school.	0.28
	5. Average Annual Drop-out Rate at Secondary level	10
4.c: By 2030, substantially increase the supply of qualified teachers, including through international cooperation for teacher training in developing countries, especially least developed countries and small island developing States.	6. Percentage of School Teachers Professionally Qualified.	100
	7. Percentage of elementary and secondary schools with Pupil Teacher Ratio less than/equal to 30.	100

Source: (NITI Aayog 2018).

8.5. Indian's SDG-4 Index Indicators, Data Source and Interpretations

The NITI *Aayog*, Government of India had collected required data from different government agencies to capture the UN SDG's target indicators as well as had framed its own indicators to justify the achievement of the SDGs. Apart from that the NITI *Aayog* had developed the computational approach of the disaggregated data as per valid methods along with the parameters of the performance; in the following tables (Table no-35, Table no-36, Table no-37, Table no-38, Table no-39, Table no-40 and Table no-41) shows the details of the above issue to develop a sense of progress of the SDG-4, entitled as 'Quality Education'.

Table No. 35: SDG-4, Indian Indicator-1

SDG-4: 'Quality Education'	**Indicator-1:** Adjusted Net Enrolment Ratio at Elementary (Class 1-8) and Secondary (Class (9-10) School (%).
Indicator data source	National Institute of Education Planning and Implementation [Unified-District-Information System for Education]
Computation approach	(Adjusted Net Enrolment Ratio at Elementary School + Adjusted Net Enrolment Ratio at Secondary School) ÷ 2
Data period (year)	2016-2017
States/UTs covered	36
Data periodicity	Annual
Relevant UN target	4.1: By 2030, ensure that all girls and boys complete free, equitable and quality primary and secondary education leading to relevant and effective learning outcomes.
Relevant UN indicator	NA
Relevant MoSPI indicator	4.1.2: Adjusted net enrolment ratio in primary, upper primary and secondary education
Indicator interpretation	Higher value means higher performance (+)

Source: (NITI Aayog 2018).

Table No. 36: SDG-4, Indian Indicator-2

SDG-4: 'Quality Education'	**Indicator-2:** Percentage corrects responses on Learning Outcomes in Language, Mathematics and Environmental Science (EVS) for Class – 5 Students.
Indicator data source	Ministry of Human Resource Development - National Council of Educational Research and Training [National Achievement Survey 2017].
Computation approach	Directly from data source
Data period (year)	2016-2017
States/UTs covered	36
Data periodicity	2 years
Relevant UN target	4.1: By 2030, ensure that all girls and boys complete free, equitable and quality primary and secondary education leading to relevant and effective learning outcomes.
Relevant UN indicator	4.1.1: Proportion of children and young people: (a) in grades 2/3; (b) at the end of primary and (c) at the end of lower secondary achieving at least a minimum proficiency level in (i) reading and (ii) mathematics, by sex.
Relevant MoSPI indicator	4.1.4: Percentage of students in grade 3, 8 and 10 achieving at least a minimum proficiency level in terms of nationally defined learning outcomes to be attained by the pupils at the end of each of above grades.
Indicator interpretation	Higher value means higher performance (+)

Source: (NITI Aayog 2018).

Table No. 37: SDG-4, Indian Indicator-3

SDG-4: 'Quality Education'	**Indicator–3:** Percentage corrects responses on Learning Outcomes in Language, Mathematics, Science and Social Science for Class 8 students.
Indicator data source	Ministry of Human Resource Development - National Council of Educational Research and Training [National Achievement Survey 2017].
Computation approach	Directly from data source
Data period (year)	2016-2017
States/UTs covered	36
Data periodicity	2 years
Relevant UN target	4.1: By 2030, ensure that all girls and boys complete free, equitable and quality primary and secondary education leading to relevant and effective learning outcomes.
Relevant UN indicator	4.1.1: Proportion of children and young people: (a) in grades 2/3; (b) at the end of primary and (c) at the end of lower secondary achieving at least a minimum proficiency level in (i) reading and (ii) mathematics, by sex.
Relevant MoSPI indicator	4.1.4: Percentage of students in grade 3, 8 and 10 achieving at least a minimum proficiency level in terms of nationally defined learning outcomes to be attained by the pupils at the end of each of above grades.
Indicator interpretation	Higher value means higher performance (+)

Source: (NITI Aayog 2018).

Table No. 38: SDG-4, Indian Indicator-4

SDG-4: 'Quality Education'	**Indicator–4:** Percentage of children in the Age-group 6-13 who are out of school.
Indicator data source	Ministry of Human Resource Development – Social and Rural Research Institute [National Sample Survey of Estimation of out-of-school].
Computation approach	Directly from data source
Data period (year)	2014
States/UTs covered	34
Data periodicity	4 years
Relevant UN target	4.1: By 2030, ensure that all girls and boys complete free, equitable and quality primary and secondary education leading to relevant and effective learning outcomes.
Relevant UN indicator	NA
Relevant MoSPI indicator	4.1.7: Out-of-school ratio (primary, upper primary, elementary, secondary and higher secondary).
Indicator interpretation	Higher value means lower performance (-)

Source: (NITI Aayog 2018).

Table No. 39: SDG-4, Indian Indicator-5

SDG-4: 'Quality Education'	**Indicator–5:** Average Annual Drop-out Rate at Secondary level.
Indicator data source	Ministry of Human Resource Development, Ministry Reports.

(Contd...)

Computation approach	Directly from data source
Data period (year)	2015-16
States/UTs covered	35
Data periodicity	2 years
Relevant UN target	4.1: By 2030, ensure that all girls and boys complete free, equitable and quality primary and secondary education leading to relevant and effective learning outcomes.
Relevant UN indicator	NA
Relevant MoSPI indicator	NA
Indicator interpretation	Higher value means lower performance (-)

Source: (NITI Aayog 2018).

Table No. 40: SDG-4, Indian Indicator-6

SDG-4: 'Quality Education'	**Indicator–6:** Percentage of School Teachers Professionally Qualified.
Indicator data source	National Institute of Education Planning and Implementation [Unified-District-Information System for Education].
Computation approach	Directly from data source
Data period (year)	2016-17
States/UTs covered	36
Data periodicity	2 years
Relevant UN target	4.c: By 2030, substantially increase the supply of qualified teachers, including through international cooperation for teacher training in developing countries, especially least developed countries and small island developing States.
Relevant UN indicator	4.c.1: Proportion of teachers in (a) pre-primary; (b) primary; (c) lower secondary; and (d) upper secondary education who have received at least the minimum organized teacher training (e. g. pedagogical training) pre-service or in-service required for teaching at the relevant level in a given country.
Relevant MoSPI indicator	4.c.1: Proportion of trained teachers, by educational level (pre-primary, primary, upper primary, elementary, secondary, and higher secondary education.
Indicator interpretation	Higher value means higher performance (+)

Source: (NITI Aayog 2018).

Table No. 41: SDG-4, Indian Indicator-7

SDG-4: 'Quality Education'	**Indicator–7:** Percentage of elementary and secondary schools with Pupil Teacher Ratio less than/equal to 30.
Indicator data source	National Institute of Education Planning and Implementation [Unified-District-Information System for Education].
Computation approach	Directly from data source
Data period (year)	2016-17
States/UTs covered	36
Data periodicity	2 years
Relevant UN target	4.c: By 2030, substantially increase the supply of qualified teachers, including through international cooperation for teacher training in developing countries, especially least developed countries and small island developing States.

(*Contd...*)

Relevant UN indicator	NA
Relevant MoSPI indicator	4.c.2: Pupil and trained teachers ratio by educational level.
Indicator interpretation	Higher value means higher performance (+)

Source: (NITI Aayog 2018).

8.6. Provisions of the Indian Constitution for SDG-4

The spirit of the unity in this diverse country, India is secured by its great Constitution; the Constitution of India not only secured its unity, announced a vision in the Preamble in the beginning of its Articles included in the Indian Constitution, *"We the people of India, having solemnly resolved to constitute India into a Sovereign Socialist Secular Democratic Republic and to secure to all its citizens: justice, social, economic and political; liberty of thought, expression, belief, faith and worship; equality of status and of opportunity; and to promote among them all fraternity assuring the dignity of the individual and the unity and integrity of the nation; in our Constituent Assembly this twenty-sixth day of November, 1949, do hereby adopt, enact and give to ourselves this Constitution* (India 1950/2015)". The mode of orientation of the Indian Constitution and the sustainable development goals of the contemporary time are given us an opportunity to make a link between these two visions of development and the author is trying to make the link.

As we know the sustainable development goals are interlinked, that means the success or failure of one is affected to other SDGs. From this perspective, this section presents the provisions in the Indian Constitution to eradicate poverty as reflected in the sustainable development agenda entitled as SDG-4, Quality Education. The linked Constitutional provisions are in the following Table no-42 -

Table No. 42: Provisions in Indian Constitution for SDG-4

SDG-4 and the Linked Articles and Schedules of the Constitution of India
Article 15-(1), (4) and (5), Article 16-(1) to (5), Article 19.1 (g), 21A, Article 29-(1) and (2), Article 30-(1), (1A) and (2), Article 38-(1) and (2), Article 41, Article 43, Article 45, Article 46, Article 51A (h) and (k), Article 309, Article 310, Article 311, Article 312, Article 313, Article 314, Article 315, Article 320, Article 323A, Article 323B and Article 351.
Article 246: Seventh Schedule, List-I: Union List No: 12, 25, 62, 63, 64, 65, 66, 67, 68, 69 and 94. List-II: State List No: 14, 15, 32 and 41. List-III: Concurrent List No: 19, 20, 24, 25, 26, 30 and 39.
Article 243G: Eleventh Schedule: Powers, Authority and Responsibilities of Panchayats. Schedule No: 17, 18, 19, 20, 24 and 25. Article 243W: Twelfth Schedule: Powers, Authority and Responsibilities of Municipalities. Schedule No: 1, 3, 12, 13 and 16.

Source: The Constitution of India, 2015 as on 9th November, 2015.

8.7. Policies of the Government of India for Targets of the SDG-4

According to the SDG India Index Base Line Report, 2018 (NITI Aayog 2018), India is proactive to achieve the target of the UN's SDGs. The Government of India initiated as well as implemented various policies to capture the indicators of the targets of each individual SDG. On the moment of preparation of SDG India Index Base Line Report, 2018, on the basis of the availability of the disaggregated data, the NITI *Aayog* framed India's own indicators of the targets of each individual SDG. For the SDG-4, that is 'Quality Education', the NITI *Aayog* framed seven indicators; which capture two out of ten UNs SDG targets. As per the report, 66 dedicated policies or schemes are in action to achieve two targets (4.1 and 4.c) of the UN's SDG-4 under the leadership and monitoring of 13 dedicated Ministries or the Departments. The policies or schemes to achieve the targets of SDG-4 and the concerned dedicated Ministries and the Departments are detailed in the -Table no-43.

Table No. 43: Policies Initiated by the Indian Government for Targets of SDG-4

<table>
<tr><th colspan="2">SDG-4, Quality Education</th></tr>
<tr><td colspan="2">SDG-4: Quality Education, that aims to ensure that all girls and boys complete free, equitable and quality primary and secondary education leading to relevant and effective learning outcomes, including technical and vocational skills for employment, decent jobs and entrepreneurship.</td></tr>
<tr><td colspan="2">Target: 4.1: By 2030, ensure that all girls and boys complete free, equitable and quality primary and secondary education leading to relevant and effective learning outcomes.</td></tr>
<tr><td>Centrally Sponsored /Central Sector Schemes (CSS)</td><td>Concerned Ministries/ Departments</td></tr>
<tr><td>1. Sarva Shiksha Abhiyan,
2. National Programme of Mid Day Meal in Schools (MDM)
3. Rashtriya Madhyamik Shiksha Abhiyan
4. National Means-cum-Merit Scholarship Scheme(NMMSS)
5. Strengthening of Teacher Training Institutions
6. Pandit Madan Mohan Malaviya National Mission on Teachers and Teaching (PMMMNMTT)
7. National Scheme for Incentive to Girl Child for Secondary Education (NSIGSE)</td><td>Ministry of Human Resource Development (School Education & Literacy)</td></tr>
<tr><td>8. Pre-matric scholarships for SC, OBC and vulnerable groups
9. Pre-matric scholarships for children of those engaged in unclean occupations and prone to health hazards
10. Pre-matric Scholarship to students with disabilities
11. Other scholarships & fellowships for SC, OBC Students
12. Free coaching for SC students
13. Hostels for SC & OBC students</td><td>Ministry of Social Justice & Empowerment</td></tr>
<tr><td>14. Pre-matric scholarships for ST students</td><td>Ministry of Tribal Affairs</td></tr>
<tr><td>15. Pre-matric scholarships for minority students</td><td>Ministry of Minority Affairs</td></tr>
</table>

(Contd...)

16. National Child Labour Project (including grants-in-aid to voluntary agencies & reimbursement of assistance to bonded labour)	Ministry of Labour and Employment
Target: 4.2: By 2030, ensure that all girls and boys have access to quality early childhood development, care and pre-primary education so that they are ready for primary education.	
Centrally Sponsored /Central Sector Schemes (CSS)	Concerned Ministries/ Departments
1. Umbrella ICDS (*Aganwadi* Services)	Ministry of Women and Child Development
Target: 4.3: By 2030, ensure equal access for all women and men to affordable and quality technical, vocational and tertiary education, including university.	
Centrally Sponsored /Central Sector Schemes (CSS)	Concerned Ministries/ Departments
1. *Rashtriya Uchhatar Shiksha Abhiyan* 2. Scholarship for College and University Students 3. Interest Subsidy and Contribution for Guarantee Funds 4. Technical Education Quality Improvement Programme (EAP)	Ministry of Human Resource Development
5. Post-matric scholarships for SC, OBC and other vulnerable community students	Ministry of Social Justice & Empowerment
6. Post-matric scholarships for ST students 7. National Fellowship and Scholarship for Higher Education of ST Students 8. Vocational Training Centres in Tribal Areas	Ministry of Tribal Affairs
9. Post-matric scholarships for minorities students 10. Merit-cum-means based scholarship for minorities students for professional and technical courses undergraduate and postgraduate 11. Free Coaching &Allied Scheme for Minorities 12. Support for minorities students clearing preliminary examinations conducted by UPSC, SSC, State PSCs, etc. 13. Interest subsidy on education loans for overseas studies for minorities students 14. *Maulana* Azad National Fellowship for minorities students 15. Multi-Sectoral Development Programme for Minorities (MsDP) i. Umbrella Programme for Skill Development of Minorities: ii. *Seekho aur Kamao* – Skill Development Initiatives for minorities iii. Upgrading Skills and Training in Traditional Arts / Crafts for Development (USTAAD) for Minorities iv. *Nai Manzil*- The Integrated educational and Livelihood initiatives	Ministry of Minority Affairs
16. *Pradhan Mantri Kaushal Vikas Yojana*: i. Development of Skills (Umbrella Scheme) ii. Development of Entrepreneurship (Umbrella Scheme) iii. National Board of Skill Certification iv. National Skill Development Agency v. Model ITIs/Multi Skill Training Institutes vi. Apprenticeship and Training (Umbrella Scheme) vii. Scheme of Polytechnics	Skill Development & Entrepreneurship
Target: 4.4: By 2030, substantially increase the number of youth and adults who have relevant skills, including technical and vocational skills, for employment, decent jobs and entrepreneurship.	
Centrally Sponsored /Central Sector Schemes (CSS)	Concerned Ministries/ Departments
16. *Pradhan Mantri Kaushal Vikas Yojana*: i. Development of Skills (Umbrella Scheme) ii. Development of Entrepreneurship (Umbrella Scheme)	Skill Development & Entrepreneurship

(*Contd...*)

iii. National Board of Skill Certification iv. National Skill Development Agency v. Model ITIs/Multi Skill Training Institutes vi. Apprenticeship and Training (Umbrella Scheme) vii. Scheme of Polytechnics	
2. Vocational Training Centres in Tribal Areas	Ministry of Tribal Affairs
3. Umbrella Programme for Skill Development of Minorities: i. *Seekho aur Kamao* – Skill Development Initiatives for minorities ii. Upgrading Skills and Training Development (USTAAD) for minorities iii. *Nai Manzil*- The Integrated educational and Livelihood initiatives	Ministry of Minority Affairs
Target: 4.5: By 2030 eliminate gender disparities in education and ensure equal access to all levels of education and vocational training for the vulnerable, including persons with disabilities, indigenous peoples and children in vulnerable situations.	
Centrally Sponsored /Central Sector Schemes (CSS)	Concerned Ministries/ Departments
1. National Scheme for Incentive to Girl Child for Secondary Education (NSIGSE) 2. Prime Minister's Girls' Hostel	Ministry of Human Resource Development (School Education & Literacy)
3. Assistance to Disabled Persons for purchase of Fitting Devices (ADIP) 4. *Deendayal* Disabled Rehabilitation Scheme (DDRS) Scholarships for students with disabilities 5. Support to Establishment/ Modernization/ Capacity augmentation of Braille Presses 6. Establishment of Colleges for Deaf 7. National Program for Persons with Disabilities 8. National Fellowship for Persons with Disabilities (PwD) 9. Pre-and post-matric Scholarship to students with disabilities 10. National Overseas Scholarship for Students with Disabilities 11. Free Coaching for SC and OBC Students 12. Boys and Girls Hostels 13. SIPDA (Schemes for the Implementation of the Persons with Disabilities (Equal Opportunities, Protection of Rights and Full Participation) Act, 1995	Ministry of Social Justice & Empowerment
14. *Pradhan Mantri Kaushal Vikas Yojana*: i. Development of Skills (Umbrella Scheme) ii. Development of Entrepreneurship (Umbrella Scheme) iii. National Board of Skill Certification iv. National Skill Development Agency v. Model ITIs/Multi Skill Training Institutes vi. Apprenticeship and Training (Umbrella Scheme) vii. Scheme of Polytechnics	Skill Development & Entrepreneurship
Target: 4.6: By 2030 ensure that all youth and a substantial proportion of adults, both men and women, achieve literacy and numeracy.	
Centrally Sponsored /Central Sector Schemes (CSS)	Concerned Ministries/ Departments
1. *Saakshar Bharat*	Ministry of Human Resource Development (School Education & Literacy)
2. *Vanbandhu Kalyan Yojana* – Development of Particularly Vulnerable Tribal Groups (PVTGs)	Ministry of Tribal Affairs

(Contd...)

3. National Service Scheme (NSS) 4. Schemes for Youth development & Education (Nehru *Yuva Kendra Sangathan*, National Programme for Youth and Adolescent Development, etc.).	Ministry of Youth Affairs and sports
Target: 4.7: By 2030 ensure that all learners acquire the knowledge and skills needed to promote sustainable development, including, among others, through education for sustainable development and sustainable lifestyles, human rights, gender equality, promotion of a culture of peace and non-violence, global citizenship and appreciation of cultural diversity and of culture's contribution to sustainable development.	
Centrally Sponsored /Central Sector Schemes (CSS)	Concerned Ministries/ Departments
1. *Saakshar Bharat*	Human Resource Development (School Education & Literacy)
2. *Vanbandhu Kalyan Yojana* – Development of Particularly Vulnerable Tribal Groups (PVTGs)	Ministry of Tribal Affairs
3. National Service Scheme (NSS) 4. Schemes for Youth development & Education (Nehru *Yuva Kendra Sangathan*, National Programme for Youth and Adolescent Development, etc.).	Ministry of Youth Affairs and sports
5. *Kala Sanskriti Vikas Yojana*	Ministry of Culture
14. *Pradhan Mantri Kaushal Vikas Yojana*: i. Development of Skills (Umbrella Scheme) ii. Development of Entrepreneurship (Umbrella Scheme) iii. National Board of Skill Certification iv. National Skill Development Agency v. Model ITIs/Multi Skill Training Institutes vi. Apprenticeship and Training (Umbrella Scheme) vii. Scheme of Polytechnics	Skill Development & Entrepreneurship
Target: 4.a: Build and upgrade education facilities that are child, disability and gender sensitive and provide safe, non-violent, inclusive and effective learning environments for all.	
Centrally Sponsored /Central Sector Schemes (CSS)	Concerned Ministries/ Departments
1. *Sarva Shiksha Abhiyan* 2. Umbrella Programme for Education of SC, ST, OBC and minorities students.	Ministry of Human Resource Development
3. Umbrella ICDS	Ministry of Women and Child Development
4. Umbrella Programme for Education of SC, OBC and vulnerable group students.	Ministry of Social Justice & Empowerment
5. Umbrella Programme for Education of ST students.	Ministry of Tribal Affairs
6. Umbrella Programme for Education of minorities students.	Ministry of Minority Affairs
Target: 4.b: By 2020, substantially expand globally the number of scholarships available to developing countries, in particular least developed countries, small island developing States and African countries, for enrolment in higher education, including vocational training and information and communications technology, technical, engineering and scientific programmes, in developed countries and other developing countries.	
Centrally Sponsored /Central Sector Schemes (CSS)	Concerned Ministries/ Departments
	School Education & Literacy,

(*Contd...*)

	Higher Education Ministry of Tribal Affairs Ministry of External Affairs
Target: 4.c: By 2030, substantially increase the supply of qualified teachers including through international cooperation for teacher training in developing countries, especially least developed countries and small island developing States.	
Centrally Sponsored /Central Sector Schemes (CSS)	Concerned Ministries/ Departments
1. *Pandit Madan Mohan Malaviya* National Mission on Teachers and Teaching 2. Teachers Training and Adult Education	Ministry of Human Resource Development Ministry of External Affairs

Source: (NITI Aayog 2018).

8.8. Initiatives, Expectation and Performance of Government of India in SDG-4

According to the SDG India Index Base Line Report, 2018 (NITI Aayog 2018), to achieving the target of the UN's SDG-4, the Government of India had framed seven indicators. The Government of India reported that, 66 dedicated policies or schemes are in action to achieve two targets (4.1 and 4.c) of the UN's SDG-4 under the leadership and monitoring of 13 dedicated Ministries or the Departments. The SDG-4 indicators are –

SDG_4_1: Adjusted Net Enrolment Ratio at Elementary (Classes 1 - 8) and Secondary (Classes 9 - 10) School [%].

SDG_4_2: Percentage of Correct Responses on Learning Outcomes in Language, Mathematics and EVS for Class 5 Students.

SDG_4_3: Percentage of Correct Responses on Learning Outcomes in Language, Mathematics, Science and Social Sciences for Class 8 Students.

SDG_4_4: Percentage of the Children in the Age-group 6 – 13 who are out of School.

SDG_4_5: Average Annual Drop-out Rate at Secondary Level (%).

SDG_4_6: Percentage of School Teachers Professionally Qualified.

SDG_4_7: Percentage of Elementary and Secondary Students with Pupil-Teacher Ratio Less or Equal to 30.

Table No. 44: India's SDG-16=71 and the Performances in SDG-4

SDG India Indicators	SDG_ 4_1	SDG_ 4_2	SDG_ 4_3	SDG_ 4_4	SDG_ 4_5	SDG_ 4_6	SDG_ 4_7
UN Target of this SDG	100	67.89	57.17	0.28	10	100	100
Performance of India	75.83	54.69	44.58	2.97	17.06	81.15	70.43
India SDG 16 Score	71	71	71	71	71	71	71
India SDG Mean Score	57	57	57	57	57	57	57
Expected Performance, When SDG 16=71	71	48.20	40.59	0.19	7.1	71	71
Indicator Interpretation	Value High - Perfor-mance High	Value High - Perfor-mance High	Value High - Perfor-mance High	Value High - Perfor-mance Low	Value High - Perfor-mance Low	Value High - Perfor-mance High	Value High - Perfor-mance High
Performance Difference, When SDG 16=71	+4.83	+6.49	+3.99	-2.78	-9.96	+10.15	-0.57

Inference: It was assumed that, 'Peace, Justice and Strong Institutions' are the pre-conditions of achievement.

Here, Expected Performance = India SDG 16 Score (UN target of this SDG / 100) and

Performance Difference = (Expected Performance - Performance of India)

From the above conditions it is explored in the table no-44.

For the SDG_4_1: That is 'Adjusted Net Enrolment Ratio at Elementary (Classes 1 - 8) and Secondary (Classes 9 - 10) School [%]', India is positively differed (75.83) from its expected score 49.7, when SDG-16 score is 71 and here performance level have to hold and increase to a far better score from the present performance 75.83. Here the performance difference is +4.83.

For the SDG_4_2: That is 'Percentage of Correct Responses on Learning Outcomes in Language, Mathematics and EVS for Class 5 Students', India is positively differed (54.69) from its expected score 48.20, when SDG-16 score is 71 and here performance level have to hold and increase to a far better score from the present performance 54.69. Here the performance difference is +6.49.

For the SDG_4_3: That is 'Percentage of Correct Responses on Learning Outcomes in Language, Mathematics, Science and Social Sciences for Class 8 Students', India is positively differed (44.58) from its expected score 40.59, when SDG-16 score is 71 and here performance level have to hold and increase to a far better score from the present performance 44.58. Here the performance difference is +3.99.

For the SDG_4_4: That is 'Percentage of the Children in the Age-group 6 – 13 who are out of School', India is negatively differed (2.97) from its expected score 0.19, when SDG-16 score is 71 and here performance have to reduce to a level of -2.78 from the present performance. So India have to devote its tools of 'Peace, Justice and Strong Institutions' in a better way for a better score. Here the performance difference is -2.78.

For the SDG_4_5: That is 'Average Annual Drop-out Rate at Secondary Level (%)', India is negatively differed (17.06) from its expected score 7.1, when SDG-16 score is 71 and here performance have to reduce to a level of -9.96 from the present performance. So India have to devote its tools of 'Peace, Justice and Strong Institutions' in a better way for a better score. Here the performance difference is -9.96.

For the SDG_4_6: 'That is Percentage of School Teachers Professionally Qualified', India is positively differed (81.15) from its expected score 71, when SDG-16 score is 71 and here performance level have to hold and increase to a far better score from the present performance 81.15. Here the performance difference is +10.15.

For the SDG_4_7: For the SDG_4_6: 'That is 'Percentage of Elementary and Secondary Students with Pupil-Teacher Ratio Less or Equal to 30', India is slight negatively differed (70.43) from its expected score 71, when SDG-16 score is 71 and here performance have to increase to a level of +0.57 from the present performance. So India have to devote its tools of 'Peace, Justice and Strong Institutions' in a better way for a better score. Here the performance difference is -0.57.

8.9. Government of India's Remaining Targets and the Indicators for SDG-4

As we know that, on the basis of the availability of the disaggregated data, the NITI *Aayog* had framed India's own indicators of the targets of each individual SDG. For the SDG-4, that is 'Quality Education', the NITI *Aayog* had framed seven indicators; which captured two (4.1.1, and 4.c.1) of eleven indicators of the ten UNs SDG targets. As per the report,

66 dedicated policies or schemes are in action to achieve two targets (4.1 and 4.c) of the UN's SDG-4; the remaining indicators of the UN's SDG-4 is to be achieve by 2030. The remaining lists of targets along with the indicators of SDG-4 are detailed in Table no-45.

Table No. 45: Government of India's Remaining Targets and the Indicators for SDG-4

Targets	Indicators
4.1: By 2030, ensure that all girls and boys complete free, equitable and quality primary and secondary education leading to relevant and effective learning outcomes [i].	4.1.1: Proportion of children and young people: (a) in grades 2/3; (b) at the end of primary; and (c) at the end of lower secondary achieving at least a minimum proficiency level in (i) reading and (ii) mathematics, by sex [i].
4.2: By 2030, ensure that all girls and boys have access to quality early childhood development, care and pre-primary education so that they are ready for primary education [ii].	4.2.1: Proportion of children under 5 years of age who are developmentally on track in health, learning and psychosocial well-being, by sex [ii].
	4.2.2: Participation rate in organized learning (one year before the official primary entry age), by sex [ii].
4.3: By 2030, ensure equal access for all women and men to affordable and quality technical, vocational and tertiary education, including university [ii].	4.3.1: Participation rate of youth and adults in formal and non-formal education and training in the previous 12 months, by sex [ii].
4.4: By 2030, substantially increase the number of youth and adults who have relevant skills, including technical and vocational skills, for employment, decent jobs and entrepreneurship [ii].	4.4.1: Proportion of youth and adults with information and communications technology (ICT) skills, by type of skill [ii].
4.5: By 2030, eliminate gender disparities in education and ensure equal access to all levels of education and vocational training for the vulnerable, including persons with disabilities, indigenous peoples and children in vulnerable situations [ii].	4.5.1: Parity indices (female/male, rural/urban, bottom/top wealth quintile and others such as disability status, indigenous peoples and conflict affected, as data become available) for all education indicators on this list that can be disaggregated [ii].
4.6: By 2030, ensure that all youth and a substantial proportion of adults, both men and women, achieve literacy and numeracy [ii].	4.6.1: Percentage of population in a given age group achieving at least a fixed level of proficiency in functional (a) literacy and (b) numeracy skills, by sex [ii].
4.7: By 2030, ensure that all learners acquire the knowledge and skills needed to promote sustainable development, including, among others, through education for sustainable development and sustainable lifestyles, human rights, gender equality, promotion of a culture of peace and non-violence, global citizenship and appreciation of cultural diversity and of culture's contribution to sustainable development [ii].	4.7.1: Extent to which (i) global citizenship education and (ii) education for sustainable development, including gender equality and human rights, are mainstreamed at all levels in: (a) national education policies, (b) curricula, (c) teacher education and (d) student assessment [ii].

(Contd...)

4.a: Build and upgrade education facilities that are child, disability and gender sensitive and provide safe, non-violent, inclusive and effective learning environments for all [ii].	4.a.1: Proportion of schools with access to: (a) electricity; (b) the Internet for pedagogical purposes; (c) computers for pedagogical purposes; (d) adapted infrastructure and materials for students with disabilities; (e) basic drinking water; (f) single sex basic sanitation facilities; and (g) basic handwashing facilities (as per the WASH indicator definitions) [ii].
4.b: By 2020, substantially expand globally the number of scholarships available to developing countries, in particular least developed countries, small island developing States and African countries, for enrolment in higher education, including vocational training and information and communications technology, technical, engineering and scientific programmes, in developed countries and other developing countries [ii].	4.b.1: Volume of official development assistance flows for scholarships by sector and type of study [ii].
4.c: By 2030, substantially increase the supply of qualified teachers, including through international cooperation for teacher training in developing countries, especially least developed countries and small island developing States [i].	4.c.1: Proportion of teachers in: (a) pre-primary; (b) primary; (c) lower secondary; and (d) upper secondary education who have received at least the minimum organized teacher training (e.g. pedagogical training) pre-service or in-service required for teaching at the relevant level in a given country [i].
Notes of the Table: i. Target indicators captured and analysed. ii. Remaining.	

The Ministries and the Departments associate with indicators of this SDG such as, External Affairs, Higher Education, Human Resource Development, Human Resource Development (School Education and Literacy), Labour and Employment, Ministry of Culture, Minority Affairs, School Education and Literacy, Skill Development and Entrepreneurship, Social Justice and Empowerment, Tribal Affairs, Women and Child Development and Youth Affairs and sports have to concentrate to monitor on the above issues to achieve the target by 2030 through the provisions of Indian Constitution such as Article 15-(1), (4) and (5), Article 16-(1) to (5), Article 19.1 (g), 21A, Article 29-(1) and (2), Article 30-(1), (1A) and (2), Article 38-(1) and (2), Article 41, Article 43, Article 45, Article 46, Article 51A (h) and (k), Article 309, Article 310, Article 311, Article 312, Article 313, Article 314, Article 315, Article 320, Article 323A, Article 323B and Article 351; Article 246 - Seventh Schedule, List-I-Union List No 12, 25, 62, 63, 64, 65, 66, 67, 68, 69 and 94; List-I-State List No 14, 15, 32 and 41; List-III-Concurrent List No 19, 20, 24, 25, 26, 30 and 39; Article 243G - Eleventh Schedule - Powers, Authority and Responsibilities of Panchayats – Schedule No – 17, 18, 19, 20, 24 and 25; Article 243W - Twelfth Schedule - Powers, Authority and Responsibilities of Municipalities - Schedule No – 1, 3, 12, 13 and 16 - if we could not monitor, we would not be able to stand in front of the future generation with a smile.

Chapter – IX

Initiative and Performance of India in SDG-5, Gender Equality

The Global Agenda of goal-5 is 'Gender Equality', it is a fundamental human right and is a prerequisite for sustainable development. Goal-5 was aimed to achieve gender equality by ending all forms of discrimination, violence and harmful practices, including trafficking and sexual exploitation against women and girls.

It calls for valuing women's unpaid care and domestic work. In addition it calls for full and effective participation and equal opportunities for leadership at all levels of decision-making in political, economic and public life for women.

9.1. The Global Targets and Indicators for SDG-5

The global indicator framework was developed by the Inter-Agency and Expert Group on SDG Indicators (IAEG-SDGs) and agreed to, as a practical starting point at the 47th session of the UN Statistical Commission held in March 2016. The report of the Commission, which included the global indicator framework, was then taken note of by ECOSOC at its 70th session in June 2016 (NITI Aayog 2018). The global targets and the indicator of this SDG are tabled (Table No – 46) bellow –

Table No. 46: UNDP-DDGs Targets and Indicators of SDG-5

SDG-5, Achieve gender equality and empower all women and girls[1]	
Targets	**Indicators**
5.1: End all forms of discrimination against all women and girls everywhere.	5.1.1: Whether or not legal frameworks are in place to promote, enforce and monitor equality and non-discrimination on the basis of sex.

(Contd...)

1. Data Source: SDG India Index Baseline Report, 2018, NITI *Aayog*, Government of India, New Delhi.

5.2: Eliminate all forms of violence against all women and girls in the public and private spheres, including trafficking and sexual and other types of exploitation.	5.2.1: Proportion of ever-partnered women and girls aged 15 years and older subjected to physical, sexual or psychological violence by a current or former intimate partner in the previous 12 months, by form of violence and by age.
	5.2.2: Proportion of women and girls aged 15 years and older subjected to sexual violence by persons other than an intimate partner in the previous 12 months, by age and place of occurrence.
5.3: Eliminate all harmful practices, such as child, early and forced marriage and female genital mutilation.	5.3.1: Proportion of women aged 20-24 years who were married or in a union before age 15 and before age 18.
	5.3.2: Proportion of girls and women aged 15-49 years who have undergone female genital mutilation/cutting, by age.
5.4: Recognize and value unpaid care and domestic work through the provision of public services, infrastructure and social protection policies and the promotion of shared responsibility within the household and the family as nationally appropriate.	5.4.1: Proportion of time spent on unpaid domestic and care work, by sex, age and location.
5.5: Ensure women's full and effective participation and equal opportunities for leadership at all levels of decision-making in political, economic and public life.	5.5.1: Proportion of seats held by women in national parliaments and local governments.
	5.5.2-Proportion of women in managerial positions.
5.6: Ensure universal access to sexual and reproductive health and reproductive rights as agreed in accordance with the Programme of Action of the International Conference on Population and Development and the Beijing Platform for Action and the outcome documents of their review conferences.	5.6.1: Proportion of women aged 15-49 years who make their own informed decisions regarding sexual relations, contraceptive use and reproductive health care.
	5.6.2: Number of countries with laws and regulations that guarantee women aged 15-49 years access to sexual and reproductive health care, information and education.
5.a: Undertake reforms to give women equal rights to economic resources, as well as access to ownership and control over land and other forms of property, financial services, inheritance and natural resources, in accordance with national laws.	5.a.1: Proportion of total agricultural population with ownership or secure rights over agricultural land, by sex; and (b) share of women among owners or rights-bearers of agricultural land, by type of tenure.
	5.a.2: Proportion of countries where the legal framework (including customary law) guarantees women's equal rights to land ownership and/or control.
5.b: Enhance the use of enabling technology, in particular information and communications technology, to promote the empowerment of women.	5.b.1: Proportion of individuals who own a mobile telephone, by sex.
5.c: Adopt and strengthen sound policies and enforceable legislation for the promotion of gender equality and the empowerment of all women and girls at all levels.	5.c.1: Proportion of countries with systems to track and make public allocations for gender equality and women's empowerment.

9.3. The National Context of SDG-5:

The SDG-5's global agenda, 2030 is to empower all women to live dignified lives, contributing as equal partners in the growth and development of the country, in an environment free from violence and discrimination. Women and girls in India experience inequalities in access to healthcare, education, nutrition, employment and asset ownership. Decision making at home and in public sphere is another area where women lag behind. This is reflected in the indicators such as child (0-6 years) sex ratio which was 919 females per 1000 males in 2011, declining from 927 in 2001. Women continue to lag behind in education as reflected in literacy rate for women being 65 percent compared to 82 percent for males in 2011.

Overall intensive efforts are being made towards eliminating gender inequality by focusing on education of the girl child, providing access to health care facilities to girls and women, and ensuring access to livelihood opportunities. The participation of women in *Panchayati Raj* Institutions is having a positive impact on decision making opportunities for women in public sphere. India's commitment towards undertaking reforms to ensure gender equality is reflected in number of legislations enacted for ensuring equal opportunities and dignity of life for women, namely, *Protection of Women from Domestic Violence Act, 2005; Sexual Harassment of Women at Workplace (Prevention, Prohibition and Redressal) Act, 2013; Prohibition of Child Marriage Act, 2006; Medical Termination of Pregnancy Act, 1971* and the *Equal Remuneration Act, 1976.*

Targeted national level schemes and programmes, such as the *Beti Bachao, Beti Padhao* campaign, *SukanyaSamridhi Yojana*, *MUDRA Yojana* and *Pradhan Mantri Ujjwala Yojana,* have been launched – all aimed at achieving the targets of Goal-5. Besides these, there are a number of State level schemes as well, aimed at providing welfare, support and building capacity of women and girls.

India is committed, both constitutionally and through its policies, to achieving gender equality in all spheres of life. The Constitution of India prohibits discrimination based on gender, upholds women's right to participate in political and decision-making processes and also reiterates the country's commitments towards the socio-economic well-being of women in India. To further efforts towards this goal, India has also launched several national level schemes and programmes. The Gender Budget Statement was introduced in the government budget of 2005-06 to highlight the differential impact of budgets on men and women by dissecting allocations and utilisations under government schemes and programmes by sex. The *Beti Bachao, Beti Padhao,* campaign aims to ensure girls are born, nurtured and educated without discrimination to become empowered citizens of this country. Schemes like *Sukanya Samridhi Yojan*a and the *Janani Suraksha Yojanai* ensure the well-being and the prosperity of the girl child and the mother. Under the MUDRA initiative, financial assistance is provided to female entrepreneurs. One Stop Centre aims to ensure the safety and integrity of women. *Pradhan Mantri Ujjwala Yojana* (PMUY) is aimed at safeguarding the health of rural women by providing them 'clean-cooking-fuel'.

The evidence explored that the, India experienced a sex ratio at birth in India is 898 females per 1000 males. The national target is to achieve the natural sex ratio at birth of 954 females for 1000 males. Two States, namely Chhattisgarh and Kerala have achieved this target with a sex ratio at birth of 963 and 959 respectively.

The discrimination in paying equal wage is marked downhearted in India. Average wages and salaries of females is 70 percent of that of males for regular wage and salaried employees in the age-group 15-59 years in India. The national goal is to achieve equal pay for men and women. Only the UTs of Dadra and Nagar Haveli the female wage rate is higher than that of male and in Andaman and Nicobar islands the female wage rate is equal to that of male.

Another downhearted is domestic violence, as per the National Family Health Survey of 2015-16 (NFHS-4), one in every three ever-married women aged between 15 to 49 years experienced physical, sexual or emotional form of spousal violence. The survey highlights that spousal violence reduces with a rise in education and wealth control amongst women. This shows this Goal's interlinkage with 'Quality Education (SDG-4) and 'Decent Work and Economic Growth' (SDG-8).

The women in leadership are expected or not, are a big question in Indian democracy and it reflected in all other managerial segments as well. The evidence shows that only 8.7 percent of seats in the State Legislative Assemblies are held by women. The national target is to have 50 percent of the seats to be held by men and women each. No State or Union Territories has achieved this target yet. Amongst all the legislative assemblies in the country, the legislative assemblies of Rajasthan and West Bengal have the highest representation of women at 14 percent and 13.95 percent respectively.

Labour force participation only when it was converted by wages is counted or recorded not the domestic as well as household agriculture or the industries are not in India. After all the report explored that the labour force participation rate of women in India is only 32 percent of the labour force participation rate of men. The national target for 2030 is to have equal labour force participation rate for both women and men. While no State in India has achieved this target yet, Nagaland has the highest performance with women's labour force participation rate being 76 percent of that of men. Mizoram is the runner up with 73 percent.

The question is the family planning depends on the desire of the women when the socio-cultural-economic factors play a vital role into planning and framing the private life of the couple; and the country like India where poverty, illiteracy, lack of awareness about health and hygiene and unwilling to disclose about the private life are common nature of the women along with unavailability of modern methods of family planning in the location even by provided by the health care centre and even unable to buy when they want, due to lack of marketing facilities in the area. Even though, as per report, almost half of currently married women aged between 15-49 years are using modern methods of family planning. Female sterilization is the most popular contraceptive method. The use of modern family planning methods is the highest in Punjab among States, and in Chandigarh among Union Territories.

In the next part of this chapter we tried to visualized the performance level of India through the SDG's targets and the SDG India Index Base Line Report, 2018 along with the Constitutional provisions in India to explore citizen's responsibility along with the its institutions through the mirror of indexed score on 'peace, justice and strong institutions' (SDG-16).

9.4. SDG-5 Targets, National Indicators and Target Values of India

India in its SDG India Index Base Line Report, 2018 (NITI Aayog 2018), India had measured the performance of India on the goal of 'Gender Equality', India had identified six national level indicators, which captured four (5.1, 5.2, 5.5 and 5.6) out of the nine UN's SDG targets for 2030. These indicators have been selected based on availability of data at national level; these are in (Table – 47).

Table No. 47: SDG-5 Targets, National Indicators and Target Values of India

SDG-5 Global Target	Indicator Selected for SDG India Index	National Target Value for 2030
5.1: End all forms of discrimination against all women and girls everywhere.	1. Sex Ratio at Birth (Female per 1000 Male).	954
	2. Average Female to Male Ratio of Average Wages/Salaries Received per Day by Regular Wages/Salaried Employees of Age 15-59 for Rural and Urban.	1
5.2: Eliminate all forms of violence against all women and girls in the public and private spheres, including trafficking, sexual and other type of exploitations.	3. Percentage of Ever Married Women Aged 15 - 49 years who have ever Experienced Spousal Violence.	0
5.5: Ensure women's full and effective participation and equal opportunities for leadership at all levels of decision-making in political, economic and public life.	4. Percentage of Seats Won by Women in the General Elections to State Legislative Assembly.	50
	5. Ratio of Female Labour Force Participation Rate to Male Labour Force Participation Rate.	1
5.6: Ensure universal access to sexual and reproductive health and reproductive rights as agreed in accordance with the Programme of Action of the International Conference on Population and Development and the Beijing Platform for Action and the outcome documents of their review conference.	6. Percentage of Women in the Age Group of 15 - 49 Years Using Modern Method of Family Planning	100

Source: (NITI Aayog 2018).

9.5. Indian's SDG-5 Index Indicators, Data Source and Interpretations

The NITI *Aayog*, Government of India had collected required data from different government agencies to capture the UN SDG's target indicators as well as had framed its own indicators to justify the achievement of the SDGs. Apart from that the NITI *Aayog* had developed the computational approach of the disaggregated data as per valid methods along with the parameters of the performance; in the following tables (Table no-48, Table no-49, Table no-50, Table no-51, Table no-52 and Table no-53) shows the details of the above issue to develop a sense of progress of the SDG-5, entitled as 'Gender Equality'.

Table No. 48: SDG-5, Indian Indicator-1

SDG-5: 'Gender Equality'	**Indicator-1:** Sex Ratio at Birth (Female per 1000 Male).
Indicator data source	Ministry of Home Affairs-Office of the Registrar General of India [Sample Registration System]
Computation approach	Directly from data source
Data period (year)	2014-2016
States/UTs covered	22
Data periodicity	3 years
Relevant UN target	5.1: End all forms of discrimination against all women and girls everywhere.
Relevant UN indicator	NA
Relevant MoSPI indicator	5.1.3: Sex Ratio at birth
Indicator interpretation	Higher value means higher performance (+)

Source: (NITI Aayog 2018).

Table No. 49: SDG-5, Indian Indicator-2

SDG-5: 'Gender Equality'	**Indicator-2:** Average Female to Male Ratio of Average Wages/Salaries Received per Day by Regular Wages/Salaried Employees of Age 15-59 for Rural and Urban.
Indicator data source	Ministry of Statistics and Programme Implementation [Employment and Unemployment Situation in India, National Sample Survey 68th round]
Computation approach	Average of urban and rural wages/salaries received per day by regular wages/salaried employees of age 15-59 years was calculated for females and males. Using these, ratio was computed as follows - Average female wages/salaries received per day by ÷ Average male wages/salaries received per day by
Data period (year)	2011-2012
States/UTs covered	35
Data periodicity	5 years
Relevant UN target	5.1: End all forms of discrimination against all women and girls everywhere.
Relevant UN indicator	NA
Relevant MoSPI indicator	NA
Indicator interpretation	Higher value means higher performance (+)

Source: (NITI Aayog 2018).

Table No. 50: SDG-5, Indian Indicator-3

SDG-5: 'Gender Equality'	**Indicator-3:** Percentage of Ever Married Women Aged 15 - 49 years who have ever Experienced Spousal Violence.
Indicator data source	Ministry of Health and Family Welfare [National Family Health Survey - 4]
Computation approach	Directly from data source
Data period (year)	2015-2016

(Contd...)

States/UTs covered	36
Data periodicity	3 years
Relevant UN target	5.2: Eliminate all forms of violence against all women and girls in the public and private spheres, including trafficking, sexual and other type of exploitations.
Relevant UN indicator	5.2.1: Proportion of ever-partnered women and girls aged 15 years and older subjected to physical, sexual or psychological violence by a current or former intimate partner in the previous 12 months, by form of violence and by age.
Relevant MoSPI indicator	5.2.3: Proportion of cruelty/ physical violence on women by husband or his relative to total crime against women during the calendar year.
Indicator interpretation	Higher value means lower performance (-).

Source: (NITI Aayog 2018).

Table No. 51: SDG-5, Indian Indicator-4

SDG-5: 'Gender Equality'	**Indicator-4:** Percentage of Seats won by women in the General Elections to State Legislative Assembly.
Indicator data source	Election Commission of India [Electoral Statistics Document]
Computation approach	Directly from data source
Data period (year)	2016-2017
States/UTs covered	30
Data periodicity	Annual
Relevant UN target	5.5: Ensure women's full and effective participation and equal opportunities for leadership at all levels of decision-making in political, economic and public life.
Relevant UN indicator	5.5.1: Proportion of seat held by women in (a) national parliaments and (b) State Legislation and Local Self Government.
Relevant MoSPI indicator	5.2.3: Proportion of cruelty/physical violence on women by husband or his relative to total crime against women during the calendar year.
Indicator interpretation	Higher value means higher performance (+).

Source: (NITI Aayog 2018).

Table No. 52: SDG-5, Indian Indicator-5

SDG-5: 'Gender Equality'	**Indicator-5:** Ratio of Female Labour Force Participation Rate to Male Labour Force Participation Rate.
Indicator data source	Labour Bureau [Labour Bureau Report]
Computation approach	Female labour force participation ÷ male labour force participation
Data period (year)	2015-2016
States/UTs covered	35
Data periodicity	Annual
Relevant UN target	5.5: Ensure women's full and effective participation and equal opportunities for leadership at all levels of decision-making in political, economic and public life.
Relevant UN indicator	NA
Relevant MoSPI indicator	NA
Indicator interpretation	Higher value means higher performance (+).

Source: (NITI Aayog 2018).

Table No. 53: SDG-5, Indian Indicator-6

SDG-5: 'Gender Equality'	**Indicator-6:** Percentage of Women in the Age Group of 15 - 49 Years Using Modern Method of Family Planning.
Indicator data source	Ministry of Health and Family Welfare [National Family Health Survey - 4]
Computation approach	Direct from data source
Data period (year)	2015-2016
States/UTs covered	36
Data periodicity	3 years
Relevant UN target	5.6: Ensure universal access to sexual and reproductive health and reproductive rights as agreed in accordance with the Programme of Action of the International Conference on Population and Development and the Beijing Platform for Action and the outcome documents of their review conference.
Relevant UN indicator	5.6.1: Proportion of women aged 15-49 years who make their own informed decisions regarding sexual relations, contraceptive use and reproductive health care.
Relevant MoSPI indicator	5.6.1: Percentage of currently married women (15-49 years) who use modern methods of family planning.
Indicator interpretation	Higher value means higher performance (+).

Source: (NITI Aayog 2018).

9.6. Provisions of the Indian Constitution for SDG-5

The spirit of the unity in this diverse country, India is secured by its great Constitution; the Constitution of India not only secured its unity, announced a vision in the Preamble in the beginning of its Articles included in the Indian Constitution, *"We the people of India, having solemnly resolved to constitute India into a Sovereign Socialist Secular Democratic Republic and to secure to all its citizens: justice, social, economic and political; liberty of thought, expression, belief, faith and worship; equality of status and of opportunity; and to promote among them all fraternity assuring the dignity of the individual and the unity and integrity of the nation; in our Constituent Assembly this twenty-sixth day of November, 1949, do hereby adopt, enact and give to ourselves this Constitution* (India 1950/2015)". The mode of orientation of the Indian Constitution and the sustainable development goals of the contemporary time are given us an opportunity to make a link between these two visions of development and the author is trying to make the link.

As we know the sustainable development goals are interlinked, that means the success or failure of one is affected to other SDGs. From this perspective, this section presents the provisions in the Indian Constitution to eradicate poverty as reflected in the sustainable development agenda entitled as SDG-5, Gender Equality. The linked Constitutional provisions are in the following Table no-54 -

Table No. 54: Provisions in Indian Constitution for SDG-5

SDG-5 and the Linked Articles and Schedules of the Constitution of India
Article 14, Article 15-(1) to (5), Article 16-(1) to (5), Article 17, Article 18, Article 19, Article 20, Article 21A, Article 23, Article 24, Article 28, Article 30-(1), (1A) and (2), Article 38-(1) and (2), Article 39-(a) to (f), Article 39A, Article 41, Article 42, Article 43, Article 43A, Article 44, Article 45, Article 46, Article 47, Article 51A (a) to (k) Article 243D (2), Article 243T (2), Article 301, Article 309, Article 310, Article 311, Article 312, Article 313, Article 314, Article 315, Article 320, Article 323A, Article 323B, Article 325, Article 326, Article 350A, Article 350B, and Article 351.
Article 246: Seventh Schedule, List-I: Union List No: 12, 25, 62, 63, 64, 65, 66, 67, 68, 69 and 94. List-II: State List No: 5, 6, 9 and 12. List-III: Concurrent List No: 5, 20, 22, 23 24, 25, 26, 30 and 39.
Article 243G: Eleventh Schedule: Powers, Authority and Responsibilities of Panchayats. Schedule No: 1-5, 8, 9, 10, 11, 12, 14, 16, 17, 18, 19, 20, 21 and 23 to 28. Article 243W: Twelfth Schedule: Powers, Authority and Responsibilities of Municipalities. Schedule No: 1, 3, 6, 8, 9, 10, 11, 12, 13, 14, 16 and 17.

Source: The Constitution of India, 2015 as on 9th November, 2015.

9.7. Policies of the Government of India for Targets of the SDG-5

According to the SDG India Index Base Line Report, 2018 (NITI Aayog 2018), India is proactive to achieve the target of the UN's SDGs. The Government of India initiated as well as implemented various policies to capture the indicators of the targets of each individual SDG. On the moment of preparation of SDG India Index Base Line Report, 2018, on the basis of the availability of the disaggregated data, the NITI *Aayog* framed India's own indicators of the targets of each individual SDG. For the SDG-5, that is 'Gender Equality', the NITI *Aayog* framed six indicators; which capture four out of nine UNs SDG targets. As per the report, 19 dedicated policies or schemes are in action to achieve four targets (5.1, 5.2, 5.5 and 5.6) of the UN's SDG-5 under the leadership and monitoring of 14 dedicated Ministries or the Departments. The policies or schemes to achieve the targets of SDG-5 and the concerned dedicated Ministries and the Departments are detailed in the - Table no-55.

Table No. 55: Policies Initiated by the Indian Government for Targets of SDG-5

SDG-5, Gender Equality
SDG-5: *Gender Equality* as Goal-1 emphasises creation of gender sensitive development strategies, and equal rights and access to economic resources, as well as ownership and control over land and other forms of property, inheritance, natural resources and financial resources, including micro-finance.

(Contd...)

Target: 5.1: End all forms of discrimination against all women and girls everywhere.	
Centrally Sponsored /Central Sector Schemes (CSS)	Concerned Ministries/ Departments
1. Mission for Protection and Empowerment of Women - *Beti Bachao Beti Padhao, Pradhan Mantri Mahila Shakti Kendra* (PMMSK), *Ujjawala*, One Stop Centre, Women Helpline, hostels, SWADHAR *Greh*, gender budgeting etc. 2. *Pradhan Mantri Matru Vandana Yojana* (PMMVY) 3. Umbrella ICDS 4. Support to Training and Employment Programme (STEP)	Ministry of Women and Child Development
5. National Scheme for Incentive to Girl Child for Secondary Education (NSIGSE) 6. PRAGATI (Providing Assistance for Girls' Advancement in Technical Education Initiative)	Ministry of Human Resource Development
Target: 5.2: Eliminate all forms of violence against all women and girls in the public and private spheres, including trafficking, sexual and other type of exploitations.	
Centrally Sponsored /Central Sector Schemes (CSS)	Concerned Ministries/ Departments
1. Mission for Protection and Empowerment of Women - *Beti Bachao Beti Padhao, Pradhan Mantri Mahila Shakti Kendra* (PMMSK), *Ujjawala*, One Stop Centre, Women Helpline, hostels, SWADHAR *Greh*, gender budgeting etc. 2. Umbrella ICDS	Ministry of Women and Child Development
Target: 5.3: Eliminate all harmful practices, such as child, early and forced marriage and female genital mutilation.	
Centrally Sponsored /Central Sector Schemes (CSS)	Concerned Ministries/ Departments
1. Mission for Protection and Empowerment of Women - *Beti Bachao Beti Padhao, Pradhan Mantri Mahila Shakti Kendra* (PMMSK), *Ujjawala*, One Stop Centre, Women Helpline, hostels, SWADHAR *Greh*, gender budgeting etc. 2. Umbrella ICDS	Ministry of Women and Child Development
Target: 5.4: Recognize and value unpaid care and domestic work through the provision of public services, infrastructure and social protection policies and the promotion of shared responsibility within the household and the family as nationally appropriate.	
Centrally Sponsored /Central Sector Schemes (CSS)	Concerned Ministries/ Departments
1. Mission for Protection and Empowerment of Women	Ministry of Women and Child Development
2. *Pradhan Mantri Ujjwala Yojana*	Ministry of Petroleum & Natural Gas
3. Labour and Employment Statistical System (LESS)	Ministry of Labour & Employment
Target: 5.5: Ensure women's full and effective participation and equal opportunities for leadership at all levels of decision-making in political, economic and public life.	
Centrally Sponsored /Central Sector Schemes (CSS)	Concerned Ministries/ Departments
1. Support to Training and Employment Programme (STEP)	Ministry of Women and Child Development
2. *Rashtriya Gram Swaraj Abhiyan* (RGSA)	Ministry of *Panchayati Raj*

(Contd...)

Target: 5.6: Ensure universal access to sexual and reproductive health and reproductive rights as agreed in accordance with the Programme of Action of the International Conference on Population and Development and the Beijing Platform for Action and the outcome documents of their review conference.	
Centrally Sponsored /Central Sector Schemes (CSS)	Concerned Ministries/ Departments
1. National Health Mission 2. National AIDS Control Programme	Ministry of Health and Family Welfare
3. *Pradhan Mantri Matru Vandana Yojana* (PMMVY)	Ministry of Women and Child Development
Target: 5.a: Undertake reforms to give women equal rights to economic resources, as well as access to ownership and control over land and other forms of property, financial services, inheritance and natural resources, in accordance with national laws.	
Centrally Sponsored /Central Sector Schemes (CSS)	Concerned Ministries/ Departments
1. *Deen Dayal Antyodaya Yojana* (DAY) - National Rural Livelihood Mission (NRLM)	Ministry of Rural Development
2. *Deen Dayal Antyodaya Yojana* (DAY) -National Urban Livelihood Mission (NULM)	Housing and Urban Affairs
3. *Pradhan Mantri Jan Dhan Yojana*	Ministry of Finance Ministry of Land Resource Ministry of Women and Child Development
Target: 5.b: Enhance the use of enabling technology, in particular information and communications technology, to promote the empowerment of women.	
Centrally Sponsored /Central Sector Schemes (CSS)	Concerned Ministries/ Departments
1. Science &Technology Institutional and Human Capacity Building	Ministry of Science and Technology Telecommunication Ministry of Women and Child Development
Target: 5.c: Adopt and strengthen sound policies and enforceable legislation for the promotion of gender equality and the empowerment of all women and girls at all levels.	
Centrally Sponsored /Central Sector Schemes (CSS)	Concerned Ministries/ Departments
1. Mission for Protection and Empowerment of Women - *Beti Bachao Beti Padhao, Pradhan Mantri Mahila Shakti Kendra* (PMMSK), Ujjawala, One Stop Centre, Women Helpline, hostels, SWADHAR *Greh*, gender budgeting etc. 2. Gender Budgeting	Ministry of Social Justice and Empowerment

Source: (NITI Aayog 2018).

9.8. Initiatives, Expectation and Performance of Government of India in SDG-5

According to the SDG India Index Base Line Report, 2018 (NITI Aayog 2018), to achieving the target of the UN's SDG-5, the Government of India had framed six indicators. The Government of India reported that, 19 dedicated policies or schemes are in action to achieve four targets

(5.1, 5.2, 5.5 and 5.6) of the UN's SDG-5 under the leadership and monitoring of 14 dedicated Ministries or the Departments. The SDG-5 indicators are –

SDG_5_1: Sex Ratio at Birth (Female per 1000 Male).

SDG_5_2: Average Female to Male Ratio of Average Wages/Salaries Received per Day by Regular Wages/Salaried Employees of Age 15-59 for Rural & Urban.

SDG_5_3: Percentage of Ever Married Women Aged 15 - 49 who have ever Experienced Spousal Violence.

SDG_5_4: Percentage of Seats Won by Women in the General Elections to State Legislative Assembly.

SDG_5_5: Ratio of Female Labour Force Participation Rate to Male Labour Force Participation Rate.

SDG_5_6: Percentage of Women in the Age Group of 15 - 49 Years Using Modern Method of Family Planning.

Inference: It was assumed that, 'Peace, Justice and Strong Institutions' are the pre-conditions of achievement.

Here, Expected Performance = India SDG 16 Score (UN target of this SDG / 100) and

Performance Difference = (Expected Performance - Performance of India)

From the above conditions it is explored in the table no-56.

Table No. 56: India's SDG-16=71 and the Performances in SDG-5

SDG India Indicators	SDG_5_1	SDG_5_2	SDG_5_3	SDG_5_4	SDG_5_5	SDG_5_6
UN Target of this SDG	954	1	0	50	1	100
Performance of India	898	0.7	33.3	8.7	0.32	53.5
India SDG 16 Score	71	71	71	71	71	71
India SDG Mean Score	57	57	57	57	57	57
Expected Performance, When SDG 16=71	677.34	0.71	0	35.5	0.71	71
Indicator Interpretation	Value High-Performance High	Value High-Performance High	Value High-Performance Low	Value High-Performance High	Value High-Performance High	Value High-Performance High
Performance Difference, When SDG 16=71	+220.66	-0.01	-33.3	-26.8	-0.39	-17.5

Data Source: NITI *Aayog*, 2018 and Inference drawn by the author.

For the SDG_5_1: That is 'Sex Ratio at Birth (Female per 1000 Male)'; here, India is positively differed (898) from its expected score 677.34, when SDG-16 score is 71 and here performance level have to hold and increase to a far better score from the present performance 898. Here the performance difference is +220.66.

For the SDG_5_2: That is 'Average Female to Male Ratio of Average Wages/Salaries Received per Day by Regular Wages/Salaried Employees of Age 15-59 for Rural & Urban'; here, India is slight negatively differed (0.7) from its expected score 0.71, when SDG-16 score is 71 and here performance have to increase to a level of 0.01 from the present performance. So India have to devote its tools of 'Peace, Justice and Strong Institutions' in a better way for a better score. Here the performance difference is -0.01.

For the SDG_5_3: That is 'Percentage of Ever Married Women Aged 15 - 49 who have ever Experienced Spousal Violence'; here, India is negatively differed (33.3) from its expected score '0', when SDG-16 score is 71 and here performance have to reduce to a level of -33.3 from the present performance. So India have to devote its tools of 'Peace, Justice and Strong Institutions' in a better way for a better score. Here the performance difference is -33.3.

For the SDG_5_4: That is 'Percentage of Seats won by women in the General Elections to State Legislative Assembly'; here, India is negatively differed (8.7) from its expected score 35.5, when SDG-16 score is 71 and here performance have to increase to a level of 26.8 from the present performance. So India have to devote its tools of 'Peace, Justice and Strong Institutions' in a better way for a better score. Here the performance difference is -26.8.

For the SDG_5_5: That is 'Ratio of Female Labour Force Participation Rate to Male Labour Force Participation Rate'; here, India is negatively differed (0.32) from its expected score 0.71, when SDG-16 score is 71 and here performance have to increase to a level of 0.39 from the present performance. So India have to devote its tools of 'Peace, Justice and Strong Institutions' in a better way for a better score. Here the performance difference is -0.39.

For the SDG_5_6: That is 'Percentage of Women in the Age Group of 15 - 49 Years Using Modern Method of Family Planning'; here, India is negatively differed (53.5) from its expected score 71, when SDG-16 score is 71 and here performance have to increase to a level of 17.5 from the present performance. So India have to devote its tools of 'Peace, Justice and Strong Institutions' in a better way for a better score. Here the performance difference is -17.5.

9.9. Government of India's Remaining Targets and the Indicators for SDG-5

As we know that, on the basis of the availability of the disaggregated data, the NITI *Aayog* had framed India's own indicators of the targets of each individual SDG. For the SDG-5, that is 'Gender Equality', the NITI *Aayog* had framed six indicators; which captured three (5.2.1, 5.5.1 and 5.6.1) of fourteen indicators of the nine UNs SDG targets. As per the report, 19 dedicated policies or schemes are in action to achieve four targets (5.1, 5.2, 5.5 and 5.6) of the UN's SDG-5; the remaining indicators of the UN's SDG-5 is to be achieve by 2030. The remaining lists of targets along with the indicators of SDG-5 are detailed in Table no-57.

Table No. 57: Government of India's Remaining Targets and the Indicators for SDG-5

India's Remaining Targets and the Indicators for SDG-5	
Targets	**Indicators**
5.1: End all forms of discrimination against all women and girls everywhere [i].	5.1.1: Whether or not legal frameworks are in place to promote, enforce and monitor equality and non-discrimination on the basis of sex [i].
5.2: Eliminate all forms of violence against all women and girls in the public and private spheres, including trafficking and sexual and other types of exploitation [i].	5.2.1: Proportion of ever-partnered women and girls aged 15 years and older subjected to physical, sexual or psychological violence by a current or former intimate partner in the previous 12 months, by form of violence and by age [i].
	5.2.2: Proportion of women and girls aged 15 years and older subjected to sexual violence by persons other than an intimate partner in the previous 12 months, by age and place of occurrence [iii].
5.3: Eliminate all harmful practices, such as child, early and forced marriage and female genital mutilation [iii].	5.3.1: Proportion of women aged 20-24 years who were married or in a union before age 15 and before age 18 [iii].
	5.3.2: Proportion of girls and women aged 15-49 years who have undergone female genital mutilation/cutting, by age [iii].
5.4: Recognize and value unpaid care and domestic work through the provision of public services, infrastructure and social protection policies and the promotion of shared responsibility within the household and the family as nationally appropriate [iii].	5.4.1: Proportion of time spent on unpaid domestic and care work, by sex, age and location [iii].

5.5: Ensure women's full and effective participation and equal opportunities for leadership at all levels of decision-making in political, economic and public life [i].	5.5.1: Proportion of seats held by women in national parliaments and local governments [i].
	5.5.2: Proportion of women in managerial positions [iii].
5.6: Ensure universal access to sexual and reproductive health and reproductive rights as agreed in accordance with the Programme of Action of the International Conference on Population and Development and the Beijing Platform for Action and the outcome documents of their review conferences [ii].	5.6.1: Proportion of women aged 15-49 years who make their own informed decisions regarding sexual relations, contraceptive use and reproductive health care [i].
	5.6.2: Number of countries with laws and regulations that guarantee women aged 15-49 years access to sexual and reproductive health care, information and education [iii].
5.a: Undertake reforms to give women equal rights to economic resources, as well as access to ownership and control over land and other forms of property, financial services, inheritance and natural resources, in accordance with national laws [iii].	5.a.1: Proportion of total agricultural population with ownership or secure rights over agricultural land, by sex; and (b) share of women among owners or rights-bearers of agricultural land, by type of tenure [iii].
	5.a.2: Proportion of countries where the legal framework (including customary law) guarantees women's equal rights to land ownership and/or control [iii].
5.b: Enhance the use of enabling technology, in particular information and communications technology, to promote the empowerment of women [iii].	5.b.1: Proportion of individuals who own a mobile telephone, by sex [iii].
5.c: Adopt and strengthen sound policies and enforceable legislation for the promotion of gender equality and the empowerment of all women and girls at all levels [iii].	5.c.1: Proportion of countries with systems to track and make public allocations for gender equality and women's empowerment [iii].
Notes of the Table: i. Target indicators captured and analysed. ii. Not captured all the indicators. iii. Remaining.	

The Ministries and the Departments associate with indicators of this SDG such as, DeiTy, Finance, Health and Family Welfare, Housing and Urban Affairs, Human Resource Development, Labour & Employment, Land Resource, *Panchayati Raj*, Petroleum & Natural Gas, Rural Development, Science and Technology, Social Justice and Empowerment, Telecommunication and Women and Child Development have to concentrate to monitor on the above issues to achieve the target by 2030 through the provisions of Indian Constitution such as Article 14, Article 15-(1) to (5), Article 16-(1) to (5), Article 17, Article 18, Article 19, Article

20, Article 21A, Article 23, Article 24, Article 28, Article 30-(1), (1A) and (2), Article 38-(1) and (2), Article 39-(a) to (f), Article 39A, Article 41, Article 42, Article 43, Article 43A, Article 44, Article 45, Article 46, Article 47, Article 51A (a) to (k) Article 243D (2), Article 243T (2), Article 301, Article 309, Article 310, Article 311, Article 312, Article 313, Article 314, Article 315, Article 320, Article 323A, Article 323B, Article 325, Article 326, Article 350A, Article 350B, and Article 351; Article 246 - Seventh Schedule, List-I-Union List No 12, 25, 62, 63, 64, 65, 66, 67, 68, 69 and 94; List-II-State List No 5, 6, 9 and 12; List-III-Concurrent List 5, 20, 22, 23 24, 25, 26, 30 and 39; Article 243G - Eleventh Schedule - Powers, Authority and Responsibilities of Panchayats – Schedule No – 1-5, 8, 9, 10, 11, 12, 14, 16, 17, 18, 19, 20, 21 and 23 to 28; Article 243W - Twelfth Schedule - Powers, Authority and Responsibilities of Municipalities - Schedule No – 1, 3, 6, 8, 9, 10, 11, 12, 13, 14, 16 and 17 - if we could not monitor, we would not be able to stand in front of the future generation with a smile.

Chapter – X

Initiative and Performance of India in SDG-6, Clean Water and Sanitation

The Global Agenda of SDG-6 is 'clean water and sanitation' which aimed to ensure availability and sustainable management of water and sanitation for all. Water has been considered as the life support of the human civilization. Water is not essential for only human survival, it requires for supportive environment of human civilization; that is human-ecology to for agriculture, industrial use and domestic purposes. Availability of clean water is heavily dependent on appropriate waste management. Again, SDG-6 on 'clean water and sanitation' aims to improve water quality by reducing pollution, substantially increasing water-use efficiency across all sectors and supporting and strengthening the participation of local communities in improving water and sanitation management.

10.1. The Global Targets and Indicators for SDG-6

The global indicator framework was developed by the Inter-Agency and Expert Group on SDG Indicators (IAEG-SDGs) and agreed to, as a practical starting point at the 47th session of the UN Statistical Commission held in March 2016. The report of the Commission, which included the global indicator framework, was then taken note of by ECOSOC at its 70th session in June 2016 (NITI Aayog 2018). The global targets and the indicator of this SDG are tabled (Table no-58) bellow –

Table No. 58: UNDP-DDGs Targets and Indicators of SDG-6

SDG-6, Ensure availability and sustainable management of water and sanitation for all[1]	
Targets	**Indicators**
6.1: By 2030, achieve universal and equitable access to safe and affordable drinking water for all.	6.1.1: Proportion of population using safely managed drinking water services.

(*Contd...*)

1. Data Source: SDG India Index Baseline Report, 2018, NITI *Aayog*, Government of India, New Delhi.

6.2: By 2030, achieve access to adequate and equitable sanitation and hygiene for all and end open defecation, paying special attention to the needs of women and girls and those in vulnerable situations.	6.2.1: Proportion of population using safely managed sanitation services, including a hand-washing facility with soap and water.
6.3: By 2030, improve water quality by reducing pollution, eliminating dumping and minimizing release of hazardous chemicals and materials, halving the proportion of untreated wastewater and substantially increasing recycling and safe reuse globally.	6.3.1: Proportion of wastewater safely treated.
	6.3.2: Proportion of bodies of water with good ambient water quality.
6.4: By 2030, substantially increase water-use efficiency across all sectors and ensures sustainable withdrawals and supply of freshwater to address water scarcity and substantially reduce the number of people suffering from water scarcity.	6.4.1: Change in water-use efficiency over time.
	6.4.2: Level of water stress: freshwater withdrawal as a proportion of available freshwater resources.
6.5: By 2030, implement integrated water resources management at all levels, including through transboundary cooperation as appropriate.	6.5.1: Degree of integrated water resources management implementation (0-100).
	6.5.2-Proportion of transboundary basin area with an operational arrangement for water cooperation.
6.6: By 2020, protect and restore water-related ecosystems, including mountains, forests, wetlands, rivers, aquifers and lakes.	6.6.1: Change in the extent of water-related ecosystems over time.
6.a: By 2030, expand international cooperation and capacity-building support to developing countries in water- and sanitation-related activities and programmes, including water harvesting, desalination, water efficiency, wastewater treatment, recycling and reuse technologies.	6.a.1: Amount of water- and sanitation-related official development assistance that is part of a government-coordinated spending plan.
6.b: Support and strengthen the participation of local communities in improving water and sanitation management.	6.b.1: Proportion of local administrative units with established and operational policies and procedures for participation of local communities in water and sanitation management.

10.3. The National Context of SDG-6

Provide to access safe drinking water and sanitation is one of the most pressing challenges in the country and is being addressed by the government on a priority basis. As per 2011 Census data, 85.5 percent population had access to safe drinking water whereas only 30.8 percent of the households in rural areas had toilet facilities. While striving to ensure full access to water for all, robust efforts are being taken to optimise water resource endowments in the country. It is important to take an integrated, balanced approach to managing water resources towards effective water governance. The allocation of water among various uses needs to be carefully planned to ensure sustainability. Research and development efforts need to be targeted at improving water use efficiency as fresh water becomes a scarce resource. As per report the Government of India is committed to providing safe drinking water and access to sanitation to all habitations by 2022. Along with existing policies, national initiatives like the *Swachh Bharat* Mission, National Rural Drinking Water Programme and National Mission for Clean Ganga - *Namami Gange* have provided the necessary thrust to India's commitment on providing universal access to clean water and sanitation to all.

According to the reported result of the *Swachh Bharat* Mission, as of November 2018, 96 percent of the targeted household toilets have been constructed and 3.9 lakh villages across India have been verified to be open defecation free (ODF). However, sanitation in India is a major challenge where the government has a mammoth task, of not only constructing toilets for all but also of raising awareness and influencing behaviour change so that people understand the risks of open defecation and begin to use these toilets.

To capture the United Nations indicators of SDG-6, the national indicators for this goal cover various dimensions which include providing adequate safe and clean drinking water for all, substantially increasing water use efficiency and providing access to sustainable sanitation practices for all. India has been actively working in this arena through multi-sector interventions.

National Rural Drinking Water Programme (NRDWP) is aimed at providing every rural household with adequate safe water for drinking, cooking and other basic domestic needs on a sustainable basis, with a minimum water quality standard. 80.34 percent rural habitations have been fully covered with access to 40 litres of drinking water per capita per day being provided through this scheme. Further, 56 percent rural population has access to piped water supply. As far as the urban households are concerned, more than 90 percent have drinking water supply within or nearby their premises. The National Water Quality Sub-Mission (NWQSM) aimed to eliminate water quality issues related to excessive Arsenic and Fluoride in the country by 2021. The *Namami Gange* is an integrated conservation mission related to water management to accomplish the multiple objectives of effective abatement of pollution, conservation and rejuvenation of the river Ganga along with sustainable withdrawal and supply of freshwater. The *Swachh Bharat* Mission - *Gramin* is a cleanliness mission of the Government of India which ensures access to sanitation and aims to make the whole country be Open Defecation Free (ODF) by 2019. Again, the estimation was that, 32 percent of the districts have been verified to be ODF as of March 2018.

To provide safe and adequate drinking water in rural areas is commitment of the union government and the policies are framed to meet the commitment. While the national target is to provide safe and adequate drinking water to all, currently only 71.8 percent of the rural population in India has access to safe and adequate drinking water. Goa, Gujrat and Maharashtra are close to achieving universal coverage in rural areas. Uttar Pradesh follows with coverage of about 98 percent.

To provide toilets to each needy Rural Household, it will not only meet this goal; the dignity as well as violence of and against the women may reduce. As per report, 82.72 percent of rural households had individual household toilets constructed as of March 2018. The target is to have 100 percent of the rural households with individual toilets. Thirteen States and four Union Territories had achieved this target till March 2018. Andhra Pradesh is the runner up with 99 percent coverage.

The open defecation considered as the carrier of diseases as well as the violence of and against the women. Approximately 32 percent of districts in India have been verified to be open defecation free (ODF). The target of the country is to have all districts to be ODF. Seven States and three Union Territories have achieved the target (they are verified to be ODF under the *Swatchh Bharat* Mission).

Installation of sewage treatment capacity is a major initiative of the union government. The installed sewage treatment capacity of urban India as a percent of sewage generated is 37.58 percent. The 2030 target is to take this ratio to 68.79 percent. Four States – Gujarat, Himachal Pradesh, Punjab and Sikkim, and the UT of Chandigarh have already achieved it. On the account of Ground Water Withdrawal, as per report about 62 percent of the net available groundwater in India is withdrawn. The national upper limit is 70 percent so that the ground water is replenished at a normal rate. Haryana, Punjab, Rajasthan and Delhi need to improve these ratios which have far surpassed the maximum limit.

In the next part of this chapter we tried to visualized the performance level of India through the SDG's targets and the SDG India Index Base Line Report, 2018 along with the Constitutional provisions in India to explore citizen's responsibility along with the its institutions through the mirror of indexed score on 'peace, justice and strong institutions' (SDG-16).

10.4. SDG-6 Targets, National Indicators and Target Values of India

India in its SDG India Index Base Line Report, 2018 (NITI Aayog 2018), India had measured the performance of India on the goal of 'Clean Water and Sanitation', India had identified five national level indicators, which captured three (6.1, 6.2 and 6.4) out of the eight UN' SDG targets for 2030. These indicators have been selected based on availability of data at national level these are in Table no-59.

Table No. 59: SDG-6 Targets, National Indicators and Target Values of India

SDG-6 Global Target	Indicator Selected for SDG India Index	National Target Value for 2030
6.1: By 2030, achieve universal and equitable access to safe and affordable drinking water for all.	1.Percentage of population having safe and adequate drinking water in rural areas	100
6.2: By 2030, achieve access to adequate and equitable sanitation and hygiene for all and end open defecation, paying special attention to the needs of women and girls and those in vulnerable situations.	2. Percentage of rural households with individual household toilets.	100
	3. Percentage of districts to be verified open defecation free.	100
	4. Installed sewage treatment capacity as a proportion of sewage generated in urban areas.	68.79
6.4: By 2030, substantially increase water-use efficiency across all sectors and ensure sustainable withdrawals and supply of freshwater to address water scarcity and substantially reduce the number of people suffering from water scarcity.	5. Percentage annual ground water withdrawal against NET annual availability.	70

Source: (NITI Aayog 2018).

10.5. Indian's SDG-6 Index Indicators, Data Source and Interpretations

The NITI *Aayog*, Government of India had collected required data from different government agencies to capture the UN SDG's target indicators as well as had framed its own indicators to justify the achievement of the SDGs. Apart from that the NITI *Aayog* had developed the computational approach of the disaggregated data as per valid methods along with the parameters of the performance; in the following tables (Table no-60, Table no-61, Table no-62, Table no-63 and Table no-64) shows the details of the above issue to develop a sense of progress of the SDG-6, entitled as 'Clean Water and Sanitation'.

Table No. 60: SDG-6, Indian Indicator-1

SDG-6: 'Clean Water and Sanitation'	**Indicator-1:** Percentage of population having safe and adequate drinking water in rural areas.
Indicator data source	Ministry of Drinking Water and Sanitation [National Drinking Water Programme]
Computation approach	Directly from data source
Data period (year)	2018
States/UTs covered	31
Data periodicity	Annual
Relevant UN target	6.1: By 2030, achieve universal and equitable access to safe and affordable drinking water for all.
Relevant UN indicator	6.1.1: Proportion of population using safely managed drinking water services.
Relevant MoSPI indicator	6.1.1: Percentage of population having safe and adequate drinking water within their premises.
Indicator interpretation	Higher value means higher performance (+).

Source: (NITI Aayog 2018).

Table No. 61: SDG-6, Indian Indicator-2

SDG-6: 'Clean Water and Sanitation'	**Indicator-2:** Percentage of rural households with individual household toilets.
Indicator data source	Ministry of Drinking Water and Sanitation [*Swachh Bharat* Mission *Gramin* - Dashboard]
Computation approach	Directly from data source
Data period (year)	2018
States/UTs covered	34
Data periodicity	Daily
Relevant UN target	6.2: By 2030, achieve access to adequate and equitable sanitation and hygiene for all and end open defecation, paying special attention to the needs of women and girls and those in vulnerable situations.
Relevant UN indicator	6.2.1: Proportion of population using safely managed sanitation services, including a hand-washing facility with soap and water.
Relevant MoSPI indicator	6.2.1: Proportion of households having access to toilet facility (Urban and Rural).
Indicator interpretation	Higher value means higher performance (+).

Source: (NITI Aayog 2018).

Table No. 62: SDG-6, Indian Indicator-3

SDG-6: 'Clean Water and Sanitation'	**Indicator-3:** Percentages of districts to be verified open defecation free (ODF).
Indicator data source	Ministry of Drinking Water and Sanitation [*Swachh Bharat* Mission *Gramin* - Dashboard]
Computation approach	Directly from data source
Data period (year)	2018
States/UTs covered	34
Data periodicity	Daily

(*Contd...*)

Relevant UN target	6.2: By 2030, achieve access to adequate and equitable sanitation and hygiene for all and end open defecation, paying special attention to the needs of women and girls and those in vulnerable situations.
Relevant UN indicator	NA
Relevant MoSPI indicator	6.2.2: Percentage of districts achieving ODF target.
Indicator interpretation	Higher value means higher performance (+).

Source: (NITI Aayog 2018).

Table No. 63: SDG-6, Indian Indicator-4

SDG-6: 'Clean Water and Sanitation'	**Indicator-4:** Installed sewage treatment capacity as a proportion of sewage generated in urban areas (%).
Indicator data source	Ministry of Environment, Forest and Climate Change [Lok Sabha Unstirred Question 1723]
Computation approach	Directly from data source
Data period (year)	2016
States/UTs covered	29
Data periodicity	Non-periodic
Relevant UN target	6.2: By 2030, achieve access to adequate and equitable sanitation and hygiene for all and end open defecation, paying special attention to the needs of women and girls and those in vulnerable situations.
Relevant UN indicator	NA
Relevant MoSPI indicator	NA
Indicator interpretation	Higher value means higher performance (+)

Source: (NITI Aayog 2018).

Table No. 64: SDG-6, Indian Indicator-5

SDG-6: 'Clean Water and Sanitation'	**Indicator-5:** Percentage annual ground water withdrawal against net annual availability.
Indicator data source	Ministry of Water Resources [Dynamic Ground Water Resource of India]
Computation approach	Directly from data source
Data period (year)	2012-13
States/UTs covered	35
Data periodicity	5 years
Relevant UN target	6.4: By 2030, substantially increase water-use efficiency across all sectors and ensure sustainable withdrawals and supply of freshwater to address water scarcity and substantially reduce the number of people suffering from water scarcity.
Relevant UN indicator	6.4.1: Change in water-use efficiency over time.
Relevant MoSPI indicator	6.4.1: Percentage ground water withdrawal against availability.
Indicator interpretation	Higher value means lower performance (-).

Source: (NITI Aayog 2018).

10.6. Provisions of the Indian Constitution for SDG-6

The spirit of the unity in this diverse country, India is secured by its great Constitution; the Constitution of India not only secured its unity, announced a vision in the Preamble in the beginning of its Articles included in the Indian Constitution, *"We the people of India, having solemnly resolved to constitute India into a Sovereign Socialist Secular Democratic Republic and to secure to all its citizens: justice, social, economic and political; liberty of thought, expression, belief, faith and worship; equality of status and of opportunity; and to promote among them all fraternity assuring the dignity of the individual and the unity and integrity of the nation; in our Constituent Assembly this twenty-sixth day of November, 1949, do hereby adopt, enact and give to ourselves this Constitution* (India 1950/2015)". The mode of orientation of the Indian Constitution and the sustainable development goals of the contemporary time are given us an opportunity to make a link between these two visions of development and the author is trying to make the link.

As we know the sustainable development goals are interlinked, that means the success or failure of one is affected to other SDGs. From this perspective, this section presents the provisions in the Indian Constitution to eradicate poverty as reflected in the sustainable development agenda entitled as SDG-6, Clean Water and Sanitation. The linked Constitutional provisions are in the following Table no-65 -

Table No. 65: Provisions in Indian Constitution for SDG-6

SDG-6 and the Linked Articles and Schedules of the Constitution of India
Article 15-(2).(a), Article 15-(3), (4) and (5), Article 16-(1) to (5), Article 21, Article 21A, Article 38-(1) and (2), Article 39 – (a) to (f), Article 41, Article 42, Article 43, Article 45, Article 47, Article 48, Article 51A, Article 309, Article 310, Article 311, Article 312, Article 313, Article 314, Article 315, Article 320, Article 323A and Article 323B.
Article 246: Seventh Schedule, List-I: Union List No: 12, 13, 15, 25, 55, 56, 64, 65, 66, 68, 69 and 94. List-II: State List No: 6, 13 and 17. List-III: Concurrent List No: 18, 20, 20A, 24, 25, 26, 30 and 33.
Article 243G: Eleventh Schedule: Powers, Authority and Responsibilities of Panchayats. Schedule No: 3, 11, 16, 17, 18, 19 and 23, 24, 25, 26, 27, 28 and 29. Article 243W: Twelfth Schedule: Powers, Authority and Responsibilities of Municipalities. Schedule No: 1, 3, 4, 5, 6, 8, 9, 10, and 16.

Source: The Constitution of India, 2015 as on 9th November, 2015.

10.7. Policies of the Government of India for Targets of the SDG-6

According to the SDG India Index Base Line Report, 2018 (NITI Aayog 2018), India is proactive to achieve the target of the UN's SDGs. The

Government of India has initiated as well as implemented various policies to capture the indicators of the targets of each individual SDG. On the moment of preparation of SDG India Index Base Line Report, 2018, on the basis of the availability of the disaggregated data, the NITI *Aayog* framed India's own indicators of the targets of each individual SDG. For the SDG-6, that is 'Clean Water and Sanitation'; the NITI *Aayog* framed five indicators; which capture three out of eight UNs SDG targets. As per the report, 22 dedicated policies or schemes are in action to achieve three targets (6.1, 6.2 and 6.4) of the UN's SDG-6 under the leadership and monitoring of 9 dedicated Ministries or the Departments. The policies or schemes to achieve the targets of SDG-6 and the concerned dedicated Ministries and the Departments are detailed in the - Table no-66.

Table No. 66: Policies of the Government of India for Targets of the SDG-6

SDG-6, Clean Water and Sanitation	
SDG-6: Clean *Water and Sanitation* which aims to achieve universal and equitable access to safe and affordable drinking water and sanitation and hygiene for all.	
Target: 6.1: By 2030 achieve universal and equitable access to safe and affordable drinking water for all.	
Centrally Sponsored /Central Sector Schemes (CSS)	Concerned Ministries/ Departments
1. National Rural Drinking Water Programme (NRDWP)	Drinking Water & Sanitation Ministry of Women and Child Development
Target: 6.2: By 2030 achieve access to adequate and equitable sanitation and hygiene for all and end open defecation, paying special attention to the needs of women and girls and those in vulnerable situations.	
Centrally Sponsored /Central Sector Schemes (CSS)	Concerned Ministries/ Departments
1. *Swachh Bharat* Mission (Rural)	Drinking Water & Sanitation
2. *Swachh Bharat* Mission (Urban)	Ministry of Housing and Urban Affairs
3. Mission for Protection and Empowerment of Women	Ministry of Women and Child Development Ministry of Rural Development, Ministry of *Panchayati Raj*
Target: 6.3: By 2030 improve water quality by reducing pollution, eliminating dumping and minimising release of hazardous chemicals and materials, halving the proportion of untreated wastewater and substantially increasing recycling and safe reuse globally.	
Centrally Sponsored /Central Sector Schemes (CSS)	Concerned Ministries/ Departments
1. National River Conservation Programme (NRCP)	Ministry of Forest, Environment and Climate Change
2. Atal Mission for Rejuvenation and Urban Transformation (AMRUT) 3. Smart Cities Mission	Ministry of Housing and Urban Affairs
4. National Ganga Plan and *Ghat* Works	Ministry of Water Resource, Rural Development and Green Revolution

(*Contd...*)

<table>
<tr><td colspan="2">Target: 6.4: By 2030, substantially increase water-use efficiency across all sectors and ensure sustainable withdrawals and supply of freshwater to address water scarcity and substantially reduce the number of people suffering from water scarcity.</td></tr>
<tr><td>Centrally Sponsored /Central Sector Schemes (CSS)</td><td>Concerned Ministries/ Departments</td></tr>
<tr><td>1. Ground Water Management and Regulation
2. Pradhan Mantri Krishi Sinchayee Yojana (PMKSY)
3. Development of Water Resources Information System</td><td>Ministry of Water Resource, Rural Development and Green Revolution Agriculture & Cooperation, Land Resources</td></tr>
<tr><td colspan="2">Target: 6.5: By 2030, implement integrated water resources management at all levels, including through transboundary cooperation as appropriate.</td></tr>
<tr><td>Centrally Sponsored /Central Sector Schemes (CSS)</td><td>Concerned Ministries/ Departments</td></tr>
<tr><td>1. River Basin Management
2. National Water Mission
3. Interlinking of Rivers
4. Flood Management & Border Areas Programme
5. National Hydrology Project</td><td>Ministry of Water Resource, Rural Development and Green Revolution Agriculture & Cooperation, Land Resources</td></tr>
<tr><td colspan="2">Target: 6.6: By 2030, implement integrated water resources management at all levels, including through transboundary cooperation as appropriate.</td></tr>
<tr><td>Centrally Sponsored /Central Sector Schemes (CSS)</td><td>Concerned Ministries/ Departments</td></tr>
<tr><td>1. Conservation of Natural Resources and Ecosystems
2. National River Conservation Programme
3. Environment Protection, Management and Sustainable Development
4. Decision Support System for Environmental Policy, Planning and Outcome Evaluation</td><td>Ministry of Forest, Environment and Climate Change</td></tr>
<tr><td>5. Ground Water Management and Regulation</td><td>Ministry of Water Resource, Rural Development and Green Revolution Agriculture & Cooperation, Land Resources</td></tr>
<tr><td></td><td></td></tr>
<tr><td colspan="2">Target: 6.6.a: By 2030, expand international cooperation and capacity-building support to developing countries in water-and sanitation-related activities and programmes, including water harvesting, desalination, water efficiency, waste water treatment, recycling and rescue technologies.</td></tr>
<tr><td>Centrally Sponsored /Central Sector Schemes (CSS)</td><td>Concerned Ministries/ Departments</td></tr>
<tr><td>1. Research & Development and Implementation of National Water Mission
2. National Ganga Plan
3. Dam Rehabilitation and Improvement Programme
4. Human Resources Development and Capacity Building in NERIWALM, National Water Academy, RGI-Groundwater, MoWR and IEC</td><td>Ministry of Water Resource, Rural Development and Green Revolution</td></tr>
<tr><td></td><td>Drinking Water & Sanitation, Ministry of Housing and Urban Affairs, Ministry of External Affairs</td></tr>
<tr><td colspan="2">Target: 6.6.b: Support and strengthen the participation of local communities in improving water and sanitation management.</td></tr>
<tr><td>Centrally Sponsored /Central Sector Schemes (CSS)</td><td>Concerned Ministries/ Departments</td></tr>
</table>

(*Contd...*)

	Panchayati Raj, Ministry of Water Resource, Rural Development and Green Revolution Drinking Water & Sanitation, Ministry of Housing and Urban Affairs

Source: (NITI Aayog 2018).

10.8. Initiatives, Expectation and Performance of Government of India in SDG-6

According to the SDG India Index Base Line Report, 2018 (NITI Aayog 2018), to achieving the target of the UN's SDG-6, the Government of India had framed five indicators. The Government of India reported that, 22 dedicated policies or schemes are in action to achieve three targets (6.1, 6.2 and 6.4) of the UN's SDG-6 under the leadership and monitoring of 9 dedicated Ministries or the Departments. The SDG-6 indicators are –

SDG_6_1: Percentage of population having safe and adequate drinking water in rural areas.

SDG_6_2: Percentage of rural households with individual household toilets.

SDG_6_3: Percentage of districts to be verified open defecation free.

SDG_6_4: Installed sewage treatment capacity as a proportion of sewage generated in urban areas.

SDG_6_5: Percentage annual ground water withdrawal against NET annual availability.

Inference: It was assumed that, 'Peace, Justice and Strong Institutions' are the pre-conditions of achievement.

Here, Expected Performance = India SDG 16 Score (UN target of this SDG / 100) and

Performance Difference = (Expected Performance - Performance of India)

From the above conditions it is explored in the table no-67.

Table No. 67: India's SDG-16=71 and the Performances in SDG-6

Table No-67: India's SDG-16=71 and the Performances in SDG-6					
SDG India Indicators	SDG_6_1	SDG_6_2	SDG_6_3	SDG_6_4	SDG_6_5
UN Target of this SDG	100	100	100	68.79	70
Performance of India	71.8	82.72	31.95	37.58	61.53
India SDG 16 Score	71	71	71	71	71
India SDG Mean Score	57	57	57	57	57
Expected Performance, When SDG 16=71	71	71	71	48.84	49.7
Indicator Interpretation	Value High-Performance High	Value High-Performance High	Value High-Performance High	Value High-Performance High	Value High-Performance Low
Performance Difference, When SDG 16=71	+0.8	+11.72	-39.05	-11.26	-11.83

Data Source: NITI *Aayog*, 2018 and Inference drawn by the author.

For the SDG_6_1: That is 'Percentage of population having safe and adequate drinking water in rural areas'; here, India is slight positively differed (71.8) from its expected score 71, when SDG-16 score is 71 and here performance level have to hold and increase to a far better score from the present performance 71.8. Here the performance difference is +0.8.

For the SDG_6_2: That is 'Percentage of rural households with individual household toilets'; here, India is positively differed (82.72) from its expected score 71, when SDG-16 score is 71 and here performance level have to hold and increase to a far better score from the present performance 82.72. Here the performance difference is +11.72.

For the SDG_6_3: That is 'Percentage of districts to be verified open defecation free'; here, India is negatively differed (31.95) from its expected score 71, when SDG-16 score is 71 and here performance level have to increase to a level of 39.05 from the present performance. So India have to devote its tools of 'Peace, Justice and Strong Institutions' in a better way for a better score. Here the performance difference is -39.05.

For the SDG_6_4: That is 'Installed sewage treatment capacity as a proportion of sewage generated in urban areas'; here, India is negatively differed (37.58) from its expected score 48.84, when SDG-16 score is 71 and here performance level have to increase to a level of 11.26 from the present performance. So India have to devote its tools of 'Peace, Justice and Strong Institutions' in a better way for a better score. Here the performance difference is -11.26.

For the SDG_6_5: That is 'Percentage annual ground water withdrawal against NET annual availability'; here, India is negatively differed (61.53) from its expected score 49.7, when SDG-16 score is 71 and here performance have to reduce to a level of -11.83 from the present performance. So India have to devote its tools of 'Peace, Justice and Strong Institutions' in a better way for a better score. Here the performance difference is -11.83.

10.9. Government of India's Remaining Targets and the Indicators for SDG-6

As we know that, on the basis of the availability of the disaggregated data, the NITI *Aayog* had framed India's own indicators of the targets of each individual SDG. For the SDG-6, that is 'Clean Water and Sanitation', the NITI *Aayog* had framed five indicators; which captured three (6.1.1, 6.2.1 and 6.4.1) of eleven indicators of the eight UNs SDG targets. As per the report, 22 dedicated policies or schemes are in action to achieve three targets (6.1, 6.2 and 6.4) of the UN's SDG-6; the remaining indicators of the UN's SDG-6 is to be achieve by 2030. The remaining lists of targets along with the indicators of SDG-6 are detailed in Table no-68.

Table No. 68: Government of India's Remaining Targets and the Indicators for SDG-6

India's Remaining Targets and the Indicators for SDG-6	
Targets	**Indicators**
6.1: By 2030, achieve universal and equitable access to safe and affordable drinking water for all [i].	6.1.1: Proportion of population using safely managed drinking water services [i].
6.2: By 2030, achieve access to adequate and equitable sanitation and hygiene for all and end open defecation, paying special attention to the needs of women and girls and those in vulnerable situations [i].	6.2.1: Proportion of population using safely managed sanitation services, including a hand-washing facility with soap and water [i].
6.3: By 2030, improve water quality by reducing pollution, eliminating dumping and minimizing release of hazardous chemicals and materials, halving the proportion of untreated wastewater and substantially increasing recycling and safe reuse globally [iii].	6.3.1: Proportion of wastewater safely treated [iii].
	6.3.2: Proportion of bodies of water with good ambient water quality [iii].
6.4: By 2030, substantially increase water-use efficiency across all sectors and ensures sustainable withdrawals and supply of freshwater to address water scarcity and substantially reduce the number of people suffering from water scarcity [ii].	6.4.1: Change in water-use efficiency over time [i].
	6.4.2: Level of water stress: freshwater withdrawal as a proportion of available freshwater resources [iii].
6.5: By 2030, implement integrated water resources management at all levels, including through transboundary cooperation as appropriate [iii].	6.5.1-Degree of integrated water resources management implementation (0-100) [iii].
	6.5.2: Proportion of transboundary basin area with an operational arrangement for water cooperation [iii].

(Contd...)

6.6: By 2020, protect and restore water-related ecosystems, including mountains, forests, wetlands, rivers, aquifers and lakes [iii].	6.6.1: Change in the extent of water-related ecosystems over time [iii].
6.a: By 2030, expand international cooperation and capacity-building support to developing countries in water- and sanitation-related activities and programmes, including water harvesting, desalination, water efficiency, wastewater treatment, recycling and reuse technologies [iii].	6.a.1: Amount of water- and sanitation-related official development assistance that is part of a government-coordinated spending plan [iii].
6.b: Support and strengthen the participation of local communities in improving water and sanitation management [iii].	6.b.1: Proportion of local administrative units with established and operational policies and procedures for participation of local communities in water and sanitation management [iii].
Notes of the Table: i. Target indicators captured and analysed. ii. Not captured all the indicators. iii. Remaining.	

The Ministries and the Departments associate with indicators of this SDG such as, Agriculture & Cooperation, Land Resources; Drinking Water & Sanitation, Drinking Water & Sanitation, HUA, MEA; Housing and Urban Affairs, Ministry of Forest, Environment and Climate Change; Ministry of Water Resource, Rural Development and Green Revolution; *Panchayati Raj*, Rural Development, Women and Child Development have to concentrate to monitor on the above issues to achieve the target by 2030 through the provisions of Indian Constitution such as Article 15-(2).(a), Article 15-(3), (4) and (5), Article 16-(1) to (5), Article 21, Article 21A, Article 38-(1) and (2), Article 39 – (a) to (f), Article 41, Article 42, Article 43, Article 45, Article 47, Article 48 and Article 51A, Article 309, Article 310, Article 311, Article 312, Article 313, Article 314, Article 315,Article 320, Article 323A and Article 323B; Article 246 - Seventh Schedule, List-I-Union List No 12, 13, 15, 25, 55, 56, 64, 65, 66, 68, 69 and 94; List-II-State List No 6, 13 and 17 and List-III-Concurrent List No 18, 20, 20A, 24, 25, 26, 30 and 33; Article 243G - Eleventh Schedule - Powers, Authority and Responsibilities of Panchayats – Schedule No – 3, 11, 16, 17, 18, 19 and 23, 24, 25, 26, 27, 28 and 29; Article 243W - Twelfth Schedule - Powers, Authority and Responsibilities of Municipalities - Schedule No – 1, 3, 4, 5, 6, 8, 9, 10, and 16 - if we could not monitor, we would not be able to stand in front of the future generation with a smile.

Chapter – XI

Initiative and Performance of India in SDG-7, Affordable and Clean Energy

Arrangement and providing affordable and clean energy is a big challenges for the developing populous countries like India. The global agenda of SDG-7 is aimed to ensure universal access to affordable, reliable and modern energy services for all. Energy has recognized as necessary pre-requisite for development of societies and for them to flourish. Access to energy enables people to augment their income and improve their productivity, enhancing their access to healthcare, water and education and improving their overall well-being. In this connection SDG-7 aimed to ensure universal access to affordable, reliable and modern energy services by the year 2030.

11.1. The Global Targets and Indicators for SDG-7

The global indicator framework was developed by the Inter-Agency and Expert Group on SDG Indicators (IAEG-SDGs) and agreed to, as a practical starting point at the 47th session of the UN Statistical Commission held in March 2016. The report of the Commission, which included the global indicator framework, was then taken note of by ECOSOC at its 70th session in June 2016 (NITI Aayog 2018). The global targets and the indicator of this SDG are tabled (Table no-67) bellow -

Table No. 69: UNDP-DDGs Targets and Indicators of SDG-7

SDG-7, Ensure access to affordable, reliable, sustainable and modern energy for all[1]	
Targets	**Indicators**
7.1: By 2030, ensure universal access to affordable, reliable and modern energy services.	7.1.1: Proportion of population with access to electricity.
	7.1.2: Proportion of population with primary reliance on clean fuels and technology.
7.2: By 2030, increase substantially the share of renewable energy in the global energy mix.	7.2.1: Renewable energy share in the total final energy consumption.

1. Data Source: SDG India Index Baseline Report, 2018, NITI *Aayog*, Government of India, New Delhi.

7.3: By 2030, double the global rate of improvement in energy efficiency.	7.3.1: Energy intensity measured in terms of primary energy and GDP.
7.a: By 2030, enhance international cooperation to facilitate access to clean energy research and technology, including renewable energy, energy efficiency and advanced and cleaner fossil-fuel technology, and promote investment in energy infrastructure and clean energy technology.	7.a.1: Mobilized amount of United States dollars per year starting in 2020 accountable towards the $100 billion commitment.
7.b: By 2030, expand infrastructure and upgrade technology for supplying modern and sustainable energy services for all in developing countries, in particular least developed countries, small island developing States and landlocked developing countries, in accordance with their respective programmes of support.	7.b.1: Investments in energy efficiency as a percentage of GDP and the amount of foreign direct investment in financial transfer for infrastructure and technology to sustainable development services.

11.2. Interlinkage of SDG-7 with other SDGs

This section presents the linkage of the SDG-7 to other SDGs, that is, the success of this SDG habitually will influence the success of the linked SDGs; according to the SDG India Index, Baseline Report, 2018 (NITI Aayog 2018), the SDG-7 linked with the following SDGs –

SDG-1, that is *No Poverty*, which aims to reduce poverty in all its dimensions, which includes ensuring access to safe, nutritious and sufficient food all year round, particularly for the poor.

SDG-2, that is *Zero Hunger*, which aims to end all forms of malnutrition and ensures access to safe, nutritious and sufficient food for all, in particular the poor and vulnerable, and support small scale food producers.

SDG-3, is *Good Health and Well-being*, which aims to end epidemics and preventable deaths and achieve universal health coverage, including financial risk protection and access to quality essential health care services, medicines and vaccines for all.

SDG-4, is *Quality Education* that aims to ensure that all girls and boys complete free, equitable and quality primary and secondary education leading to relevant and effective learning outcomes, including technical and vocational skills for employment, decent jobs and entrepreneurship.

SDG-5, is *Gender Equality* as Goal 1 emphasises creation of gender sensitive development strategies, and equal rights and access to economic resources, as well as ownership and control over land and other forms of property, inheritance, natural resources and financial resources, including microfinance.

SDG-6, is *Clean Water and Sanitation*, which aims to achieve universal and equitable access to safe and affordable drinking water and sanitation and hygiene for all.

SDG-8, is *Decent Work and Economic Growth* which aims to promote development oriented policies that support productive activities, decent job creation, entrepreneurship, and encourage the formalization and growth of micro-, small - and medium-sized enterprises through access to financial services.

SDG-9, is *Industry, Innovation and Infrastructure* aims at building quality, reliable and resilient infrastructures. It further aims at promoting resource-use efficiency and greater adoption of clean and environmentally sound technologies and industrial processes, to support economic development and human well-being. Investment in innovation is an important pillar of this goal.

SDG-10, is *Reduced Inequalities* that aims to adopt policies, especially fiscal wage and social protection policies and progressively achieve and sustain income growth of the bottom 40 percent of the population at a rate higher than the national average, leading to greater equality.

SDG-11, is *Sustainable Cities and Communities* which aims to ensure access for all to adequate, safe and affordable housing and basic services and upgrade slums, and significantly reduce the numbers of deaths and people affected by disasters, with focus on protecting the poor and vulnerable.

SDG-12, *Sustainable Consumption and Production* aiming to halve per capita global food waste at consumer level and reduce food losses along production and supply chains.

SDG-13, is *Climate Action* which aims to develop resilience and adaptive capacity of the poor to climate related hazards and natural disasters.

11.3. The National Context of SDG-7

India has positively accepted the challenges which was associated with the SDG-7 entitled as 'affordable and clean energy' when nearly 40 percent of the population use the biomass as the prime source of cooking energy. The SDG-7 aimed to ensuring access to affordable, reliable, sustainable and modern energy for all for a prerequisite for socio-economic development. Accordingly, energy policies of India have over the years directly aims to raise per capita energy, especially the electricity consumption. Ensuring access to clean energy will be a precondition for the country to meet its ambitious target of double digit economic growth.

As per the SDG India Index Base Line Report, 2018, nearly 200 million Indians without access to electricity, and about 264 million people, still depends on solid biomass for cooking, it may be acknowledged that the country has a long way to go in securing its energy security objective. Considering India's rapid economic growth, rise in per capita consumption and increase in the coverage of villages with access to energy, the total energy demand is likely to rise sharply over the next few years. As per the energy modelling exercise undertaken by the NITI *Aayog* — India Energy Security Scenarios (IESS), 2047, the energy demands of India is likely to go up by 1.5 to 1.7 times between 2017 and 2030, with the electricity component itself rising 2.3 times .

The objective of providing clean and affordable energy for all is India's priority and can be seen clearly from the multiple programmes and schemes that are being run in the country at national and sub-national level. In April 2018, India achieved the milestone of providing electricity to all the Census villages and aims to achieve universal electrification at the household level by 31st March, 2019; but till June 2019, there is no any report in this regard.

In order to promote use of clean energy Petroleum and Natural Gas aimed to reduce oil imports by 10 percent from 2014-15 to 2021-22 mix to above 40 percent by 2030. Additionally, according to National Determined Contributions (NDCs) targets, India aims to (i) reduce emissions intensity by 33 percent to 35 percent over 2005 to 2030, (ii) achieve a 175 GW renewable energy capacity by 2022 and (iii) increase the share of non-fossil-fuel-based capacity in the electricity mix to above 40 percent by 2030. India has taken vast strides in provision of clean energy and is currently running one of the largest renewable capacity expansion programmes in the world.

The Government of India has set total renewable capacity targets at 175 GW by the end of 2022, which includes 100 GW from solar power, 60 GW from wind power, 10 GW from biomass power, and 5 GW from small hydro-power, while committing to have 40 percent of non-fossil fuel sources by 2030, towards energy security and meeting the NDCs.

With 69 GW installed capacity at the end of March 2018, the renewable energy accounts for a little over 20 percent of total installed capacity. Thus, the renewable energy installed capacity has grown by 77 percent from 38.9 GW on 31st March 2015, in a period of three years.

The installed capacity in the renewable energy Sector has been growing at a Combine Annual Growth Rate (CAGR) of 19 percent in the last 6 years that is Financial Year 2012 to Financial Year 2017, capacity growing at 36 percent in the last one year of 2017. Currently, In terms of renewable energy installed capacity, India ranks 4th globally after China, USA and Germany.

India aims to achieve the dual objective of affordable and clean energy by providing access to energy for all at affordable prices and by lying emphasis on de-carbonization through improve energy efficiency and shift towards renewable energy. The Government of India has prepared the National Electricity Plan and the National Energy Policy which aim to chart a clear roadmap to meet these ambitious targets in the energy domain.

The Government of India has launched various schemes which are aimed at creating awareness, making clean energy accessible to all, and sustainable usage by reducing wastage.

The National Solar Mission has set the ambitious target of deploying 20,000 MW of grid connected solar power by 2022, aimed at reducing the cost of solar power generation in the country. Dedicated Green Energy Corridor has been constructed in the country to improve inter-State transmission system to evacuate approximately 20.000 MW of large scale renewable power. The Off-Grid and Decentralized Solar Photovoltaic (DSPV) Application Programmes was launched with the objective to demonstrate and promote off-grid applications of Solar Photovoltaic (SPV) systems for meeting lighting and electricity requirements of individuals, institutions, communities, commercial and industrial establishments.

The National Biogas and Manure Management Programme was started with the objective of providing fuel for cooking purposes and organic manure to rural households through family type biogas plants. It aims to mitigate the drudgery of firewood collection by rural women, reduce the pressure on forests and accentuates social benefits of improved sanitation in villages by linking toilets to biogas plants.

To achieve 100 percent electrification in India the *Pradhan Mantri Sahaj Bijli Har Ghar Yojana Saubhagya*, that is Prime Minister's Programme for Easy electricity for Each Household was launched for provide electricity connection to all households in rural and urban areas. As of October 2018, 95 percent of the households have been electrified under this scheme.

The LPG subsidy, under PAHAL, aims at reducing the cost of LPG by providing subsidy on the gas cylinders through Direct Benefit Transfer

(DBT) to all households. The *Deen Dayal Upadhyaya Gram Jyoti Yojana* scheme focuses on providing continuous power supply to rural households and to agricultural consumers. The high dependency of nearly 40 percent of India's population on biomass for cooking has been a key challenge, which has been sought to be corrected by the *Pradhan Mantri Ujjwala Yojana* that aims at providing Liquefied Petroleum Gas (LPG) connection to 50 million women from poor families over a 3 year period (2016-19). So far, 50 million LPG connections have already been provided and the target has been increased to 80 million. The number of families using clean cooking fuel has shown an upward trend (increasing from 25.5 percent in 2005-06 to 43.8 percent in 2015-16), which is being further boosted by this initiative.

The National Programme for Energy Efficiency Appliances has been launched in 2015 with the aim of cutting emissions significantly. UJALA, the programme for distributing low-cost LEDs, the Energy Efficient Bulb Code, labelling of appliances for energy efficiency are some such targeted interventions. Apart from these, India has played a leading role in the International Renewable Energy Community and has facilitated the formation of International Solar Alliance along with France, involving 121 countries, whose Secretariat is housed in New Delhi.

On the account of household electrification, India has shown strong intent and performance towards household electrification. India is soon set to achieve the target of providing access to electricity to every household in the country. By the end of October 2018, nearly 95 percent of households were electrified. Six States along with the Union Territory Puducherry have achieved universal access to electricity.

According to the National Family Health Survey-4 2015-16, 43.8 percent of Indian households use clean cooking fuels. There is a significant divide between rural and urban households, with only 24 percent of rural households using clean cooking fuels compared to 81 percent urban households. Goa at 84.1 percent and Delhi at 97.7 percent are the best performing among States and Union Territories respectively. In the case of renewable energy, the report explored that, the renewable energy sources are 17.51 percent of the total installed electricity generating capacity of India. Among the installed electricity sources of utilities, renewables grew at the highest rate during 2006-07 and 2015-16. Wind power has the highest share among all renewable power sources (March, 2016). Renewable sources constitute 100 percent of total installed generating capacity of electricity in three States and four Union Territories.

In the next part of this chapter we tried to visualized the performance level of India through the SDG's targets and the SDG India Index Base Line Report, 2018 along with the Constitutional provisions in India to explore citizen's responsibility along with the its institutions through the mirror of indexed score on 'peace, justice and strong institutions' (SDG-16).

11.4. SDG-7 Targets, National Indicators and Target Values of India

India in its SDG India Index Base Line Report, 2018 (NITI Aayog 2018), India had measured the performance of India on the goal of 'Affordable and Clean Energy', India had identified three national level indicators, which was captured two (7.1 and 7.2) out of five UN's SDG targets for 2030. These indicators have been selected based on availability of data at national level; these are in Table No – 70.

Table No. 70: SDG-7 Targets, National Indicators and Target Values of India

SDG-7 Global Target	Indicator Selected for SDG India Index	National Target Value for 2030
7.1: By 2030, ensure universal access to affordable, reliable and modern energy services.	1. Percentage of households electrified.	100
	2. Percentage of households using Clean Cooking Fuel	100
7.2: By 2030, increase substantially the share of renewable energy in the global energy mix.	3. Percentage of renewable share of installed generation capacity.	40

Source: (NITI Aayog 2018).

11.5. Indian's SDG-7 Index Indicators, Data Source and Interpretations

The NITI *Aayog*, Government of India had collected required data from different government agencies to capture the UN SDG's target indicators as well as had framed its own indicators to justify the achievement of the SDGs. Apart from that the NITI *Aayog* had developed the computational approach of the disaggregated data as per valid methods along with the parameters of the performance; in the following tables (Table no-71, Table no-72 and Table no-73) shows the details of the above issue to develop a sense of progress of the SDG-7, entitled as 'Affordable and Clean Energy'.

Table No. 71: SDG-7, Indian Indicator-1

SDG-7: 'Affordable and Clean Energy'	**Indicator-1:** Percentage of households electrified.
Indicator data source	Ministry of Power [*Saubhagya* Dashboard]
Computation approach	Directly from data source
Data period (year)	2018
States/UTs covered	30
Data periodicity	Daily
Relevant UN target	7.1: By 2030, ensure universal access to affordable, reliable and modern energy services.
Relevant UN indicator	7.1.1: Proportion of population with access to electricity.
Relevant MoSPI indicator	7.1.1: Percentage of households electrified.
Indicator interpretation	Higher value means higher performance (+).

Source: (NITI Aayog 2018).

Table No. 72: SDG-7, Indian Indicator-2

SDG-7: 'Affordable and Clean Energy'	**Indicator-2**: Percentage of households using Clean Cooking Fuel.
Indicator data source	Ministry of Health and Family Welfare [National Family Health Survey-4]
Computation approach	Directly from data source
Data period (year)	2015-16
States/UTs covered	36
Data periodicity	3 years
Relevant UN target	7.1: By 2030, ensure universal access to affordable, reliable and modern energy services.
Relevant UN indicator	7.1.2: Proportion of population with primary reliance on clean fuels and technology.
Relevant MoSPI indicator	7.1.2: Percentage of households using Clean Cooking Fuel.
Indicator interpretation	Higher value means higher performance (+).

Source: (NITI Aayog 2018).

Table No. 73: SDG-7, Indian Indicator-3

SDG-7: 'Affordable and Clean Energy'	**Indicator-3**: Percentage of renewable share of installed generation capacity.
Indicator data source	Ministry of Statistics and Programme Implementation [Energy Statistics 2018]
Computation approach	Directly from data source
Data period (year)	2017
States/UTs covered	36
Data periodicity	Annual
Relevant UN target	7.2: By 2030, increase substantially the share of renewable energy in the global energy mix.

(*Contd...*)

Relevant UN indicator	7.2.1: Renewable energy share in the total final energy consumption.
Relevant MoSPI indicator	7.2.1: Renewable energy share in the total final energy mix.
Indicator interpretation	Higher value means higher performance (+).

Source: (NITI Aayog 2018).

11.6. Provisions of the Indian Constitution for SDG-7

The spirit of the unity in this diverse country, India is secured by its great Constitution; the Constitution of India not only secured its unity, announced a vision in the Preamble in the beginning of its Articles included in the Indian Constitution, *"We the people of India, having solemnly resolved to constitute India into a Sovereign Socialist Secular Democratic Republic and to secure to all its citizens: justice, social, economic and political; liberty of thought, expression, belief, faith and worship; equality of status and of opportunity; and to promote among them all fraternity assuring the dignity of the individual and the unity and integrity of the nation; in our Constituent Assembly this twenty-sixth day of November, 1949, do hereby adopt, enact and give to ourselves this Constitution* (India 1950/2015)". The mode of orientation of the Indian Constitution and the sustainable development goals of the contemporary time are given us an opportunity to make a link between these two visions of development and the author is trying to make the link.

As we know the sustainable development goals are interlinked, that means the success or failure of one is affected to other SDGs. From this perspective, this section presents the provisions in the Indian Constitution to eradicate poverty as reflected in the sustainable development agenda entitled as SDG-7, Affordable and Clean Energy. The linked Constitutional provisions are in the following Table no-74 -

Table No. 74: Provisions in Indian Constitution for SDG-7

SDG-7 and the Linked Articles and Schedules of the Constitution of India
Article 15-(2).(a), Article 15-(3), (4) and (5), Article 21, Article 21A, Article 38-(1) and (2), Article 39 – (a) to (f), Article 41, Article 42, Article 43, Article 46, Article 47, Article 48A, Article 51A, Article 309, Article 310, Article 311, Article 312, Article 313, Article 314, Article 315, Article 320, Article 323A and Article 323B.
Article 246 - Seventh Schedule, List-I: Union List No: 6, 12, 13, 14, 15, 42, 55, 58, 64, 65, 66, 68, 69 and 94. List-II: State List No: 6, 9, 10, 13 and 25. List-III: Concurrent List No: 20, 21, 22, 23, 24, 25, 26, 30, 33, 34, 35, 36, 37 and 38.
Article 243G: Eleventh Schedule Powers, Authority and Responsibilities of Panchayats. Schedule No: 2, 6, 7, 12, 16, 17, 18, 19 and 23, 24, 25, 26, 27, 28 and 29. Article 243W: Twelfth Schedule: Powers, Authority and Responsibilities of Municipalities. Schedule No: 1, 3, 4, 6, 7, 8, 9, 10, 11, 14, and 16.

Source: The Constitution of India, 2015 as on 9th November, 2015.

11.7. Policies of the Government of India for Targets of the SDG-7

According to the SDG India Index Base Line Report, 2018 (NITI Aayog 2018), India is proactive to achieve the target of the UN's SDGs. The Government of India initiated as well as implemented various policies to capture the indicators of the targets of each individual SDG. On the moment of preparation of SDG India Index Base Line Report, 2018, on the basis of the availability of the disaggregated data, the NITI *Aayog* framed India's own indicators of the targets of each individual SDG. For the SDG-7, that is 'Affordable and Clean Energy'; the NITI *Aayog* framed three indicators; which capture two out of five UNs SDG targets. As per the report, 17 dedicated policies or schemes are in action to achieve two targets (7.1 and 7.2) of the UN's SDG-7 under the leadership and monitoring of 5 dedicated Ministries or the Departments. The policies or schemes to achieve the targets of SDG-7 and the concerned dedicated Ministries and the Departments are detailed in the - Table no-75.

Table No. 75: Policies Initiated by the Indian Government for Targets of SDG-7

<table>
<tr><th colspan="2">SDG-7, Affordable and Clean Energy</th></tr>
<tr><td colspan="2">SDG-7: Affordable and Clean Energy aims to ensure universal access to affordable, reliable and modern energy services for all.</td></tr>
<tr><td colspan="2">Target: 7.1: By 2030 ensure universal access to affordable, reliable and modern energy services for all.</td></tr>
<tr><td>Centrally Sponsored /Central Sector Schemes (CSS)</td><td>Concerned Ministries/ Departments</td></tr>
<tr><td>1. Deen Dayal Upadhyaya Gram Jyoti Yojana
2. Sahaj Bijli Har Ghar Yojana (Urban)-Saubhagya
3. Integrated Power Development Scheme
4. Strengthening of Power Systems
5. Smart Grids
6. Green Energy Corridor</td><td>Ministry of Power</td></tr>
<tr><td>7. Grid Interactive Renewable Power
8. Off-Grid Distributed and Decentralized Renewable Power
9. Research & Development</td><td>Ministry of New and Renewable Energy</td></tr>
<tr><td>10. LPG Subsidy
11. Pradhan Mantri Ujjwala Yojana</td><td>Ministry of Petroleum and Natural Gas</td></tr>
<tr><td></td><td>Ministry of Coal,
Ministry of Tribal Affairs</td></tr>
<tr><td colspan="2">Target: 7.2: By 2030, increase substantially the share of renewable energy in the global energy mix.</td></tr>
<tr><td>Centrally Sponsored /Central Sector Schemes (CSS)</td><td>Concerned Ministries/ Departments</td></tr>
<tr><td>7. Grid Interactive Renewable Power
8. Off-Grid Distributed and Decentralized Renewable Power
9. Research & Development</td><td>Ministry of New and Renewable Energy</td></tr>
</table>

(Contd...)

Target: 7.3: By 2030, double the global rate of improvement in energy efficiency.	
Centrally Sponsored /Central Sector Schemes (CSS)	Concerned Ministries/ Departments
1. Bureau of Energy Efficiency 2. Energy Conservation 3. UJALA	Ministry of Power
4. Human Resources Development and Training 5. Information, Education and Communication	Ministry of New and Renewable Energy
6. *Pradhan Mantri Ujjwala Yojana*	Ministry of Petroleum and Natural Gas
	Ministry of Coal
Target: 7.a: By 2030, enhance international cooperation to facilitate access to clean energy research and technology, including renewable energy, energy efficiency and advanced and cleaner fossil-fuel technology, and promote investment in energy infrastructure and clean energy technology.	
Centrally Sponsored /Central Sector Schemes (CSS)	Concerned Ministries/ Departments
7. Research, Development and International Cooperation	Ministry of New and Renewable Energy
8.Bureau of Energy Efficiency 9. Energy Conservation	Ministry of Power
	Ministry of Coal, Petroleum and Natural Gas
Target: 7.b: By 2030, expand infrastructure and upgrade technology for supplying modern and sustainable energy services for all in developing countries, in particular least developed countries, small island developing States and landlocked developing countries, in accordance with their respective programmes of support.	
Centrally Sponsored /Central Sector Schemes (CSS)	Concerned Ministries/ Departments
	Ministry of Power, Petroleum and Natural

Source: (NITI Aayog 2018).

11.8. Initiatives, Expectation and Performance of Government of India in SDG-7

According to the SDG India Index Base Line Report, 2018 (NITI Aayog 2018), to achieving the target of the UN's SDG-7, the Government of India had framed five indicators. The Government of India reported that, 17 dedicated policies or schemes are in action to achieve two targets (7.1 and 7.2) of the UN's SDG-7 under the leadership and monitoring of 5 dedicated Ministries or the Departments. The SDG-7 indicators are –

SDG_7_1: Percentage of households electrified.

SDG_7_2: Percentage of households using Clean Cooking Fuel.

SDG_7_3: Percentage of renewable share of installed generation capacity.

Inference: It was assumed that, 'Peace, Justice and Strong Institutions' are the pre-conditions of achievement.

Here, Expected Performance = India SDG 16 Score (UN target of this SDG / 100) and

Performance Difference = (Expected Performance - Performance of India)

From the above conditions it is explored in table no-76.

Table No. 76: India's SDG-16=71 and the Performances in SDG-7

SDG India Indicators	SDG_7_1	SDG_7_2	SDG_7_3
UN Target of this SDG	100	100	40
Performance of India	94.57	43.8	17.51
India SDG 16 Score	71	71	71
India SDG Mean Score	57	57	57
Expected Performance, When SDG 16=71	71	71	28.4
Indicator Interpretation	Value High - Performance High	Value High - Performance High	Value High - Performance High
Performance Difference, When SDG 16=71	+23.57	-27.2	-10.89

For the SDG_7_1: That is 'Percentage of households electrified'; here, India is positively differed (94.57) from its expected score 71, when SDG-16 score is 71 and here performance level have to hold and increase to a far better score from the present performance 94.57. Here the performance difference is +23.57.

For the SDG_7_2: That is 'Percentage of households using Clean Cooking Fuel'; here, India is negatively differed (23.8) from its expected score 71, when SDG-16 score is 71 and here performance level have to increase to a level of 27.2 from the present performance. So India have to devote its tools of 'Peace, Justice and Strong Institutions' in a better way for a better score. Here the performance difference is -27.2.

For the SDG_7_3: That is 'Percentage of renewable share of installed generation capacity; here, India is negatively differed (17.51) from its expected score 28.4, when SDG-16 score is 71 and here performance level have to increase to a level of 10.89 from the present performance. So India have to devote its tools of 'Peace, Justice and Strong Institutions' in a better way for a better score. Here the performance difference is -10.89.

11.9. Government of India's Remaining Targets and the Indicators for SDG-7

As we know that, on the basis of the availability of the disaggregated data, the NITI *Aayog* had framed India's own indicators of the targets of each individual SDG. For the SDG-7, that is 'Affordable and Clean Energy', the NITI *Aayog* had framed three indicators; which captured three (7.1.1, 7.1.2 and 7.2.1) of six indicators of the five UNs SDG targets. As per the report, 17 dedicated policies or schemes are in action to achieve two targets (7.1 and 7.2) of the UN's SDG-7; the remaining indicators of the UN's SDG-7 is to be achieve by 2030. The remaining lists of targets along with the indicators of SDG-7 are detailed in Table no-77.

Table No. 77: Government of India's Remaining Targets and the Indicators for SDG-7

Targets	Indicators
7.1: By 2030, ensure universal access to affordable, reliable and modern energy services [i].	7.1.1: Proportion of population with access to electricity [i].
	7.1.2: Proportion of population with primary reliance on clean fuels and technology [i].
7.2: By 2030, increase substantially the share of renewable energy in the global energy mix [i].	7.2.1: Renewable energy share in the total final energy consumption [i].
7.3: By 2030, double the global rate of improvement in energy efficiency [ii].	7.3.1: Energy intensity measured in terms of primary energy and GDP [ii].
7.a By 2030, enhance international cooperation to facilitate access to clean energy research and technology, including renewable energy, energy efficiency and advanced and cleaner fossil-fuel technology, and promote investment in energy infrastructure and clean energy technology [ii].	7.a.1: Mobilized amount of United States dollars per year starting in 2020 accountable towards the $100 billion commitment [ii].
7.b: By 2030, expand infrastructure and upgrade technology for supplying modern and sustainable energy services for all in developing countries, in particular least developed countries, small island developing States and landlocked developing countries, in accordance with their respective programmes of support [ii].	7.b.1: Investments in energy efficiency as a percentage of GDP and the amount of foreign direct investment in financial transfer for infrastructure and technology to sustainable development services [ii].

Notes of the Table:

i. Target indicators captured and analysed.

ii. Remaining.

The Ministries and the Departments associate with indicators of this SDG such as, Ministry of Coal, Ministry of Power, Ministry of Tribal Affairs, New and Renewable Energy and Petroleum and Natural Gas have to concentrate to monitor on the above issues to achieve the target by

2030 through the provisions of Indian Constitution such as Article 15-(2).(a), Article 15-(3), (4) and (5), Article 21, Article 21A, Article 38-(1) and (2), Article 39 – (a) to (f), Article 41, Article 42, Article 43, Article 46, Article 47, Article 48A and Article 51A, Article 309, Article 310, Article 311, Article 312, Article 313, Article 314, Article 315, Article 320, Article 323A and Article 323B; Article 243G - Eleventh Schedule - Powers, Authority and Responsibilities of Panchayats – Schedule No – 2, 6, 7, 12, 16, 17, 18, 19 and 23, 24, 25, 26, 27, 28 and 29; Article 243W - Twelfth Schedule - Powers, Authority and Responsibilities of Municipalities - Schedule No – 1, 3, 4, 6, 7, 8, 9, 10, 11, 14, and 16. Article 246 - Seventh Schedule; List-I: Union List No: 6, 12, 13, 14, 15, 42, 55, 58, 64, 65, 66, 68, 69 and 94; List-II: State List No: 6, 9, 10, 13 and 25 and List-III: Concurrent List No: 20, 21, 22, 23, 24, 25, 26, 30, 33, 34, 35, 36, 37 and 38; Article 243G - Eleventh Schedule - Powers, Authority and Responsibilities of Panchayats – Schedule No – 2, 6, 7, 12, 16, 17, 18, 19 and 23, to 29; Article 243W - Twelfth Schedule - Powers, Authority and Responsibilities of Municipalities - Schedule No – 1, 3, 4, 6, 7, 8, 9, 10, 11, 14, and 16 - if we could not monitor, we would not be able to stand in front of the future generation with a smile.

Chapter – XII

Initiative and Performance of India in SDG-8, Decent Work and Economic Growth

The global agenda of SDG-8 is 'Decent Work and Economic Growth'; which is aimed to promote development oriented policies that support productive activities, decent job creation, entrepreneurship, and encourage the formalization and growth of micro-, small - and medium-sized enterprises through access to financial services. The 'Goal of Decent Work and Economic Growth' is also aims to achieve higher levels of economic productivity through diversification and technological upgradation and also promote develop-oriented policies that support decent job creation, entrepreneurship and creativity and innovation. It also seeks to protect labour rights and promote safe and secure working environments for all workers.

12.1. The Global Targets and Indicators for SDG-8

The global indicator framework was developed by the Inter-Agency and Expert Group on SDG Indicators (IAEG-SDGs) and agreed to, as a practical starting point at the 47th session of the UN Statistical Commission held in March 2016. The report of the Commission, which included the global indicator framework, was then taken note of by ECOSOC at its 70th session in June 2016. The global targets and the indicator of this SDG are tabled (Table no-78) bellow –

Table No. 78: UNDP-DDGs Targets and Indicators of SDG-8

SDG-8, Promote sustained, inclusive and sustainable economic growth, full and productive employment and decent work for all[1]	
Targets	**Indicators**
8.1: Sustain per capita economic growth in accordance with national circumstances and, in particular, at least 7 per cent gross domestic product growth per annum in the least developed countries.	8.1.1: Annual growth rate of real GDP per capita.
8.2: Achieve higher levels of economic productivity through diversification, technological upgrading and innovation, including through a focus on high-value added and labour-intensive sectors.	8.2.1: Annual growth rate of real GDP per employed person.
8.3: Promote development-oriented policies that support productive activities, decent job creation, entrepreneurship, creativity and innovation, and encourage the formalization and growth of micro-, small- and medium-sized enterprises, including through access to financial services.	8.3.1: Proportion of informal employment in non-agriculture employment, by sex.
8.4: Improve progressively, through 2030, global resource efficiency in consumption and production and endeavour to decouple economic growth from environmental degradation, in accordance with the 10-Year Framework of Programmes on Sustainable Consumption and Production, with developed countries taking the lead.	8.4.1: Material footprint, material footprint per capita, and material footprint per GDP.
	8.4.2: Domestic material consumption, domestic material consumption per capita, and domestic material consumption per GDP.
8.5: By 2030, achieve full and productive employment and decent work for all women and men, including for young people and persons with disabilities, and equal pay for work of equal value.	8.5.1: Average hourly earnings of female and male employees, by occupation, age and persons with disabilities.
	8.5.2: Unemployment rate, by sex, age and persons with disabilities.
8.6: By 2020, substantially reduce the proportion of youth not in employment, education or training.	8.6.1: Proportion of youth (aged 15-24 years) not in education, employment or training.
8.7: Take immediate and effective measures to eradicate forced labour, end modern slavery and human trafficking and secure the prohibition and elimination of the worst forms of child labour, including recruitment and use of child soldiers, and by 2025 end child labour in all its forms.	8.7.1: Proportion and number of children aged 5-17 years engaged in child labour, by sex and age.
8.8: Protect labour rights and promote safe and secure working environments for all workers, including migrant workers, in particular women migrants, and those in precarious employment.	8.8.1: Frequency rates of fatal and non-fatal occupational injuries, by sex and migrant status.
	8.8.2 Increase in national compliance of labour rights (freedom of association and collective bargaining) based on International Labour Organization (ILO) textual sources and national legislation, by sex and migrant status.

1. Data Source: SDG India Index Baseline Report, 2018, NITI *Aayog*, Government of India, New Delhi.

8.10: Strengthen the capacity of domestic financial institutions to encourage and expand access to banking, insurance and financial services for all.	8.10.1: Number of commercial bank branches and automated teller machines (ATMs) per 100,000 adults.
	8.10.2: Proportion of adults (15 years and older) with an account at a bank or other financial institution or with a mobile-money-service provider.
8.a: Increase Aid for Trade support for developing countries, in particular least developed countries, including through the Enhanced Integrated Framework for Trade-related Technical Assistance to Least Developed Countries.	8.a.1: Aid for Trade commitments and disbursements.
8.b: By 2020, develop and operationalize a global strategy for youth employment and implement the Global Jobs Pact of the International Labour Organization.	8.b.1: Total government spending in social protection and employment programmes as a proportion of the national budgets and GDP.

12.2. Interlinkage of SDG-8 with other SDGs

This section presents the linkage of the SDG-8 to other SDGs, that is, the success of this SDG habitually will influence the success of the linked SDGs; according to the SDG India Index, Baseline Report, 2018 (NITI Aayog 2018), the SDG-8 linked with the following SDGs –

SDG-1, that is *No Poverty*, which aims to reduce poverty in all its dimensions, which includes ensuring access to safe, nutritious and sufficient food all year round, particularly for the poor.

SDG-2, that is *Zero Hunger*, which aims to end all forms of malnutrition and ensures access to safe, nutritious and sufficient food for all, in particular the poor and vulnerable, and support small scale food producers.

SDG-3, is *Good Health and Well-being*, which aims to end epidemics and preventable deaths and achieve universal health coverage, including financial risk protection and access to quality essential health care services, medicines and vaccines for all.

SDG-4, is *Quality Education* that aims to ensure that all girls and boys complete free, equitable and quality primary and secondary education leading to relevant and effective learning outcomes, including technical and vocational skills for employment, decent jobs and entrepreneurship.

SDG-5, is *Gender Equality* as Goal 1 emphasises creation of gender sensitive development strategies, and equal rights and access to economic resources, as well as ownership and control over land and other forms of property, inheritance, natural resources and financial resources, including microfinance.

SDG-7, is *Affordable and Clean Energy* that aims to ensure universal access to affordable, reliable and modern energy services.

SDG-9, is *Industry, Innovation and Infrastructure* aims at building quality, reliable and resilient infrastructures. It further aims at promoting resource-use efficiency and greater adoption of clean and environmentally sound technologies and industrial processes, to support economic development and human well-being. Investment in innovation is an important pillar of this goal.

SDG-10, is *Reduced Inequalities* that aims to adopt policies, especially fiscal wage and social protection policies and progressively achieve and sustain income growth of the bottom 40 percent of the population at a rate higher than the national average, leading to greater equality.

SDG-12, *Sustainable Consumption and Production* aiming to halve per capita global food waste at consumer level and reduce food losses along production and supply chains.

SDG-14, is *Life Bellow Water* which aims to increase benefits to Small Island Developing States (SIDs) and Least Developed Countries (LDCs) from sustainable use of marine resources.

SDG-16: *Peace, Justice and Strong Institutions* which aims to build accountable and transparent economic institutions.

12.3. The National Context of SDG-8

A stable macroeconomic environment is a precursor to growth. India has variously demonstrated and resolved to achieve fiscal consolidation, complemented with aggressive measures for improving the business and skill ecosystem, and continues to make progress with a slew of policy reforms and initiatives. The GDP growth at 6.5 percent in Financial Year 2017-18 and continues to see an upward trend. Stable macro-economic indicators, structural reforms improving business ecosystem, thrust on infrastructure development, and liberal FDI regime have resulted in the estimation that India's GDP continues to rise to 7.4 percent in 2018-19, 7.8 percent in 2019-20 and 2020-21 making it one of the world's fastest growing economy.

India has been recording the highest growth rate amongst the BRICS economies. The progress of the Indian economy is evident from India's significant jump of 33 places in the World Bank's Ease of Doing Business Rankings, 2018, from 100th rank in 2017 to 77th rank in 2018. India is the only nation to have made it to the list of top 10 improvers for the second consecutive year.

Government programmes like Start-Up India, Make in India, Digital India, MUDRA *Yojana*, Skill India and Prime Ministers Employment Generation Programme, Prime Minister *Jan Dhan Yojana*, focus on Micro, Small and Medium Enterprises (MSMEs), among others, are all directed towards promoting and encouraging entrepreneurship, creativity and innovation and inclusive business.

According to the report, by the end of 2030, every citizen of the country, male or female, including persons with disabilities should have decent work contributing towards the GDP of the country. India's MSMEs are likely to play a greater role than before in achieving this goal of holistic, sustainable and inclusive growth. To meet this target, government has initiated several programmes for generating employment opportunities, enhancing skill development and accelerating economic growth for the masses.

On the account of the GDP growth, it was reported that, the annual growth rate of India's GDP per capita stands at 6.5 percent. The target is to take this rate to 10 percent. Sixteen States and three UTs have annual per capita GDP growth rate more than the national average. Among the States and UTs, the best performance is shown by Jammu and Kashmir and Delhi respectively.

The unemployment rate is one of the big challenge India facing, the average unemployment rate per 1000 person stands at 63.5. The 2030 target is to reduce this figure to 14.83. Among the States, Gujrat has the least number of unemployed persons per 1000 (10/1000). Among the Union Territories, the best performance is shown by Daman and Diu (18/1000).

On the account to access the banking facility, as per report, 99.99 percent households in the country have bank accounts. This was made possible because of the *Pradhan Mantri Jan Dhan Yojana*. Only nine States – Assam, Chhattisgarh, Jammu and Kashmir, Karnataka, Manipur, Mizoram, Nagaland, Odisha and Rajasthan fall short of 100 percent achievement on this indicator. Along with banking facility, 16.84 Bank's ATMs are available in the country for per 100000 populations. The 2030 target is to take this figure to 50.95. Goa is the best performing State on this indicator with 65.42 Bank's ATMs are available for per 100000 populations. Among the Union Territories, Chandigarh leads with 45.23 Bank's ATMs are available for the same population.

Towards the employment generation, India initiated Prime Minister's Employment Generation Programme (PMEGP) along with the existing policies, is a central sector scheme administered by the Ministry of Micro, Small and Medium Enterprises, which aims to generate employment opportunities by establishing micro enterprises in rural as well as urban areas. It is a credit linked subsidy programme where Self Help Groups registered under Societies Registration Act, 1860 are eligible for subsidies to setup projects under PMEGP.

The government of India initiated the 'Start-up India'. It was launched by the government to foster an environment for nurturing innovation and start-ups in the country, aimed at driving economic growth and generating large scale employment opportunities. The scheme facilitated bank loans between Rs.10 lakh and Rs.1 Crore, from Scheduled Commercial Banks (SCBs), to at least on Scheduled Caste (SC) or Scheduled Tribe (ST) and one women per bank branch for setting up a Greenfield enterprise in trading, services or the manufacturing sector. The scheme is expected to benefit at least 2.5 lakh borrowers.

Skill India is an encouraging initiative accepted by the government of India. It seeks to provide institutional capacity to train a minimum of 400 million skilled people by 2022 (PIB, 2015). It focuses on short-term vocational education programmes, with the mission to scale-up skill development efforts by creating an end to end, outcome focused implementation framework, which aligns demands of the market with a well-trained and skilled workforce. Specific programmes under this umbrella are the National Apprenticeship Promotion Scheme, and the *Pradhan Mantri Kaushal Vikas Yojana*. These programmes will bolster the growth of Indian MSMEs.

In the next part of this chapter we tried to visualized the performance level of India through the SDG's targets and the SDG India Index Base Line Report, 2018 along with the Constitutional provisions in India to explore citizen's responsibility along with the its institutions through the mirror of indexed score on 'peace, justice and strong institutions' (SDG-16).

12.4. SDG-8 Targets, National Indicators and Target Values of India

India in its SDG India Index Base Line Report, 2018 (NITI Aayog 2018), India had measured the performance of India on the goal of 'Decent Work end Economic Growth', India had identified four national level indicators, which captured three (8.1, 8.5 and 8.10) out of twelve UN's SDG targets. These indicators have been selected based on availability of data at national level; these are in Table no-79.

Table No 79: SDG-8 Targets, National Indicators and Target Values of India

SDG-8 Global Target	Indicator Selected for SDG India Index	National Target Value for 2030
8.1: Sustain per capita economic growth in accordance with national circumstances and, in particular, at least 7% Gross Domestic Product (GDP) growth per annum in the least developed countries.	1. Annual growth rate of GDP per capita (at constant price of 2011-12).	10
8.5: By 2030, achieve full and productive employment and decent work for all women and men, including for young people and persons with disabilities, and equal pay for work of equal value.	2. Average unemployment rate per 1000 persons for males and females.	14.83
8.10: Strengthen the capacity of domestic financial institutions to encourage and expand access to banking, insurance and financial services to all.	3. Percentage of households with a Bank account.	100
	4. Number of ATMs per 100000 populations.	50.95

Source: (NITI Aayog 2018).

12.5. Indian's SDG-8 Index Indicators, Data Source and Interpretations

The NITI *Aayog*, Government of India had collected required data from different government agencies to capture the UN SDG's target indicators as well as had framed its own indicators to justify the achievement of the SDGs. Apart from that the NITI *Aayog* had developed the computational approach of the disaggregated data as per valid methods along with the parameters of the performance; in the following tables (Table no-80, Table no-81, Table no-82 and Table no-83) shows the details of the above issue to develop a sense of progress of the SDG-8, entitled as 'Decent Work and Economic Growth'.

Table No. 80: SDG-8, Indian Indicator-1

SDG-8: 'Decent Work and Economic Growth'	**Indicator-1:** Annual growth rate of GDP per capita (at constant price of 2011-12).
Indicator data source	Ministry of Statistics and Programme Implementation [Ministry Reports]
Computation approach	Directly from data source
Data period (year)	2017-18

(Contd...)

Data periodicity	Annual
Relevant UN target	8.1: Sustain per capita economic growth in accordance with national circumstances and, in particular, at least 7% Gross Domestic Product (GDP) growth per annum in the least developed countries.
Relevant UN indicator	8.1.1: Annual growth rate of real GDP per capita.
Relevant MoSPI indicator	8.1.1: Annual growth rate of GDP (adjusted to price changes) per capita.
Indicator interpretation	Higher value means higher performance (+).

Source: (NITI Aayog 2018).

Table No. 81: SDG-8, Indian Indicator-2

SDG-8: 'Decent Work and Economic Growth'	**Indicator-2:** Average unemployment rate per 1000 persons for males and females.
Indicator data source	Labour Bureau [Labour Bureau Report]
Computation approach	Directly from data source
Data period (year)	2015-16
States/UTs covered	36
Data periodicity	Annual
Relevant UN target	8.5: By 2030, achieve full and productive employment and decent work for all women and men, including for young people and persons with disabilities, and equal pay for work of equal value.
Relevant UN indicator	8.5.2: Unemployment rate, by sex, age and persons with disabilities.
Relevant MoSPI indicator	8.5.1: Unemployment rate.
Indicator interpretation	Higher value means lower performance (-).

Source: (NITI Aayog 2018).

Table No. 82: SDG-8, Indian Indicator-3

SDG-8: 'Decent Work and Economic Growth'	**Indicator-3:** Percentage of households with a Bank account.
Indicator data source	Ministry of Finance [Progress Report on *Pradhan Mantri Jan Dhan Yojna*]
Computation approach	Directly from data source
Data period (year)	2018
States/UTs covered	36
Data periodicity	Weekly
Relevant UN target	8.10: Strengthen the capacity of domestic financial institutions to encourage and expand access to banking, insurance and financial services to all.
Relevant UN indicator	8.10.2: Proportion of adults (15 years and older) with an account at a bank or other financial institution or with a mobile-money-service provider.
Relevant MoSPI indicator	8.10.2: Proportion of population having Bank accounts
Indicator interpretation	Higher value means higher performance (+).

Source: (NITI Aayog 2018).

Table No.83: SDG-8, Indian Indicator-4

SDG-8: 'Decent Work and Economic Growth'	**Indicator-4:** Number of ATMs per 100000 populations.
Indicator data source	Reserve Bank of India [RBI Reports]
Computation approach	Directly from data source
Data period (year)	2018
States/UTs covered	36
Data periodicity	3 months
Relevant UN target	8.10: Strengthen the capacity of domestic financial institutions to encourage and expand access to banking, insurance and financial services to all.
Relevant UN indicator	8.10.1: (a) Number of commercial bank branches per 100000 adults and (b) Number of ATMs per 100000 adults.
Relevant MoSPI indicator	8.10.4: ATMS per 100000 populations.
Indicator interpretation	Higher value means higher performance (+).

Source: (NITI Aayog 2018).

12.6. Provisions of the Indian Constitution for SDG-8

The spirit of the unity in this diverse country, India is secured by its great Constitution; the Constitution of India not only secured its unity, announced a vision in the Preamble in the beginning of its Articles included in the Indian Constitution, "*We the people of India, having solemnly resolved to constitute India into a Sovereign Socialist Secular Democratic Republic and to secure to all its citizens: justice, social, economic and political; liberty of thought, expression, belief, faith and worship; equality of status and of opportunity; and to promote among them all fraternity assuring the dignity of the individual and the unity and integrity of the nation; in our Constituent Assembly this twenty-sixth day of November, 1949, do hereby adopt, enact and give to ourselves this Constitution* (India 1950/2015)". The mode of orientation of the Indian Constitution and the sustainable development goals of the contemporary time are given us an opportunity to make a link between these two visions of development and the author is trying to make the link.

As we know the sustainable development goals are interlinked, that means the success or failure of one is affected to other SDGs. From this perspective, this section presents the provisions in the Indian Constitution to eradicate poverty as reflected in the sustainable development agenda entitled as SDG-8, Decent Work and Economic Growth. The linked Constitutional provisions are in the following Table no-84 -

Table No. 84: Provisions in Indian Constitution for SDG-8

SDG-8 and the Linked Articles and Schedules of the Constitution of India
Article 14, Article 15-(2).(a), (b), Article 15-(3), (4) and (5), Article 16 (1) to (5), Article 21, Article 21A, Article 23 (1) and (2), Article 24, Article 29 (2), Article 38-(1) and (2), Article 39 – (a) to (f), Article 39 A, Article 41, Article 42, Article 43, Article 43 (A), Article 44, Article 45, Article 46, Article 47, Article 48, Article 48A, Article 51 (a) Article 51A, Article 301, Article 302, Article 303, Article 304, Article 305, Article 307, Article 309, Article 310, Article 311, Article 312, Article 313, Article 314, Article 315, Article 320, Article 323A and Article 323B.
Article 246 - Seventh Schedule, List-I: Union List No: 12, 13, 22, 23, 24, 27, 29, 30, 31, 39, 42 to 62 to 66, 76, 82 to 92B and 94. List-II: State List No: 8, 9, 13, 14, 10, 11, 12, 13, 14, 15, 16,17, 18, 21, 23, 24, 25, 26, 27, 28, 30, 31, 32, 34, 35 and 55, 56, 57, 58, 59, 60, 61, 62 and 63. List-III: Concurrent List No: 7, 20, 21, 22, 23, 24, 25 26, 30, 31, 32, 33, 34, 35, 36, 37, 38, 39 and 45.
Article 243G: Eleventh Schedule: Powers, Authority and Responsibilities of Panchayats. Schedule No: 1 to 5, 8, 9, 12, 13, 14, 15, 16, 17, 18, 19, 22 and 26. Article 243W: Twelfth Schedule: Powers, Authority and Responsibilities of Municipalities. Schedule No: 1 to 5, 7, 9, 10, 11 and 16.

Source: The Constitution of India, 2015 as on 9th November, 2015.

12.7. Policies of the Government of India for Targets of the SDG-8

According to the SDG India Index Base Line Report, 2018 (NITI Aayog 2018), India is proactive to achieve the target of the UN's SDGs. The Government of India initiated as well as implemented various policies to capture the indicators of the targets of each individual SDG. On the moment of preparation of SDG India Index Base Line Report, 2018, on the basis of the availability of the disaggregated data, the NITI *Aayog* framed India's own indicators of the targets of each individual SDG. For the SDG-8, that is 'Decent Work and Economic Growth'; the NITI *Aayog* framed four indicators; which capture three out of twelve UNs SDG targets. As per the report, 55 dedicated policies or schemes are in action to achieve three targets (8.1, 8.5 and 8.10) of the UN's SDG-8 under the leadership and monitoring of 22 dedicated Ministries or the Departments. The policies or schemes to achieve the targets of SDG-8 and the concerned dedicated Ministries and the Departments are detailed in the - Table no-85.

Table No. 85: Policies Initiated by the Indian Government for Targets of SDG-8

SDG-8, Decent Work and Economic Growth
SDG-8: *Decent Work and Economic Growth* which aims to promote development oriented policies that support productive activities, decent job creation, entrepreneurship, and encourage the formalization and growth of micro-small-and medium-sized enterprises through access to financial services.

(*Contd...*)

Target: 8.1: By 2030 ensure universal access to affordable, reliable and modern energy services for all. 8.1 Sustain per capita economic growth in accordance with national circumstances and, in particular, at least 7% Gross Domestic Product (GDP) growth per annum in the least developed countries.	
Centrally Sponsored /Central Sector Schemes (CSS)	Concerned Ministries/ Departments
	Ministry of Labour & Employment, Ministry of Finance, MoSPI, Ministry of Rural Development, Ministry of Housing and urban Affairs,
Target: 8.2: Achieve higher level of economic productivity through diversification, technological upgrading and innovation, including through a focus on high-value added and labour intensive-sectors.	
Centrally Sponsored /Central Sector Schemes (CSS)	Concerned Ministries/ Departments
1. *Pradhan Mantri Rojgar Protsahan Yojana* 2. Employment Promotion Scheme 3. National Career Services	Ministry of Labour and Employment
4. Prime Minister's Employment Generation Programme (PMEGP) and other Credit Support Schemes	MSME
5. Innovation, Technology Development and Deployment	Department of Science and Technology
6. Green Revolution 7. White Revolution	Agriculture and Cooperation
	MoSPI
Target: 8.3: Promote development-oriented policies that support productive activities, decent job creation, entrepreneurship, creativity and innovation and encourage the formalization and growth of micro-small and medium-sized enterprises, including through access of financial services.	
Centrally Sponsored /Central Sector Schemes (CSS)	Concerned Ministries/ Departments
1. *Deendayal Antyodaya Yojana*-National Rural Livelihood Mission (DAY-NRLM)	Ministry of Rural Development
2. *Deendayal Antyodaya Yojana*-National Urban Livelihood Mission (DAY-NULM)	Ministry of Housing and urban Affairs
3. Make in India (Scheme for Investment Promotion, Scheme for implementation of National Manufacturing Policy, etc.) 4. Ease of Doing Business (e-Biz Project) 5. Start up India	Ministry of Commerce & Industry (DIPP)
6. Stand-Up India 7. *Pradhan Mantri Mudra Yojana* (PMMY) and allied initiatives 8. Credit Guarantee Funds	Ministry of Finance
9. Prime Minister Employment Generation Programme and Other Credit Support Schemes 10. Development of Khadi, Village and Coir Industries 11. Modified Market Development Assistance (MMDA) & setting up of Khadi plazas 12. Technology Upgradation and Quality Certification 13. Entrepreneurship and Skill Development. 14. Infrastructure Development Programme	MSME

(*Contd...*)

15. Social Security Schemes for Workers 16. Schemes to implement labour laws	Ministry of Labour and Employment
	Ministry of Tribal Affairs
Target: 8.4: Improve progressively, through 2030, global resource efficiency in consumption and production and endeavour to decouple economic growth from environmental degradation, in accordance with the 10-year framework of programmes on sustainable consumption and production, with developed countries taking the lead.	
Centrally Sponsored /Central Sector Schemes (CSS)	Concerned Ministries/ Departments
1. *Swachh Bharat* Mission-Rural	Ministry of Rural Development
2. *Swachh Bharat* Mission-Urban 3. Smart Cities Mission 4. Atal Mission for Rejuvenation and Urban Transformation (AMRUT)	Ministry of Housing and urban Affairs
5. National River Conservation Programme	MoEF&CC
6. Grid Interactive Renewable Power 7. Off-Grid Distributed and Decentralized Renewable Power 8. Research & Development	New and Renewable Energy
Target: 8.5: By 2030 achieve full and productive employment and decent work for all women and men, including for young people and persons with disabilities, and equal pay for work of equal value.	
Centrally Sponsored /Central Sector Schemes (CSS)	Concerned Ministries/ Departments
4. *Pradhan Mantri Kaushal Vikas Yojana*	Ministry of Skill Development & Entrepreneurship
5. Vocational Training Centres in Tribal Areas 6. National Schedule Caste/Schedule Tribe Hub Centre	Ministry of Labour & Employment
7. Integrated Skill Development Scheme (textiles)	Ministry of Textiles
8. Mission for Protection and Empowerment of Women and Girls	Ministry of Women and Child Development
9. Umbrella Programme for Skill Development of Minorities: i. *Seekho aur Kamao* – Skill Development Initiatives for minorities ii. Upgrading Skills and Training in Traditional Arts/Crafts for Development (USTAAD) for minorities iii. *Nai Manzil*- The Integrated educational and Livelihood initiatives	Ministry of Minority Affairs
10. National Program for the Welfare of Persons with Disabilities 11. Umbrella Programme for Development of Other Vulnerable Groups	Ministry of Social Justice and Empowerment
12. Umbrella Programme for Skill Development of ST communities Vulnerable Groups	Ministry of Tribal Affairs
Target: 8.6: By 2030 substantially reduce the proportion of youth not in employment, education or training.	
Centrally Sponsored /Central Sector Schemes (CSS)	Concerned Ministries/ Departments
1. *Pradhan Mantri Kaushal Vikas Yojana*	Ministry of Skill Development & Entrepreneurship,

(*Contd...*)

2. *Pradhan Mantri Rojgar Protsahan Yojana* 3. National Career Services (NCS) 4. Employment Promotion Scheme	Ministry of Labour & Employment,
5. National Service Scheme 6. Schemes for Youth development & Education (Nehru *Yuva Kendra Sangathan*, National Programme for Youth and Adolescent Development, etc.)	Ministry of Youth Affairs and Sports
7. Umbrella Programme for Development of STs	Ministry of Tribal Affairs
Target: 8.7: Take immediate and effective measures to eradicate forced labour, end modern slavery and human trafficking and secure the prohibition and elimination of the worst forms of child labour, including recruitment and use of child soldiers, and by 2025 end child labour in all its forms.	
Centrally Sponsored /Central Sector Schemes (CSS)	Concerned Ministries/ Departments
1. National Child Labour Project 2. Rehabilitation of Bonded Labourers	Ministry of Labour & Employment
	Ministry of Home Affairs, Ministry of Women and Child Development
Target: 8.8: Protect labour rights and promote safe and secure working environments for all workers, including migrant workers, in particular women migrants, and those in precarious employment.	
Centrally Sponsored /Central Sector Schemes (CSS)	Concerned Ministries/ Departments
1. Labour Welfare Scheme 2. Social Security for Unorganised Workers 3. Schemes for awareness generation, occupational health and enforcement of labour laws, etc.	Ministry of Labour & Employment
Target: 8.9: By 2030 devise and implement policies to promote sustainable tourism that creates jobs and promotes local culture and products.	
Centrally Sponsored /Central Sector Schemes (CSS)	Concerned Ministries/ Departments
1. Tourism Infrastructure 2. Promotion and Publicity 3. Training and Skill Development	Ministry of Tourism
4. Integrated Skill Development Scheme (textiles)	Ministry of Textiles
Target: 8.10: Strengthen the capacity of domestic financial institutions to encourage and expand access to banking, insurance and financial services to all.	
Centrally Sponsored /Central Sector Schemes (CSS)	Concerned Ministries/ Departments
1. Recapitalisation of Public Sector Banks 2. Support to Financial Institutions	Ministry of Finance
Target: 8.a: Increase Aid for Trade support for developing countries, in particular least developed countries, through the Enhanced Integrated Framework for Trade-Related Technical Assistance to Least Developed Countries.	
Centrally Sponsored /Central Sector Schemes (CSS)	Concerned Ministries/ Departments
	Ministry of Commerce
Target: 8.b: By 2020, develop and operationalize a global strategy for youth employment and implement the Global Jobs Pact of the International Labour Organization.	
1. *Pradhan Mantri Rojgar Protsahan Yojana* 2. National Career Services (NCS)	Ministry of Labour & Employment,

(*Contd*...)

3. Employment Promotion Scheme	
4. National Service Scheme 5. Schemes for Youth development & Education (Nehru *Yuva Kendra Sangathan,* National Programme for Youth and Adolescent Development, etc.)	Ministry of Youth Affairs and Sports

Source: (NITI Aayog 2018).

12.8. Initiatives, Expectation and Performance of Government of India in SDG-8

According to the SDG India Index, Baseline Report, 2018 (NITI Aayog 2018), to achieving the target of the UN's SDG-8, the Government of India had framed four indicators. The Government of India has reported that, 55 dedicated policies or schemes are in action to achieve three targets (8.1, 8.5 and 8.10) of the UN's SDG-8 under the leadership and monitoring of 22 dedicated Ministries or the Departments. The SDG-8 indicators are –

SDG_8_1: Annual growth rate of GDP per capita (at constant price of 2011-12).

SDG_8_2: Average unemployment rate per 1000 persons for males and females.

SDG_8_3: Percentage of households with a Bank account.

SDG_8_4: Number of ATMs per 100000 populations.

Inference: It was assumed that, 'Peace, Justice and Strong Institutions' are the pre-conditions of achievement.

Here, Expected Performance = India SDG 16 Score (UN target of this SDG / 100) and

Performance Difference = (Expected Performance - Performance of India)

From the above conditions it is explored in the table no-86.

Table No. 86: India's SDG-16=71 and the Performances in SDG-8

	SDG_8_1	SDG_8_2	SDG_8_3	SDG_8_4
UN Target of this SDG	10	14.83	100	50.95
Performance of India	6.5	63.5	99.99	16.84
India SDG 16 Score	71	71	71	71
India SDG Mean Score	57	57	57	57
Expected Performance, When SDG 16=71	7.1	10.53	71	36.17

(Contd...)

Indicator Interpretation	Value High - Performance High	Value High - Performance Low	Value High - Performance High	Value High - Performance High
Performance Difference, When SDG 16=71	-0.6	-52.97	+28.99	-19.33

Data Source: NITI *Aayog*, 2018 and Inference drawn by the author.

For the SDG_8_1: That is 'Annual growth rate of GDP per capita (at constant price of 2011-12)'; here, India is slight negatively differed (6.5) from its expected score 7.1, when SDG-16 score is 71 and here performance level have to increase to a level of 0.6 from the present performance. So India have to devote its tools of 'Peace, Justice and Strong Institutions' in a better way for a better score. Here the performance difference is -0.6.

For the SDG_8_2: That is 'Average unemployment rate per 1000 persons for males and females'; here, India is negatively differed (63.5) from its expected score 10.53, when SDG-16 score is 71 and here performance level have to increase to a level of 52.97 from the present performance. So India have to devote its tools of 'Peace, Justice and Strong Institutions' in a better way for a better score. Here the performance difference is -52.97.

For the SDG_8_3: That is 'Percentage of households with a Bank account'; here, India is positively differed (99.99) from its expected score 71, when SDG-16 score is 71 and here performance level have to hold with demographic changes according with the present performance. So India have to devote its tools of 'Peace, Justice and Strong Institutions' in a better way for a better score. Here the performance difference is +28.99.

For the SDG_8_4: That is 'Number of ATMs per 100000 populations'; here, India is negatively differed (16.84) from its expected score 36.17, when SDG-16 score is 71 and here performance level have to increase to a level of 19.33 from the present performance. So India have to devote its tools of 'Peace, Justice and Strong Institutions' in a better way for a better score. Here the performance difference is -19.33.

12.9. Government of India's Remaining Targets and the Indicators for SDG-8

As we know that, on the basis of the availability of the disaggregated data, the NITI *Aayog* had framed India's own indicators of the targets of each individual SDG. For the SDG-8, that is 'Decent Work and Economic Growth', the NITI *Aayog* had framed four indicators; which captured four (7.1.1, 7.1.2 and 7.2.1) of seventeen indicators of the twelve UNs SDG targets. As per the report, 55 dedicated policies or schemes are in action to achieve three targets (8.1, 8.5 and 8.10) of the UN's SDG-8; the remaining indicators of the UN's SDG-8 is to be achieve by 2030. The remaining lists of targets along with the indicators of SDG-8 are detailed in Table no-87.

Table No. 87: Government of India's Remaining Targets and the Indicators for SDG-8

India's Remaining Targets and the Indicators for SDG-8	
Targets	**Indicators**
8.1: Sustain per capita economic growth in accordance with national circumstances and, in particular, at least 7 per cent gross domestic product growth per annum in the least developed countries [i].	8.1.1: Annual growth rate of real GDP per capita [i].
8.2: Achieve higher levels of economic productivity through diversification, technological upgrading and innovation, including through a focus on high-value added and labour-intensive sectors [iii].	8.2.1: Annual growth rate of real GDP per employed person [iii].
8.3: Promote development-oriented policies that support productive activities, decent job creation, entrepreneurship, creativity and innovation, and encourage the formalization and growth of micro-, small- and medium-sized enterprises, including through access to financial services [iii].	8.3.1: Proportion of informal employment in non-agriculture employment, by sex [iii].
8.4: Improve progressively, through 2030, global resource efficiency in consumption and production and endeavour to decouple economic growth from environmental degradation, in accordance with the 10-Year Framework of Programmes on Sustainable Consumption and Production, with developed countries taking the lead [iii].	8.4.1: Material footprint, material footprint per capita, and material footprint per GDP [iii]. 8.4.2: Domestic material consumption, domestic material consumption per capita, and domestic material consumption per GDP [iii].
8.5: By 2030, achieve full and productive employment and decent work for all women and men, including for young people and persons with disabilities, and equal pay for work of equal value [ii].	8.5.1: Average hourly earnings of female and male employees, by occupation, age and persons with disabilities [iii]. 8.5.2: Unemployment rate, by sex, age and persons with disabilities [i].
8.6: By 2020, substantially reduce the proportion of youth not in employment, education or training [iii].	8.6.1: Proportion of youth (aged 15-24 years) not in education, employment or training [iii].
8.7: Take immediate and effective measures to eradicate forced labour, end modern slavery and human trafficking and secure the prohibition and elimination of the worst forms of child labour, including recruitment and use of child soldiers, and by 2025 end child labour in all its forms [iii].	8.7.1: Proportion and number of children aged 5-17 years engaged in child labour, by sex and age [iii].

(Contd...)

8.8: Protect labour rights and promote safe and secure working environments for all workers, including migrant workers, in particular women migrants, and those in precarious employment [iii].	8.8.1: Frequency rates of fatal and non-fatal occupational injuries, by sex and migrant status [iii].
	8.8.2: Increase in national compliance of labour rights (freedom of association and collective bargaining) based on International Labour Organization (ILO) textual sources and national legislation, by sex and migrant status [iii].
8.9: By 2030, devise and implement policies to promote sustainable tourism that creates jobs and promotes local culture and products [iii].	8.9.1: Tourism direct GDP as a proportion of total GDP and in growth rate [iii].
	8.9.2: Number of jobs in tourism industries as a proportion of total jobs and growth rate of jobs, by sex [3].
8.10: Strengthen the capacity of domestic financial institutions to encourage and expand access to banking, insurance and financial services for all [i].	8.10.1: Number of commercial bank branches and automated teller machines (ATMs) per 100,000 adults [i].
	8.10.2: Proportion of adults (15 years and older) with an account at a bank or other financial institution or with a mobile-money-service provider [i].
8.a: Increase Aid for Trade support for developing countries, in particular least developed countries, including through the Enhanced Integrated Framework for Trade-related Technical Assistance to Least Developed Countries [iii].	8.a.1: Aid for Trade commitments and disbursements [iii].
8.b: By 2020, develop and operationalize a global strategy for youth employment and implement the Global Jobs Pact of the International Labour Organization [iii].	8.b.1: Total government spending in social protection and employment programmes as a proportion of the national budgets and GDP [iii].

Notes of the Table:

i. Target indicators captured and analysed.
ii. Not captured all the indicators.
iii. Remaining.

The Ministries and the Departments associate with indicators of this SDG such as Agriculture & Cooperation, Commerce, Commerce & Industry (DIPP), Finance, Home Affairs, Housing and Urban Affairs, Tribal Affairs, Labour & Employment, Minority Affairs, MoEF&CC, MoSPI, MSME, New and Renewable Energy, Rural Development, Science and Technology, Skill Development & Entrepreneurship, Social Justice and Empowerment, Textiles, Tourism, Tribal Affairs, Women and Child Development, Youth Affairs and Sports have to concentrate to monitor on the above issues to achieve the target by 2030 through the provisions of Indian Constitution such as Article 14, Article 15-(2).(a), (b), Article 15-(3), (4) and (5), Article 16 (1) to (5), Article 21, Article 21A, Article 23 (1) and (2), Article 24, Article 29 (2), Article 38-(1) and

(2), Article 39 – (a) to (f), Article 39 A, Article 41, Article 42, Article 43, Article 43 (A), Article 44, Article 45, Article 46, Article 47, Article 48, Article 48A, Article 51 (a) Article 51A, Article 301, Article 302, Article 303, Article 304, Article 305, Article 307, Article 309, Article 310, Article 311, Article 312, Article 313, Article 314, Article 315, Article 320, Article 323A and Article 323B; Article 243G - Eleventh Schedule - Powers, Authority and Responsibilities of Panchayats – Schedule No – 1 to 5, 8, 9, 12, 13, 14, 15, 16, 17, 18, 19, 22 and 26; Article 243W - Twelfth Schedule - Powers, Authority and Responsibilities of Municipalities - Schedule No – 1 to 5, 7, 9, 10, 11 and 16; Article 246 - Seventh Schedule, List-I: Union List No: 12, 13, 22, 23, 24, 27, 29, 30, 31, 39, 42 to 62 to 66, 76, 82 to 92B and 94; List-II: State List No: 8, 9, 13, 14, 10, 11, 12, 13, 14, 15, 16,17, 18, 21, 23, 24, 25, 26, 27, 28, 30, 31, 32, 34, 35 and 55, 56, 57, 58, 59, 60, 61, 62 and 63 and List-III: Concurrent List No: 7, 20, 21, 22, 23, 24, 25 26, 30, 31, 32, 33, 34, 35, 36, 37, 38, 39 and 45 - if we could not monitor, we would not be able to stand in front of the future generation with a smile.

Chapter – XIII

Initiative and Performance of India in SDG–9, Industry, Innovation and Infrastructure

The industry, innovation and infrastructure development is the global agenda of SDG-8. The industry, innovation and infrastructure development has been aimed at building quality, reliable and resilient infrastructures. It further it was aimed at promoting resource-use efficiency and greater adoption of clean and environmentally sound technologies and industrial processes, to support economic development and human well-being. Investment in innovation is an important pillar of this goal that is build resilient infrastructure, promote inclusive and sustainable industrialization and foster innovation.

13.1. The Global Targets and Indicators for SDG-9

The global indicator framework was developed by the Inter-Agency and Expert Group on SDG Indicators (IAEG-SDGs) and agreed to, as a practical starting point at the 47th session of the UN Statistical Commission held in March 2016. The report of the Commission, which included the global indicator framework, was then taken note of by ECOSOC at its 70th session in June 2016 (NITI Aayog 2018). The global targets and the indicator of this SDG are tabled (Table no-88) bellow –

Table No. 88: UNDP-DDGs Targets and Indicators of SDG-9

SDG-9, Build resilient infrastructure, promote inclusive and sustainable industrialization and foster innovation[1]	
Targets	**Indicators**
9.1: Develop quality, reliable, sustainable and resilient infrastructure, including regional and trans-border infrastructure, to support economic development and human well-being, with a focus on affordable and equitable access for all.	9.1.1: Proportion of the rural population who live within 2 km of an all-season road.
	9.1.2: Passenger and freight volumes, by mode of transport.

1. Data Source: SDG India Index Baseline Report, 2018, NITI *Aayog*, Government of India, New Delhi.

9.2: Promote inclusive and sustainable industrialization and, by 2030, significantly raise industry's share of employment and gross domestic product, in line with national circumstances, and double its share in least developed countries.	9.2.1: Manufacturing value added as a proportion of GDP and per capita. 9.2.2: Manufacturing employment as a proportion of total employment.
9.3: Increase the access of small-scale industrial and other enterprises, in particular in developing countries, to financial services, including affordable credit, and their integration into value chains and markets.	9.3.1: Proportion of small-scale industries in total industry value added. 9.3.2: Proportion of small-scale industries with a loan or line of credit.
9.4: By 2030, upgrade infrastructure and retrofit industries to make them sustainable, with increased resource-use efficiency and greater adoption of clean and environmentally sound technologies and industrial processes, with all countries taking action in accordance with their respective capabilities.	9.4.1: CO_2 emission per unit of value added.
9.5: Enhance scientific research, upgrade the technological capabilities of industrial sectors in all countries, in particular developing countries, including, by 2030, encouraging innovation and substantially increasing the number of research and development workers per 1 million people and public and private research and development spending.	9.5.1: Research and development expenditure as a proportion of GDP. 9.5.2: Researchers (in full-time equivalent) per million inhabitants.
9.a: Facilitate sustainable and resilient infrastructure development in developing countries through enhanced financial, technological and technical support to African countries, least developed countries, landlocked developing countries and small island developing States.	9.a.1: Total official international support (official development assistance plus other official flows) to infrastructure.
9.b: Support domestic technology development, research and innovation in developing countries, including by ensuring a conducive policy environment for, inter alia, industrial diversification and value addition to commodities.	9.b.1: Proportion of medium and high-tech industry value added in total value added.
9.c: Significantly increase access to information and communications technology and strive to provide universal and affordable access to the Internet in least developed countries by 2020.	9. c.1: Proportion of population covered by a mobile network, by technology.

13.2. Interlinkage of SDG-9 with other SDGs

While industrialization, innovation and infrastructure are the three main drivers of economic growth, inclusive resilience and sustainability must be of paramount significance to enable sustainable development. This section presents the linkage of the SDG-9 to other SDGs, that is said, that the success of this SDG habitually will influence the success of the linked SDGs; according to the SDG India Index, Baseline Report, 2018 (NITI Aayog 2018), the SDG-9 linked with the following SDGs –

SDG-5, is *Gender Equality* as Goal 1 emphasises creation of gender sensitive development strategies, and equal rights and access to economic resources, as well as ownership and control over land and other forms of property, inheritance, natural resources and financial resources, including microfinance.

SDG-6, is *Clean Water and Sanitation*, which aims to achieve universal and equitable access to safe and affordable drinking water and sanitation and hygiene for all.

SDG-7, is *Affordable and Clean Energy* that aims to ensure universal access to affordable, reliable and modern energy services.

SDG-8, is *Decent Work and Economic Growth* which aims to promote development oriented policies that support productive activities, decent job creation, entrepreneurship, and encourage the formalization and growth of micro-, small - and medium-sized enterprises through access to financial services.

SDG-10, is *Reduced Inequalities* that aims to adopt policies, especially fiscal wage and social protection policies and progressively achieve and sustain income growth of the bottom 40 percent of the population at a rate higher than the national average, leading to greater equality.

SDG-11, is *Sustainable Cities and Communities* which aims to ensure access for all to adequate, safe and affordable housing and basic services and upgrade slums, and significantly reduce the numbers of deaths and people affected by disasters, with focus on protecting the poor and vulnerable.

SDG-12, *Sustainable Consumption and Production* aiming to halve per capita global food waste at consumer level and reduce food losses along production and supply chains.

SDG-13, is *Climate Action* which aims to develop resilience and adaptive capacity of the poor to climate related hazards and natural disasters.

13.3. The National Context of SDG-9

As we know that, the Infrastructure is a critical determinant of economic growth as it has a direct bearing on investment, manufacturing sector, logistics and productivity. It is equally important for social sectors – investment in appropriate infrastructure is critical for positive outcomes in education and health. It is so vital and important for promoting inclusive development and poverty reduction. India aimed to build resilient infrastructure, achieve sustainable industrialization and promote innovation and research.

India is taking forward an unprecedented reform agenda to trigger manufacturing, spur industrialization, promotes investment and foster innovation. Major structural reforms such as Goods and Services Tax (GST) implementation, ease of doing business reforms and introduction of insolvency and bankruptcy code have been rolled out. Focus on digital revolution; internet penetration and financial inclusion are contributing to fuelling growth and investment. Flagship initiative like 'Make in India', '*Startup* India', '*Standup* India', and 'Skill India' have been launched and are playing an important role in augmenting the collective growth impact. These reforms are fast creating a highly conducive ecosystem accelerating the growth of innovation, creativity, entrepreneurship and business within a fast growing formal economy.

As per reports, the transformational impact on the Indian economy is evident from India's significant jump of 33 places in the World Bank's ease of doing business rankings, 2018, from 100th rank in 2017 to 77th rank in 2018. India is the only nation to have made it to the list of top 10 improvers for the second consecutive year. India undertook more than seven thousand reforms in the 36 States and Union Territories (UTs) to simplify business regime. India has also made progress on other international indices. India raised five spots over a year to secure the 58th spot in the 2018 Global Competitiveness Index. India climbed one spot, to 8th rank in the 2017 at A. T. Kearney Foreign Direct Investment (FDI) confidence index, because of simplified and transparent business environment but due to investors worry about rising political and economic risks within these markets, India fall down 5th spot from the 2018 and ranked 16 with a score of 1.54 when the top that is United States of America scored 2.10.

On the account of economic growth, the government of India is taking several initiatives to boost the infrastructure sector. The PMGSY was launched by the Government of India to provide connectivity to remote habitations as part of a poverty reduction strategy. The total funds allocated to PMGSY in the Union Budget 2018-19 is about Rs. 19000 crore. *Bharatmala*, the ambitious project to link India with world class highways and the *Sagarmala* programme to facilitate port-led industrialization are giving a renewed thrust to the development of infrastructure and integrated logistics framework in the country.

The Make in India campaign has been launched with the objective of attracting foreign and domestic investments so as to develop the country as a global hub for manufacturing, innovation and design. The Digital India is a flagship programme launched with an aim to transform India into a digitally powered society and prepare India as a knowledge economy by focusing on technology to enable change. It is an umbrella programme which covers various sectors under its purview to lay emphasis on National e-Governance Plan. The *Aadhaar* programme, wherein every resident of the country is provided with a unique identification number, is one of the key pillars of Digital India.

The development of road connectivity is considered one among the good determinants of economic growth. Good connectivity is a fundamental requirement for industrialization and development. To ensure equitable spread of industrial growth, all regions, including each and every habitation in villages and small towns, must be connected by all-weather roads. To make this possible, the Government of India has initiated a programme *Pradhan Mantri Gram Sadak Yojana* (PMGSY). At the national level, 47.38 percent of targeted habitations have been covered. Gujarat is the only State that has achieved 100 percent connectivity under PMGSY. Rajasthan has achieved the second highest connectivity at 81.88 percent.

In the contemporary world, Internet density and mobile tele-density are playing a major role to economic growth by speedy paperless communication. India aimed to achieve the target of providing at least one mobile connection and one internet connection per person by 2030. The mobile density per 100 persons is more than 100 percent in six States and one Union Territory. In the issue of telecommunication that is number of user of mobile, at the national level, mobile density is roughly 83 per 100 persons. Internet access is significantly lower in comparison to mobile access. There are about 33 internet subscribers per 100 persons nationally. Delhi has the highest internet density in the country, with 126 internet connections per 100 persons.

The government of India initiated 'Bharat Net' coverage with a holistic goal. 'Bharat Net' has been launched to develop infrastructure to spread the reach of mobile and internet access to the remotest *Gram Panchayats* (GPs) in the country. Currently 42.43 percent of the Gram Panchayats in India are covered under Bharat Net, as against the national target of 100 percent. Two States and one Union Territory, namely Karnataka, Kerala and Puducherry have achieved this target.

In the next part of this chapter we tried to visualized the performance level of India through the SDG's targets and the SDG India Index Base Line Report, 2018 along with the Constitutional provisions in India to explore citizen's responsibility along with the its institutions through the mirror of indexed score on 'peace, justice and strong institutions' (SDG-16).

13.4. SDG-9 Targets, National Indicators and Target Values of India

India in its SDG India Index Base Line Report, 2018 (NITI Aayog 2018), India had measured the performance of India on the goal of 'Industry, Innovation and Infrastructure', India had identified four national level indicators, which captured two (9.1 and 9.c) out of eight UN's SDG targets. These indicators have been selected based on availability of data at national level; these are in Table no-89.

Table No. 89: SDG-9 Targets, National Indicators and Target Values of India

SDG-9 Global Target	Indicator Selected for SDG India Index	National Target Value for 2030
9.1: Develop quality, reliable, sustainable and resilient infrastructure, including regional and trans-border infrastructure, to support economic development and human well-being, with a focus on affordable and equitable access for all.	1. Percentage of targeted habitations connected by all-weather roads under *Pradhan Mantri Gram Sadak Yojana.*	100
9. c: Significantly increase access to information and communications technology and strive to provide universal and affordable access to the Internet in least developed countries by 2020.	2. Number of mobile connections per 100 persons in rural and urban areas (Mobile tele Density).	100
	3. Number of Internet Subscribers per 100 population.	100
	4. Percentage of Gram Panchayats covered under Bharat Net.	100

Source: (NITI Aayog 2018).

13.5. Indian's SDG-9 Index Indicators, Data Source and Interpretations

The NITI *Aayog*, Government of India had collected required data from different government agencies to capture the UN SDG's target indicators as well as had framed its own indicators to justify the achievement of the SDGs. Apart from that the NITI *Aayog* had developed the computational approach of the disaggregated data as per valid methods along with the parameters of the performance; in the following tables (Table no-90, Table no-91, Tableno-92 and Table no-93) shows the details of the above issue to develop a sense of progress of the SDG-9, entitled as 'Industry, Innovation and Infrastructure'.

Table No. 90: SDG-9, Indian Indicator-1

SDG-9: 'Industry, Innovation and Infrastructure'	**Indicator-1:** Percentage of targeted habitations connected by all-weather roads under *Pradhan Mantri Gram Sadak Yojana*.
Indicator data source	National Rural Roads Development Organisation [*Pradhan Mantri Gram Sadak Yojana* Dashboard]
Computation approach	Directly from data source
Data period (year)	2017-18
States/UTs covered	29
Data periodicity	Monthly
Relevant UN target	9.1: Develop quality, reliable, sustainable and resilient infrastructure, including regional and trans-border infrastructure, to support economic development and human well-being, with a focus on affordable and equitable access for all.
Relevant UN indicator	9.1.1: Proportion of the rural population who live within 2 KM of an all-season road.
Relevant MoSPI indicator	9.1.1: Proportion of the rural population who live within 2 KM of an all-season road.
Indicator interpretation	Higher value means higher performance (+).

Source: (NITI Aayog 2018).

Table No. 91: SDG-9, Indian Indicator-2

SDG-9: 'Industry, Innovation and Infrastructure'	**Indicator-2:** Number of mobile connections per 100 persons in rural and urban areas (Mobile tele Density).
Indicator data source	Numerator: Department of Telecommunications [DoT Reports] Denominator: Ministry of Home Affairs, [Census 2011]
Computation approach	Number of mobile connections per 100 persons in rural and urban areas calculated as – (Total number of mobile connections ÷ total population multiplied) × 100. Population for 2016 was estimated based on Census 2011.

(*Contd...*)

Data period (year)	2016-17
States/UTs covered	18
Data periodicity	Annual
Relevant UN target	9.c: Significantly increase access to information and communication technology and strive to provide universal and affordable access to the internet to least developed countries by 2030.
Relevant UN indicator	9. c.1: Proportion of population covered by a mobile network, by technology.
Relevant MoSPI indicator	9. c.1: Proportion of population covered by a mobile network, by technology.
Indicator interpretation	Higher value means higher performance (+).

Source: (NITI Aayog 2018).

Table No. 92: SDG-9, Indian Indicator-3

SDG-9: 'Industry, Innovation and Infrastructure'	**Indicator-3:** Number of Internet Subscribers per 100 populations.
Indicator data source	Telecom Regulatory Authority of India [The Indian Telecom Services Performance Indicators]
Computation approach	Directly from data source
Data period (year)	June, 2017
States/UTs covered	18
Data periodicity	Annual
Relevant UN target	9.c: Significantly increase access to information and communication technology and strive to provide universal and affordable access to the internet to least developed countries by 2030.
Relevant UN indicator	NA
Relevant MoSPI indicator	9. c.2: Number of broadband subscribers per 10000 persons.
Indicator interpretation	Higher value means higher performance (+).

Source: (NITI Aayog 2018).

Table No. 93: SDG-9, Indian Indicator-4

SDG-9: 'Industry, Innovation and Infrastructure'	**Indicator-4**: Percentage of Gram Panchayats covered under Bharat Net.
Indicator data source	Numerator: Department of Telecommunications, [DoT Reports] Denominator: Ministry of *Panchayati Raj* [Lok Sabha Unstarred Questions 1863]
Computation approach	Percentage of Gram Panchayats covered under Bharat Net calculated as – (Gram Panchayats covered by Bharat Net ÷ number of Gram Panchayats) × 100.
Data period (year)	June, 2017

(*Contd*...)

States/UTs covered	18
Data periodicity	Annual
Relevant UN target	9.c: Significantly increase access to information and communication technology and strive to provide universal and affordable access to the internet to least developed countries by 2030.
Relevant UN indicator	NA
Relevant MoSPI indicator	NA
Indicator interpretation	Higher value means higher performance (+).

Source: (NITI Aayog 2018).

13.6. Provisions of the Indian Constitution for SDG-9

The spirit of the unity in this diverse country, India is secured by its great Constitution; the Constitution of India not only secured its unity, announced a vision in the Preamble in the beginning of its Articles included in the Indian Constitution, *"We the people of India, having solemnly resolved to constitute India into a Sovereign Socialist Secular Democratic Republic and to secure to all its citizens: justice, social, economic and political; liberty of thought, expression, belief, faith and worship; equality of status and of opportunity; and to promote among them all fraternity assuring the dignity of the individual and the unity and integrity of the nation; in our Constituent Assembly this twenty-sixth day of November, 1949, do hereby adopt, enact and give to ourselves this Constitution* (India 1950/2015)". The mode of orientation of the Indian Constitution and the sustainable development goals of the contemporary time are given us an opportunity to make a link between these two visions of development and the author is trying to make the link.

As we know the sustainable development goals are interlinked, that means the success or failure of one is affected to other SDGs. From this perspective, this section presents the provisions in the Indian Constitution to eradicate poverty as reflected in the sustainable development agenda entitled as SDG-9, Industry, Innovation and Infrastructure. The linked Constitutional provisions are in the following Table no-94 -

Table No. 94: Provisions in Indian Constitution for SDG-9

SDG-9 and the Linked Articles and Schedules of the Constitution of India
Article 14, Article 16 (1) to (5), Article 21, Article 21A, Article 38-(1) and (2), Article 39 – (a) to (f), Article 39A, Article 41, Article 42, Article 43, Article 43 (A), Article 44, Article 46, Article 48, Article 48A, Article 51A, Article 301, Article 302, Article 303. Article 304, Article 304, Article 307, Article 309, Article 310, Article 311, Article 312, Article 313, Article 314, Article 315, Article 320, Article 323A, Article 323B Article 364 and 365.

(Contd...)

Article 246 - Seventh Schedule, List-I: Union List No: 7, 12, 13, 22, 23, 24, 25, 27, 28, 29, 30, 31, 36, 38, 39, 41, 42, 43, 44, 45, 46, 47, 48, 49, 50, 51, 52, 53, 54, 55, 56, 57, 58, 59, 60, 61, 62, 63, 64, 65, 66, 67 , 68, 69, 76, 82, 83, 84, 85, 86, 87, 88, 89, 90, 91, 92, 92A, 92B and 94. List-II State List No: 8, 9, 13, 14 to 18, 21, 23, 24, 25, 26, 27, 28, 30, 31, 32, 34, 35 and 37, 38, 39, 40, 41, 42, 43, 44, 45, 46, 47, 48, 49, 50, 51, 52, 53, 54, 55, 56, 57, 58, 59, 60, 61, 62, 63, 64, 65 and 66. List-III: Concurrent List No: 6, 7, 10, 20, 21, 22, 23, 24, 25, 26 and 31, 32, 33, 34, 35, 36, 37, 38, 39, 40, 41, 42, 43, 44, 45, 46 and 47.
Article 243G: Eleventh Schedule: Powers, Authority and Responsibilities of Panchayats. Schedule No: 1, 2, 3, 4, 5, 8, 9, 12, 13, 14, 15, 16, 17, 18, 19, 20, 21, 22, 26 and 27. Article 243W: Twelfth Schedule: Powers, Authority and Responsibilities of Municipalities. Schedule No: 1, 2, 3, 4, 5, 6, 7, 8, 9, 10, 11, 12, 16 and 17.

Source: The Constitution of India, 2015 as on 9th November, 2015.

13.7. Policies of the Government of India for Targets of the SDG-9

According to the SDG India Index Base Line Report, 2018, India is proactive to achieve the target of the UN's SDGs. The Government of India initiated as well as implemented various policies to capture the indicators of the targets of each individual SDG. On the moment of preparation of SDG India Index Base Line Report, 2018, on the basis of the availability of the disaggregated data, the NITI *Aayog* framed India's own indicators of the targets of each individual SDG. For the SDG-9, that is 'Industry, Innovation and Infrastructure'; the NITI *Aayog* framed four indicators; which capture two out of eight UNs SDG targets. As per the report, 45 dedicated policies or schemes are in action to achieve two targets (9.1 and 9.2) of the UN's SDG-9 under the leadership and monitoring of 22 dedicated Ministries or the Departments. The policies or schemes to achieve the targets of SDG-9 and the concerned dedicated Ministries and the Departments are detailed in the - Table no – 95.

Table No. 95: Policies Initiated by the Indian Government for Targets of SDG-9

SDG-9, Industry, Innovation and Infrastructure	
SDG-9, is *Industry, Innovation and Infrastructure* aims at building quality, reliable and resilient infrastructures. It further aims at promoting resource-use efficiency and greater adoption of clean and environmentally sound technologies and industrial processes, to support economic development and human well-being. Investment in innovation is an important pillar of this goal.	
Target: 9.1: Develop quality, reliable, sustainable and resilient infrastructure, including regional and trans-border infrastructure, to support economic development and human well-being, with a focus on affordable and equitable access for all	
Centrally Sponsored /Central Sector Schemes (CSS)	Concerned Ministries/ Departments
1. *Pradhan Mantri Gram Sadak Yojana* (PMGSY) 2. *Shyama Prasad Mukherjee Rurban* Mission	Ministry of Rural Development,
1. *Bharatmala Pariyojana* 2. Special Accelerated Road Development Programme for North Eastern Region (SARDP-NE)	Ministry of Road Transport and Highways

(*Contd...*)

3. Railways, Mass Rapid Transit System (MRTS) and Metro Projects	Ministry of Railways
4. Border Area Development Programme (BADP)	Ministry of Home Affairs
5. Development of Industrial Corridors 6.Modified Industrial Infrastructure Upgradation Scheme (MIIUS) 7. North East Industrial Development Scheme (NEIDS) 8. Industrial Development Scheme for Himalayan States - Jammu & Kashmir, Himachal Pradesh and Uttarakhand 9. Indian Footwear, Leather & Accessories Development Programme	DIPP
10. Schemes for upgradation of Airport Infrastructure 11. Schemes for Regional Connectivity	Ministry of Civil Aviation
12. National Handloom Development Programme 13. Catalytic Development Programme under Sericulture	Ministry of Textiles
14. Digital India 15. Promotion of Electronics and IT HW manufacturing (MSIPS, EDF and Manufacturing Clusters)	Ministry of Electronics & Information Technology
16. *Sagarmala* Programme	Ministry of Shipping
17. MPLADS	Ministry of Statistics & Programme Implementation
Target: 9.2: Promote inclusive and sustainable development and by 2030 significantly raise industry's share of employment and gross domestic product, in line with national circumstances, and double its share in least developed countries.	
Centrally Sponsored /Central Sector Schemes (CSS)	Concerned Ministries/ Departments
1. Science and Technology Institutional and Human Capacity Building 2. Research and Development 3. Innovation, Technology Development and Deployment 4. Biotechnology Research &Development 5. Industrial and Entrepreneurship Development	Department of Science & Technology
6. Environment Protection, Management and Sustainable Development	MoEF&CC
7. Industrial Infrastructure Upgradation Scheme	DIPP
8. Technology Upgradation and Quality Certification 9. Entrepreneurship and Skill Development 10. Infrastructure Development Programme	MSME
	Ministry of Corporate Affairs, Heavy Industry
Target: 9.3: Increase the access of small-scale industrial and other enterprises, in particular in developing countries, to financial services, including affordable credit, and their integration into value chains and markets.	
Centrally Sponsored /Central Sector Schemes (CSS)	Concerned Ministries/ Departments
1. Make in India (Scheme for Investment Promotion, Scheme for implementation of National Manufacturing Policy, etc.) 2. Ease of Doing Business (e-Biz Project) 3. Start-up India	DIPP
4. Stand-Up India	Ministry of Finance
5. Development of Khadi, Village and Coir Industries 6. Technology Upgradation and Quality 7. Entrepreneurship and Skill Development. 8. Infrastructure Development Programme	MSME

(Contd...)

<table>
<tr><td>9. Pradhan Mantri Mudra Yojana (PMMY) and allied initiatives
10. Credit Guarantee Funds</td><td>Ministry of Finance</td></tr>
<tr><td>11. Umbrella Programme for Development of Scheduled Tribes</td><td>Ministry of Tribal Affairs</td></tr>
<tr><td colspan="2">Target: 9.4: By 2030, upgrade infrastructure and retrofits industries to make them sustainable, with increased resource-use efficiency and greater adoption of clean and environmentally sound technologies and industrial processes, with all countries taking action in accordance with their respective capabilities.</td></tr>
<tr><td>Centrally Sponsored /Central Sector Schemes (CSS)</td><td>Concerned Ministries/ Departments</td></tr>
<tr><td>1. Digital India</td><td>Department of Science & Technology</td></tr>
<tr><td>2. Railways, Mass Rapid Transit System (MRTS) and Metro Projects</td><td>Ministry of Housing and Urban Affairs</td></tr>
<tr><td>3. Scheme for Faster Adoption and Manufacturing of (Hybrid and) Electric Vehicle in India - (FAME - India).
4. Research and Development project for development of Advanced Ultra Super Critical (AUSC) Technology for Thermal Power Plants</td><td></td></tr>
<tr><td>5. National Handloom Development Programme
6. Catalytic Development Programme under Sericulture</td><td>Ministry of Textiles</td></tr>
<tr><td>7. Make in India</td><td>DIPP</td></tr>
<tr><td colspan="2">Target: 9.5: Enhance scientific researches, upgrade the technological capabilities of industrial sectors in all countries, in particular developing countries, including, by 2030, encouraging innovation and substantially increasing the number of research and development workers per 1 million people and public and private research and development spending.</td></tr>
<tr><td>Centrally Sponsored /Central Sector Schemes (CSS)</td><td>Concerned Ministries/ Departments</td></tr>
<tr><td>1. Science and Technology Institutional and Human Capacity Building
2. Research and Development
3. Innovation, Technology Development and Deployment
4. Biotechnology Research and Development
5. Industrial and Entrepreneurship Development</td><td>Department of Science & Technology</td></tr>
<tr><td>6. Atal Innovation Mission (AIM) including Self Employment and Talent Utilization (SETU)</td><td>Planning</td></tr>
<tr><td>7. Implementation of the IMPRINT Research Initiative</td><td>Ministry of Human Resource Development</td></tr>
<tr><td colspan="2">Target: 9.a: Facilitate sustainable and resilient infrastructure development in developing countries through enhanced financial, technological and technical support to African countries, least developed countries, landlocked developing countries and small island developing States.</td></tr>
<tr><td>Centrally Sponsored /Central Sector Schemes (CSS)</td><td>Concerned Ministries/ Departments</td></tr>
<tr><td></td><td>Ministry of Rural Development, Ministry of External Affairs</td></tr>
<tr><td colspan="2">Target: 9.b: Support domestic technology development, research and innovation in developing countries, including by ensuring a conductive policy environment for, inter alia, industrial diversification and value addition to commodities.</td></tr>
<tr><td>Centrally Sponsored /Central Sector Schemes (CSS)</td><td>Concerned Ministries/ Departments</td></tr>
<tr><td>1. Science and Technology Institutional and Human Capacity Building
2. Research and Development
3. Innovation, Technology Development and Deployment
4. Biotechnology Research &Development
5. Industrial and Entrepreneurship Development</td><td>Department of Science & Technology</td></tr>
</table>

(*Contd...*)

6. *Shyama Prasad Mukherjee Rurban* Mission	Ministry of Rural Development,
7. Modified Industrial Infrastructure Upgradation Scheme (MIIUS)	DIPP
8. National Handloom Development Programme 9. Catalytic Development Programme under Sericulture	Ministry of Textile
10. Atal Innovation Mission	Planning
11. Railways, Mass Rapid Transit System (MRTS)and Metro Projects	Ministry of Housing and Urban Affairs
12. Digital India 13. Promotion of Electronics and IT HW manufacturing (MSIPS, EDF and Manufacturing Clusters)	Ministry of Electronics & Information Technology
14. MPLADS	Ministry of Statistics & Programme Implementation
Target: 9.c: Significantly increase access to information and communication technology and strive to provide universal and affordable access to the internet to least developed countries by 2030.	
Centrally Sponsored /Central Sector Schemes (CSS)	Concerned Ministries/ Departments
1. Digital India including Promotion of Electronics and IT HW manufacturing (MSIPS, EDF and Manufacturing Clusters	Ministry of Electronics & Information Technology
2. *Bharatnet* 3. Compensation to Telecom Service Providers	Telecommunication

Source: (NITI Aayog 2018).

13.8. Initiatives, Expectation and Performance of Government of India in SDG-9

According to the India SDG Index, Baseline Report, 2018 (NITI Aayog 2018), to achieving the target of the UN's SDG-9, the Government of India had framed four indicators. The Government of India reported that, 45 dedicated policies or schemes are in action to achieve two targets (9.1 and 9.2) of the UN's SDG-9 under the leadership and monitoring of 22 dedicated Ministries or the Departments. The SDG-9 indicators are –

SDG_9_1: Percentage of targeted habitations connected by all-weather roads under *Pradhan Mantri Gram Sadak Yojana*.

SDG_9_2: Number of mobile connections per 100 persons in rural and urban areas (Mobile tele Density).

SDG_9_3: Number of Internet Subscribers per 100 populations.

SDG_9_4: Percentage of Gram Panchayats covered under Bharat Net.

Inference: It was assumed that, 'Peace, Justice and Strong Institutions' are the pre-conditions of achievement.

Here, Expected Performance = India SDG 16 Score (UN target of this SDG / 100) and

Performance Difference = (Expected Performance - Performance of India)

From the above conditions it is explored in the table no-96.

Table No. 96: India's SDG-16=71 and the Performances in SDG-9

SDG India Indicators	SDG_9_1	SDG_9_2	SDG_9_3	SDG_9_4
UN Target of this SDG	100	100	100	100
Performance of India	47.38	82.97	33.47	42.43
India SDG 16 Score	71	71	71	71
India SDG Mean Score	57	57	57	57
Expected Performance, When SDG 16=71	71	71	71	71
Indicator Interpretation	Value High - Performance High	Value High - Performance High	Value High - Performance High	Value High - Performance High
Performance Difference, When SDG 16=71	-23.62	+11.97	-37.53	-28.57

Data Source: NITI *Aayog*, 2018 and Inference drawn by the author.

For the SDG_9_1: That is 'Percentage of targeted habitations connected by all-weather roads under *Pradhan Mantri Gram Sadak Yojana*'; here, India is negatively differed (47.38) from its expected score 71, when SDG-16 score is 71 and here performance level have to increase to a level of 23.62 from the present performance. So India have to devote its tools of 'Peace, Justice and Strong Institutions' in a better way for a better score. Here the performance difference is -23.62.

For the SDG_9_2: That is 'Number of mobile connections per 100 persons in rural and urban areas (Mobile tele Density)'; here, India is positively differed (82.97) from its expected score 71, when SDG-16 score is 71 and here performance level have to hold with demographic changes according with the present performance. So India have to devote its tools of 'Peace, Justice and Strong Institutions' in a better way for a better score. Here the performance difference is +11.97.

For the SDG_9_3: That is 'Number of Internet Subscribers per 100 populations'; here, India is negatively differed (33.47) from its expected score 71, when SDG-16 score is 71 and here performance level have to increase to a level of 37.53 from the present performance. So India have to devote its tools of 'Peace, Justice and Strong Institutions' in a better way for a better score. Here the performance difference is -37.53.

For the SDG_9_4: That is 'Percentage of Gram Panchayats covered under Bharat Net'; here, India is negatively differed (42.43) from its expected score 71, when SDG-16 score is 71 and here performance level have to increase to a level of 28.57 from the present performance. So India have to devote its tools of 'Peace, Justice and Strong Institutions' in a better way for a better score. Here the performance difference is -28.57.

13.9. Government of India's Remaining Targets and the Indicators for SDG-9

As we know that, on the basis of the availability of the disaggregated data, the NITI *Aayog* had framed India's own indicators of the targets of each individual SDG. For the SDG-9, that is 'Industry, Innovation and Infrastructure', the NITI *Aayog* had framed four indicators; which captured two (9.1.1 and 9.c.1) of twelve indicators of the eight UNs SDG targets. As per the report, 45 dedicated policies or schemes are in action to achieve two targets (9.1 and 9.2) of the UN's SDG-9; the remaining indicators of the UN's SDG-9 is to be achieve by 2030. The remaining lists of targets along with the indicators of SDG-9 are detailed in Table no-97.

Table No. 97: Government of India's Remaining Targets and the Indicators for SDG-9

India's Remaining Targets and the Indicators for SDG-9	
Targets	**Indicators**
9.1:Develop quality, reliable, sustainable and resilient infrastructure, including regional and trans-border infrastructure, to support economic development and human well-being, with a focus on affordable and equitable access for all [i].	9.1.1: Proportion of the rural population who live within 2 km of an all-season road [ii].
	9.1.2: Passenger and freight volumes, by mode of transport [iii].
9.2: Promote inclusive and sustainable industrialization and, by 2030, significantly raise industry's share of employment and gross domestic product, in line with national circumstances, and double its share in least developed countries [iii].	9.2.1: Manufacturing value added as a proportion of GDP and per capita [iii].
	9.2.2: Manufacturing employment as a proportion of total employment [iii].
9.3: Increase the access of small-scale industrial and other enterprises, in particular in developing countries, to financial services, including affordable credit, and their integration into value chains and markets [iii].	9.3.1: Proportion of small-scale industries in total industry value added [iii].
	9.3.2: Proportion of small-scale industries with a loan or line of credit [iii].
9.4: By 2030, upgrade infrastructure and retrofit industries to make them sustainable, with increased resource-use efficiency and	9.4.1: CO_2 emission per unit of value added [iii].

(Contd...)

9.4: By 2030, upgrade infrastructure and retrofit industries to make them sustainable, with increased resource-use efficiency and greater adoption of clean and environmentally sound technologies and industrial processes, with all countries taking action in accordance with their respective capabilities [iii].	9.4.1: CO_2 emission per unit of value added [iii].
9.5: Enhance scientific research, upgrade the technological capabilities of industrial sectors in all countries, in particular developing countries, including, by 2030, encouraging innovation and substantially increasing the number of research and development workers per 1 million people and public and private research and development spending [iii].	9.5.1: Research and development expenditure as a proportion of GDP [iii]. 9.5.2: Researchers (in full-time equivalent) per million inhabitant [iii].
9.a: Facilitate sustainable and resilient infrastructure development in developing countries through enhanced financial, technological and technical support to African countries, least developed countries, landlocked developing countries and small island developing States [iii].	9.a.1: Total official international support (official development assistance plus other official flows) to infrastructure [iii].
9.b: Support domestic technology development, research and innovation in developing countries, including by ensuring a conducive policy environment for, inter alia, industrial diversification and value addition to commodities [iii].	9.b.1: Proportion of medium and high-tech industry value added in total value added [iii].
9.c:-Significantly increase access to information and communications technology and strive to provide universal and affordable access to the Internet in least developed countries by 2020 [ii].	9.c.1: Proportion of population covered by a mobile network, by technology [ii].
Notes of the Table: i. Not captured all the indicators. ii. Target indicators captured and analysed. iii. Remaining.	

The Ministries and the Departments associate with indicators of this SDG such as Civil Aviation, Corporate Affairs, DIPP, Electronics & Information Technology, External Affairs, Finance, Heavy Industry, Home Affairs, Housing and Urban Affairs, Human Resource Development, MoEF&CC, MSME, Planning, Railways, Road Transport and Highways, Rural Development, Science & Technology, Shipping, Statistics & Programme Implementation, Telecommunication, Textiles and Tribal Affairs have to concentrate to monitor on the above issues to achieve the target by 2030 through the provisions of Indian Constitution such as Article

14, Article 16 (1) to (5), Article 21, Article 21A, Article 38-(1) and (2), Article 39 – (a) to (f), Article 39A, Article 41, Article 42, Article 43, Article 43 (A), Article 44, Article 46, Article 48, Article 48A, Article 51A, Article 301, Article 302, Article 303. Article 304, Article 304, Article 307, Article 309, Article 310, Article 311, Article 312, Article 313, Article 314, Article 315, Article 320, Article 323A, Article 323B Article 364 and 365; Article 243G - Eleventh Schedule - Powers, Authority and Responsibilities of Panchayats – Schedule No – 1, 2, 3, 4, 5, 8, 9, 12, 13, 14, 15, 16, 17, 18, 19, 20, 21, 22, 26 and 27; Article 243W - Twelfth Schedule - Powers, Authority and Responsibilities of Municipalities - Schedule No – 1, 2, 3, 4, 5, 6, 7, 8, 9, 10, 11, 12, 16 and 17; Article 246 - Seventh Schedule, List-I: Union List No: 7, 12, 13, 22, 23, 24, 25, 27, 28, 29, 30, 31, 36, 38, 39, 41, 42, 43, 44, 45, 46, 47, 48, 49, 50, 51, 52, 53, 54, 55, 56, 57, 58, 59, 60, 61, 62, 63, 64, 65, 66, 67 , 68, 69, 76, 82, 83, 84, 85, 86, 87, 88, 89, 90, 91, 92, 92A, 92B and 94; List-II: State List No: 8, 9, 13, 14 to 18, 21, 23, 24, 25, 26, 27, 28, 30, 31, 32, 34, 35 and 37, 38, 39, 40, 41, 42, 43, 44, 45, 46, 47, 48, 49, 50, 51, 52, 53, 54, 55, 56, 57, 58, 59, 60, 61, 62, 63, 64, 65 and 66 and List-III: Concurrent List No: 6, 7, 10, 20, 21, 22, 23, 24, 25, 26 and 31, 32, 33, 34, 35, 36, 37, 38, 39, 40, 41, 42, 43, 44, 45, 46 and 47 - if we could not monitor, we would not be able to stand in front of the future generation with a smile.

Chapter – XIV

Initiative and Performance of India in SDG-10, Reduced Inequalities

Reducing inequalities is a big challenge around the world, which is reflected in the SDGs and to be achieve by 2030; but reducing inequalities in a country like India is a double-barrelled challenge – economic as well as social; where, the discrimination as well as bias attitude towards women, sometimes cruel behaviour towards low caste origin are deep rooted; almost both are the mentally settled in India. The global agenda of SDG-10 is to 'Reduced Inequalities'; it calls for progressively reducing not only income inequalities but also inequalities of outcome by ensuring access to equal opportunities and promoting social, economic and political inclusion of all, irrespective of age, sex, disability, race, ethnicity, religion or other status relevant within a society. The Goal also aims to enhance representation and voice for developing countries in decision making in international institutions. Along with these, reducing inequality within and among countries that aims to adopt policies, especially fiscal wage and social protection policies and progressively achieve and sustain income growth of the bottom 40 percent of the population at a rate higher than the national average, leading to greater equality.

14.1 The Global Targets and Indicators for SDG-10

The global indicator framework was developed by the Inter-Agency and Expert Group on SDG Indicators (IAEG-SDGs) and agreed to, as a practical starting point at the 47th session of the UN Statistical Commission held in March 2016. The report of the Commission, which included the global indicator framework, was then taken note of by ECOSOC at its 70th session in June 2016 (NITI Aayog 2018). The global targets and the indicator of this SDG are tabled (Table no-96) bellow –

Table No. 98: UNDP-DDGs Targets and Indicators of SDG-10

SDG-10, Reduce inequality within and among countries[1]	
Targets	**Indicators**
10.1: By 2030, progressively achieve and sustain income growth of the bottom 40 per cent of the population at a rate higher than the national average.	10.1.1: Growth rates of household expenditure or income per capita among the bottom 40 per cent of the population and the total population.
10.2: By 2030, empower and promote the social, economic and political inclusion of all, irrespective of age, sex, disability, race, ethnicity, origin, religion or economic or other status.	10.2: By 2030, empower and promote the social, economic and political inclusion of all, irrespective of age, sex, disability, race, ethnicity, origin, religion or economic or other status.
10.3: Ensure equal opportunity and reduce inequalities of outcome, including by eliminating discriminatory laws, policies and practices and promoting appropriate legislation, policies and action in this regard.	10.3.1: Proportion of the population reporting having personally felt discriminated against or harassed within the previous 12 months on the basis of a ground of discrimination prohibited under international human rights law.
10.4: Adopt policies, especially fiscal, wage and social protection policies, and progressively achieve greater equality.	10.4.1: Labour share of GDP, comprising wages and social protection transfers.
10.5: Improve the regulation and monitoring of global financial markets and institutions and strengthen the implementation of such regulations.	10.5.1: Financial Soundness Indicator.
10.6: Ensure enhanced representation and voice for developing countries in decision-making in global international economic and financial institutions in order to deliver more effective, credible, accountable and legitimate institutions.	10.6.1: Proportion of members and voting rights of developing countries in international organizations.
10.7: Facilitate orderly, safe, regular and responsible migration and mobility of people, including through the implementation of planned and well-managed migration policies.	10.7.1: Recruitment cost borne by employee as a proportion of yearly income earned in country of destination.
	10.7.2: Number of countries that have implemented well-managed migration policies.
10.a: Implement the principle of special and differential treatment for developing countries, in particular least developed countries, in accordance with World Trade Organization agreements.	10.a.1: Proportion of tariff lines applied to imports from least developed countries and developing countries with zero-tariff.
10.b: Encourage official development assistance and financial flows, including foreign direct investment, to States where the need is greatest, in particular least developed countries, African countries, small island developing States and landlocked developing countries, in accordance with their national plans and programmes.	10.b.1: Total resource flows for development, by recipient and donor countries and type of flow (e.g. official development assistance, foreign direct investment and other flows).
10.c: By 2030, reduce to less than 3 per cent the transaction costs of migrant remittances and eliminate remittance corridors with costs higher than 5 per cent.	10.c.1: Remittance costs as a proportion of the amount remitted.

1. Data Source: SDG India Index Baseline Report, 2018, NITI *Aayog*, Government of India, New Delhi.

14.2. Interlinkage of SDG-10 with other SDGs

This section presents the linkage of the SDG-10 to other SDGs, that is, the success of this SDG habitually will influence the success of the linked SDGs; according to the SDG India Index, Baseline Report, 2018 (NITI Aayog 2018), the SDG-10 linked with the following SDGs –

SDG-1, that is *No Poverty*, which aims to reduce poverty in all its dimensions, which includes ensuring access to safe, nutritious and sufficient food all year round, particularly for the poor.

SDG-2, that is *Zero Hunger*, which aims to end all forms of malnutrition and ensures access to safe, nutritious and sufficient food for all, in particular the poor and vulnerable, and support small scale food producers.

SDG-3, is *Good Health and Well-being*, which aims to end epidemics and preventable deaths and achieve universal health coverage, including financial risk protection and access to quality essential health care services, medicines and vaccines for all.

SDG-4, is *Quality Education* that aims to ensure that all girls and boys complete free, equitable and quality primary and secondary education leading to relevant and effective learning outcomes, including technical and vocational skills for employment, decent jobs and entrepreneurship.

SDG-5, is *Gender Equality* as Goal 1 emphasises creation of gender sensitive development strategies, and equal rights and access to economic resources, as well as ownership and control over land and other forms of property, inheritance, natural resources and financial resources, including microfinance.

SDG-6, is *Clean Water and Sanitation*, which aims to achieve universal and equitable access to safe and affordable drinking water and sanitation and hygiene for all.

SDG-7, is *Affordable and Clean Energy* that aims to ensure universal access to affordable, reliable and modern energy services.

SDG-8, is *Decent Work and Economic Growth* which aims to promote development oriented policies that support productive activities, decent job creation, entrepreneurship, and encourage the formalization and growth of micro-, small - and medium-sized enterprises through access to financial services.

SDG-9, is *Industry, Innovation and Infrastructure* aims at building quality, reliable and resilient infrastructures. It further aims at promoting resource-use efficiency and greater adoption of clean and environmentally sound technologies and industrial processes, to support economic development and human well-being. Investment in innovation is an important pillar of this goal.

SDG-11, is *Sustainable Cities and Communities* which aims to ensure access for all to adequate, safe and affordable housing and basic services and upgrade slums, and significantly reduce the numbers of deaths and people affected by disasters, with focus on protecting the poor and vulnerable.

Goal-15, *Life on Land* that aims to promote fair and equitable utilization of genetic resources.

SDG-16, *Peace, Justice and Strong Institutions* which aims to build accountable and transparent economic institutions. Since Goal 10 aims to ensure enhanced representation and voice for developing countries in decision making in global and international institutions.

14.3. The National Context of SDG-10

Inequality takes on many forms in a large and diverse country like India. There are inequalities in income and consumption; structural inequalities which take the form of inequalities based on gender, religion, caste and social groups as well as regional inequalities, all of which manifest in inequalities of opportunities and access.

India has a number of legislations and programmes for empowerment and socio-economic development of women and different social groups. There are several programmes in place which aim to provide equal opportunity in education to girls and children from vulnerable sections of the society.

The Government of India's emphasis on the JAM trinity *(Jan Dhan Aadhaar*-Mobile) presents a broad strategy of inclusion, financial security and social empowerment. India has several national level schemes like *Pradhan Mantri Jan Dhan Yojana, Deen Dayal Upadhyay Grameen Kaushal Yojana* and employment schemes like Prime Minister Employment Generation Programme, which are aimed at reducing social, economic and political gaps and progressively achieving greater equality in the country.

To reduce socio-economic inequalities, the government of India initiated several schemes some directly and some indirectly, are aimed at reducing inequalities. Very recently *Pradhan Mantri Jan Dhan Yojana* (PMJDY) was launched in 2014 to promote an inclusive growth agenda and strives to attain financial inclusion of all by providing universal access to banking and other financial services. The plan envisions facilitating the opening of at least one bank account per households, and empowering all through financial literacy, access to credit, insurance and pension facilities. In addition, beneficiaries will be given a RuPay debit card with inbuilt accident insurance cover of Rs.1 lakh.

The Prime Minister Employment Generation Programme (PMEGP), the programme is another such a scheme aimed at generating continuous and sustainable employment opportunities in rural as well as in urban areas. It is a major credit-linked subsidy programme, aimed at generating self-employment opportunities through establishment of micro-enterprises in the non-farm sector by helping traditional artisans and unemployed youth.

The Mahatma Gandhi National Rural Employment Guarantee Act (MGNREGA) enacted in 2005 provides a legal guarantee for 100 days of employment in every financial year, to adult members of any rural household willing to do un-skilled manual work related to public-works, at the statutory minimum wage. It aims to bridge the gap between the rich and the poor and increase the purchasing power of the poorest of the poor.

The *Deen Dayal Upadhyaya Grameen Kaushalya Yojana* (DDU-GKY) focuses on rural youth from poor families, between the ages of 15 and 35 years, with the objective of equipping them for better employment opportunities and income enhancement through skill development, since lack of formal education and marketable skills prevent them from competing on an equitable basis. DDU-GKY attempts to bridge this gap by funding training projects benchmarked to global standards, with an emphasis on placement, retention, career progression and foreign placement.

The *Stand-Up India Scheme* was launched on 5 April 2016, to give new and promising entrepreneurs a chance at making it big. The scheme aims to provide a special thrust to entrepreneurship among women and scheduled castes and tribes. The scheme is anchored at the Department of Financial Services (DFS), Ministry of Finance Government of India. Under this scheme, bank loans between Rs.10 lakh to Rs. 1 Crore are provided for setting up a Greenfield enterprise. This scheme is being made available to at least one Scheduled Caste or Scheduled Tribe borrower and at least one women borrower, per bank branch. The objective of the scheme is to support SC, ST and women entrepreneurs, who face numerous challenges, in setting up enterprises, obtaining loans and other needs from time to time. The scheme therefore endeavours to create an ecosystem which facilitates and continues to foster a supportive environment for ease of doing business.

Globally the trend of urban inequality is increasing. In urban India, the top 10 percent of the households have a monthly consumption expenditure that is 1.41 times the monthly consumption expenditure of the bottom 40 percent. Among the States, urban inequality is the lowest in Manipur with the Palma Ratio at 0.68, and is the highest in Karnataka and Uttar Pradesh at 1.83. Among the Union Territories, it is the lowest in Daman and Diu at 0.74 and the highest in Andaman and Nicobar Islands at 1.76.

The rural inequality in India is depicted painful in nature and it accelerated by the discrimination attitude towards women, girls and the biasness as well as the cruel attitude towards low caste origin. In rural India, the top 10 percent spend 0.92 times the bottom 40 percent households on monthly consumption. Among the States, rural inequality is lowest in Meghalaya with Palma Ratio at 0.61and highest in Arunachal Pradesh at 1.34. Among the Union Territories, rural inequality is lowest in Delhi and Puducherry at 0.63 and highest in Chandigarh at 1.18.

On the issue of transgender labour force participation, the 2030 target is to have the labour force participation rate of the transgender population to be equal to the labour force participation rate of the male population. The current ratio of former to latter in India stands lower than the target ratio of 1 at 0.64. Five States in India have surpassed the target, namely, Arunachal Pradesh, Himachal Pradesh, Meghalaya, Mizoram and Telangana.

On the account of social inclusion of Scheduled Caste, the governments initiated laws, schemes and it is a constitutional provision to sanction funds for their welfare. The utilization of funds sanctioned for this ground, three States and two Union Territories namely Kerala, Manipur, West Bengal, Chandigarh and Daman & Diu utilized 100 percent of their Scheduled Caste Sub Plan (SCSP) funds while States of Goa and Uttarakhand utilized less than half. On an average in the country, 77.67 percent of the fund allocated for the Scheduled Caste population has been utilized. Again on the account of social inclusion of Scheduled Tribe, the governments initiated laws, schemes and it is a constitutional provision to sanction funds for their welfare. The utilization of funds sanctioned for this ground, three States and two UTs namely, Karnataka, Kerala, West Bengal, Andaman and Nicobar Island, and Daman & Diu utilized 100 percent of their Tribal Sub Plan (TSP) funds while Goa and Uttar Pradesh utilized less than half. On an average in the country, 82.98

percent of the fund allocated towards the Scheduled Tribe population has been utilized.

In the next part of this chapter we tried to visualized the performance level of India through the SDG's targets and the SDG India Index Base Line Report, 2018 along with the Constitutional provisions in India to explore citizen's responsibility along with the its institutions through the mirror of indexed score on 'peace, justice and strong institutions' (SDG-16).

14.4. SDG-10 Targets, National Indicators and Target Values of India

To measure India's performance towards the Goal of 'Reduced Inequality', India had identified five national level indicators, which captured three (10.1, 10.2 and 10.4) out of ten UN's SDG targets. These indicators have been selected based on availability of data at national level; these are in Table no-99.

Table No. 99: SDG-10 Targets, National Indicators and Target Values of India

SDG-10 Global Target	Indicator Selected for SDG India Index	National Target Value for 2030
10.1: By 2030, progressively achieve and sustain income growth of the bottom 40 percent of the population at a rate higher than the national average.	1. Palma ratio of Household Expenditure in Urban India.[1]	1
	2. Palma ratio of Household Expenditure in Rural India.*	1
10.2: By 2030, empower and promote the social, economic and political inclusion of all, irrespective is age, sex, disability, race, ethnicity, origin, religion or economic or other status.	3. Ratio of Transgender Labour force participation rate to Male labour force participation rate.	1
10.4: Adopt policies, especially fiscal, wage protection policies, and progressively achieve greater equality.	4. Percentage of Scheduled Caste Sub Plan Funds Utilized.	100
	5. Percentage of Scheduled Caste Sub Plan Funds Utilized.	100
*. Measured as the ratio of the monthly consumption expenditure of the top 10 percent households to the monthly consumption expenditure of the bottom 40 percent households.		

Source: (NITI Aayog 2018).

14.5. Indian's SDG-10 Index Indicators, Data Source and Interpretations

The NITI *Aayog*, Government of India had collected required data from different government agencies to capture the UN SDG's target indicators as well as had framed its own indicators to justify the achievement of the

SDGs. Apart from that the NITI *Aayog* had developed the computational approach of the disaggregated data as per valid methods along with the parameters of the performance; in the following tables (Table no-100, Table no-101, Table no-102, Table no-103 and Table no-104) shows the details of the above issue to develop a sense of progress of the SDG-10, entitled as 'Reduced Inequality'.

Table No. 100: SDG-10, Indian Indicator-1

SDG-10: 'Reduced Inequality'	**Indicator-1:** Palma ratio of Household Expenditure in Urban India.
Indicator data source	Numerator: Ministry of Statistics and Programme Implementation [Household Consumer Expenditure Reports 2011] Denominator: Ministry of Home Affairs, [Census 2011]
Computation approach	Ratio of total monthly consumption expenditure of the richest 10% households to that of the poorest 40% households in urban areas calculated as – Monthly consumption expenditure of the richest 10% households ÷ Monthly consumption expenditure of the poorest 40% households
Data period (year)	2011
States/UTs covered	35
Data periodicity	10 Years
Relevant UN target	10.1: By 2030, progressively achieve and sustain income growth of the bottom 40 percent of the population at a rate higher than the national average.
Relevant UN indicator	NA
Relevant MoSPI indicator	10.1.2: Gini coefficient of household expenditure.
Indicator interpretation	Higher value means lower performance (-).

Source: (NITI Aayog 2018).

Table No-101: SDG-10, Indian Indicator-2

SDG-10: 'Reduced Inequality'	**Indicator-2:** Palma ratio of Household Expenditure in Rural India.
Indicator data source	Numerator: Ministry of Statistics and Programme Implementation [Household Consumer Expenditure Reports 2011] Denominator: Ministry of Home Affairs, [Census 2011]
Computation approach	Ratio of total monthly consumption expenditure of the richest 10% households to that of the poorest 40% households in urban areas calculated as – Monthly consumption expenditure of the richest 10% households ÷ Monthly consumption expenditure of the poorest 40% households
Data period (year)	2011
States/UTs covered	35
Data periodicity	10 Years

(*Contd*...)

Relevant UN target	10.1: By 2030, progressively achieve and sustain income growth of the bottom 40 percent of the population at a rate higher than the national average.
Relevant UN indicator	NA
Relevant MoSPI indicator	10.1.2: Gini coefficient of household expenditure.
Indicator interpretation	Higher value means lower performance (-).

Source: (NITI Aayog 2018).

Table No. 102: SDG-10, Indian Indicator-3

SDG-10: 'Reduced Inequality'	**Indicator-3:** Ratio of Transgender Labour force participation rate to Male labour force participation rate.
Indicator data source	Labour Bureau [Labour Bureau Report]
Computation approach	Transgender labour force participation rate ÷ Male labour force participation rate
Data period (year)	2015-16
States/UTs covered	27
Data periodicity	Annual
Relevant UN target	10.2: By 2030, empower and promote the social, economic and political inclusion of all, irrespective is age, sex, disability, race, ethnicity, origin, religion or economic or other status.
Relevant UN indicator	NA
Relevant MoSPI indicator	NA
Indicator interpretation	Higher value means higher performance (+).

Source: (NITI Aayog 2018).

Table No. 103: SDG-10, Indian Indicator-4

SDG-10: 'Reduced Inequality'	**Indicator-4**: Percentage of Scheduled Caste Sub Plan Funds Utilized.
Indicator data source	NITI *Aayog*, [State Reports to NITI *Aayog*]
Computation approach	Directly from data source
Data period (year)	2013-14
States/UTs covered	25
Data periodicity	Non-periodic
Relevant UN target	10.4: Adopt policies, especially fiscal, wage protection policies, and progressively achieve greater equality.
Relevant UN indicator	NA
Relevant MoSPI indicator	NA
Indicator interpretation	Higher value means higher performance (+).

Source: (NITI Aayog 2018).

Table No. 104: SDG-10, Indian Indicator-5

SDG-10: 'Reduced Inequality'	**Indicator-5:** Percentage of Scheduled Caste Sub Plan Funds Utilized.
Indicator data source	NITI *Aayog*, [State Reports to NITI *Aayog*]
Computation approach	Directly from data source
Data period (year)	2013-14
States/UTs covered	22
Data periodicity	Non-periodic
Relevant UN target	10.4: Adopt policies, especially fiscal, wage protection policies, and progressively achieve greater equality.
Relevant UN indicator	NA
Relevant MoSPI indicator	NA
Indicator interpretation	Higher value means higher performance (+).

14.6. Provisions of the Indian Constitution for SDG-10

The spirit of the unity in this diverse country, India is secured by its great Constitution; the Constitution of India not only secured its unity, announced a vision in the Preamble in the beginning of its Articles included in the Indian Constitution, *"We the people of India, having solemnly resolved to constitute India into a Sovereign Socialist Secular Democratic Republic and to secure to all its citizens: justice, social, economic and political; liberty of thought, expression, belief, faith and worship; equality of status and of opportunity; and to promote among them all fraternity assuring the dignity of the individual and the unity and integrity of the nation; in our Constituent Assembly this twenty-sixth day of November, 1949, do hereby adopt, enact and give to ourselves this Constitution* (India 1950/2015)". The mode of orientation of the Indian Constitution and the sustainable development goals of the contemporary time are given us an opportunity to make a link between these two visions of development and the author is trying to make the link.

As we know the sustainable development goals are interlinked, that means the success or failure of one is affected to other SDGs. From this perspective, this section presents the provisions in the Indian Constitution to eradicate poverty as reflected in the sustainable development agenda entitled as SDG-10, Reduced Inequality. The linked Constitutional provisions are in the following Table no-105 -

Table No. 105: Provisions in Indian Constitution for SDG-10

SDG-10 and the Linked Articles and Schedules of the Constitution of India
Article 14, Article 15-*1* to *5*, Article 16 (1) to (5), Article 17 to Article 31, Article 38-(1) and (2), Article 39 – (a) to (f), Article 39A, Article 41 to Article 48, Article 51A, Article 243D and Article 243T, Article 301 to Article 305, Article 307, Article 309, Article 310, Article 311, Article 312, Article 313, Article 314, Article 315, Article 320, Article 323A, Article 323B, Article 325 and 326, Article 333, Article 334, Article 335, Article 336, Article 337, Article 338, 338A 364, Article 340, Article 341, Article 342, Article 350A, Article 350B and Article 351.
Article 246 - Seventh Schedule, List-I: Union List No: 12, 13, 22, 23, 24, 25, 27, 28, 29, 30, 31, 32, 33, 34, 35, 36, 37, 38, 39, 40, 41, 42, 43, 44, 45, 46, 47, 48, 49, 50, 51, 52, 53, 54, 55, 56, 57, 58, 59, 60, 61, 62, 63, 64, 65, 66, 67, 68, 69 and 94. List-II: State List No: 6, 7, 12, 13, 14, 15, 16, 17, 18, 22, 23, 24, 25, 26, 27, 28, 30, 31, 32, 33, 34 and 35. List-III: Concurrent List: No – 6, 7, 10, 20, 21, 22, 23, 24, 25, 26, 27, 28, 29, 30, 31, 32, 33, 33A, 34, 35, 36, 37, 38, 39, 40, 41, 42, 43, 44, 45, 46 and 47.
Article 243G - Eleventh Schedule - Powers, Authority and Responsibilities of Panchayats – Schedule No – 1, 2, 3, 4, 5, 6, 7, 8, 9, 10,11 12, 13, 14, 15, 16, 17, 18, 19, 20, 21, 22, 23, 24, 25, 26, 27, 28 and 29. Article 243W - Twelfth Schedule - Powers, Authority and Responsibilities of Municipalities - Schedule No – 1, 2, 3, 4, 5, 6, 7, 8, 9, 10, 11, 12, 13, 14 and 16.

Source: The Constitution of India, 2015 as on 9th November, 2015.

14.7. Policies of the Government of India for Targets of the SDG-10

According to the SDG India Index Base Line Report, 2018 (NITI Aayog 2018), India is proactive to achieve the target of the UN's SDGs. The Government of India initiated as well as implemented various policies to capture the indicators of the targets of each individual SDG. On the moment of preparation of SDG India Index Base Line Report, 2018, on the basis of the availability of the disaggregated data, the NITI *Aayog* framed India's own indicators of the targets of each individual SDG. For the SDG-10, that is 'Reduced Inequality'; the NITI *Aayog* framed five indicators; which capture three out of ten UNs SDG targets. As per the report, 24 dedicated policies or schemes are in action to achieve three targets (10.1, 10.2 and 10.4) of the UN's SDG-10 under the leadership and monitoring of 16 dedicated Ministries or the Departments. The policies or schemes to achieve the targets of SDG-10 and the concerned dedicated Ministries and the Departments are detailed in the - Table no-106.

Table No. 106: Policies Initiated by the Indian Government for Targets of SDG-10

Table No-106: SDG-10, Reduced Inequality	
SDG-10, is *Reduced Inequalities* that aims to adopt policies, especially fiscal wage and social protection policies and progressively achieve and sustain income growth of the bottom 40 percent of the population at a rate higher than the national average, leading to greater equality.	
Target: 10.1: By 2030, progressively achieve and sustain income growth of the bottom 40 percent of the population at a rate higher than the national average.	
Centrally Sponsored /Central Sector Schemes (CSS)	Concerned Ministries/ Departments
1. Umbrella Scheme for Development of Scheduled Castes (Scholarships for educational empowerment, protection of civil rights, promotion of livelihoods, Special Assistance, etc.) 2. Umbrella Programme for Development of Other Vulnerable Groups including OBCs 3. Schemes for implementation of Persons with Disability Act, as a part of the Umbrella Programme for Development of Other Vulnerable Groups 4. National Programme for the Welfare of Persons with Disabilities 5. *Deendayal* Disabled Rehabilitation Scheme (DDRS) Scholarships for students with disabilities	Ministry of Social Justice and Empowerment
6. Umbrella Programme for Development of Scheduled Tribes (Tribal Education, *Vanbandhu Kalyan Yojana*, Special Central Assistance, etc.)	Ministry of Tribal Affairs
7. Umbrella Programme for Development of Minorities (education empowerment, skill development & Livelihoods, etc.)	Ministry of Minority Affairs
8. Stand-Up India	Ministry of Finance
9. Prime Minister's Employment Generation Programme & allied credit support schemes	MSME
10. *Pradhan Mantri Kaushal Vikas Yojana*	Skill Development and Entrepreneurship
11. *Deendayal Antyodaya Yojana* National Rural Livelihood Mission (DAY-NRLM)	Ministry of Rural Development
12. *Deendayal Antyodaya Yojana* National Urban Livelihood Mission (DAY-NULM)	Ministry of Housing and Urban Affairs
Target: 10.2: By 2030, empower and promote the social, economic and political inclusion of all, irrespective is age, sex, disability, race, ethnicity, origin, religion or economic or other status.	
Centrally Sponsored /Central Sector Schemes (CSS)	Concerned Ministries/ Departments
1. Mahatma Gandhi National Rural Employment Guarantee Act (MGNREGA) 2. *Deendayal Antyodaya Yojana* National Rural Livelihood Mission (DAY-NRLM)	Ministry of Rural Development
3. *Pradhan Mantri Rojgar Protsahan Yojana* 4. Employment Promotion Scheme 5. National Career Services	Ministry of Labour and Employment
6. Prime Minister's Employment Generation Programme (PMEGP) and other Credit Support Schemes	MSME
7. Coaching and Guidance for SC and Other Backward Classes 8. Scheme for educational and economic OF Denotified Nomadic Tribes	Ministry of Social Justice and Empowerment
9. Umbrella scheme for development of ST communities	Ministry of Tribal Affairs
10. Umbrella scheme for development of minority communities	Ministry of Minority Affairs

(*Contd...*)

11. *Pradhan Mantri Mudra Yojana* (PMMY)	Ministry of Finance
12. North East Region Livelihood Project (NERLP)	Ministry of Development of North Eastern Region
Target: 10.3: Ensure equal opportunity and reduce inequalities of outcome, including by eliminating discriminatory laws, policies and practices and promoting appropriate legislation, policies and action in this regard.	
Centrally Sponsored /Central Sector Schemes (CSS)	Concerned Ministries/ Departments
1. Schemes for awareness generation, occupational health and enforcement of labour laws, etc. 2. Common Registration under relevant Central Labour Acts (relating to contract and migrant labours and benefits to workers like Provident Fund, insurance, etc.)	Ministry of Labour and Employment
	Ministry of Social Justice and Empowerment, Law and Justice, Tribal Affairs Ministry of Human Resource Development
Target: 10.4: Adopt policies, especially fiscal, wage protection policies, and progressively achieve greater equality.	
Centrally Sponsored /Central Sector Schemes (CSS)	Concerned Ministries/ Departments
	Ministry of Social Justice and Empowerment, Ministry of Tribal Affairs
Target: 10.5: Improve the regulation and monitoring of global financial markets and institutions and strengthen the implementation of such regulations.	
Centrally Sponsored /Central Sector Schemes (CSS)	Concerned Ministries/ Departments
	Ministry of Finance
Target: 10.6: Ensure enhanced representation and voice for developing countries in decision making in global international economic and financial institutions in order to deliver more effective, credible accountable and legitimate institutions.	
Centrally Sponsored /Central Sector Schemes (CSS)	Concerned Ministries/ Departments
	Ministry of Finance
Target: 10.7: Facilitate orderly, safe, regular and responsible migration and mobility of people, including through the implementation of planned and well-managed migration policies.	
Centrally Sponsored /Central Sector Schemes (CSS)	Concerned Ministries/ Departments
	Ministry of Overseas Indian Affairs, Ministry of Labour and Employment
Target: 10.a: Implement the principle of special and differential treatment for developing countries, in particular least developed countries, in accordance with World Trade Organization agreements.	
Centrally Sponsored /Central Sector Schemes (CSS)	Concerned Ministries/ Departments
	Ministry of External Affairs, Ministry of Commerce, DIPP

(*Contd...*)

Target: 10. b: Encourage official development assistance and financial flows, including foreign direct investment, to States where the need is greatest, in particular least developed countries, African countries, Small Island Developing States and landlocked developing countries, in accordance with their national plans and programmes.	
Centrally Sponsored /Central Sector Schemes (CSS)	Concerned Ministries/ Departments
	Ministry of Finance
Target: 10.c: By 2030, reduce to less than 3 percent the transaction costs of migrant remittances and eliminate remittance corridors with costs higher than 5 percent.	
Centrally Sponsored /Central Sector Schemes (CSS)	Concerned Ministries/ Departments
	Ministry of Finance

Source: (NITI Aayog 2018).

14.8. Initiatives, Expectation and Performance of Government of India in SDG-10

According to the India SDG Index, Baseline Report, 2018 (NITI Aayog 2018), to achieving the target of the UN's SDG-10, the Government of India had framed five indicators, which captured three out of ten UN's SDG targets. The Government of India reported that, 24 dedicated policies or schemes are in action to achieve two targets (10.1, 10.2 and 10.4) of the UN's SDG-10 under the leadership and monitoring of 16 dedicated Ministries or the Departments. The SDG-10 indicators are –

SDG_10_1: Palma ratio of Household Expenditure in Urban India.

SDG_10_2: Palma ratio of Household Expenditure in Rural India.

SDG_10_3: Ratio of Transgender Labour force participation rate to Male labour force participation rate.

SDG_10_4: Percentage of Scheduled Caste Sub Plan Funds Utilized.

SDG_10_5: Percentage of Scheduled Caste Sub Plan Funds Utilized.

Inference: It was assumed that, 'Peace, Justice and Strong Institutions' are the pre-conditions of achievement.

Here, Expected Performance = India SDG 16 Score, that is 71 × (UN target of this SDG ÷ 100), and

Performance Difference = (Expected Performance - Performance of India)

From the above conditions it is explored in the table no-107.

Table No. 107: India's SDG-16=71 and the Performances in SDG-10

SDG India Indicators	SDG_10_1	SDG_10_2	SDG_10_3	SDG_10_4	SDG_10_5
UN Target of this SDG	1	1	1	100	100
Performance of India	1.41	0.92	0.64	77.67	82.98
India SDG 16 Score	71	71	71	71	71
India SDG Mean Score	57	57	57	57	57
Expected Performance, When SDG 16=71	0.71	0.71	0.71	71	71
Indicator Interpretation	Value High - Performance Low	Value High - Performance Low	Value High - Performance High	Value High - Performance High	Value High - Performance High
Performance Difference, When SDG 16=71	-0.7	-0.21	-0.07	+6.67	+11.98

Data Source: NITI *Aayog*, 2018 and Inference drawn by the author.

For the SDG_10_1: That is 'Palma ratio of Household Expenditure in Urban India'; here, India is negatively differed (1.41) from its expected score 0.71, when SDG-16 score is 71 and here performance level have to decrease to a level of 0.7 from the present performance. So India have to devote its tools of 'Peace, Justice and Strong Institutions' in a better way for a better score. Here the performance difference is -0.7.

For the SDG_10_2: That is 'Palma ratio of Household Expenditure in Rural India'; here, India is negatively differed (0.92) from its expected score 0.71, when SDG-16 score is 71 and here performance level have to decrease to a level of 0.21 from the present performance. So India have to devote its tools of 'Peace, Justice and Strong Institutions' in a better way for a better score. Here the performance difference is -0.21.

For the SDG_10_3: That is 'Ratio of Transgender Labour force participation rate to Male labour force participation rate'; here, India is slight negatively differed (0.64) from its expected score 0.71, when SDG-16 score is 71 and here performance level have to increase to a level of 0.07 from the present performance. So India have to devote its tools of 'Peace, Justice and Strong Institutions' in a better way for a better score. Here the performance difference is -0.07.

For the SDG_10_4: That is 'Percentage of Scheduled Caste Sub Plan Funds Utilized'; here, India is slight positively differed (77.67) from its expected score 71, when SDG-16 score is 71 and here performance level have to hold and perform according to the demographic changes with the present performance 77.67. So India have to devote its tools of 'Peace, Justice and Strong Institutions' in a better way for a better score. Here the performance difference is +6.67.

For the SDG_10_5: That is 'Percentage of Scheduled Caste Sub Plan Funds Utilized'; here, India is positively differed (82.98) from its expected score 71, when SDG-16 score is 71 and here performance level have to hold and perform according to the demographic changes with the present performance 82.98. So India have to devote its tools of 'Peace, Justice and Strong Institutions' in a better way for a better score. Here the performance difference is +11.98.

14.9. Government of India's Remaining Targets and the Indicators for SDG-10

As we know that, on the basis of the availability of the disaggregated data, the NITI *Aayog* had framed India's own indicators of the targets of each individual SDG. For the SDG-10, that is 'Reduced Inequality', the NITI *Aayog* had framed five indicators; which not captured any of eleven indicators of the ten UNs SDG targets. As per the report, 24 dedicated policies or schemes are in action to achieve three targets (10.1, 10.2 and 10.4) of the UN's SDG-10; the remaining indicators of the UN's SDG-10 is to be achieve by 2030. The remaining lists of targets along with the indicators of SDG-10 are detailed in Table no-108.

Table No. 108: Government of India's Remaining Targets and the Indicators for SDG-10

Table No-108: India's Remaining Targets and the Indicators for SDG-10	
Targets	**Indicators**
10.1: By 2030, progressively achieve and sustain income growth of the bottom 40 per cent of the population at a rate higher than the national average [i].	10.1.1: Growth rates of household expenditure or income per capita among the bottom 40 per cent of the population and the total population [ii].
10.2: By 2030, empower and promote the social, economic and political inclusion of all, irrespective of age, sex, disability, race, ethnicity, origin, religion or economic or other status [i].	10.2: By 2030, empower and promote the social, economic and political inclusion of all, irrespective of age, sex, disability, race, ethnicity, origin, religion or economic or other status [ii].
10.3: Ensure equal opportunity and reduce inequalities of outcome, including by eliminating discriminatory laws, policies and practices and promoting appropriate legislation, policies and action in this regard [ii].	10.3.1: Proportion of the population reporting having personally felt discriminated against or harassed within the previous 12 months on the basis of a ground of discrimination prohibited under international human rights law [ii].
10.4: Adopt policies, especially fiscal, wage and social protection policies, and progressively achieve greater equality [i].	10.4.1: Labour share of GDP, comprising wages and social protection transfers [ii].
10.5: Improve the regulation and monitoring of global financial markets and institutions and strengthen the implementation of such regulations [ii].	10.5.1: Financial Soundness Indicator [ii].

(Contd...)

10.6: Ensure enhanced representation and voice for developing countries in decision-making in global international economic and financial institutions in order to deliver more effective, credible, accountable and legitimate institutions [ii].	10.6.1: Proportion of members and voting rights of developing countries in international organizations [ii].
10.7: Facilitate orderly, safe, regular and responsible migration and mobility of people, including through the implementation of planned and well-managed migration policies [ii].	10.7.1: Recruitment cost borne by employee as a proportion of yearly income earned in country of destination [ii].
	10.7.2-Number of countries that have implemented well-managed migration policies [ii].
10.a: Implement the principle of special and differential treatment for developing countries, in particular least developed countries, in accordance with World Trade Organization agreements [ii].	10.a.1: Proportion of tariff lines applied to imports from least developed countries and developing countries with zero-tariff [ii].
10.b: Encourage official development assistance and financial flows, including foreign direct investment, to States where the need is greatest, in particular least developed countries, African countries, small island developing States and landlocked developing countries, in accordance with their national plans and programmes [ii].	10.b.1: Total resource flows for development, by recipient and donor countries and type of flow (e.g. official development assistance, foreign direct investment and other flows) [ii].
10.c: By 2030, reduce to less than 3 per cent the transaction costs of migrant remittances and eliminate remittance corridors with costs higher than 5 per cent [ii].	10.c.1: Remittance costs as a proportion of the amount remitted [ii].
Notes of the Table: i. Only the target captured. ii. Remaining.	

The Ministries and the Departments associate with indicators of this SDG such as Commerce, DIPP, External Affairs, Finance, Housing and Urban Affairs, Human Resource Development, Labour and Employment, Law and Justice, Ministry of Development of North Eastern Region, Minority Affairs, MSME, Overseas Indian Affairs, Rural Development, Skill Development and Entrepreneurship, Social Justice and Empowerment and Tribal Affairs have to concentrate to monitor on the above issues to achieve the target by 2030 through the provisions of Indian Constitution such as Article 14, Article 15-*1* to *5*, Article 16 (1) to (5), Article 17 to Article 31, Article 38-(1) and (2), Article 39 – (a) to (f), Article 39A, Article 41 to Article 48, Article 51A, Article 243D and Article 243T, Article 301 to Article 305, Article 307, Article 309, Article 310, Article 311, Article 312, Article 313, Article 314, Article 315, Article 320, Article 323A, Article 323B, Article 325 and 326, Article 333, Article 334, Article 335, Article 336, Article 337, Article 338, 338A

364, Article 340, Article 341, Article 342, Article 350A, Article 350B and Article 351; Article 246 - Seventh Schedule, List-I: Union List No: 12, 13, 22, 23, 24, 25, 27, 28, 29, 30, 31, 32, 33, 34, 35, 36, 37, 38, 39, 40, 41, 42, 43, 44, 45, 46, 47, 48, 49, 50, 51, 52, 53, 54, 55, 56, 57, 58, 59, 60, 61, 62, 63, 64, 65, 66, 67, 68, 69 and 94; List-II: State List No: 6, 7, 12, 13, 14, 15, 16, 17, 18, 22, 23, 24, 25, 26, 27, 28, 30, 31, 32, 33, 34 and 35 and the List-III: Concurrent List No: 6, 7, 10, 20, 21, 22, 23, 24, 25, 26, 27, 28, 29, 30, 31, 32, 33, 33A, 34, 35, 36, 37, 38, 39, 40, 41, 42, 43, 44, 45, 46 and 47; Article 243G - Eleventh Schedule - Powers, Authority and Responsibilities of Panchayats – Schedule No – 1, 2, 3, 4, 5, 6, 7, 8, 9, 10,11 12, 13, 14, 15, 16, 17, 18, 19, 20, 21, 22, 23, 24, 25, 26, 27, 28 and 29and Article 243W - Twelfth Schedule - Powers, Authority and Responsibilities of Municipalities - Schedule No – 1, 2, 3, 4, 5, 6, 7, 8, 9, 10, 11, 12, 13, 14 and 16 - if we could not monitor, we would not be able to stand in front of the future generation with a smile.

Chapter – XV

Initiative and Performance of India in SDG-11, Sustainable Cities and Communities

The population concentration in the cities is accelerated by infrastructure and overall development throughout the world; the limited urban are demanding it expansion; but the global leaders thinks about the future and its generation by a sustainable manner. The United Nation's SDG-11, that is *Sustainable Cities and Communities* aimed to make cities and human settlements inclusive, safe, resilient and sustainable as well as aimed to ensure access for all to adequate, safe and affordable housing and basic services and upgrade slums, and significantly reduce the numbers of deaths and people affected by disasters, with focus on protecting the poor and vulnerable and to promote inclusive and sustainable urbanization by providing access to affordable housing, public transport, basic services and green public spaces through improved urban planning and management. The Goal also aims to reduce the adverse per capita environmental impact of cities, and also the number of deaths and direct economic losses caused by disasters.

15.1. The Global Targets and Indicators for SDG-11

The global indicator framework was developed by the Inter-Agency and Expert Group on SDG Indicators (IAEG-SDGs) and agreed to, as a practical starting point at the 47th session of the UN Statistical Commission held in March 2016. The report of the Commission, which included the global indicator framework, was then taken note of by ECOSOC at its 70th session in June 2016 (NITI Aayog 2018). The global targets and the indicator of this SDG are tabled (Table no-109) bellow –

Table No. 109: UNDP-DDGs Targets and Indicators of SDG-11

SDG-11, Make cities and human settlements inclusive, safe, resilient and sustainable[1]	
Targets	**Indicators**
11.1: By 2030, ensure access for all to adequate, safe and affordable housing and basic services and upgrade slums.	11.1.1: Proportion of urban population living in slums, informal settlements or inadequate housing.
11.2: By 2030, provide access to safe, affordable, accessible and sustainable transport systems for all, improving road safety, notably by expanding public transport, with special attention to the needs of those in vulnerable situations, women, children, persons with disabilities and older persons.	11.2.1: Proportion of population that has convenient access to public transport, by sex, age and persons with disabilities.
11.3: By 2030, enhance inclusive and sustainable urbanization and capacity for participatory, integrated and sustainable human settlement planning and management in all countries.	11.3.1: Ratio of land consumption rate to population growth rate.
	11.3.2: Proportion of cities with a direct participation structure of civil society in urban planning and management that operate regularly and democratically.
11.4: Strengthen efforts to protect and safeguard the world's cultural and natural heritage.	11.4.1: Total expenditure (public and private) per capita spent on the preservation, protection and conservation of all cultural and natural heritage, by type of heritage (cultural, natural, mixed and World Heritage Centre designation), level of government (national, regional and local/municipal), type of expenditure (operating expenditure/investment) and type of private funding (donations in kind, private non-profit sector and sponsorship).
11.5: By 2030, significantly reduce the number of deaths and the number of people affected and substantially decrease the direct economic losses relative to global gross domestic product caused by disasters, including water-related disasters, with a focus on protecting the poor and people in vulnerable situations.	11.5.1: Number of deaths, missing persons and persons affected by disaster per 100,000 people [a].
	11.5.2: Direct disaster economic loss in relation to global GDP, including disaster damage to critical infrastructure and disruption of basic services [a].
11.6: By 2030, reduce the adverse per capita environmental impact of cities, including by paying special attention to air quality and municipal and other waste management.	11.6.1: Proportion of urban solid waste regularly collected and with adequate final discharge out of total urban solid waste generated, by cities.
	11.6.2: Annual mean levels of fine particulate matter (e.g. PM2.5 and PM10) in cities (population weighted).
11.7: By 2030, provide universal access to safe, inclusive and accessible, green and public spaces, in particular for women and children, older persons and persons with disabilities.	11.7.1: Average share of the built-up area of cities that is open space for public use for all, by sex, age and persons with disabilities.
	11.7.2: Proportion of person victim of physical or sexual harassment, by sex, age, disability status and place of occurrence, in the previous 12 months.

(*Contd...*)

1. Data Source: SDG India Index Baseline Report, 2018, NITI *Aayog*, Government of India, New Delhi.

11.a: Support positive economic, social and environmental links between urban, peri-urban and rural areas by strengthening national and regional development planning.	11.a.1: Proportion of population living in cities that implement urban and regional development plans integrating population projections and resource needs, by size of city.
11.b: By 2020, substantially increase the number of cities and human settlements adopting and implementing integrated policies and plans towards inclusion, resource efficiency, mitigation and adaptation to climate change, resilience to disasters, and develop and implement, in line with the Sendai Framework for Disaster Risk Reduction 2015-2030, holistic disaster risk management at all levels.	11.b.1: Proportion of local governments that adopt and implement local disaster risk reduction strategies in line with the Sendai Framework for Disaster Risk Reduction 2015-2030 [a].
	11.b.2: Number of countries with national and local disaster risk reduction strategies [a].
11.c: Support least developed countries, including through financial and technical assistance, in building sustainable and resilient buildings utilizing local materials.	11.c.1: Proportion of financial support to the least developed countries that is allocated to the construction and retrofitting of sustainable, resilient and resource-efficient buildings utilizing local materials.
Note: [a] - An open-ended intergovernmental expert working group on indicators and terminology relating to disaster risk reduction established by the General Assembly (resolution 69/284) is developing a set of indicators to measure global progress in the implementation of the Sendai Framework. These indicators will eventually reflect the agreements on the Sendai Framework indicators.	

15.2. Interlinkage of SDG-11 with other SDGs

This section presents the linkage of the SDG-11 to other SDGs, that is, the success of this SDG habitually will influence the success of the linked SDGs; according to the SDG India Index, Baseline Report, 2018 (NITI Aayog 2018), the SDG-11 linked with the following SDGs –

SDG-1, that is *No Poverty*, which aims to reduce poverty in all its dimensions, which includes ensuring access to safe, nutritious and sufficient food all year round, particularly for the poor.

SDG-3, is *Good Health and Well-being*, which aims to end epidemics and preventable deaths and achieve universal health coverage, including financial risk protection and access to quality essential health care services, medicines and vaccines for all.

SDG-5, is *Gender Equality* as Goal 1 emphasises creation of gender sensitive development strategies, and equal rights and access to economic resources, as well as ownership and control over land and other forms of property, inheritance, natural resources and financial resources, including microfinance.

SDG-6, is *Clean Water and Sanitation*, which aims to achieve universal and equitable access to safe and affordable drinking water and sanitation and hygiene for all.

SDG-9, is *Industry, Innovation and Infrastructure* aims at building quality, reliable and resilient infrastructures. It further aims at promoting resource-use efficiency and greater adoption of clean and environmentally sound technologies and industrial processes, to support economic development and human well-being. Investment in innovation is an important pillar of this goal.

SDG-10, is *Reduced Inequalities* that aims to adopt policies, especially fiscal wage and social protection policies and progressively achieve and sustain income growth of the bottom 40 percent of the population at a rate higher than the national average, leading to greater equality.

SDG-12, *Sustainable Consumption and Production* aiming to halve per capita global food waste at consumer level and reduce food losses along production and supply chains.

SDG-16, *Peace, Justice and Strong Institutions* which aims to build accountable and transparent economic institutions. Since Goal 10 aims to ensure enhanced representation and voice for developing countries in decision making in global and international institutions.

15.3. The National Context of SDG-11

Along with the world trends, India is a fast urbanizing country and is witnessing a steady increase in migration from rural areas to urban centres due to multiple factors and of course, opportunities in the urban space and the overcrowded labour concentration in the rural area which resulted unemployment and bound to migrate in the urban space. This poses stress on the already overburdened infrastructure of the cities, such as housing, and services related to transportation, provision of clean water and sewage treatment. It is therefore essential to promote inclusive and sustainable urbanization as well develop capacity for participatory, integrated and sustainable human settlement planning and management.

To capture this ground reality, the government of India adopted various government schemes and strategies have been formulated for achieving targets enlisted under SDG-11. Atal Mission for Rejuvenation and Urban Transformation (AMRUT) is one among the schemes aimed to provide basic services and amenities such as water supply, sewerage, urban transport in the cities to improve quality of life, especially of the poor and the vulnerable. For the urban needy, the government of India adopted

Pradhan Mantri Awas Yojana - urban seeks to address housing requirements of the urban poor, including the slum dwellers. The mission will support construction of houses with up to 30 square meter carpet area with basic civic infrastructure. It is proposed to be taken up through various programme channels like the rehabilitation of slum dwellers with participation of private developers using land as a resource. It aims at promotion of affordable housing through credit linked subsidy or through partnership with public and private sectors. Apart from this government of India adopted Smart Cities Mission (SCM) is a step in the direction of achieving the vision of improving the ease of living, particularly for poor, women, elderly and differently abled people. The strategic component of area-based development in the Smart Cities Mission are city improvement (retrofitting), city renewal (redevelopment) and city extension (Greenfield development) as well as applying of smart solutions covering larger parts of the city.

To achieve indicators of the SDG-11, the government of India sets its own indicator to capture the base of this SDG through houses completed under PMAY. The target is to meet 100 percent of housing demand under PMAY. While India has to go a long way to achieve this ambitious target with the current achievement at 3.32 percent, a few States and Union Territories have done relatively better. Among the States, Goa has met 35.71 percent of its housing demand. Among the UTs, Dadra and Nagar Haveli leads with 17.48 percent of its housing demand met. On the account of slum households in India, 5.41 percent of the urban households in India live in slums. Among the States, Andhra Pradesh has the highest percentage of its urban population living in slums (12.4 percent). Among the Union Territories Puducherry has the highest slum rate with 11.58 percent of its urban households living in slums. The State closest to the target is Kerala.

To create sustainable environment, the government of India initiated 'door to door waste collection' it's recycle and reuse with supporting managements and technologies. Proper and established waste management is an important criterion for sustainable cities. Five States and four Union Territories have achieved the target of 100 percent door to door waste collection. On an average, across India, 73.58 percent of the wards are collecting 100 percent of the waste from door to door.

Waste processing is another step ahead initiative to sustainable environment, which considered by the government of India. The installed capacity of waste treatment in the country is not at par with the amount of waste generated. Only 24.8 percent of the total waste generated gets treated. The best performer among the States is Chhattisgarh with 74 percent of its waste getting processed. Among the UTs, Delhi leads with processing 55 percent of its waste.

In the next part of this chapter we tried to visualized the performance level of India through the SDG's targets and the SDG India Index Base Line Report, 2018 along with the Constitutional provisions in India to explore citizen's responsibility along with the its institutions through the mirror of indexed score on 'peace, justice and strong institutions' (SDG-16).

15.4. SDG-11 Targets, National Indicators and Target Values of India

India in its SDG India Index Base Line Report, 2018 (NITI Aayog 2018), India had measured the performance of India on the goal of 'Sustainable Cities and Communities', India had identified four national level indicators, which captured two (11.1and 11.6) out of ten UN's SDG targets. These indicators have been selected based on availability of data at national level; these are in Table no-110.

Table No. 110: SDG-11 Targets, National Indicators and Target Values of India

SDG-11 Global Target	Indicator Selected for SDG India Index	National Target Value for 2030
11.1: By 2030, ensure access to all for adequate, safe affordable housing and basic services and upgrade slums.	1. Houses completed under *Pradhan Mantri Awas Yojana* (PMAY) as a percentage of net demand assessment for houses.	100
	2. Percentage of urban households living in slums.	0
11.6: By 2030, reduce the adverse per capita environmental impact of cities, including by paying special attention to air quality, municipal and other waste management.	3. Percentage of wards 100 percent door to door waste collection.	100
	4. Percentage of waste processed.	100

Source: (NITI Aayog 2018).

15.5. SDG India Index Indicators, Data Source and Interpretations of SDG-11

The NITI *Aayog*, Government of India had been collected required data from different government agencies to capture the UN SDG's target indicators as well as had framed its own indicators to justify the achievement of the SDGs. Apart from that the NITI *Aayog* had developed the computational approach of the disaggregated data as per valid methods along with the parameters of the performance; in the following tables (Table no-111, Table no-112, Table no-113 and Table no-114) shows the details of the above issue to develop a sense of progress of the SDG-11, entitled as 'Sustainable Cities and Communities'.

Table No. 111: SDG-11, Indian Indicator-1

SDG-11: 'Sustainable Cities and Communities'	**Indicator-1:** Houses completed under *Pradhan Mantri Awas Yojana* (PMAY) as a percentage of net demand assessment for houses.
Indicator data source	Ministry of Housing and Urban Affairs [*Pradhan Mantri Awas Yojana* progress report]
Computation approach	Directly from data source
Data period (year)	2018
States/UTs covered	34
Data periodicity	Quarterly
Relevant UN target	11.1: By 2030, ensure access to all for adequate, safe affordable housing and basic services and upgrade slums.
Relevant UN indicator	NA
Relevant MoSPI indicator	11.1.1: Percentage of slums / Economically Weaker Sections (EWS) households covered through formal / affordable housing.
Indicator interpretation	Higher value means higher performance (+).

Source: (NITI Aayog 2018).

Table No. 112: SDG-11, Indian Indicator-2

SDG-11: 'Sustainable Cities and Communities'	**Indicator-2:** Percentage of urban households living in slums.
Indicator data source	Ministry of Home Affairs, (Census – 2011)
Computation approach	Directly from data source
Data period (year)	2011
States/UTs covered	31
Data periodicity	10 years
Relevant UN target	11.3: By 2030, ensure access to all for adequate, safe affordable housing and basic services and upgrade slums.
Relevant UN indicator	11.1.1: Proportion of urban population living in slums, informal settlements or inadequate Housing.
Relevant MoSPI indicator	11.1.3: Proportion of urban population living in slums, informal settlements or inadequate Housing.
Indicator interpretation	Higher value means lower performance (-).

Source: (NITI Aayog 2018).

Table No. 113: SDG-11, Indian Indicator-3

SDG-11: 'Sustainable Cities and Communities'	**Indicator-3:** Percentage of wards 100 percent door to door waste collection.
Indicator data source	Ministry of Housing and Urban Affairs, [*Swachh Bharat* Mission Urban – Dashboard]
Computation approach	Directly from data source
Data period (year)	March 2018
States/UTs covered	35
Data periodicity	Quarterly
Relevant UN target	11.6: By 2030, reduce the adverse per capita environmental impact of cities, including by paying special attention to air quality, municipal and other waste management.
Relevant UN indicator	11.6.1: Proportion of urban solid waste regularly collected and with adequate final discharge out of total urban solid waste generated, by cities.
Relevant MoSPI indicator	11.6.1: Proportion of urban solid waste regularly collected and with adequate final discharge out of total urban solid waste generated, by cities.
Indicator interpretation	Higher value means higher performance (+).

Source: (NITI Aayog 2018).

Table No. 114: SDG-11, Indian Indicator-4

SDG-11: 'Sustainable Cities and Communities'	**Indicator-4:** Percentage of waste processed.
Indicator data source	Ministry of Housing and Urban Affairs, [*Swachh Bharat* Mission Urban – Dashboard]
Computation approach	Directly from data source
Data period (year)	March 2018
States/UTs covered	35
Data periodicity	Quarterly
Relevant UN target	11.6: By 2030, reduce the adverse per capita environmental impact of cities, including by paying special attention to air quality, municipal and other waste management.
Relevant UN indicator	11.6.1: Proportion of urban solid waste regularly collected and with adequate final discharge out of total urban solid waste generated, by cities.
Relevant MoSPI indicator	11.6.1: Proportion of urban solid waste regularly collected and with adequate final discharge out of total urban solid waste generated, by cities.
Indicator interpretation	Higher value means higher performance (+).

Source: (NITI Aayog 2018).

15.6. Provisions of the Indian Constitution for SDG-11

The spirit of the unity in this diverse country, India is secured by its great Constitution; the Constitution of India not only secured its unity, announced a vision in the Preamble in the beginning of its Articles included in the Indian Constitution, *"We the people of India, having solemnly resolved to constitute India into a Sovereign Socialist Secular Democratic Republic and to secure to all its citizens: justice, social, economic and political; liberty of thought, expression, belief, faith and worship; equality of status and of opportunity; and to promote among them all fraternity assuring the dignity of the individual and the unity and integrity of the nation; in our Constituent Assembly this twenty-sixth day of November, 1949, do hereby adopt, enact and give to ourselves this Constitution* (India 1950/2015)". The mode of orientation of the Indian Constitution and the sustainable development goals of the contemporary time are given us an opportunity to make a link between these two visions of development and the author is trying to make the link.

As we know the sustainable development goals are interlinked, that means the success or failure of one is affected to other SDGs. From this perspective, this section presents the provisions in the Indian Constitution to eradicate poverty as reflected in the sustainable development agenda entitled as SDG-11, Sustainable Cities and Communities. The linked Constitutional provisions are in the following Table no-115 -

Table No. 115: Provisions in Indian Constitution for SDG-11

SDG-11 and the Linked Articles and Schedules of the Constitution of India
Article 14, Article 15 1 to 5, Article 21 to Article 21A, Article 31A, Article 38-(1) and (2), Article 39 – (a) to (f), Article 39A, Article 44 to Article 48A, Article 51, Article 51A, Article 309, Article 310, Article 311, Article 312, Article 313, Article 314, Article 315, Article 320, Article 323A and Article 323B.
Article 246 - Seventh Schedule, List-I: Union List No: 6, 12, 13, 20, 22, 23, 24, 25, 27, 28, 29, 30, 31, 52, 53, 54, 55, 56, 57, 58, 59, 60, 61, 62, 63, 64, 65, 66, 67, 68, 69, 81 and 94. List-II: State List No: 6, 7, 8, 10, 12, 13, 14, 15, 16, 17, 18, 23, 24, 25, 26, 27, 28, and 35. List-III: Concurrent List No: 9, 15, 20, 21, 22, 23, 24, 25, 26, 29, 30, 31, 32, 33, 33A, 34, 35, 36, 37, 38, 39, 40, 41, 42, 43, 44, 45, 46 and 47.
Article 243W: Twelfth Schedule: Powers, Authority and Responsibilities of Municipalities. Schedule No: 1, 2, 3, 4, 5, 6, 7, 8, 9, 10, 11, 12, 13, 14, 15, 16 and 17.

Source: The Constitution of India, 2015 as on 9th November, 2015.

15.7. Policies of the Government of India for Targets of the SDG-11

According to the SDG India Index Base Line Report, 2018 (NITI Aayog 2018), India is proactive to achieve the target of the UN's SDGs. The Government of India initiated as well as implemented various policies to capture the indicators of the targets of each individual SDG. On the moment of preparation of SDG India Index Base Line Report, 2018, on the basis of the availability of the disaggregated data, the NITI *Aayog* framed India's own indicators of the targets of each individual SDG. For the SDG-11, that is 'Sustainable Cities and Communities'; the NITI *Aayog* framed four indicators; which capture two out of ten UNs SDG targets. As per the report, 24 dedicated policies or schemes are in action to achieve two targets (11.1and 11.6) of the UN's SDG-11 under the leadership and monitoring of 15 dedicated Ministries or the Departments. The policies or schemes to achieve the targets of SDG-11 and the concerned dedicated Ministries and the Departments are detailed in the - Table no-116.

Table No. 116: Policies Initiated by the Indian Government for Targets of SDG-11

SDG-11, Sustainable Cities and Communities	
SDG-11, is *Sustainable Cities and Communities* to make cities and human settlements inclusive, safe, resilient and sustainable; which aimed to ensure access for all for adequate, safe and affordable housing and basic services and upgrade slums, and significantly reduce the numbers of deaths and people affected by disasters, with focus on protecting the poor and vulnerable.	
Target: 11.1: By 2030, ensure access to all for adequate, safe affordable housing and basic services and upgrade slums.	
Centrally Sponsored /Central Sector Schemes (CSS)	Concerned Ministries/ Departments
1. *Pradhan Mantri Awas Yojana* (PMAY) - Urban 2. Atal Mission for Rejuvenation and Urban Transformation (AMRUT) 3. Smart Cities Mission	Ministry of Housing and Urban Affairs
4. *Pradhan Mantri Awas Yojana* (PMAY) - Rural	Ministry of Rural Development
Target: 11.2: By 2030, provide access to safe affordable, accessible and sustainable transport systems for all, improving road safety, notably by expanding public transport, with special attention to the needs of those in vulnerable situations, women, children, persons with disabilities and older persons.	
Centrally Sponsored /Central Sector Schemes (CSS)	Concerned Ministries/ Departments
1. Atal Mission for Rejuvenation and Urban Transformation (AMRUT) 2. Smart Cities Mission 3. MRTS and Metro Project	Ministry of Housing and Urban Affairs
4. *Bharatmala Pariyojan*	Road Transport and Highways
5. Schemes for Railway Infrastructure Development	Ministry of Railways
6. *Shyama Prasad Mukherjee* RURBAN Mission	Rural Development
Target: 11.3: By 2030 enhance inclusive and sustainable urbanization and capacities for participatory, integrated and sustainable human settlement planning and management in all countries.	
Centrally Sponsored /Central Sector Schemes (CSS)	Concerned Ministries/ Departments
1. Atal Mission for Rejuvenation and Urban Transformation (AMRUT) 2. Smart Cities Mission 3. *Swachh Bharat* Mission	Ministry of Housing and Urban Affairs

4. *Bharatmala Pariyojan*	Road Transport and Highways
5. Schemes for Railway Infrastructure Development	Ministry of Railways
6. *Shyama Prasad Mukherjee* RURBAN Mission	Rural Development
Target: 11.3: By 2030 enhance inclusive and sustainable urbanization and capacities for participatory, integrated and sustainable human settlement planning and management in all countries.	
Centrally Sponsored /Central Sector Schemes (CSS)	Concerned Ministries/ Departments
1. Atal Mission for Rejuvenation and Urban Transformation (AMRUT) 2. Smart Cities Mission 3. *Swachh Bharat* Mission	Ministry of Housing and Urban Affairs
Target: 11.4 Strengthen the efforts to protect and safeguard the world's cultural and natural heritage.	
Centrally Sponsored /Central Sector Schemes (CSS)	Concerned Ministries/ Departments
1. *Kala Sanskriti Vikas Yojana* 2. National Heritage City Development and Augmentation *Yojana* (HRIDAY)	Ministry of Culture
Target: 11.5: By 2030, significantly reduce the number of deaths and the number of people affected and substantially decrease the direct economic losses relative to global gross domestic product caused by disasters, including water-related disasters with a focus on protecting the poor and people in vulnerable situations.	
Centrally Sponsored /Central Sector Schemes (CSS)	Concerned Ministries/ Departments
1. Infrastructure of Disaster Management 2. National Cyclone Risk Mitigation Project (NCRMP) 3. Other Disaster Management Schemes	Ministry of Home Affairs
4. Flood Management & Border Areas Programme 5. Development of Water Resources Information System	Ministry of Water Resources Rural Development and Green Revolution
6. Atmosphere and Climate Research – Modelling, Observing Systems and Services (ACROSS) 7. Ocean Services, Technology, Observations, Resources, Modelling and Science (OSTORMS) 8. Seismology and Geosciences (SAGE)	Department of Earth Sciences
9. Design & Development of Applications for EO, Communication, Disaster Management, etc.	Department of Space
Target: 11.6: By 2030, reduce the adverse per capita environmental impact of cities, including by paying special attention to air quality, municipal and other waste management.	
Centrally Sponsored /Central Sector Schemes (CSS)	Concerned Ministries/ Departments
1. Atal Mission for Rejuvenation and Urban Transformation (AMRUT) 2. Smart Cities Mission 3. *Swachh Bharat* Mission-Urban	Ministry of Housing and Urban Affairs
4. Environment Protection, Management and Sustainable Development	Ministry of Environment, Forest and Climate Change
Target: 11.7: By 2030, provide universal access to safe, inclusive and accessible, green and public spaces, particularly for women and children, older persons and persons with disabilities.	
Centrally Sponsored /Central Sector Schemes (CSS)	Concerned Ministries/ Departments
1. Atal Mission for Rejuvenation and Urban Transformation (AMRUT)	Ministry of Housing and Urban Affairs

(*Contd...*)

Target: 11.a: Support positive economic, social and environmental links between urban, peri-urban and rural areas by strengthening national and regional development planning.	
Centrally Sponsored /Central Sector Schemes (CSS)	Concerned Ministries/ Departments
1. *Shyama Prasad Mukherjee* RURBAN Mission	Ministry of Rural Development
2. North Eastern Regional Urban Development Project (NERUDP) and other projects in the North Eastern Region	Ministry of Housing and Urban Affairs
1. *Rastriya Gram Swaraj Abhiyan* (RGSA)	Ministry of *Panchayati Raj*
Target: 11.b: By 2020, substantially increase the number of cities and human settlements adopting and implementing integrated policies and plans towards inclusion, resource efficiency, mitigation and adaptation to climate change, resilience to disasters, and develop and implement, in line with the Sendai Framework for Disaster Risk Reduction 2015-2030, holistic disaster risk management at all levels.	
Centrally Sponsored /Central Sector Schemes (CSS)	Concerned Ministries/ Departments
1. Atal Mission for Rejuvenation and Urban Transformation (AMRUT)	Ministry of Housing and Urban Affairs
2. Infrastructure of Disaster Management 3. National Cyclone Risk Mitigation Project (NCRMP) 4. Other Disaster Management Schemes	Ministry of Home Affairs
5. Flood Management & Border Areas Programme 6. Development of Water Resources Information System	Ministry of Water Resources Rural Development and Green Revolution
7. Atmosphere and Climate Research – Modelling, Observing Systems and Services (ACROSS) 8. Ocean Services, Technology, Observations, Resources, Modelling and Science (OSTORMS) 9. Seismology and Geosciences (SAGE).	Department of Earth Sciences
10. Design & Development of Applications for EO, Communication, Disaster Management, etc.	Department of Space
Target: 11.c: Support least developed countries, including through financial and technical assistance, for sustainable and resilient buildings utilizing local materials.	
Centrally Sponsored /Central Sector Schemes (CSS)	Concerned Ministries/ Departments
	Ministry of Finance, Ministry of External Affairs

Source: (NITI Aayog 2018).

15.8. Initiatives, Expectation and Performance of Government of India in SDG-11

According to the India SDG Index, Baseline Report, 2018 (NITI Aayog 2018), to achieving the target of the UN's SDG-11, the Government of India had framed four indicators, which capture two out of ten UN's SDG targets. The Government of India reported that, 24 dedicated policies or schemes are in action to achieve two targets (11.1 and 11.6) of the UN's SDG-11under the leadership and monitoring of 15 dedicated Ministries or the Departments. The SDG-11 indicators are –

SDG_11_1: Houses completed under *Pradhan Mantri Awas Yojana* (PMAY) as a percentage of net demand assessment for houses.

SDG_11_2: Percentage of urban households living in slums.

SDG_11_3: Percentage of wards 100 percent door to door waste collection.

SDG_11_4: Percentage of waste processed.

Inference: It was assumed that, 'Peace, Justice and Strong Institutions' are the pre-conditions of achievement.

Here, Expected Performance = India SDG 16 Score, that is 71 × (UN target of this SDG ÷ 100), and

Performance Difference = (Expected Performance - Performance of India)

From the above conditions it is explored in the table no-117.

Table No. 117: India's SDG-16=71 and the Performances in SDG-11

SDG India Indicators	SDG_11_1	SDG_11_2	SDG_11_3	SDG_11_4
UN Target of this SDG	100	0	100	100
Performance of India	3.32	5.41	73.58	24.8
India SDG 16 Score	71	71	71	71
India SDG Mean Score	57	57	57	57
Expected Performance, When SDG 16=71	71	0	71	71
Indicator Interpretation	Value High - Performance High	Value High - Performance Low	Value High - Performance High	Value High - Performance High
Performance Difference, When SDG 16=71	-67.68	-5.41	+2.58	-46.2

Data Source: NITI *Aayog*, 2018 and Inference drawn by the author.

For the SDG_11_1: That is 'Houses completed under *Pradhan Mantri Awas Yojana* (PMAY) as a percentage of net demand assessment for houses'; here, India is negatively differed (3.32) from its expected score 71, when SDG-16 score is 71 and here performance level have to increase to a level of 67.68 from the present performance. So India have to devote its tools of 'Peace, Justice and Strong Institutions' in a better way for a better score. Here the performance difference is -67.68.

For the SDG_11_2: That is 'Percentage of urban households living in slums'; here, India is negatively differed (5.41) from its expected score '0', when SDG-16 score is 71 and here performance level have to decrease to a level of 5.41from the present performance. So India have to devote its tools of 'Peace, Justice and Strong Institutions' in a better way for a better score. Here the performance difference is -5.41.

For the SDG_11_3: That is 'Percentage of wards 100 percent door to door waste collection'; here, India is slight positively differed (73.58) from its expected score 71, when SDG-16 score is 71 and here performance level have to hold and perform according to the demographic changes with the present performance 73.58. So India have to devote its tools of 'Peace, Justice and Strong Institutions' in a better way for a better score. Here the performance difference is +2.58.

For the SDG_11_4: That is 'Percentage of waste processed'; here, India is negatively differed (24.8) from its expected score 71, when SDG-16 score is 71 and here performance level have to increase to a level of 46.2 from the present performance. So India have to devote its tools of 'Peace, Justice and Strong Institutions' in a better way for a better score. Here the performance difference is -46.2.

15.9. Government of India's Remaining Targets and the Indicators for SDG-11

As we know that, on the basis of the availability of the disaggregated data, the NITI *Aayog* had framed India's own indicators of the targets of each individual SDG. For the SDG-11, that is 'Sustainable Cities and Communities', the NITI *Aayog* had framed four indicators; which captured two (11.1.1 and 11.6.1) of fifteen indicators of the ten UNs SDG targets. As per the report, 24 dedicated policies or schemes are in action to achieve two targets (11.1and 11.6) of the UN's SDG-11; the remaining indicators of the UN's SDG-11 is to be achieve by 2030. The remaining lists of targets along with the indicators of SDG-11 are detailed in Table no-118.

Table No. 118: Government of India's Remaining Targets and the Indicators for SDG-11

India's Remaining Targets and the Indicators for SDG-11	
Targets	**Indicators**
11.1: By 2030, ensure access for all to adequate, safe and affordable housing and basic services and upgrade slums [i].	11.1.1: Proportion of urban population living in slums, informal settlements or inadequate housing [i].
11.2: By 2030, provide access to safe, affordable, accessible and sustainable transport systems for all, improving road safety, notably by expanding public transport, with special attention to the needs of those in vulnerable situations, women, children, persons with disabilities and older persons [iii].	11.2.1: Proportion of population that has convenient access to public transport, by sex, age and persons with disabilities [iii].

(*Contd...*)

11.3: By 2030, enhance inclusive and sustainable urbanization and capacity for participatory, integrated and sustainable human settlement planning and management in all countries [iii].	11.3.1: Ratio of land consumption rate to population growth rate [iii].
	11.3.2: Proportion of cities with a direct participation structure of civil society in urban planning and management that operate regularly and democratically [iii].
11.4: Strengthen efforts to protect and safeguard the world's cultural and natural heritage [iii].	11.4.1: Total expenditure (public and private) per capita spent on the preservation, protection and conservation of all cultural and natural heritage, by type of heritage (cultural, natural, mixed and World Heritage Centre designation), level of government (national, regional and local/municipal), type of expenditure (operating expenditure /investment) and type of private funding (donations in kind, private non-profit sector and sponsorship) [iii].
11.5: By 2030, significantly reduce the number of deaths and the number of people affected and substantially decrease the direct economic losses relative to global gross domestic product caused by disasters, including water-related disasters, with a focus on protecting the poor and people in vulnerable situations [iii].	11.5.1: Number of deaths, missing persons and persons affected by disaster per 100,000 people [a, iii].
	11.5.2: Direct disaster economic loss in relation to global GDP, including disaster damage to critical infrastructure and disruption of basic services [a, iii].
11.6: By 2030, reduce the adverse per capita environmental impact of cities, including by paying special attention to air quality and municipal and other waste management [ii].	11.6.1: Proportion of urban solid waste regularly collected and with adequate final discharge out of total urban solid waste generated, by cities [i].
	11.6.2: Annual mean levels of fine particulate matter (e.g. PM2.5 and PM10) in cities (population weighted) [iii].
11.7: By 2030, provide universal access to safe, inclusive and accessible, green and public spaces, in particular for women and children, older persons and persons with disabilities [iii].	11.7.1: Average share of the built-up area of cities that is open space for public use for all, by sex, age and persons with disabilities [iii].
	11.7.2: Proportion of person victim of physical or sexual harassment, by sex, age, disability status and place of occurrence, in the previous 12 months [iii].
11.a: Support positive economic, social and environmental links between urban, peri-urban and rural areas by strengthening national and regional development planning [iii].	11.a.1: Proportion of population living in cities that implement urban and regional development plans integrating population projections and resource needs, by size of city [iii].
11.b: By 2020, substantially increase the number of cities and human settlements adopting and implementing integrated policies and plans towards inclusion, resource efficiency, mitigation and adaptation to climate change, resilience to disasters, and develop and implement, in line with the Sendai Framework for Disaster Risk Reduction 2015-2030, holistic disaster risk management at all levels [iii].	11.b.1: Proportion of local governments that adopt and implement local disaster risk reduction strategies in line with the Sendai Framework for Disaster Risk Reduction 2015-2030 [a, iii].
	11.b.2: Number of countries with national and local disaster risk reduction strategies [a, iii].

(*Contd...*)

11.c: Support least developed countries, including through financial and technical assistance, in building sustainable and resilient buildings utilizing local materials [iii].	11.c.1: Proportion of financial support to the least developed countries that is allocated to the construction and retrofitting of sustainable, resilient and resource-efficient buildings utilizing local materials [iii].

Notes of the Table:

[a] - An open-ended intergovernmental expert working group on indicators and terminology relating to disaster risk reduction established by the General Assembly (resolution 69/284) is developing a set of indicators to measure global progress in the implementation of the Sendai Framework. These indicators will eventually reflect the agreements on the Sendai Framework indicators.

i. Target indicators captured and analysed.
ii. Not captured all the indicators.
iii. Remaining.

The Ministries and the Departments associate with indicators of this SDG such as Housing and Urban Affairs, Rural Development, Road Transport and Highways, Railways, Ministry of Culture, Home Affairs, Ministry of Water Resources, Rural Development and Green Revolution, Earth Sciences, Space, *Panchayati Raj*, External Affairs, Ministry of Environment, Forest and Climate Change, Ministry of Water Resources, Rural Development and Green Revolution have to concentrate to monitor on the above issues to achieve the target by 2030 through the provisions of Indian Constitution such as Article 14, Article 15 1 to 5, Article 21 to Article 21A, Article 31A, Article 38-(1) and (2), Article 39 – (a) to (f), Article 39A, Article 44 to Article 48A, Article 51, Article 51A, Article 309, Article 310, Article 311, Article 312, Article 313, Article 314, Article 315, Article 320, Article 323A and Article 323B; Article 246 - Seventh Schedule, List-I: Union List No: 6, 12, 13, 20, 22, 23, 24, 25, 27, 28, 29, 30, 31, 52, 53, 54, 55, 56, 57, 58, 59, 60, 61, 62, 63, 64, 65, 66, 67, 68, 69, 81 and 94; List-II: State List No: 6, 7, 8, 10, 12, 13, 14, 15, 16, 17, 18, 23, 24, 25, 26, 27, 28, and 35; List-III: Concurrent List No: 9, 15, 20, 21, 22, 23, 24, 25, 26, 29, 30, 31, 32, 33, 33A, 34, 35, 36, 37, 38, 39, 40, 41, 42, 43, 44, 45, 46 and 47. Article 243W - Twelfth Schedule - Powers, Authority and Responsibilities of Municipalities - Schedule No – 1, 2, 3, 4, 5, 6, 7, 8, 9, 10, 11, 12, 13, 14, 15, 16 and 17 - if we could not monitor, we would not be able to stand in front of the future generation with a smile.

Chapter – XVI

Initiative and Performance of India in SDG-12, Sustainable Consumption and Production

The sustainable consumption and production is the one of the best humanistic approach of sustainable development ever framed. The SDG-12 is entitled as '*Sustainable Consumption and Production*' aiming to halve per capita global food waste at consumer level and reduce food losses along production and supply chains to ensure sustainable consumption and production patterns. The global agenda of SDG-12 on *Sustainable Consumption and Production* emphasizes on "doing more with less" thereby ensuring that the needs of the present generation are fulfilled by without compromising the needs of the future generation. The goal emphasizes promoting resources efficiency, green economies and sustainable infrastructure. It also focusses on reducing degradation and pollution, and minimising waste. It calls for environmentally sound management of chemicals and all wastes throughout their life cycle, efficient use of natural resources, as well as ensuring spread of information and awareness on sustainable practices and lifestyles.

According to the UN, should the global population reach 9.6 billion by 2050, the equivalent of almost three planets will be required to provide the natural resources needed to sustain current lifestyles.

16.1. The Global Targets and Indicators for SDG-12

The global indicator framework was developed by the Inter-Agency and Expert Group on SDG Indicators (IAEG-SDGs) and agreed to, as a practical starting point at the 47th session of the UN Statistical Commission held in March 2016 (NITI Aayog 2018). The report of the Commission, which included the global indicator framework, was then taken note of by ECOSOC at its 70th session in June 2016. The global targets and the indicator of this SDG are tabled (Table no-119) bellow –

Table No. 119: UNDP-DDGs Targets and Indicators of SDG-12

SDG-12, Ensure sustainable consumption and production patterns[1]	
Targets	**Indicators**
12.1: Implement the 10-Year Framework of Programmes on Sustainable Consumption and Production Patterns, all countries taking action, with developed countries taking the lead, taking into account the development and capabilities of developing countries.	12.1.1: Number of countries with sustainable consumption and production (SCP) national action plans or SCP mainstreamed as a priority or a target into national policies.
12.2: By 2030, achieve the sustainable management and efficient use of natural resources.	12.2.1: Material footprint, material footprint per capita, and material footprint per GDP.
	12.2.2: Domestic material consumption, domestic material consumption per capita, and domestic material consumption per GDP.
12.3: By 2030, halve per capita global food waste at the retail and consumer levels and reduce food losses along production and supply chains, including post-harvest losses.	12.3: Global food loss index.
12.4: By 2020, achieve the environmentally sound management of chemicals and all wastes throughout their life cycle, in accordance with agreed international frameworks, and significantly reduce their release to air, water and soil in order to minimize their adverse impacts on human health and the environment.	12.4.1: Number of parties to international multilateral environmental agreements on hazardous waste, and other chemicals that meet their commitments and obligations in transmitting information as required by each relevant agreement.
	12.4.2: Hazardous waste generated per capita and proportion of hazardous waste treated, by type of treatment.
12.5: By 2030, substantially reduce waste generation through prevention, reduction, recycling and reuse.	12.5.1: National recycling rate, tons of material recycled.
12.6: Encourage companies, especially large and transnational companies, to adopt sustainable practices and to integrate sustainability information into their reporting cycle.	12.6.1: Number of companies publishing sustainability reports.
12.7: Promote public procurement practices that are sustainable, in accordance with national policies and priorities.	12.7.1: Number of countries implementing sustainable public procurement policies and action plans.
12.8: By 2030, ensure that people everywhere have the relevant information and awareness for sustainable development and lifestyles in harmony with nature.	12.8.1: Extent to which (i) global citizenship education and (ii) education for sustainable development (including climate change education) are mainstreamed in (a) national education policies; (b) curricula; (c) teacher education; and (d) student assessment.

(Contd...)

1. Data Source: SDG India Index Baseline Report, 2018, NITI *Aayog*, Government of India, New Delhi.

12.a: Support developing countries to strengthen their scientific and technological capacity to move towards more sustainable patterns of consumption and production.	12.a.1: Amount of support to developing countries on research and development for sustainable consumption and production and environmentally sound technologies.
12.b: Develop and implement tools to monitor sustainable development impacts for sustainable tourism that creates jobs and promotes local culture and products.	12.b.1: umber of sustainable tourism strategies or policies and implemented action plans with agreed monitoring and evaluation tools.
12.c: Rationalize inefficient fossil-fuel subsidies that encourage wasteful consumption by removing market distortions, in accordance with national circumstances, including by restructuring taxation and phasing out those harmful subsidies, where they exist, to reflect their environmental impacts, taking fully into account the specific needs and conditions of developing countries and minimizing the possible adverse impacts on their development in a manner that protects the poor and the affected communities.	12.c.1: Amount of fossil-fuel subsidies per unit of GDP (production and consumption) and as a proportion of total national expenditure on fossil fuels.

16.2. Interlinkage of SDG-12 with other SDGs

This section presents the linkage of the SDG-12 to other SDGs, that is, the success of this SDG habitually will influence the success of the linked SDGs; according to the SDG India Index, Baseline Report, 2018 (NITI Aayog 2018), the SDG-12 linked with the following SDGs –

SDG-2, that is *Zero Hunger*, which aims to end all forms of malnutrition and ensures access to safe, nutritious and sufficient food for all, in particular the poor and vulnerable, and support small scale food producers.

SDG-3, is *Good Health and Well-being*, which aims to end epidemics and preventable deaths and achieve universal health coverage, including financial risk protection and access to quality essential health care services, medicines and vaccines for all.

SDG-4, is *Quality Education* that aims to ensure that all girls and boys complete free, equitable and quality primary and secondary education leading to relevant and effective learning outcomes, including technical and vocational skills for employment, decent jobs and entrepreneurship.

SDG-6, is *Clean Water and Sanitation*, which aims to achieve universal and equitable access to safe and affordable drinking water and sanitation and hygiene for all.

SDG-7, is *Affordable and Clean Energy* that aims to ensure universal access to affordable, reliable and modern energy services.

SDG-8, is *Decent Work and Economic Growth* which aims to promote development oriented policies that support productive activities, decent job creation, entrepreneurship, and encourage the formalization and growth of micro-, small - and medium-sized enterprises through access to financial services.

SDG-9, is *Industry, Innovation and Infrastructure* aims at building quality, reliable and resilient infrastructures. It further aims at promoting resource-use efficiency and greater adoption of clean and environmentally sound technologies and industrial processes, to support economic development and human well-being. Investment in innovation is an important pillar of this goal.

SDG-11, is *Sustainable Cities and Communities* which aims to ensure access for all to adequate, safe and affordable housing and basic services and upgrade slums, and significantly reduce the numbers of deaths and people affected by disasters, with focus on protecting the poor and vulnerable.

SDG-13, is *Climate Action* which aims to develop resilience and adaptive capacity of the poor to climate related hazards and natural disasters.

SDG-14, is *Life Bellow Water* which aims to increase benefits to Small Island Developing States (SIDs) and Least Developed Countries (LDCs) from sustainable use of marine resources.

Goal-15, *Life on Land* that aims to promote fair and equitable utilization of genetic resources.

16.3. The National Context of SDG-12

India, being the second most populous country in the world, is home to about 17.5 percent of the world population with a meagre 2.4 percent of the world's area. This makes it necessary to have a comprehensive policy framework aimed at achieving resource efficiency, reduction in waste and pollutant activities, and adoption of technologies focusing on renewable resources. To encourage sustainable practices requires cultural and attitudinal shifts supported by national policies. Government of India's policies like the National Policy on Biofuels aims to achieve sustainable consumption and production.

There are several Government of India schemes aimed at improving and achieving efficiency in the management of natural resources and encouraging sustainable consumption and production. National Policy on Biofuels was introduced in 2009 by the Ministry of New and Renewable

Energy to promote use of biofuels in the country. The aim is to accelerate use of biofuels as a substitute to fossil fuels for transportation and other stationary applications as well. This is envisaged to contribute towards building energy security, mitigating climate change, as well as creating new employment opportunities, while leading to environmentally sustainable development (National Policy on Biofuels, 2018).

National Clean Energy Fund was created in 2010-11to promote research and facilitate investment in projects on development of clean energy technologies, renewable and alternate energy initiatives and environmental management in the areas surrounding energy sector projects. The fund was created by levying a clean energy cess (Rs. 50) on every ton of coal produced or imported. The cess, collected by the Central Board of Excises and Customs, has grown over the years, as the cess levied has been steadily increased – Rs.100 per ton in 2014, Rs.200 per ton in 2015 and Rs.400 per ton in the 2016 budget. This shows the country's commitment towards adopting clean technologies and ensuring sustainable consumption and production patterns.

As per the SDG India Index Base Line Report, 2018, India is not in a position to directly address the issue and measure due to unavailability of supporting data on the issue. It is tough to capture also. The seeds of consumption patterns, especially for the food components are rooted into the disparities in income, along with that the cultural patterns in India, such as life-cycle rituals from conception of baby to normal death of the people and religious festivals are full of friends and relative centric intimacy and the arrangement of their at least one time food sometimes more is the basic feature of the sub-continent of India irrespective of caste, religion and income. Most of the cases expected invited 100 percent of the guests are unable to attend the house of the host but their arrangement is their – this is way of food wasting culture of India. It is so tough to capture in figure. But the persons with needs and fulfilment of their needs must be prioritized by searching the ways and the Indian think tanks adopt few policies to address the issues without framing any indicators to address the issues associated with the SDG-12 be captured.

16.4. Provisions of the Indian Constitution for SDG-12

The spirit of the unity in this diverse country, India is secured by its great Constitution; the Constitution of India not only secured its unity, announced a vision in the Preamble in the beginning of its Articles included in the Indian Constitution, *"We the people of India, having solemnly resolved to constitute India into a Sovereign Socialist Secular Democratic Republic and to secure to all its citizens: justice, social, economic and political; liberty of thought, expression, belief, faith and worship; equality of status and of opportunity; and to promote among them all fraternity assuring the dignity of the individual and the unity and integrity of the nation; in our Constituent Assembly this twenty-sixth day of November, 1949, do hereby adopt, enact and give to ourselves this Constitution* (India 1950/2015)". The mode of orientation of the Indian Constitution and the sustainable development goals of the contemporary time are given us an opportunity to make a link between these two visions of development and the author is trying to make the link.

As we know the sustainable development goals are interlinked, that means the success or failure of one is affected to other SDGs. From this perspective, this section presents the provisions in the Indian Constitution to eradicate poverty as reflected in the sustainable development agenda entitled as SDG-12, Sustainable Consumption and Production. The linked Constitutional provisions are in the following Table no-20 -

Table No. 120: Provisions in Indian Constitution for SDG-12

SDG-12 and the Linked Articles and Schedules of the Constitution of India
Article 14, 15-(2).(a), (b), -(3), (4) and (5), Article 16 (1) to (5), Article 19-1.(a) to (g), Article 21, Article 21A, Article 29-(1) and (2), Article 30-(1), (1A) and (2), Article 31A, Article 32, Article 38-(1) and (2), Article 39 – (a) to (f), Article 39 A, Article 41, Article 42, Article 43, Article 44, Article 45, Article 46, Article 47, Article 48, Article 48A, Article 50, Article 51, Article 51A, Article 301, Article 302, Article 303, Article 304, Article 305, Article 307, Article 309, Article 310, Article 311, Article 312, Article 313, Article 314, Article 315, Article 320, Article 323A, Article 323B Article 351, Article 364 and Article 365.
Article 246 - Seventh Schedule, List-I: Union List No: 6, 7, 12, 13, 14, 15, 20, 22, 23, 24, 25, 27, 28, 29, 30, 31, 36, 38, 39, 41, 42, 43, 44, 45, 46, 47, 48, 49, 50, 51, 52, 53, 54, 55, 56, 57, 58, 59, 60, 61, 62, 63, 64, 65, 66, 67, 68, 69, 76, 81, 82, 83, 84, 85, 86, 87, 88, 89, 90, 91, 92, 92A to 92B and 94. List-II: State List No: 6, 7, 8, 9, 13, 14, 15, 16, 17, 18, 22, 23, 24, 25, 26, 27, 28, 30, 31 and 32. List-III: Concurrent List No: 15, 17, 17A.17B, 18, 19, 20, 20A, 21, 22, 23, 24, 25, 26, 30, 31, 32, 33, 33A, 34, 35, 36, 37, 38, 39, 40, 41, 42, 43, 44, 45, 46 and 47.
Article 243G: Eleventh Schedule: Powers, Authority and Responsibilities of Panchayats. Schedule No: 1, 2, 3, 4, 5, 6, 7, 8, 9, 10, 11, 12, 13, 14, 14, 16, 17, 18, 19, 20, 21, 22, 23, 24, 25, 26, 27, 28 and 29. Article 243W: Twelfth Schedule: Powers, Authority and Responsibilities of Municipalities. Schedule No: 1, 2, 3, 4, 5, 6, 7, 8, 9, 10, 11, 12, 13, 14, 15, 16, 17 and 18.

Source: The Constitution of India, 2015 as on 9th November, 2015.

16.5. Policies of the Government of India for Targets of the SDG-12

According to the SDG India Index Base Line Report, 2018 (NITI Aayog 2018), India is proactive to achieve the target of the UN's SDGs. The Government of India initiated as well as implemented various policies to capture the indicators of the targets of each individual SDG. On the moment of preparation of SDG India Index Base Line Report, 2018, on the basis of the availability of the disaggregated data, the NITI *Aayog* framed India's own indicators of the targets of each individual SDG. For the SDG-12, that is 'Sustainable Consumption and Production'; the NITI *Aayog* unable to manage the data to frame any measurable indicators; which capture the UNs SDG targets. Even though, as per the report, 21 dedicated policies or schemes are in action to achieve the targets of the UN's SDG-12 under the leadership and monitoring of 18 dedicated Ministries or the Departments. The policies or schemes to achieve the targets of SDG-12 and the concerned dedicated Ministries and the Departments are detailed in the - Table no-121.

Table No. 121: Policies Initiated by the Indian Government for Targets of SDG-12

SDG-12, Sustainable Consumption and Production	
SDG-12, is Sustainable Consumption and Production aiming to halve per capita global food waste at consumer level and reduce food losses along production and supply chains.	
Target: 12.1: Implement the 10-year framework of programmes on sustainable consumption and production, all countries taking action, with developed countries taking the lead, taking into account the development and capabilities of developing countries.	
Centrally Sponsored /Central Sector Schemes (CSS)	Concerned Ministries/ Departments
	Agriculture & Cooperation Ministry of Environment, Forest and Climate Change Commerce and Industry, Ministry of New and Renewable Energy
Target: 12.2: By 2030 achieve the sustainable management and efficient use of natural resources.	
Centrally Sponsored /Central Sector Schemes (CSS)	Concerned Ministries/ Departments
1. National Mission for a Green India 2. Conservation of Natural Resources and Eco-systems 3. National River Conservation Programme 4. Environment Protection, Management and Sustainable Development	Ministry of Environment, Forest and Climate Change
5. Science &Technology Programme (Mines)	Ministry of Mines

(*Contd...*)

Target12.3: By 2030, halve per capita global food waste at the retail and consumer levels and reduce food losses along production and supply chains, including post-harvest losses.	
Centrally Sponsored /Central Sector Schemes (CSS)	Concerned Ministries/ Departments
1. Consumer Protection (including consumer awareness development)	Ministry of Consumer Affairs Food and Public Distribution
2. *Pradhan Mantri Kisan* SAMPADA *Yojana* 3. Storage and Go-downs	Food Processing Industries
Target: 12.4: By 2020, achieve the environmentally sound management of chemicals and all wastes throughout their life cycle, in accordance with agreed international frameworks, and significantly reduce their release to air, water and soil in order to minimise their adverse impacts on human health and the environment.	
Centrally Sponsored /Central Sector Schemes (CSS)	Concerned Ministries/ Departments
1. Environment Protection, Management and Sustainable Development 2. Decision Support System for Environmental Policy, Planning and Outcome Evaluation	Ministry of Environment, Forest and Climate Change
3. *Shyama Prasad Mukherjee* RURBAN Mission	Ministry of Rural Development
4. *Swachh Bharat* Mission – Rural	Drinking Water and Sanitation
5. *Swachh Bharat* Mission – Urban	Ministry of Housing and Urban Affairs
	Agriculture and Cooperation Chemicals and Fertilisers
Target: 12.5: By 2030, substantially reduce waste generation through prevention, reduction, recycling and reuse.	
Centrally Sponsored /Central Sector Schemes (CSS)	Concerned Ministries/ Departments
11. Atal Mission for Rejuvenation and Urban Transformation (AMRUT) 12. *Swachh Bharat Mission*-Urban	Ministry of Urban Development
13. *Shyama Prasad Mukherjee* RURBAN Mission	Rural Development
14. Environment Protection, Management and Sustainable Development 15. Decision Support System for Environmental Policy, Planning and Outcome Evaluation	Ministry of Environment, Forest and Climate Change
Target: 12.6: Encourage companies, especially large and transnational companies, to adopt sustainable practices and to integrate sustainability information into their reporting cycle.	
Centrally Sponsored /Central Sector Schemes (CSS)	Concerned Ministries/ Departments
	Ministry of Environment, Forest and Climate Change Corporate Affairs
Target: 11.7: By 2030, provide universal access to safe, inclusive and accessible, green and public spaces, particularly for women and children, older persons and persons with disabilities.	
Centrally Sponsored /Central Sector Schemes (CSS)	Concerned Ministries/ Departments
1. Atal Mission for Rejuvenation and Urban Transformation (AMRUT)	Ministry of Housing and Urban Affairs

(*Contd...*)

Target: 12.7: Promote public procurement practices that are sustainable, in accordance with national policies and priorities.	
Centrally Sponsored /Central Sector Schemes (CSS)	Concerned Ministries/ Departments
	Ministry of Finance
Target: 12.8: By 2030, ensure that people everywhere have the relevant information and awareness for sustain able development and lifestyles in harmony with nature.	
Centrally Sponsored /Central Sector Schemes (CSS)	Concerned Ministries/ Departments
1. Environment Protection, Management and Sustainable Development 2. Decision Support System for Environmental Policy, Planning and Outcome Evaluation	Ministry of Environment, Forest and Climate Change
	Ministry of Information and Broadcasting
Target: 12.a: Support developing countries to strengthen their scientific and technological capacity to move towards more sustainable patterns of consumption and production.	
Centrally Sponsored /Central Sector Schemes (CSS)	Concerned Ministries/ Departments
	Ministry of Environment, Forest and Climate Change, Department of Science and Technology
Target: 12.b: Develop and implement tools to monitor sustainable development impacts for sustainable tourism that creates jobs and promotes local culture and products.	
Centrally Sponsored /Central Sector Schemes (CSS)	Concerned Ministries/ Departments
1. Tourism Infrastructure 2. *Swadesh Darshan* – Integrated Development of Tourist Circuits 3. PRASAD - Pilgrimage Rejuvenation and Spiritual Augmentation Drive 4. Assistance to Central Agencies for Tourism Infrastructure Development 5. Promotion and Publicity 6. Domestic Promotion and Publicity including Hospitality 7. Overseas Promotion and Publicity including Market Development Assistance 8. Training for Entrepreneurship Development, etc.	Ministry of Tourism
Target: 12.c: Rationalize inefficient fossil-fuel subsidies that encourage wasteful consumption by removing market distortions, in accordance with national circumstances, including by restructuring taxation and phasing out those harmful subsidies, where they exist, to reflect their environmental impacts, taking fully into account the specific needs and conditions of developing countries and minimizing the possible adverse impacts on their development in a manner that protects the poor and the affected communities.	
Centrally Sponsored /Central Sector Schemes (CSS)	Concerned Ministries/ Departments
	Ministry of Finance, Ministry of Petroleum and Natural Gas

Source: (NITI Aayog 2018).

16.6. Initiatives, Expectation and Performance of Government of India in SDG-12

According to the India SDG Index, Baseline Report, 2018, to achieving the target of the UN's SDG-12, the Government of India unable to frame any indicator, which not capture any of the UN's SDG targets; but, as per report, the Government of India initiated 21 dedicated policies or schemes which are in action to achieve the targets of the UN's SDG-12 under the leadership and monitoring of 18 dedicated Ministries or the Departments without any performance details on this SDG-12.

16.7. Government of India's Remaining Targets and the Indicators for SDG-12

As we know that, on the basis of the availability of the disaggregated data, the NITI *Aayog* had framed India's own indicators of the targets of each individual SDG. For thc SDG-12, that is 'Sustainablc Citics and Communities', the NITI *Aayog* unable to collect and manage the data as required to capture the indicators of the UNs SDG-12 targets. As per the report, 21 dedicated policies or schemes are in action to achieve the UN's SDG-12. As per report, all the indicators of the SDG-12 remained as it is but is to be achieve by 2030. The remaining lists of targets along with the indicators of SDG-12 are detailed in Table no-122.

Table No. 122: Government of India's Remaining Targets and the Indicators for SDG-12

India's Remaining Targets and the Indicators for SDG-12	
Targets	**Indicators**
12.1: Implement the 10-Year Framework of Programmes on Sustainable Consumption and Production Patterns, all countries taking action, with developed countries taking the lead, taking into account the development and capabilities of developing countries.	12.1.1: Number of countries with sustainable consumption and production (SCP) national action plans or SCP mainstreamed as a priority or a target into national policies.
12.2: By 2030, achieve the sustainable management and efficient use of natural resources.	12.2.1: Material footprint, material footprint per capita, and material footprint per GDP.
	12.2.2: Domestic material consumption, domestic material consumption per capita, and domestic material consumption per GDP.
12.3: By 2030, halve per capita global food waste at the retail and consumer levels and reduce food losses along production and supply chains, including post-harvest losses.	12:3: Global food loss index.

(*Contd...*)

12.3: By 2030, halve per capita global food waste at the retail and consumer levels and reduce food losses along production and supply chains, including post-harvest losses.	12.3: Global food loss index.
12.4: By 2020, achieve the environmentally sound management of chemicals and all wastes throughout their life cycle, in accordance with agreed international frameworks, and significantly reduce their release to air, water and soil in order to minimize their adverse impacts on human health and the environment.	12.4.1: Number of parties to international multilateral environmental agreements on hazardous waste, and other chemicals that meet their commitments and obligations in transmitting information as required by each relevant agreement.
	12.4.2: Hazardous waste generated per capita and proportion of hazardous waste treated, by type of treatment.
12.5: By 2030, substantially reduce waste generation through prevention, reduction, recycling and reuse.	12.5.1: National recycling rate, tons of material recycled.
12.6: Encourage companies, especially large and transnational companies, to adopt sustainable practices and to integrate sustainability information into their reporting cycle.	12.6.1: Number of companies publishing sustainability reports.
12.7: Promote public procurement practices that are sustainable, in accordance with national policies and priorities.	12.7.1: Number of countries implementing sustainable public procurement policies and action plans.
12.8: By 2030, ensure that people everywhere have the relevant information and awareness for sustainable development and lifestyles in harmony with nature.	12.8.1: Extent to which (i) global citizenship education and (ii) education for sustainable development (including climate change education) are mainstreamed in (a) national education policies; (b) curricula; (c) teacher education; and (d) student assessment.
12.a: Support developing countries to strengthen their scientific and technological capacity to move towards more sustainable patterns of consumption and production.	12.a.1: Amount of support to developing countries on research and development for sustainable consumption and production and environmentally sound technologies.
12.b: Develop and implement tools to monitor sustainable development impacts for sustainable tourism that creates jobs and promotes local culture and products.	12.b.1: Number of sustainable tourism strategies or policies and implemented action plans with agreed monitoring and evaluation tools.
12.c: Rationalize inefficient fossil-fuel subsidies that encourage wasteful consumption by removing market distortions, in accordance with national circumstances, including by restructuring taxation and phasing out those harmful subsidies, where they exist, to reflect their environmental impacts, taking fully into account the specific needs and conditions of developing countries and minimizing the possible adverse impacts on their development in a manner that protects the poor and the affected communities.	12.c.1: Amount of fossil-fuel subsidies per unit of GDP (production and consumption) and as a proportion of total national expenditure on fossil fuels.
Note of the Table: • Remaining to capture the data of targets and indicators.	

The Ministries or the Departments are - Agriculture & Cooperation, Chemicals & Fertilisers, Commerce and Industry, Consumer Affairs Food and Public Distribution, Corporate Affairs, Drinking Water and Sanitation, Finance, Food Processing Industries, Housing and Urban Affairs, Information and Broadcasting, Mines, Ministry of Environment, Forest and Climate Change, Ministry of Tourism, New and Renewable Energy, Petroleum and Natural Gas, Rural Development, Science and Technology and Urban Development.

Apart from the above policies, Ministries and the active governmental Departments; there in the Indian Constitution are ample options to capture the issues associated with the SDG-12. The Ministries or the Departments have to concentrate to monitor on the above issues to achieve the target by 2030 through the provisions of Indian Constitution such as - Article 14, 15-(2).(a), (b), -(3), (4) and (5), Article 16 (1) to (5), Article 19-1.(a) to (g), Article 21, Article 21A, Article 29-(1) and (2), Article 30-(1), (1A) and (2), Article 31A, Article 32, Article 38-(1) and (2), Article 39 – (a) to (f), Article 39 A, Article 41, Article 42, Article 43, Article 44, Article 45, Article 46, Article 47, Article 48, Article 48A, Article 50, Article 51, Article 51A, Article 301, Article 302, Article 303, Article 304, Article 305, Article 307, Article 309, Article 310, Article 311, Article 312, Article 313, Article 314, Article 315, Article 320, Article 323A, Article 323B Article 351, Article 364 and Article 365; Article 246 - Seventh Schedule, List-I: Union List No: 6, 7, 12, 13, 14, 15, 20, 22, 23, 24, 25, 27, 28, 29, 30, 31, 36, 38, 39, 41, 42, 43, 44, 45, 46, 47, 48, 49, 50, 51, 52, 53, 54, 55, 56, 57, 58, 59, 60, 61, 62, 63, 64, 65, 66, 67, 68, 69, 76, 81, 82, 83, 84, 85, 86, 87, 88, 89, 90, 91, 92, 92A to 92B and 94; List-II: State List No: – 6, 7, 8, 9, 13, 14, 15, 16, 17, 18, 22, 23, 24, 25, 26, 27, 28, 30, 31 and 32; List-III: Concurrent List No: 15, 17, 17A.17B, 18, 19, 20, 20A, 21, 22, 23, 24, 25, 26, 30, 31, 32, 33, 33A, 34, 35, 36, 37, 38, 39, 40, 41, 42, 43, 44, 45, 46 and 47; Article 243G - Eleventh Schedule - Powers, Authority and Responsibilities of Panchayats – Schedule No – 1, 2, 3, 4, 5, 6, 7, 8, 9, 10, 11, 12, 13, 14, 14, 16, 17, 18, 19, 20, 21, 22, 23, 24. 25, 26, 27, 28 and 29; Article 243W - Twelfth Schedule - Powers, Authority and Responsibilities of Municipalities - Schedule No – 1, 2, 3, 4, 5, 6, 7, 8, 9, 10, 11, 12, 13, 14, 15, 16, 17 and 18 - if we could not monitor, we would not be able to stand in front of the future generation with a smile.

Chapter – XVII

Initiative and Performance of India in SDG-13, Climate Action

The changed climate is such an issue, we the common people may not be interested in it but the issue itself very much interested to us, because of its influence in our socio-economic, socio-environmental, socio-political, socio-cultural lifestyles. Along with these it has a threaten attitude towards the wellbeing of the future generations. In these perspectives, the world leaders has been considered in the SDG-13 entitled 'Climate Action', is to take urgent action to combat climate change and its impacts; which was aimed to develop resilience and adaptive capacity of the poor to climate related hazards and natural disasters. The global agenda of SDG-13 on climate change was aimed to integrate climate change measures into national policies and strategies; and further aims to plan and promote mechanism for riding capacity effective climate change-related planning and management. Nations across the world are experiencing effects of climate change. Global warming is a concern with 2016 being the third consecutive year in which temperatures were more than 1 degree Celsius above late 19th century level. Thus, a detrimental effects on crop productivity that is, each 1^{0} Celsius rise in global temperature is estimated to reduce average global yields of wheat by 6 percent, rice yields by 3.2 percent, and maize yields by 7.4 percent (United Nations 2018). Absolute sea levels are rising faster since 1993 than the long term trend. Greenhouse gas emissions continue to rise, and are now more than 50 percent higher than their 1990 level. It is estimated that the annual average losses from tsunamis, tropical cyclones and flooding amounts hundreds of billions of dollars, requiring an investment of $6 billion annually in disaster risk management alone (United Nations 2018).

A comprehensive strategy is required to combats the effects of climate change. Efforts at the national level for adopting green technologies, promoting use of clean and modern source of energy, advocating for behaviour change for sustainable use of resources have to be complimented by international cooperation on climate change since the causes and effects of climate change transcends the national boundaries.

The United Nations Framework Convention on Climate Change (UNFCCC) provides technical expertise and assists in the analysis and review of climate change information and in the implementation of the Kyoto mechanism (UNFCCC). The Green Climate Funds (GCF), which aims to jointly mobilize $100 billion annually by 2030, has emerged as a viable source of long-term climate finance internationally.

17.1. The Global Targets and Indicators for SDG-13

The global indicator framework was developed by the Inter-Agency and Expert Group on SDG Indicators (IAEG-SDGs) and agreed to, as a practical starting point at the 47th session of the UN Statistical Commission held in March 2016 (NITI Aayog 2018). The report of the Commission, which included the global indicator framework, was then taken note of by ECOSOC at its 70th session in June 2016. The global targets and the indicator of this SDG are tabled (Table no-123) bellow –

Table No. 123: UNDP-DDGs Targets and Indicators of SDG-13

SDG-13, Take urgent action to combat climate change and its impacts[1, a]	
Targets	**Indicators**
13.1: Strengthen resilience and adaptive capacity to climate-related hazards and natural disasters in all countries.	13.1.1: Number of countries with national and local disaster risk reduction strategies [b].
	13.1.2: Number of deaths, missing persons and persons affected by disaster per 100,000 people [a].
13.2: Integrate climate change measures into national policies, strategies and planning.	13.2.1: Number of countries that have communicated the establishment or operationalization of an integrated policy/strategy/plan which increases their ability to adapt to the adverse impacts of climate change, and foster climate resilience and low greenhouse gas emissions development in a manner that does not threaten food production (including a national adaptation plan, nationally determined contribution, national communication, biennial update report or other).

(*Contd*...)

1. Data Source: SDG India Index Baseline Report, 2018, NITI *Aayog*, Government of India, New Delhi.

13.3: Improve education, awareness-raising and human and institutional capacity on climate change mitigation, adaptation, impact reduction and early warning.	13.3.1: Number of countries that have integrated mitigation, adaptation, impact reduction and early warning into primary, secondary and tertiary curricula.
	13.3.2: Number of countries that have communicated the strengthening of institutional, systemic and individual capacity-building to implement adaptation, mitigation and technology transfer, and development actions.
13.a: Implement the commitment undertaken by developed-country parties to the United Nations Framework Convention on Climate Change to a goal of mobilizing jointly $100 billion annually by 2020 from all sources to address the needs of developing countries in the context of meaningful mitigation actions and transparency on implementation and fully operationalize the Green Climate Fund through its capitalization as soon as possible.	13.a.1: Mobilized amount of United States dollars per year starting in 2020 accountable towards the $100 billion commitment.
13.b; Promote mechanisms for raising capacity for effective climate change-related planning and management in least developed countries and small island developing States, including focusing on women, youth and local and marginalized communities.	13.b.1: Number of least developed countries and small island developing States that are receiving specialized support, and amount of support, including finance, technology and capacity-building, for mechanisms for raising capacities for effective climate change-related planning and management, including focusing on women, youth and local and marginalized communities.

Notes of the Table:

- Remaining to capture the data of targets and indicators.

[a] - Acknowledging that the United Nations Framework Convention on Climate Change is the primary international, intergovernmental forum for negotiating the global response to climate change.

[b] - An open-ended intergovernmental expert working group on indicators and terminology relating to disaster risk reduction established by the General Assembly (resolution 69/284) is developing a set of indicators to measure global progress in the implementation of the Sendai Framework. These indicators will eventually reflect the agreements on the Sendai Framework indicators.

17.2. Interlinkage of SDG-13 with other SDGs

This section presents the linkage of the SDG-13 to other SDGs, that is, the success of this SDG habitually will influence the success of the linked SDGs; according to the SDG India Index, Baseline Report, 2018 (NITI Aayog 2018), the SDG-13 linked with the following SDGs –

SDG-2, that is *Zero Hunger*, which aims to end all forms of malnutrition and ensures access to safe, nutritious and sufficient food for all, in particular the poor and vulnerable, and support small scale food producers.

SDG-3, is *Good Health and Well-being*, which aims to end epidemics and preventable deaths and achieve universal health coverage, including financial risk protection and access to quality essential health care services, medicines and vaccines for all.

SDG-4, is *Quality Education* that aims to ensure that all girls and boys complete free, equitable and quality primary and secondary education leading to relevant and effective learning outcomes, including technical and vocational skills for employment, decent jobs and entrepreneurship.

SDG-6, is *Clean Water and Sanitation*, which aims to achieve universal and equitable access to safe and affordable drinking water and sanitation and hygiene for all.

SDG-7, is *Affordable and Clean Energy* that aims to ensure universal access to affordable, reliable and modern energy services.

SDG-8, is *Decent Work and Economic Growth* which aims to promote development oriented policies that support productive activities, decent job creation, entrepreneurship, and encourage the formalization and growth of micro-, small - and medium-sized enterprises through access to financial services.

SDG-9, is *Industry, Innovation and Infrastructure* aims at building quality, reliable and resilient infrastructures. It further aims at promoting resource-use efficiency and greater adoption of clean and environmentally sound technologies and industrial processes, to support economic development and human well-being. Investment in innovation is an important pillar of this goal.

SDG-11, is *Sustainable Cities and Communities* which aims to ensure access for all to adequate, safe and affordable housing and basic services and upgrade slums, and significantly reduce the numbers of deaths and people affected by disasters, with focus on protecting the poor and vulnerable.

SDG-12, *Sustainable Consumption and Production* aiming to halve per capita global food waste at consumer level and reduce food losses along production and supply chains.

SDG-14, is *Life Bellow Water* which aims to increase benefits to Small Island Developing States (SIDs) and Least Developed Countries (LDCs) from sustainable use of marine resources.

Goal – 15, *Life on Land* that aims to promote fair and equitable utilization of genetic resources.

17.3. The National Context of SDG-13

India has great geographic diversity, and a variety of climate regimes and regional and local weather conditions, which are vulnerable to climate change. This is manifested in floods droughts as well as the risk from tsunamis and cyclones experienced in coastal areas.

India is vulnerable to climate induced risks; it was one of the three countries most-hit-by-disaster in 2015, with economic losses amounting to $3.30 billion (United Nations, 2016). India's National Action Plan on climate change is an example of the government's commitment to building adaptive capacity to climate-related hazards.

The Government of India has been proactive and has adopted many interventions to address the issue of climate change in the country, some of which are discussed below:

National Action Plan on Climate Change (NAPCC) outlines a comprehensive strategy to deal with climate change related issues and events and builds on the development and use of advanced technologies. At the core of NAPCC are eight national missions: - National Solar Mission (NSM), National Mission for Enhanced Energy Efficiency (NMEEE), National Mission on Sustainable Habitats (NMSH), National Water Mission (NWM), National Mission for Sustaining the Himalayan Ecosystem (NMSHE), National Mission for a Green India (NMGI), National Mission for Sustainable Agriculture (NMSA) and National Mission on Strategic Knowledge on Climate Change (NMSKCC).

National Air Quality Monitoring Programme (NAMP) is another initiative, the Central Pollution Control Board (CPCB), in association with State Pollution Control Boards (SPCBs) / Pollution Control Committees (PCCs), monitor air quality across the country under National Air Quality Monitoring Programme (NAMP). The National Air Quality Monitoring Programme (NAMP) network comprises 680 monitoring stations located in 300 cities/towns, covering 29 States and 6 Union Territories (UTs). Under this scheme grants are being provided to SPCBs, Environment Departments, Central/State Research Institutions, and other government agencies/ organizations with the aim of strengthening their technical capabilities to achieve the objective of management and control of pollution.

As per the SDG India Index Base Line Report, 2018, India is not in a position to directly address the issue and measure due to unavailability of supporting data on the issue. It is tough to capture also. The seeds of climate change lie in the unaccounted consumption as well as use and exploitations of natural resources by diverse industrially developed areas and the burdens are borne by the industrially less developed areas and its inhabitants variously. It is so tough to capture in figure. But the persons, whose needs are affected, must be prioritized first by searching the ways and the Indian think tanks adopt few policies to address the issues without framing any indicators to address the issues associated with the SDG-13 be captured.

17.4. Provisions of the Indian Constitution for SDG-13

The spirit of the unity in this diverse country, India is secured by its great Constitution; the Constitution of India not only secured its unity, announced a vision in the Preamble in the beginning of its Articles included in the Indian Constitution, *"We the people of India, having solemnly resolved to constitute India into a Sovereign Socialist Secular Democratic Republic and to secure to all its citizens: justice, social, economic and political; liberty of thought, expression, belief, faith and worship; equality of status and of opportunity; and to promote among them all fraternity assuring the dignity of the individual and the unity and integrity of the nation; in our Constituent Assembly this twenty-sixth day of November, 1949, do hereby adopt, enact and give to ourselves this Constitution* (India 1950/2015)". The mode of orientation of the Indian Constitution and the sustainable development goals of the contemporary time are given us an opportunity to make a link between these two visions of development and the author is trying to make the link.

As we know the sustainable development goals are interlinked, that means the success or failure of one is affected to other SDGs. From this perspective, this section presents the provisions in the Indian Constitution to eradicate poverty as reflected in the sustainable development agenda entitled as SDG-13, Climate Action. The linked Constitutional provisions are in the following Table no-124 -

Table No. 124: Provisions in Indian Constitution for SDG-13

SDG-13 and the Linked Articles and Schedules of the Constitution of India
Article 14, 15-(2).(a), (b), -(3), (4) and (5), Article 16 (1) to (5), Article 19-1.(a) to (g), Article 21, Article 21A, Article 38-(1) and (2), Article 39 – (a) to (f), Article 39 A, Article 41, Article 42, Article 43, Article 43A, Article 44, Article 45, Article 47, Article 48, Article 48A, Article 50, Article 51, Article 51A, Article 243D (2), Article 243T (2), Article 302, Article 303, Article 304, Article 305, Article 307, Article 309, Article 310, Article 311, Article 312, Article 313, Article 314, Article 315, Article 320, Article 323A and Article 323B.

(Contd...)

Article 246 - Seventh Schedule, List-I: Union List No: 5, 6, 7, 10, 12, 13, 14, 15, 16, 22 to 31, 41, 42, 43, 44, 52, 53, 54, 55, 56, 57, 58, 59, 60, 61, 64, 65, 66, 68, 69 and 94. List-II: State List No: 5, 6, 10, 13, 14, 15, 16, 17, 18, 21, 22, 23, 24, 25, 26, 27, 28, 30, 31, 32, 33, 34 and 35. List-III: Concurrent List No: – 7, 10, 17, 17A.17B, 18, 19, 20, 20A, 21, 22, 23, 24, 25, 26, 29, 30, 31, 32, 36, 37, 38, 40 and 47.
Article 243G: Eleventh Schedule: Powers, Authority and Responsibilities of Panchayats. Schedule No: 1, 2, 3, 4, 5, 6, 7, 8, 9, 10, 11, 12, 13, 14, 14, 16, 17, 18, 19, 20, 21, 22, 23, 24, 25, 26, 27, 28 and 29. Article 243W: Twelfth Schedule: Powers, Authority and Responsibilities of Municipalities. Schedule No: 1, 2, 3, 4, 5, 6, 7, 8, 9, 10, 11, 12, 13, 14, 15, 16, 17 and 18.

Source: The Constitution of India, 2015 as on 9th November, 2015.

17.5. Policies of the Government of India for Targets of the SDG-13

According to the SDG India Index Base Line Report, 2018 (NITI Aayog 2018), India is proactive to achieve the target of the UN's SDGs. The Government of India initiated as well as implemented various policies to capture the indicators of the targets of each individual SDG. On the moment of preparation of SDG India Index Base Line Report, 2018, on the basis of the availability of the disaggregated data, the NITI *Aayog* framed India's own indicators of the targets of each individual SDG. For the SDG-13, that is 'Climate Action'; the NITI *Aayog* unable to manage the data to frame any measurable indicators; which capture the UNs SDG targets. Even though, as per the report, 12 dedicated policies or schemes are in action to achieve the targets of the UN's SDG-13 under the leadership and monitoring of 5 dedicated Ministries or the Departments. The policies or schemes to achieve the targets of SDG-13 and the concerned dedicated Ministries and the Departments are detailed in the - Table no-125.

Table No. 125: Policies Initiated by the Indian Government for Targets of SDG-13

SDG-13, Climate Action	
SDG-13, is *Climate Action* which aims to develop resilience and adaptive capacity of the poor to climate related hazards and natural disasters.	
Target: 13.1: Strengthen resilience and adaptive capacity-related hazards and natural disaster in all countries.	
Centrally Sponsored /Central Sector Schemes (CSS)	Concerned Ministries/ Departments
1. National Mission for a Green India 2. Conservation of Natural Resources and Eco-systems 3. National River Conservation Programme 4. Environment Protection, Management and Sustainable Development	Ministry of Environment, Forest and Climate Change

(Contd...)

	Ministry of Home Affairs
Target: 13.2: Integrate climate change measures into national policies, strategies and planning.	
Centrally Sponsored /Central Sector Schemes (CSS)	Concerned Ministries/ Departments
1. National Mission for a Green India 2. Conservation of Natural Resources and Eco-systems 3. National River Conservation Programme 4. Environment Protection, Management and Sustainable Development	Ministry of Environment, Forest and Climate Change
5. Grid-Interactive Renewable Power (solar, wind, small hydro and biopower, and green energy corridor) 6. Off-Grid / Distributed Renewable Power (solar, wind, small hydro and biopower, biogas and other renewable energy applications) 7. Research and Development	Ministry of New and Renewable Energy
8. Power system improvement, Smart Grids, etc.	Ministry of Power
Target: 13.3: Improve education, awareness-rising and human and institutional capacity on climate change mitigation, adaptation, impact reduction and early warning.	
Centrally Sponsored /Central Sector Schemes (CSS)	Concerned Ministries/ Departments
1. Decision Support System for Environmental Policy, Planning and Outcome Evaluation 2. Environmental Knowledge and Capacity Building 3. Human Resources Development and Training 4. Information, Education and Communication	Ministry of Environment, Forest and Climate Change
	Ministry of New and Renewable Energy, Ministry of Information and Broadcasting
Target: 13.a: Implement the commitment undertaken by developed county parties to the United Nations Framework Convention on Climate Change to a goal of mobilising jointly $100 billion annually by 2020 from all sources to address the needs of developing countries in the context of meaningful mitigation actions and transparency on implementation and fully operationalize the Green Climate fund through its capitalization as soon as possible.	
Centrally Sponsored /Central Sector Schemes (CSS)	Concerned Ministries/ Departments
	Ministry of Environment, Forest and Climate Change
Target: 13.b: Promote mechanisms for rising capacity for effective climate change-related planning and management in least developed countries and small island developing States, including focusing on women, youth and local and marginalised communities.	
Centrally Sponsored /Central Sector Schemes (CSS)	Concerned Ministries/ Departments
	Ministry of Environment, Forest and Climate Change

Source: (NITI Aayog 2018).

17.6. Initiatives, Expectation and Performance of Government of India in SDG-13

According to the India SDG Index, Baseline Report, 2018 (NITI Aayog 2018), to achieving the target of the UN's SDG-13, the Government of

India not framed any indicator, which capture the UN's SDG targets; but, as per report, the Government of India initiated 12 dedicated policies or schemes which are in action to achieve the targets of the UN's SDG-13 under the leadership and monitoring of 5 dedicated Ministries or the Departments without any performance details on this SDG-13.

17.7. Government of India's Remaining Targets and the Indicators for SDG-13

As we know that, on the basis of the availability of the disaggregated data, the NITI *Aayog* framed India's own indicators of the targets of each individual SDG. For the SDG-13, that is 'Climate Action', the NITI *Aayog* unable to collect and manage the data as required to capture the indicators of the UNs SDG-13 targets. As per the report, 12 dedicated policies or schemes are in action to achieve the UN's SDG-13. As a result, all the indicators of the SDG-13 remained uncaptured but indicators of the UN's SDG-13 is to be achieve by 2030. The remaining lists of targets along with the indicators of SDG-13 are detailed in Table no-126.

Table No. 126: Government of India's Remaining Targets and the Indicators for SDG-13

India's Remaining Targets and the Indicators for SDG-13	
Targets	**Indicators**
13.1: Strengthen resilience and adaptive capacity to climate-related hazards and natural disasters in all countries.	13.1.1: Number of countries with national and local disaster risk reduction strategies [a].
	13.1.2: Number of deaths, missing persons and persons affected by disaster per 100,000 people [a].
13.2: Integrate climate change measures into national policies, strategies and planning.	13.2.1: Number of countries that have communicated the establishment or operationalization of an integrated policy/strategy/plan which increases their ability to adapt to the adverse impacts of climate change, and foster climate resilience and low greenhouse gas emissions development in a manner that does not threaten food production (including a national adaptation plan, nationally determined contribution, national communication, biennial update report or other).
13.3: Improve education, awareness-raising and human and institutional capacity on climate change mitigation, adaptation, impact reduction and early warning.	13.3.1: Number of countries that have integrated mitigation, adaptation, impact reduction and early warning into primary, secondary and tertiary curricula.

(*Contd...*)

	13.3.2: Number of countries that have communicated the strengthening of institutional, systemic and individual capacity-building to implement adaptation, mitigation and technology transfer, and development actions.
13.a: Implement the commitment undertaken by developed-country parties to the United Nations Framework Convention on Climate Change to a goal of mobilizing jointly $100 billion annually by 2020 from all sources to address the needs of developing countries in the context of meaningful mitigation actions and transparency on implementation and fully operationalize the Green Climate Fund through its capitalization as soon as possible.	13.a.1: Mobilized amount of United States dollars per year starting in 2020 accountable towards the $100 billion commitment.
13.b: Promote mechanisms for raising capacity for effective climate change-related planning and management in least developed countries and small island developing States, including focusing on women, youth and local and marginalized communities.	13.b.1: Number of least developed countries and small island developing States that are receiving specialized support, and amount of support, including finance, technology and capacity-building, for mechanisms for raising capacities for effective climate change-related planning and management, including focusing on women, youth and local and marginalized communities.

Notes of the Table:

[a] - An open-ended intergovernmental expert working group on indicators and terminology relating to disaster risk reduction established by the General Assembly (resolution 69/284) is developing a set of indicators to measure global progress in the implementation of the Sendai Framework. These indicators will eventually reflect the agreements on the Sendai Framework indicators.

[b] - Acknowledging that the United Nations Framework Convention on Climate Change is the primary international, intergovernmental forum for negotiating the global response to climate change.

The Ministries or the Departments are - Home Affairs, Information and Broadcasting, Ministry of Environment, Forest and Climate Change, Ministry of Power and the New and Renewable Energy. Apart from the above policies, Ministries and the active governmental Departments; there in the Indian Constitution are ample options to capture the issues associated with the SDG-13. The Ministries or the Departments have to concentrate to monitor on the above issues to achieve the target by 2030 through the provisions of Indian Constitution such as - Article 14, 15-(2).(a), (b), -(3), (4) and (5), Article 16 (1) to (5), Article 19-1.(a) to (g), Article 21, Article 21A, Article 38-(1) and (2), Article 39 – (a) to (f), Article 39 A, Article 41, Article 42, Article 43, Article 43A, Article 44, Article 45, Article 47, Article 48, Article 48A, Article 50, Article 51, Article 51A, Article 243D (2), Article 243T (2), Article 302, Article 303, Article 304, Article 305, Article 307, Article 309, Article 310, Article 311, Article

312, Article 313, Article 314, Article 315, Article 320, Article 323A and Article 323B; Article 246 - Seventh Schedule, List-I: Union List No; 5, 6, 7, 10, 12, 13, 14, 15, 16, 22 to 31, 41, 42, 43, 44, 52, 53, 54, 55, 56, 57, 58, 59, 60, 61, 64, 65, 66, 68, 69 and 94; List-II: State List No: 5, 6, 10, 13, 14, 15, 16, 17, 18, 21, 22, 23, 24, 25, 26, 27, 28, 30, 31, 32, 33, 34 and 35; List-III: Concurrent List No: 7, 10, 17, 17A.17B, 18, 19, 20, 20A, 21, 22, 23, 24, 25, 26, 29, 30, 31, 32, 36, 37, 38, 40 and 47; Article 243G - Eleventh Schedule - Powers, Authority and Responsibilities of Panchayats – Schedule No – 1, 2, 3, 4, 5, 6, 7, 8, 9, 10, 11, 12, 13, 14, 14, 16, 17, 18, 19, 20, 21, 22, 23, 24. 25, 26, 27, 28 and 29; Article 243W - Twelfth Schedule - Powers, Authority and Responsibilities of Municipalities - Schedule No – 1, 2, 3, 4, 5, 6, 7, 8, 9, 10, 11, 12, 13, 14, 15, 16, 17 and 18 - if we could not monitor, we would not be able to stand in front of the future generation with a smile.

Chapter – XVIII

Initiative and Performance of India in SDG-14, Life Bellow Water

The coastal ecology is one among the non industrial economy base of billions of people throughout the world. The global leaders feels and had resolved to protect and it had included in its agenda, that is SDG-4, entitled as *'Life Bellow Water'*, which is aimed to increase benefits to Small Island Developing States (SIDs) and Least Developed Countries (LDCs) from sustainable use of marine resources; that is conserve and sustainably use the oceans, seas and marine resources for sustainable development. The global agenda of SDG-14 is commitment to the present and for the future generations. It focuses on preventing marine pollution, ending illegal and destructive fishing practices, and sustainably managing and protecting marine and coastal ecosystems while increasing scientific knowledge research and transfer of marine technology to improve marine health.

Over three billion people worldwide depend on marine and coastal ecosystems for their livelihood. Sustainable use of oceans is indispensable for habitation on earth, given the fact that oceans cover three quarters of the earth's surface, contain 97 percent of the earth's water, and represent 99 percent of the living space on the planet by volume.

Marine ecosystems play a huge role in maintaining healthy life-cycles on land. Oceans absorb about 30 percent of the carbon dioxide produced by humans and serve as the world's largest source of protein. Economically, the market value of marine and coastal resources and industries is estimated at $ 3 trillion per year or about 5 percent of global GDP. However, reckless exploitation of ocean resources and irresponsible human activities have caused almost 40 percent of world's oceans to be heavily affected, including depleted fisheries, ocean acidification and loss of coastal habitants (United Nations, 2018).

18.1. The Global Targets and Indicators for SDG-14

The global indicator framework was developed by the Inter-Agency and Expert Group on SDG Indicators (IAEG-SDGs) and agreed to, as a practical starting point at the 47th session of the UN Statistical Commission held in March 2016 (NITI Aayog 2018). The report of the Commission, which included the global indicator framework, was then taken note of by ECOSOC at its 70th session in June 2016. The global targets and the indicator of this SDG are tabled (Table no-127) bellow –

Table No. 127: UNDP-DDGs Targets and Indicators of SDG-14

SDG-14, Conserve and sustainably use the oceans, seas and marine resources for sustainable development[1]	
Targets	**Indicators**
14.1: By 2025, prevent and significantly reduce marine pollution of all kinds, in particular from land-based activities, including marine debris and nutrient pollution.	14.1.1: Index of coastal eutrophication and floating plastic debris density.
14.2 By 2020, sustainably manage and protect marine and coastal ecosystems to avoid significant adverse impacts, including by strengthening their resilience, and take action for their restoration in order to achieve healthy and productive oceans.	14.2.1: Proportion of national exclusive economic zones managed using ecosystem-based approaches.
14.3: Minimize and address the impacts of ocean acidification, including through enhanced scientific cooperation at all levels.	14.3.1: Average marine acidity (pH) measured at agreed suite of representative sampling stations.
14.4: By 2020, effectively regulate harvesting and end overfishing, illegal, unreported and unregulated fishing and destructive fishing practices and implement science-based management plans, in order to restore fish stocks in the shortest time feasible, at least to levels that can produce maximum sustainable yield as determined by their biological characteristics.	14.4.1: Proportion of fish stocks within biologically sustainable levels.
14.5: By 2020, conserve at least 10 per cent of coastal and marine areas, consistent with national and international law and based on the best available scientific information.	14.5.1: Coverage of protected areas in relation to marine areas.
14.6: By 2020, prohibit certain forms of fisheries subsidies which contribute to overcapacity and overfishing, eliminate subsidies that contribute to illegal, unreported and unregulated fishing and refrain from introducing new such subsidies, recognizing that appropriate and effective special and differential treatment for developing and least developed countries should be an integral part of the World Trade Organization fisheries subsidies negotiation [a].	14.6.1: Progress by countries in the degree of implementation of international instruments aiming to combat illegal, unreported and unregulated fishing.

14.7: By 2030, increase the economic benefits to small island developing States and least developed countries from the sustainable use of marine resources, including through sustainable management of fisheries, aquaculture and tourism.	14.7.1: Sustainable fisheries as a percentage of GDP in small island developing States, least developed countries and all countries.
14.a: Increase scientific knowledge, develop research capacity and transfer marine technology, taking into account the Intergovernmental Oceanographic Commission Criteria and Guidelines on the Transfer of Marine Technology, in order to improve ocean health and to enhance the contribution of marine biodiversity to the development of developing countries, in particular small island developing States and least developed countries.	14.a.1: Proportion of total research budget allocated to research in the field of marine technology.
14.b: Provide access for small-scale artisanal fishers to marine resources and markets.	14.b.1: Progress by countries in the degree of application of a legal/ regulatory/ policy/institutional framework which recognizes and protects access rights for small-scale fisheries.
14.c: Enhance the conservation and sustainable use of oceans and their resources by implementing international law as reflected in the United Nations Convention on the Law of the Sea, which provides the legal framework for the conservation and sustainable use of oceans and their resources, as recalled in paragraph 158 of "The future we want".	14.c.1: Number of countries making progress in ratifying, accepting and implementing through legal, policy and institutional frameworks, ocean-related instruments that implement international law, as reflected in the United Nation Convention on the Law of the Sea, for the conservation and sustainable use of the oceans and their resources.
Note – [a] - Taking into account ongoing World Trade Organization negotiations, the Doha Development Agenda and the Hong Kong ministerial mandate.	

18.2. Interlinkage of SDG-14 with other SDGs

This section presents the linkage of the SDG-14 to other SDGs, that is, the success of this SDG habitually will influence the success of the linked SDGs; according to the SDG India Index, Baseline Report, 2018 (NITI Aayog 2018), the SDG-14 linked with the following SDGs –

SDG-1, that is *No Poverty*, which aims to reduce poverty in all its dimensions, which includes ensuring access to safe, nutritious and sufficient food all year round, particularly for the poor.

SDG-2, that is *Zero Hunger*, which aims to end all forms of malnutrition and ensures access to safe, nutritious and sufficient food for all, in particular the poor and vulnerable, and support small scale food producers.

SDG-8, is *Decent Work and Economic Growth* which aims to promote development oriented policies that support productive activities, decent job creation, entrepreneurship, and encourage the formalization and growth of micro-, small - and medium-sized enterprises through access to financial services.

SDG-9, is *Industry, Innovation and Infrastructure* aims at building quality, reliable and resilient infrastructures. It further aims at promoting resource-use efficiency and greater adoption of clean and environmentally sound technologies and industrial processes, to support economic development and human well-being. Investment in innovation is an important pillar of this goal.

SDG-12, *Sustainable Consumption and Production* aiming to halve per capita global food waste at consumer level and reduce food losses along production and supply chains.

SDG-13, is *Climate Action* which aims to develop resilience and adaptive capacity of the poor to climate related hazards and natural disasters.

Goal-15, *Life on Land* that aims to promote fair and equitable utilization of genetic resources.

SDG-16: *Peace, Justice and Strong Institutions* which aims to build accountable and transparent economic institutions.

18.3. The National Context of SDG-14

Apart from agriculture, the marine base is a very important economy base in India. India has taken various steps to protect and enhance the coastal and marine ecosystem. Marine sector in India has been the backbone of the country's trade and has grown manifold over the years. The First Maritime Summit was organized in the country in 2016. More than 4500 delegates from across 40 countries participated in the Summit.

To harness India's 7,500 km long coastline, 14,500 km of potentially navigable waterways and strategic location on key international maritime trade routes, the Government of India is laying emphasis on promoting Blue Economy through ambitious projects like the *Sagarmala,* which aim to promote port-led development and sustainable development of coastal communities through skill development and livelihood generation activities, fisheries development, coastal tourism, etc.

As per, SDG India Index Base Line Report, 2018, the Government of India has taken interventions to sustainably manage the oceans given the 7,500km long coastline of the country; National Plan for Conservation of Aquatic Eco-systems is a common regulatory framework, launched in 2013, the principal objective of which is holistic conservation, restoration, and sustainable use of resources of lakes and wetlands, adopting an integrated and multidisciplinary approach.

Project *SAGARMALA* is a part of the National Perspective Plan (NPP) for the comprehensive development of India's coastline and maritime sector which was unveiled in April, 2016 at the Maritime India Summit. The project has four broad objectives; namely, modernizing port infrastructure, enhancing their capacity and adding new ports; improving port connectivity through rail corridors, freight-friendly expressways and inland waterways; developing port-proximate industrial clusters and Coastal Economic Zones to reduce logistics cost and time of EXIM and domestic cargo; and promoting sustainable development of coastal communities through skill development and livelihood generation activities, fisheries development, coastal tourism etc.

India has a long history of mangrove forest management. The Sundarbans mangroves, located in the Bay of Bengal, were first in the world to be put under scientific management. Government of India supports research and development activities with an emphasis on mangrove bio diversity. There has been a net increase of 112 square km in the mangrove cover of the country as compared to the previous assessment. Further in Gujarat, more than 15,000 Ha of mangroves have been planted through active participation of local communities under the Integrated Coastal Zone Management Project. India is a part of the regional initiative 'Mangroves for the future', being coordinated by the United Nations Development Programme and the International Union for Conservation of Nature.

India has 25 Marine Protected Areas in the peninsular region and 106 in islands, collectively covering approximately 10,000 square km of the country's geographical areas. Four major coral reefs have also been identified in the country for intensive conservation and management.

Various national and subnational legislations are in place for the management and protection of the coastal and marine environment. India has also ratified numerous international conventions related to the use of oceans and their resources, including the United Nations Convention on the Law of the Sea. An online mechanism for predicting the movement of oil spills, the Online Oil Spill Advisory System, was launched in 2015. In addition, the revised National Oil Spill Disaster Contingency Plan, 2015 reflects the important national regulations as well as the current international norms.

Further, levels of marine pollution are being monitored by the government at various locations along the country's coastline through the Coastal Ocean Monitoring and Prediction System. India is also setting up a Marine Observation System along the Coast to gain a better understanding of coastal processes and monitor water quality.

As per the SDG India Index Base Line Report, 2018 (NITI Aayog 2018), India is not in a position to directly address the issue and measure due to unavailability of supporting data on the issue. It is tough to capture also. But, as per the commitment of the United Nations General Assembly, India have to devote to capture the data to address the issues associated with the SDG-14 in a scientific manner and the priority must be given by searching the ways. The Indian think tanks adopt few policies to address the issues without framing any indicators to address the issues associated with the SDG-14.

18.4. Provisions of the Indian Constitution for SDG-14

The spirit of the unity in this diverse country, India is secured by its great Constitution; the Constitution of India not only secured its unity, announced a vision in the Preamble in the beginning of its Articles included in the Indian Constitution, *"We the people of India, having solemnly resolved to constitute India into a Sovereign Socialist Secular Democratic Republic and to secure to all its citizens: justice, social, economic and political; liberty of thought, expression, belief, faith and worship; equality of status and of opportunity; and to promote among them all fraternity assuring the dignity of the individual and the unity and integrity of the nation; in our Constituent Assembly this twenty-sixth day of November, 1949, do hereby adopt, enact and give to ourselves this Constitution* (NITI Aayog 2018)". The mode of orientation of the Indian Constitution and the sustainable development goals of the contemporary time are given us an opportunity to make a link between these two visions of development and the author is trying to make the link.

As we know the sustainable development goals are interlinked, that means the success or failure of one is affected to other SDGs. From this perspective, this section presents the provisions in the Indian Constitution to eradicate poverty as reflected in the sustainable development agenda entitled as SDG-14, Life Bellow Water. The linked Constitutional provisions are in the following Table no-128 -

Table No. 128: Provisions in Indian Constitution for SDG-14

SDG-14 and the Linked Articles and Schedules of the Constitution of India
Article 16 (1) to (5), Article 21, Article 21A, Article 38-(1) and (2), Article 39 – (a) to (f), Article 39A, Article 41, Article 42, Article 43, Article 43A, Article 44, Article 47, Article 48A, Article 51, Article 51A, Article 243D (2), Article 243T (2), Article 301, Article 302, Article 303, Article 304, Article 305, Article 307, Article 309, Article 310, Article 311, Article 312, Article 313, Article 314, Article 315, Article 320, Article 323A and Article 323B.

Article 246 - Seventh Schedule, List-I: Union List No: 2, 3, 8, 10, 12, 13, 14, 21, 24, 25, 27, 28, 30, 53, 54, 57, 64, 65, 66, 68, 69, 89, and 94. List-II: State List No: 6, 17, 21 and 32. List-III: Concurrent List No: 20, 23, 24, 25 and 34.
Article 243G: Eleventh Schedule: Powers, Authority and Responsibilities of Panchayats. Schedule No: 5, 13, 16, 17, 18 and 19. Article 243W: Twelfth Schedule: Powers, Authority and Responsibilities of Municipalities. Schedule No: 1, 3, 5, 7, 8, 11 and 16.

Source: The Constitution of India, 2015 as on 9th November, 2015.

18.5. Policies of the Government of India for Targets of the SDG-14

According to the SDG India Index Base Line Report, 2018 (NITI Aayog 2018), India is proactive to achieve the target of the UN's SDGs. The Government of India initiated as well as implemented various policies to capture the indicators of the targets of each individual SDG. On the moment of preparation of SDG India Index Base Line Report, 2018, on the basis of the availability of the disaggregated data, the NITI *Aayog* framed India's own indicators of the targets of each individual SDG. For the SDG-14, that is 'Life Bellow Water'; the NITI *Aayog* unable to manage the data to frame any measurable indicators; which capture the UNs SDG targets. Even though, as per the report, 8 dedicated policies or schemes are in action to achieve the targets of the UN's SDG-14 under the leadership and monitoring of 6 dedicated Ministries or the Departments. The policies or schemes to achieve the targets of SDG-14 and the concerned dedicated Ministries and the Departments are detailed in the Table no-129.

Table No. 129: Policies Initiated by the Indian Government for Targets of SDG-14

SDG-14, Life Bellow Water	
SDG-14, is *Life Bellow Water* which aims to increase benefits to Small Island Developing States (SIDs) and Least Developed Countries (LDCs) from sustainable use of marine resources.	
Target: 14.1: By 2030, prevent and significantly reduce marine pollution of all kinds, in particular from land-based activities, including marine debris and nutrient pollution.	
Centrally Sponsored /Central Sector Schemes (CSS)	Concerned Ministries/ Departments
1. Environment Protection, Management and Sustainable Development 2. National Coastal Management Programme	Ministry of Environment, Forest and Climate Change
3. *Neel Kranti* Mission (Blue Revolution) – Marine Fisheries and aquaculture Related Components	Agriculture and Cooperation
4. Ocean Services, Technology, Observations, Resources Modelling and Science (O-STORMS)	Department of Earth Sciences

(*Contd...*)

Target: 14.2: By 2030, sustainably manage and protect marine and coastal ecosystems to avoid significant adverse impacts, including by strengthening their resilience, and take action for their restoration in order to achieve healthy and productive oceans.	
Centrally Sponsored /Central Sector Schemes (CSS)	Concerned Ministries/ Departments
1. Conservation of Natural Resources and Eco-systems 2. National Coastal Management Programme 3. Environment Protection, Management and Sustainable Development	Ministry of Environment, Forest and Climate Change
	Department of Earth Sciences
Target: 14.3: Minimise and address the impacts of ocean acidification, including through enhanced scientific cooperation at all levels.	
Centrally Sponsored /Central Sector Schemes (CSS)	Concerned Ministries/ Departments
1. National Coastal Management Programme	Ministry of Environment, Forest and Climate Change
2. Ocean Services, Technology, Observations, Resources Modelling and Science (O-STORMS) 3. ESSO - Indian National Centre for Ocean Information Services	Department of Earth Sciences
Target: 14.4: By 2030, effectively regulate harvesting and end overfishing, illegal, unreported and un regulated fishing and destructive fishing practices and implement science-based management plans, in order to restore fish stocks in the shortest time feasible at least two levels that can produce maximum sustainable yield as determined by their biological characteristics.	
Centrally Sponsored /Central Sector Schemes (CSS)	Concerned Ministries/ Departments
1. *Neel Kranti* Mission (Blue Revolution): Integrated Development and Management of Fisheries) (Core) 2. Fishery Science	Department of Animal Husbandry, Dairying & Fisheries (DADF)
Target: 14.5: By 2020, conserve at least 10 percent of coastal and marine areas, consistent with national and international law and based on the best available scientific information.	
Centrally Sponsored /Central Sector Schemes (CSS)	Concerned Ministries/ Departments
1. National Coastal Management Programme 2. Conservation of Natural Resources and Eco-systems	Ministry of Environment, Forest and Climate Change
3. Ocean Services, Technology, Observations, Resources Modelling and Science (O-STORMS)	Department of Earth Sciences
	Department of Animal Husbandry, Dairying & Fisheries (DADF), Department of Science and Technology
Target: 14.6: By 2030, prohibit certain forms of fisheries subsidies which contribute to overcapacity and overfishing, eliminate subsidies that contribute to illegal, unreported and un regulated fishing and refrain from introducing new such subsidies, recognizing that, appropriate and effective special and differential treatment for developing and least developed countries should be an integral part of the World Trade Organization fisheries subsidies negotiation.	
Centrally Sponsored /Central Sector Schemes (CSS)	Concerned Ministries/ Departments
	Department of Animal Husbandry, Dairying & Fisheries (DADF),

(*Contd...*)

Target: 14.7: By 2030, increase the economic benefits to Small Island Developing States and least developed countries from the sustainable use of marine resources, including through sustainable management of fisheries, aquaculture and tourism.	
Centrally Sponsored /Central Sector Schemes (CSS)	Concerned Ministries/ Departments
	Ministry of Tourism, Department of Animal Husbandry, Dairying & Fisheries (DADF)
Target: 14.a: Increase scientific knowledge, develop research capacity and transfer marine technology takin into account the Intergovernmental Oceanographic Commission Criteria and Guidelines on the transfer on marine technology, in order to improve ocean health and to enhance the contribution of marine biodiversity to the development of developing countries, in particular Small Island Developing States and least developed countries.	
Centrally Sponsored /Central Sector Schemes (CSS)	Concerned Ministries/ Departments
1. National Coastal Management Programme	Ministry of Environment, Forest and Climate Change
2. Ocean Services, Technology, Observations, Resources Modelling and Science (O-STORMS) 3. ESSO - Indian National Centre for Ocean Information Services	Department of Earth Sciences
Target: 14.b: Provide access for small-scale artisanal fishers to marine resources and markets.	
Centrally Sponsored /Central Sector Schemes (CSS)	Concerned Ministries/ Departments
1. *Neel Kranti* Mission (Blue Revolution): Marine Fisheries and aquaculture Related Components	Department of Animal Husbandry, Dairying & Fisheries (DADF)
Target: 14.c: Enhance the conservation and sustainable use of oceans and their resources by implementing international laws as reflected in UNCLOS, which provides the legal framework for the conservation and sustainable use of oceans and their resources, as recalled in paragraph 158 of "The Future We Want".	
Centrally Sponsored /Central Sector Schemes (CSS)	Concerned Ministries/ Departments
1. Ocean Services, Technology, Observations, Resources Modelling and Science (O-STORMS) 2. ESSO - Indian National Centre for Ocean Information Services	Department of Earth Sciences

Source: (NITI Aayog 2018).

18.6. Initiatives, Expectation and Performance of Government of India in SDG-14

According to the India SDG Index, Baseline Report, 2018 (NITI Aayog 2018), to achieving the target of the UN's SDG-14, the Government of India has not framed any indicator, which capture the UN's SDG targets; but, as per report, the Government of India initiated 8 dedicated policies or schemes which are in action to achieve the targets of the UN's SDG-14 under the leadership and monitoring of 6 dedicated Ministries or the Departments without any performance details on this SDG-14.

18.7. Government of India's Remaining Targets and the Indicators for SDG-14

As we know that, on the basis of the availability of the disaggregated data, the NITI *Aayog* framed India's own indicators of the targets of each individual SDG. For the SDG-14, that is 'Climate Action', the NITI *Aayog* unable to collect and manage the data as required to capture the indicators of the UNs SDG-14 targets. As per the report, 8 dedicated policies or schemes are in action to achieve the UN's SDG-14. As a result, all the indicators of the SDG-14 remained uncaptured but indicators of the UN's SDG-14 is to be achieve by 2030. The remaining lists of targets along with the indicators of SDG-14 are detailed in Table no-130.

Table No. 130: Government of India's Remaining Targets and the Indicators for SDG-14

India's Remaining Targets and the Indicators for SDG-14	
Targets	**Indicators**
14.1: By 2025, prevent and significantly reduce marine pollution of all kinds, in particular from land-based activities, including marine debris and nutrient pollution.	14.1.1: Index of coastal eutrophication and floating plastic debris density.
14.2: By 2020, sustainably manage and protect marine and coastal ecosystems to avoid significant adverse impacts, including by strengthening their resilience, and take action for their restoration in order to achieve healthy and productive oceans.	14.2.1: Proportion of national exclusive economic zones managed using ecosystem-based approaches.
14.3: Minimize and address the impacts of ocean acidification, including through enhanced scientific cooperation at all levels.	14.3.1: Average marine acidity (pH) measured at agreed suite of representative sampling stations.
14.4: By 2020, effectively regulate harvesting and end overfishing, illegal, unreported and unregulated fishing and destructive fishing practices and implement science-based management plans, in order to restore fish stocks in the shortest time feasible, at least to levels that can produce maximum sustainable yield as determined by their biological characteristics.	14.4.1: Proportion of fish stocks within biologically sustainable levels.
14.5: By 2020, conserve at least 10 per cent of coastal and marine areas, consistent with national and international law and based on the best available scientific information.	14.5.1: Coverage of protected areas in relation to marine areas.
14.6: By 2020, prohibit certain forms of fisheries subsidies which contribute to overcapacity and overfishing, eliminate subsidies that contribute to illegal, unreported and unregulated fishing and	14.6.1: Progress by countries in the degree of implementation of international instruments aiming to combat illegal, unreported and unregulated fishing.

(Contd...)

introducing new such subsidies, recognizing that appropriate and effective special and differential treatment for developing and least developed countries should be an integral part of the World Trade Organization fisheries subsidies negotiation [a].	
14.7: By 2030, increase the economic benefits to small island developing States and least developed countries from the sustainable use of marine resources, including through sustainable management of fisheries, aquaculture and tourism.	14.7.1: Sustainable fisheries as a percentage of GDP in small island developing States, least developed countries and all countries.
14.a: Increase scientific knowledge, develop research capacity and transfer marine technology, taking into account the Intergovernmental Oceanographic Commission Criteria and Guidelines on the Transfer of Marine Technology, in order to improve ocean health and to enhance the contribution of marine biodiversity to the development of developing countries, in particular small island developing States and least developed countries.	14.a.1: Proportion of total research budget allocated to research in the field of marine technology.
14.b: Provide access for small-scale artisanal fishers to marine resources and markets.	14.b.1: Progress by countries in the degree of application of a legal/regulatory/ policy/ institutional framework which recognizes and protects access rights for small-scale fisheries.
14.c: Enhance the conservation and sustainable use of oceans and their resources by implementing international law as reflected in the United Nations Convention on the Law of the Sea, which provides the legal framework for the conservation and sustainable use of oceans and their resources, as recalled in paragraph 158 of "The future we want".	14.c.1: Number of countries making progress in ratifying, accepting and implementing through legal, policy and institutional frameworks, ocean-related instruments that implement international law, as reflected in the United Nation Convention on the Law of the Sea, for the conservation and sustainable use of the oceans and their resources.

Notes of the Table:

- Remaining to capture the data of targets and indicators.

[a] - Taking into account ongoing World Trade Organization negotiations, the Doha Development Agenda and the Hong Kong ministerial mandate.

Apart from the above policies, the Ministries or the Departments such as, Agriculture and Cooperation, Department of Animal Husbandry, Dairying & Fisheries (DADF), Earth Sciences, Ministry of Environment, Forest and Climate Change, Ministry of Tourism and Science and Technology, along with ample options to capture the issues associated with the SDG-14 in the Constitution of India. The Ministries or the Departments have to concentrate to monitor on the above issues to achieve the target by 2030 through the provisions of Indian Constitution such as - Article 16 (1) to (5), Article 21, Article 21A, Article 38-(1) and (2),

Article 39 – (a) to (f), Article 39A, Article 41, Article 42, Article 43, Article 43A, Article 44, Article 47, Article 48A, Article 51, Article 51A, Article 243D (2), Article 243T (2), Article 301, Article 302, Article 303, Article 304, Article 305, Article 307, Article 309, Article 310, Article 311, Article 312, Article 313, Article 314, Article 315, Article 320, Article 323A and Article 323B; Article 246 - Seventh Schedule, List-I: Union List No: 2, 3, 8, 10, 12, 13, 14, 21, 24, 25, 27, 28, 30, 53, 54, 57, 64, 65, 66, 68, 69, 89, and 94; List-II: State List No: 6, 17, 21 and 32; List-III: Concurrent List No: 20, 23, 24, 25 and 34; Article 243G - Eleventh Schedule - Powers, Authority and Responsibilities of Panchayats – Schedule No – 5, 13, 16, 17, 18 and 19; Article 243W - Twelfth Schedule - Powers, Authority and Responsibilities of Municipalities - Schedule No – 1, 3, 5, 7, 8, 11 and 16 - if we could not monitor, we would not be able to stand in front of the future generation with a smile.

Chapter – XIX

Initiative and Performance of India in SDG-15, Life and Land

The life in the concrete and in the polluted environment cannot be the future history of civilization. The evolution of the civilization has variously depicted that, it starts from the water base and expanded into the soil-centric base of the world; the present call is, use of soil-centric base must be scanned for the future generations. The SDG-15, entitled as '*Life on Land'*, that aimed to promote fair and equitable utilization of genetic resources. The global agenda of SDG-15 was to protect, restore and promote sustainable use of terrestrial ecosystems, sustainably manage forests, combat desertification, and halt and reverse land degradation and halt biodiversity loss. The SDG also aimed to integrating ecosystem and biodiversity into national and local planning, development processes, poverty reduction strategies and national accounts. It also seeks to promote fair and equitable sharing of benefits arising from the utilization of genetic resources, promote appropriate access to such resources, and poaching and trafficking of protected species of flora and fauna.

19.1. The Global Targets and Indicators for SDG-15

The global indicator framework was developed by the Inter-Agency and Expert Group on SDG Indicators (IAEG-SDGs) and agreed to, as a practical starting point at the 47th session of the UN Statistical Commission held in March 2016 (NITI Aayog 2018). The report of the Commission, which has been included the global indicator framework, was then taken note of by ECOSOC at its 70th session in June 2016. The global targets and the indicator of this SDG are tabled (Table no-131) bellow –

Table No. 131: UNDP-DDGs Targets and Indicators of SDG-15

Table No-131: SDG-15, Protect, restore and promote sustainable use of terrestrial ecosystems, sustainably manage forests, combat desertification, and halt and reverse land degradation and halt biodiversity loss[1]	
Targets	**Indicators**
15.1: By 2020, ensure the conservation, restoration and sustainable use of terrestrial and inland freshwater ecosystems and their services, in particular forests, wetlands, mountains and drylands, in line with obligations under international agreements.	15.1.1: Forest area as a proportion of total land area.
	15.1.2: Proportion of important sites for terrestrial and freshwater biodiversity that are covered by protected areas, by ecosystem type.
15.2: By 2020, promote the implementation of sustainable management of all types of forests, halt deforestation, restore degraded forests and substantially increase afforestation and reforestation globally.	15.2.1: Progress towards sustainable forest management.
15.3: By 2030, combat desertification, restore degraded land and soil, including land affected by desertification, drought and floods, and strive to achieve a land degradation-neutral world.	15.3.1: Proportion of land that is degraded over total land area.
15.4: By 2030, ensure the conservation of mountain ecosystems, including their biodiversity, in order to enhance their capacity to provide benefits that are essential for sustainable development.	15.4.1: Coverage by protected areas of important sites for mountain biodiversity.
	15.4.2-Mountain Green Cover Index.
15.5: Take urgent and significant actions to reduce the degradation of natural habitats, halt the loss of biodiversity and, by 2020, protect and prevent the extinction of threatened species.	15.5.1: Red List Index.
15.6: Promote fair and equitable sharing of the benefits arising from the utilization of genetic resources and promote appropriate access to such resources, as internationally agreed.	15.6.1: Number of countries that have adopted legislative, administrative and policy frameworks to ensure fair and equitable sharing of benefits.
15.7: Take urgent action to end poaching and trafficking of protected species of flora and fauna and address both demand and supply of illegal wildlife products.	15.7.1: Proportion of traded wildlife that was poached or illicitly trafficked.
15.8: By 2020, introduce measures to prevent the introduction and significantly reduce the impact of invasive alien species on land and water ecosystems and control or eradicate the priority species.	15.8.1: Proportion of countries adopting relevant national legislation and adequately resourcing the prevention or control of invasive alien species.
15.9: By 2020, integrate ecosystem and biodiversity values into national and local planning, development processes, poverty reduction strategies and accounts.	15.9.1: Progress towards national targets established in accordance with Aichi Biodiversity Target 2 of the Strategic Plan for Biodiversity 2011-2020.

(Contd...)

1. Data Source: SDG India Index Baseline Report, 2018, NITI *Aayog*, Government of India, New Delhi.

15.a: Mobilize and significantly increase financial resources from all sources to conserve and sustainably use biodiversity and ecosystems.	15.a.1: Official development assistance and public expenditure on conservation and sustainable use of biodiversity and ecosystems.
15.b: Mobilize significant resources from all sources and at all levels to finance sustainable forest management and provide adequate incentives to developing countries to advance such management, including for conservation and reforestation.	15.b.1: Official development assistance and public expenditure on conservation and sustainable use of biodiversity and ecosystems.
15.c: Enhance global support for efforts to combat poaching and trafficking of protected species, including by increasing the capacity of local communities to pursue sustainable livelihood opportunities.	15.c.1: Proportion of traded wildlife that was poached or illicitly trafficked.

19.2. Interlinkage of SDG-15 with other SDGs

This section presents the linkage of the SDG-15 to other SDGs, that is, the success of this SDG habitually will influence the success of the linked SDGs; according to the SDG India Index, Baseline Report, 2018 (NITI Aayog 2018), the SDG-15 linked with the following SDGs –

SDG-1, that is *No Poverty*, which aims to reduce poverty in all its dimensions, which includes ensuring access to safe, nutritious and sufficient food all year round, particularly for the poor.

SDG-2, that is *Zero Hunger*, which aims to end all forms of malnutrition and ensures access to safe, nutritious and sufficient food for all, in particular the poor and vulnerable, and support small scale food producers.

SDG-3, is *Good Health and Well-being*, which aims to end epidemics and preventable deaths and achieve universal health coverage, including financial risk protection and access to quality essential health care services, medicines and vaccines for all.

SDG-5, is *Gender Equality* as Goal 1 emphasises creation of gender sensitive development strategies, and equal rights and access to economic resources, as well as ownership and control over land and other forms of property, inheritance, natural resources and financial resources, including microfinance.

SDG-6, is *Clean Water and Sanitation*, which aims to achieve universal and equitable access to safe and affordable drinking water and sanitation and hygiene for all.

SDG-10, is *Reduced Inequalities* that aims to adopt policies, especially fiscal wage and social protection policies and progressively achieve and sustain income growth of the bottom 40 percent of the population at a rate higher than the national average, leading to greater equality.

SDG-12, *Sustainable Consumption and Production* aiming to halve per capita global food waste at consumer level and reduce food losses along production and supply chains.

SDG-13, is *Climate Action* which aims to develop resilience and adaptive capacity of the poor to climate related hazards and natural disasters.

19.3. The National Context of SDG-15

Millions of people are depended in the terrestrial ecosystem in India. As per report, land that provides habitat to more than 80 percent of all terrestrial species of animals, plants and insects, is an essential and irreplaceable resource of the world. However, unsustainable developmental activities like deforestation and desertification pose a threat to the ecosystem and affect the lives of the millions of people. India's forest cover is presently 21 percent and secured territories make up almost 5 percent of the nation's aggregate land area (MEF&CC, 2017). Millions of people in India depend on land resources for their livelihood. Therefore, India aims to integrate ecosystem and biodiversity values into local planning, development processes and poverty reduction strategies.

India's progress on this goal is important globally, since the country is home to 8 percent of the world's biodiversity, including numerous species that are unique to the country. India's global leadership on biodiversity is reflected in the pivotal role it played in facilitating the implementation of the Nagoya Protocol — one of the global Aichi Biodiversity Targets. The Nagoya Protocol on Access to Genetic Resources and the Fair and Equitable Sharing of Benefits Arising from their Utilization; translates and gives practical effects to the equity provisions of the Convention on Biological Diversity.

As per, SDG India Index Base Line Report, 2018, the Government of India has taken various initiatives towards meeting the targets set under SDG-15. At the policy level, the National Environment Policy, 2006 and National Agroforestry Policy, 2014, aimed to mainstream environmental concerns into all developmental activities and address the problems faced by the agroforestry sector. The Green Highways Policy, 2015 was launched to promote greening of National Highway corridors across the country. The National afforestation Programme targets development of forest resources with the involvement of people, with a focus on sustainability and improvement in livelihoods of the forest-fringe communities and especially the poor.

The Integrated Development of Wildlife Habitats programme, which includes Project Tiger and Project Elephant, focuses on capacity building of staffs, wildlife research and evaluation, anti-poaching activities, wildlife veterinary care, addressing man animal conflicts and promoting eco-tourism. The programme on Conservation of Natural Resources and Eco-systems, through its different sob-programmes, aims at conserving biosphere reserves, natural resources and the ecosystems of the country.

The total forest cover of India is 7, 08,273 sq. km., which is 21.54 percent of the geographic area of the country. The national target is to have at least 33 percent of the area covered under forest. In terms of forest cover with respect to total geographic area, Mizoram leads among the States with 86.27 percent of its area covered with forest, and Lakshadweep among the Union Territories with 90.33 percent of its area covered with forest. In terms of total area of forest cover Madhya Pradesh has the largest forest cover spanning across an area of 77,414 sq. km.

The increase in water bodies within forest areas of the country clearly brings out the positive effects of forest in augmenting water resources. Highest increase in the extent of water bodies within forest areas has been observed in Manipur (81.25 percent) followed by Mizoram 72 percent, Tamil Nadu 62 percent and Nagaland 59 percent.

Between 2015 and 2017, the forest cover increased nationally 6, 778 sq. km. (0.21 percent) due to an increase in plantation and conservation activities, and improvement in data interpretation. Among the States, major decline in forest cover was observed in Nagaland, followed Mizoram and Meghalaya. Among the Union Territories, Puducherry has been the highest decline in area under forest cover.

As per SDG India Index Base Line Report, 2018, since elephants have high dietary requirements, their population can be supported only by forests that are under optimal conditions. So, the status of elephants is the best indicator of the status of forests. The population of wild elephants in India is estimated to have risen by 20 percent over the five-year period between 2012 and 2017. Nagaland has witnessed a 110.38 percent increase.

In the next part of this chapter we tried to visualized the performance level of India through the SDG's targets and the SDG India Index Base Line Report, 2018 along with the Constitutional provisions in India to explore citizen's responsibility along with the its institutions through the mirror of indexed score on 'peace, justice and strong institutions' (SDG-16).

19.4. SDG-15 Targets, National Indicators and Target Values of India

India in its SDG India Index Base Line Report, 2018 (NITI Aayog 2018), India had measured the performance of India on the goal of 'Land and Life', India had identified four national level indicators, which captured three (15.1, 15.2 and 15.7) out of twelve UN's SDG targets. These indicators have been selected based on availability of data at national level; these are in Table no-132.

Table No. 132: SDG-15 Targets, National Indicators and Target Values of India

SDG-16 Global Target	Indicator Selected for SDG India Index	National Target Value for 2030
15.1: By 2030, ensure the conservation, restoration and sustainable use of terrestrial and inland fresh water ecosystem and the services, in particular forests, wetlands, mountains and drylands, in line with obligations under international agreements.	1. Percentage of total land area covered under forest.	33
	2. Decadal change in extent of water bodies within forests from 2005 to 2015 (%).	0
15.2: By 2020, promote the implementation of sustainable management of all types of forests, halt globally.	3. Change in forest area from 2015 to 2017 (%).	0
15.7: Take urgent action to end poaching and trafficking of protected species of flora and fauna and address both demand and supply of illegal wildlife products.	4. Percentage change in estimated population of wild elephants over 5 year period.	0

Source: (NITI Aayog 2018).

19.5. Indian's SDG-15 Index Indicators, Data Source and Interpretations

The NITI *Aayog*, Government of India had collected required data from different government agencies to capture the UN SDG's target indicators as well as had framed its own indicators to justify the achievement of the SDGs. Apart from that the NITI *Aayog* had developed the computational approach of the disaggregated data as per valid methods along with the parameters of the performance; in the following tables (Table no-133, Table no-134, Table no-135 and Table no-136) shows the details of the above issue to develop a sense of progress of the SDG-15, entitled as 'Life and Land'.

Table No. 133: SDG-15, Indian Indicator-1

SDG-15: 'Life and Land'	**Indicator-1: Percentage of total land area covered under forest.**
Indicator data source	Ministry of Environment, Forest and Climate Change [Forest Survey of India 2017]
Computation approach	Directly from data source
Data period (year)	2017
States/UTs covered	36
Data periodicity	2 years
Relevant UN target	15.1: By 2030, ensure the conservation, restoration and sustainable use of terrestrial and inland fresh water ecosystem and the services, in particular forests, wetlands, mountains and drylands, in line with obligations under international agreements.
Relevant UN indicator	15.1.1: Forest area as a proportion of total land area.
Relevant MoSPI indicator	15.1.1: Forest area as a proportion of total land area.
Indicator interpretation	Higher value means higher performance (+).

Source: (NITI Aayog 2018).

Table No. 134: SDG-15, Indian Indicator-2

SDG-15: 'Life and Land'	**Indicator-2:** Decadal change in extent of water bodies within forests from 2005 to 2015 (%).
Indicator data source	Ministry of Environment, Forest and Climate Change [Forest Survey of India 2017]
Computation approach	Directly from data source
Data period (year)	2017
States/UTs covered	34
Data periodicity	2 years
Relevant UN target	15.1: By 2030, ensure the conservation, restoration and sustainable use of terrestrial and inland fresh water ecosystem and the services, in particular forests, wetlands, mountains and drylands, in line with obligations under international agreements.
Relevant UN indicator	NA
Relevant MoSPI indicator	NA
Indicator interpretation	Higher value means higher performance (+).

Source: (NITI Aayog 2018).

Table No. 135: SDG-15, Indian Indicator-3

SDG-15: 'Life and Land'	**Indicator-3:** Change in forest area from 2015 to 2017 (%).
Indicator data source	Ministry of Environment, Forest and Climate Change [Forest Survey of India 2017]
Computation approach	Directly from data source
Data period (year)	2017
States/UTs covered	36
Data periodicity	2 years
Relevant UN target	15.2: By 2020, promote the implementation of sustainable management of all types of forests, halt globally.

(*Contd...*)

Relevant UN indicator	15.2.1: Progress towards sustainable forest management.
Relevant MoSPI indicator	15.2.1: Percentage change in forest area coverage.
Indicator interpretation	Higher value means higher performance (+).

Source: (NITI Aayog 2018).

Table No. 136: SDG-15, Indian Indicator-4

SDG-15: 'Life and Land'	**Indicator-4:** Percentage change in estimated population of wild elephants over 5 year period.
Indicator data source	Ministry of Environment, Forest and Climate Change [Elephant population estimation, Project Elephant Division]
Computation approach	Directly from data source [Since elephants have high dietary requirements, their population can be supported only by forests that are under optimal conditions. So, the status of elephants is the best indicator of the status of forests.]
Data period (year)	2017
States/UTs covered	36
Data periodicity	5 years
Relevant UN target	15.7: Take urgent action to end poaching and trafficking of protected species of flora and fauna and address both demand and supply of illegal wildlife products.
Relevant UN indicator	15.7.1: Proportion of traded wildlife that was poached or illicitly trafficked.
Relevant MoSPI indicator	15.7.1: Percentage of reduction in traded wildlife that was poached or illicitly trafficked.
Indicator interpretation	Higher value means higher performance (+).

Source: (NITI Aayog 2018).

19.6. Provisions of the Indian Constitution for SDG-15

The spirit of the unity in this diverse country, India is secured by its great Constitution; the Constitution of India not only secured its unity, announced a vision in the Preamble in the beginning of its Articles included in the Indian Constitution, *"We the people of India, having solemnly resolved to constitute India into a Sovereign Socialist Secular Democratic Republic and to secure to all its citizens: justice, social, economic and political; liberty of thought, expression, belief, faith and worship; equality of status and of opportunity; and to promote among them all fraternity assuring the dignity of the individual and the unity and integrity of the nation; in our Constituent Assembly this twenty-sixth day of November, 1949, do hereby adopt, enact and give to ourselves this Constitution* (India 1950/2015)". The mode of orientation of the Indian Constitution and the sustainable development goals of the contemporary time are given us an opportunity to make a link between these two visions of development and the author is trying to make the link.

As we know the sustainable development goals are interlinked, that means the success or failure of one is affected to other SDGs. From this perspective, this section presents the provisions in the Indian Constitution to eradicate poverty as reflected in the sustainable development agenda entitled as SDG-15, Life and Land. The linked Constitutional provisions are in the following Table no-137 -

Table No. 137: Provisions in Indian Constitution for SDG-15

SDG-15 and the Linked Articles and Schedules of the Constitution of India
Article 14, Article 15 *1* to *5*, Article 16, Article 21A, Article 38-(1) and (2), Article 41, Article 44, Article 46, Article 47, Article 48, Article 48A, Article 51, Article 51A, Article 304, Article 307, Article 309, Article 310, Article 311, Article 312, Article 313, Article 314, Article 315, Article 320, Article 323A and Article 323B.
Article 246 - Seventh Schedule, List-I: Union List No: 4, 7, 10, 12, 13, 14, 24, 25, 26, 27, 28, 30, 41, 42, 52, 53, 54, 55, 56, 57, 58, 64, 65, 66, 89, and 94. List-II: State List No: 13, 14, 15, 16, 17, 18, 22, 23, 24, 25, 26, 27 and 58. List-III: Concurrent List No: 17, 17A, 17B, 18, 19, 25, 26, 30, 31, 32 and 33.
Article 243G: Eleventh Schedule: Powers, Authority and Responsibilities of Panchayats. Schedule No: 1, 2, 3, 4, 5, 6, 7, 8, 9, 16, 17, 18, 19, 20, 21, 22, 26, 27, 28 and 29. Article 243W: Twelfth Schedule: Powers, Authority and Responsibilities of Municipalities. Schedule No: 1, 2, 3, 5, 8, 9, 10, 11, 12, 13, 14, 15, 16 and 18.

Source: The Constitution of India, 2015 as on 9th November, 2015.

19.7. Policies of the Government of India for Targets of the SDG-15

According to the SDG India Index Base Line Report, 2018 (NITI Aayog 2018), India is proactive to achieve the target of the UN's SDGs. The Government of India initiated as well as implemented various policies to capture the indicators of the targets of each individual SDG. On the moment of preparation of SDG India Index Base Line Report, 2018, on the basis of the availability of the disaggregated data, the NITI *Aayog* framed India's own indicators of the targets of each individual SDG. For the SDG-15, that is 'Life and Land'; the NITI *Aayog* framed four indicators; which capture three out of twelve UNs SDG targets. As per the report, 17 dedicated policies or schemes are in action to achieve three targets (15.1, 15.2 and 15.7) of the UN's SDG-15 under the leadership and monitoring of 9 dedicated Ministries or the Departments. The policies or schemes to achieve the targets of SDG-15 and the concerned dedicated Ministries and the Departments are detailed in the - Table no-138.

Table No. 138: Policies Initiated by the Indian Government for Targets of SDG-15

SDG-15, Life and Land	
SDG-15, is *Life and Land* is aimed to integrating ecosystem and biodiversity into national and local planning, development processes, poverty reduction strategies and national accounts. It also seeks to promote fair and equitable sharing of benefits arising from the utilization of genetic resources, promote appropriate access to such resources, and poaching and trafficking of protected species of flora and fauna.	
Target: 15.1: By 2030, ensure the conservation, restoration and sustainable use of terrestrial and inland fresh water ecosystem and the services, in particular forests, wetlands, mountains and drylands, in line with obligations under international agreements.	
Centrally Sponsored /Central Sector Schemes (CSS)	Concerned Ministries/ Departments
1. National Mission for a Green India 2. Integrated Development for Wildlife Habitat (Project Tiger, Project Elephant etc. 3. Conservation of Natural Resources and Ecosystem 4. National River Conservation Programme. 5. Environment Protection, Management and Sustainable Development 6. Decision Support System for Environmental Policy, Planning and Outcome Evaluation 7. Environmental Knowledge and Capacity Building	Ministry of Environment, Forest and Climate Change
1. River Basin Management 2. Flood Management & Border Areas Programme	Agriculture and Cooperation
Target: 15.2: By 2020, promote the implementation of sustainable management of all types of forests, halt globally.	
Centrally Sponsored /Central Sector Schemes (CSS)	Concerned Ministries/ Departments
1. National Mission for a Green India 2. Integrated Development for Wildlife Habitat (Project Tiger, Project Elephant etc. 3. Conservation of Natural Resources and Ecosystem 4. Environment Protection, Management and Sustainable Development 5. Decision Support System for Environmental Policy, Planning and Outcome Evaluation 6. Environmental Knowledge and Capacity Building	Ministry of Environment, Forest and Climate Change
	Ministry of Tribal Affairs
Target: 15.3: By 2030, combat desertification, restore degraded land and soil, including land affected by desertification, drought and floods, strive to achieve a land-degradation neutral world.	
Centrally Sponsored /Central Sector Schemes (CSS)	Concerned Ministries/ Departments
1. National Mission for a Green India 2. Conservation of Natural Resources and Ecosystem 3. Environment Protection, Management and Sustainable Development 4. Decision Support System for Environmental Policy, Planning and Outcome Evaluation	Ministry of Environment, Forest and Climate Change
5. Ground Water Management and Regulation National Hydrology Project 6. Water Resources Information System 7. River Basin management	Ministry of Water Resource, Rural Development and Green Revolution
8. PMKSY – Watershed component	Ministry of Land Resources

(*Contd*...)

<table>
<tr><td colspan="2">Target: 15.4: By 2030, ensure the conservation of mountain ecosystems, including their biodiversity, in order to enhance their capacity to provide benefits that are essential for sustainable development.</td></tr>
<tr><td>Centrally Sponsored /Central Sector Schemes (CSS)</td><td>Concerned Ministries/ Departments</td></tr>
<tr><td>1. Conservation of Natural Resources and Ecosystem
2. Integrated Development for Wildlife Habitat (Project Tiger, Project Elephant etc.)
3. Environment Protection, Management and Sustainable Development
4. Environmental Knowledge and Capacity Building</td><td>Ministry of Environment, Forest and Climate Change</td></tr>
<tr><td colspan="2">Target: 15.5: Take urgent and significant action to reduce the degradation of natural habitats, that the loss of biodiversity and, by 2020, protect and prevent the extinction of threatened species.</td></tr>
<tr><td>Centrally Sponsored /Central Sector Schemes (CSS)</td><td>Concerned Ministries/ Departments</td></tr>
<tr><td>1. Conservation of Natural Resources and Ecosystem
2. Integrated Development for Wildlife Habitat (Project Tiger, Project Elephant etc.)</td><td>Ministry of Environment, Forest and Climate Change</td></tr>
<tr><td colspan="2">Target: 15.6: Promote fair and equitable sharing of benefits arising from the utilizing of genetic resources and promote appropriate access to such resources, as internationally agreed.</td></tr>
<tr><td>Centrally Sponsored /Central Sector Schemes (CSS)</td><td>Concerned Ministries/ Departments</td></tr>
<tr><td>1. Green Revolution (umbrella scheme)
2. White Revolution (the umbrella scheme includes National Livestock Mission (NLM), National Programme for Bovine Breeding and Dairy Development, etc.
3. Crop science,
4. Animal science,
5. Fishery science</td><td>Agriculture and Cooperation</td></tr>
<tr><td>6. Conservation of Natural Resources and Ecosystem
7. Integrated Development for Wildlife Habitat (Project Tiger, Project Elephant etc.)</td><td>Ministry of Environment, Forest and Climate Change</td></tr>
<tr><td></td><td>Ministry of Tribal Affairs</td></tr>
<tr><td colspan="2">Target: 15.7: Take urgent action to end poaching and trafficking of protected species of flora and fauna and address both demand and supply of illegal wildlife products.</td></tr>
<tr><td>Centrally Sponsored /Central Sector Schemes (CSS)</td><td>Concerned Ministries/ Departments</td></tr>
<tr><td>1. Integrated Development for Wildlife Habitat (Project Tiger, Project Elephant etc.)</td><td>Ministry of Environment, Forest and Climate Change</td></tr>
<tr><td colspan="2">Target: 15.8: By 2030 Introduce measures to prevent the introduction and significantly reduce the impact of invasive alien species on land and water ecosystems and control or eradicate the priority species.</td></tr>
<tr><td>Centrally Sponsored /Central Sector Schemes (CSS)</td><td>Concerned Ministries/ Departments</td></tr>
<tr><td>1. Conservation of Natural Resources and Ecosystem</td><td>Ministry of Environment, Forest and Climate Change</td></tr>
<tr><td colspan="2">Target: 15.9: By 2030, integrate ecosystem and biodiversity values into national and local planning, development process, poverty reduction strategies and accounts.</td></tr>
<tr><td>Centrally Sponsored /Central Sector Schemes (CSS)</td><td>Concerned Ministries/ Departments</td></tr>
<tr><td>1. Conservation of Natural Resources and Ecosystem
2. Environmental Knowledge and Capacity Building</td><td>Ministry of Environment, Forest and Climate Change</td></tr>
</table>

(*Contd...*)

3. *Rashtriya Gram Swaraj Abhiyan* (RGSA)	Ministry of Home Affairs
	Ministry of Rural Development, Ministry of Tribal Affairs
Target: 15.a: Mobilize and significantly increase financial resources from all sources to conserve and sustainably use biodiversity and ecosystems.	
Centrally Sponsored /Central Sector Schemes (CSS)	Concerned Ministries/ Departments
	Ministry of Environment, Forest and Climate Change, Ministry of Finance
Target: 15.b: Mobilize and significant sources from all sources and all levels to finance sustainable forest management and provide adequate incentives to developing countries to advance such management, including for conservation and reforestation.	
Centrally Sponsored /Central Sector Schemes (CSS)	Concerned Ministries/ Departments
	Ministry of Environment, Forest and Climate Change, Ministry of Finance, Ministry of Tribal Affairs
Target: 15.c: Enhance global support for efforts to combat poaching and trafficking of protected species, including by increasing the capacity of local communities to pursue sustainable livelihood opportunities.	
Centrally Sponsored /Central Sector Schemes (CSS)	Concerned Ministries/ Departments
1. Integrated Development for Wildlife Habitat (Project Tiger, Project Elephant etc.) 2. Conservation of Natural Resources and Ecosystem	Ministry of Environment, Forest and Climate Change

Source: (NITI Aayog 2018).

19.8. Initiatives, Expectation and Performance of Government of India in SDG-15

According to the India SDG Index, Baseline Report, 2018 (NITI Aayog 2018), to achieving the target of the UN's SDG-15, the Government of India had framed four indicators, which capture three out of twelve UN's SDG targets. The Government of India reported that, 17 dedicated policies or schemes are in action to achieve three targets (15.1, 15.2 and 15.7) of the UN's SDG-15 under the leadership and monitoring of 9 dedicated Ministries or the Departments. The SDG-15 indicators are –

SDG_15_1: Percentage of total land area covered under forest.

SDG_15_2: Decadal change in extent of water bodies within forests from 2005 to 2015 (%).

SDG_15_3: Change in forest area from 2015 to 2017 (%).

SDG_15_4: Percentage change in estimated population of wild elephants over 5 year period.

Inference: It was assumed that, 'Peace, Justice and Strong Institutions' are the pre-conditions of achievement.

Here, Expected Performance = India SDG 16 Score, that is 71 × (UN target of this SDG ÷ 100), and

Performance Difference = (Expected Performance - Performance of India)

From the above conditions it is explored in the table no-139.

Table No. 139: India's SDG-16=71 and the Performances in SDG-15

SDG India Indicators	SDG_15_1	SDG_15_2	SDG_15_3	SDG_15_4
UN Target of this SDG	33	0	0	0
Performance of India	21.54	18.24	0.21	19.53
India SDG 16 Score	71	71	71	71
India SDG Mean Score	57	57	57	57
Expected Performance, When SDG 16=71	23.43	0	0	0
Indicator Interpretation	Value High - Performance High	Value High - Performance Low	Value High - Performance Low	Value High - Performance Low
Performance Difference, When SDG 16=71	-1.89	-18.24	-0.21	-19.53

Data Source: NITI *Aqyog*, 2018 and Inference drawn by the author.

For the SDG_15_1: That is 'Percentage of total land area covered under forest'; here, India is slight negatively differed (21.54) from its expected score 23.43, when SDG-16 score is 71 and here performance level have to increase to a level of 1.89 from the present performance. So India have to devote its tools of 'Peace, Justice and Strong Institutions' in a better way for a better score. Here the performance difference is -1.89.

For the SDG_15_2: That is 'Decadal change in extent of water bodies within forests from 2005 to 2015 (%)'; here, India is negatively differed (18.24) from its expected score '0', when SDG-16 score is 71 and here performance level have to decrease to a level of 18.24 from the present performance. So India have to devote its tools of 'Peace, Justice and Strong Institutions' in a better way for a better score. Here the performance difference is -18.24.

For the SDG_15_3: That is 'Change in forest area from 2015 to 2017 (%)'; here, India is slight negatively differed (0.21) from its expected score '0', when SDG-16 score is 71 and here performance level have to decrease to a level of 0.21 from the present performance. So India have to devote its tools of 'Peace, Justice and Strong Institutions' in a better way for a better score. Here the performance difference is -0.21.

For the SDG_15_4: That is 'Percentage change in estimated population of wild elephants over 5 year period'; here, India is slight negatively differed (19.53) from its expected score '0', when SDG-16 score is 71 and here performance level have to decrease to a level of 19.53 from the present performance. So India have to devote its tools of 'Peace, Justice and Strong Institutions' in a better way for a better score. Here the performance difference is -19.53.

19.9. Government of India's Remaining Targets and the Indicators for SDG-15

As we know that, on the basis of the availability of the disaggregated data, the NITI *Aayog* had been framed India's own indicators of the targets of each individual SDG. For the SDG-15, that is 'Life and Land', the NITI *Aayog* had framed four indicators; which captured three (15.1.1, 15.2.1 and 15.7.1) of fourteen indicators of the twelve UNs SDG targets. As per the report, 17 dedicated policies or schemes are in action to achieve three targets (15.1, 15.2 and 15.7) of the UN's SDG-15; the remaining indicators of the UN's SDG-15 is to be achieved by 2030. The remaining lists of targets along with the indicators of SDG-15 are detailed in Table no-140.

Table No. 140: Government of India's Remaining Targets and the Indicators for SDG-15

India's Remaining Targets and the Indicators for SDG-15	
Targets	**Indicators**
15.1: By 2020, ensure the conservation, restoration and sustainable use of terrestrial and inland freshwater ecosystems and their services, in particular forests, wetlands, mountains and drylands, in line with obligations under international agreements [i].	15.1.1: Forest area as a proportion of total land area [ii].
	15.1.2: Proportion of important sites for terrestrial and freshwater biodiversity that are covered by protected areas, by ecosystem type [iii].
15.2: By 2020, promote the implementation of sustainable management of all types of forests, halt deforestation, restore degraded forests and substantially increase afforestation and reforestation globally [ii].	15.2.1: Progress towards sustainable forest management [ii].
15.3: By 2030, combat desertification, restore degraded land and soil, including land affected by desertification, drought and floods, and strive to achieve a land degradation-neutral world [iii].	15.3.1: Proportion of land that is degraded over total land area [iii].

15.4: By 2030, ensure the conservation of mountain ecosystems, including their biodiversity, in order to enhance their capacity to provide benefits that are essential for sustainable development [iii].	15.4.1: Coverage by protected areas of important sites for mountain biodiversity [iii]. 15.4.2: Mountain Green Cover Index [iii].
15.5: Take urgent and significant actions to reduce the degradation of natural habitats, halt the loss of biodiversity and, by 2020, protect and prevent the extinction of threatened species [iii].	15.5.1: Red List Index [iii].
15.6: Promote fair and equitable sharing of the benefits arising from the utilization of genetic resources and promote appropriate access to such resources, as internationally agreed [iii].	15.6.1: Number of countries that have adopted legislative, administrative and policy frameworks to ensure fair and equitable sharing of benefits [iii].
15.7: Take urgent action to end poaching and trafficking of protected species of flora and fauna and address both demand and supply of illegal wildlife products [ii].	15.7.1: Proportion of traded wildlife that was poached or illicitly trafficked [ii].
15.8: By 2020, introduce measures to prevent the introduction and significantly reduce the impact of invasive alien species on land and water ecosystems and control or eradicate the priority species [iii].	15.8.1: Proportion of countries adopting relevant national legislation and adequately resourcing the prevention or control of invasive alien species [iii].
15.9: By 2020, integrate ecosystem and biodiversity values into national and local planning, development processes, poverty reduction strategies and accounts [iii].	15.9.1: Progress towards national targets established in accordance with Aichi Biodiversity Target 2 of the Strategic Plan for Biodiversity 2011-2020 [iii].
15.a: Mobilize and significantly increase financial resources from all sources to conserve and sustainably use biodiversity and ecosystems [iii].	15.a.1: Official development assistance and public expenditure on conservation and sustainable use of biodiversity and ecosystems [iii].
15.b: Mobilize significant resources from all sources and at all levels to finance sustainable forest management and provide adequate incentives to developing countries to advance such management, including for conservation and reforestation [iii].	15.b.1: Official development assistance and public expenditure on conservation and sustainable use of biodiversity and ecosystems [iii].
15.c: Enhance global support for efforts to combat poaching and trafficking of protected species, including by increasing the capacity of local communities to pursue sustainable livelihood opportunities [iii].	15.c.1: Proportion of traded wildlife that was poached or illicitly trafficked [iii].

Notes of the Table:

i. Not captured all the indicators.
ii. Target indicators captured and analysed.
iii. Remaining.

The Ministries and the Departments associate with indicators of this SDG such as Ministry of Environment, Forest and Climate Change, Agriculture and Cooperation, Tribal Affairs, Ministry of Water Resource,

Rural Development and Green Revolution, Land Resources, *Panchayati Raj*, Rural Development and Ministry of Finance have to concentrate to monitor on the above issues to achieve the target by 2030 through the provisions of Indian Constitution such as Article 14, Article 15 *1* to *5*, Article 16, Article 21A, Article 38-(1) and (2), Article 41, Article 44, Article 46, Article 47, Article 48, Article 48A, Article 51, Article 51A, Article 304, Article 307, Article 309, Article 310, Article 311, Article 312, Article 313, Article 314, Article 315, Article 320, Article 323A and Article 323B; Article 246 - Seventh Schedule, List-I: Union List No: 4, 7, 10, 12, 13, 14, 24, 25, 26, 27, 28, 30, 41, 42, 52, 53, 54, 55, 56, 57, 58, 64, 65, 66, 89, and 94; List-II: State List No: 13, 14, 15, 16, 17, 18, 22, 23, 24, 25, 26, 27 and 58; List-III: Concurrent List No: 17, 17A, 17B, 18, 19, 25, 26, 30, 31, 32 and 33; Article 243G - Eleventh Schedule - Powers, Authority and Responsibilities of Panchayats – Schedule No – 1, 2, 3,4, 5, 6, 7, 8, 9, 16, 17, 18, 19, 20, 21, 22, 26,27, 28 and 29; Article 243W - Twelfth Schedule - Powers, Authority and Responsibilities of Municipalities - Schedule No – 1, 2, 3, 5, 8, 9, 10, 11, 12, 13, 14, 15, 16 and 18 - if we could not monitor, we would not be able to stand in front of the future generation with a smile.

Chapter – XX

Initiative and Performance of India in SDG-16, Peace, Justice and Strong Institutions

The society seeks a social structure composed of stable mechanism of peace, justice and strong institutions. The global leaders has been prescribed for the peace, justice and strong institutions; even though many countries have its required level, but their contributions to the remaining parts of the world are very significant in this regard. The SDG-16 which was entitled as 'Peace, Justice and Strong Institutions' framed to promote peaceful and inclusive societies for Sustainable development, provide access to justice for all and build effective, accountable and inclusive institutions at all levels; which aims to build accountable and transparent economic institutions. The global agenda of SDG-16 peace, security effective governance based on rule of law and upholding principles of equality, human tights and justice are prerequisite for sustainable development. Cycles of conflict, violence, crime and exploitation undermine and reverse development gains.

The goal primarily focuses on significantly reducing all forms of violence and promoting the rule of law to the national and international levels to ensure equal access to justice for all. It not only aims to find enduring solutions to conflict and insecurity but also aims to end abuse, exploitation, trafficking, corruption, bribery; develop effective, accountable and transparent institutions and ensures inclusive and representative decision making at all levels.

20.1. The Global Targets and Indicators for SDG-16

The global indicator framework was developed by the Inter-Agency and Expert Group on SDG Indicators (IAEG-SDGs) and agreed to, as a practical starting point at the 47th session of the UN Statistical Commission held in March 2016 (NITI Aayog 2018). The report of the Commission, which included the global indicator framework, was then taken note of by ECOSOC at its 70th session in June 2016. The global targets and the indicator of this SDG are tabled (Table no-141) bellow –

Table No. 141: UNDP-DDGs Targets and Indicators of SDG-16

SDG, Promote peaceful and inclusive societies for sustainable development, provide access to justice for all and build effective, accountable and inclusive institutions at all levels[1]	
Targets	**Indicators**
16.1: Significantly reduce all forms of violence and related death rates everywhere.	16.1.1: Number of victims of intentional homicide per 100,000 populations, by sex and age.
	16.1.2: Conflict-related deaths per 100,000 populations, by sex, age and cause.
	16.1.3: Proportion of population subjected to physical, psychological or sexual violence in the previous 12 months.
	16.1.4: Proportion of population that feel safe walking alone around the area they live.
16.2: End abuse, exploitation, trafficking and all forms of violence against and torture of children.	16.2.1: Proportion of children aged 1-17 years who experienced any physical punishment and/or psychological aggression by caregivers in the past month.
	16.2.2: Number of victims of human trafficking per 100,000 populations, by sex, age and form of exploitation.
	16.2.3: Proportion of young women and men aged 18-29 years who experienced sexual violence by age 18.
16.3: Promote the rule of law at the national and international levels and ensure equal access to justice for all.	16.3.1: Proportion of victims of violence in the previous 12 months who reported their victimization to competent authorities or other officially recognized conflict resolution mechanisms.
	16.3.2: Un-sentenced detainees as a proportion of overall prison population.
16.4: By 2030, significantly reduce illicit financial and arms flows, strengthen the recovery and return of stolen assets and combat all forms of organized crime.	16.4.1: Total value of inward and outward illicit financial flows (in current United States dollars).
	16.4.2: Proportion of seized small arms and light weapons that are recorded and traced, in accordance with international standards and legal instruments.
16.5: Substantially reduce corruption and bribery in all their forms.	16.5.1: Proportion of persons who had at least one contact with a public official and who paid a bribe to a public official, or were asked for a bribe by those public officials, during the previous 12 months.
	16.5.2: Proportion of businesses that had at least one contact with a public official and that paid a bribe to a public official, or were asked for a bribe by those public officials during the previous 12 months.

(Contd...)

1. Data Source: SDG India Index Baseline Report, 2018, NITI *Aayog*, Government of India, New Delhi.

16.6: Develop effective, accountable and transparent institutions at all levels.	16.6.1: Primary government expenditures as a proportion of original approved budget, by sector (or by budget codes or similar).
	16.6.2: Proportion of the population satisfied with their last experience of public services.
16.7-Ensure responsive, inclusive, participatory and representative decision-making at all levels.	16.7.1: Proportions of positions (by sex, age, persons with disabilities and population groups) in public institutions (national and local legislatures, public service, and judiciary) compared to national distributions.
	16.7.2: Proportion of population who believe decision-making is inclusive and responsive, by sex, age, disability and population group.
16.8: Broaden and strengthen the participation of developing countries in the institutions of global governance.	16.8.1: Proportion of members and voting rights of developing countries in international organizations.
16.9: By 2030, provide legal identity for all, including birth registration.	16.9.1: Proportion of children under 5 years of age whose births have been registered with a civil authority, by age.
16.10: Ensure public access to information and protect fundamental freedoms, in accordance with national legislation and international agreements.	16.10.1: Number of verified cases of killing, kidnapping, enforced disappearance, arbitrary detention and torture of journalists, associated media personnel, trade unionists and human rights advocates in the previous 12 months.
	16.10.2: Number of countries that adopt and implement constitutional, statutory and/or policy guarantees for public access to information.
16.a: Strengthen relevant national institutions, including through international cooperation, for building capacity at all levels, in particular in developing countries, to prevent violence and combat terrorism and crime.	16.a.1: Existence of independent national human rights institutions in compliance with the Paris Principles.
16.b: Promote and enforce non-discriminatory laws and policies for sustainable development.	16.b.1: Proportion of population reporting having personally felt discriminated against or harassed in the previous 12 months on the basis of a ground of discrimination prohibited under international human rights law.

20.2. Interlinkage of SDG-16 with other SDGs

The SDG-16 is closely interrelated to the success of all the SDGs, as it is related to strengthening the institutions and rule of law that affects all the goals. This section presents the linkage of the SDG-16 to other SDGs, that is, the success of this SDG habitually will influence the success of the linked SDGs; according to the SDG India Index, Baseline Report, 2018 (NITI Aayog 2018), the SDG-16 linked with the following SDGs –

SDG-1, that is *No Poverty*, which aims to reduce poverty in all its dimensions, which includes ensuring access to safe, nutritious and sufficient food all year round, particularly for the poor.

SDG-4, is *Quality Education* that aims to ensure that all girls and boys complete free, equitable and quality primary and secondary education leading to relevant and effective learning outcomes, including technical and vocational skills for employment, decent jobs and entrepreneurship.

SDG-5, is *Gender Equality* as Goal 1 emphasises creation of gender sensitive development strategies, and equal rights and access to economic resources, as well as ownership and control over land and other forms of property, inheritance, natural resources and financial resources, including microfinance.

SDG-8, is *Decent Work and Economic Growth* which aims to promote development oriented policies that support productive activities, decent job creation, entrepreneurship, and encourage the formalization and growth of micro-, small - and medium-sized enterprises through access to financial services.

SDG-10, is *Reduced Inequalities* that aims to adopt policies, especially fiscal wage and social protection policies and progressively achieve and sustain income growth of the bottom 40 percent of the population at a rate higher than the national average, leading to greater equality.

SDG-11, is *Sustainable Cities and Communities* which aims to ensure access for all to adequate, safe and affordable housing and basic services and upgrade slums, and significantly reduce the numbers of deaths and people affected by disasters, with focus on protecting the poor and vulnerable.

SDG-17, is Partnerships for the Goals aimed for strengthen the means of implementation and revitalize the global partnership for sustainable development.

20.3. The National Context of SDG-16

India is one of the largest democracies of the world with principles of justice, liberty and equality enshrined in the Constitution of the country. There is a strong network of institutions at the national and State level that are transparent and effective.

Government of India's Unique Identity Number *Aadhaar* along with the Right to Information Act, 2005, are key steps to strengthen national institutions for effective and non-discriminatory public service delivery and to empower citizens with access to information.

Legal framework for protection against child abuse has been made more stringent. Free legal aid to vulnerable sections of the society is provided through legal aid societies. With regard to inclusive and participatory decision making, the 73rd and 74th Constitutional Amendment Acts have ushered in democracy at the grassroots levels by strengthening local governance.

Since independence and adoption of its Constitution, India aimed to foster an environment of peace, justice and good governance through transparent and accountable institutions at all levels. To achieve its targets India has taken various initiatives. The Constitution of India provides for transparent and effective institutions. The 73rd and 74th Constitutional Amendment Acts provide for democratic institutions of local governance in rural and urban areas respectively.

India empowers its citizens through a strong system of rights based legislation. The Right to Information Act, 2005, is one such legislation that allows citizens to access information from public authorities, thus ensuring transparency and accountability of institutions. The *Aadhaar* is one of the world's largest unique national identification projects. Besides creating a biometric-based legal identity system, it also assists in providing direct benefits transfers of government subsidies to its beneficiaries. This has resulted in efficient service delivery and reducing corruption.

For achieving effective, accountable and transparent implantation of government schemes and programmes across sectors, appropriate rules, mechanisms and decentralised decision-making processes have been put in place, for example, the Panchayats are the nodal agencies with decision making powers for several developmental programmes. India has prioritized strengthening and spreading the reach of its judicial infrastructure by developing local judicial bodies like the *Gram Nyayalays* in villages and through initiatives like the *Pragati* platform, which is a public grievance redressal system.

As per report, the number of murders reported per lakh population in India is 2.4. There is an acknowledged need to strengthen under reporting of murders. Lakshadweep one among the Union Territories reported no murder case in 2015-2016. The crimes against children is another issue associated with SDG-16, the target for 2030 is to eradicate all forms of violence against children. There were 24 cases reported for every one lakh children in 5015-2016. None of the States or Union Territories in India has achieved the national target.

Providing legal aid is the spirit of peace, justice and strong institution. At present there are about 13 courts per 10 lakh population in India. India has the highest number of pending court cases in the world. There is a dire need for increasing the number of judicial institutions. Goa and Chandigarh have the highest court density among States and Union Territories respectively.

The corruption is avital threat to any kind of developmental initiative; it may consider as the violator of 'fundamental rights' of the citizens of India provisioned by the Constitution of India. The corruption is a crime; its rate must be reduced. As per SDG India Index Base Line Report, 2018, for every 1 crore people in India, 34 corruption cases have been reported. It is worth noting that the actual number of cases may differ from the reported number pf cases. Manipur and Meghalaya among the States reported no corruption cases in 2015-2016.

Births Registration is required for future plan for the social units. While the target is to have 100 percent births registered, the country's average in 2015 was 88.3 percent on this indicator. 15 States/ Union Territories have 100 percent registered births. Punjab is the runner up at 99.2 percent, followed by Gujarat and Rajasthan at 98.7 percent.

On the account of providing unique identity to its citizen India is playing a leading role by covering it namely by *Aadhaar*. India is the leading nation in providing universally accepted legal identity to all its citizens. In eight States/ Union Territories, 100 percent of the population is covered under *Aadhaar*. Overall, about 90 percent of the country's population is under *Aadhaar* coverage, as against the 2030 national target of 100 percent.

In the next part of this chapter we tried to visualized the performance level of India through the SDG's targets and the SDG India Index Base Line Report, 2018 along with the Constitutional provisions in India to explore citizen's responsibility along with the its institutions through the mirror of indexed score on 'peace, justice and strong institutions' (SDG-16).

20.4. SDG-16 Targets, National Indicators and Target Values of India

India in its SDG India Index Base Line Report, 2018 (NITI Aayog 2018), India has been measured the performance of India on the goal of 'Peace, Justice and Strong Institutions', India had identified six national level indicators, which captured five (16.1, 16.2, 16.3, 16.5 and 16.9) out of twelve UN's SDG targets. These indicators has been selected based on availability of data at national level; these are in Table no-142.

Table No. 142: SDG-16 Targets, National Indicators and Target Values of India

SDG-16 Global Target	Indicator Selected for SDG India Index	National Target Value for 2030
16.1: Significantly reduce all forms of violence and related death rates everywhere.	1. Reported murders per 1 lakh population.	1.2
16.2: End abuse, exploitation, trafficking and all forms of violence against and torture of children.	2. Reported cognizable crimes against children per 1 lakh population.	0
16.3: Promote the rule of law at the national and international levels and ensure equal access to justice for all.	3. Estimated number of courts per 10 lakh persons.	33.76
16.5: Substantially reduce corruption and bribery in all their forms.	4. Estimated reported corruption crimes per 1 crore population.	17
16.9: By 2030, provide legal identity for all, including birth registration.	5. Percentage of births registered.	100
	6. Percentage of population covered under *Aadhaar*.	100

Source: (NITI Aayog 2018).

20.5. Indian's SDG-16 Index Indicators, Data Source and Interpretations

The NITI *Aayog*, Government of India had collected required data from different government agencies to capture the UN SDG's target indicators as well as had framed its own indicators to justify the achievement of the SDGs. Apart from that the NITI *Aayog* had developed the computational approach of the disaggregated data as per valid methods along with the parameters of the performance; in the following tables (Table no-143, Table no-144, Table no-145, Table no-146, Table no-147 and Table no-148) shows the details of the above issue to develop a sense of progress of the SDG-16, entitled as 'Peace, Justice and Strong Institutions'.

Table No. 143: SDG-16, Indian Indicator-1

SDG-16: 'Peace, Justice and Strong Institutions'	**Indicator-1:** Reported murders per 1 lakh population.
Indicator data source	National Crime Record Bureau [NCRB Reports]
Computation approach	Directly from data source
Data period (year)	2015-16
States/UTs covered	36
Data periodicity	Annual

(*Contd...*)

Relevant UN target	16.2: End abuse, exploitation, trafficking and all forms of violence against and torture of children.
Relevant UN indicator	16.2.2: Number of victims of human trafficking per 100,000 populations, by sex, age of exploitation.
Relevant MoSPI indicator	16.2.2: Proportion of crime committed against children during the year (per lakh children).
Indicator interpretation	Higher value means lower performance (-).

Source: (NITI Aayog 2018).

Table No. 144: SDG-16, Indian Indicator-2

SDG-16: 'Peace, Justice and Strong Institutions'	**Indicator-2:** Reported cognizable crimes against children per 1 lakh population.
Indicator data source	National Crime Record Bureau [NCRB Reports]
Computation approach	Directly from data source
Data period (year)	2015-16
States/UTs covered	36
Data periodicity	Annual
Relevant UN target	16.2: End abuse, exploitation, trafficking and all forms of violence against and torture of children.
Relevant UN indicator	16.2.2: Number of victims of human trafficking per 100,000 populations, by sex, age of exploitation.
Relevant MoSPI indicator	16.2.2: Proportion of crime committed against children during the year (per lakh children).
Indicator interpretation	Higher value means lower performance (-).

Source: (NITI Aayog 2018).

Table No. 145: SDG-16, Indian Indicator-3

SDG-16: 'Peace, Justice and Strong Institutions'	**Indicator-3:** Estimated number of courts per 10 lakh persons.
Indicator data source	Numerator: Ministry of Justice, [Lok Sabha Unstarred Question 1111] Denominator: Ministry of Home Affairs, [Census 2011]
Computation approach	(Number of courts ÷ Estimated population size) × 10,00,000 Population for 2017 was estimated based on Census 2011.
Data period (year)	2017
States/UTs covered	32
Data periodicity	Non-periodic
Relevant UN target	16.3: Promote the rule of law at the national and international levels and ensure equal access to justice for all.
Relevant UN indicator	16.3.1: Proportion of victims of violence in the previous 12 months who reported their victimization to competent authorities or other officially recognized conflict resolution mechanisms.
Relevant MoSPI indicator	16.3.1: Number of courts per lakh population
Indicator interpretation	Higher value means higher performance (+).

Source: (NITI Aayog 2018).

Table No. 146: SDG-16, Indian Indicator-4

SDG-16: 'Peace, Justice and Strong Institutions'	**Indicator-4:** Estimated reported corruption crimes per 1 crore population.
Indicator data source	Numerator: National Crime Record Bureau, [NCRB Reports] Denominator: Ministry of Home Affairs, [Census 2011]
Computation approach	[(Reported corruption crimes ÷ Estimated population size) × 1,00,00,000] Population for 2015-16 was estimated based on Census 2011.
Data period (year)	2015-16
States/UTs covered	32
Data periodicity	Annual
Relevant UN target	16.5: Substantially reduce corruption and bribery in all their forms.
Relevant UN indicator	16.5.1: Proportion of persons who had at least one contact with a public official, or were ask for a bribe by those public officials, during the previous 12 months.
Relevant MoSPI indicator	16.5.1: Persons arrested in total cognizable crime cases under offenses Under Prevention of Corruption Act and Related Sections of Indian Penal Code (IPC).
Indicator interpretation	Higher value means lower performance (-).

Source: (NITI Aayog 2018).

Table No. 147: SDG-16, Indian Indicator-5

SDG-16: 'Peace, Justice and Strong Institutions'	**Indicator-5:** Percentage of births registered.
Indicator data source	Registrar General of India [RGI Report]
Computation approach	Directly from data source
Data period (year)	2015
States/UTs covered	36
Data periodicity	3 years
Relevant UN target	16.9: By 2030, provide legal identity for all, including birth registration.
Relevant UN indicator	16.9.1: Proportion of children under 5 years of age whose births have been registered with a civil authority, by age.
Relevant MoSPI indicator	16.9.1: Percentage of births registered
Indicator interpretation	Higher value means higher performance (+).

Source: (NITI Aayog 2018).

Table No. 148: SDG-16, Indian Indicator-6

SDG-16: 'Peace, Justice and Strong Institutions'	**Indicator-6:** Percentage of population covered under *Aadhaar*
Indicator data source	Unique Identification Authority of India [*Aadhar* Progress Report]
Computation approach	Directly from data source
Data period (year)	2018

(*Contd...*)

States/UTs covered	36
Data periodicity	Annual
Relevant UN target	16.9: By 2030, provide legal identity for all, including birth registration.
Relevant UN indicator	NA
Relevant MoSPI indicator	16.9.2: Proportion of population covered under *Aadhaar*
Indicator interpretation	Higher value means higher performance (+)

Source: (NITI Aayog 2018).

20.6. Provisions of the Indian Constitution for SDG-16

The spirit of the unity in this diverse country, India is secured by its great Constitution; the Constitution of India not only secured its unity, announced a vision in the Preamble in the beginning of its Articles included in the Indian Constitution, *"We the people of India, having solemnly resolved to constitute India into a Sovereign Socialist Secular Democratic Republic and to secure to all its citizens: justice, social, economic and political; liberty of thought, expression, belief, faith and worship; equality of status and of opportunity; and to promote among them all fraternity assuring the dignity of the individual and the unity and integrity of the nation; in our Constituent Assembly this twenty-sixth day of November, 1949, do hereby adopt, enact and give to ourselves this Constitution* (India 1950/2015)". The mode of orientation of the Indian Constitution and the sustainable development goals of the contemporary time are given us an opportunity to make a link between these two visions of development and the author is trying to make the link.

As we know the sustainable development goals are interlinked, that means the success or failure of one is affected to other SDGs. From this perspective, this section presents the provisions in the Indian Constitution to eradicate poverty as reflected in the sustainable development agenda entitled as SDG-16, Peace, Justice and Strong Institutions. The linked Constitutional provisions are in the following Table no-149 -

Table No. 149: Provisions in Indian Constitution for SDG-16

SDG-16 and the Linked Articles and Schedules of the Constitution of India
Article 14, Article 15 *1* to *5*, Article 16, Article 17, Article 19, Article 20, Article 21, Article 21A, Article 22, Article 23, Article 24, Article 25, Article 26, Article 27, Article 28, Article 29, Article 30, Article 31A, Article 31.B, Article 31C, Article 32A, Article 33, Article 34, Article 35, Article 38-(1) and (2), Article 39, Article 39A, Article 40, Article 41, Article 42, Article 43, Article 43A, Article 44, Article 45, Article 46, Article 47, Article 48, Article 48A, Article 50, Article 51, Article 51A, Article 243D, Article 243T, Article 301, Article 302, Article 303, Article 304, Article 307, Article 309, Article 310, Article 311, Article 312, Article 313, Article 314, Article 315, Article 320, Article 323A, Article 323B Articles 325, Article 326, Article 333, Article 334, Article 335, Article 336, Article 337, Article 338, Article 338A, Article 340, Article 341, Article 342, Article 350A, Article 350B, Article 351, Article 364 and Article 365

Article 246 - Seventh Schedule, List-I: Union List No: 1, 2, 3, 4, 5, 6, 7, 8, 9, 10, 11, 12, 13, 14, 15, 16, 17, 18, 19, 20, 21, 22, 23, 24, 25, 26, 27, 28, 30, 31, 32, 34, 35, 36, 37, 38, 39, 40, 41, 42, 43, 44, 45, 46, 47, 48, 49, 50, 51, 52, 53, 54, 55, 56, 57, 58, 59, 60, 61, 63, 64, 65, 66, 67, 68, 69, 70, 71, 72, 73, 74, 75, 76, 77, 78, 80, 81, 82, 83, 84, 85, 86, 87, 88, 89, 90, 91, 92, 92A, 92B, 93, 94, 95, 96 and 97. List-II: State List No: 1, 2, 3, 4, 5, 6, 7, 8, 9, 10, 12, 13, 14, 15, 16, 17, 18, 21, 22, 23, 24, 25, 26, 27, 28, 30, 31, 32, 33, 34, 35, 37, 38, 39, 40, 41, 42, 43, 44, 45,,46, 47, 48, 49, 50, 51, 52, 53, 54, 55, 56, 57, 58, 59, 60, 61, 62, 63, 64, 65, 66. List-III: Concurrent List No: 1, 2, 3, 4, 5, 6, 7, 8, 9, 10, 11, 12, 13, 14, 15, 16, 17, 17A, 17B, 18, 19, 20, 21, 22, 23, 24, 25, 26, 27, 28, 29, 30, 31, 32, 33, 33A, 34, 35, 36, 37, 38, 39, 40, 41, 42, 43, 44, 45, 46 and 47.
Article 243G: Eleventh Schedule: Powers, Authority and Responsibilities of Panchayats. Schedule No: 1, 2, 3, 4, 5, 6, 7, 8, 9, 10, 11, 12, 13, 14, 15, 16, 17, 18, 19, 20, 21, 22, 23, 24, 25, 26, 27, 28 and 29. Article 243W: Twelfth Schedule: Powers, Authority and Responsibilities of Municipalities. Schedule No: 1, 2, 3, 4, 5, 6, 7, 8, 9, 10, 11, 12, 13, 14, 15, 16, 17 and 18.

Source: The Constitution of India, 2015 as on 9th November, 2015.

20.7. Policies of the Government of India for Targets of the SDG-16

According to the SDG India Index Base Line Report, 2018 (India 1950/ 2015), India is proactive to achieve the target of the UN's SDGs. The Government of India has been initiated as well as implemented various policies to capture the indicators of the targets of each individual SDG. On the moment of preparation of SDG India Index Base Line Report, 2018, on the basis of the availability of the disaggregated data, the NITI *Aayog* has been framed India's own indicators of the targets of each individual SDG. For the SDG-16, that is 'Peace, Justice and Strong Institutions'; the NITI *Aayog* framed six indicators; which has been captured five out of twelve UNs SDG targets. As per the report, 7 dedicated policies or schemes are in action to achieve five targets (16.1, 16.2, 16.3, 16.5 and 16.9) of the UN's SDG-16 under the leadership and monitoring of 11 dedicated Ministries or the Departments. The policies or schemes to achieve the targets of SDG-16 and the concerned dedicated Ministries and the Departments are detailed in the - Table no-150.

Table No. 150: Policies Initiated by the Indian Government for Targets of SDG-16

150: SDG-16, Peace, Justice and Strong Institutions
SDG-16, is The SDG-16 that is Peace, Justice and Strong Institutions promote peaceful and inclusive societies for Sustainable development; provide access to justice for all and build effective, accountable and inclusive institutions at all levels; which aims to build accountable and transparent economic institutions. The global agenda of SDG-16 peace, security effective governance based on rule of law and upholding principles of equality, human tights and justice are prerequisite for sustainable development. Cycles of conflict, violence, crime and exploitation undermine and reverse development gains.

(*Contd...*)

Target: 16.1: Significantly reduce all forms of violence and related death rates everywhere.	
Centrally Sponsored /Central Sector Schemes (CSS)	Concerned Ministries/ Departments
	Ministry of Home Affairs
Target: 16.2: End abuse, exploitation, trafficking and all forms of violence against and torture of children.	
Centrally Sponsored /Central Sector Schemes (CSS)	Concerned Ministries/ Departments
1. Umbrella ICDS 2. National Labour Project	Ministry of Home Affairs, Ministry of Labour and Employment
Target: 16.3: Promote the rule of law at the national and international levels and ensure equal access to justice for all.	
Centrally Sponsored /Central Sector Schemes (CSS)	Concerned Ministries/ Departments
	Ministry of Home Affairs, Ministry of Law and Justice
Target: 16.4: By 2030, significantly reduce illicit financial and arms flows, strengthen the recovery and return of stolen assets and combat all forms of organized crime.	
Centrally Sponsored /Central Sector Schemes (CSS)	Concerned Ministries/ Departments
	Ministry of Home Affairs
Target: 16.5: Substantially reduce corruption and bribery in all their forms.	
Centrally Sponsored /Central Sector Schemes (CSS)	Concerned Ministries/ Departments
	Ministry of Home Affairs
Target: 16.6: Develop effective, accountable and transparent institutions at all levels.	
Centrally Sponsored /Central Sector Schemes (CSS)	Concerned Ministries/ Departments
1. Digital India 2. Digital India Land Record Modernization Programme	Department of Science and Technology
3. *Rashtriya Gram Swaraj Abhiyan* (RGSA)	Ministry of *Panchayati Raj*
4. Modernisation of Police Forces (including Security Related Expenditure)	Ministry of Home Affairs
5. Development of Infrastructure Facilities for Judiciary including *Gram Nyayalayas* and e-courts	Ministry of Law and Justice
Target: 16.7: Ensure responsive, inclusive, participatory and representative decision-making at all levels.	
Centrally Sponsored /Central Sector Schemes (CSS)	Concerned Ministries/ Departments
	Personnel, Public Grievances and Pensions, Ministry of Housing and Urban Affairs, Ministry of Rural Development, Ministry of *Panchayati Raj*
Target: 16.8: Broaden and strengthen the participation of developing countries in the institutions of global governance.	
Centrally Sponsored /Central Sector Schemes (CSS)	Concerned Ministries/ Departments
	Ministry of External Affairs

(*Contd...*)

Target: 16.9: By 2030, provide legal identity for all, including birth registration.	
Centrally Sponsored /Central Sector Schemes (CSS)	Concerned Ministries/ Departments
Aadhaar Card	UIDAI, Ministry of Home Affairs, Ministry of *Panchayati Raj*
Target: 16.10: Ensure public access to information and protect fundamental freedoms, in accordance with national legislation and international agreements.	
Centrally Sponsored /Central Sector Schemes (CSS)	Concerned Ministries/ Departments
	Ministry of External Affairs, Ministry of Home Affairs,
Target: 16.a: Strengthen relevant national institutions, including through international cooperation, for building capacity at all levels, in particular in developing countries, to prevent violence and combat terrorism and crime.	
Centrally Sponsored /Central Sector Schemes (CSS)	Concerned Ministries/ Departments
	Ministry of External Affairs, Ministry of Home Affairs,
Target: 16.b: Promote and enforce non-discriminatory laws and policies for sustainable development.	
Centrally Sponsored /Central Sector Schemes (CSS)	Concerned Ministries/ Departments
	Ministry of Home Affairs

Source: (NITI Aayog 2018).

20.8. Initiatives, Expectation and Performance of Government of India in SDG-16

According to the India SDG Index, Baseline Report, 2018 (NITI Aayog 2018), to achieving the target of the UN's SDG-16, the Government of India had framed six indicators, which capture five out of twelve UN's SDG targets. The Government of India reported that, 7 dedicated policies or schemes are in action to achieve five targets (16.1, 12.2, 16.3, 16.5 and 16.9) of the UN's SDG-16 under the leadership and monitoring of 11 dedicated Ministries or the Departments. The SDG-15 indicators are –

SDG_16_1: Reported murders per 1 lakh population.

SDG_16_2: Reported cognizable crimes against children per 1 lakh population.

SDG_16_3: Estimated number of courts per 10 lakh persons.

SDG_16_4: Estimated reported corruption crimes per 1 crore population.

SDG_16_5: Percentage of births registered.

SDG_16_6: Percentage of population covered under *Aadhaar.*

Inference: It was assumed that, 'Peace, Justice and Strong Institutions' are the pre-conditions of achievement.

Here, Expected Performance = India SDG 16 Score, that is 71 × (UN target of this SDG ÷ 100), and

Performance Difference = (Expected Performance - Performance of India)

From the above conditions it is explored in table no-151.

Table No. 151: India's SDG-16=71 and the Performances in SDG-16

SDG India Indicators	SDG_16_1	SDG_16_2	SDG_16_3	SDG_16_4	SDG_16_5	SDG_16_6
UN Target of this SDG	1.2	0	33.76	17	100	100
Performance of India	2.4	24	12.83	34.01	88.3	89.5
India SDG 16 Score	71	71	71	71	71	71
India SDG Mean Score	57	57	57	57	57	57
Expected Performance, When SDG 16=71	0.85	0	23.97	12.07	71	71
Indicator Interpretation	Value High - Performance Low	Value High - Performance Low	Value High - Performance High	Value High - Performance Low	Value High - Performance High	Value High - Performance High
Performance Difference, When SDG 16=71	-1.55	-24	-11.14	-21.94	+17.3	+18.5

Data Source: NITI *Aayog*, 2018 and Inference drawn by the author.

For the SDG_16_1: That is 'Reported murders per 1 lakh population'; here, India is negatively differed (2.4) from its expected score 0.85, when SDG-16 score is 71 and here performance level have to decrease to a level of 1.55 from the present performance. So India have to devote its tools of 'Peace, Justice and Strong Institutions' in a better way for a better score. Here the performance difference is -1.55.

For the SDG_16_2: That is 'Reported cognizable crimes against children per 1 lakh population'; here, India is negatively differed (24) from its expected score '0', when SDG-16 score is 71 and here performance level have to decrease to a level of 24 from the present performance. So India have to devote its tools of 'Peace, Justice and Strong Institutions' in a better way for a better score. Here the performance difference is -24.

For the SDG_16_3: That is 'Estimated number of courts per 10 lakh persons'; here, India is negatively differed (12.83) from its expected score 23.97, when SDG-16 score is 71 and here performance level have to increase to a level of 11.14 from the present performance. So India have to devote its tools of 'Peace, Justice and Strong Institutions' in a better way for a better score. Here the performance difference is -11.14.

For the SDG_16_4: That is 'Estimated reported corruption crimes per 1 crore population'; here, India is negatively differed (34.01) from its expected score 12.07, when SDG-16 score is 71 and here performance level have to decrease to a level of 21.94 from the present performance. So India have to devote its tools of 'Peace, Justice and Strong Institutions' in a better way for a better score. Here the performance difference is -21.94.

For the SDG_16_5: That is 'Percentage of births registered'; here, India is positively differed (88.3) from its expected score 71, when SDG-16 score is 71 and here performance level have to hold with demographic changes according with the present performance. So India have to devote its tools of 'Peace, Justice and Strong Institutions' in a better way for a better score. Here the performance difference is +17.3.

For the SDG_16_6: That is 'Percentage of population covered under *Aadhaar*'; here, India is positively differed (89.5) from its expected score 71, when SDG-16 score is 71 and here performance level have to hold with demographic changes according with the present performance. So India have to devote its tools of 'Peace, Justice and Strong Institutions' in a better way for a better score. Here the performance difference is +18.5.

20.9. Government of India's Remaining Targets and the Indicators for SDG-16

As we know that, on the basis of the availability of the disaggregated data, the NITI *Aayog* had framed India's own indicators of the targets of each individual SDG. For the SDG-16, that is 'Peace, Justice and Strong Institutions, the NITI *Aayog* had framed five indicators; which captured five (16.1.1, 16.2.2, 16.3.1, 16.5.1 and 16.9.2) of twenty three indicators of the twelve UNs SDG targets. As per the report, 7 dedicated policies or schemes are in action to achieve five targets (16.1, 16.2, 16.3, 16.5 and 16.9) of the UN's SDG-16; the remaining indicators of the UN's SDG-16 is to be achieve by 2030. The remaining lists of targets along with the indicators of SDG-16 are detailed in Table no-152.

Table No. 152: Government of India's Remaining Targets and the Indicators for SDG-16

India's Remaining Targets and the Indicators for SDG-16	
Targets	**Indicators**
16.1: Significantly reduce all forms of violence and related death rates everywhere [i].	16.1.1: Number of victims of intentional homicide per 100,000 populations, by sex and age [ii].
	16.1.2: Conflict-related deaths per 100,000 populations, by sex, age and cause [iii].
	16.1.3: Proportion of population subjected to physical, psychological or sexual violence in the previous 12 months [iii].
	16.1.4: Proportion of population that feel safe walking alone around the area they live [iii].
16.2: End abuse, exploitation, trafficking and all forms of violence against and torture of children [i].	16.2.1: Proportion of children aged 1-17 years who experienced any physical punishment and/or psychological aggression by caregivers in the past month [iii].
	16.2.2: Number of victims of human trafficking per 100,000 populations, by sex, age and form of exploitation [ii].
	16.2.3: Proportion of young women and men aged 18-29 years who experienced sexual violence by age 18 [iii].
16.3: Promote the rule of law at the national and international levels and ensure equal access to justice for all [i].	16.3.1: Proportion of victims of violence in the previous 12 months who reported their victimization to competent authorities or other officially recognized conflict resolution mechanisms [ii].
	16.3.2: Un-sentenced detainees as a proportion of overall prison population [iii].
16.4: By 2030, significantly reduce illicit financial and arms flows, strengthen the recovery and return of stolen assets and combat all forms of organized crime [iii].	16.4.1: Total value of inward and outward illicit financial flows (in current United States dollars) [iii].
	16.4.2: Proportion of seized small arms and light weapons that are recorded and traced, in accordance with international standards and legal instruments [iii].
16.5: Substantially reduce corruption and bribery in all their forms [i].	16.5.1: Proportion of persons who had at least one contact with a public official and who paid a bribe to a public official, or were asked for a bribe by those public officials, during the previous 12 months [ii].
	16.5.2: Proportion of businesses that had at least one contact with a public official and that paid a bribe to a public official, or were asked for a bribe by those public officials during the previous 12 months [iii].

(Contd...)

16.6: Develop effective, accountable and transparent institutions at all levels [iii].	16.6.1: Primary government expenditures as a proportion of original approved budget, by sector (or by budget codes or similar) [iii].
	16.6.2: Proportion of the population satisfied with their last experience of public services [iii].
16.7: Ensure responsive, inclusive, participatory and representative decision-making at all levels [iii].	16.7.1: Proportions of positions (by sex, age, persons with disabilities and population groups) in public institutions (national and local legislatures, public service, and judiciary) compared to national distributions [iii].
	16.7.2: Proportion of population who believe decision-making is inclusive and responsive, by sex, age; disability and population group [iii].
16.8: Broaden and strengthen the participation of developing countries in the institutions of global governance [iii].	16.8.1: Proportion of members and voting rights of developing countries in international organizations [iii].
16.9: By 2030, provide legal identity for all, including birth registration [ii].	16.9.1: Proportion of children under 5 years of age whose births have been registered with a civil authority, by age [ii].
16.10: Ensure public access to information and protect fundamental freedoms, in accordance with national legislation and international agreements [iii].	16.10.1: Number of verified cases of killing, kidnapping, enforced disappearance, arbitrary detention and torture of journalists, associated media personnel, trade unionists and human rights advocates in the previous 12 months [iii].
	16.10.2: Number of countries that adopt and implement constitutional, statutory and/or policy guarantees for public access to information [iii].
16.a: Strengthen relevant national institutions, including through international cooperation, for building capacity at all levels, in particular in developing countries, to prevent violence and combat terrorism and crime [iii].	16.a.1: Existence of independent national human rights institutions in compliance with the Paris Principles [iii].
16.b: Promote and enforce non-discriminatory laws and policies for sustainable development [iii].	16.b.1: Proportion of population reporting having personally felt discriminated against or harassed in the previous 12 months on the basis of a ground of discrimination prohibited under international human rights law [iii].

Notes of the Table:

i. Not captured all the indicators.
ii. Target indicators captured and analysed.
iii. Remaining.

The Ministries and the Departments associate with indicators of this SDG such as Housing and Urban Affairs, Labour and Employment, Ministry of Externa Affairs, Ministry of Home Affairs, Ministry of Law and Justice, *Panchayati Raj*, Personnel, Public Grievances and Pensions, Rural Development, Science and Technology and UIDAI, have to concentrate to monitor on the above issues to achieve the target by 2030 through the provisions of Indian Constitution such as Article 14, Article 15 *1* to *5*, Article 16, Article 17, Article 19, Article 20, Article 21, Article 21A, Article 22, Article 23, Article 24, Article 25, Article 26, Article 27, Article 28, Article 29, Article 30, Article 31A, Article 31.B, Article 31C, Article 32A, Article 33, Article 34, Article 35, Article 38-(1) and (2), Article 39, Article 39A, Article 40, Article 41, Article 42, Article 43, Article 43A, Article 44, Article 45, Article 46, Article 47, Article 48, Article 48A, Article 50, Article 51, Article 51A, Article 243D, Article 243T, Article 301, Article 302, Article 303, Article 304, Article 307, Article 309, Article 310, Article 311, Article 312, Article 313, Article 314, Article 315, Article 320, Article 323A, Article 323B, Articles 325, Article 326, Article 333, Article 334, Article 335, Article 336, Article 337, Article 338, Article 338A, Article 340, Article 341, Article 342, Article 350A, Article 350B, Article 351, Article 364 and Article 365; Article 246 - Seventh Schedule; List-I: Union List: 1, 2, 3, 4, 5, 6, 7, 8, 9, 10, 11, 12, 13, 14, 15, 16, 17, 18, 19, 20, 21, 22, 23, 24, 25, 26, 27, 28, 30, 31, 32, 34, 35, 36, 37, 38, 39, 40, 41, 42, 43, 44, 45, 46, 47, 48, 49, 50, 51, 52, 53, 54, 55, 56, 57, 58, 59, 60, 61, 63, 64, 65, 66, 67, 68, 69, 70, 71, 72, 73, 74, 75, 76, 77, 78, 80, 81, 82, 83, 84, 85, 86, 87, 88, 89, 90, 91, 92, 92A, 92B, 93, 94, 95, 96 and 97; List-II: State List No: 1, 2, 3, 4, 5, 6, 7, 8, 9, 10, 12, 13, 14, 15, 16, 17, 18, 21, 22, 23, 24, 25, 26, 27, 28, 30, 31, 32, 33, 34, 35, 37, 38, 39, 40, 41, 42, 43, 44, 45,,46, 47, 48, 49, 50, 51, 52, 53, 54, 55, 56, 57, 58, 59, 60, 61, 62, 63, 64, 65, 66; List-III: Concurrent List No: 1, 2, 3, 4, 5, 6, 7, 8, 9, 10, 11, 12, 13, 14, 15, 16, 17, 17A, 17B, 18, 19, 20, 21, 22, 23, 24, 25, 26, 27, 28, 29, 30, 31, 32, 33, 33A, 34, 35, 36, 37, 38, 39, 40, 41, 42, 43, 44, 45, 46 and 47; Article 243G - Eleventh Schedule - Powers, Authority and Responsibilities of Panchayats – Schedule No – 1, 2, 3,4, 5, 6, 7, 8, 9, 10, 11, 12, 13, 14, 15, 16, 17, 18, 19, 20, 21, 22, 23, 24, 25, 26,27, 28 and 29; Article 243W - Twelfth Schedule - Powers, Authority and Responsibilities of Municipalities - Schedule No – 1, 2, 3, 4, 5, 6, 7, 8, 9, 10, 11, 12, 13, 14, 15, 16, 17 and 18 - if we could not monitor, we would not be able to stand in front of the future generation with a smile.

Chapter – XXI

Initiative and Performance of India in SDG-17, Partnerships for the Goals

As per the resolution of the United Nations General Assembly, the Global Partnership for Sustainable Data is global network of governments, NGOs and businesses working together to strengthen the inclusivity, trust and innovation in the way that data is used to address the world's sustainable development efforts. It works to bring the resources of national governments, independent non-profits, and private companies to bear on the world's development data poverty. Official statistical systems are the building block for understanding poverty and how to address it. The global partnership seeks to map data gaps at a national level, the channel funding to strengthen those systems. Thus, the partnership aims to bring the best data, analytical skills and ideas to solve data problems - from using satellites capture to monitor agriculture efforts, to citizen engagement tools to understand sanitation requirements in villages in remote parts of the world. It works to ensure that governments are given the tools they need to ensure they leave no-one behind in these development efforts.

So, the SDGs can only be realized with strong global partnerships and cooperation. Official Development Assistance remained steady but below target, at US$147 billion in 2017. While humanitarian crises brought on by conflict or natural disasters continue to demand more financial resources and aid. Many countries also require Official Development Assistance to encourage growth and trade.

The world is more interconnected than ever. Improving access to technology and knowledge is an important way to share ideas and foster innovation. Coordinating policies to help developing countries manage their debt, as well as promoting investment for the least developed, is vital for sustainable growth and development.

The goals aim to enhance North-South and South-South cooperation by supporting national plans to achieve all the targets. Promoting international trade, and helping developing countries increase their exports is all part of achieving a universal rules-based and equitable trading system that is fair and open and benefits all.

The UN Conference on Trade and Development (UNCTAD) says achieving SDGs will require US$5 trillion to $7 trillion in annual investment; total official development assistance reached US$147.2 billion in 2017; in 2017, international remittances totalled US$613 billion; 76 percent of it went to developing countries; in 2016, 6 countries met the international target to keep official development assistance at or above 0.7 percent of gross national income; sustainable and responsible investments represent high-potential sources of capital for SDGs; as of 2016, US$18.2 trillion was invested in this asset class and the bond market for sustainable business is growing. In 2018 global green bonds reached US$155.5billion, up 78 percent from previous year (UNDP. 2016. SDG 17).

21.1. The Global Targets and Indicators for SDG-17

The global indicator framework was developed by the Inter-Agency and Expert Group on SDG Indicators (IAEG-SDGs) and agreed to, as a practical starting point at the 47th session of the UN Statistical Commission held in March 2016 (NITI Aayog 2018). The report of the Commission, which included the global indicator framework, was then taken note of by ECOSOC at its 70th session in June 2016. The global targets and the indicator of this SDG are tabled (Table no-153) bellow –

Table No. 153: UNDP-DDGs Targets and Indicators of SDG-17

SDG-17, Strengthen the means of implementation and revitalize the Global Partnership for Sustainable Development[1]	
Finance	
Targets	**Indicators**
17.1: Strengthen domestic resource mobilization, including through international support to developing countries, to improve domestic capacity for tax and other revenue collection.	17.1.1: Total government revenue as a proportion of GDP, by source.
	17.1.2-Proportion of domestic budget funded by domestic taxes.
17.2: Developed countries to implement fully their official development assistance commitments, including the commitment by many developed countries to achieve the target of 0.7 per cent of gross national income for official development assistance (ODA/GNI) to	17.2.1: Net official development assistance, total and to least developed countries, as a proportion of the Organization for Economic Cooperation and Development (OECD) Development Assistance Committee

(*Contd...*)

1. Data Source: SDG India Index Baseline Report, 2018, NITI *Aayog*, Government of India, New Delhi.

ODA/GNI to least developed countries; ODA providers are encouraged to consider setting a target to provide at least 0.20 per cent of ODA/GNI to least developed countries.	donors' gross national income (GNI).
17.3: Mobilize additional financial resources for developing countries from multiple sources.	17.3.1: Foreign direct investments (FDI), official development assistance and South-South Cooperation as a proportion of total domestic budget.
	17.3.2: Volume of remittances (in United States dollars) as a proportion of total GDP.
17.4: Assist developing countries in attaining long-term debt sustainability through coordinated policies aimed at fostering debt financing, debt relief and debt restructuring, as appropriate, and address the external debt of highly indebted poor countries to reduce debt distress.	17.4.1: Debt service as a proportion of exports of goods and services.
17.5: Adopt and implement investment promotion regimes for least developed countries.	17.5.1: Number of countries that adopt and implement investment promotion regimes for least developed countries.
Technology	
17.6: Enhance North-South, South-South and triangular regional and international cooperation on and access to science, technology and innovation and enhance knowledge-sharing on mutually agreed terms, including through improved coordination among existing mechanisms, in particular at the United Nations level, and through a global technology facilitation mechanism.	17.6.1: Number of science and/or technology cooperation agreements and programmes between countries, by type of cooperation.
	17.6.2: Fixed Internet broadband subscriptions per 100 inhabitants, by speed.
17.7: Promote the development, transfer, dissemination and diffusion of environmentally sound technologies to developing countries on favourable terms, including on concessional and preferential terms, as mutually agreed.	17.7.1: Total amount of approved funding for developing countries to promote the development, transfer, dissemination and diffusion of environmentally sound technologies.
17.8: Fully operationalize the technology bank and science, technology and innovation capacity-building mechanism for least developed countries by 2017 and enhance the use of enabling technology, in particular information and communications technology.	17.8.1: Proportion of individuals using the Internet.
Capacity building	
17.9: Enhance international support for implementing effective and targeted capacity-building in developing countries to support national plans to implement all the Sustainable Development Goals, including through North-South, South-South and triangular cooperation.	17.9.1: Dollar value of financial and technical assistance (including through North-South, South-South and triangular cooperation) committed to developing countries.
Trade	
17.10: Promote a universal, rules-based, open, non-discriminatory and equitable multilateral trading system under the World Trade Organization, including through the conclusion of negotiations under its Doha Development Agenda.	17.10.1: Worldwide weighted tariff-average.

(*Contd...*)

17.11: Significantly increase the exports of developing countries, in particular with a view to doubling the least developed countries' share of global exports by 2020.	17.11.1: Developing countries' and least developed countries' share of global exports.
17.12: Realize timely implementation of duty-free and quota-free market access on a lasting basis for all least developed countries, consistent with World Trade Organization decisions, including by ensuring that preferential rules of origin applicable to imports from least developed countries are transparent and simple, and contribute to facilitating market access.	17.12.1: Average tariffs faced by developing countries, least developed countries and small island developing States.
Systemic issues, Policy and institutional coherence	
17.13: Enhance global macroeconomic stability, including through policy coordination and policy coherence.	17.13.1: Macroeconomic Dashboard.
17.14: Enhance policy coherence for sustainable development.	17.14.1: Number of countries with mechanisms in place to enhance policy coherence of sustainable development.
17.15: Respect each country's policy space and leadership to establish and implement policies for poverty eradication and sustainable development.	17.15.1: Extent of use of country-owned results frameworks and planning tools by providers of development cooperation.
Multi-stakeholder partnerships	
17.16: Enhance the Global Partnership for Sustainable Development, complemented by multi-stakeholder partnerships that mobilize and share knowledge, expertise, technology and financial resources, to support the achievement of the Sustainable Development Goals in all countries, in particular developing countries.	17.16.1: Number of countries reporting progress in multi-stakeholder development effectiveness monitoring frameworks that support the achievement of the sustainable development goals.
17.17: Encourage and promote effective public, public-private and civil society partnerships, building on the experience and resourcing strategies of partnerships.	17.17.1: Amount of United States dollars committed to public-private and civil society partnerships.
Data, monitoring and accountability	
17.18: By 2020, enhance capacity-building support to developing countries, including for least developed countries and small island developing States, to increase significantly the availability of high-quality, timely and reliable data disaggregated by income, gender, age, race, ethnicity, migratory status, disability, geographic location and other characteristics relevant in national contexts.	17.18.1: Proportion of sustainable development indicators produced at the national level with full disaggregation when relevant to the target, in accordance with the Fundamental Principles of Official Statistics.
	17.18.2: Number of countries that have national statistical legislation that complies with the Fundamental Principles of Official Statistics.
	17.18.3: Number of countries with a national statistical plan that is fully funded and under implementation, by source of funding.
17.19-By 2030, build on existing initiatives to develop measurements of progress on sustainable development that complement gross domestic	17.19.1: Dollar value of all resources made available to strengthen statistical capacity in developing countries.

(*Contd...*)

development that complement gross domestic product, and support statistical capacity-building in developing countries.	capacity in developing countries.
	17.19.2: Proportion of countries that (a) have conducted at least one population and housing census in the last 10 years; and (b) have achieved 100 per cent birth registration and 80 per cent death registration.

21.2. The National Context of SDG-17

As per SDG India Index Base Line Report, 2018 (NITI Aayog 2018), while working towards revitalizing the global partnership for the achievement of the SDGs, India reaffirms the principle of common but differentiated responsibilities. Despite significant efforts for domestic resource mobilisation, India is unlikely to gather sufficient revenues for achieving the SDGs. Therefore, India reiterates that the developed countries have an essential obligation to provide financial assistance to the developing countries, especially for global public goods such as climate change mitigation and control of pandemics, so that they can fully achieve the SDGs. India also highlights the need for international cooperation for curbing illicit financial flows, defining aid unambiguously and establishing robust systems for monitoring commitments made by donor countries. Against this background, India is making all necessary efforts to raise its own revenue resources as described below.

21.2.1. Improving Taxation Capacity and Compliance: The tax-GDP ratio in India is significantly lower than the average for the BRICS countries. Thus, there is considerable scope for boosting domestic resources by expanding the tax base as well as strengthening the tax administration system.

The Indian government has committed to the implementation of an ambitious tax reform agenda, including the Goods and Services Tax (GST) as well as direct tax reforms to increase domestic resource mobilization, while committing to keeping public debt at sustainable levels in the medium term. An innovative tax like the *Swachh Bharat* Cess (Clean India Cess) has also been levied for mobilizing resources for the Clean India Mission. Additionally, implementation of the budget responsibility legislation is ensuring predictable and sustainable budgeting as well as long-term debt sustainability. In India's efforts to improve the efficacy of tax collection, a critical constraint is the absence of adequate global cooperation on capping money laundering and poor progress on mutual administrative assistance in tax matters. Global cooperation that alleviates this constraint will boost the ability of India and the entire developing world to secure the means of implementation for achieving the SDGs.

It is estimated that developing countries lose nearly USD 1 trillion every year on account of illicit financial flows (black money generated through money laundering and adverse practices in financial transactions like under or over invoicing). International tax havens and tax evasion make it very difficult for countries to mobilize the resources domestically.

India has on several occasions highlighted the scale of revenue loss in developing countries on account of profit shifting practices of multinationals (transfer pricing). One of the important challenges is that developing countries are often required to adhere to standards that have been defined by the developed world. India with support from G77 and China had proposed stronger international tax rules and advocated for an intergovernmental tax body. However, this endeavour did not fructify. The modest achievement for India (hailed as significant in diplomatic circles) has been to introduce new modalities in the constitution of the UN promoted international tax committee (Committee of Experts on International Cooperation in Tax Matters under the Economic and Social Council of the UN).

21.2.2. Strengthening Sub-National Governments: The states and local bodies will be at the frontline of operationalizing the SDG strategy in India. The fiscal relationship between the national government and the sub-national governments is undergoing a paradigm shift. The Fourteenth Finance Commission increased the share of tax devolution to states from 32% to 42% of the divisible pool. In addition, special purpose grants to secure universal primary education, health, employment, affordable housing, and urbanization provide a solid collaborative fiduciary basis for securing the SDGs. In addition, the Centre also supplements Local Body finances by providing them with appropriate fiscal space. Targeted and adequately financed initiatives to promote inclusion and gender empowerment and addressing the special needs of vulnerable groups are key to India's development strategy.

21.2.3. Enhancing Efficiency of Expenditures: On the expenditure front, the government has comprehensively restructured the framework of the expenditure budget. This restructuring will enable the government to monitor the results of different public expenditure initiatives in terms of their impact on the SDGs and undertake course corrections when necessary. The introduction of sunset clauses for all public expenditure programmes will allow the government to divest itself from unproductive "legacy" expenditures and deploy the freed resources towards programmes that will contribute to securing the SDGs. A comprehensive public financial management system is now operational that allows the government to track expenditure flows to end objectives in real time, thereby contributing to increased effectiveness in public expenditure management. These significant improvements in efficiency and predictability of public expenditure will play an important role in securing financing for the SDGs.

21.2.4. Establishing Strong Partnerships with the Private Sector: India has had one of the largest Public-Private Partnership (PPP) programmes globally. Given the substantial financing requirement for SDGs, a continued focus on PPP initiatives as well as addressing challenges in their rollout is crucial.

Given the vast financing needs, it is important that the private sector has access to global finance. To this end, the government has embarked on a comprehensive set of reforms to attract FDI, including opening up key sectors like defence and railways to such investment. Increased private investment will be key to securing high growth, employment and improved productive efficiency. Thus, India has framed consistent policies that open up the economy to FDI so as to accelerate financing from this source; India has over the past year witnessed an increase of 36 % in FDI inflows despite a 5 % reduction in global FDI flows. Here too India faces a challenge that requires international action. Subjective assessments of the Indian policy and regulatory environment by global financial institutions and rating agencies raise the costs of private financial flows to India by positing a highly subjective "regulatory risk premium". This particularly affects long-term finance for infrastructure and other investments that are crucial for achieving the SDGs. It would be helpful to the cause of the Indian and global SDGs achievement, if this impediment to the means of implementation were to be addressed through global action.

21.2.5. Promoting South-South Cooperation: To achieve the objectives of SDGs in a framework of shared prosperity and destiny, particularly in the region to which it belongs, India has been following the principles of South-South Cooperation in its bilateral and multilateral engagements. This helps to foster the southern narrative on development and sustainability at multilateral forums. South-South Cooperation is particularly beneficial on sharing of best practices, sustainable use of resources available regionally and joint development projects on common challenges.

21.2.6. Reforming the Aid System and Honouring Existing ODA Commitments: While domestic resource mobilization is becoming increasingly important, high-income nations that are a part of the Development Assistance Committee (DAC) also need to honour their commitments of providing 0.7% of GNI as ODA. ODA is especially important in the context of global public goods such as climate change mitigation, ecosystems and biodiversity as well as pandemics. For instance, at the 21st Conference of the Parties of the UN Framework Convention on Climate Change, developed countries reiterated their commitment to mobilizing additional resources to the tune of USD 100 billion every year by 2020 through the Green Climate Fund for meeting the requirements of developing nations.

On average, DAC members only provide 0.3% of GNI with a handful of countries meeting or exceeding the 0.7% level. Ironically, the highest ODA-to-GNI ratio in 2016 was of a non-DAC member, the United Arab Emirates (1.12%). During 2013, it was estimated that if all DAC members had met the 0.7% target, it would have been possible to mobilize an additional USD 184 billion.

Further, there is a need for setting clear eligibility standards and ensuring greater transparency with respect to ODA. Currently, there is considerable ambiguity about what counts as aid. For instance, contrary to the spirit of the Cancun agreement, a substantial share of ODA is often counted twice – as climate finance as well as ODA. Moreover, robust systems for monitoring of aid commitments made by donor countries have not been put in place.

21.2.7. Technology Facilitation Mechanism (TFM) for SDGs: The Addis Ababa Action Agenda established a new mechanism for making technologies available to developing countries for implementing the SDGs known as TFM. India, through its submissions, has highlighted that urgent delivery of technology development, deployment, dissemination and transfer to developing countries requires a suitable response. This includes a continued emphasis by all countries on the enhancement of enabling environments, facilitating access to technology and financing that leverages private sector resources.

21.2.8. Data, Monitoring and Accountability: The Indian Statistical System functions within the overall administrative framework of the country. Central and state ministries are responsible for collecting statistics on a subject depending on whether it is a part of the central, state or concurrent lists of the Constitution. MoSPI has overall responsibility for statistical coordination in the country including defining standards as well as ensuring quality and timeliness of statistics. At the state-level, the Directorate of Economics and Statistics performs a similar function in alignment with the overall standards determined by MoSPI.

21.2.9. Legal Framework for Data Collection: Primary statistical information is collected under the legal provision of various Acts and Rules. In addition, MoSPI has notified Survey Guidelines in 2011 for conducting all-India Surveys. It is mandatory for government agencies to follow these guidelines while conducting nationwide surveys so that consistency in quality can be ensured. In May 2016, the Government of India notified the 'Fundamental Principles of Official Statistics' adopted by the UN Statistical Commission in 2014. Data collected by a private agency under the 'Fundamental Principles of Official Statistics' and the Survey Guidelines notified by MoSPI may be considered for SDG monitoring purposes, following validation by a government Ministry. MoSPI regularly organizes conferences with data producers and users to provide updates; identify gaps in data and statistical methods and initiate necessary course correction.

21.2.10. Monitoring Framework for SDGs: Efforts are underway at the national-level for finalizing the indicators that will enable monitoring of the progress made on the SDGs. Additionally, there is an emphasis on assessing and improving the availability of data as well as putting in place transparent monitoring systems. India appreciates that tracking the SDGs effectively will require mechanisms to be established for generating a set of data that is broader, more disaggregated and available at shorter intervals of time as compared to the data that is currently utilized for reviewing development efforts. Disaggregated data is vital as it enables the formulation of effective policies for targeting specific disadvantaged groups and geographical areas in the country.

Through a series of technical workshops conducted by NITI *Aayog* in which MoSPI was an active participant, the draft indicators for SDG monitoring were assessed based on regularity of data generation and availability of disaggregated data. Civil Society Organizations and other stakeholders are also providing significant inputs towards the development of the measurement framework. Moreover, the government plans to strengthen the mechanisms for SDG monitoring and reporting through a dashboard currently under development, with technical support from the UNDP.

A number of goals in the SDGs do not require the government to deliver public services, but instead to develop and enforce the necessary policy and regulatory frameworks. Given the interrelatedness of the goals and targets, the government is also considering setting up a high-level Committee headed by the Chief Statistician of India to oversee the monitoring framework for SDGs at the national-level.

Steps are being taken to strengthen the statistical system in the country through adequate financial and human resource investments. There is also a focus on bridging the gaps and identifying new sources for meeting the growing data requirements. For instance, it has been decided that Labour Force surveys providing employment/unemployment estimates will be conducted on a quarterly basis for urban India and annually for the country as a whole.

Additionally, it is proposed to carry out Time Use Surveys, which will serve as an important source of data for assessing gender-related economic disparities. Further, several initiatives are being launched for modernizing the data system including e-collection, e-dissemination and use of space technology for household surveys. While national efforts are paramount, global technical support is also important in various areas including developing methodologies for data collection as well as monitoring and evaluation. This is especially relevant in the context of the fact that a number of the indicators for tracking SDGs at the global level are not necessarily readily measurable at the country level. In its VNR last year, Estonia had highlighted that following their initial review of 231 global sustainable development indicators; only 14% were found to be measurable.

21.3. Provisions of the Indian Constitution for SDG-17

The spirit of the unity in this diverse country, India is secured by its great Constitution; the Constitution of India not only secured its unity, announced a vision in the Preamble in the beginning of its Articles included in the Indian Constitution, *"We the people of India, having solemnly resolved to constitute India into a Sovereign Socialist Secular Democratic Republic and to secure to all its citizens: justice, social, economic and political; liberty of thought, expression, belief, faith and worship; equality of status and of opportunity; and to promote among them all fraternity assuring the dignity of the individual and the unity and integrity of the nation; in our Constituent Assembly this twenty-sixth day of November, 1949, do hereby adopt, enact and give to ourselves this Constitution* (India 1950/2015)". The mode of orientation of the Indian Constitution and the sustainable development goals of the contemporary time are given us an opportunity to make a link between these two visions of development and the author is trying to make the link.

As we know the sustainable development goals are interlinked, that means the success or failure of one is affected to other SDGs. From this perspective, this section presents the provisions in the Indian Constitution to eradicate poverty as reflected in the sustainable development agenda entitled as SDG-17, Partnerships for the Goals. The linked Constitutional provisions are in the following Table no-154 -

Table No. 154: Provisions in Indian Constitution for SDG-17

SDG-17 and the Linked Articles and Schedules of the Constitution of India
Article-15-1, 2-a, 2-b, 3, 4 and 5; Article-16-(1) to (5); Article-19-1. (a) to (e); Article 21-A, Article-38-(1) and (2); Article-43A, Article-46, Article-51A that is (a) to (j); Article-243, Article-243A, Article-243B, Article-243C, Article-243D, Article-243P, Article-243Q, Article-243R, Article-243S, Article-243T, Article-309, Article-310, Article-311, Article-312, Article-313, Article-314, Article-315, Article-320, Article-323A and Article-323B.
Article 246 - Seventh Schedule, List-I: Union List No: 12, 13, 14, 15, 16, 17, 19, 20, 21, 22, 23, 24, 25, 27, 29, 30, 31, 38, 42, 51,62, 63, 64, 65, 66, 67, 68, 69, and 94. List-II: State List No: 1, 2, 3, 4, 5, 6, 12, 13, and 26. List-III: Concurrent List No: 10, 25, 26, 27, 28, 29, 30 and 33.
Article 243G: Eleventh Schedule: Powers, Authority and Responsibilities of Panchayats. Schedule No: 1, 2, 3, 4, 5, 6, 7, 8, 9, 10, 11, 12, 13, 14, 15, 16, 17, 18, 19, 20, 21, 22, 23, 24, 25, 26, 2, 28 and 29. Article 243W: Twelfth Schedule: Powers, Authority and Responsibilities of Municipalities. Schedule No: 1, 2, 3, 4, 5, 6, 7, 8, 9, 10, 11, 12, 13, 14, 15,16, 17 and 18.

Source: The Constitution of India, 2015 as on 9th November, 2015.

21.4. Policies of the Government of India for Targets of the SDG-17

According to the SDG India Index Base Line Report, 2018, India is proactive to achieve the target of the UN's SDGs. The Government of India initiated as well as implemented various policies to capture the indicators of the targets of each individual SDG. On the moment of preparation of SDG India Index Base Line Report, 2018, on the basis of the availability of the disaggregated data, the NITI *Aayog* had framed India's own indicators of the targets of each individual SDG. For the SDG-17, that is 'Partnerships for the Goals'; the NITI *Aayog* unable to manage the data to frame any measurable indicators; which capture the UNs SDG targets. Even though, as per the report, 13 dedicated Ministries or the Departments are in action to achieve the targets of the UN's SDG-17, details are in the - Table no-155.

Table No. 155: Policies Initiated by the Indian Government for Targets of SDG-17

SDG-17, Partnerships for the Goals	
SDG-17, is Partnerships for the Goals aiming to strengthen the means of implementation and revitalize the global partnership for sustainable development.	
Target: 17.1: Strengthen domestic resource mobilization, including through international support to developing countries, to improve domestic capacity for tax and other revenue collection.	
Centrally Sponsored /Central Sector Schemes (CSS)	Concerned Ministries/ Departments
	Ministry of Finance, Ministry of Corporate Affairs

(*Contd...*)

Target: 17.2: Developed countries to implement fully their official development assistance commitments, including the commitment by many developed countries to achieve the target of 0.7 per cent of gross national income official for development assistance (ODA/GNI) to developing countries and 0.15 to 0.20 per cent of ODA/GNI to least developed countries; ODA providers are encouraged to consider setting a target to provide at least 0.20 per cent of ODA/GNI to least developed countries.	
Centrally Sponsored /Central Sector Schemes (CSS)	Concerned Ministries/ Departments
	Ministry of Finance, Ministry of External Affairs
Target: 17.3: Mobilize additional financial resources for developing countries from multiple sources.	
Centrally Sponsored /Central Sector Schemes (CSS)	Concerned Ministries/ Departments
	Ministry of Finance,
Target: 17.4: Assist developing countries in attaining long-term debt sustainability through coordinated policies aimed at fostering debt financing, debt relief and debt restructuring, as appropriate, and address the external debt of highly indebted poor countries to reduce debt distress.	
Centrally Sponsored /Central Sector Schemes (CSS)	Concerned Ministries/ Departments
	Ministry of Finance, Ministry of External Affairs
Target: 17.5: Adopt and implement investment promotion regimes for least developed countries.	
Centrally Sponsored /Central Sector Schemes (CSS)	Concerned Ministries/ Departments
	Ministry of Finance, Ministry of External Affairs
Target: 17.6: Enhance North-South, South-South and triangular regional and international cooperation on and access to science, technology and innovation and enhance knowledge sharing on mutually agreed terms, including through improved coordination among existing mechanisms, in particular at the United Nations Level, and through a global technology facilitation mechanism, knowledge sharing on mutually agreed terms, including through improved coordination among existing mechanisms, in particular at the United Nations level, and through a global technology facilitation mechanism when agreed upon.	
Centrally Sponsored /Central Sector Schemes (CSS)	Concerned Ministries/ Departments
	Ministry of External Affairs, Ministry of Information and Technology, Broadcasting
Target: 17.7: Promote the development, transfer, dissemination and diffusion of environmentally sound technologies to developing countries on favourable terms, including on concessional and preferential terms, as mutually agreed.	
Centrally Sponsored /Central Sector Schemes (CSS)	Concerned Ministries/ Departments
	Ministry of Environment, Forest and Climate Change, Information and Technology,
Target: 17.8: Fully operationalize the technology bank and science, technology and innovation capacity building mechanism for least developed countries by 2017 and enhance the use of enabling technology, in particular information and communications technology.	
Centrally Sponsored /Central Sector Schemes (CSS)	Concerned Ministries/ Departments

(*Contd*...)

Centrally Sponsored /Central Sector Schemes (CSS)	Concerned Ministries/ Departments
	Ministry of Science and Technology, Telecommunication
Target: 17.9: Enhance international support for implementing effective and targeted capacity-building in developing countries to support national plans to implement all the sustainable development goals, including through North-South, South-South and triangular cooperation.	
Centrally Sponsored /Central Sector Schemes (CSS)	Concerned Ministries/ Departments
	Ministry of External Affairs, Ministry of Rural Development
Target: 17.10: Promote a universal, rules-based, open, non-discriminatory and equitable multilateral trading system under the World Trade Organization, including through the conclusion of negotiations under its Doha Development Agenda.	
Centrally Sponsored /Central Sector Schemes (CSS)	Concerned Ministries/ Departments
	Ministry of Commerce and Trade
Target: 17.11: Significantly increase the exports of developing countries, in particular with a view to doubling the least developed countries' share of global exports by 2020.	
Centrally Sponsored /Central Sector Schemes (CSS)	Concerned Ministries/ Departments
	Ministry of Commerce
Target: 17.12: Realise timely implementation of duty-free and quota-free market access on a lasting basis for all least developed countries, consistent with World Trade Organization decisions, including by ensuring that preferential rules of origin applicable to imports from least developed countries are transparent and simple, and contribute to facilitating market access.	
Centrally Sponsored /Central Sector Schemes (CSS)	Concerned Ministries/ Departments
	Ministry of Commerce, DIPP
Target: 17.13: Enhance global macroeconomic stability, including through policy coordination and policy.	
Centrally Sponsored /Central Sector Schemes (CSS)	Concerned Ministries/ Departments
	Ministry of Finance, MoSPI
Target: 17.14: Enhance policy coherence for sustainable development.	
Centrally Sponsored /Central Sector Schemes (CSS)	Concerned Ministries/ Departments
	Ministry of Environment, Forest and Climate Change
Target: 17.15: Respect each country's policy space and leadership to establish and implement policies for poverty eradication and sustainable development.	
	Ministry of External Affairs, Ministry of Rural Development
Target: 17.16: Enhance the global partnership for sustainable development, complemented by multi-stakeholder partnerships that mobilize and share knowledge, expertise, technology and financial resources, to support the achievement of the sustainable development goals in all countries, in particular developing countries.	
Centrally Sponsored /Central Sector Schemes (CSS)	Concerned Ministries/ Departments

(*Contd*...)

	Ministry of Environment, Forest and Climate Change, Information and Broadcasting
Target: 17.17: Encourage and promote effective public, public-private and civil society partnerships, building on the experience and resourcing strategies of partnerships.	
Centrally Sponsored /Central Sector Schemes (CSS)	Concerned Ministries/ Departments
	Ministry of Finance
Target: 17.18: By 2030, enhance capacity-building support to developing countries, including for least developed countries and small Island Developing States, to increase significantly the availability of high-quality, timely and reliable data disaggregated by income, gender, age, race, ethnicity, migratory status, disability, geographic location and other characteristics relevant in national contexts.	
Centrally Sponsored /Central Sector Schemes (CSS)	Concerned Ministries/ Departments
	MoSPI
Target: 17.19: By 2030, build on existing initiatives to develop measurements of progress on sustainable development that complement gross domestic product, and support statistical capacity-building in developing countries.	
Centrally Sponsored /Central Sector Schemes (CSS)	Concerned Ministries/ Departments
	MoSPI

Source: (NITI Aayog 2018).

21.5. Government of India's Remaining Targets and the Indicators for SDG-17

As we know that, on the basis of the availability of the disaggregated data, the NITI *Aayog* had framed India's own indicators of the targets of each individual SDG. For the SDG-17, that is 'Partnerships for the Goals', the NITI *Aayog* unable to collect and manage the data as required to capture the indicators of the UNs SDG-17 targets. As per the report, 13 dedicated Ministries or the Departments are in action to achieve the UN's SDG-17. As a result, all the indicators of the SDG-17 remained uncaptured but indicators of the UN's SDG-17 is to be achieve by 2030. The remaining lists of targets along with the indicators of SDG-17 are detailed in Table no-156.

Table No- 156: Government of India's Remaining Targets and the Indicators for SDG-17

India's Remaining Targets and the Indicators for SDG-17	
Finance	
Targets	**Indicators**
17.1: Strengthen domestic resource mobilization, including through international support to developing countries, to improve domestic capacity for tax and other revenue collection.	17.1.1: Total government revenue as a proportion of GDP, by source.
	17.1.2: Proportion of domestic budget funded by domestic taxes.

(Contd...)

17.2: Developed countries to implement fully their official development assistance commitments, including the commitment by many developed countries to achieve the target of 0.7 per cent of gross national income for official development assistance (ODA/GNI) to developing countries and 0.15 to 0.20 per cent of ODA/GNI to least developed countries; ODA providers are encouraged to consider setting a target to provide at least 0.20 per cent of ODA/GNI to least developed countries.	17.2.1: Net official development assistance, total and to least developed countries, as a proportion of the Organization for Economic Cooperation and Development (OECD) Development Assistance Committee donors' gross national income (GNI).
17.3: Mobilize additional financial resources for developing countries from multiple sources.	17.3.1: Foreign direct investments (FDI), official development assistance and South-South Cooperation as a proportion of total domestic budget.
	17.3.2: Volume of remittances (in United States dollars) as a proportion of total GDP.
17.4: Assist developing countries in attaining long-term debt sustainability through coordinated policies aimed at fostering debt financing, debt relief and debt restructuring, as appropriate, and address the external debt of highly indebted poor countries to reduce debt distress.	17.4.1: Debt service as a proportion of exports of goods and services.
17.5: Adopt and implement investment promotion regimes for least developed countries.	17.5.1: Number of countries that adopt and implement investment promotion regimes for least developed countries.
Technology	
17.6: Enhance North-South, South-South and triangular regional and international cooperation on and access to science, technology and innovation and enhance knowledge-sharing on mutually agreed terms, including through improved coordination among existing mechanisms, in particular at the United Nations level, and through a global technology facilitation mechanism.	17.6.1: Number of science and/or technology cooperation agreements and programmes between countries, by type of cooperation.
	17.6.2: Fixed Internet broadband subscriptions per 100 inhabitants, by speed.
17.7: Promote the development, transfer, dissemination and diffusion of environmentally sound technologies to developing countries on favourable terms, including on concessional and preferential terms, as mutually agreed.	17.7.1: Total amount of approved funding for developing countries to promote the development, transfer, dissemination and diffusion of environmentally sound technologies.
17.8: Fully operationalize the technology bank and science, technology and innovation capacity-building mechanism for least developed countries by 2017 and enhance the use of enabling technology, in particular information and communications technology.	17.8.1: Proportion of individuals using the Internet.

(Contd...)

Capacity-building	
17.9: Enhance international support for implementing effective and targeted capacity-building in developing countries to support national plans to implement all the Sustainable Development Goals, including through North-South, South-South and triangular cooperation.	17.9.1: Dollar value of financial and technical assistance (including through North-South, South-South and triangular cooperation) committed to developing countries.
Trade	
17.10: Promote a universal, rules-based, open, non-discriminatory and equitable multilateral trading system under the World Trade Organization, including through the conclusion of negotiations under its Doha Development Agenda.	17.10.1: Worldwide weighted tariff-average.
17.11: Significantly increase the exports of developing countries, in particular with a view to doubling the least developed countries' share of global exports by 2020.	17.11.1: Developing countries' and least developed countries' share of global exports.
17.12: Realize timely implementation of duty-free and quota-free market access on a lasting basis for all least developed countries, consistent with World Trade Organization decisions, including by ensuring that preferential rules of origin applicable to imports from least developed countries are transparent and simple, and contribute to facilitating market access.	17.12.1: Average tariffs faced by developing countries, least developed countries and small island developing States.
Systemic issues, Policy and institutional coherence	
17.13: Enhance global macroeconomic stability, including through policy coordination and policy coherence.	17.13.1: Macroeconomic Dashboard.
17.14: Enhance policy coherence for sustainable development.	17.14.1: Number of countries with mechanisms in place to enhance policy coherence of sustainable development.
17.15-Respect each country's policy space and leadership to establish and implement policies for poverty eradication and sustainable development.	17.15.1-Extent of use of country-owned results frameworks and planning tools by providers of development cooperation.
Multi-stakeholder partnerships	
17.16: Enhance the Global Partnership for Sustainable Development, complemented by multi-stakeholder partnerships that mobilize and share knowledge, expertise, technology and financial resources, to support the achievement of the Sustainable Development Goals in all countries, in particular developing countries.	17.16.1: Number of countries reporting progress in multi-stakeholder development effectiveness monitoring frameworks that support the achievement of the sustainable development goals.
17.17: Encourage and promote effective public, public-private and civil society partnerships, building on the experience and resourcing strategies of partnerships.	17.17.1: Amount of United States dollars committed to public-private and civil society partnerships.

(*Contd...*)

Data, monitoring and accountability	
17.18: By 2020, enhance capacity-building support to developing countries, including for least developed countries and small island developing States, to increase significantly the availability of high-quality, timely and reliable data disaggregated by income, gender, age, race, ethnicity, migratory status, disability, geographic location and other characteristics relevant in national contexts.	17.18.1: Proportion of sustainable development indicators produced at the national level with full disaggregation when relevant to the target, in accordance with the Fundamental Principles of Official Statistics.
	17.18.2: Number of countries that have national statistical legislation that complies with the Fundamental Principles of Official Statistics.
	17.18.3: Number of countries with a national statistical plan that is fully funded and under implementation, by source of funding.
17.19: By 2030, build on existing initiatives to develop measurements of progress on sustainable development that complement gross domestic product, and support statistical capacity-building in developing countries.	17.19.1: Dollar value of all resources made available to strengthen statistical capacity in developing countries.
	17.19.2: Proportion of countries that (a) have conducted at least one population and housing census in the last 10 years; and (b) have achieved 100 per cent birth registration and 80 per cent death registration.
Note of the Table: • Remaining to capture the data of targets and indicators.	

If we look the SDG-17, 'Partnerships for the Goals' targets, there are seven-point partnership making approach, these are Finance, Technology, Capacity-building, Trade, Systemic issues - Policy and institutional coherence, Multi-stakeholder partnerships and Data, monitoring and accountability under each point there are several targets and its indicator – as per the goal all the points, targets and the indicators are the requisite to achieve the SDG as a whole.

While working towards revitalizing the global partnership for the achievement of the SDGs, India reaffirms the principle of common but differentiated responsibilities. Despite significant efforts for domestic resource mobilisation, India is unlikely to gather sufficient revenues for achieving the SDGs. Therefore, India reiterates that the developed countries have an essential obligation to provide financial assistance to the developing countries, especially for global public goods such as climate change mitigation and control of pandemics, so that they can fully achieve the SDGs. India also highlights the need for international cooperation for curbing illicit financial flows, defining aid unambiguously and establishing robust systems for monitoring commitments made by donor countries.

Towards implementation of the above local as well as global partnership making initiatives to achieving the SDG's targets, the

Government of India with its dedicated Ministries or the Departments such as Ministry of Corporate Affairs, DIPP, External Affairs, Information and Broadcasting, Information and Technology, Ministry of Commerce, Ministry of Commerce and Trade, Ministry of Environment, Forest and Climate Change, Ministry of Finance, Ministry of Rural Development, Ministry of Science and Technology, MoSPI and Telecommunication for this SDG are a proactive role; these role and initiatives are accelerated the Indian Constitution, there are ample options to capture the issues associated with the SDG-17 in the Constitution of India.

As the Government of India had been played a vital role to formation as well as framing the issues of SDG; in a similar manner, India have to play a vital role to making 'partnership for the goals' within as well as between its territorial area to achieve the SDG as a whole by effective use and monitoring of its mechanism of 'peace, justice and strong institutions' (SDG-16); unless we will be liable on the ground of violation the commitment as agreed in the United Nations General Assembly on implementation of SDGs as well as violation of the linked provisions which has been reflected on SDG-17 in the Indian Constitution; the Constitutional provisions associated with the SDG-17 are as - Article-15-1, 2-a and b, 3, 4 and 5; Article-16-(1) to (5); Article-19-1. (a) to (e); Article 21-A, Article-38-(1) and (2); Article-43A, Article-46, Article-51A that is (a) to (j); Article-243, Article-243A, Article-243B, Article-243C, Article-243D, Article-243P, Article-243Q, Article-243R, Article-243S, Article-243T, Article-309, Article-310, Article-311, Article-312, Article-313, Article-314, Article-315, Article-320, Article-323A and Article-323B; Article 246 - Seventh Schedule; List-I: Union List No: 12, 13, 14, 15, 16, 17, 19, 20, 21, 22, 23, 24, 25, 27, 29, 30, 31, 38, 42, 51,62, 63, 64, 65, 66, 67, 68, 69, and 94; List-II: State List No: 1, 2, 3, 4, 5, 6, 12, 13, 26; List-III: Concurrent List No:10, 25, 26, 27, 28, 29, 30 and 33; Article 243G - Eleventh Schedule - Powers, Authority and Responsibilities of Panchayats – Schedule No – 1, 2, 3,4, 5, 6, 7, 8, 9, 10, 11, 12, 13, 14, 15, 16, 17, 18, 19, 20, 21, 22, 23, 24, 25, 26,27, 28 and 29; Article 243W - Twelfth Schedule - Powers, Authority and Responsibilities of Municipalities - Schedule No – 1, 2, 3, 4, 5, 6, 7, 8, 9, 10, 11, 12, 13, 14, 15, 16, 17 and 18. So, we have to concentrate to monitor on the above issues to achieve the target by 2030 through the provisions of Indian Constitution, if we could not monitor, we would not be able to stand in front of the future generation with a smile.

Chapter – XXII

Conclusion

It was assumed that, *'Peace, Justice and Strong Institutions'* are the pre-conditions of achievement of SDGs. In SDG-16, that is *Peace, Justice and Strong Institutions*, India has been scored 71 and overall performance mean score is 57. In this regard, the author must want to saying that, the analysis in the above chapters are the reported facts in the way which may point a citizen's responsibility towards the development of the future generation of India.

Please consider the issues as your own future generations for whom you wish a better life than the past. So this initiative is by a citizen for the citizens of India which was developed by the world citizens. Engage in debating for the bettering of future generation. Rise your voice for the lacks in the execution to eradicate every confusion towards the proper implementation of Sustainable Development Goals.

At the end, we are not hopeless, as a citizen of India, this is our commitment to our future generation, and we shall create the future 'India' under the guidance of dynamic Constitution of India. We shall create the India for the future generation as it imagined by the global leaders during formation of the agenda of SDGs. We have all the supporting components to execute the 'targets' of the Sustainable Development Goals. We have few gaps or lack of effectiveness in different levels of executional statutory organization of the Constitutional institutions but it must be said that we have the efficient executives at all level of these statutory organization of the Indian Constitution. We have to overcome these kind of lacunas because time is limited; we have bound to complete the agendas of SDGs execution by 2030.

If we recall the initiatives of the Government of India for each individual SDG, we would see that there are 485 policies under the head of 211 dedicated Ministries or the departments. But these initiatives has only able to captured only 39 targets of the SDGs; in percentage it is 23.08; but 130 targets of the SDGs; in percentage it is 76.92 are still remaining. In this point there is another point to be remember, the NITI *Aayog* unable to gather valid data of few indicators from few Ministries or the departments. In this connection the author is strongly recommending to digitize all the policies and details of the policies for the citizens of India which would be create the better world for the future generation. In this regard, the author believe the words of Shri Ravi Shankar Prasad; Hon'ble Minister of Electronics & Information Technology and Law & Justice, Government of India portrayed in the website of *'Digital India'* that, the *"Digital India is more for the poor and underprivileged. It aims to bridge the gap between the digital haves or have-nots by using technology for citizen* (Prasad 2021)*"*.

Because, the gaps are lies in the availability of the disaggregated data, so that the NITI *Aayog* has been framed India's own indicators of the targets of each individual SDG. For the SDG-1, that is 'No Poverty', the NITI *Aayog* had framed five indicators; which captured two (1.2.1 and 1.3.1) of twelve indicators from the seven UNs SDG targets and there are 68 dedicated policies or schemes to achieve only three targets (1.2, 1.3 and 1.4) of the UN's SDG-1. The Constitution of India opened wide provision for

SDG-1 in its Article 15-(2).(a), Article 15-(4) and (5), Article 16-(1) to (5), Article 19-1.(a) to (g), Article 21A, Article 38-(1) and (2), Article 39-(a) to (f), Article 39A, Article 41, Article 42, Article 43, Article 46 and Article 47, Article 309, Article 310, Article 311, Article 312, Article 313, Article 314, Article 315, Article 320, Article 323A and Article 323B; Article 246 - Seventh Schedule, List-I-Union List 12, 15, 55, 65, 65, 66, 68, 69, and 94; List-II-State List No 6, 9, 14 to 18, 21, 23 and 27; List-III-Concurrent List No - 24, 25, 26 and 30; Article 243G - Eleventh Schedule - Powers, Authority and Responsibilities of Panchayats – Schedule No – 1,2, 3, 4, 5, 10, 11, 12, 16, 17, 18, 19, 23, 25, 26, 27 and 28; Article 243W - Twelfth Schedule - Powers, Authority and Responsibilities of Municipalities - Schedule No – 1, 3, 6, 9, 11 and 16 to monitor the rest of the targets and indicators of SDG-1.

For the SDG-2, that is 'Zero Hunger', the NITI *Aayog* had framed four indicators; which captured only three (2.1.2, 2.2.1 and 2.3.1) of fourteen indicators of the eight UNs SDG targets. As per the report, 37 dedicated policies or schemes to achieve three targets (2.1, 2.2 and 2.3) of the UN's SDG-2. The Constitution of India opened wide provision for SDG-2 in its Article 15-(2).(a), Article 15-(4) and (5), Article 16-(1) to

(5), Article 19-1.(a) to (g), Article 21A, Article 38-(1) and (2), Article 39-(a) to (f), Article 39A, Article 41, Article 42, Article 43, Article 45, Article 46, Article 47, Article 48, Article 309, Article 310, Article 311, Article 312, Article 313, Article 314, Article 315, Article 320, Article 323A and Article 323B; Article 246 - Seventh Schedule; List-I-Union List 12, 15, 55, 65, 66, 68, 69 and 94; List-II-State List No 6, 9, 14 to 18, 21, 23 and 27; List-III-Concurrent List No-24, 25, 26 and 30; Article 243G - Eleventh Schedule - Powers, Authority and Responsibilities of Panchayats – Schedule No – 1, 2, 3, 4, 5, 6, 8, 9, 10, 11, 12, 16, 17, 18, 19, 23, 24. 25, 26, 27, 28 and 29 and Article 243W - Twelfth Schedule - Powers, Authority and Responsibilities of Municipalities - Schedule No – 1, 3, 6, 8, 9, 10, 11 and 16 to monitor the rest of the targets and indicators of SDG-2.

For the SDG-3, that is 'Good Health and Well-being', the NITI *Aayog* had framed five indicators; which has only captured three (3.1.1, 3.2.1 and 3.3.2) of twenty six indicators of the thirteen UNs SDG targets. As per the report, 45 dedicated policies or schemes to achieve four targets (3.1, 3.2, 3.3 and 3.8) of the UN's SDG-3. The Constitution of India opened wide provision for SDG-3 in its Article 15-(2).(a), Article 15-(3), (4) and (5), Article 16-(1) to (5), Article 21A, Article 38-(1) and (2), Article 41, Article 42, Article 43, Article 45, Article 47, Article 48, Article 51A (g), Article 309, Article 310, Article 311, Article 312, Article 313, Article 314, Article 315, Article 320, Article 323A and Article 323B; Article 246 - Seventh Schedule, List-I-Union List No 12, 15, 55, 65, 66, 68, 69 and 94; List-II-State List No 6, 9, 14 to 17, 21 and 23; List-III-Concurrent List No 19, 20, 20A, 24, 25, 26 and 30; Article 243G - Eleventh Schedule - Powers, Authority and Responsibilities of Panchayats – Schedule No – 3, 6, 7, 8, 10, 11, 12, 16, 17 and 23 to 29 and Article 243W - Twelfth Schedule - Powers, Authority and Responsibilities of Municipalities - Schedule No – 1, 3, 4, 5, 6, 8, 9, 10, 11 and 16 to monitor the rest of the targets and indicators of SDG-3.

For SDG-4, that is 'Quality Education', the NITI *Aayog* had framed seven indicators; which captured only two (4.1.1, and 4.c.1) of eleven indicators out of the ten UNs SDG targets. As per the report, 66 dedicated policies or schemes to achieve two targets (4.1 and 4.c) of the UN's SDG-4. The Constitution of India opened wide provision for SDG-4 in its Article 15-(1), (4) and (5), Article 16-(1) to (5), Article 19.1 (g), 21A, Article 29-(1) and (2), Article 30-(1), (1A) and (2), Article 38-(1) and (2), Article 41, Article 43, Article 45, Article 46, Article 51A (h) and (k), Article 309, Article 310, Article 311, Article 312, Article 313, Article 314, Article 315, Article 320, Article 323A, Article 323B and Article 351; Article 246

- Seventh Schedule, List-I-Union List No 12, 25, 62, 63, 64, 65, 66, 67, 68, 69 and 94; List-I-State List No 14, 15, 32 and 41; List-III-Concurrent List No 19, 20, 24, 25, 26, 30 and 39; Article 243G - Eleventh Schedule - Powers, Authority and Responsibilities of Panchayats – Schedule No – 17, 18, 19, 20, 24 and 25; Article 243W - Twelfth Schedule - Powers, Authority and Responsibilities of Municipalities - Schedule No – 1, 3, 12, 13 and 16 to monitor the rest of the targets and indicators of SDG-4.

For the SDG-5, that is 'Gender Equality', the NITI *Aayog* had framed six indicators; which captured only three (5.2.1, 5.5.1 and 5.6.1) out of fourteen indicators of the nine UNs SDG targets. As per the report, 19 dedicated policies or schemes to achieve four targets (5.1, 5.2, 5.5 and 5.6) of the UN's SDG-5. The Constitution of India opened wide provision SDG-5 in its Article 14, Article 15-(1) to (5), Article 16-(1) to (5), Article 17, Article 18, Article 19, Article 20, Article 21A, Article 23, Article 24, Article 28, Article 30-(1), (1A) and (2), Article 38-(1) and (2), Article 39-(a) to (f), Article 39A, Article 41, Article 42, Article 43, Article 43A, Article 44, Article 45, Article 46, Article 47, Article 51A (a) to (k) Article 243D (2), Article 243T (2), Article 301, Article 309, Article 310, Article 311, Article 312, Article 313, Article 314, Article 315, Article 320, Article 323A, Article 323B, Article 325, Article 326, Article 350A, Article 350B, and Article 351; Article 246 - Seventh Schedule, List-I-Union List No 12, 25, 62, 63, 64, 65, 66, 67, 68, 69 and 94; List-II-State List No 5, 6, 9 and 12; List-III-Concurrent List 5, 20, 22, 23 24, 25, 26, 30 and 39; Article 243G - Eleventh Schedule - Powers, Authority and Responsibilities of Panchayats – Schedule No – 1-5, 8, 9, 10, 11, 12, 14, 16, 17, 18, 19, 20, 21 and 23 to 28; Article 243W - Twelfth Schedule - Powers, Authority and Responsibilities of Municipalities - Schedule No – 1, 3, 6, 8, 9, 10, 11, 12, 13, 14, 16 and 17 to monitor the rest of the targets and indicators of SDG-5.

For the SDG-6, that is 'Clean Water and Sanitation', the NITI *Aayog* had framed five indicators; which captured only three (6.1.1, 6.2.1 and 6.4.1) of eleven indicators of the eight UNs SDG targets. As per the report, 22 dedicated policies or schemes to achieve three targets (6.1, 6.2 and 6.4) of the UN's SDG-6. The Constitution of India opened wide provision for SDG-6 in its Article 15-(2).(a), Article 15-(3), (4) and (5), Article 16-(1) to (5), Article 21, Article 21A, Article 38-(1) and (2), Article 39 – (a) to (f), Article 41, Article 42, Article 43, Article 45, Article 47, Article 48 and Article 51A, Article 309, Article 310, Article 311, Article 312, Article 313, Article 314, Article 315,Article 320, Article 323A and Article 323B; Article 246 - Seventh Schedule, List-I-Union List No 12, 13, 15, 25, 55,

56, 64, 65, 66, 68, 69 and 94; List-II-State List No 6, 13 and 17 and List-III-Concurrent List No 18, 20, 20A, 24, 25, 26, 30 and 33; Article 243G - Eleventh Schedule - Powers, Authority and Responsibilities of Panchayats – Schedule No – 3, 11, 16, 17, 18, 19 and 23, 24, 25, 26, 27, 28 and 29; Article 243W - Twelfth Schedule - Powers, Authority and Responsibilities of Municipalities - Schedule No – 1, 3, 4, 5, 6, 8, 9, 10, and 16 to monitor the rest of the targets and indicators of SDG-6.

For the SDG-7, that is 'Affordable and Clean Energy', the NITI *Aayog* had framed three indicators; which captured three (7.1.1, 7.1.2 and 7.2.1) of six indicators of the five UNs SDG targets. As per the report, 17 dedicated policies or schemes to achieve two targets (7.1 and 7.2) of the UN's SDG-7. The Constitution of India opened wide provision for SDG-7 in its Article 15-(2).(a), Article 15-(3), (4) and (5), Article 21, Article 21A, Article 38-(1) and (2), Article 39 – (a) to (f), Article 41, Article 42, Article 43, Article 46, Article 47, Article 48A and Article 51A, Article 309, Article 310, Article 311, Article 312, Article 313, Article 314, Article 315, Article 320, Article 323A and Article 323B; Article 243G - Eleventh Schedule - Powers, Authority and Responsibilities of Panchayats – Schedule No – 2, 6, 7, 12, 16, 17, 18, 19 and 23, 24, 25, 26, 27, 28 and 29; Article 243W - Twelfth Schedule - Powers, Authority and Responsibilities of Municipalities - Schedule No – 1, 3, 4, 6, 7, 8, 9, 10, 11, 14, and 16. Article 246 - Seventh Schedule; List-I: Union List No: 6, 12, 13, 14, 15, 42, 55, 58, 64, 65, 66, 68, 69 and 94; List-II: State List No: 6, 9, 10, 13 and 25 and List-III: Concurrent List No: 20, 21, 22, 23, 24, 25, 26, 30, 33, 34, 35, 36, 37 and 38; Article 243G - Eleventh Schedule - Powers, Authority and Responsibilities of Panchayats – Schedule No – 2, 6, 7, 12, 16, 17, 18, 19 and 23, to 29; Article 243W - Twelfth Schedule - Powers, Authority and Responsibilities of Municipalities - Schedule No – 1, 3, 4, 6, 7, 8, 9, 10, 11, 14, and 16 to monitor the rest of the targets and indicators of SDG-7.

For the SDG-8, that is 'Decent Work and Economic Growth', the NITI *Aayog* had framed four indicators; which captured only four (7.1.1, 7.1.2 and 7.2.1) of seventeen indicators of the twelve UNs SDG targets. As per the report, 55 dedicated policies or schemes to achieve three targets (8.1, 8.5 and 8.10) of the UN's SDG-8. The Constitution of India opened wide provision for SDG-8 in its Article 14, Article 15-(2).(a), (b), Article 15-(3), (4) and (5), Article 16 (1) to (5), Article 21, Article 21A, Article 23 (1) and (2), Article 24, Article 29 (2), Article 38-(1) and (2), Article 39 – (a) to (f), Article 39 A, Article 41, Article 42, Article 43, Article 43 (A), Article 44, Article 45, Article 46, Article 47, Article 48, Article 48A,

Article 51 (a) Article 51A, Article 301, Article 302, Article 303, Article 304, Article 305, Article 307, Article 309, Article 310, Article 311, Article 312, Article 313, Article 314, Article 315, Article 320, Article 323A and Article 323B; Article 243G - Eleventh Schedule - Powers, Authority and Responsibilities of Panchayats – Schedule No – 1 to 5, 8, 9, 12, 13, 14, 15, 16, 17, 18, 19, 22 and 26; Article 243W - Twelfth Schedule - Powers, Authority and Responsibilities of Municipalities - Schedule No – 1 to 5, 7, 9, 10, 11 and 16; Article 246 - Seventh Schedule, List-I: Union List No: 12, 13, 22, 23, 24, 27, 29, 30, 31, 39, 42 to 62 to 66, 76, 82 to 92B and 94; List-II: State List No: 8, 9, 13, 14, 10, 11, 12, 13, 14, 15, 16,17, 18, 21, 23, 24, 25, 26, 27, 28, 30, 31, 32, 34, 35 and 55, 56, 57, 58, 59, 60, 61, 62 and 63 and List-III: Concurrent List No: 7, 20, 21, 22, 23, 24, 25 26, 30, 31, 32, 33, 34, 35, 36, 37, 38, 39 and 45 to monitor the rest of the targets and indicators of SDG-8.

For the SDG-9, that is 'Industry, Innovation and Infrastructure', the NITI *Aayog* had framed four indicators; which captured only two (9.1.1 and 9.c.1) of twelve indicators of the eight UNs SDG targets. As per the report, 45 dedicated policies or schemes to achieve two targets (9.1 and 9.2) of the UN's SDG-9. The Constitution of India opened wide provision for SDG-9 in its Article 14, Article 16 (1) to (5), Article 21, Article 21A, Article 38-(1) and (2), Article 39 – (a) to (f), Article 39A, Article 41, Article 42, Article 43, Article 43 (A), Article 44, Article 46, Article 48, Article 48A, Article 51A, Article 301, Article 302, Article 303. Article 304, Article 304, Article 307, Article 309, Article 310, Article 311, Article 312, Article 313, Article 314, Article 315, Article 320, Article 323A, Article 323B Article 364 and 365; Article 243G - Eleventh Schedule - Powers, Authority and Responsibilities of Panchayats – Schedule No – 1, 2, 3, 4, 5, 8, 9, 12, 13, 14, 15, 16, 17, 18, 19, 20, 21, 22, 26 and 27; Article 243W - Twelfth Schedule - Powers, Authority and Responsibilities of Municipalities - Schedule No – 1, 2, 3, 4, 5, 6, 7, 8, 9, 10, 11, 12, 16 and 17; Article 246 - Seventh Schedule, List-I: Union List No: 7, 12, 13, 22, 23, 24, 25, 27, 28, 29, 30, 31, 36, 38, 39, 41, 42, 43, 44, 45, 46, 47, 48, 49, 50, 51, 52, 53, 54, 55, 56, 57, 58, 59, 60, 61, 62, 63, 64, 65, 66, 67 , 68, 69, 76, 82, 83, 84, 85, 86, 87, 88, 89, 90, 91, 92, 92A, 92B and 94; List-II: State List No: 8, 9, 13, 14 to 18, 21, 23, 24, 25, 26, 27, 28, 30, 31, 32, 34, 35 and 37, 38, 39, 40, 41, 42, 43, 44, 45, 46, 47, 48, 49, 50, 51, 52, 53, 54, 55, 56, 57, 58, 59, 60, 61, 62, 63, 64, 65 and 66 and List-III: Concurrent List No: 6, 7, 10, 20, 21, 22, 23, 24, 25, 26 and 31, 32, 33, 34, 35, 36, 37, 38, 39, 40, 41, 42, 43, 44, 45, 46 and 47 to monitor the rest of the targets and indicators of SDG-9.

For the SDG-10, that is 'Reduced Inequality', the NITI *Aayog* had framed five indicators; which not captured any of the eleven indicators out of the ten UNs SDG targets. As per the report, 24 dedicated policies or schemes are in action to achieve three targets (10.1, 10.2 and 10.4) of the UN's SDG-10. The Constitution of India opened wide provision in its Article 14, Article 15-*1* to *5*, Article 16 (1) to (5), Article 17 to Article 31, Article 38-(1) and (2), Article 39 – (a) to (f), Article 39A, Article 41 to Article 48, Article 51A, Article 243D and Article 243T, Article 301 to Article 305, Article 307, Article 309, Article 310, Article 311, Article 312, Article 313, Article 314, Article 315, Article 320, Article 323A, Article 323B, Article 325 and 326, Article 333, Article 334, Article 335, Article 336, Article 337, Article 338, 338A 364, Article 340, Article 341, Article 342, Article 350A, Article 350B and Article 351; Article 246 - Seventh Schedule, List-I: Union List No: 12, 13, 22, 23, 24, 25, 27, 28, 29, 30, 31, 32, 33, 34, 35, 36, 37, 38, 39, 40, 41, 42, 43, 44, 45, 46, 47, 48, 49, 50, 51, 52, 53, 54, 55, 56, 57, 58, 59, 60, 61, 62, 63, 64, 65, 66, 67, 68, 69 and 94; List-II: State List No: 6, 7, 12, 13, 14, 15, 16, 17, 18, 22, 23, 24, 25, 26, 27, 28, 30, 31, 32, 33, 34 and 35 and the List-III: Concurrent List No: 6, 7, 10, 20, 21, 22, 23, 24, 25, 26, 27, 28, 29, 30, 31, 32, 33, 33A, 34, 35, 36, 37, 38, 39, 40, 41, 42, 43, 44, 45, 46 and 47; Article 243G - Eleventh Schedule - Powers, Authority and Responsibilities of Panchayats – Schedule No – 1, 2, 3, 4, 5, 6, 7, 8, 9, 10,11 12, 13, 14, 15, 16, 17, 18, 19, 20, 21, 22, 23, 24, 25, 26, 27, 28 and 29and Article 243W - Twelfth Schedule - Powers, Authority and Responsibilities of Municipalities - Schedule No – 1, 2, 3, 4, 5, 6, 7, 8, 9, 10, 11, 12, 13, 14 and 16 to monitor the rest of the targets and indicators of SDG-10.

For the SDG-11, that is 'Sustainable Cities and Communities', the NITI *Aayog* had framed four indicators; which captured two (11.1.1 and 11.6.1) of fifteen indicators of the ten UNs SDG targets. As per the report, 24 dedicated policies or schemes to achieve only two targets (11.1and 11.6) of the UN's SDG-11. The Constitution of India opened wide provision in its Article 14, Article 15 1 to *5*, Article 21 to Article 21A, Article 31A, Article 38-(1) and (2), Article 39 – (a) to (f), Article 39A, Article 44 to Article 48A, Article 51, Article 51A, Article 309, Article 310, Article 311, Article 312, Article 313, Article 314, Article 315, Article 320, Article 323A and Article 323B; Article 246 - Seventh Schedule, List-I: Union List No: 6, 12, 13, 20, 22, 23, 24, 25, 27, 28, 29, 30, 31, 52, 53, 54, 55, 56, 57, 58, 59, 60, 61, 62, 63, 64, 65, 66, 67, 68, 69, 81 and 94; List-II: State List No: 6, 7, 8, 10, 12, 13, 14, 15, 16, 17, 18, 23, 24, 25, 26, 27, 28, and 35; List-III: Concurrent List No: 9, 15, 20, 21, 22, 23, 24, 25,

26, 29, 30, 31, 32, 33, 33A, 34, 35, 36, 37, 38, 39, 40, 41, 42, 43, 44, 45, 46 and 47. Article 243W - Twelfth Schedule - Powers, Authority and Responsibilities of Municipalities - Schedule No – 1, 2, 3, 4, 5, 6, 7, 8, 9, 10, 11, 12, 13, 14, 15, 16 and 17 to monitor the rest of the targets and indicators of SDG-11.

For the SDG-12, that is 'Sustainable Cities and Communities', here significantly noted that, the NITI *Aayog* unable to collect and manage the data as required to capture the indicators of the UNs SDG-12 targets. As per the report, 21 dedicated policies or schemes to achieve the UN's SDG-12. As a result, all the indicators of the SDG-12 remained uncaptured. The Constitution of India opened wide provision in its Article 14, 15-(2).(a), (b), -(3), (4) and (5), Article 16 (1) to (5), Article 19-1.(a) to (g), Article 21, Article 21A, Article 29-(1) and (2), Article 30-(1), (1A) and (2), Article 31A, Article 32, Article 38-(1) and (2), Article 39 – (a) to (f), Article 39 A, Article 41, Article 42, Article 43, Article 44, Article 45, Article 46, Article 47, Article 48, Article 48A, Article 50, Article 51, Article 51A, Article 301, Article 302, Article 303, Article 304, Article 305, Article 307, Article 309, Article 310, Article 311, Article 312, Article 313, Article 314, Article 315, Article 320, Article 323A, Article 323B Article 351, Article 364 and Article 365; Article 246 - Seventh Schedule, List-I: Union List No: 6, 7, 12, 13, 14, 15, 20, 22, 23, 24, 25, 27, 28, 29, 30, 31, 36, 38, 39, 41, 42, 43, 44, 45, 46, 47, 48, 49, 50, 51, 52, 53, 54, 55, 56, 57, 58, 59, 60, 61, 62, 63, 64, 65, 66, 67, 68, 69, 76, 81, 82, 83, 84, 85, 86, 87, 88, 89, 90, 91, 92, 92A to 92B and 94; List-II: State List No: – 6, 7, 8, 9, 13, 14, 15, 16, 17, 18, 22, 23, 24, 25, 26, 27, 28, 30, 31 and 32; List-III: Concurrent List No: 15, 17, 17A.17B, 18, 19, 20, 20A, 21, 22, 23, 24, 25, 26, 30, 31, 32, 33, 33A, 34, 35, 36, 37, 38, 39, 40, 41, 42, 43, 44, 45, 46 and 47; Article 243G - Eleventh Schedule - Powers, Authority and Responsibilities of Panchayats – Schedule No – 1, 2, 3, 4, 5, 6, 7, 8, 9, 10, 11, 12, 13, 14, 14, 16, 17, 18, 19, 20, 21, 22, 23, 24. 25, 26, 27, 28 and 29; Article 243W - Twelfth Schedule - Powers, Authority and Responsibilities of Municipalities - Schedule No – 1, 2, 3, 4, 5, 6, 7, 8, 9, 10, 11, 12, 13, 14, 15, 16, 17 and 18 to monitor the rest of the targets and indicators of SDG-12.

For the SDG-13, that is 'Climate Action', significantly here also, the NITI *Aayog* unable to collect and manage the data as required to capture the indicators of the UNs SDG-13 targets. As per the report, 12 dedicated policies or schemes to achieve the UN's SDG-13. As a result, all the indicators of the SDG-13 remained uncaptured. The Constitution of India opened wide provision in its Article 14, 15-(2).(a), (b), -(3), (4) and (5),

Article 16 (1) to (5), Article 19-1.(a) to (g), Article 21, Article 21A, Article 38-(1) and (2), Article 39 – (a) to (f), Article 39 A, Article 41, Article 42, Article 43, Article 43A, Article 44, Article 45, Article 47, Article 48, Article 48A, Article 50, Article 51, Article 51A, Article 243D (2), Article 243T (2), Article 302, Article 303, Article 304, Article 305, Article 307, Article 309, Article 310, Article 311, Article 312, Article 313, Article 314, Article 315, Article 320, Article 323A and Article 323B; Article 246 - Seventh Schedule, List-I: Union List No; 5, 6, 7, 10, 12, 13, 14, 15, 16, 22 to 31, 41, 42, 43, 44, 52, 53, 54, 55, 56, 57, 58, 59, 60, 61, 64, 65, 66, 68, 69 and 94; List-II: State List No: 5, 6, 10, 13, 14, 15, 16, 17, 18, 21, 22, 23, 24, 25, 26, 27, 28, 30, 31, 32, 33, 34 and 35; List-III: Concurrent List No: 7, 10, 17, 17A.17B, 18, 19, 20, 20A, 21, 22, 23, 24, 25, 26, 29, 30, 31, 32, 36, 37, 38, 40 and 47; Article 243G - Eleventh Schedule - Powers, Authority and Responsibilities of Panchayats – Schedule No – 1, 2, 3, 4, 5, 6, 7, 8, 9, 10, 11, 12, 13, 14, 14, 16, 17, 18, 19, 20, 21, 22, 23, 24. 25, 26, 27, 28 and 29; Article 243W - Twelfth Schedule - Powers, Authority and Responsibilities of Municipalities - Schedule No – 1, 2, 3, 4, 5, 6, 7, 8, 9, 10, 11, 12, 13, 14, 15, 16, 17 and 18 to monitor the rest of the targets and indicators of SDG-13.

For the SDG-14, that is 'Climate Actión', again the remarkable point is that, the NITI *Aayog* unable to collect and manage the data as required to capture the indicators of the UNs SDG-14 targets. As per the report, 8 dedicated policies or schemes to achieve the UN's SDG-14. As a result, all the indicators of the SDG-14 remained uncaptured. The Constitution of India opened wide provision in its Article 16 (1) to (5), Article 21, Article 21A, Article 38-(1) and (2), Article 39 – (a) to (f), Article 39A, Article 41, Article 42, Article 43, Article 43A, Article 44, Article 47, Article 48A, Article 51, Article 51A, Article 243D (2), Article 243T (2), Article 301, Article 302, Article 303, Article 304, Article 305, Article 307, Article 309, Article 310, Article 311, Article 312, Article 313, Article 314, Article 315, Article 320, Article 323A and Article 323B; Article 246 - Seventh Schedule, List-I: Union List No: 2, 3, 8, 10, 12, 13, 14, 21, 24, 25, 27, 28, 30, 53, 54, 57, 64, 65, 66, 68, 69, 89, and 94; List-II: State List No: 6, 17, 21 and 32; List-III: Concurrent List No: 20, 23, 24, 25 and 34; Article 243G - Eleventh Schedule - Powers, Authority and Responsibilities of Panchayats – Schedule No – 5, 13, 16, 17, 18 and 19; Article 243W - Twelfth Schedule - Powers, Authority and Responsibilities of Municipalities - Schedule No – 1, 3, 5, 7, 8, 11 and 16 to monitor the rest of the targets and indicators of SDG-14.

For the SDG-15, that is 'Life and Land', the NITI *Aayog* had framed four indicators; which captured only three (15.1.1, 15.2.1 and 15.7.1) of fourteen indicators of the twelve UNs SDG targets. As per the report, 17 dedicated policies or schemes to achieve three targets (15.1, 15.2 and 15.7) of the UN's SDG-15. The Constitution of India opened wide provision in its Article 14, Article 15 *1* to *5*, Article 16, Article 21A, Article 38-(1) and (2), Article 41, Article 44, Article 46, Article 47, Article 48, Article 48A, Article 51, Article 51A, Article 304, Article 307, Article 309, Article 310, Article 311, Article 312, Article 313, Article 314, Article 315, Article 320, Article 323A and Article 323B; Article 246 - Seventh Schedule, List-I: Union List No: 4, 7, 10, 12, 13, 14, 24, 25, 26, 27, 28, 30, 41, 42, 52, 53, 54, 55, 56, 57, 58, 64, 65, 66, 89, and 94; List-II: State List No: 13, 14, 15, 16, 17, 18, 22, 23, 24, 25, 26, 27 and 58; List-III: Concurrent List No: 17, 17A, 17B, 18, 19, 25, 26, 30, 31, 32 and 33; Article 243G - Eleventh Schedule - Powers, Authority and Responsibilities of Panchayats – Schedule No – 1, 2, 3,4, 5, 6, 7, 8, 9, 16, 17, 18, 19, 20, 21, 22, 26,27, 28 and 29; Article 243W - Twelfth Schedule - Powers, Authority and Responsibilities of Municipalities - Schedule No – 1, 2, 3, 5, 8, 9, 10, 11, 12, 13, 14, 15, 16 and 18 to monitor the rest of the targets and indicators of SDG-15.

For the SDG-16, that is 'Peace, Justice and Strong Institutions, the NITI *Aayog* had framed five indicators; which captured five (16.1.1, 16.2.2, 16.3.1, 16.5.1 and 16.9.2) of twenty three indicators of the twelve UNs SDG targets. As per the report, 7 dedicated policies or schemes to achieve five targets (16.1, 16.2, 16.3, 16.5 and 16.9) of the UN's SDG-16. The Constitution of India opened wide provision in its Article 14, Article 15 *1* to *5*, Article 16, Article 17, Article 19, Article 20, Article 21, Article 21A, Article 22, Article 23, Article 24, Article 25, Article 26, Article 27, Article 28, Article 29, Article 30, Article 31A, Article 31.B, Article 31C, Article 32A, Article 33, Article 34, Article 35, Article 38-(1) and (2), Article 39, Article 39A, Article 40, Article 41, Article 42, Article 43, Article 43A, Article 44, Article 45, Article 46, Article 47, Article 48, Article 48A, Article 50, Article 51, Article 51A, Article 243D, Article 243T, Article 301, Article 302, Article 303, Article 304, Article 307, Article 309, Article 310, Article 311, Article 312, Article 313, Article 314, Article 315, Article 320, Article 323A, Article 323B, Articles 325, Article 326, Article 333, Article 334, Article 335, Article 336, Article 337, Article 338, Article 338A, Article 340, Article 341, Article 342, Article 350A, Article 350B, Article 351, Article 364 and Article 365; Article 246 - Seventh Schedule; List-I: Union List: 1, 2, 3, 4, 5, 6, 7, 8, 9, 10, 11, 12,

13, 14, 15, 16, 17, 18, 19, 20, 21, 22, 23, 24, 25, 26, 27, 28, 30, 31, 32, 34, 35, 36, 37, 38, 39, 40, 41, 42, 43, 44, 45, 46, 47, 48, 49, 50, 51, 52, 53, 54, 55, 56, 57, 58, 59, 60, 61, 63, 64, 65, 66, 67, 68, 69, 70, 71, 72, 73, 74, 75, 76, 77, 78, 80, 81, 82, 83, 84, 85, 86, 87, 88, 89, 90, 91, 92, 92A, 92B, 93, 94, 95, 96 and 97; List-II: State List No: 1, 2, 3, 4, 5, 6, 7, 8, 9, 10, 12, 13, 14, 15, 16, 17, 18, 21, 22, 23, 24, 25, 26, 27, 28, 30, 31, 32, 33, 34, 35, 37, 38, 39, 40, 41, 42, 43, 44, 45,,46, 47, 48, 49, 50, 51, 52, 53, 54, 55, 56, 57, 58, 59, 60, 61, 62, 63, 64, 65, 66; List-III: Concurrent List No: 1, 2, 3, 4, 5, 6, 7, 8, 9, 10, 11, 12, 13, 14, 15, 16, 17, 17A, 17B, 18, 19, 20, 21, 22, 23, 24, 25, 26, 27, 28, 29, 30, 31, 32, 33, 33A, 34, 35, 36, 37, 38, 39, 40, 41, 42, 43, 44, 45, 46 and 47; Article 243G - Eleventh Schedule - Powers, Authority and Responsibilities of Panchayats – Schedule No – 1, 2, 3,4, 5, 6, 7, 8, 9, 10, 11, 12, 13, 14, 15, 16, 17, 18, 19, 20, 21, 22, 23, 24, 25, 26,27, 28 and 29; Article 243W - Twelfth Schedule - Powers, Authority and Responsibilities of Municipalities - Schedule No – 1, 2, 3, 4, 5, 6, 7, 8, 9, 10, 11, 12, 13, 14, 15, 16, 17 and 18 to monitor the rest of the targets and indicators of SDG-16.

Finally for the SDG-17, that is 'Partnerships for the Goals', the NITI *Aayog* here also unable to collect and manage the data as required to capture the indicators of the UNs SDG-17 targets. As per the report, 13 dedicated Ministries or the Departments engaged to achieve the UN's SDG-17. As a result, all the indicators of the SDG-17 remained uncaptured. If we look the SDG-17, 'Partnerships for the Goals' targets, there are seven-point partnership making approach, these are Finance, Technology, Capacity-building, Trade, Systemic issues - Policy and institutional coherence, Multi-stakeholder partnerships and Data, monitoring and accountability under each point there are several targets and its indicator – as per the goal all the points, targets and the indicators are the requisite to achieve the SDG as a whole.

While working towards revitalizing the global partnership for the achievement of the SDGs, India reaffirms the principle of common but differentiated responsibilities. Despite significant efforts for domestic resource mobilisation, India is unlikely to gather sufficient revenues for achieving the SDGs. Therefore, India reiterates that the developed countries have an essential obligation to provide financial assistance to the developing countries, especially for global public goods such as climate change mitigation and control of pandemics, so that they can fully achieve the SDGs. India also highlights the need for international cooperation for curbing illicit financial flows, defining aid unambiguously and establishing robust systems for monitoring commitments made by donor countries.

Towards implementation of the above local as well as global partnership making initiatives to achieving the SDG's targets, the Government of India with its dedicated Ministries or the Departments such as Ministry of Corporate Affairs, DIPP, External Affairs, Information and Broadcasting, Information and Technology, Ministry of Commerce, Ministry of Commerce and Trade, Ministry of Environment, Forest and Climate Change, Ministry of Finance, Ministry of Rural Development, Ministry of Science and Technology, MoSPI and Telecommunication for this SDG are a proactive role; these role and initiatives are accelerated the Indian Constitution, there are ample options to capture the issues associated with the SDG-17 in the Constitution of India.

As the Government of India had been played a vital role to formation as well as framing the issues of SDG; in a similar manner, India have to play a vital role to making 'partnership for the goals' within as well as between its territorial area to achieve the SDG as a whole by effective use and monitoring of its mechanism of 'peace, justice and strong institutions' (SDG-16); unless we will be liable on the ground of violation the commitment as agreed in the United Nations General Assembly on implementation of SDGs as well as violation of the linked provisions reflected on SDG-17 in the Indian Constitution. In this regard, the Constitution of India opened wide provision in its - Article-15-1, 2-a, 2-b, 3, 4 and 5; Article-16-(1) to (5); Article-19-1. (a) to (e); Article 21-A, Article-38-(1) and (2); Article-43A, Article-46, Article-51A that is (a) to (j); Article-243, Article-243A, Article-243B, Article-243C, Article-243D, Article-243P, Article-243Q, Article-243R, Article-243S, Article-243T, Article-309, Article-310, Article-311, Article-312, Article-313, Article-314, Article-315, Article-320, Article-323A and Article-323B; Article 246 - Seventh Schedule; List-I: Union List No: 12, 13, 14, 15, 16, 17, 19, 20, 21, 22, 23, 24, 25, 27, 29, 30, 31, 38, 42, 51,62, 63, 64, 65, 66, 67, 68, 69, and 94; List-II: State List No: 1, 2, 3, 4, 5, 6, 12, 13, 26; List-III: Concurrent List No:10, 25, 26, 27, 28, 29, 30 and 33; Article 243G - Eleventh Schedule - Powers, Authority and Responsibilities of Panchayats – Schedule No – 1, 2, 3,4, 5, 6, 7, 8, 9, 10, 11, 12, 13, 14, 15, 16, 17, 18, 19, 20, 21, 22, 23, 24, 25, 26,27, 28 and 29; Article 243W - Twelfth Schedule - Powers, Authority and Responsibilities of Municipalities - Schedule No – 1, 2, 3, 4, 5, 6, 7, 8, 9, 10, 11, 12, 13, 14, 15, 16, 17 and 18 to monitor the rest of the targets and indicators of SDG-17.

Table No. 157: Summary of Performance of India in UNDP-SDGs Targets

SDGs	No of UN-SDG Targets	Expected Target when SDG-16=71	India Captured of UN-SDG Target	Reaming UN- SDG's Target
SDG-1, End Poverty	7	4.97	3	4
SDG-2, Zero Hunger	8	5.68	3	5
SDG-3, Good Health and Well-being	13	9.23	4	9
SDG-4, Quality Education	10	7.1	2	8
SDG-5, Gender Equality	9	6.39	4	5
SDG-6, Clean Water and Sanitation	8	5.68	3	5
SDG-7, Affordable and Clean Energy	5	3.55	2	3
DG-8, Decent Work and Economic Growth	12	8.52	3	9
SDG-9, Industry, Innovation and Infrastructure	8	5.68	2	6
SDG-10, Reduce Inequality	10	7.1	3	7
SDG-11, Sustainable Cities and Communities	10	7.1	2	8
SDG-12, Sustainable Consumption and Production	11	7.81	0	11
SDG-13, Climate Action	5	3.55	0	5
SDG-14, Life Bellow Water	10	7.1	0	10
SDG-15, Life and Land	12	8.52	3	9
SDG-16, Peace, Justice and Strong Institutions	12	8.52	5	7
SDG-17, Partnerships for the Goals	19	13.49	0	19
Total	169	119.99	39	130
Percentage			23.08	76.92

Finally if we a look into the table no-157, as per the score of SDG-16, that is *Peace, Justice and Strong Institutions,* it is expected that India will able to capture at least 199.99 targets of the UN-SDGs but unexpectedly it is happened only for 39, in percentage it is 23.08 and 76.92 percent targets are still remain untouched.

Table No. 158: Summary of Performance of India in UNDP-SDGs Indicators

SDGs	No of UN-SDG Indicators	Expected Indicators when SDG-16=71	No. of India's Indicators	Reaming UN- SDG's Indicators
SDG-1, End Poverty	12	8.52	5	7
SDG-2, Zero Hunger	14	9.94	4	10
SDG-3, Good Health and Well-being	26	18.46	5	21
SDG-4, Quality Education	11	7.81	7	4

(*Contd...*)

SDG-5, Gender Equality	14	9.94	6	8
SDG-6, Clean Water and Sanitation	11	7.81	5	6
SDG-7, Affordable and Clean Energy	6	4.26	3	3
DG-8, Decent Work and Economic Growth	17	12.07	4	13
SDG-9, Industry, Innovation and Infrastructure	12	8.52	4	8
SDG-10, Reduce Inequality	11	7.81	5	6
SDG-11, Sustainable Cities and Communities	14	9.94	4	10
SDG-12, Sustainable Consumption and Production	13	9.23	0	13
SDG-13, Climate Action	7	4.97	0	7
SDG-14, Life Bellow Water	10	7.1	0	10
SDG-15, Life and Land	13	9.23	4	9
SDG-16, Peace, Justice and Strong Institutions	22	15.62	6	16
SDG-17, Partnerships for the Goals	25	17.75	0	25
Total	238	168.98	62	176
Percentage			26.05	73.95

Again if we a look into the table no-158, as per the score of SDG-16, that is *Peace, Justice and Strong Institutions,* it is expected that India will able to capture at least 168.98 indicators of the UN-SDGs but unexpectedly it is happened only for 62, in percentage it is 26.0 and 73.95 percent indicators are still remain untouched.

Table No. 159: Summary of Nature of Performance of India for UNDP-SDGs

Table No-159				
SDGs	**Dedicated Policies**	**Policies under No. of Head**	**No. of Positive Performance Indicators**	**No. of Negativities Performance Indicators**
SDG-1, End Poverty	68	12	1	4
SDG-2, Zero Hunger	37	15	1	3
SDG-3, Good Health and Well-being	45	19	0	5
SDG-4, Quality Education	64	13	4	3
SDG-5, Gender Equality	19	14	1	5
SDG-6, Clean Water and Sanitation	22	9	2	3
SDG-7, Affordable and Clean Energy	17	5	1	2
DG-8, Decent Work and Economic Growth	55	22	1	3
SDG-9, Industry, Innovation and Infrastructure	45	22	1	3
SDG-10, Reduce Inequality	24	16	2	3
SDG-11, Sustainable Cities and Communities	24	15	1	3

(Contd...)

SDG-12, Sustainable Consumption and Production	21	18	0	0
SDG-13, Climate Action	12	5	0	0
SDG-14, Life Bellow Water	8	6	0	0
SDG-15, Life and Land	17	9	0	4
SDG-16, Peace, Justice and Strong Institutions	7	11	2	4
SDG-17, Partnerships for the Goals	0	0	0	0
Total	485	211	17	45
Percentage			27.42	72.58

Finally if we a look into the table no-159, as per the score of SDG-16, that is *Peace, Justice and Strong Institutions,* it is expected that India will able to make positive score at least 71 percent (as SDG-16 score=71) but unfortunately India in performed negatively in 72.58 percent of the indicators.

The agenda of the UNDP-SDGs are a pious initiatives for the future generation which is favouring for 'leave one no behind' from these initiatives. India is a country which conceiving almost 17.40 percent of world population; which is 1381.59 million in number. These huge numbers of population are differently stratified. They are diversified in many forms in its varied geographical area.

Including all the people of India in a development approach like Sustainable Development Goals is a great challenge to India along with the UNDP. As India played great role to formulate the SDGs targets and indicators by incorporation its own social issues, so as leading country, India have to play a more pro-active role to achieving the targets of the SDGs. To proper implementation of the agenda of UNDP-SDGs, as a responsible citizen of India we cannot ignore our duties and responsibilities to play a vital role as a stakeholders of the society for the future generation. We must play the significant role under the provisions of Indian Constitution for future generations.

We have to find out the gaps, it is the matter of our future generation. We have trained and efficient human resources at our all kind of educational institutions, most of the multinational companies are depends on efficient Indian talent to expansion of their productivities and the India talents has been effectively doing this. So, we have to rise our voice to there where lies the root of effective use of efficient Indian talent for the Indian future generation. Unless, we the experts of different sectors who are thinking they are working for the people will be remain into the painful memories of the future generation of India.

References

NITI Aayog. 2018. *SDG India Index Baseline Report, 2018.* New Delh: NITI Aayog, Government of India.

Basu, Kaushik. 2007. *India's demographic dividend.* United Kingdom: BBC News.

Cullen-Dupont, K. 2009. *Human Trafficking (1st ed.).* New York: Infobase Publishing.

Dietrich Wolfgang. 2012. *Interpretations of Peace in History and Culture.* London: Palgrave Macmillan.

Dietrich, Wolfgang. 2011. *The Palgrave International Handbook of Peace Studies. A Cultural Approach (Edited).* London: Palgrave MacMillan.

Dutt, S. 1998. "Identities and the Indian State: An Overview." *Third World Quarterly* 19 (3): 411–434.

Echeverri-Gent, J. 2002. *Politics in India's Decentred Polity", in Ayres, A.; Oldenburg, P. (eds.), Quickening the Pace of Change, India Briefing.* London: M. E. Sharpe.

Express India. 2009. *Indian Car Exports Surge 36%".* New Delhi: Express India, 13 October 2009.

GAIL. 2018. *Annual Report 2017-2018 of GAIL.* New Delhi: GAIL India Limited, Government of India.

Galtung, Johan. 1967. *Theories of Peace - A Synthetic Approach To Peace Thinking.* Oslo: International Peace Research Institute.

Gargan, Edward A. 1992. *India Stumbles in Rush to a Free Market Economy.* New York: The New York Times, 15 August.

Gilbert, Martin. 2002. *A History of the Twentieth Century.* New York: HarperCollins,.

Gledhill, A. 1970. *The Republic of India: The Development of its Laws and Constitution.* Westport, USA: Greenwood, .

Heehs, P. 2002. *Indian Religions: A Historical Reader of Spiritual Expression and Experience (Edited).* New York : New York University Press.

IBEF. 2021. *Foreign Trade Policy of India.* New Delhi: India Brand Equity Foundation (IBEF).

IEP. 2018. *Positive Peace Report 2018: Analysing the Factors that Sustain Peace.* Sydney: Institute for Economics and Peace (IEP).

ILO. 2017. *Global estimates of child labour: Results and trends, 2012-2016.* Geneva: International Labour Organizatio (ILO).

India, Government of. 1950/2015. *The Constitution of India.* New Delhi: Ministry of Law and Justice, (Legislative Department), Government of India.

Jones, G. and Ramdas, K. 2005. *(Un)tying the Knot: Ideal and Reality in Asian Marriage, .* Singapore: National University of Singapore Press.

Khan, Danish. 2017. *Indian smartphone market grows 23% to overtake US in Q3; Samsung, Xiaomi drive shipments.* New Delhi: The Economic Times.

Kothari, Ashish. 2018. *Development and Ecological Sustainability in India: Possibilities for the Post-2015 Framework.* Mumbai: OXFAM India.

Kuipe, Kathleen. 2010. *The Culture of India.* New York: The Rosen Publishing Group.

Makar, E. M. 2007. *An American's Guide to Doing Business in India.* Greeneville, USA: Adams.

Matsoukas, David G. Mahal and Ianis G. 2018. "The Geographic Origins of Ethnic Groups in the Indian Subcontinent: Exploring Ancient Footprints with Y-DNA Haplogroups." *Frontiers in Genetics* (Frontiers in Genetics) 1.

Medora, N. 2003. *Mate Selection in Contemporary India: Love Marriages Versus Arranged Marriages", in Hamon, R. R.; Ingoldsby, B. B. (eds.), Mate Selection Across Cultures.* New Delhi: SAGE Publications.

Messner, W. 2009. *Working with India. The Softer Aspects of a Successful Collaboration with the Indian IT & BPO Industry.* New York: Springer.

Metcalf, B. and Metcalf, T. R. 2006. *A Concise History of Modern India (2nd ed.).* Cambridge: Cambridge University Press.

MoSPI. 2017. *Millennium Development Goals – Final Country Report of India.* Nes Delhi: Ministry of Statistics and Programme Implementation (MoSPI), Government of India.

Nagar, Bimal N. Patel and Ranita. 2018. *Sustainable Development and India: Convergence of Law, Economics, Science, and Politics.* Oxford: Oxford University Press.

Nakamura, H. 1999. *Indian Buddhism: A Survey with Bibliographical Notes, Buddhist Tradition Series (12th ed.).* New Delhi: Motilal Banarsidass.

Nayak, P. B., B. Goldar, and P. Agrawal. 2010. *India's Economy and Growth: Essays in Honour of V. K. R. V. Rao, .* New Delhi: SAGE Publications.

Neuborne, B. 2003. "The Supreme Court of India ." *International Journal of Constitutional Law* 1 (1): 476–510.

NITI Aayog. 2017. *Voluntary National Review Report on Implementation of Sustainable Development Goals.* New Delhi: NITI Aayog, Government of India.

OECD. 2007. *Economic Surveys India.* Paris: Organisation for Economic Co-Operation and Development (OECD).

Pal, P., and J Ghosh. 2007. *Inequality in India: A Survey of Recent Trends" (PDF),Economic and Social Affairs: DESA Working Paper No. 45* . California: United Nations.

Pereira, Ignatius. 2013. *Rising number of dowry deaths in India: NCRB.* Kollam: The Hindu.

Perkovich, G. 2001. *India's Nuclear Bomb: The Impact on Global Proliferation.* California : University of California Press.

Pylee, M. V. 2003. *The Union Judiciary: The Supreme Court", Constitutional Government in India (2nd ed.).* New Delhi: S. Chand.

Registrar General & Census Commissioner. 2011. *The Census of India, 2011.* New Delhi: Office of the Registrar General & Census Commissioner, Government of India.

Rothermund, D. 2000. *The Routledge Companion to Decolonization, Routledge Companions to History (1st ed.)*. London: Routledge.

Schwab, Klaus. 2010. *The Global Competitiveness Report*. Geneva: World Economic Forum.

Sharma, B. K. 2007. *SIntroduction to the Constitution of India (4th ed.)*. New Delhi: Prentice Hall.

Sharma, R. 1950. "Cabinet Government in India." *Parliamentary Affairs* 4 (1): 116–126.

Sharma, S. R. 1999. *India-USSR Relations, 1947-1971: From Ambivalence to Steadfastness, Volume 1*. New Dilhi: Discovery Publishing House.

Simi Mehta, Vikash Kumar and Arjun Kumar. 2018. *Lessons in Sustainable Development from Bangladesh and India*. London: Palgrave Macmillan.

Sinha, A. 2004. "The Changing Political Economy of Federalism in India." *India Review* 3 (1): 25–63.

Sisodia, N. S., and G. V. C Naidu. 2005. *Changing Security Dynamic in Eastern Asia: Focus on Japan*. New Delhi: Promilla.

Sripati, V. 1998. "Toward Fifty Years of Constitutionalism and Fundamental Rights in India: Looking Back to See Ahead (1950–2000)." *American University International Law Review* 14(2): 413–496.

TERI-GGGI. 2015. *Green Growth and Sustainable Development in India*. New Delhi: The Energy and Resources Institute (TERI) and Global Green Growth Institute (GGGI).

The Economist. 2017. *Measuring the cost of living worldwide*. London: The Economist, 21 March 2017.

UN-DESA-PD. 2017. *World Population Prospects: The 2017 Revision, Key Findings and Advance*. New York: United Nations, Department of Economic and Social Affairs, Population Division (UN-DESA-PD).

UN-RIS. 2016. *India and Sustainable Development Goals: The Way Forward*. New Delhi: United Nation's Research and Information System for Developing Countries (UN-RIS).

Wheare, K. C. 1980. *Federal Government (4th ed.), Oxford University Press, ISBN 978-0-313-22702-8*. Oxford: Oxford University Press.

Wolpert, S. 2003. *A New History of India (7th ed.), Oxford University Press,*. Oxford: Oxford University Press.

World Bank. 2006. *Inclusive Growth and Service Delivery: Building on India's Success*. Washington DC: World Bank.

World Bank. 2011. *PERSPECTIVES ON POVERTY IN INDIA*. Washington DC: World Bank.

INTERNET REFERENCES

1. Behera, L. K. 2011. *India's Defence Budget 2011-12*, March 7, 2011, accessed on 05.04.2021, https://idsa.in/idsacomments/IndiasDefenceBudget2011-12_lkbehera_070311

2. Behera, L. K. 2012. *India's Defence Budget 2012-13,* March 20, 2012, accessed on 05.04.2021, https://idsa.in/idsacomments/IndiasDefenceBudget2012-13_LaxmanBehera_200312

3. Bonner Bill. 2010. *Make way, world. India is on the move,* March 20, 2010, accessed on 05.04.2021, https://www.csmonitor.com/Business/The-Daily-Reckoning/2010/0320/Make-way-world.-India-is-on-the-move

4. Business Standard. 2019. *India's industrial production growth rebounds to 4.3% in July 2019,* September 12, 2019, accessed on 05.04.2021, https://www.business-standard.com/article/news-cm/india-s-industrial-production-growth-rebounds-to-4-3-in-july-2019-119091201141_1.html#:~:text=India's%20industrial%20production%20growth%20rebounds%20to%204.3%25%20in%20July%202019,-Capital%20Market%20%7C%20%7C%20Last&text=India's%20industrial%20production%20(base%20year,of%201.2%25%20in%20June%202019.

5. Business Standard, 2020: *India retains position of 3rd-largest economy on PPP basis for 2017,* June 24, 2020, accessed on 05.04.2021, https://www.business-standard.com/article/economy-policy/india-retains-position-of-3rd-largest-economy-on-ppp-basis-for-2017-120062301724_1.html#:~:text=%22India%20is%20also%20third%2Dlargest,National%20Statistical%20Office%20(NSO).

6. Business Standard, 2020: *India will slip to seventh largest economy in 2021, shows IMF data,* October 23, 2020, accessed on 05.04.2021, https://www.business-standard.com/article/economy-policy/india-will-slip-to-seventh-largest-economy-in-2021-shows-imf-data-120102300060_1.html#:~:text=The%20International%20Monetary%20Fund%20(IMF,to%20No%207%20in%202021.

7. Dalai Lama. 2018. XIV > Quotes > Quotable Quote, accessed on 04.04.2021, https://www.goodreads.com/quotes/11559-world-peace-must-develop-from-inner-peace-peace-is-not

8. Deccan Herald. 2015. *ISRO-SAARC satellite to be a communication vehicle,* January 12, 2015, accessed on 05.04.2021, https://www.deccanherald.com/content/452938/isro-saarc-satellite-communication-vehicle.html

9. Diana Farrell and Eric Beinhocker. 2007. *Next Big Spenders: India's middle class,* May 19, 2007, accessed on 05.04.2021, https://www.mckinsey.com/mgi/overview/in-the-news/next-big-spenders-indian-middle-class#

10. Etymonline. 2015. *Online Etymology Dictionary,* accessed on 05.04.2021, https://web.archive.org/web/20140329072421/http://etymonline.com/index.php?term=peace&allowed_in_frame=0

11. Freman S. P and Elisabeth S. 2008. *Arms production,* accessed on 05.04.2021, https://www.sipri.org/sites/default/files/YB08%20255%2006.pdf

12. GHI. 2020. *Global Hunger Index,* accessed on 05.04.2021, https://www.globalhungerindex.org/india.html#:~:text=In%20the%202020%20Global%20Hunger,See%20overview%20of%20GHI%20calculation%5D.

13. Hindustan Times, 2016: *Bonded labourers, sex workers, forced beggars: India leads world in slavery,* May 31, 2016, accessed on 05.04.2021, https://www.hindustantimes.com/india/india-has-the-largest-population-of-modern-day-slaves/story-PVP1mAQlFqLwOXFtE9EsII.html

14. Jeff A. Benner. 2018. *Ancient Hebrew Word Meanings Peace – shalom,* accessed on 04.04.2021, https://web.archive.org/web/20140426232655/http://www.ancient-hebrew.org/27_peace.html
15. Kumar, Vinod A. 2010. *Reforming the NPT to include India,* May 1, 2010, accessed on 05.04.2021, https://thebulletin.org/2010/05/reforming-the-npt-to-include-india/
16. Library of Congress. 2004. *Country Profile: India,* Library of Congress – Federal Research Division, accessed on 05.04.2021, https://www.loc.gov/rr/frd/cs/profiles/India.pdf
17. Sengupta. D. 2017. *"Pakistan, Afghanistan fare better than India on women's representation in parliament",* The New Indian Express, 16.03. 2017, https://www.newindianexpress.com/nation/2017/mar/16/pakistan-afghanistan-fare-better-than-india-on-womens-representation-in-parliament-1581960.html
18. Sharma Raktim. 2021. *How many people in India actually pay income tax? How this affects the economy?* Yahoo Finance, February 9, 2021, accessed on 05.04.2021, https://in.finance.yahoo.com/news/how-many-people-in-india-actually-pay-income-tax-how-this-affects-the-economy-114734612.html#:~:text=How%20this%20affects%20the%20economy%3F,-article&text=The%20number%20of%20taxpayers%20in,of%20130%20crore%20into%20perspective.
19. PWC.2017. *The World in 2050, The long view: how will be the global economic change by 2050?* February, 2017, accessed on 09.04.2021, https://www.pwc.com/gx/en/research-insights/economy/the-world-in-2050.html
20. Sherani Sakib. 2015. *Worker remittances to Pakistan have increased sharply since the launch of the Pakistan Remittance Initiative (PRI) in 2009,* Dawn, April 17, 2015, https://www.dawn.com/news/1176411
21. Niraj Sheth. 2009. *Outlook for Outsourcing Spending Brightens,* The Wall Street Journal, May 28, 2009, accessed on 05.04.2021, https://www.wsj.com/articles/SB124344190542659025
22. Prasad R. S. 2021. *Digital India,* accessed on 10.04.2021, https://www.digitalindia.gov.in/
23. Shob, Kishan. 2020. *National Nutrition Month 2020: An Analysis of India's Nutritional Status,* Dailyrounds, September 9, 2020, accessed on 05.04.2021, https://www.dailyrounds.org/blog/national-nutrition-month-2020-an-analysis-of-indias-nutritional-status/#:~:text=Despite%20the%20status%2C%2014%20per,five%20in%20India%20are%20stunted.
24. Shukla, A. 2011. *China matches India's expansion in military spending,* Broadsword, March 5, 2011, accessed on 05.04.2021, https://www.ajaishukla.com/2011/03/china-matches-indias-expansion-in.html?m=0
25. Statista. 2021. *Number of reported dowry death cases in India 2005-2019,* February 25, 2021, accessed on 05.04.2021, https://www.statista.com/statistics/632553/reported-dowry-death-cases-india/
26. The Economic Times. 2014. *India's rank improves to 55th position on global hunger index, October 13, 2014,* accessed on 05.04.2021, https://economictimes.indiatimes.com/news/economy/indicators/indias-rank-improves-to-55th-position-on-global-hunger-index/articleshow/44802193.cms?from=mdr

27. The Economic Times. 2021. *India's rank slips to 86th in corruption perception index 2020*, January 28, 2021, accessed on 05.04.2021, https://economictimes.indiatimes.com/news/economy/indicators/indias-rank-slips-to-86th-in-corruption-perception-index-2020/articleshow/80512814.cms
28. The Economist. 2011. Not just rubies and polyester shirts, October 8, 2011, accessed on 05.04.2021, https://www.economist.com/finance-and-economics/2011/10/08/not-just-rubies-and-polyester-shirts
29. The Guardian. 2011. *India's missing women,* July 22, 2011, accessed on 05.04.2021, https://www.theguardian.com/global-development/poverty-matters/2011/jul/22/india-sex-selection-missing-women
30. The Times of India. 2009. *Exporters get wider market reach,* August 28, 2009, accessed on 05.04.2021, https://timesofindia.indiatimes.com/business/india-business/Exporters-get-wider-market-reach/articleshow/4942892.cms?referral=PM
31. The Times of India. 2017. *India's population to surpass that of China around 2024: UN*, January 21, 2017, accessed on 05.04.2021, https://timesofindia.indiatimes.com/india/indias-population-to-surpass-that-of-chinas-around-2024-un/articleshow/59257045.cms#:~:text=The%20new%20estimates%20released%20here,population%20of%201.44%20billion%20each.
32. The Times of India. 2018. *India Russia S-400 missile deal: All you need to know*, October 5, 2018, accessed on 05.04.2021, https://timesofindia.indiatimes.com/india/india-russia-s-400-missile-deal-all-you-need-to-know/articleshow/66066460.cms
33. The World Bank. 2013. *End Extreme Poverty by 2030 Promote Shared Prosperity*, accessed on 04.04.2021. https://www.worldbank.org/en/news/feature/2013/04/17/ending_extreme_poverty_and_promoting_shared_prosperity
34. The World Bank. 2019. *World Population Prospects: 2019 Revision,* accessed on 05.04.2021, *https://data.worldbank.org/indicator/SP.POP.GROW*
35. The World Bank. 2021. *Labour Force –Total India,* January 29, 2021, accessed on 05.04.2021, https://data.worldbank.org/indicator/SL.TLF.TOTL.IN?locations=IN
36. Times Now News. 2018. *No ties with Pakistan at India's cost, relations with New kDelhi long-term: Russia,* October 11, 2018, accessed on 05.04.2021, https://www.timesnownews.com/india/article/will-not-develop-relations-with-pakistan-at-cost-of-india-ties-with-new-delhi-long-term-russia-narendra-modi-vladimir-putin/298009
37. UNDP. 2012. *Background on the goals*, accessed on 04.04.2021 https://www.undp.org/content/undp/en/home/sustainable-development-goals/background.html
38. UNDP. 2016. *SDG 1: No Poverty,* accessed on 04.04.2021, *https://www.undp.org/content/undp/en/home/sustainable-development-goals/goal-1-no-poverty.html*
39. UNDP. 2016 *SDG 10: Reduced Inequalities,* accessed on 04.04.2021, https://www.undp.org/content/undp/en/home/sustainable-development-goals/goal-10-reduced-inequalities.html

40. UNDP. 2016UNDP. 2016 *SDG 11: Sustainable Cities and Communities,* accessed on 04.04.2021, https://www.undp.org/content/undp/en/home/sustainable-development-goals/goal-11-sustainable-cities-and-communities.html
41. UNDP. 2016*SDG 12:Responsible Consumption and Production,* accessed on 04.04.2021, https://www.undp.org/content/undp/en/home/sustainable-development-goals/goal-12-responsible-consumption-and-production.html
42. UNDP. 2016. *SDG 13:Climate Action,* accessed on 04.04.2021, https://www.undp.org/content/undp/en/home/sustainable-development-goals/goal-13-climate-action.html
43. UNDP. 2016. *SDG 14:Life Below Water,* accessed on 04.04.2021, https://www.undp.org/content/undp/en/home/sustainable-development-goals/goal-14-life-below-water.html
44. UNDP. 2016. *SDG 15:Life on Land,* accessed on 04.04.2021, https://www.undp.org/content/undp/en/home/sustainable-development-goals/goal-15-life-on-land.html
45. UNDP. 2016. *SDG 16: Peace, Justice and Strong Institutions,* accessed on 04.04.2021, https://www.undp.org/content/undp/en/home/sustainable-development-goals/goal-16-peace-justice-and-strong-institutions.html
46. UNDP. 2016. *SDG 17: Partnerships for the Goals,* accessed on 04.04.2021, https://www.undp.org/content/undp/en/home/sustainable-development-goals/goal-17-partnerships-for-the-goals.html
47. UNDP. 2016. *SDG 2: Zero Hunger,* accessed on 04.04.2021, https://www.undp.org/content/undp/en/home/sustainable-development-goals/goal-2-zero-hunger.html
48. UNDP. 2016. *SDG 3: Good health and Well-being,* accessed on 04.04.2021, https://www.undp.org/content/undp/en/home/sustainable-development-goals/goal-3-good-health-and-well-being.html
49. UNDP. 2016. *SDG 4: Quality Education,* accessed on 04.04.2021, https://www.undp.org/content/undp/en/home/sustainable-development-goals/goal-4-quality-education.html
50. UNDP. 2016. *SDG 5: Gender Equality,* accessed on 04.04.2021, https://www.undp.org/content/undp/en/home/sustainable-development-goals/goal-5-gender-equality.html
51. UNDP. 2016. *SDG 6: Clean water and Sanitation,* accessed on 04.04.2021, https://www.undp.org/content/undp/en/home/sustainable-development-goals/goal-6-clean-water-and-sanitation.html
52. UNDP. 2016. *SDG 7: Affordable and Clean Energy,* accessed on 04.04.2021, https://www.undp.org/content/undp/en/home/sustainable-development-goals/goal-7-affordable-and-clean-energy.html
53. UNDP. 2016. *SDG 8: Decent Work and Economic Growth,* accessed on 04.04.2021, https://www.undp.org/content/undp/en/home/sustainable-development-goals/goal-8-decent-work-and-economic-growth.html
54. UNDP. 2016. *SDG 9: Industry, Innovation and Infrastructure,* accessed on 04.04.2021, https://www.undp.org/content/undp/en/home/sustainable-development-goals/goal-9-industry-innovation-and-infrastructure.html

55. UNDP. 2017. *The Millennium Development Goals Report 2015,* accessed on 04.04.2021, https://www.undp.org/content/undp/en/home/librarypage/mdg/the-millennium-development-goals-report-2015.html
56. USCIRF 2012. *India,* accessed on 05.04.2021, https://www.uscirf.gov/sites/default/files/resources/2012ARChapters/india%202012.pdf
57. WTO. 2016. *Members and Observers,* July 29, 2016, accessed on 05.04.2021, https://www.wto.org/english/thewto_e/whatis_e/tif_e/org6_e.htm

Index

E

F

J

K

L

M

U

V

W